THE SHORES OF LIGHT

The Shores of Light

A Literary Chronicle
of the Twenties and Thirties

BY
EDMUND WILSON

With a Foreword by Daniel Aaron

NORTHEASTERN UNIVERSITY PRESS
Boston

Northeastern University Press edition 1985

Library of Congress Cataloging in Publication Data

Wilson, Edmund, 1895–1972.
The shores of light.

Reprint. Originally published: New York: Farrar,
Straus and Young, c1952.
Includes index.
1. American literature—20th century—History and
criticism—Addresses, essays, lectures. 2. Literature,
Modern—History and criticism—Addresses, essays,
lectures.   I. Title.
PS223.W54   1985   810'.9'0052   85-3122
ISBN 0-930350-68-5 (pbk.: alk. paper)

Printed and bound by The Alpine Press,
Stoughton, Massachusetts. The paper
is Warren's 1854, an acid-free sheet.

MANUFACTURED IN THE UNITED STATES OF AMERICA
90 89 88 87 86 85   5 4 3 2 1

CONTENTS

CONTENTS

CONTENTS

CONTENTS

THIS BOOK was originally planned as a companion volume to my *Classics and Commercials: A Literary Chronicle of the Forties:* a similar selection from my literary articles published during the twenties and thirties; but it has turned into something rather different. I have aimed in the present collection to present a kind of panorama of the books and the ideas, the movements and the literary life, of a period that was very much livelier and had a much more exciting development than the war-darkened years of the forties. I have therefore included some youthful stuff that can only, if at all, be of interest from an historical point of view—in showing how it looked to a contemporary; and I have not confined myself, as in the earlier volume, to essays and reviews, but have admitted dialogues, jeux d'esprit, satires, short sketches and personal letters. I have even put in a few pieces that do not deal with writing at all, but these, too, are intended to contribute to a general picture of the culture of a recklessly unspecialized era, when minds and imaginations were exploring in all directions. I have suppressed the worst of my aberrations, and I have thoroughly revised almost everything, sometimes trimming and toning down what I originally wrote and sometimes expanding it with material taken from my old notes. In the case of some articles that had been hastily written, I have found it a satisfaction to get them into better shape, even after twenty or thirty years. In this volume, I have not arranged the pieces in strictly chronological order, but have sometimes grouped them in such a way as to put together pieces on the same subject or to bring out some special aspect of the period.

The reader may find here, as I have done, attitudes that surprise or amuse him; but I have generally refrained from comment and leave him to do his own discounting. The self-assertive approach of the twenties, which seems rather brash today, I have not always been able to eliminate. We had grown up on the journalism of Shaw and Chesterton, Belloc and Max Beerbohm, and later, in the United States, of the Mencken and Nathan of the *Smart Set* and the Woollcott and Broun of the *World*. All these writers were everlastingly saying "I": the exploitation of personality had become an integral part of criticism. It all stemmed, I suppose, from Oscar Wilde, who had a genius for self-dramatization and who was imitated in this respect by Bernard Shaw. In the twenties a young man who was still nobody made a point of saying "I"— "I don't like so-and-so," "I can't read so-and-so," "I have always thought so-and-so,"—in the hope of being taken for somebody. Now the habit has gone out of fashion. Aside from this personal emphasis, however, I have not reprinted here very much that I disapprove of, as of the date when it was first written—though, of course, I see some things today in a somewhat different perspective: in the light of the author's subsequent work or of my own better information. I have sometimes had to leave in passages that are more or less duplicated in my other books, but I do not suppose that this will worry anybody. I apologize for printing documents in which other writers pay me compliments, but this is part of this ancient history, too, and I have offset them by putting in others in which I am taken to task. I have added a few pieces of later date, whose presence explains itself.

Of these ninety-seven pieces, seventy-three first appeared in the *New Republic*. *Christian Gauss as a Teacher of Literature* was first printed in the *American Scholar*; *The Literary Worker's Polonius* in the *Atlantic Monthly*; *F. Scott Fitzgerald* in the *Bookman*; *Marxism at the End of the Thirties* in the New York *Call*; *The Classics on the Soviet Stage* in the Moscow *Daily News*; *Mr. E. A. Robinson's Moonlight*, "*A Lost Lady*," *Byron and His Biographers*, *Late Violets from the Nineties*, *Sherwood Anderson's "Many Marriages," Ring Lardner's American Characters*, *Mr. Hemingway's Dry-Points* and "*The Seven Lively Arts*" in the *Dial*; *The Pleasures of Literature* and *Edna St. Vincent Millay* in the *Nation*; "*The Great Audience*," "*Things As They Are*," *Dream Poetry* and the second article, of which part is given under *Talking United States*, in the *New Yorker*; *The New Byron Letters* in the New York *Tribune*; and "*One of Ours*" and *Eugene O'Neill as Prose Writer* in *Vanity Fair*. The following pieces were included, after their first periodical publication, in collections of essays by various hands: *F. Scott Fitzgerald* in *The Literary Spotlight*, published by George H. Doran in 1924; *The All-Star Literary Vaudeville* in *American Criticism*, published by Harcourt, Brace in 1926; and *Notes on Babbitt and More* in *The Critique of Humanism*, published by Brewer & Warren in 1930. *The Satire of Samuel Butler* appeared in my book *The Triple Thinkers*, published by Harcourt, Brace in 1938, but was removed in a later edition to make room for new material. The two *Imaginary Dialogues* are reprinted from a book of mine, *Discordant Encounters*, published by Albert & Charles Boni in 1926.

I have to thank Mr. Ernest Hemingway, Mr. Henry Miller, M. André Malraux and Mr. John Crowe Ransom for permission to print their letters; Mr. Leonard Woolf for permission to reprint a letter of Virginia Woolf; Miss

Norma Millay for permission to print two letters of Edna St. Vincent Millay; Mr. Harold R. Medina for permission to reprint his tribute to Christian Gauss from the Princeton *Alumni Weekly*; Brandt & Brandt for permission to include *To Love Impuissant* from *A Few Figs From Thistles*, published by Harper & Brothers, copyright 1920, 1948, by Edna St. Vincent Millay, and *Portrait* from *The Buck in the Snow*, published by Harper & Brothers, copyright 1928 by Edna St. Vincent Millay; and Mr. Philip Horton for permission to include a quotation from a letter of Hart Crane included in his biography *Hart Crane*. The words and music of *Wedding Joy* are reprinted by permission from the *Botsford Collection of Folk Songs*, copyright 1929 by G. Schirmer, Inc.

FOREWORD

i

IN THE fall of 1949, Edmund Wilson began to sort out reviews and articles he had contributed in the twenties to various magazines and newspapers. Two years later, he mentioned in a letter to Vladimir Nabokov that his as yet untitled "gigantic book" (it by then included pieces from the thirties) was turning into "a sort of volume of literary memoirs." He described its contents more precisely in his preface to *The Shores of Light*, published in 1952: "a general history of the culture of a recklessly unspecialized era, when minds and imaginations were exploring in all directions." Given his pessimistic view of a post-World War II society dominated, he felt, by intellectual pitchmen and shallow entertainers, it is no wonder that he should have looked with a certain nostalgia, if on the whole unsentimentally, to a period made golden by distance when he and his friends were full of great expectations for literature and America.

No one else of his generation was better qualified to undertake this "history." He had been in the vortex of it, had participated in and monitored cultural campaigns, adjudicated literary debates, and composed political and aesthetic manifestos. He had seen the literary hopes of his generation drowned in politics and war. In fact, all his previous training and experience had prepared him for the role he confidently assumed in the early twenties. The magisterial man of letters was presaged in the Hill School adolescent (1909–1912) absorbed in acquiring Latin and Greek and precociously savoring Shaw, Chesterton, Kipling, Bennett, and Wilde; in the Princeton undergraduate

(1912–1916) deep in French and Italian classics and holding forth to his friends on a hodgepodge of authors from Emerson, Zola, Tolstoy, Ibsen, Dickens, Macaulay, and Disraeli to Henry James, Edith Wharton, and Compton Mackenzie; in the enlisted soldier who read the wedding hymns of Catullus in the military camp at the Detroit fairgrounds, and Romain Rolland, Anatole France, Robert Browning, H. L. Mencken, and James Joyce during the last German offensives.

Back from the war, Wilson quickly found his place in the New York cultural scene. Young and old regarded him with an awe inspired, perhaps, one editor opined, "by his extraordinary fund of knowledge, his gift for writing poetry, his mastery of four languages." He seemed to have read everything. When he later dug up his early writing, prompted, he said, by "my scholarly instincts" and "literary vanity," he dismissed much of it as "sick-making puerilia"; but whatever its faults, it is generally dextrous and firmly knit and free of ostentation, pedantry, and slickness. In the two decades covered by *The Shores of Light*, Wilson was understandably reckoned the most erudite and readable of American critics, a literary force renowned for his lively intelligence and powers of analysis.

What distinguished him from the majority of his journalist competitors was the serious intent that tempered his lightheartedness and his readiness to welcome every expression of the new American idiom without jettisoning tradition. Matthew Josephson, one of many self-appointed spokesmen for the "Younger Generation" and the new modernism, charged him with embracing defunct forms of genteel Victorian culture. He was quite wrong. Wilson had no truck with the so-called "Uplift School" and joined the Menckenian assault against the "unexamined prejudices of a bigoted Puritan heritage." On the other hand, he parodied Josephson's rambunctious modernism in a dialogue reprinted here. A kind of acolyte of literature and

committed to its civilizing function, Wilson reminded the
celebrators of skyscrapers, subway racket, dadaism, and
advertising copy that even original artists built on the
achievements of their predecessors, and that the genteel
custodians were in many instances more disciplined and
better educated than their irreverent assailants.

Wilson's seriousness in no way inhibited his enjoyment
of new tendencies in the popular arts. His review of
Gilbert Seldes' work (pp. 156–173) and comparable essays
in *The Shores of Light* are tributes to the artistry of the
great clowns, magicians, and cartoonists, to the inspired
antics of burlesque and vaudeville performers, and to the
humor of Mr. Dooley, Ring Lardner, and H. L. Mencken.
They also demonstrate Wilson's discerning eye and extraordinary memory for the telling verbal detail and nu-
ances of voice and gesture. According to Seldes, he might
have become a master critic of the performing arts had he
chosen to follow that particular bent, but too many other
subjects compelled his attention, not only the poets, novelists, and critics he judged in his article, "The All-Star
Literary Vaudeville," but also political writers, historians,
philosophers, and scientists. The Index, bristling with the
names and titles associated with a dozen cultures, measures the extent and depth of his intellectual curiosity.

A gradual darkening—and a testier attitude toward national institutions—can be observed in Wilson's essays and
reviews after the execution of Sacco and Vanzetti in 1927.
Never reconciled to the commercial obsessions of the Cool-
idge years and increasingly sympathetic to the conviction
of his friend John Dos Passos "that there is something
lacking, something wrong in America," he then more out-
spokenly than ever before chided his fellow writers' "unwillingness or incapacity to come to terms with the world
they live in" and scorned their resort to social and religious
nostrums. No sudden conversion marked Wilson's left-
ward turn at the beginning of the thirties. Midway

through *The Shores of Light*, however, in "The Literary Consequences of the Crash," he offers a postmortem on the "mad hilarity and heartbreak" of the Jazz Age. Believers in perpetual prosperity and the infallibility of the "Big Business Man" had seen their dreams disintegrate, and Wilson recalls the savage satisfaction he took in the collapse of a rotten financial structure and its, to him, immoral architects.

Caught up in political and industrial events between 1930 and 1940 and searching for clues to the economic debacle in the writings of Karl Marx, he paid less attention to purely literary subjects than he had in the twenties. A good many of his articles, no matter what he was writing about, betray his social and economic preoccupations. He commented without much enthusiasm on the literary wars of the thirties and admonished both the left-wing skirmishers and their adversaries. His attitude toward the Soviet "experiment" changed from sympathetic interest to skepticism to violent dislike. One can sense his growing dismay as partisan ideological squabbles divided the Republic of Letters, souring his hope, once so ebulliently advanced, of an America at last "beginning to express itself in something like an idiom of her own." Throughout the Depression years, Wilson's humanistic values remained his real concern: he came to recognize that, at bottom, his loyalties were with the literary men of the twenties, not with the new class of "intellectuals" who had supplanted them.

ii

In 1943, Wilson glanced back to the times when he felt liberated and stimulated, and the United States appeared to be moving "out of its complacent provinciality on to the larger stage of the world." The twenties had already acquired a special charm for him despite their fancy dress atmosphere and "frantic self-advertisement." At least it was a good time for writers and writing. The "intellectuals" of the thirties, on the other hand, had produced "a new political culture but no distinctive artistic culture." Beguiled at first by the vision of a truly just society, and then disenchanted by the suffocation of art and thought in Stalin's Russia, they had finally yielded to the lures of the Luce publications or Hollywood (sacrificing their individuality in the process), or else sought refuge in the teaching profession. "The scholarship of Marxism," he observed, "in some cases shaded easily into the scholarship of the English Department; and the inquest on literary culture from the social-economic view was contracted to a simple ambition to get the whole thing under glass."

The Shores of Light is his testament to the days when literary journalism was a serious and tough profession. To maintain his standards and still survive as a freelance writer, the practitioner, as Wilson put it, had "to learn to load solid matter into notices of ephemeral happenings" and to smuggle into these random pieces ideas and points of view usually uncongenial to fashion-oriented editors. To do all this without being dull took skill and hard work. Wilson made it his practice to review books or wangle assignments on subjects of particular interest to him. He regarded his articles as "preliminary" or "tentative" exercises, later to be collected and revised for publication— that is to say, trimmed or expanded, with blunders corrected, and grouped to underscore a specific theme.

The Shores of Light opens with Wilson's tribute to his Princeton mentor, Christian Gauss, a cultivated and cosmopolitan humanist. It closes with an elegiac meditation on the poet Edna St. Vincent Millay. Both prologue and epilogue are dated 1952, and the two figures they commemorate set the boundaries of the book.

Gauss is presented as the ideal teacher and surrogate father, undogmatic, tolerant, encouraging yet demanding "scrupulous precision." He becomes Wilson's model for the scholar-artist, a man steeped in Mediterranean culture, a lover of languages, at home in the world and able to dip at will into his capacious memory to enforce a point with apt quotation or anecdote. Wilson's strong sense of the writer's civic obligations, his continuing interest in literary and historical personalities, his assumption "that the world was real and that we ourselves may find some sense in it and make ourselves happy in it" derive in part from the influences of his teacher and friend.

Thought and feeling are seldom kept apart in *The Shores of Light*, but insofar as they are, Gauss might be said to stand for the former and Edna Millay for the latter. The epilogue unconvincingly acclaims her greatness as a poet. In the context of the essay, however, she is plainly no "mere individual with a birthplace and a legal residence," but an embodiment of the Muse herself. She is also a "pseudonym" for the romantic spirit of the twenties that haunted Wilson and other members of his gin-drinking company, and a reminder of the days "when everything had seemed possible and they had been able to treat their genius as an unlimited checking account." While still alive, she had figured as a central character in his autobiographical novel, *I Thought of Daisy* (1929). In a poem Wilson wrote after her death, she shares "the fate of souls who have not died./Buried in sullen shadows underground—/That reach for ever toward the shores of light."

Wilson's literary chronicle artfully preserves the spontaneity and flavor of a time when he was most responsive to cultural reverberations. At once an objective report and a critique of what he heard and saw and read, it furnishes an invaluable overview of an era still imperfectly understood but entirely engrossing.

DANIEL AARON

THE SHORES OF LIGHT

PROLOGUE, 1952

Christian Gauss as a Teacher of Literature

WHEN Christian Gauss of Princeton died on November 1, 1951, I was asked by the Princeton *Alumni Weekly* to write something for a set of tributes that were to appear in the issue of December 7. I sent the editor, who wanted a column, only part of what I had written in response to this request, and even this was much cut before it was printed. I have now further elaborated my original memoir, and I am including it here to serve as a sort of prologue, for it indicates to some extent the point of view from which I started off in my criticism of the twenties.

I have been asked to write about Christian Gauss as an influence on my generation at Princeton. Since we knew him as a teacher of literature only—I was in the class of 1916, and he did not become dean of the college till 1925—I shall speak mainly of this side of his activity.

As a professor of French and Italian, then, one of the qualities that distinguished Gauss was the unusual fluidity of mind that he preserved through his whole career. A teacher like Irving Babbitt was a dogmatist who either imposed his dogma or provoked a strong opposition. Christian Gauss was a teacher of a different kind—the kind who starts trains of thought that he does not him-

3

self guide to conclusions but leaves in the hands of his students to be carried on by themselves. The student might develop, extend them, transpose them into different terms, build out of them constructions of his own. Gauss never imposed, he suggested; and his own ideas on any subject were always taking new turns: the light in which he saw it would be shifted, it would range itself in some new context. It bored him, in his course on French Romanticism, to teach the same texts year after year; and with the writers that he could not get away from, he would vary the works read. With the less indispensable ones, he would change the repertory altogether. If Alfred de Vigny, for example, had been featured in the course when you took it, you might come back a few years later and find that he had been pushed into the background by Stendhal. Christian would have been reading up Stendhal, and his interest in him would seem almost as fresh as if he had never read him before. He would have some new insights about him, and he would pass these on to you when you came to see him, as he was doing to his students in class. I know from my own experience how the lightly dropped seeds from his lectures could take root and unfold in another's mind; and, while occupied in writing this memoir, I have happened to find striking evidence of the persistence of this vital gift in the testimony of a student of Romance languages who sat under Gauss twenty years later, and who has told me that, in preparing his doctor's thesis, he had at first been exhilarated by an illusion of developing original ideas, only to find the whole thing in germ in his old notes on Gauss's lectures. But though his influence on his students was so penetrating, Gauss founded no school of teaching—not even, I suppose, an academic tradition—because, as one of his colleagues pointed out to me, he had no communicable body of doctrine and no pedagogical method that other teachers could learn to apply. If one went back to Princeton to see him, as I more or less regularly did, after one had got out of college, one's memory of his old preceptorials (relatively informal discussions with groups of five or six students) would seem prolonged, without interruptions, into one's more recent conversations, as if it had all been a long conversation that had extended, off and on, through the years: a commentary that, on Christian's part, never seemed to be trying to prove anything in any overwhelming way, a voyage of speculation that aimed rather to survey the world than to fix a convincing vision. In his role of the least didactic of sages, the most accessible of talkers, he seemed a part of that good eighteenth-century Princeton which has always managed to flourish between the pressures of a narrow Presbyterianism and a rich man's suburbanism. It is probable that Christian was at home in Princeton as he would not have been anywhere else. He was delightful in the days of his deanship, in the solid and compact and ample yellow-and-white Joseph Henry house, built in 1837, where there was always, during the weekends, a constant going and coming of visitors, who could pick up with him any topic, literary, historical or collegiate, and pursue it till someone else came and the thread was left suspended. Though by this time so important a local figure, he seemed always, also, international. He had been born of German parents in Michigan, and German had been his first language. In his youth he had spent a good deal of time in France. He had no foreign accent in English, and, so far as I was able to judge, spoke all his languages correctly and fluently; but French, Italian and English, at any rate, with a deliberate articulation, never running the words together, as if they were not native to him. One did not learn a bad accent from him, but one did not learn to speak the

Romance languages as they are spoken in their own countries. On the other hand, the very uniformity of his candid tone, his unhurried pace and his scrupulous precision, with his slightly drawling intonations, made a kind of neutral medium in which everything in the world seemed soluble. I have never known anyone like him in any academic community. He gave the impression of keeping in touch, without the slightest effort—he must have examined all the printed matter that came into the university library—with everything that was going on everywhere, as well as everything that had ever gone on. It used to amuse me sometimes to try him out on unlikely subjects. If one asked him a question about the Middle Ages, one absolutely got the impression that he had lived in Europe then and knew it at firsthand.

This extreme flexibility and enormous range were, of course, a feature of his lectures. He was able to explain and appreciate almost any kind of work of literature from almost any period. He would show you what the author was aiming at and the methods he had adopted to achieve his ends. He was wonderful at comparative literature, for his reading had covered the whole of the West, ancient, medieval and modern, and his memory was truly Macaulayan (an adjective sometimes assigned too cheaply). He seemed to be able to summon almost anything he wanted in prose or verse, as if he were taking down the book from the shelf. (He told me once that, in his younger days, he had set out to write something about Rabelais and had presently begun to grow suspicious of what he saw coming out. On looking up Taine's essay on Rabelais, he found that he had been transcribing whole paragraphs from it, his unconscious doing the work of translation.) He was brilliant at revealing the assumptions, social, aesthetic and moral, implicit in, say, a scene from a romantic play as contrasted with a scene from a Greek tragedy, or in the significance of a character in

Dante as distinguished from the significance of a character in Shakespeare. I remember his later quoting with approval A. N. Whitehead's statement, in *Science and the Modern World*, that, "when you are criticizing the philosophy of an epoch," you should "not chiefly direct your attention to those intellectual positions which its exponents feel it necessary explicitly to defend. There will be some fundamental assumptions which adherents of all the variant systems within the epoch unconsciously presuppose. Such assumptions appear so obvious that people do not know what they are assuming because no other way of putting things has ever occurred to them." Gauss had always had a special sense of this. But he was interested also in individuals and liked to bring out the traits of a literary personality. His commentary on a poem of Victor Hugo's—*Le Mendiant* from *Les Contemplations*—would run along something like this: "A poor man is passing in the frost and rain, and Victor Hugo asks him in. He opens the door *'d'une façon civile'* —he is always democratic, of course. *'Entrez, brave homme,'* he says, and he tells the man to warm himself and has a bowl of milk brought him—as anybody, of course, would do. He makes him take off his cloak— *'tout mangé des vers, et jadis bleu'*—and he hangs it on a nail, where the fire shines through its holes, so that it looks like a night illumined by stars.

> Et, pendant qu'il séchait ce haillon désolé
> D'où ruisselaient le pluie et l'eau des fondrières,
> Je songeais que cet homme était plein de prières.
> Et je regardais, sourd à ce que nous disions,
> Sa bure où je voyais des constellations.

"This sounds impressive, but what does it mean? Not a thing. We have not been told anything that would indicate that the old man is full of prayers. It is a gratuitous assumption on the part of Hugo. That the cloak with its holes reminded him of a heaven with constellations has no moral significance whatever. Yet with his mastery of verse and his rhetoric, Victor Hugo manages to carry it off. —I don't mean," he would add, "that he was insincere. Rather than live under Louis Napoleon, he went into voluntary exile—at considerable personal inconvenience—for almost twenty years. He lived up to his democratic principles, but he was always a bit theatrical, and he was not very profound."

I include such reminiscences of the classroom in the hope that they may be of interest in putting on record Gauss's methods as a teacher, for the work of a great teacher who is not, as Gauss was not, a great writer is almost as likely to be irrecoverable as the work of a great actor. Not that Christian was ever in the least histrionic, as some of the popular professors of the time were. On the contrary, for all the friendliness of one's relations with him outside class when one eventually got to know him, his tone was sober and quiet, his attitude detached and impersonal. This was partly due to shyness, no doubt; but the impression he made was formidable. He would come into the classroom without looking at us, and immediately begin to lecture, with his eyes dropped to his notes, presenting a mask that was almost Dantesque and levelling on us only occasionally the clear gaze that came through his eyeglasses. When he made us recite in Dante, he would sometimes pace to and fro between the desk and the window, with his hands behind his back, rarely consulting the text, which he apparently knew by heart. In the case of some appalling error, he would turn with a stare of ironic amazement and remonstrate in a tone of mock grief: "You thought that barretry was the same as banditry? O-o-oh, Mr. X, that's too-oo ba-a-ad!" This last exclamation, drawled out, was his only way of indicating disapproval. His voice was always low and even, except at those moments when he became aware that the class was falling asleep, when he would turn on another voice, loud, nasal, declamatory and pitilessly distinct, which would be likely to begin in the middle of a sentence for the sake of the shock-value, I think, and in order to dissociate this special effect from whatever he happened to be saying—which might be something no more blood-curdling than a statement that André Chénier had brought to the classical forms a nuance of romantic feeling. When this voice would be heard in the class next door—for it penetrated the partition like a fire-siren—it always made people laugh; but for the students in Gauss's own room, it seemed to saw right through the base of the spine and made them sit forward intently. When it had had this effect, it would cease. He was never sarcastic and never bullied; but the discipline he maintained was perfect. Any signs of disorder were silenced by one straight and stern look.

Nevertheless, though Christian's methods were nondramatic, he had a knack of fixing in one's mind key passages and key facts. His handling of Rousseau, for example, was most effective in building up the importance of a writer whom we might otherwise find boring. (In this case, he *has* left something that can be used by his successors in his volume of *Selections* from Rousseau, published by the Princeton University Press—though, as usual with Gauss's writing, the introduction and notes have little of the peculiar effectiveness of his lecture-room presentation.) He would start off by planting, as it were, in our vision of the panorama of history that critical moment of Rousseau's life which, since he did not include it in the *Confessions*, having already described it in the first of his letters to M. de Malesherbes, is likely to be overlooked or insufficiently emphasized (compare

Saintsbury's slurring-over of this incident and its consequences for Western thought, in his *Encyclopaedia
Britannica* article): the moment, almost as momentous as
that of Paul's conversion on the road to Damascus,
when Jean-Jacques, then thirty-seven, was walking from
Paris to Vincennes, where he was going to see Diderot in
prison, and happened to read the announcement that the
Academy of Dijon was offering a prize for the best essay
on the question, "Has the progress of the arts and sciences
contributed to corrupt or to purify society?" Such an
incident Gauss made memorable, invested with reverber-
ating significance, by a series of incisive strokes that involved no embroidery or dramatics. It was, in fact, as if
the glamor of legend, the grandeur of history, had evaporated and left him exposed to our passing gaze, the
dusty and sunstruck Jean-Jacques—the clockmaker's son
of Geneva, the ill-used apprentice, the thieving lackey,
the vagabond of the roads—sinking down under a tree
and dazzled by the revelation that all the shames and misfortunes of his life had been the fault of the society that
had bred him—that "man is naturally good and that it is
only through institutions that men have become wicked."
In the same way, he made us feel the pathos and the
psychological importance of the moment when the six-
teen-year-old apprentice, returning from a walk in the
country, found for the third time the gates of Geneva
locked against him, and decided that he would never go
back.

Christian admired the romantics and expounded them
with the liveliest appreciation; but the romantic ideal in
literature was not his own ideal. In spite of his imaginative gift for entering into other people's points of
view, he was devoted to a certain conception of art that
inevitably asserted itself and that had a tremendous influence on the students with literary interests who were

exposed to Gauss's teaching. Let me try to define this ideal. Christian had first known Europe at firsthand as a foreign correspondent in the Paris of the late nineties, and he had always kept a certain loyalty to the "aestheticism" of the end of the century. There was a legend that seemed almost incredible of a young Christian Gauss with long yellow hair—in our time he was almost completely bald—who had worn a green velvet jacket;* and he would surprise you from time to time by telling you of some conversation he had had with Oscar Wilde or describing some such bohemian character as Bibi-La-Purée. It was rumored—though I never dared ask him about this—that he had once set out to experiment one by one with all the drugs mentioned in Baudelaire's *Les Paradis Artificiels*. He rather admired Wilde, with whom he had talked in cafés, where the latter was sitting alone and running up high piles of saucers. He had given Christian copies of his books, inscribed; and Christian used to tell me, with evident respect, that Wilde in his last days had kept only three volumes: a copy of Walter Pater's *The Renaissance* that had been given him by Pater, Flaubert's *La Tentation de Saint Antoine* and Swinburne's *Atalanta in Calydon*. And it was always Gauss's great advantage over the school of Babbitt and More that he understood the artist's morality as something that expressed itself in different terms than the churchgoer's or the citizen's morality; the fidelity to a kind of truth that is rendered by the discipline of aesthetic form, as distinct from that of the professional moralist: the explicit communication of a "message." But there was nothing in his attitude of the truculent pose, the defiance of the bourgeoisie, that had been characteristic

* I learn from Mrs. Gauss, who has shown me a photograph, that the realities behind this legend were a head of blond bushy hair and a jacket which, though green, was not velvet.

of the fin de siècle and that that other professor of the Romance languages, Gauss's near-contemporary, Ezra Pound, was to sustain through his whole career. How fundamental to his point of view, how much a thing to be taken for granted, this attitude had become, was shown clearly in a conversation I had with him, on some occasion when I had come back after college, when, in reply to some antinomian attitude of mine, or one that he imputed to me, he said, "But you were saying just now that you would have to rewrite something before it could be published. That implies a moral obligation." And his sense of the world and the scope of art was, of course, something very much bigger than was common among the aesthetes and the symbolists.

Partly perhaps as a heritage from the age of Wilde but, more deeply, as a logical consequence of his continental origin and culture, he showed a pronounced though discreet parti pris against the literature of the Anglo-Saxon countries. In our time, he carried on a continual feud—partly humorous, yet basically serious —with the canons of the English department. I remember his telling me, with sly satisfaction, about a visiting French professor, who had asked, when it was explained to him that someone was an authority on Chaucer, *"Il est intelligent tout de même?"* Certain classical English writers he patronized—in some cases, rightly, I think. Robert Browning, in particular, he abominated. The author of *Pippa Passes* was one of the very few writers about whom I thought his opinions intemperate. "That Philistine beef-eating Englishman," he would bait his colleagues in English, "—what did he know about art? He writes lines like 'Irks care the crop-full bird? Frets doubt the maw-crammed beast?'" When I tried to find out once why Browning moved Christian to such special indignation, he told me, a little darkly, that he had greatly admired him in boyhood and had learned from him "a lot of bad doctrine." He said that the irregular love affairs in Browning were made to seem too jolly and simple, and insisted that the situation of the self-frustrated lovers of *The Statue and the Bust* had never been faced by Browning: If "the end in sight was a vice," the poet should not have wanted to have them get together; if he wanted them to get together, he ought not to have described it as a vice, but, on the other hand, he ought to have foreseen a mess. "He is one of the most immoral poets because he makes moral problems seem easy. He tells you that the good is sure to triumph." He would suggest to you an embarrassing picture of a Browning offensively hearty—"not robust," he would say slily, "but robustious"—bouncing and booming in Italy, while the shades of Leopardi and Dante looked on, as Boccaccio said of the latter, *"con isdegnoso occhio."* The kind of thing he especially hated was such a poem as the one, in *James Lee's Wife,* that begins, "O good gigantic smile o' the brown old earth." . . . Of Byron—though Byron's writing was certainly more careless than Browning's—he had a much better opinion, because, no doubt, of Byron's fondness for the Continent as well as his freer intelligence and his experience of the ills of the world. He accepted Byron's love affairs—he had nothing of the prig or the Puritan— because Byron knew what he was doing and was not misleading about it. As for Shakespeare, though Christian was, of course, very far from the point of view of Voltaire, there was always just a suggestion of something of the kind in the background. He knew Shakespeare well and quoted him often, but Shakespeare was not one of the authors whom Christian had lived in or on; and he always made us feel that that sort of thing could never come up to literature that was polished and carefully planned and that knew how to make its points and the meaning of the points it was making. He was certainly unfair to Shakespeare in insisting that the Shakespearean characters all talk the same language, whereas Dante's all express themselves differently. For Christian, the great poet was Dante, and he gradually convinced you of this in his remarkable Dante course. He made us see the objectivity of Dante and the significance of his every stroke, so that even the geographical references have a moral and emotional force (the Po that finds peace with its tributaries in the Paolo and Francesca episode, the mountain in the Ugolino canto that prevents the Pisans from seeing their neighbors of Lucca); the vividness of the scenes and the characters (he liked to point out how Farinata's arrogant poise was thrown into dramatic relief by the passionate interruption of Cavalcanti); and the tremendous intellectual power by which all sorts of men and women exhibiting all sorts of passions have been organized in an orderly vision that implies, also, a reasoned morality. No Englishman, he made us feel, could ever have achieved this; it would never have occurred to Shakespeare. Nor could any English novelist have even attempted what Gustave Flaubert had achieved—a personal conception of the world, put together, without a visible seam, from apparently impersonal descriptions, in which, as in Dante, not a stroke was wasted. He admired the Russians, also, for their sober art of implication. I remember his calling our attention to one of the church scenes in Tolstoy's *Resurrection*, in which, as he pointed out, Tolstoy made no overt comment, yet caused you to loathe the whole thing by describing the ceremony step by step. This non-English, this classical and Latin ideal, became indissolubly associated in our minds with the summits of literature. We got from Gauss a good many things, but the most important things we

CHRISTIAN GAUSS　　　　　　　　　　15

got were probably Flaubert and Dante. John Peale Bishop, who came to Princeton intoxicated with Swinburne and Shelley, was concentrating, by the time he graduated, on hard images and pregnant phrases. Ezra Pound and the imagists, to be sure, had a good deal to do with this, but Gauss's courses were important, too, and such an early poem of Bishop's as *Losses*, which contrasts Verlaine with Dante, was directly inspired by them. Less directly, perhaps, but no less certainly, the development of F. Scott Fitzgerald from *This Side of Paradise* to *The Great Gatsby*, from a loose and subjective conception of the novel to an organized impersonal one, was also due to Christian's influence. He made us all want to write something in which every word, every cadence, every detail, should perform a definite function in producing an intense effect.

Gauss's special understanding of the techniques of art was combined, as is not always the case, with a highly developed sense of history, as well as a sense of morality (he admirably prepared us for Joyce and Proust). If he played down—as I shall show in a moment—the Thomist side of Dante to make us see him as a great artist, he brought out in Flaubert the moralist and the bitter critic of history. And so much, at that period, was all his thought pervaded by the *Divine Comedy* that even his own version of history had at moments a Dantesque touch. It would not have been difficult, for example, to transpose such a presentation as the one of Rousseau that I have mentioned above into the sharp concise self-description of a character in the *Divina Commedia*: "I am the clockmaker's son of Geneva who said that man has made man perverse. When for the third time the cruel captain closed the gates, I made the sky my roof, and found in Annecy the love Geneva had denied" . . .

With this sense of history of Christian's was involved another strain in his nature that had nothing to do with the aestheticism of the nineties and yet that lived in his mind with it quite comfortably. His father, who came from Baden—he was a relative of the physicist Karl Friedrich Gauss—had taken part in the unsuccessful German revolution of 1848 and come to the United States with the emigration that followed it. The spirit of '48 was still alive in Christian, and at the time of the first World War an hereditary hatred of the Prussians roused him to a passionate championship of the anti-German cause even before the United States declared war. Later on, when Prohibition was imposed on the nation, the elder Gauss, as Christian told me, was so much infuriated by what he regarded as an interference nothing short of Prussian with the rights of a free people that he could not talk calmly about it, and, even when dean of the college and obliged to uphold the law, the American-born Christian continued in public to advocate its repeal, which required a certain courage in Presbyterian Princeton. It was this old-fashioned devotion to liberty that led him to admire Hugo for his refusal to live under the Second Empire, and Byron for his willingness to fight for Italian and Greek liberation. "Everywhere he goes in Europe," Christian would say of Byron, "it is the places, such as the prison of Chillon, where men have been oppressed, that arouse him." When he lectured on Anatole France, he would point out the stimulating contrast between the early France of *Sylvestre Bonnard*, who always wrote, as he said, like a kindly and bookish old man, and the France who defended Dreyfus, made a tour of the provinces to speak for him and remained for the rest of his life a social satirist and a radical publicist. In the years when I was first at Princeton, Gauss called himself, I believe, a socialist; and during the years of depression in the thirties, he gravitated again toward the Left and, in *A Primer for Tomorrow* (1934), he made some serious attempt to criticize the financial-industrial system. In an inscription in the copy he sent me, he said that my stimulation had counted for something in his writing the book. But I was never able to persuade him to read Marx and Engels at firsthand: he read Werner Sombart instead; and I noted this, like the similar reluctance of Maynard Keynes to look into Marx, as a curious confirmation of the theory of the Marxists that the "bourgeois intellectuals" instinctively shy away from Marxist thought to the extent of even refusing to find out what it really is. Yet Christian had read Spengler with excitement—it was from him that I first heard of *The Decline of the West*—immediately after the war; and he never, in these later years, hesitated, in conversation, to indulge the boldest speculations as to the destiny of contemporary society.

He was a member of the National Committee of the American Civil Liberties Union, and he made a point, after the second war, of speaking to Negro audiences in the South. On my last visit to Princeton when I saw him, in the spring of 1951, he talked to me at length about his adventures in the color-discrimination states—how the representatives of some Negro organization under whose auspices he had been speaking had been unable to come to see him in his white hotel, and how, as he told me with pride, he had succeeded, for the first time in the history of Richmond, in assembling—in a white church, to which, however, he found the Negroes were only admitted on condition of their sitting in the back pews—a mixed black and white audience. As he grew older, he became more internationalist. He foresaw, and he often insisted, at the end of the first World War, that nothing but trouble could come of creating more small European states, and, at the end of the second war, he was bitterly opposed to what he regarded as the development of American nationalism. He complained much, in this connection, of the intensive cultivation, in the colleges, of American literature, which had been carried on since sometime in the middle thirties with a zeal that he thought more and more menacing to sound international values. I did not, on the whole, agree with him in disapproving of the growth of American studies; but I could see that, with his relative indifference to English literature, he must have conceived, at the end of the century, an extremely low opinion of American. He took no interest in Henry James and not very much in Walt Whitman. He told me once that Henry Ford had said, "Cut your own wood and it will warm you twice," not knowing that Ford had been quoting Thoreau. For Christian, the level of American writing was more or less represented by William Dean Howells, the presiding spirit of the years of his youth, for whom he felt hardly the barest respect. It was absolutely incredible to him— and in this I did agree with him—that *The Rise of Silas Lapham* should ever have been thought an important novel. "It wasn't much of a rise," he would say. Yet the "renaissance" of the twenties—unlike Paul Elmer More —he followed with sympathetic, if critical, interest.

Christian Gauss was a complex personality as well as a subtle mind, and one finds it in some ways difficult to sort out one's impressions of him. I want to try to deal now with the moral qualities which, combined with his unusual intellectual powers, gave him something of the stature of greatness. In some sense, he was a moral teacher as well as a literary one; but his teaching, in the same way as his criticism, was conveyed by throwing out suggestions and dropping incidental comments. If this connection, I want to quote here the tribute of Mr. Harold R. Medina, the distinguished federal judge, from the symposium in the *Alumni Weekly*. It expresses a good deal better than anything I was able to write myself, when I drafted this memoir for the first time, the penetrating quality of Gauss's power, and it interesting to me in describing an experience that closely parallels my own on the part of an alumnus of an earlier class—1909—who was to work in a different field yet who had known Christian Gauss, as I had, not as dean of the college, but as teacher of literature.

"Of all the men whom I have met," Mr. Medina writes, "only four have significantly influenced my life. Dean Gauss was the second of these; the first, my father. From freshman year on I had many courses and precepts with Dean Gauss and during my senior year I was with him almost daily. He attracted me as he did everyone else; and I sensed that he had something to impart which was of infinitely greater importance than the mere content of the courses in French Literature. It was many years after I left Princeton before I realized that it was he who first taught me how to think. How strange it is that so many people have the notion that they are thinking when they are merely repeating the thoughts of others. He dealt in ideas without seeming to do so; he led and guided with so gentle a touch that one began to think almost despite oneself. The process once started, he continued in such fashion as to instil into my very soul the determination to be a seeker after truth, the elusive, perhaps never to be attained, complete and utter truth, no matter where it led or whom it hurt. How he did it I shall never know; but that it was he I have not the slightest doubt. His own intellectual integrity was a constant example for me to follow. And to this precious element he added another. He gave me the vision of language and literature as something representing the continuous and never-ending flow of man's struggle to think the thoughts which, when put into action, constitute in the aggregate the advance of civilization. Whatever I may be today or may ever hope to be is largely the result of the germination of the seeds he planted. The phenomena of cause and effect are not to be denied. With Dean Gauss there were so many hundreds of persons, like myself, whom he influenced and whose innate talents he developed that the ripples he started in motion were multiplied again and again. In critical times I always wondered whether he approved or would approve of things I said and did. And this went on for over forty years."

"To instil into my very soul the determination to be a seeker after truth . . . no matter where it led or whom it hurt." I remember my own thrilled response when, in taking us through the seventeenth canto of the *Paradiso*, Christian read without special emphasis yet in a way that brought out their conviction some lines that remained from that moment engraved, as they say, on my mind:

> E s'io al vero son timido amico,
>> Temo di perder viver tra coloro
>> Che questo tempo chiameranno antico.

—"If to the truth I prove a timid friend, I fear to lose my life [to fail of survival] among those who will call this time ancient." The truth about which Dante is speaking is his opinion of certain powerful persons, who will, as he has just been forewarned in Heaven, retaliate by sending him into exile—a truth which, as Heaven approves, he will not be deterred from uttering. Another moment in the classroom comes back to me from one of Christian's preceptorials. He had put up to us the issue created by the self-assertive type of romantic, who followed his own impulse in defiance of conventional morality and with indifference to social consequences; and he called upon me to supply him with an instance of moral conflict between social or personal duty and the duty of self-realization. I gave him the case of a problem with which I had had lately to deal as editor of the *Nassau Lit*, when I had not been able to bring myself to tell a friend who had set his heart upon contributing that the manuscripts he brought me were hopeless. "That's not an impulse," said Christian, "to do a humane thing: it's a temptation to do a weak thing." I was struck also by what seemed to me the unusual line that he took one day in class when one of his students complained that he hadn't been able to find out the meaning of a word. "What did you call it?" asked Christian. "Didn't you call it something?" The boy confessed that he hadn't. "That's bad intellectual form," said Christian. "Like going out in the morning with your face unwashed. In reading a foreign language, you must never leave a gap or a blur. If you can't find out what something means, make the best supposition you can. If it's wrong, the chances are that the context will show it in a moment or that you'll see, when the word occurs again, that it couldn't have meant that." This made such an impression on me that—just as Mr. Medina says he has been asking himself all his life whether Christian would approve of his actions—I still make an effort to live up to it.

I love to remember, too, how Christian began one of his lectures as follows: "There are several fundamental philosophies that one can bring to one's life in the world—or rather, there are several ways of taking life. One of these ways of taking the world is not to have any

philosophy at all—that is the way that most people take
it. Another is to regard the world as unreal and God as
the only reality; Buddhism is an example of this. Another
may be summed up in the words *Sic transit gloria mundi*
—that is the point of view you find in Shakespeare." He
then went on to an explanation of the eighteenth-century
philosophy which assumed that the world was real
and that we ourselves may find some sense in it and
make ourselves happy in it. On another occasion, in
preceptorial, Christian asked me, "Where do you think
our ideals come from—justice, righteousness, beauty and
so on?" I replied, "Out of the imaginations of men"; and
he surprised me by answering, "That is correct." This
made an impression on me, because he usually confined
himself to a purely Socratic questioning, in which he did
not often allow himself to express his own opinions. I
felt that I had caught him off guard: what he had evidently been expecting to elicit was either Platonic idealism or Christian revelation.

It was only outside class and at secondhand that I
learned that he said of himself at this time that his only
religion was Dante; yet it could not escape us in the long
run that the Dante we were studying was a secular
Dante—or rather, perhaps, a Dante of the Reformation—
the validity of whose art and morality did not in the least
depend on one's acceptance or non-acceptance of the
faith of the Catholic Church. Christian would remind
us from time to time of Dante's statement, in his letter
to Can Grande, that his poem, though it purported to
describe a journey to the other world, really dealt with
men's life in this, and we were shown that the conditions
of the souls in Hell, Purgatory and Heaven were metaphors for our moral situation here. The principle of salvation that we learned from Dante was not the Catholic
surrender to Jesus—who plays in the *Divine Comedy* so

significantly small a role—but the vigilant cultivation of *"il ben del intelletto."*

Some of those who had known Christian Gauss in his great days as a teacher of literature were sorry, after the war, to see him becoming involved in the administrative side of the University. I remember his saying to me one day, in the early stages of this, "I've just sent off a lot of letters, and I said to myself as I mailed them, 'There are seventeen letters to people who don't interest me in the least.'" But the job of the Dean's office did interest him— though it seemed to us that it did not take a Gauss to rule on remiss or refractory students. He had never liked repeating routine, and I suppose that his department was coming to bore him. He made, by all accounts, a remarkable dean—for his card-catalogue memory kept all names and faces on file even for decades after the students had left, and the sensitive feeling for character that had been hidden behind his classroom mask must have equipped him with a special tact in dealing with the difficult cases. His genius for moral values had also a new field now in which it could exercise itself in an immediate and practical way, and the responsibilities of his office—especially in the years just after the war, when students were committing suicide and getting into all sorts of messes— sometimes put upon him an obvious strain. Looking back since his death, it has seemed to me that the Gauss who was dean of Princeton must have differed almost as much from the Gauss with whom I read French and Italian as this austere teacher had done from the young correspondent in Paris, who had paid for Oscar Wilde's drinks. The Gauss I had known in my student days, with his pale cheeks and shuttered gaze, his old raincoat and soft flat hat, and a shabby mongrel dog named Baudelaire which had been left with him by the Jesse Lynch Wil-

liamses and which sometimes accompanied him into
class—the Gauss who would pass one on the campus
without speaking, unless you attracted his attention, in
an abstraction like that of Dante in Hell and who seemed
to meet the academic world with a slightly constrained
self-consciousness at not having much in common with
it—this figure warmed up and filled out, became recognizably Princetonian in his neckties and shirts and a
touch of that tone that combines a country-club self-
assurance with a boyish country-town homeliness. He
now met the college world, unscreened, with his humorous and lucid green eyes. He wore golf stockings and
even played golf. He interested himself in the football
team and made speeches at alumni banquets. Though
I know that his influence as dean was exerted in favor of
scholarships, higher admission requirements and the sal-
vaging of the Humanities—I cannot do justice here to
this whole important phase of his career—the only
moments of our long friendship when I was ever at all
out of sympathy with him occurred during these years
of officialdom; for I felt that he had picked up a little the
conventional local prejudices when I would find him protesting against the advent in Princeton of the Institute
for Advanced Study or, on one occasion, censoring the
Lit for publishing a "blasphemous" story. One was always
impressed, however, by the way in which he seemed to
have absorbed the whole business of the University.

We used to hope that he would eventually be president; but, with the domination of business in the boards
of trustees of the larger American colleges, it was almost
as improbable that Christian would be asked to be president of Princeton as it would have been that Santayana
should be asked to be president of Harvard. Not, of
course, that it would ever have occurred to anyone to
propose such a post for Santayana, but it was somehow

characteristic of Christian's career that the idea should have entered the minds of his friends and that nothing should ever have come of it. There appeared in the whole line of Christian's life a certain diversion of purpose, an unpredictable ambiguity of aim, that corresponded to the fluid indeterminate element in his teaching and conversation. He had originally been a newspaper correspondent and a writer of reviews for the literary journals, who hoped to become a poet. He was later a college professor who had developed into a brilliant critic—by far the best, so far as I know, in our academic world of that period— and who still looked forward to writing books; I once found him, in one of his rare moments of leisure, beginning an historical novel. Then, as dean, in the late twenties and thirties, he came to occupy a position of intercollegiate distinction rather incongruous with that usually prosaic office. Was he a "power" in American education? I do not believe he was. That kind of role is possible only for a theorist like John Dewey or an administrator like Charles W. Eliot. Though he was offered the presidency of another college, he continued at Princeton as dean and simply awaited the age of retirement. When that came, he seemed at first depressed, but later readjusted himself. I enjoyed him in these post-official years. He was no longer overworked and he no longer had to worry about the alumni. He returned to literature and started an autobiography, with which, however, he said he was unsatisfied. In October of 1951, he had been writing an introduction for a new edition of Machiavelli's *Prince,* and he was pleased with it when he had finished. He took Mrs. Gauss for a drive in the car, and they talked about a trip to Florida. He had seemed in good spirits and health, though he had complained the Saturday before, after going to the Cornell game, where he had climbed to one of the top tiers of seats, that he was feeling the effects of age—he was now seventy-three. The day after finishing his introduction, he took the manuscript to his publisher in New York and attended there a memorial service for the Austrian novelist Hermann Broch, whom he had known when the latter lived in Princeton. While waiting outside the gates for the train to take him back to Princeton, with the evening paper in his pocket, his heart failed and he suddenly fell dead.

One had always still expected something further from Christian, had hoped that his character and talents would arrive at some final fruition. But—what seems to one still incredible—one's long conversation with him was simply forever suspended. And one sees now that the career was complete, the achievement is all there. He has left no solid body of writing; he did not remake Princeton (as Woodrow Wilson in some sense was able to do); he was not really a public man. He was a spiritual and intellectual force—one does not know how else to put it— of a kind that it may be possible for a man to do any of those other things without in the least becoming. His great work in his generation was unorganized and unobtrusive; and *Who's Who* will tell you nothing about it; but his influence was vital for those who felt it.

> Chè in la mente m'è fitta, ed or m'accora,
>   La cara e buona imagine paterna
>   Di voi, quando nel mondo ad ora ad ora
> M'insegnavate come l'uom s'eterna. . . .

F. SCOTT FITZGERALD

IT HAS BEEN SAID by a celebrated person* that to meet F. Scott Fitzgerald is to think of a stupid old woman with whom someone has left a diamond; she is extremely proud of the diamond and shows it to everyone who comes by, and everyone is surprised that such an ignorant old woman should possess so valuable a jewel; for in nothing does she appear so inept as in the remarks she makes about the diamond.

The person who invented this simile did not know Fitzgerald very well and can only have seen him, I think, in his more diffident or uninspired moods. The reader must not suppose that there is any literal truth in the image. Scott Fitzgerald is, in fact, no old woman, but a very good-looking young man, nor is he in the least stupid, but, on the contrary, exhilaratingly clever. Yet there *is* a symbolic truth in the description quoted above: it is true that Fitzgerald has been left with a jewel which he doesn't know quite what to do with. For he has been given imagination without intellectual control of it; he has been given the desire for beauty without an aesthetic ideal; and he has been given a gift for expression without very many ideas to express.

Consider, for example, the novel—*This Side of Para-*

* This was Edna St. Vincent Millay, who met Scott Fitzgerald in Paris in the spring of 1921.

27

dise—with which he founded his reputation. It has almost every fault and deficiency that a novel can possibly have. It is not only highly imitative but it imitates an inferior model. Fitzgerald, when he wrote the book, was drunk with Compton Mackenzie, and it sounds like an American attempt to rewrite *Sinister Street*. Now, Mackenzie, in spite of his gift for picturesque and comic invention and the capacity for pretty writing that he says he learned from Keats, lacks both the intellectual force and the emotional imagination to give body and outline to the material which he secretes in such enormous abundance. With the seeds he took from Keats's garden, one of the best-arranged gardens in England, he exfloreated so profusely that he blotted out the path of his own. Michael Fane, the hero of *Sinister Street*, was swamped in the forest of description; he was smothered by creepers and columbine. From the time he went up to Oxford, his personality began to grow dimmer, and, when he last turned up (in Belgrade) he seemed quite to have lost his identity. As a consequence, Amory Blaine, the hero of *This Side of Paradise*, had a very poor chance of coherence: Fitzgerald did endow him, to be sure, with a certain emotional life which the phantom Michael Fane lacks; but he was quite as much a wavering quantity in a phantasmagoria of incident that had no dominating intention to endow it with unity and force. In short, one of the chief weaknesses of *This Side of Paradise* is that it is really not *about* anything: its intellectual and moral content amounts to little more than a gesture—a gesture of indefinite revolt. The story itself, furthermore, is very immaturely imagined: it is always just verging on the ludicrous. And, finally, *This Side of Paradise* is one of the most illiterate books of any merit ever published (a fault which the publisher's proofreader seems to have made no effort to remedy). Not only is it ornamented with bogus ideas and faked literary references, but it is full of literary words tossed about with the most reckless inaccuracy.

I have said that *This Side of Paradise* commits almost every sin that a novel can possibly commit: but it does not commit the unpardonable sin: it does not fail to live. The whole preposterous farrago is animated with life. It is rather a fluttering and mercurial life: its emotions do not move you profoundly; its drama does not make you hold your breath; but its gaiety and color and movement did make it come as something exciting after the realistic heaviness and dinginess of so much serious American fiction. If one recalls the sort of flavorless fodder of which Ernest Poole's *The Harbor* was an example, one can understand the wild enthusiasm with which *This Side of Paradise* was hailed. The novel was also well-written— well-written in spite of its illiteracies. It is true, as I have said above, that Fitzgerald mishandles words; his works are full of malapropisms of the most disconcerting kind. You will find: "Whatever your flare [sic] proves to be— religion, architecture, literature"; "the Juvenalia of my collected editions"; "There were nice things in it [the room] . . . offsprings of a vicarious [vagarious] impatient taste"; "a mind like his, lucrative in intelligence, intuition and lightning decision"; etc., etc. It reminds one rather of:

> Agib, who could readily, at sight,
> Strum a march upon the loud Theodolite.
>   He would diligently play
>   On the Zoetrope all day,
> And blow the gay Pantechnicon all night.

It is true that Scott Fitzgerald plays the language entirely by ear. But his instrument, for all that, is no mean one.

He has an instinct for graceful and vivid prose that some of his more pretentious fellows might envy.

In regard to the man himself, there are perhaps two things worth knowing, for the influence they have had on his work. In the first place, he comes from the Middle West—from St. Paul, Minnesota. Fitzgerald is as much of the Middle West of large cities and country clubs as Sinclair Lewis is of the Middle West of the prairies and little towns. What we find in him is much what we find in the more prosperous strata of these cities: sensitivity and eagerness for life without a sound base of culture and taste; a structure of millionaire residences, brilliant expensive hotels and exhilarating social activities built not on the eighteenth century but simply on the flat Western land. And it seems to me rather a pity that he has not written more of the West: it is perhaps the only milieu that he thoroughly understands. When Fitzgerald approaches the East, he brings to it the standards of the wealthy West—the preoccupation with display, the appetite for visible magnificence and audible jamboree, the vigorous social atmosphere of amiable flappers and youths comparatively untainted as yet by the snobbery of the East. In *The Beautiful and Damned*, for example, we feel that he is moving in a vacuum; the characters have no real connection with the background to which they have been assigned; they are not part of the organism of New York as the characters, in, say, the short story *Bernice Bobs Her Hair* are a part of the organism of St. Paul. Surely F. Scott Fitzgerald should some day do for Summit Avenue what Lewis has done for Main Street.

But you are not to suppose from all this that the author of *This Side of Paradise* is merely a typical well-to-do Middle Westerner, with correct clothes and clear skin, who has been sent to the East for college. The second thing one should know about him is that Fitzgerald is partly Irish and that he brings both to life and to fiction certain qualities that are not Anglo-Saxon. For, like the Irish, Fitzgerald is romantic, but also cynical about romance; he is bitter as well as ecstatic; astringent as well as lyrical. He casts himself in the role of playboy, yet at the playboy he incessantly mocks. He is vain, a little malicious, of quick intelligence and wit, and has an Irish gift for turning language into something iridescent and surprising. He often reminds one, in fact, of the description that a great Irishman, Bernard Shaw, has written of the Irish: "An Irishman's imagination never lets him alone, never convinces him, never satisfies him; but it makes him that he can't face reality nor deal with it nor handle it nor conquer it: he can only sneer at them that do . . . and imagination's such a torture that you can't bear it without whisky. . . . And all the while there goes on a horrible, senseless, mischievous laughter."

For the rest, F. Scott Fitzgerald is a rather childlike fellow, very much wrapped up in his dream of himself and his projection of it on paper. For a person of his mental agility, he is extraordinarily little occupied with the general affairs of the world: like a woman, he is not much given to abstract or impersonal thought. Conversations about politics or general ideas have a way of snapping back to Fitzgerald. But this seldom becomes annoying; he is never pretentious or boring. He is quite devoid of affectation and takes the curse off his relentless egoism by his readiness to laugh at himself and his boyish uncertainty of his talent. And he exhibits, in his personality as well as in his writings, a quality rare today among even the youngest American writers: he is almost the only one among them who is capable of lighthearted high spirits. Where a satirist like Sinclair Lewis would stew "the Problem of Salesmanship" in acrid rancorous fumes, Fitzgerald, in *The Beautiful and Damned*, has made of it hilarious farce. His characters—and he—are actors in an elfin harlequinade; they are as nimble, as gay and as lovely—and as hardhearted—as fairies: Columbine elopes with Harlequin on a rope ladder dropped from the Ritz and both go morris-dancing amuck on a case of bootleg liquor; Pantaloon is pinked with an epigram that withers him up like a leaf; the Policeman is tripped by Harlequin and falls into the Pulitzer Fountain. Just before the curtain falls, Harlequin puts on false whiskers and pretends to be Bernard Shaw; he gives reporters an elaborate interview on politics, religion and history; a hundred thousand readers see it and are more or less impressed; Columbine nearly dies laughing; Harlequin sends out for a case of gin.

Let me quote a characteristic incident in connection with *The Beautiful and Damned*. Since writing *This Side of Paradise*—on the inspiration of Wells and Mackenzie—Fitzgerald has become acquainted with a different school of fiction: the ironical-pessimistic. In college, he had supposed that the thing to do was to write biographical novels with a burst of ideas toward the close; since his advent in the literary world, he has discovered that another genre has recently come into favor: the kind which makes much of the tragedy and what Mencken has called "the meaninglessness of life." Fitzgerald had imagined, hitherto, that the thing to do in a novel was to bring out a meaning in life; but he now set bravely about it to contrive a shattering tragedy that should be, also, a hundred-percent meaningless. As a result of this determination, the first version of *The Beautiful and Damned* culminated in an orgy of horror for which the reader was imperfectly prepared. Fitzgerald destroyed his characters with a succession of catastrophes so arbitrary that, beside them, the perversities of Hardy seemed the working of natural laws. The heroine was to lose her beauty at a prematurely early age, and her character was to go to pieces with it; Richard Carmel, a writer of promise, was to lose his artistic ideals and prostitute himself to the popular taste; and the wealthy Anthony Patch was not only to lose his money but, finding himself unable to make a living, abjectly to succumb to drink and eventually to go insane. But the bitterest moment of the story was to come at the very end, when Anthony was to be wandering the streets of New York in an attempt to borrow some money. After several humiliating failures, he finally approaches an old friend whom he sees with an elegant lady just getting into a cab. This is the brilliant Maury Noble, a cynic, an intellectual and a man of genuine parts. Maury cuts Anthony dead and drives away in the taxi. "But," the author explains, "he really had not seen Anthony. For Maury had indulged his appetite for alcoholic beverage once too often: he was now stone-blind!" But the point of my story is this: though Fitzgerald had been perfectly serious in writing this bathetic passage, he did not hesitate, when he heard people laugh at it, to laugh about it himself, and with as much surprise and delight as if he had just come across it in Max Beerbohm. He at once improvised a burlesque: "It seemed to Anthony that Maury's eyes had a fixed glassy stare; his legs moved stiffly as he walked and when he spoke his voice was lifeless. When Anthony came nearer, he saw that Maury was dead."

To conclude, it would be quite unfair to subject Scott Fitzgerald, who is still in his twenties and has presumably most of his work before him, to a rigorous overhauling. His restless imagination may yet produce something durable. For the present, however, this imagination is certainly not seen to the best advantage: it suffers badly from lack of discipline and poverty of aesthetic ideas. Fitzgerald is a dazzling extemporizer, but his stories have a way of petering out: he seems never to have planned them completely or to have thought out his themes from the beginning. This is true even of some of his most suc- cessful fantasies, such as *The Diamond as Big as the Ritz* or his comedy, *The Vegetable*. On the other hand, *The Beautiful and Damned*, imperfect though it is, marks an advance over *This Side of Paradise*: the style is more nearly mature and the subject more solidly unified, and there are scenes that are more convincing than any in his previous fiction.

But, in any case, even the work that Fitzgerald has done up to date has a certain moral importance. In his very expression of the anarchy by which he finds himself bewildered, of his revolt which cannot fix on an object, he is typical of the war generation—the generation so memorably described on the last page of *This Side of Paradise* as "grown up to find all gods dead, all wars fought, all faiths in men shaken." There is a moral in *The Beautiful and Damned* that the author did not per- haps intend to point. The hero and the heroine of this giddy book are creatures without method or purpose: they give themselves up to wild debaucheries and do not, from beginning to end, perform a single serious act; yet somehow you get the impression that, in spite of their fantastic behavior, Anthony and Gloria Patch are the most rational people in the book. Wherever they come in contact with institutions, with the serious life of their time, these are made to appear ridiculous, they are sub- jects for scorn or mirth. We see the army, finance and business successively and casually exposed as completely without point or dignity. The inference we are led to draw is that, in such a civilization as this, the sanest and most honorable course is to escape from organized society and live for the excitement of the moment. It cannot be merely a special reaction to a personal situation which gives rise to the paradoxes of such a book. It may be that we cannot demand too high a degree of moral balance from young men, however able or brilliant, who write books in the year 1921: we must remember that they have had to grow up in, that they have had to derive their chief stimulus from the wars, the society and the commerce of the Age of Confusion itself.

March, 1922

MR. E. A. ROBINSON'S MOONLIGHT

The Poetry of Edwin Arlington Robinson, by Mr. Lloyd Morris, "was written to commemorate an award" and "attempts to express the appreciative attitude of the Authors' Club toward Mr. Robinson's work." It is, therefore, rather like a speech at a birthday dinner: except for an interesting and valuable chapter on Robinson's philosophic sources, it has little importance as criticism, and one should not perhaps expect too much of it. Yet one cannot but boggle at the wholesale way in which Mr. Morris has swallowed his subject. There is no word of the poet's limitations; no candid effort to gauge his stature. To read Mr. Morris's monograph, you would think that all Robinson's poems had achieved an equally consummate success.

That this is very far from the case is indicated all too clearly by *Roman Bartholow*, Mr. Robinson's new long poem. This is one of the most arid products of a mind which has always run much into the sands. I will admit, à la rigueur, that the novel in verse is a practicable form—I suppose that *The Ring and the Book* has still some claims to distinction. And I will grant that Mr. Robinson's shadowy world has an authentic relation to the real one: with the examples of Hawthorne and Henry James, we cannot refuse credence to shadows. It seems to be characteristic of the genius of the New England writers that their shrewdness is combined with shyness—that they are occupied with casuistry rather than with action and prefer ghosts to carnal men. To appreciate the fiction of New England, it is necessary to accept this world of phantoms. But what I cannot forgive Robinson the poet is the absence in *Roman Bartholow* of poetry. Surely a poem should be beautiful as well as interesting: it is beauty which makes it a poem. But *Roman Bartholow*, though it sometimes interests, almost never rises to beauty.

Yet Edwin Arlington Robinson began as a real poet—and a poet of a very rare sort. He was the last, and probably the greatest, of the line of the New England poets. To the countryside and the coast of Longfellow, Lowell and Whittier, the lone farm houses and sea-scoured towns, the thin air of the northern hills and the blackness of the northern nights, he brought a more sophisticated point of view and a far greater artistic seriousness. Luke Havergal and Aaron Stark are even better than Floyd Ireson. And the moral ideas of *The Man Against the Sky* are a marked advance on *The Psalm of Life*.

But Robinson, even in youth, was a poet of regrets and failures. He was preoccupied with New England in decay. In the moonlight of an eternal autumn, he sat brooding on the poor ghosts of men—but in sadness rather than grief, for time has calmed that passion like the others. Through a long contemplation of life, he has learned to what end are doomed our loves and our worldly ambitions. One can only fix one's eye on "the gleam," which drifts faintly on the weedy dunes—pale green like an *ignis fatuus*—and which must surely be the most spectral and unluminous beacon that has ever kept a poet from despairing. We can hardly be warmed by this gleam, but the landscape itself may enchant us. When the red western gates have been locked, the moonlight strips the world to white bones, and among them dim forms of the dead move faintly in unfinished gestures.

Mr. Robinson began with the autumn, and he has

never had his rightful spring. He was old in spirit from the very first; and now that he is old in years, not merely are his branches bare: they are blurred by the moon's waning. As he told us in his poems of the nineties, he arrived on the poetic scene to find Amaryllis "grown old" and the flutes of Arcady "broken"; and though he has written of their ruin with poignance, he has not brought them back to their prime. He himself has felt the pinch of sterility. Even his poignance has lately been failing. I do not say that his later long poems—*Avenel Gray* and *Avon's Harvest*—have no fine lines or moving moments; but I cannot, like Mr. Morris, accept the Arthurian series as Robinson's crowning glories. Except for an occasional passage, they seem to me among the flattest of latter-day blank-verse deserts. The earlier blank-verse idylls that dealt with New England subjects had far more flavor and life. And when it comes to *Roman Bartholow* and the later historical monologues, the old charm has been quite left behind. In *Roman Bartholow*, for example, we, as usual, hear much of moonlight: the culmination of the poem is enveloped in it. But this is not the moonlight we used to know. It no longer possesses radiance. It leaves glamorless the situation, sufficiently unpleasing in itself, that the poet intends it to bathe. That situation, understood subtly and skillfully presented though it is, never undergoes the transmutation that can make an idea into a work of art.

Yet one ought not to complain too much of the dreariness of the later Robinson. He has already given us enough to put us forever in his debt. He is one of the few first-rate artists of the older generation, and even his artistic failures could only have been produced by a distinguished and original mind.

May, 1923

TWO NOVELS OF WILLA CATHER

I. *One of Ours*

CAN H. L. MENCKEN have been mistaken when he decided that Willa Cather was a great novelist? I have not read *My Ántonia*—which is said to be her best book —but I have not been able to find anything in her last two that seemed to bear out this description. Miss Cather's new novel—*One of Ours*—seems to me a pretty flat failure. She has taken what might, if it had been better handled, have provided a very interesting theme— the career of an imaginative Nebraska boy, who, though charged with the energy for great achievements, is balked and imprisoned first by the necessity of running his father's farm, and then by his marriage with a pious and prosaic Prohibition worker; but whose noble and romantic impulses are finally freed by the war. The publishers hint that Claude Wheeler is a symbol of the national character, and one can see that Miss Cather has aimed to make her people American types: the money-making farmer father, jocular and lacking in intelligence; the sympathetic religious mother; the son made wretched by passions which are outlawed among his neighbors and for which he can find no fit objects, which he is finally obliged to extinguish in the dubious crusade of the war. And this theme might indeed have served for a tragedy of national significance. But I feel, in the case of this book as I did with her collection of short stories, *Youth and the Bright Medusa*, that it has cost Miss Cather too much effort to summon her people from the void and that, even when she has got them before us, they appear less like human beings, or even the phantoms of human beings, than like pale unfeatured silhouettes, pasted on cardboard backs and, skillfully but a little mechanically, put through the paces of puppets. Even in incidents that might be convincing—as in the first night of Claude Wheeler's wedding trip, when his new bride coldly tells him she is ill and requests him not to share her state-room—the emotions of the hero are not created: we do not *experience* the frustration of Claude when his wife will not return his love, and in the latter part of the book, where Miss Cather has imposed on herself the special handicap of having to imagine her hero in rela-tion to the ordeal of the war, we feel that she has told us with commendable accuracy almost everything about the engagements she describes except the thing that is vital to the novel—what they did to the soul of Claude.

Admirers of Willa Cather will declare that this kind of criticism is based on a misunderstanding; that her method is not to get inside her characters—as Dostoevsky does, for example—and depict their emotions directly, but rather, in the manner of Turgenev, to tell you how people behave and to let the inner blaze of their glory or grief shine through the simple recital. But the reader, in either case, must demand that the characters come to life. In this novel, they never do. Flaubert, by a single phrase— a notation of some commonplace object—can convey all the poignance of human desire, the pathos of human defeat; his description of some homely scene will close with a dying fall that reminds one of great verse or music. But Miss Cather never finds this phrase.

Let it be counted to her for righteousness, however, that, like Flaubert, she has devoted her life to her art;

that—even though her colors are faint and the characters she animates shadowy—she understands how fine work should be done. She knows that in a decent novel every word should be in its place and every figure in its right perspective, that every incident should be presented with its appropriate economy of detail. If *One of Ours* only had more vitality, it might figure as a standard and a stimulus, as, for the limited number of people who have read it, James Joyce's *Ulysses* has done. It might serve to shame the "younger novelists" from their sloppiness and their facility; but, as it is, they can evade the moral of Willa Cather's example by complaining that her books are dull. And, unfortunately, one cannot deny it.

October, 1922

II. *A Lost Lady*

Willa Cather's new novel—*A Lost Lady*—does something to atone for *One of Ours*. Miss Cather seems to suffer from a disability like that of Henry James: it is almost impossible for her to describe an emotion or an action except at secondhand. When Henry James, in *The Wings of the Dove*, wants to present his heroine, Milly Theale, who is supposed to be dying for lack of love, he abandons the direct record of her psychological processes as soon as the situation becomes acute, and allows the reader to watch her only through the eyes of the fortune-hunter Merton Densher, and when the relation between Milly and Densher begins to be really dramatic, he sidesteps it altogether and passes on the culmination of the tragedy to the insight of a second observer who talks with Densher after Milly's death. I am aware of the aesthetic advantages on which Henry James insisted in favor of this use of reflectors, but I am inclined to believe he arrived at it by way of his limitations.

It had always been his tendency to admit us to only so much of the drama of his more daring and sophisticated protagonists as might have been observed or guessed at by some timid or inexperienced person who happened to be looking on. If the most satisfactory of James's novels is perhaps *What Maisie Knew*, it is because here the person who is looking on and whose consciousness is to be laid before us is not even a grown-up person, but merely a little girl, who in consequence makes a minimum demand for experience or adult emotion on the part of the author himself. *One of Ours*, for a converse reason, was one of Miss Cather's least satisfactory performances: she had to deal directly with the problem of rendering not only the cramping of the passions and aspirations of a young Middle Westerner on a farm, but also his eventual self-realization as a soldier in the war.

In *A Lost Lady*, however, Miss Cather falls back on the indirect method of James—who was a great artist, as novelists go, for all his not infrequent incapacity to fill in with adequate color the beautiful line and composition of his pictures; and she achieves something of James's success. Here her problem is to present the vicissitudes of a young and attractive woman, with a vigorous capacity for life, in the course of her marriage, during the pioneering period after the Civil War, with an elderly contractor of the "railroad aristocracy," who has brought her from California to live somewhere between Omaha and Denver. For this purpose, she invents another of those limpid and sensitive young men to whom she has always been rather addicted and makes him the Jamesian glass through which we are to look at her heroine. It is significant that on the only two important occasions when the author tries to show us something that was not directly witnessed by young Niel Herbert, she strikes, in the first case—the brief scene between the lady and her lover that takes place in the house at night—perhaps the only false melodramatic note to be found in the whole story ("'Be careful,' she murmured as she approached him, 'I have a distinct impression that there is someone on the enclosed stairway. . . . Ah, but kittens have claws, these days!'"); and in the second—the expedition in the sleigh—is able to save the situation only by introducing a subsidiary limpid young man whose function is to witness phenomena unmanageable for the first.

In any case, A Lost Lady is a charming sketch performed with exceptional skill. Willa Cather is, in fact, one of the only writers who has been able to bring any real distinction to the life of the Middle West. Other writers have more enthusiasm or animation or color or humor, but Miss Cather is perhaps unique in her art of imposing a patina on that meager and sprawling scene. There are exquisite pages of landscape in A Lost Lady, and the portrait of the veteran railroad man is surely one of the most sensitive and accurate that has ever been put into a novel of the best type of old-fashioned American of the post-Civil War period—a type greatly preferable, I grant Miss Cather, in its straightness and simplicity and honor, for all its cultural limitations, to the sharpers who superseded it.

Not, however, that Willa Cather sentimentalizes the Middle West or represents it as spiritually richer than it is—as Mr. Vachel Lindsay, for example, seems to do. There run through Miss Cather's work two currents of profound feeling—one for the beauty of those lives lived out between the sky and the prairie; the other—most touchingly in A Wagner Concert, my favorite among her short stories, and now in certain scenes of A Lost Lady—for the pathos of the human spirit making the effort to send down its roots and to flower in that barren soil.

January, 1924

EZRA POUND'S PATCHWORK

EZRA POUND's new book of poems—*Poems 1918-21*—is as unsatisfactory as his previous ones. He still spends two-thirds of his time translating or quoting other poets, and a good deal of the rest of it in imitating them (where it used to be Browning and Yeats, it now seems to be T. S. Eliot*), and he has not even yet, in his original work, really mastered his own style, which still remains patchy and uneven and acutely self-conscious. The failure of Pound as a poet is a curious literary phenomenon. Ezra Pound's aesthetic ideal is probably one of the highest in contemporary poetry in English. Indifferent to public approval, he has labored conscientiously and fiercely to reduce the vague substance of words to a sharp hard residuum of beauty which should have nothing in common with the comparatively loose rhetoric of even such a good poet as Masefield. From Catullus to Yeats, his masters (with the possible exception of Browning) have been the severest and the most durable in the whole range of poetry. And for a line or two at a time he has sometimes crystallized this beauty. In his newest book— which, nonetheless, has far fewer fine things in it than *Lustra*, his best collection up to date—we find: "Dawn, to our waking, drifts in the green cool light"; "But today,

* I did not know at that time that both Eliot and Yeats had been influenced by Pound.

44

Garonne is thick like paint, beyond Dorada"; "That he may free her—who sheds such light in the air." Such isolated lines as these have certainly an authentic ring; but the trouble is that all his lines are isolated lines. His poems do not hang together. His eye for a general effect is poor. It is as if he could not fix any picture squarely in his imagination and reproduce it for the reader, but could only try to piece it out with separate details and aspects, conceived and perhaps jotted down without proper regard for the whole. It is all like a pile of fragments from a collection of objets d'art: there are the foot of a Chinese jade god, the hand of a Tanagra statuette, a green, gold and blue initial from a medieval book and a pale nearly perfect amethyst engraved with a Renaissance Apollo. None of them is complete, and they do not go together.

There is a strange discrepancy between Pound's ideals and his ability to embody them in his work. It is as if his conception of style had matured while his taste had remained immature: not only has he never learned to deal with large problems, he has never been able to out-grow a certain beguilement with preciosity and mystifica-tion. For, in spite of the parade of cultures and the pontifical pretenses which have terrified the more naïve of the American intelligentsia, Ezra Pound is really at heart a very boyish fellow and an incurable provincial. It is true that he was driven to Europe by a thirst for romance and color that he could scarcely have satisfied in America, but he took to Europe the simple faith and the pure enthusiasms of his native Idaho. And he took, also, the fresh cavalier spirit which remains his greatest charm. His early poems were full of gallant and simply felt emo-tions; but they were already tainted with an obsession which has cursed him all his life: the frantic desire to flee as far from Idaho as possible, the itching to prove to Main Street that he has extirpated it from his soul.

That he has remained unsuccessful to this day is sufficiently attested by the fact that he still spends so much time insulting the United States. He seeks refuge in bawdiness, in obscurity, in recondite erudition, in the most extravagant of the modern movements, such as dadaism and vorticism, but he can never slough off his self-consciousness at having settled in the Sacred Grove. "Look at me!" he says in effect to his compatriots at home. "See how cultured and cosmopolitan I have become since I've left America—how different from you over there! I'll bet there's not a man among you who knows about Pratinas and Gaudier-Brzeska. I can read half a dozen languages! I am a friend of Francis Picabia!" But his sophistication is still juvenile, his ironies are still clumsy and obvious; when he ridicules Americans in Europe not very much simpler than himself, he reveals the callowness of the hunter by the pettiness of the game he pursues.

One fears that Ezra Pound has repeated the recurrent and oft-told tragedy of the artistic American fled to Europe. What the American flees to in Europe is the Europe he has read about, and unfortunately it is all too often exclusively the Europe of books in which he finds himself forced to continue to live. I take this as a way of accounting for Ezra Pound's peculiar deficiencies of experience and feeling. His contacts seem still to remain almost exclusively literary contacts. Consider, for example, the long poem of which he has now published seven cantos. The first six cantos of this work are occupied with literary reminiscences; it is apparently a cross-section of the poet's mind; odds and ends of old reading seem to float in and out—the Latin poets, Homer, a Latin translation of Homer, fragments of Chinese poetry, tags from the annals of Provence. At last, with the seventh canto, he seems to arrive at something that has been part of his own life: he remembers a girl called Eleanor, but the name immediately recalls to him the Aeschylean puns about Helen; and from this point on, in the first twenty-four lines, we have quotations from five languages and have presently lost our way altogether. Toward the end, we seem to get our bearings and find ourselves in a classroom of some sort; but the poet is bored with the class, and his mind begins to run on Lorenzaccio and Dante. So everything in life only serves to remind him of something in literature.

There exist without doubt in Ezra Pound some of the elements of a bold personality, a first-rate modern poet; but, for some reason, champion and poet have never quite rounded themselves out or stood on their own feet. One of the symptoms of his incompleteness is his continual recourse to translation: he tries to realize his own personality by putting on the costumes of other poets with whom he seems to himself to have some kinship. As Propertius, as Arnaut Daniel, as Guido Cavalcanti, he tries to attain his full stature. But even with the material they give him to supplement his defective experience and the solid and clear-cut personalities that they lend him to prop up his own, he still reveals his fatal inadequacy in the lameness of his rendering of them. In his hands they somehow become (with the possible exception of the Chinese poets) uncertain and unsatisfactory like Ezra Pound himself.

The truth about Ezra Pound is no doubt, as I have already suggested, that he merely presents a new instance of the now familiar dilemma of the clever and sensitive man in the United States of his day: his case has something in common with that of Henry James. America could not supply Pound with the society and the tradition he needed to develop a very special and very delicate talent; but Europe, of which he has never been part, cannot supply him with it either. He is a case for Mr. Van Wyck Brooks, that expert in American artistic failures. But let us, at least, do him honor for having failed in so high a cause.

April 19, 1922

WALLACE STEVENS AND E. E. CUMMINGS

THE POEMS OF Mr. Wallace Stevens have now been collected in a volume, with the title *Harmonium*. Mr. Stevens is the master of a style: that is the most remarkable thing about him. His gift for combining words is baffling and fantastic but sure: even when you do not know what he is saying, you know that he is saying it well. He derives plainly from several French sources of the last fifty years, but—except for an occasional fleeting phrase—he never really sounds like any of them. You could not mistake even a title by Wallace Stevens for a title by anyone else: *Invective Against Swans; Hibiscus on the Sleeping Shores; A High-Toned Old Christian Woman; The Emperor of Ice-Cream; Exposition of the Contents of a Cab; The Bird with the Coppery Keen Claws; Two Figures in Dense Violet Night; Hymn from a Watermelon Pavilion;* and *Frogs Eat Butterflies. Snakes Eat Frogs. Hogs Eat Snakes. Men Eat Hogs.*

These titles also represent Mr. Stevens's curious ironic imagination at its very best. The poems themselves—ingenious, charming and sometimes beautiful though they are—do not always quite satisfy the expectations aroused by the titles. If you read only a few poems by Mr. Stevens, you get the impression from the richness of his verbal imagination that he is a poet of rich personality, but when you come to read the whole volume through, you are struck by a sort of aridity. Mr. Stevens, who is so observant and displays so distinguished a fancy, seems to possess emotion neither in abundance nor in intensity. He is ironic a little in Mr. Eliot's manner; but not poignantly, not tragically ironic. Emotion seems to emerge only furtively in the cryptic images of his poetry, as if it had been driven, as he seems to hint, into the remotest crannies of sleep or disposed of by being dexterously converted into exquisite amusing words. Nothing could be more perfect in its tone and nothing by itself could be more satisfactory than such a thing as *Last Looks at the Lilacs*. But when we have gone all through Mr. Stevens, we find ourselves putting to him the same question that he himself, in the last poem of his book, puts *To a Roaring Wind*:

> What syllable are you seeking,
> Vocallissimus,
> In the distances of sleep?
> Speak it.

Mr. E. E. Cummings, on the other hand, in his volume *Tulips and Chimneys*, does not show himself, like Mr. Stevens, a master in a peculiar vein; a master is precisely, as yet, what Mr. Cummings is not. Cummings's style is an eternal adolescent, as fresh and often as winning but as half-baked as boyhood. A poet with a real gift for language, for a melting music a little like Shelley's, which rhapsodizes and sighs in soft vowels disembarrassed of their baggage of consonants, he strikes often on ethereal measures of a singular purity and charm—his best poems seem to dissolve on the mind like the flakes of a lyric dew; but he never seems to know when he is writing badly and when he is writing well. He has apparently no faculty for self-criticism. One imagines him giving off his poems as spontaneously as perspiration and

with as little application of the intellect. One imagines
him chuckling with the delight of a schoolboy when he
has invented an adverb like "sayingly" or hit upon the
idea of writing capitals in the middles of words instead
of at the beginnings. One imagines him just as proud to
have written:

> last   we
> on the groaning flame of neat huge
> trudging kiss moistly climbing hideously with
> large
> minute
> hips, O
>
>> press

as:

> on such a night the sea through her blind miles
> of crumbling silence

or the sonnet about the little dancer:

>> abslatively posolutely dead,
>> like Coney Island in winter

And there is really, it seems to me, a certain amateurish-
ness about even the better of these specimens as well as
about the worse. Just as, in the first example, he takes one
of the lines of least resistance with a complex and difficult
sensation by setting down indiscriminately all the
ideas it suggests to him without focussing it for the
reader, so he succumbs, in the second, to an overindulgence in the beautiful English long *i* which, from
Shelley's "I arise from dreams of thee" to Mr. T. S.
Eliot's nightingale filling "all the desert with inviolable
voice," has been reserved for effects of especial brightness

or clearness. Mr. Cummings has cheapened it a little by too much reiteration. One or two of these *i*'s, rightly placed and combined with other long vowels, is enough to illuminate a passage, but Mr. Cummings cannot resist them, and he likes to turn them on all over till his poems are lit up like Christmas trees.

Mr. Cummings's eccentric punctuation is, also, I believe, a symptom of his immaturity as an artist. It is not here merely a question of an unconventional usage: unconventional punctuation may very well gain its effect. But though the methods of Mr. Cummings have been explained to me by one of his friends and though I have made a sincere effort to appreciate them, I still feel that his punctuation does not gain the effects he intends. It is, I learn, Mr. Cummings's theory that punctuation marks, capitalization and arrangement of words on the page should not be used by the poet as conventional indications of structure that make it easier for the reader to follow the meaning of the words themselves but as instruments of expression, susceptible, like the words, of infinite variation. Thus he refuses to make use of capitals for the purposes for which they were invented—to announce the beginnings of sentences and the occurrence of proper names—but presses them into service for purposes of special emphasis; and he even demotes the first person singular of the pronoun by writing it with a small *i*, only restoring its stature as a capital when he desires to give it salience—not, apparently, aware of the fact that, since the reader is accustomed to the capital, the poet makes it more instead of less conspicuous by writing it with a dot. But the really serious case against Mr. Cummings's punctuation is that the results which it yields are ugly. His poems on the page are hideous. He insists upon breaking up even the least unconventional of his verses, which would be more appropriately printed as neat little blocks of type like the prose poems of Logan Pearsall Smith, into systems of exploded fragments, and this, so far from making the cadences plainer, only involves us in a jigsaw puzzle of putting the lines together again. I think it may be said that a writer is obliged to depend on the words themselves, through the order in which they are written, to carry his cadence and emphasis. The extent to which punctuation and typography can supplement this is certainly very limited.

Behind this barrier of strange punctuation and deliberate disorganization, for which Mr. Cummings seems, unfortunately, so far to have achieved most celebrity, his emotions are familiar and simple. They occasionally even verge on the banal. You find the adoration of young love and the excitement of the coming of spring, and you find the reflection that all flesh must die and all "roses" turn to "ashes." But this is perhaps precisely where E. E. Cummings has the advantage over Wallace Stevens. Whatever Mr. Cummings is, he is not insulated or chilled; he is not indifferent to life. Eagerly and unconstrainedly, he takes what the world has to offer. His poetry is the expression of a temperament of a kind very rare in America—of a being who desires and enjoys, who reacts to everything that touches him with a tenderness or a mockery quite free from the inhibitions from which so much American writing is merely the anguish to escape. E. E. Cummings is, I suppose, one of the only American writers living who is not reacting against something. And for this—for the fact that, though not yet fully grown, he is a genuine lyric poet at a time when there is a great deal of writing of verse and very little poetic feeling—Mr. Cummings deserves well of the public.

March 19, 1924

This review in its original version was to have been called *Two American Symbolists*, and it began with the following paragraphs, in which I tried to relate Stevens and Cummings to the French symbolist school. I saw, however, that this was too large a subject to be treated in a review of this kind, and I did not deal fully with the influence of symbolism till, in 1929 and 1930, I came to write the studies that were later brought together in my book *Axel's Castle*.

Both Mr. E. E. Cummings and Mr. Wallace Stevens have reputations as innovators; and the only questions usually raised in connection with their work are based on the assumption that their technique is unconventional. So it is, perhaps, in America; but there is little in their work that is new. They are merely the latest representatives in English of a belated development of French symbolism, and what they are trying to do is, in general, as old as Mallarmé.

Nor should it be possible for symbolism in itself to inspire terror and consternation, as it seems to do in the case of so many Anglo-Saxon critics—even if one has never heard of a literary movement which is already about forty years old. Symbolism consisted, by definition, of substituting symbols for things—but it was by no means so different from any other kind of poetry as you might have thought to hear the outcry raised years ago in France over Verlaine's *Sagesse* or only the other day in New York over T. S. Eliot's *The Waste Land*. All metaphors are symbols that stand for things; and what symbolism did was merely to cut the metaphors lose from their moorings. The tendency was to present the metaphors without mentioning the subject that inspired them, to suggest it to the reader, to make him guess, without letting him know precisely what it was. Symbolism, at its most successful, contrives to communicate emotions by images whose connection with the subject and whose relevance to one another we may not always understand. Who can tell, for example, to take two fairly easy instances, precisely what Verlaine is referring to, in the poem that begins, *"L'espoir luit comme un brin de paille dans l'étable,"* when he writes *"Que crains-tu de la guêpe, ivre de son vol fou?,"* or precisely what Eliot means, in *The Waste Land*, when he suddenly begins talking about "Phlebas the Phoenician, a fortnight dead"? But who can fail to feel the effectiveness of these strange lines? We respond to their magic emotionally before our minds have propounded the riddle. In one case, we get the impression of something troublesome and rather sinister from which the poet is trying to escape; in the other, of a longing for peace, of an assuagement, if even by death, of some torturing thirst of the spirit. These images could probably have been conveyed in a perfectly conventional manner—as Dante, describing a state of mind surely not less unusual and difficult, would write in the *Paradiso* of the fading from his memory of the divine vision, "so the snow is unsealed by the sun, so the light leaves of the Sybil's message are scattered by the wind." But the method of symbolism was to cut away the links that indicated how the images grew out of the subject—even sometimes, so far as was possible, to suppress the subject itself. Along with this isolation of metaphors, there appeared also a general addiction to hiatuses of all sorts. The point was not that the emotions of, say, Jules Laforgue were necessarily more complicated than those of, say, Catullus in his sequence of poems about Lesbia, but rather that the symbolist poet—instead of disentangling a complex emotion into a series of varying moods or at least, when the mood of a single poem is allowed to change abruptly (as in Catullus's *Illa Lesbia . . .*), of

subduing the disordered feeling to the logic of consecutive statement—is in the habit of telescoping the whole
thing by a few stenographic strokes. Nor are his feelings
necessarily more difficult to render than those, say, of
Wordsworth in the most mysterious of his visions of the
natural world; but the symbolist—instead of attempting
to reduce an unearthly elusive sensation to the lucidity
of simple language—invents for it a vocabulary and a
syntax as unfamiliar as the sensation itself.

In considering the work of such American poets as
Stevens and E. E. Cummings, their technique should no
longer be made an issue. They should be judged by their
greater or less success in a tradition that can already boast
its masterpieces. It is a question, not at all of method,
but of the good artist or the bad. The good artist, in this
as in any other style, is one who can create a work that
has completeness and significance outside himself, that is
not merely a literary ectoplasm imperfectly disengaged
from his drift of consciousness. Such good artists of this
symbolist school, Verlaine and Eliot certainly are in the
poems I have quoted above, and Laforgue in his *Derniers
Vers*. Mallarmé, for all his labor and integrity, seems to
me not quite to have succeeded, and Tristan Tzara, at the
other end of the line but essentially attempting the same
sort of thing, seems to me, so far as I have read him, not
to have succeeded at all. In the first class, the logic of the
images, the association of ideas is never quite out of reach
of the reader; in the second, we are incapable of enjoying the poems—or at least this reader is—because the
key to this association is buried in the poet's mind. The
emotion, if there was an emotion, has not really been
captured and fixed; the words that the poet combines do
not bring it before the reader.

BYRON IN THE TWENTIES

I. The New Byron Letters

I CANNOT ACCEPT the opinion of Mr. Maurice Hewlett and others who have asserted that the new collection of Byron letters, *Lord Byron's Correspondence* (a supplement to the six volumes of *Letters and Journals* published at the beginning of the century) only supply more conclusive evidence that Byron was a "blackguard" and a "cad." This is to simplify the matter too much. It is to assume that when Byron writes "Maid of Athens, ere we part, Give oh give me back my heart!" in one breath and in the next tells Hobhouse that "the old woman, Theresa's mother, was mad enough to imagine I was going to marry the girl, but I have better amusement," and when he sneers at his wife in his private correspondence, not long after having written, "even though unforgiving, never 'Gainst thee shall my heart rebel," he is sincere in his cynicism but not in his warmth of emotion. It is to assume that one cannot take a personal relation with cynicism and seriousness at the same time—that Childe Harold and Manfred did not represent realities of Byron's experience as well as Don Juan. The truth is that Byron was a man of picturesque and violent moods, who reacted to life with extraordinary vividness, but without discipline or order. He never knew where he stood nor what

57

he really wanted. He was a force of enormous energy, running amuck through a world in which he could not find peace. His compromises with civilized society were doomed to disaster from the beginning, though in them he was surely sincere in seeking tranquillity or discipline. To say, as Mr. Hewlett does, that he cold-bloodedly seduced Lady Frances Webster seems to me to melo-dramatize the situation. Even if Lady Frances had not been all of a flutter from the moment Byron came into the house and in a mood of violent reaction against the clumsy and stupid husband who had boasted that she was as passionless "as Jesus Christ," these letters seem amply to prove that Byron believed himself in love with her and was ready at any moment to drop everything and run away with her.

The fact that he was an old hand at lovemaking and was amused by the humors of the situation and drama-tized the whole affair in almost daily bulletins to Lady Melbourne does not prove him to have been much more of a popinjay than the average imaginative person. In a similar fashion, it is certainly true that he was honestly seeking happiness in his marriage; he wanted, he said, some one to "govern" him—which was unquestionably what he needed. The trouble was that Annabella Mil-banke was a quite unsuitable wife for Byron. He had qualms at the last moment and was ready to give the whole thing up; but Lady Melbourne, who had been "governing" him lately and in whose judgment he seems to have trusted absolutely, had arranged the marriage herself and urged it upon him as a panacea. The relation-ship was impossible from the start. It is clear that Byron behaved abominably, but, then, he was by nature and fortune a spoiled and refractory child, while poor little Miss Milbanke was a correct jeune fille, charmless and unsophisticated, who went in for mathematics and was a little priggish about it. With the best intentions on both sides, the situation could hardly have turned out differently. "Disease or not," says Lady Byron, speaking of Byron's supposed madness, "all my recollections and reflections tend to convince me that the irritability is inseparably connected with me in a greater degree than with any other object, that my presence has been uniformly oppressive to him from the hour we married—if not before, and in his best moods he has always wished to be away from me . . . had we continued together, he *would* have gone mad."

It is, therefore, a great pity that Byron was ever persuaded to marry Miss Milbanke. He had already a sharp sense of his unfitness to play a role in English society. When Miss Milbanke finally came to accept him, he had been fully prepared to go back to the East; *there* were fighting and adventure—gaiety, color and sun; *there* was no boring politics or business; women were not taken seriously; *there* he would be able to find something like the kind of life he understood. His genius has its happiest expression in his letters to Hobhouse from the Continent and in the harlequinade of *Beppo* and *Don Juan*.

For Byron's gift was for living rather than for literature. He had neither the intensity nor the fineness to fuse, for perdurable brilliants, the shifting moods of the soul. Don Juan, after all, was always more real than Childe Harold. The windy storms of passion that were blown off in *Childe Harold* and the tragedies were never the most solid realities of that deeply sensuous life. If he had only not tried to live in England, if the women only hadn't set their hearts on him, what an amiable figure he might have been! There is nothing more exhilarating in literature than Byron's first trip to Greece—his duels and skirmishings with bandits, his heroic swimming of the Hellespont, his reception by Vely Pasha and his delight at the Pasha's present of "a very pretty horse," his defense of the Temple of Athena against the depredations of Lord Elgin and his row with the authorities at Constantinople because they would not allow him, as a Peer of the Realm, to take first place in a Turkish official reception. To read Byron is to watch a panorama of the Europe of the early nineteenth century—the morrow of the French Revolution and of the victory of Napoleon seen through the eyes of a sophisticated man who is as much alive to how people are feeling and to what sort of struggles they are waging as to how they are drinking and making love. How amusing he makes Milan and Geneva and Venice!—that Venice of which Stendahl wrote that it constituted "a distinct world, of which the gloomy society of the rest of Europe can form no conception; care is there a subject of mockery." Here as yet was neither Burbank with his Baedeker nor Bleistein with his cigar, but balconies to which one looked up to encounter romantic black eyes peeping out from behind long blinds; covered gondolas gliding at night through narrow canals of wavering water; the dancing, the delirious wines and the masqued flirtations of the Carnival; the revolutionary young countess Guiccioli with her aged and complacent husband and her English *cavalier servente*, the scandalous witty Lord Byron.

Yet this record, as we follow it further, produces an effect of depression that at last becomes almost unbearable. For one thing, life had played poor Byron not the least annoying of its tricks: by the time he had acquired enough judgment not to make any further disastrous mistakes and to be sure in what manner of life his hope for happiness lay, he had already hurt others and himself so grievously in the process of learning that both his peaceful pursuits and his pleasures were forever impaired by the wounds. Among the motley baggage of his soul, there was a sort of Calvinistic conscience (supposed to have been implanted by his early education in Edinburgh) which gnawed its nails and gnashed its teeth amid the very laughter of Venice. "It must be admitted," says Stendahl, writing of Byron at this period, "that during nearly a third of the time we passed in the poet's society he appeared to us like one laboring under an access of folly, often approaching to madness. . . . One evening, among others, the conversation turned upon a handsome Milanese female who had eagerly desired to venture her person in single combat with a lover by whom she had been abandoned; the discussion afterward changed to the story of a prince who in cold blood had murdered his mistress for an act of infidelity. Byron was instantly silent, endeavored to restrain his feelings, but, unequal to the effort, soon afterward indignantly quitted the box."

Then, Byron had by this time another remorse to stave off by champagne. Jane Claremont, a connection of the Shelleys and a romantic foolish young girl, mad to give herself to a poet, had laid violent siege to Byron and had finally nagged him into gratifying her. They had parted in Switzerland, Byron refusing implacably ever to see her again, and when Jane with the Shelleys had returned to England, she bore Byron a daughter. The new documents published here in elucidation of this affair take glamor from both Byron and Shelley. They reveal the dismal underside of that stimulating lyric revolt. One is chilled to find the price these poets paid—and that other people paid—not only in pain and grief, but in sordidness and raw distress. How much good life was plowed under in the triumph of that noble defiance! And how messy the triumph itself appears when looked at in the process of its making.

Well, art has its origin in the need to pretend that human life is something other than it is, and, in a sense, by pretending this, it succeeds to some extent in transforming it. What we see when we turn back our eyes to the age of Shelley and Byron is not the ignominy of mute broken hearts, of hurriedly muffled-up births, but a blaze of divine white light and the smoky torches of rebellion. And yet, poor Jane Claremont, to have set her heart on a love affair with a poet! Poor Annabella Milbanke, to have been so naïve and misguided as to marry an inspired rake! Poor Shelley and poor Byron, to have carried in their hearts the consciousness of such guilt as no wine could for long disguise, no songs could forever relieve. Poor male and female human beings, who, understanding life in different fashions and unfitted to live together, yet cannot leave each other alone! For a moment, as we read these letters, the very splendors of *Childe Harold* and *Prometheus* seem dwindled and insubstantial, like witch-fires above a bog.

July 2, 1922

II. Byron and His Biographers

The Political Career of Lord Byron by Dora Neill Raymond is an interesting, though not very penetrating, book, written from the point of view of the conventional admiring biographer. For Miss Raymond, all of Byron's political lampoons and parliamentary speeches, as well as his revolutionary activities in Italy and Greece, are the results of wise and well-considered opinions. Byron's motives are invariably generous, disinterested and straightforward; and the question of his complex and unsteady character does not arise at all. In discussing Byron's hatred of the radicals, to take a single example, Miss

Raymond describes the squib that he wrote about Hobhouse's relations with them as "a rollicking and somewhat sarcastic ballad"—whereas it will perhaps seem more likely to a reader of the ballad in question and of the poet's letters dealing with this period that he had merely given vent to his own irritation at the aimlessness of his life in Italy and his envy of his friend's achievements at home by an outburst less rollicking and sarcastic than jeering and ill-natured. Furthermore, it seems clear that Byron's hatred of oppression and the readiness of his sympathy with the unfortunate were somehow bound up with what would be nowadays called a sort of "inferiority complex." But it never occurs to Miss Raymond to question either the soundness of Byron's character or the exaltedness of his position, so she quite fails to understand either his personal or his social situation.

Mr. Harold Nicolson, on the other hand, in *Byron: The Last Journey*, understands these matters only too well. Mr. Nicolson is a pupil of the school of Strachey, and he has picked up the whole technique of emphasizing the idiosyncrasies and the personal imperfections that, ignored by the contemporary public, fix the shape of spectacular public careers. This enables him, if not to rival the consummate successes of the Master, at least to write such a passage as the following, which comes nearer to arriving at the truth about Byron than a biography in Miss Raymond's vein can do: "It must be realized that the life of Byron is not, as has often been imagined, a series of wasted opportunities; rather is it a catalogue of false positions. His brain was male, his character was feminine. He had genius, but it was misunderstood and misdirected; he had beauty, but it was branded by deformity; he had rank, but no position; fortune, but it came too late; fame, but it blazed for him too early. From his childhood the foreground of his life had been out of focus with the background; throughout his career this error of focus marred the sincerity, the completeness and even the meaning of the whole."

Yet this formula of Strachey's has its penalties as well as its dazzling rewards. One of these is the use or the excessive use of irony where irony is not really in order. The irony of Strachey himself always serves to convey some criticism: as Mr. Clive Bell has said, Strachey's attitude toward the Victorian Age implies a judgment derived from a study of the history of society. We do not find Lytton Strachey writing about Madame du Deffand or Racine in the same vein as about Florence Nightingale, Cardinal Manning or Dr. Arnold. Even in *Eminent Victorians*, where he is most cruel, perhaps most unfair, all his efforts are directed toward compelling us to accept a certain definite point of view. But his followers are always in danger of taking over the mocking tone without understanding this point of view. The worst offender in this regard is perhaps Mr. Philip Guedalla. The biographical writing of Mr. Guedalla is full of details and inflections that have an invidious mocking sound but which, when one comes to examine them, seem to lack any real significance. And Mr. Nicolson, in writing of Byron, is not entirely free from this vice. " 'Our visit was a long one,' records Lady Blessington. It was. They sat in the large, cool room," etc. Now, what is there ridiculous about the fact that this visit to Byron was rather long? Why does Mr. Nicolson write "It was" in such a sly knowing way? For no other reason on earth than that he has caught the tone from Lytton Strachey. There is certainly some place for irony in a biography of a figure like Byron, whose romantic reputation has been swollen by so much nonsense; but, except in his preface, Mr. Nicolson has surely leaned a little too far over backward in his endeavor to avoid the legend. For the legend, after all, was a reality as much as Byron's effeminate voice, which Mr. Nicolson is so unwilling to have us forget.

Here is a typical passage: "That in this sudden ferment of unexpected adulation Byron should have been manoeuvred into adopting the postures which were expected of him was perhaps inevitable. . . . [The provoking specter of Childe Harold] thrust upon him the exacting function of being a very dangerous and enterprising man. His slightest civility was interpreted as a seduction; his chance encounters became assignations. They persisted, all of them, in taking him at his word. For a man who, although kindly and sentimental, was only adequately sexed, all this became extremely exhausting." But, after all, it was Byron himself who had created Childe Harold and his postures. He had certainly more than half believed in them, and he succeeded in making others believe in them, and they thus became actual values, which Mr. Nicolson should have brought on the stage. "Kindly and sentimental" is a quite inadequate description of Byron in his relations with women: on the contrary, he seems always to have been ready to flare up, if only momentarily, into a fever of eager devotion, and in even the most unpromising of his love affairs, to have been able to work up at least a mood or two of something like passionate conviction. Even from the half-humorous bulletins that he sent off to Lady Melbourne, it is plain that he pursued his mistresses with an energy and an anxiety considerably more than "kindly and sentimental." Mr. Nicolson, in writing about Byron with Childe Harold left out, has illustrated the un-humanistic point of view to which Stracheyism is likely to lead. If a biographer be too wary of taking the figures of history and the heroes of literature at their own valuation and that of their contemporaries, he is likely to miss the point altogether. Every age has its complacent failures of intelligence, and we have learned in our own time to laugh at the "reason-able" point of view that was fashionable in the eighteenth century and the moral point of view of the nineteenth, but it looks as if this new sort of ironic belittlement were likely to become characteristic of our own. What should be most interesting at any time is to find out to what actuality of human ideals and adventures a creation like Childe Harold corresponded.

For the rest, Miss Raymond's book is a readable and useful one, and Mr. Nicolson's a vivid and amusing one, which has a great deal more of his own in it than his preceding biography of Tennyson, in which one found him paraphrasing, as if for a literary exercise, the whole last page of Strachey's *Queen Victoria*. Confining itself, as Mr. Nicolson's book does, to the last year of Byron's life, it cannot be expected to supply a satisfactory full-length portrait of Byron. Mr. Nicolson presupposes on the part of the reader a knowledge of most of what has gone before and concentrates on Byron's last year, of which he makes an absorbing narrative. Mr. Nicolson has unpublished documents and a firsthand knowledge of Greece, and both these books are of the picture-filling-in sort particularly valuable in connection with Byron. For Byron, in literature, presents a peculiar case: he was not a great literary artist, and it is only by familiarizing ourselves with his life as well as with his work that we come to appreciate his merits and understand why it was possible for Arnold to speak, as he did, in one breath, of "Goethe's sage mind and Byron's force." What we come to do justice to then—and both Miss Raymond's and Mr. Nicolson's books help us to do justice—is the knowledge of Europe and the world, the consciousnes of the stage upon which he was playing, that make Byron so remarkable among nineteenth-century Englishmen; the generous ideas and impulses which counterbalance his faults and his errors; and the inexhaustible capacity for experience that is so satisfactory today in its contrast with the limitations of the typical literary man who agreeably diverts the hours of a safe and regular life by turning out novels or poems.

June, 1925

LATE VIOLETS FROM THE NINETIES

MR. CARL VAN VECHTEN, in *The Blind Bow-Boy*, has tried his hand at a kind of burlesque fiction of which we have had all too little in America: the satiric iridescent novel of the type of *Zuleika Dobson* and *La Révolte des Anges*; and, though at times a little less fantastic, a little less surprising than one could wish, he gets away with it, on the whole, very well. You must remember that he has had the hardihood to go to New York for his rococo *Satyricon*; and you may imagine whether New York is recalcitrant. The result, in spite of all the green orchids and the rose-jade cysts for cosmetics that the author finds in East Nineteenth Street, may come closer to the prosaic reality—or conventional reality of fiction—than Mr. Van Vechten perhaps intended. The marriage of the hero, Harold, with the rich, boring, well-bred Alice Blake might almost have taken place in the New York of Edith Wharton. It is rather the figure of Campaspe Lorillard who exists on a high comic plane, and I am inclined to believe that the book should have centered about her rather than Harold. Campaspe craves no other activity than the luxurious enjoyment of her mind, thoughts and sensations, the play of an exquisite taste and the exercise of a ruthless intelligence; she snubs her husband with a regal kindness, yet declines any other attachment, and sees as little of her children as possible, thereby trebling their interest in her. The only member of her family who interests *her* is her mother, whom she calls by her first name. She is Mr. Van Vechten's most successful achievement.

It is not, of course, in comparison with current American novels that I call Mr. Van Vechten prosaic. Beside Floyd Dell and Willa Cather, he is Ariel, Till Eulenspiegel. But I have been reading *The Flower Beneath the Foot* by the Englishman Ronald Firbank, a writer for whom Mr. Van Vechten has expressed immense admiration and with whom he will not, I am sure, consider it inappropriate to compare him; and I am struck by how much further Mr. Firbank has got beyond the world of our commonplace fiction than even Mr. Van Vechten's Campaspe. From the first pages of *The Flower Beneath the Foot,* you find yourself closed about by a new and more vivid world, and a world so complete in itself that, for all its artificiality, one feels sure it must somewhere exist. You are moving through the high-windowed rooms of the Winter Palace of Pisuerga: silk swishes and gossip tinkles; the Queen is lounging "supine on a couch"; a Maid of Honour, looking out from a window with a fringe of green-veined bougainvilleas, at the clouds, like great knots of pink roses, that speed slowly above the town, dreams of marrying the languid Prince Yousef; all about one feels the rustle of the court, the glitter of state dinners, where the very hangings seem to be vibrant with an insatiable sensuality that provides, only a little disguised by the ceremony of office and fashion—though itself phantasmal and fragile—one of the only real incitements to activity. I have heard Ronald Firbank called trivial, and in one of his phases he is; but he is certainly more serious as an artist than he is commonly credited with being. He can create a very sharp impression—about trivial matters, if you like—with extraordinarily few words. It is not merely—though for this he is perhaps most famous—a question of suggesting the improper so inobviously and so lightly that it is difficult to put your finger on the phrase that has prompted the indecent idea; he is also able to make details, exquisitely selected and placed, tell strongly in securing effects of a certain aesthetic intensity—as when Laura looks out later at the royal wedding of the prince she had hoped to marry, from the spike-fringed walls of a convent.

What one finds in both these books is a last survival of the fin de siècle: despite their occasional dallyings with the movies and other features of the twentieth century, they belong essentially to the *Yellow Book* era. But it is curious to contemplate the change that has come over the decadence of the nineties since the heyday of Beardsley and Wilde. The school which began with Baudelaire and is now dissolving with Arthur Symons derived its principal force from its constant conviction of sin. The decadents talked much about "paganism," but their point of view was not pagan: it was a reaction against Victorian Christianity by people who were still Christians and Victorians. The fascination with which they succeeded in investing certain ideas and situations was dependent on the extent to which they could make you believe that these were sinister. They wanted you to be afraid of sin, as sin—that is, as something to be detested—yet at the same time to celebrate it as something to be desired: an impossible moral position, sure to involve insincerity on one side or the other. How can you believe that sin is "the good" and at the same time believe it to be sin? From the point of view of the person who is really convinced of the sinfulness both of the pleasures of the flesh and of the play of the intelligence, they are things to be sedulously shunned; from a point of view really pagan, they do not become an issue at all. But Baudelaire had to pretend to take the Devil seriously while he was spending his artistic life endeavoring to make him attractive; and his successors followed his example.

This is perhaps why the writers of the end of the century seem today diminished in stature. Who can read *Les Fleurs du Mal, À Rebours, The Picture of Dorian Grey* or Swinburne's *Poems and Ballads* with the enthusiasm of their contemporaries? The effectiveness of the subjects dealt with depends upon one's being shocked by them, and when the prejudices to be baited have been removed, the works of art are no longer exciting. I can think of only two writers of that period and school who escaped the moral confusion of the reaction against respectability: Aubrey Beardsley and Paul Verlaine. It is, of course, true that Beardsley very often exploited in his drawings the fascination of Evil as evil; but he also wrote the opening chapters of rather a remarkable erotic romance called *Venus and Tannhäuser,* in which he does succeed in investing a sort of pagan world with the artificial graces of the nineties without allowing it to become darkened and tragic with the fumes of a burning orthodoxy; his Venus, unlike the Venus of Swinburne or the Harlot of Oscar Wilde, is not destructive and terrible, but girlish and agreeable. The grotesqueries and orgies of her court are to her all quite natural and harmless; she really approaches much nearer to the naïve naughtiness of the eighteenth century than anything to be found in Wilde. As for Verlaine, he unquestionably vacillated between "paganism" and piety; but, unlike Baudelaire, he did not try to be pagan and pious at the same time. When Verlaine was a faun, he was wholly a faun, untroubled by moral compunction. And in these moods he created, too, a neo-eighteenth-century world, erotic, lighthearted and skeptical, not unlike the world of *Venus and Tannhäuser.*

Now, Mr. Van Vechten and Mr. Firbank are also able to take their heresies and pleasures lightly. It may be that Mr. Firbank has gone to school to Beardsley. But it is probably no longer possible for practitioners of this species of fantasy to become either worried or fervent. The generation of Beardsley and Wilde had been brought up on Ruskin and Tennyson; but the generation of Firbank and Van Vechten has been brought up on Beardsley and Wilde, and their prejudices were undermined early. The conviction of sin has been removed, and it is possible for the "sinner" to be amiable again. This fin de siècle genre may be destined to grow dimmer and dimmer, but at least it fades away with a smile.

October, 1923

GREENWICH VILLAGE IN THE
EARLY TWENTIES*

I. The Road to Greenwich Village

I NEVER went to school very much. When I was a girl, they figured out that it would be a good thing for me to do the work and to get an education—and I did the work so well they forgot about the education. My father left me at a girl's school in Greeley Valley, Colorado, but I was only there a little while. They were awfully narrow-minded there. I told the girls some things that they weren't supposed to know—my father was a doctor, and I used to read his medical books, see. I told them that a baby before it's born looks like a kind of a tadpole. Some of the girls told the teachers, and the teachers bawled me out. They told me that if I ever said anything like that again I'd have to leave. The whole school was stirred up about it—and the girls I'd told that I'd been friends with, finally got to be the worst of all—they wouldn't speak to me any more. So I couldn't stand that —I left, myself. I saw one of them afterwards and she told me that she was sorry, because, after I had gone, some of them looked it up and they found out I was right.

I was married when I was fourteen and went up to
* The first of these sketches is from life; the second, imaginary.

73

Washington. On the train when I was on my way up there, a man got in from Idaho, and when he heard I was going to Washington, he said, "You're going to Washington, are you? Well, when you've been there a little while, you'll be all covered with moss—you'll have moss growing on your eyebrows and hanging out of your ears, and your hair will be full of moss!" I didn't think that sounded very cheerful, but I went up there, and I was in the woods almost fifteen years. The camp was 'way up the mountain—from where we were, Mt. Ranier looked like you could just lean right over and touch it. When we first got there, we started out for the mountain in a buckboard: the driver was a man who had been hit by a limb, and his nose was squashed all over his face. Pretty soon, he pointed out ahead and said, "You see that loblolly over there?" I looked out and saw a great big sheet of mud. "Well," he said, "we're goin' right through it!" And he lashed up the horses and plunged right in. When we got out, I looked back and saw the poor dog that had been tied to the back of the buckboard—he was all fulla mud and almost dead. So were we. Then to go up the mountain, we had to ride. I never had ridden very much, and I made some big mistakes. I couldn't understand why the horse always had to go zigzag along the path and I decided I'd make him go straight—and the first thing I knew I was off on the ground rolling down the slope. The horse had stumbled on a cedar-snag—those cedar-snags are as slick as glass, you know. If I had left him alone, he would have avoided them. He was what they call woodsbroke, and I wasn't yet.

Well, as I say, I was up there almost fifteen years and I certainly got awfully lonesome. I used to feel like I was sunk in a deep well: it's so close with the trees up all around you that you feel like you can hardly breathe. It's so hot in the daytime you can hardly stand it and so cold at night you can hardly stand it. I almost put my eyes out reading by a lantern in the evenings. I used to sit there and hear the mice running round and round like a racetrack. The woods are fulla mice—the mice get into the walls, and the skunks go in after the mice and they get fastened there. I couldn't get very many books—all they had up there was the seed catalogue and the almanac—and I had to get them brought up from the circulating library in Seattle. I read E. P. Roe's *The Opening of a Chestnut Burr* and *He Fell in Love With His Wife*—old stories about New York, you know—but I thought they were great. I used to read them and just think it must be wonderful to live in New York. Once I cooked for a camp of sixty men where the cook had gone away. It's quite a stunt in itself to learn to cook up there. What they eat up there is sourdough—that's a kind of pancake dough that isn't affected by the cold. It's so cold up there that you can't do much with food—our Indian, Jake, used to take his bread and his bottle of potato-water to bed with him at night to keep them from freezing.

I'll never forget the first time I made bread. In the first place, they don't have any regular kind of yeast—like Fleischmann's—they only have one kind—a brand called Owl—and you have to put in about twelve cakes of that to get any results at all. I tried to knead it on a table, but I couldn't do anything with it—the bottom of the pan would just clink back and forth—it was so big and weak. Finally, the old man that was there took it and put it down on the floor and went to it with his whole strength—that was the only way you could make any impression on it. What I missed most—I never thought I would—but what I missed most was a woman. I didn't see a woman for years, and then when I did, she was more like a man than a woman. She was a woman

who had come up there with her husband, who was a
Civil War veteran and had a homestead. She helped him
cut the trees and everything—sure, she used to work on
the business end of a cross-saw! Then he drank so that
she left him and went down to Tacoma and went into
business—and she bought up the tideland flats for
twenty-five dollars an acre. They were just an expanse
of mud then, and everybody gave her the big ha-ha, but
it turned out that they were valuable for machine shops
—she evidently knew that—and she sold them for a lot
of money. Her name was Larry Larson.

Well, when she was selling out her ranch she came
over to see my husband. I couldn't take my eyes off her,
I hadn't seen a woman in so long. But she didn't notice
me—didn't know I was there, see. I was standing cooking
potato cakes over the fire—we didn't have any stove, we
just had to cook over the blaze—and I was changing my
frying pan from hand to hand and trying to hold my face
away from the fire. Pretty soon, she came over, still talking to my husband, and put on a man's old slouch hat
down over her eyes, and took the frying pan away from
me and held it right out over the blaze and kept it there
without ever changing hands and you ought to have
seen her flip the potato cakes over, holding it out like
that—still talking business all the time. Made me feel
so cheap! Finally, we had a kind of a bust-up. I got tired
of living up there, and my husband thought I was
interested in another man—but you had to be interested
in something up there—and I took my boy—he was born
up there—and went south again. I really guess it's only
a woman like Larry Larson that can succeed up there.

When I first went up to Washington, I'd see all those
wives of homesteaders with picket fences around them—
Mrs. Shafer and Mrs. Huckaby and Mrs. Smith—and I
resented that the wives always died but never the men—

all except Huckaby, and he had to be shot! One woman got so desperate one winter, when her husband was off on a spree, that she killed her four children with a butcher knife and tried to get away with herself. It seemed as if it was hearing the cougar scream that she got so she couldn't stand. They give the most awful scream that just sends the shivers right through you—just like a woman, you know. She tried to drown herself, but when she struck the cold water, it sort of knocked her sane or something. The man who told me about it thought that was funny! Only the baby survived.

My husband was mean and cruel—he said he had Indian blood. He always did have a grudge, but it was him that always brought it up himself—I don't think he had any Indian blood. His father was mean—that's why his wife left him, he was so mean—but my husband improved on his meanness. He was a teaser, and when they grow up and don't get over it, it is pretty bad. The old man got kind of crazy one winter and tried to poison me. He'd sit around in the evening and say, "John L. Sullivan's dead," when he wasn't dead at all—and then he thought that I was a spy on-um that his wife had sent. I guess he'd been up there so long alone brooding in his homestead that he finally went off-uz head. Well, anyway, one night he tried to poison me. Strychnine—they use it for traps, you know. That night was a different night from the other nights—all the days were just the same, but this day was a different day. He got up and went out for a walk after dinner, instead of going right in for a nap, like he usually did. Well, anyway, at dinner he offered me this piece of meat—deer-meat—and I didn't want it, but I wanted to be polite to the old man, so I waited till he'd went out and then put it back on the plate, and in the evening he ate it himself and was so sick! But he knew what to do. I wouldn't have and might have died—but he ate a lot of lard. Now he's my best friend: we write to each other all the time. He told me afterwards he guessed he was queer that winter. They called him Abe Lincoln up there.

I had two children up there, and the third one died before it was born—a month before it was born—and poisoned me. And I wanted to die: I was so sick, and my husband was such a mean monster. I couldn't remember anything—that was really terrible, that muddled mind I had—and whenever anybody would ask me a question, it would be just like a big blank wall up in front of me. I couldn't even remember the things I had to buy when I went to the store—I used to have to memorize them on my fingers. The doctor—Dr. Smiley, who was new up there then—came in, and he felt right away what was the matter, and he said, "You don't want to get well!," and I said, "Oh, yes, I do," and he said, "No—you don't," —so then, of course, finally, I had to admit that I didn't. And he pled with me to try to get well, because he said he was new there, and if one of his patients died, they'd figure he wasn't any good. So finally I got well. But when I went to court for the divorce, I couldn't answer any of the questions they asked me: I'd just stand there like a dumb ox.

I went down to Oklahoma where my father was—my father had set up as a doctor—I don't know if he ever knew how to give anything but calomel, but he certainly gave plenty of that—and the whole community down there got to be practically dependent on him—he learned by experimenting on them, too. That was in Eagletown, which is half way between Broken Bow, Oklahoma, and De Queen, Arkansas—that's a district they call the Sticks because there's so much timber there. The country is really beautiful: they have all these yellow pines and what they call ironwood that turns first brown and then yellow, and sort of a henna-colored soil—but the people don't do anything with it. Where we were, the Choctaw Lumber Company had come in and put them to work—somebody has to do something with them—they'd just sit and rock, otherwise. Each family owns a cow, and if they're ambitious they have a "hawg" and they'd let it go at that. I tell you, you have to go down and live among them to believe that there are such people! They won't talk—all you can get out of them is "yes" and "no" and "Ah reckon." But they watch everything you do—the first morning I was there, all the women hung around and watched me get washed. You ought to have seen their faces when they saw some of the things I did—they thought I was outlandish—they didn't have to do that, see! And when I brushed my teeth! They couldn't make out what it was. They don't have any toothbrushes down there—they use snuff-sticks instead. And the women would watch me from the house across the street when I got undressed at night. The only way they know how to amuse themselves is to play craps—that's their diversion. My father had a mechanical piano brought down to try to entertain them, and you ought to have seen the crowd around the house every night—they just stood there and stared with their mouths open. They'd never heard any music before—only just these old fiddles they have.

They played that mechanical piano every night for a month, and I couldn't stand it any longer finally. I walked out one night and said, "Golly! I can't stand this tinned music any more!" They looked at me real sore and said, "Didja ever hear any better?" Later on, they had pictures there—in the same room that was the school and the church; but most of the older people didn't go—that was kind of new, see. I used to go and see films of New York, and it would make me just wild to go there. I got in wrong with them all around.—In the first place, I didn't make my boy go to church, and they're all very moral—or claim to be. And they couldn't understand why I read books—if they saw me reading a book, they'd put me through a regular cross-examination—they'd want to know what it was and why I wanted to read it. They didn't even read the Bible—they figured they wouldn't know about it. I read Darwin and some of Haeckel down there that my father had and *The Wandering Jew* by Eugene Sue. Now I like to read D. H. Lawrence and Michael Arlen. And then another thing I did they didn't like was to speak to niggers I knew in the street—you're not supposed to do that—it's as much as your life is worth to speak to a nigger. I used to go out for long walks with a book and that made them very suspicious—they wanted to know why I wanted to go out for a walk alone.

Finally, they decided that I was some kind of a fancy woman, who was meeting men in the woods—they began to talk about me like I was a menace to the town. At the same time, when I went out, the men would always follow me. There was a man with a wooden leg who used to get on my nerves—he was the most persistent of all. I used to hear his wooden leg stomping behind me wherever I went, and I used to have to dodge him among the trees. Some of the men had been in the war, and they'd been away and weren't quite so narrow-minded as the other people—one of them told me about how he was in an attack and he saw a German coming toward him with his thumb, which had been cut off, just hanging loose by the skin. "Ah couldn't kill him," he said, "so Ah just took him to the hospital." I asked him why he had gone into the war—"Why," he said, "Ah figgered that if we didn't go over there and git them, they'd come over here and git us. That's what the newspapers said. Why? wasn't it true?" He was nice—but most of the men were the kind that tar and feather people. In fact, finally, one day I was out for a walk with an engineer, who was the only man in the community I could talk to—and we were sitting on the railroad track, and all of a sudden a man jumped out of the bushes and pointed a shotgun at us and said, "What are you doing on that railroad track?" I was mad, I can tell you! I stood up and I said, "You must think we want to go some place to make love—to go out on the railroad track! But go ahead and shoot me! Here I am! You'll never have a better target!"

That was too much for me—I decided to leave and take a chance on New York. First I lived in the Bronx, and that was terrible. But I'd heard about the Village. There was a Greenwich Village girl in Seattle—a little Roumanian Jewess. I got to know her when I left the woods and lived with her while I was sick. She had painted fans and things—I'd never seen anything like that. So finally I came to the Village. I did sewing. Now I run this little store, and I like it, because I always had a sort of an original taste in decorations and things. I make these blouses myself—they're not afraid of having them too bright down here. Another thing is that nobody cares what you do down here—nobody expects you to cook or to go to church—and you can always talk to interesting people. I tell you, the West is all right, but it's a great relief to get some place where you can feel a little bit free. I know all about those great open spaces.

April 15, 1925

II. *Fire-Alarm*

The first expressionist play we ever did at the Hole-and-Corner Playhouse was a piece called *Fire-Alarm* by

a man named DeGross Wilbur. We put it on because
the author had offered to finance it himself. The play was
in eighteen scenes and dealt with the nervous breakdown
of a worker in a paper-box factory. In the first scene, you
saw him making boxes: he and the other workers wore
pasteboard masks of the same material as the boxes and
performed monotonous movements in unison. Finally, a
gong is sounded for quitting time, and all the workers
leave except the hero (who, in the program, was called
simply The Man): he gets up and looks about him; the
lights have been turned on the scenery (which has been
hitherto left in darkness), and he realizes that he is imprisoned in a great paper box. Then the sides of the box
become transparent, and he sees the families of the officials
and the shareholders of the paper-box business parading
pompously about him. A pretty girl seems to smile at him,
and he tries to go to meet her, but finds that he is balked
by the sides of the box. A policeman threatens him, and
he falls to the ground in despair. The next scene is a
long soliloquy: the stars have come out in the sky, and
the Man can see them through the paper box. They are
red, yellow and green and are continually going on and
off (DeGross declared it was silly to have stars of the
conventional kind, when no one saw them that way any
longer: these were modern American stars and ten times
the ordinary size). The Man apostrophizes the stars:
"Oh, little jazz-babies," he says, "oh, little jazz-babies,
twinkling so bright as you dance the shimmy of the
spheres! Oh, little jazz-babies, winking, with the mascara
of night on your eyelashes!—look down on the great
smoky city and tell me where my sweetie is!" This goes
on for some time. The next scene is still in the box. The
owner of the factory appears and tries to induce the Man
to go back to work; then a member of the union comes in
and tries to induce him to strike. Both were played by

the same actor, with the same make-up but different clothes. The Man sends them both away, telling them that their aims are identical and that he has no use for either. Then the man has another long soliloquy; then a Physicist appears. The Physicist explains to the Man that he has discovered a new system of morality based on the quantum theory. He has learned to disintegrate matter, and, by the application of powerful rays, he makes the paper-box prison disappear. Thereafter, the play presents the adventures of the Man and the Professor of Physics in their pursuit of the new code of morality. This code is based on discontinuity: you suddenly do the opposite of whatever you have previously done. This enables you to rob trusting friends, to trip up people walking in the street and to put knock-out drops in the cocktails of people you have invited to dinner. The Man and the Professor of Physics experiment with all these things, but they are all very disappointing. The jewelry stolen from the trusting friends turns out to be bogus, and the drugged guests have nothing in their pockets but ragged pocket-handkerchiefs and are wearing false dress-shirt fronts and made-up hook-on ties. The people tripped up in the street turn upon the practical jokers, and one of them hurls the Man through the plate-glass window of a fashionable modiste. There he encounters the girl who smiled at him and whom he has ever since been seeking, but she turns out to be a wooden mannequin. In his chagrin at this disillusion, he promptly puts into practice the morality of the Professor by assassinating him on the spot and throwing him down a drain. But, in a moment, the Physicist reappears, made unearthly by a colder kind of light. We realize now for the first time that the Physicist represents Truth, which is unchangeable and indomitable. This is conveyed to us in a soliloquy by the Man. Toward the end of this soliloquy, a large rhomboid in the backdrop begins to glow. "Come with me," says the Physicist, "into the Light!" And both advance into the mercury-tube dawn.

When I first read the script of this play, I felt a good deal of interest in a young paper-box worker—I had been given to understand that the author was himself a worker —who had developed such a singular vein of fancy. But when I met DeGross Wilbur, I discovered that he was a pale vain young man, who not only had never seen a paper-box factory in his life, but had never even been near the textile mills where his father made bathing-suits. It was the money from the bathing-suits, however, which financed DeGross's play. I asked him how he had come to write the play, if he had had so little real feeling for the workers; and he answered that he simply believed that the time had now arrived for plays of that sort to be written. I asked him why he called his play *Fire-Alarm*, and he said that, as he had originally written it, it had ended with the Professor and the Man heading a peace delegation to the President and then setting the White House on fire; and that, even though this scene had been taken out, the title was still true to the spirit of the play, which was frankly one of revolution. Later on, however, I heard him telling someone that *Fire-Alarm* was intended to have no political significance but to be taken as a "farce for live puppets, of which the moral was a Buddhistic resignationism." "You must always play for laughs," he told us. "In the dinner scene, where the Physicist and the Man pick the pockets of the guests they have drugged, you must have the guests come to life and turn seltzer bottles on them. It is years and years since a seltzer bottle has been seen on the American stage. They have been banned by the dollar-chasing 'refinement' of the uptown commercial theater. But we shall never have a real native American Drama till the

seltzer bottle squirts again!" Three days before the opening, he told us that it had always been his idea to have
a fire bell and a siren continuously sounding between
each two scenes; otherwise, he said, the title would be
meaningless. And this we tried for awhile.

I cannot say that the play was well directed: it was
scarcely directed at all. The titular director was a fellow
named Bob Mott, who had done a little of everything
in the Village. In those days, in Greenwich Village,
wherever you went to a party, there was always an impressive person who seemed so free from affectation that
you took him for one of the distinguished artists who
sometimes lived down there. He would sit in a corner
and smoke with a homely or rugged assurance that
seemed to mask treasures of subtlety and wit, and people
would gather about him to hear his judgments on all
sorts of subjects. Bob Mott was one of these persons. He
went striding around the Village with a thick and
knobby cane, a rough-and-ready old soft hat and a large
pipe, which he usually kept in his teeth all the time he
was talking; but, when you really got to know him, you
found out that the basis of his character was a smug
invincible limpness. He was, therefore, not a very good
director. It cannot be said that Bob did not appreciate the
play: on the contrary, during the rehearsals, he spent so
much time laughing at the jokes that he never got around
to finding means for making them effective with the
audience; and, at the end of a scene which moved him
strongly, as certain scenes invariably did when the actors
remembered all the lines and went through them without halting, he would turn to the nearest bystander and,
with his pipe clenched between his teeth, whisper
loudly, "God! what a punch!" He used to watch the
rehearsals very knowingly, always puffing his pipe; but
he never gave the actors any useful instructions, except

occasionally to take them aside and hold whispered con-versations with them—conversations that were mostly in-tended to promote Bob's relations with the actresses rather than the progress of the play. He was usually more or less drunk. He and DeGross Wilbur used to have terrific quarrels.

Jane Gooch, who also designed the costumes and man-aged the publicity end, did most of the real work of direction. She made a point of looking in on the re-hearsals every other day or so to see that the actors were managing to get on and off the stage and taking each other up on their cues. But she was never able to stay very long and so could not enforce the discipline and keep the actors up to the efforts which are required for a successful production. All sorts of other people used to drift in and out while the rehearsals were going on. They would make all sorts of suggestions to Bob Mott and to the actors. There was one man who ran a book shop who was jealous of one of the actresses, a girl with whom he had been living and whom he had begun to suspect of an interest in one of the members of the cast. He would come and sit there every day, and sometimes conceal himself behind the scenes, where the actors would fall over him as they were making their exits. Bob Mott had a police-dog named Hindenburg, which he always brought to the theater with him and which barked at the fire-alarm and the scenes in which people were knocked around. There was also a Polish girl, who drank and was in love with Bob Mott. We used to hear her sobbing in the pauses. The day of the dress rehearsal, Jane Gooch, who had been overworking, arrived in the afternoon, and, after witnessing a scene or two, broke down and had hysterics. She recovered, however, and did what she could.

Fire-Alarm did not run very long, but the run was extremely varied. On some occasions, the audience would hiss; and, on others, they would sit in utter silence. At one performance, a single spectator laughed harshly at one of the satiric lines and the rest of the audience hushed him. Sometimes we could hear people weeping; and sometimes they laughed so wildly that they broke the actors up. ("I am perfectly satisfied," DeGross would say. "The play has a thousand facets.") Sometimes they had nearly all left before it was half through. Nor did this altogether depend on the accidental mood of the audience: the performances differed remarkably. The prompter, whose English was poor, had difficulty in following the lines, so that parts of the play were dropped out when the actors forgot their speeches. The soliloquies were particularly treacherous and were often abruptly telescoped by the omission of long passages, before the actors who were supposed to play the following scenes had had time to arrive in the wings and pick up their cues. Sometimes the stage manager, who was also the electrician and who was having a crisis with his wife, would forget to lower the curtain, so that the actors, at the end of an act, had to hold their positions like living statues. One night, during the final scene, when the Professor took the hero by the arm and led him toward the dawn of Truth, the electric rhomboid, at the back of the stage, instead of bursting into brightness, merely gave a momentary glow and then began to grow fainter and fainter. When the Professor delivered his exhortation, "Come with me into the Light!", the stage was entirely dark. There was a good deal of laughter at this, and DeGross asked us to do it this way every night, because it made the ending more ironic. He said that, in allowing the play to end on a note of hope, he had been subconsciously affected by the pressure of the popular taste in favor of a happy ending, and that this accident had made him realize how much finer it was to end in dark-ness. We dissuaded him from this, however.

According to a tradition of the theater, the last night of a run is a special occasion: the actors play practical jokes, which are usually unnoticed by the audience, and try to break one another up. Now, the actors in *Fire-Alarm* had been through a good deal for the play, and they felt that they had the right to express their relief at its closing by hoaxes of an exceptionally elaborate kind. The stage manager, who was feeling more cheerful because his wife had come back, also entered into the spirit of the occasion and spent hours, unknown to the actors, arranging surprises and pitfalls. Thus, for the first scene, in which the hero tries to break through the sides of the box, he made invisible slits in the gauze so that the actor put his leg and arm through and had to pull them back again. And when the Employer in a later scene picked up his silk hat from the table, a shower of pretzels fell out. The guests in the dinner scene took the wind out of the hero's indignation by wearing real dress shirts instead of false ones and having large rolls of bills in their pockets. (During this scene, Bob Mott's police-dog also wandered in from the wings and licked one of the corpses on the nose.) The stage manager's most in-genious effect occurred in one of the interior sets: the Professor was supposed to open a door and enter from the outside; but the door had been fixed so that its hinges were at the bottom instead of at the side, and it came down on the stage like a portcullis; the actor had to walk in over it. When he later tried to make his exit through the door on the other side and pushed at the knob to open it, it turned out to have been taken off its hinges al-together and, evading the Professor's grasp, was wafted away into space by someone on the other side. In the midst of the final soliloquy, which the hero delivered from a high set of steps, these steps were rolled slowly behind the scenes, carrying the soliloquy with them; and when the Professor began talking about the Light, a flash-light was set off right in front of him, which upset the actor so much that he began again several speeches back and started to play the scene over.

Most of the audience laughed: there were not very many there. But after the performance, a strange rigid woman—a spinster of about forty-five, who wore spectacles and was dressed in hideous clothes of some remote age and place—appeared at the stage door and desired to meet the author. She talked nervously, as if under intense pressure, and I thought she was a little mad. When DeGross Wilbur appeared, she complimented him on his play with a curious acid eagerness that sounded as if she were so unaccustomed to expressing herself with enthusiasm that she lacked the appropriate accents. "Tell me, please, Mr. Wilbur," she demanded, "have you ever been in Gibson, Colorado? I am sure you must have been in Gibson!" DeGross said that he had never been there. "What you have given us," she went on, "so insolently—I might almost say, so atrociously—with a defiance so categoric—is a compendium of all its laxities, its brazennesses, its eclipses, as well as of its few limpid lovelinesses. I should have said that no one could have written that play who had never been a schoolteacher in Gibson! The Employer's coarse market-mindedness, so sickeningly submerged in the foodstuffs by which alone man cannot live! All his purposes are directed toward it! Above it his thoughts cannot leap!" (She was speaking of the shower of pretzels.) "I have seen it a thousand times! And the stars that do but caricature our passions when we cry to them in their coolness and clearness—and the dreadful doors of our rooms that seem to topple inward upon us or to waver away at our touch, as we pass from cell to cell of torment!"

As I say, I thought she was mad. That was my first meeting with Isabelle Griffin. I did not know that she was eventually to become the first woman dramatist of importance in the history of the theater. And I was even further from guessing that this immature and incoherent play of Wilbur's was actually to show her the way to her own creative development. She had come on to New York for the first time and for only a very brief visit, and if she had not seen *Fire-Alarm* at the suggestion of another schoolteacher with whom she was staying in St. Luke's Place, it is unlikely—since she read almost nothing but seventeenth-century poetry—that she would ever have come into contact with the methods of German expressionism, which, imperfectly assimilated and exemplified as they were in *Fire-Alarm*, were in her case to prove so fruitful. Today, one speaks of Isabelle Griffin and Strindberg. Nor was it merely the calculated effects of the play that influenced her own technique: she was also, to some extent, happily inspired by the accidents and jokes of the final performance. The Physicist's sudden setback when the flashlight was set off at the end provided Miss Griffin, for example, with scenes of a curious effectiveness, in which whole passages of dialogue were repeated.

DeGross Wilbur himself soon sloughed off the modernist tricks which he had been at such pains to acquire and took to writing those amusing comedies which began with satiric pictures of the country-club life of industrial towns and ended on the Riviera with the international cocktail set.

April 20, 1927

SHERWOOD ANDERSON'S *MANY MARRIAGES*

I CANNOT REGARD *Many Marriages*, the new novel by Sherwood Anderson, as a quite worthy successor to *The Triumph of the Egg*. It takes the subjective method of the last story of that book, *Out of Nowhere Into Nothing* —which was already rather too long—and applies it on an even more elaborate scale. It may be that I am not in a position to judge *Many Marriages* quite fairly, because the author, at the time he was writing it, once told me the story at length. It then seemed to me fresh and surprising, like a dream that was remembered with vividness and that kept for the dreamer some strange special significance. In the telling, it had all of the quality that has often brought Anderson, at his best, closer to the art of the poet than to that of the writer of fiction. But when I came to read the story in its extended form, I found it tedious and sometimes flat. It is as if Mr. Anderson had diluted his ideas until they had lost a good deal of their force. The incident, for example, of the meeting between the girl and the boy, when both find themselves for the moment delivered from the sense of shame, and she swims to him out of sleep like a diver from profound waters, is certainly very fine; but one has to hear too much about it—or rather, what one keeps on hearing adds too little to what one has already heard. Mr.

Anderson's repetitions, which are intended to, and which do at their best, give the effect of the rhythms of living, become here indefensibly boring. We have, for example, to listen twice to a complete and detailed description of the finding of the little green stone which is to stand as a symbol of life, and whenever it is mentioned later, this description is partly repeated. It is a little like *The House That Jack Built*.

It is a habit of Mr. Anderson's to divest his characters of their incidentals, their furniture, their houses, their clothes, their ordinary social relations; and he produces in the best of his stories an impression of classic simplicity. But this feature of his writing, also, comes off badly in *Many Marriages*. The characters seem strangely pale, as if they had been stripped of their personalities, too. The wife assigned to the hero is quite inconceivable as a human being. She presents the blank face of a phantom. When her husband announces that he is leaving her, she accommodatingly poisons herself without uttering a word of remonstrance. Such a woman, however sexless, might be expected at least to have some existence in connection with her family and her household; but Mrs. Webster gives up her daughter without making the faintest struggle. It is like something in a children's charade or one of those comic-strips, in which people fall dead, amid a galaxy of stars, at some catastrophic "wisecrack." We seem to see Mrs. Webster clasping her hand to her forehead and shooting up several feet into the air. It is true, of course, that poor Mrs. Webster is intended as an example of death-in-life; but even a corpse should be human. And in the case of Nathalie Schwartz, the mistress, who is played off against the wife, this explanation cannot apply. We are repeatedly told how strong she is, yet Nathalie, too, is a specter whose voice we are never allowed to hear. We end with an irritated feeling that the hero has simply dropped one lay-figure in order to pick up another.

Yet, in spite of the feebleness, even flabbiness, of the texture of *Many Marriages*, the book is not wholly devoid of the queer and disquieting impressiveness which one feels in all Anderson's work. Here as elsewhere, we are soothed as well as disturbed by the feeling of hands thrust down among the inner organs of life—hands that are delicate and clean but still pitiless in their explorations. My only quarrel here with Mr. Anderson is that he has not thrust down so far as usual. He takes up the familiar theme of the husband who tires of his wife and goes off with someone else, and he leaves it much more nearly as he found it than it has been his wont to do with the cases with which he deals. Awakening husband and frozen wife are not quite different enough from the people in Miss Cather's *One of Ours* or Mr. Hergesheimer's *Cytherea*. Yet even when Sherwood Anderson cannot save a banal theme from banality, his banality is something distinct from the banality of other people. He has arrived at it all by himself. At his best, Sherwood Anderson functions with a natural ease and beauty on a plane in the depths of life—as if under a diving-bell submerged in the human soul—which makes the world of the ordinary novelist seem stagy and superficial. At his worst, as in *Many Marriages*, one feels, as one cannot feel in the cases of so many of his contemporaries, that he is at least, in the pursuit of his own ideal, making his own mistakes.

April, 1923

RING LARDNER'S AMERICAN
CHARACTERS

MR. RING LARDNER is a popular journalist who writes for the New York *American* and who also provides the text for a syndicated comic strip. It has therefore been thought appropriate to present his new collection of short stories as if it were a volume of popular humor. There are a preface in the vein of Bill Nye and a jocose introduction to every story, and the title page is brightened by a humorous cut that is evidently by John Held. The book itself, from its burlesque preface, is called *How to Write Short Stories*, instead of, as it ought to be, *Champion and Other Stories*.

Is all this an idea of the publishers, who do not want to forfeit the prestige of Mr. Lardner's reputation as a humorist, or is it due to Mr. Lardner, who is timid about coming forward in the role of serious writer? The fact is that this new book of his, instead of belonging to the gruesome department of, say, Irvin Cobb's *Speaking of Operations*, contains some of the most interesting work that Ring Lardner has yet produced. These stories he observes in his preface, "will illustrate in a half-hearted way what I am trying to get at." But the stories are not half-hearted: it is the jokes that he intrudes among them. The nonsense of his introductions is so far below his usual level that one suspects him of a guilty conscience

94

at attempting to disguise his talent for social observation and satire. For, aside from a very few things, such as *The Facts*, that seem a little magazine-made, what one finds in *How to Write Short Stories* is a series of studies of American types almost equal in importance to those of Sherwood Anderson and Sinclair Lewis.

It may, indeed, be said of Ring Lardner that, if we compare him with these other two writers, he shows a certain specific advantage over each of them. In those of Mr. Lardner's stories in which he attempts something rather similar to Sherwood Anderson's *The Egg* or *I'm a Fool*, he shows a firmer grasp both of the Western vernacular and of the external realities with which he is dealing. In a sense, he is closer to life. It is curious to speculate what would have happened to some of the stories in this collection if they had been written by Sherwood Anderson. Two of Lardner's baseball players— Alibi Ike and a scout who is willing to risk ruining his team for the sake of a perfect quartet—may almost be called neurotics; and a third—the demon batter in *My Roomy*—is evidently quite insane. What startling pre-occupations might not have been revealed to the reader if Anderson had X-rayed their deepest insides! Is not the mysterious Elliot, who insists upon shaving in the middle of the night and cannot sleep unless the water in the bathtub is running, a brother to John Webster of *Many Marriages*, who appeared before his daughter naked, and to the girl in *Out of Nowhere Into Nothing*, who used to listen to the water-pail slopping over? With Anderson, you are sometimes so far submerged in the spiritual sensations of these characters that you lose sight of them as actual people in an actual Western community; with Lardner's queer cases, however, you are never taken inside them; you see them only in their relations with other people. And when Lardner comes closest to Lewis, as in

the story called *The Golden Honeymoon*, he is less likely
than Lewis to caricature, and hence to falsify, because he
is primarily interested in studying a kind of person rather
than in drawing up an indictment.

But Mr. Lardner has, of course, not as yet attained the
stature of either of these men. Anderson has a poet's
sensibility; Lewis, a satirist's fury. But what Lardner may
have to match these he has never yet fully revealed. For
all his saturnine tone, his apparent scorn of vulgar values,
he seems committed to popular journalism. He does not
even care to admit that he has tried to do work on a
higher level—hence the clownish presentation of these
stories. Yet he would seem to come closer than anyone
else among living American writers to possessing the combination of qualities that made *Huckleberry Finn* a
masterpiece. For one thing, he has ready invention—
which most American realists have not; and for another—
what is even rarer—an unmistakable personal accent
which represents a special way of looking at things. Even
such important examples of recent American realism as
Sinclair Lewis's *Main Street* and *Babbitt* have been put
together largely out of literary materials that the author
found ready to hand—the pre-war English novel of Bennett and Wells. But Ring Lardner seems to have imitated
nobody, and nobody else could reproduce his essence.
You have to read the whole of a novel of Lewis to find
out that there is anything remarkable about it; but there
is scarcely a paragraph of Lardner's which, in its irony
both fresh and morose, does not convey somehow the
sense of a distinguished aloof intelligence. And he has
shown an unexcelled, a perhaps unrivalled, mastery of
what since the publication of Mencken's book, has come
to be known as the American language. Mark Twain, in
his foreword to *Huckleberry Finn*, explained that he had
taken great care to differentiate between "the Missouri

Negro dialect; the extremest form of the backwoods Southwestern dialect; the ordinary 'Pike County' dialect; and four modified varieties of this last." So Lardner has marked the distinction between the baseball player's and the prize-fighter's slang, can speak the language of the Chicago song-writer of *Some Like Them Cold,* who has come to New York to make his fortune, and has equally at his command the whole vocabulary of adolescent clichés of the young girl who writes to the songwriter, and of the quite different set of clichés of the middle-aged man from New Jersey who goes to Florida for his golden honeymoon. And he understands the difference between the spoken language of these semi-literate types and the language they will use when they write. Finally, what is most important, he writes the vernacular like an artist and not merely like a clever journalist—as George Ade or O. Henry did. There is nothing artificial or forced about the use of slang in these stories; it is as natural as it is apt. Lardner's language is the product of a philologist's ear and a born writer's relish for words.

Will Ring Lardner, then, go on to his *Huckleberry Finn* or has he already told all he knows? It may be that the mechanical repetition of a trick that one finds in such a story as *Horseshoes* and the melodramatic exaggeration of *Champion* indicate limitations. But you never know: here is a man who has had the freedom of the modern West no less than Mark Twain did of the old one, who approaches it, as Mark Twain did, with a perceptive interest in human beings instead of with the naturalist's formula—a man who lives at a time when, if one be not sold irredeemably into bondage to the *Saturday Evening Post,* it is far easier for a serious writer to get published and find a hearing than it was in Mark Twain's day. If Ring Lardner has anything more to give us, the time has now come to deliver it. He has not even popular glory to gain by pursuing any other course. His popular vein is about worked out; and he has always been too much of an artist to make the biggest kind of success as a clown; his books have never sold so well as Stephen Leacock's or Irvin Cobb's. When Lewis himself, in his earlier phase a humorist for the *Saturday Evening Post*, took a chance and composed in *Main Street* his satire upon its readers, he received unexpected support. It turned out that there were thousands of people who were ready to hear what he wanted to say. What bell might not Lardner ring if he set out to give us the works?

July, 1924

EUGENE O'NEILL AND THE NATURALISTS

I. Eugene O'Neill as Prose-Writer

THE NEW VOLUME of Eugene O'Neill's plays contains *The Hairy Ape, Anna Christie* and *The First Man*. The first of these seems to me almost the only thing that Mr. O'Neill has yet written that has very much value as literature apart from its effectiveness as drama. As a rule, the plays of O'Neill are singularly uninviting on the printed page. The dialogue is raw and prosaic, in texture quite undistinguished, and the author has made no attempt to appeal to the imagination by way of the stage directions, which are not lifted above the baldness of the prompt-book. These plays appear too often, in short, as rather second-rate naturalistic pieces that owe their eminence, not to their intrinsic greatness, but, as Marx said of John Stuart Mill, "to the flatness of the surrounding country." The dialogue of *The First Man*, which I have not seen on the stage, proves in the reading so tasteless and dreary that one does not see how one could sit through it.

But Eugene O'Neill has another vein in which he is a literary artist of genius. When he is writing the more or less grammatical dialogue of the middle-class characters of his plays, his prose is heavy and indigestible even beyond the needs of naturalism. People say the same things to one another over and over again and never succeed in saying them any more effectively than the first time; long speeches shuffle dragging feet, marking time without progressing, for pages. But as soon as Mr. O'Neill gets a character who can only talk some kind of vernacular, he begins to write like a poet. We had already had evidence of this in the Negro hero of *The Emperor Jones* and in the first act of *Anna Christie*, but when one saw *The Hairy Ape* produced by the Province-town Players, one had the feeling that Mr. O'Neill had for the first time become fully articulate. As Walter Pritchard Eton said, he wrote slang like "a sort of wild organ music." The scenes in which the non-illiterate characters talk are as clumsy and dead as ever, but the greater part of the play, in which Yank, the stoker, dis-courses, has a mouth-filling rhythmical eloquence very rare in naturalistic drama.

When the speeches came to life in this way, the drama was always more moving. One felt that Mr. O'Neill, in his gift for drawing music from humble people, had a kinship with Sherwood Anderson. For *The Hairy Ape* is the tragedy not, as in the common formula, of the American pitted against his environment nor even of the proletarian pitted against capitalism, but of the universal human being pitted against himself. It is, as Mr. O'Neill has labelled it, a play "of ancient and modern life." I have heard this disputed by people who had got the im-pression from seeing the play that the hero of *The Hairy Ape* is thwarted by the forces of society instead of by his own limitations. But I believe that if anyone will read the last scenes in the printed text, he will see that though it is a consciousness of social inferiority that gives the first impetus to Yank's débâcle and though he himself at first supposes that it is society he has to fight, the Hairy Ape's ultimate struggle for freedom takes place within the man himself. I am not sure that Mr. O'Neill always gives enough dramatic emphasis to his most important ideas. The significance of these last scenes of *The Hairy Ape* was not thrown into relief on the stage. People seemed to understand the play better when they saw it a second time. This is a reason—aside from the fact that the *Ape* is good literature—that it is useful to have it in a book.

November, 1922

II. All God's Chillun and Others

Catskill Dutch by Roscoe Brink was a long, conscientious, rather boring play about rural life on the Hudson after the Civil War. There is a good deal of this sort ot naturalism now being turned out in America. No longer than a decade ago, our critics were still complaining of the scarcity of sober realism in American fiction and drama; that was the period of the great ascendancy of the school of Arnold Bennett and Stanley Houghton, and almost nobody but Dreiser, in the United States, was doing anything of the sort for us. Now the formula has been discovered, and dozens of people are applying it. The writer had occasion recently to go through the manuscripts submitted in a magazine short-story contest and, even knowing the popularity of novels like Lewis's and Willa Cather's, was astonished by the unanimity with which this formula had been adopted: of the three ablest writers who emerged, one dealt with the Jews on the New York East Side, another with the Southern Negroes, and a third with the suburbs of San Francisco. All three, like Mr. Brink, wrote competently and sincerely; but none of them had anything much that was personal or vivid to communicate. They tended, like Mr. Brink, to be duller than the life they described.

Thus we are getting the backwash of the naturalistic movement—as we have of so many other movements—

when Europe is just leaving it behind. What in the
theater is called expressionism represents an attempt to
escape from the literal methods of realism—as the cubism
of Braque and Picasso represents an attempt to escape
from the photographic ideals of nineteenth-century painting. The expressionistic method, as Mr. Stark Young has
said, is "merely the poetic method"; but it has produced
a genre that differs from any previous dramatic poetry,
because it is practised by people who have had to break
away from naturalism. It was not a problem for Shakespeare to disregard literal realism and to have any sort
of character give vent to his inmost thoughts in the non-
colloquial language of the imagination, because Shakespeare did not have to make the effort of unlearning Ibsen
and Shaw. But the dramatic poet today has to take a
naturalistic subject and try to knock poetry into it—just
as the modern painter has to take a conventional still-life
and by main force hack it to pieces and shuffle up the
fragments in a novel pattern. Hence the discordant con-
ceits, the limping allegories, of such a play as *The Man
Who Ate the Popomack*—a pioneer English expressionistic
comedy by W. J. Turner. *The Man Who Ate the Popomack*, though it has a dash of wit and some charming
speeches (particularly in the Chinese scene), is, on the
whole, rather an unsatisfactory medley of a little Shaw,
a little Galsworthy, a little expressionism and a residuum
of jokes from *Punch* (the man who comes to dinner in a
diving suit). The difficulties of presenting a fairy-tale
mixed up with a drawing-room comedy seem acutely to
have been felt by the producers, who have radically
altered Mr. Turner's text and presented as a conventional
dream what the author, as appears from the printed
play, meant to be shown as actually happening. I don't
think they have improved matters by doing this; I prefer

Mr. Turner's version. But then it is true that the author has not solved the problem himself.

A much better play than either of these, *All God's Chillun Got Wings* by Eugene O'Neill, also shows signs of an effort to impose subjective fancies upon an idea objectively conceived. The Provincetown Players, in producing the play, have not tried to carry out the idea that appears in the author's text, of having the walls and ceiling of the interior set contract as the situation becomes more oppressive, but they have made him a present of a curious church with a waist like a human being's and flying buttresses of brick that seem to be streaming away in the wind. These devices, both author's and producer's, strike one as a little mechanical, as not quite belonging with the rest of the play; but, in any case, they are unimportant and not typical of the treatment of the whole. Mr. O'Neill has made a much more effective departure from the cumbersome naturalism of the "transcript from life" of the type of *Catskill Dutch*, by simply throwing overboard most of its detail. He has sheared away, in *All God's Chillun*, almost everything except the relation between his two central characters, and, in doing so, has gained intensity, one of the qualities our realism most needs.

For the rest, *All God's Chillun Got Wings* is one of the best things yet written about the race problem of Negro and white and one of the best of O'Neill's plays. Two of Mr. O'Neill's chief assets are, first, a nervous driving force that carries the audience inescapably along; and, second, a gift for the eloquent use of the various forms of the American vernacular. Both of these *All God's Chillun* has. It is not quite so consistently compelling or well-written as *The Emperor Jones* or *The Hairy Ape*; it has its harsh notes and its raw expanses.

But then, it has a certain advantage over either of these other plays in presenting two characters equally strong, in collision with one another, instead of one central character who only contends with himself.

Mr. O'Neill has another qualification which sets him completely apart from the other American dramatists, who have so far done very little more than modify the conventional American comedy in the direction of Shaw or Sinclair Lewis: he nearly always, with whatever crudeness, is expressing some real experience, some impact directly from life. The characters and the scene in O'Neill are sometimes forbiddingly bleak—as in the latter part of *All God's Chillun*—but they are likely at any moment, by taking on the power and the awfulness of naked natural forces, to establish a violent contact between themselves and us. This was true of even *Welded* (on the stage), a monotonous drama of marriage —which failed principally, it seems to me, through not having been well enough written. Mr. O'Neill, with this sort of subject from ordinary middle-class life, does not pay enough attention to style. A play, like anything else that is built of words, is primarily a work of literature, and even the most vigorous dramatic idea cannot be trusted to make its effect without the right words to convey it. All but the greatest of actors are liable to betray a careless text, but an accurate and brilliant text will manage to speak for itself in spite of the very worst. The expressiveness of Mr. O'Neill seems to diminish in direct proportion to his distance from the language of the people. At one pole, you have *The Hairy Ape*, certainly his best-written play; at the other *Welded*, perhaps his worst. In *All God's Chillun Got Wings*, you see his quality rising and falling—between the stale language of stock-company melodrama and the vivid, the racy, the real.   May 28, 1924

THE NEW AMERICAN COMEDY

TEN YEARS AGO people flocked to comedies like *It Pays to Advertise*, in which the heroes were breezy business men who made a great deal of money in the last act, or to sentimental dramas like *Turn to the Right*, in which the simple American home was glorified. Today, they go to the theater to see satires like *Beggar on Horseback* by Marc Connelly and George S. Kaufman, in which business is made ridiculous; or comedies like George Kelly's *The Show-Off* and J. P. McEvoy's *The Potters*, in which business is made obnoxious and the American home hideous. It is not merely that these plays find producers but that they actually become very popular. *The Potters* is now in its seventh month, and *The Show-Off* has celebrated its hundredth performance. The work of a younger generation who have served their apprenticeships to the bond-selling business and the advertising agencies, to the ideals of Main Street generally, and who, encouraged no doubt by Lewis's example, have decided to trust their instincts in caricaturing these things, these plays find, as Lewis's novels did, audiences with similar instincts, who want nothing better than a chance to guffaw at their own preposterous dullness. Such comedies and their public are a sign—if not quite indubitably that America is becoming more intelligent—at least that a good many Americans have reached a point of supersaturation with our current commercial ideals. We have at last become aware that our commercialism has certain unattractive aspects and have begun to satirize ourselves. The crass business man, indeed, as well as the romantic advertiser, are already showing signs—in the pages of *Life*, for example—of passing into the popular mind as stereotyped comic characters, like the dude or the hayseed of yesterday.

Our satirists, nevertheless, have retained a good deal of the machinery, and hence of the point of view, of the business man's comedy upon which they have improved. The homely little old mother of *Turn to the Right* still survives—though in a modified form—as a fundamental element in *The Show-Off* and even in *Expressing Willie*; and the principal male characters, however absurd or hollow, do not fail to make a great deal of money at the end of the last act, like the hero of *It Pays to Advertise*. Aubrey Piper in *The Show-Off* saves his brother-in-law from being swindled out of the profits of his invention, and Mr. Potter turns out, after all, not to have sold the valuable oil lease. Once our writers of comedy depart from the more obvious kind of satire that depends on intensifying ugliness, they gravitate toward the commonplace—nor does it seem to me that the pessimistic heresies of the last scenes of Elmer Rice's *The Adding Machine*, for example, are very much less commonplace than the reassuring conventions I have mentioned. There can, however, be no doubt whatever that in effects of ferocious ugliness our dramatists have recently distinguished themselves. The almost half-witted joviality of *The Show-Off*; the cooped-up poisoned interiors of *The Adding Machine*; and the series of messy collisions between people living too hurriedly or too close together that makes *The Potters* like a long headache: conversations shattered by the subway, meals bolted while transacting business, the love affair on the piazza that is suddenly arrested by the headlights of another pair of lovers who are parking their car in the street, the exasperated members of a family, all with mutually conflicting aims, continually coming and going to the din of the door bell, the telephone, the phonograph and the radio—it is in such heightenings of the surface horrors of modern American life that our theater at present excels.

What one misses, however, in these plays, even at their strongest as satire, is a feeling for literary style. Our American dramatists do not write very well. Marc Connelly and George S. Kaufman deal more fancifully and more gaily than these others with the office building and the suburban sitting-room, but they do not write any better. Zona Gale, who writes well in her novels, loses most of her distinction when she works for the stage. Rachel Crothers, who, in *Expressing Willie*, presents the successful business man going in for culture, has invented some amusing patter for the conversational artist and the psychoanalytic siren into whose hands her hero has fallen, and shows in general a gift for dialogue. Scott Fitzgerald, in his play *The Vegetable*, which has been published and tried out on the stage but never yet brought to New York, has applied to this comedy of commercial mediocrity an imagination further from the commonplace than that of anyone else who has tried it, but his uncertain grasp of his subjects, more dangerous in a play than a novel, seems unpropitious to its success on the stage.

What might we not get, one asks oneself, if Ring Lardner were to write a play? He has already done several amusing sketches, and there is a rumor that he is now composing, in collaboration with George Gershwin, a version of *Carmen* in "the American language." His new book of short stories seems to me to establish him as something much nearer an artist than either Mr. Kelly or Mr.

McEvoy—I might almost say than Mr. Rice. He has a charming imagination and he writes Americanese with a real sense of style. If anyone is capable of doing a one-hundred-percent American comedy that would also be dramatic literature, it is probably Mr. Lardner. But in the meantime, he is busy supplying the text for a syndicated daily comic strip—just as Mr. McEvoy has recently taken the Potters into the comic section with a daily strip of his own. That is the trouble with American comedy. If, on the one hand, it still stays too close to the comedy of yesterday, it is drawn, when it pulls away, toward the slapstick of the funny papers. The dramatists I have mentioned above put before us the materials for a national comedy but they apply to them the methods of the comic strip. What is needed is someone to color them with the temperament of the artist.

June 18, 1924

A VORTEX IN THE NINETIES:
STEPHEN CRANE

MR. THOMAS BEER's *Stephen Crane: A Study in American Letters* is the latest and not one of the least satisfactory additions to the twentieth-century portrait gallery of nineteenth-century celebrities inaugurated five years ago by Mr. Lytton Strachey. Since *Eminent Victorians*, biography in English has become what it has long been in France: a form of literary art. "Those two fat volumes," at seven-fifty a set, which Mr. Strachey deplored in 1918, have already begun to disappear, and instead we have, if not always masterpieces of Stracheyan compression and point, at least narratives that are critical and selective and of dimensions appropriate to their subjects.

Mr. Beer, however, differs from most of his fellows in not imitating Strachey's style as well as his economy and form. Mr. Beer has gone for his style to a writer who had already before Strachey brought something of Strachey's accent to the chronicle of the nineteenth century: he has gone to our own Henry Adams. He patronizes American politics in very much Adams's manner and even imitates those curious transitions—the result, perhaps, in Adams's case, of the effort to impose a unity on a set of historical phenomena that appalled him by their apparent inconsequence—which in his *History of the United States* and *The Education of Henry Adams* suggest sometimes that

the smooth-flowing garment of style has been arranged
with a view to draping rather vague intellectual contours.
We find Mr. Beer writing: "This jape [a bon mot of
Mark Twain's at the expense of Henry James] was in
London six months later, but Crane, a few blocks to the
north of its making, was far from well," or, "He had
read with appreciation Knut Hamsun's *Hunger* when
Karl Harriman brought the book to Brede in summer,
but appetite ceased and Mrs. Crane had agitated con-
ferences with friends as to Switzerland and the Black
Forest." Was there really any point to be made by com-
bining in the same sentence Hamsun's *Hunger* and
Crane's illness?

But Mr. Beer, in spite of this and some other defects
of style, has written an incredibly entertaining book about
one of the most unpromising of periods. The eighties and
nineties in America appear—at least to one who was
born on the hither edge of them—perhaps the most
provincial and uninspired moment in the history of American society. It sometimes seems to me that it is even
possible to detect a distinct intellectual decline between
Americans educated in the seventies and Americans educated in the eighties. In the seventies, men were still living
on the culture and believing in the social ideal which had
survived from the founding of the Republic. The doctors,
the professors, the lawyers and the churchmen who were
graduated from college in the seventies had at once a
certain all-around humanism and a serious and dignified
attitude toward life; they were carrying on an integrity of
moral ideal. But by the eighties Business was flooding in
and ideals were in confusion: the old-fashioned lawyer
was on his way to becoming a corporation lawyer whose
principal function was to keep Business from going to jail;
the doctor was on his way to becoming a modern "specialist" and sending Business to a sanitarium; and the church

and the university were beginning to be abandoned by first-rate men altogether. In the meantime, the men of the eighties, with whatever sound culture and honest aims, were finding themselves launched in a world where there was a great deal of money to be made and most people were trying to make money. Humanism went by the board; moral scruples were put to rout; and seriousness about man and his problems was abrogated entirely in favor of the seriousness of Business about things that were not serious. The State became identified with Business; ideas were shot on sight. The people who acquired money had a pretty good time, one supposes; at least they spent a great deal of money. But life, in the long run, by the turn of the century, seemed to many unsatisfactory. What was a man to do who had been educated for the old America and who once might have served the Republic or followed an interesting profession in a society which offered stability and leisure? Become the slave of Business at one extreme or drink himself to death at the other, but in any case absorb, perhaps unconsciously, enough of the commercial ideal to neutralize any others with which he might have started out. For one of the most depressing features of the American world of this period was that it hardly knew what was the matter with it. It was only at a later date that people like Edith Wharton and Van Wyck Brooks began to diagnose and describe.

Now, Mr. Thomas Beer's success with this unselfconscious epoch has been attained in this book not merely through his minute knowledge of it and his exquisite appreciation of its humors, but from the fact that he has found in the sprawling and unorganized, the prosaic and Philistine America of the end of the nineteenth century a point of intellectual dignity from which it is possible to focus it. Stephen Crane was a vortex of intensity in a generally stagnant sea. He was an artist not as the age understood that word but as the world at large understands it. I do not say that he was a great artist or that he was even of the first rank, but what he had was the real thing and he adulterated it with nothing else.* Stephen Crane had arrived in prose, apparently without having read Maupassant or knowing anything of the school of Flaubert, at precisely their objective method and their ironic point of view, and in poetry, at a terse vers libre which at its best has scarcely been surpassed by any of the more profuse vers librists who have since received more liberal publicity; and he managed to practice his art without any journalistic infection. Mr. Beer says, in fact, that Crane, after years of newspaper training, was never able to write copy successfully: he could no more suspend his artistic sincerity to turn out a half-column on a fire than he was able, in *Active Service*, to concoct a popular novel. And, as a result of this undeviating devotion to a purpose which was, in that period, as little comprehensible to Richard Watson Gilder as it would have been to Mrs. Astor, he seems to have been regarded with almost universal suspicion. Joseph Conrad, who knew him well and who contributes an introduction to Mr. Beer's study, and Mr. Beer, who has been at pains to investigate, both bear witness that Crane could never really have been described as dissipated; and his writing is certainly the product of a mind of unblunted edge. Yet Stephen Crane, in the United States, at the time of

* I should certainly say today that Stephen Crane was an artist of the first rank, but I have left this opinion of the twenties as typical of our contemptuous attitude toward the nineties and our diffidence in making claims for the American writers of the past. It will be noted that, when I mention Crane later in *The All-Star Literary Vaudeville*, my opinion of him has already gone up; and still later, in *The Critic Who Does Not Exist*, I give him a place among American classics.

his great reputation, was accused of every vice and crime from drug-taking and dying in delirium tremens to seducing country girls and attempting to burn James Gordon Bennett's yacht. As he remarked, in 1896: "When people see a banker taking a glass of beer in a café, they say, 'There is Smith.' When they behold a writer taking a glass of beer, they say, 'Send for the police!'"

The effect of Mr. Beer's study is, however, as I have suggested, to bring out in these barren decades in which Stephen Crane lived a certain importance and interest which they owe to Stephen Crane's having lived in them. The happenings and habits of the era—the Bowery, the Cuban War, Clyde Fitch and Lillian Russell, the debaucheries of the Haymarket and the racing days on the Jersey coast—though they may have for us a charm of memory, do not usually wear for us the aspect of having been in themselves enchanting; but they take on a certain literary glamor when we watch them through Stephen Crane's eyes. What is exciting is to see this life experienced and criticized by a man of first-rate intelligence who was also living in the thick of it— to see its literature tried by the touchstone of a practicing artist who could feel the hollowness of Stevenson and the value of Henry James, who realized that *Huckleberry Finn* was spoiled as a perfect novel by its final pages of farce and—as I learn from another source than the biography of Mr. Beer—sometimes amused himself by trying to cut down specimens of contemporary American poetry to the minimum of idea or emotion that, on scrutiny, he found them to contain. What is touching, and perhaps most startling of all, to an American young enough to remember the banter and slang of the nineties as the language of a lost world, of an innocently rakish youth that had nothing to do with art or ideas, is to hear that language mordantly talked by an intensely serious man: "I will bet my marbles and my best top that Walter Besant is forgotten in twenty years"; "Mr. Yeats is the only man I have met who talks of Wilde with any sense. The others talk like a lot of little girls at a Sunday School party when a kid says a wicked word in a corner." Other personal qualities come through in a letter to a runaway boy whom he had found without money in San Antonio: "Dear Deadeye Dick: Thanks for sending back my money so fast. The hotel trun me out, as my friends of the Bowery say. . . . Now, old man, take some advice from a tough jay from back East. You say your family is all right and nobody bothers you. Well, it struck me that you were too young a kid and too handsome to be free and easy around where a lot of bad boys and girls will take your pennies. So better stay home and grow a mustache before you rush out into the red universe any more."

In any case, Mr. Beer has put Stephen Crane squarely back in his place on the literary map. He was partially excluded by his own time and has remained something of an outlaw even in ours. His biographer has shown him here as one of the most intellectually respectable Americans of the latter part of the century; and his works, if they are republished now, as there is a rumor they are to be, will have a lesson of artistic discipline to teach an age of easy writing.

January 2, 1924

EMERGENCE OF ERNEST HEMINGWAY

ON OCTOBER 21, 1923, the following note appeared in Burton Rascoe's *A Bookman's Daybook*, a feature of the Sunday edition of the New York *Tribune*, of which Rascoe was at that time literary editor:

Called upon Mary and Edmund Wilson late in the afternoon, and Wilson called my attention to some amusing stuff by Ernest Hemingway in the new issue of the *Little Review*.* [Lewis] Galantière sent me a copy of Hemingway's *Three Stories and Ten Poems*, which was published in Paris, and said that I would find it interesting, but I have not yet got around to reading it. Wilson was ill with a cold and complained that the difficulty with New York is that it is hard to keep feeling well here, that it ties one up nervously and residents of Manhattan are always having colds.

I presently had the following letter from Hemingway, who was then working on a newspaper in Canada:

November 11, 1923

Dear Mr. Wilson:

In Burton Rascoe's Social and Literary Notes I saw you had drawn his attention to some writing of mine in the *Little Review*.

* These contributions were *In Our Time*, comprising six of the little vignettes that afterward appeared in the two books of that title, and a satirical prose poem called *They Made Peace— What Is Peace?*

I am sending you *Three Stories and Ten Poems*. As far as I know it has not yet been reviewed in the States. Gertrude Stein writes me she has done a review but I don't know whether she has gotten it published yet.

You don't know anything in Canada.

I would like to send out some for review but do not know whether to put a dedication, as compulsory in France, or what. Being an unknown name and the books unimposing they would probably be received as by Mr. Rascoe who has not yet had time, after three months, to read the copy Galantière sent him. (He could read it all in an hour and a half.)

The Contact Publishing Co. is McAlmon. It has published Wm. Carlos Williams, Mina Loy, Marsden Hartley and McAlmon.

I hope you like the book. If you are interested could you send me the names of four or five people to send it to to get it reviewed? It would be terribly good of you. This address will be good until January when we go back to Paris.

Thanking you very much whether you have the time to do it or not.

Yours sincerely,
Ernest Hemingway

1599 Bathurst Street
Toronto, Canada

I acknowledged the book when I got it, mentioning that I might do a note on it in the *Dial*, and had from him the following reply:

November 25
1599 Bathurst Street
Toronto

Dear Mr. Wilson:

Thank you ever so much for the letter. It was awfully good of you.

The book is a silly size. McAlmon wanted to get out a series of small books with Mina Loy, W. C. Williams, etc. and wanted me in it. I gave him the stories and poems. I am glad to have it out and once it is published it is back of you.

I am very glad you liked some of it. As far as I can think at the minute yours is the only critical opinion in the States I have any respect for. Mary Colum is sometimes sound. Rascoe was intelligent about Eliot. There are probably good ones that I don't know.

No I don't think *My Old Man* derives from Anderson. It is about a boy and his father and race-horses. Sherwood has written about boys and horses. But very differently. It derives from boys and horses. Anderson derives from boys and horses. I don't think they're anything alike. I know I wasn't inspired by him.

I know him pretty well but have not seen him for several years. His work seems to have gone to hell, perhaps from people in New York telling him too much how good he was. Functions of criticism. I am very fond of him. He has written good stories.

Would it perhaps be better to postpone the "Briefer Mentions" in the *Dial* until *In Our Time* comes out sometime next month and I will send it to you. You can get from it what I am trying to get at and the two of them together could make one review.

I am awfully glad you liked the *In Our Time* stuff in the *Little Review* and it is where I think I have gotten hold of it.

There is no use trying to explain it without the book.

It is very sporting of you to offer to help me get a book before the publishers. I don't know any of them.

Edward O'Brien wrote me the other day asking formal permission to reprint *My Old Man* in his *Best Short*

Stories of 1923 and asking if he could dedicate the book to me. As the book isn't out that is confidential. He prints bum ones and good ones. He asked me if I had enough stories for a Boni and Liveright book. I don't know whether that means he could get them to publish it. I will write and ask you about it when the time comes if you don't mind.

E. E. Cummings' *Enormous Room* was the best book published last year that I read. Somebody told me it was a flop. Then look at *One of Ours*. Prize, big sale, people taking it seriously. You were in the war weren't you? Wasn't that last scene in the lines wonderful? Do you know where it came from? The battle scene in *Birth of a Nation*. I identified episode after episode, Catherized. Poor woman she had to get her war experience somewhere.

The thing in the *L.R.* was a joke.* I wrote it in the wagon-restaurant going back to Lausanne, had been at a very fine lunch at Gertrude Stein's and talked there all afternoon and read a lot of her new stuff and then drank a big bottle of Beaune myself in the dining car. Facing opening the wire again in the morning I tried to analyse the conference.

Her method is invaluable for analysing anything or making notes on a person or a place. She has a wonderful head. I would like to write a review of an old book of hers sometime. She is where Mencken and Mary Colum fall down and skin their noses.

Please excuse this very long letter and thanks again ever so much for your letter and the good advice. I would like to see you very much when we go through N. Y.

Very sincerely,
Ernest Hemingway.

* *They Made Peace—What Is Peace?*

He looked me up on his next visit to New York and sent me the first *In Our Time* (lower-cased *in our time*), which was published in the spring of 1924 in an edition of a hundred and seventy copies by the Three Mountains Press in Paris. This contained only eleven of the fifteen stories that appeared in the Boni and Liveright edition of 1925.

I wrote a review of *in our time* and *Three Stories and Ten Poems*, which appeared in the *Dial* of October, 1924. Though it is not of much interest in itself, I am proud of it because it is, so far as I know, the first criticism of Hemingway that appeared in print. (It is not, however, listed by Louis Henry Cohn in his *Bibliography of the Works of Ernest Hemingway*. The first article noted by him is of November, 1925: a review by Burton Rascoe of the expanded *In Our Time*.)

Mr. Hemingway's Dry-Points

Three Stories and Ten Poems. By Ernest Hemingway. 12mo. 58 pages. Contact Publishing Company. Paris. $1.50.

In Our Time. By Ernest Hemingway. 12mo. 30 pages. The Three Mountains Press. Paris. $2.

Mr. Hemingway's poems are not particularly important, but his prose is of the first distinction. He must be counted as the only American writer but one—Mr. Sherwood Anderson—who has felt the genius of Gertrude Stein's *Three Lives* and has evidently been influenced by it. Indeed, Miss Stein, Mr. Anderson and Mr. Hemingway may now be said to form a school by themselves. The characteristic of this school is a naïveté of language, often passing into the colloquialism of the character dealt with, which serves actually to convey profound emotions and complex states of mind. It is a distinctively American development in prose—as opposed to more or less successful American achievements in the traditional style of English prose—which has artistically justified itself at its best as a limpid shaft into deep waters.

Not, however, that Mr. Hemingway is imitative. On the contrary, he is rather strikingly original, and in the dry compressed little vignettes of *In Our Time,* has al· most invented a form of his own:

"They shot the six cabinet ministers at half-past six in the morning against the wall of a hospital. There were pools of water in the courtyard. There were dead leaves on the paving of the courtyard. It rained hard. All the shutters of the hospital were nailed shut. One of the ministers was sick with typhoid. Two soldiers carried him downstairs and out into the rain. They tried to hold him up against the wall but he sat down in a puddle of water. The other five stood very quietly against the wall. Finally the officer told the soldiers it was no good trying to make him stand up. When they fired the first volley he was sitting down in the water with his head on his knees."

Mr. Hemingway is remarkably successful in suggesting moral values by a series of simple statements of this sort. His more important book is called *In Our Time,* and, behind its cool objective manner, it constitutes a harrowing record of the barbarities of the period in which we live: you have not only political executions, but hangings of criminals, bull-fights, assassinations by the police and the cruelties and horrors of the war. Mr. Hemingway is unperturbed as he tells us about these things:

be is not a propagandist even for humanity. His bull-fight sketches have the dry sharpness and elegance of the bull-fight lithographs of Goya. And, like Goya, he is concerned first of all with making a fine picture. Too proud an artist to simplify in the interests of conventional pretenses, he is showing you what life is like. And I am inclined to think that his little book has more artistic dignity than anything else about the period of the war that has as yet been written by an American.

Not perhaps the most vivid book, but the soundest. Mr. Hemingway, who can make you feel the poignancy of the Italian soldier deciding in his death agony that he will "make a separate peace," has no anti-militarist parti pris which will lead him to suppress from his record the exhilaration of the men who had "jammed an absolutely perfect barricade across the bridge" and who were "frightfully put out when we heard the flank had gone, and we had to fall back." It is only in the paleness, the thinness of some of his effects that Mr. Hemingway sometimes fails. I am thinking especially of the story called *Up in Michigan*, which should have been a masterpiece, but has the curious defect of dealing with rude and primitive people yet leaving them rather shadowy.

In Our Time has a pretty and very amusing cover designed from scrambled newspaper clippings. The only objection I have to its appearance is that the titles are printed throughout without capitals—thus: "in our time by ernest hemingway—paris." This device, which had a certain effectiveness when the modernists used it first to call attention to the newness of what they were offering, is now becoming a bore. The American advertisers have taken it over as one of their stock tricks. And it is so unsightly in itself that one does not like to see it become—as in the case of Mr. Hemingway's book and

Mr. Hueffer's* *trans-atlantic review*—a kind of badge for all that is freshest and most interesting in contemporary writing.

October, 1924

In connection with this review, Hemingway wrote me the following letter:

113 Rue Notre Dame des Champs
Paris VII
October 18, 1924

Dear Wilson:

Thank you so much for writing the review in the October *Dial*. I liked it very much. You are very right about the lack of capital letters—which seemed very silly and affected to me—but Bird had put them in and as he was printing the *In Our Time* himself and that was all the fun he was getting out of it I thought he could go ahead and be a damn fool in his own way if it pleased him. So long as he did not fool with the text.

I'm awfully glad you liked it.

How are you anyway? and did you ever get Chaplin for your ballet?

We have lived very quietly, working hard, except for a trip to Spain, Pamplona, where we had a fine time and I learned a lot about bull fighting, the inside the ring scene. We had a lot of minor adventures.

I've worked like hell most of the time and think the stuff gets better. Finished the book of 14 stories with a chapter on *In Our Time* between each story—that is the way they were meant to go—to give the picture of the whole between examining it in detail. Like looking with your eyes at something, say a passing coast line, and

* Ford Madox Ford, who changed his family name from Hueffer.

then looking at it with 15X binoculars. Or rather, maybe, looking at it and then going in and living in it—and then coming out and looking at it again.

I sent the book to Don Stewart* at the Yale Club about three weeks ago. When he was here he offered to try and sell it for me. I think you would like it, it has a pretty good unity. In some of the stories since the *In Our Time* I've gotten across both the people and the scene. It makes you feel good when you can do it. It feels now as though I had gotten on top of it.

Will you get over here this winter do you think? We will probably be in Paris all winter. Not enough money to get out. The baby is very well and husky. Hadley is working on the piano.

She sends her best regards to you and Mrs. Wilson.

Hope everything is going well with you and that you have a good winter. I would like to hear from you and I did appreciate the review. It was cool and clear minded and decent and impersonal and sympathetic. Christ how I hate this terrible personal stuff. Do you remember my writing from Toronto wanting some reviews and publicity? and then got some and it turned me sick.

I think there's nothing more discouraging than unintelligent appreciation. Not really discouraging; but just driving something back inside of you. Some bright guy said *In Our Time* was a series of thumbnail sketches showing a great deal of talent but obviously under the influence of Ring Lardner. Yeah! That kind of stuff is fine. It doesn't bother. But these wordy, sentimental bastards. You are the only man writing criticism who or whom I can read when the book being criticized is one I've read or know something about. I can read almost anybody when they write on things I don't know about.

* Donald Ogden Stewart.

Intelligence is so damn rare and the people who have it often have such a bad time with it that they get bitter or propagandistic and then it's not much use.

With best wishes to you and to your wife,

> Very sincerely,
> Ernest Hemingway

Is this *What Price Glory?* really a good play. I don't mean a good *play*—it sounds fine over here.

I have learned, since the above was written, that my review of *In Our Time* was not the first. An earlier one, signed M. R., had appeared in Paris in the April, 1924, issue of *the transatlantic review*. 1953.

IMAGINARY DIALOGUES

I. The Poet's Return

Mr. Paul Rosenfeld and Mr. Matthew Josephson

MR. ROSENFELD. I was very much interested, Mr. Josephson, to read in a recent number of *Broom* your review of Elinor Wylie's poetry. I had never precisely understood your position before, but you have now made it quite clear.

MR. JOSEPHSON. It is a point of view of which a plain statement has, I think, been long overdue in America; it is the only point of view, I am sure, which will make it possible for Americans to realize themselves creatively. I was really very much surprised on my return from a prolonged absence abroad to find that none of the professional literary people had had the boldness or the intelligence to formulate it—though the necessity for it is perfectly obvious. Gilbert Seldes, in his articles on the movies, the jazz-band and the comic strip, has come nearer to it than anyone else; but even he is still somewhat intimidated by the pretensions of the officially "artistic": he insists upon trying to believe in Bugs Baer and Sherwood Anderson both at the same time; he will not admit that Irving Berlin has rendered Schoenberg uninteresting and unnecessary.

MR. ROSENFELD. I see; but it seems to me that Seldes's

position is easier to defend than yours. For whereas Seldes merely wants to call attention to the neglected virtues of the vulgar, you are attempting also to discredit things that are fine. You say, for example, in your review of Mrs. Wylie, "The large imaginative, daring, formidable people in America are mostly to be found on the vaudeville stage, in the movies, the advertising business, prizefighting, railroads, Wall Street. One is led to this conclusion by observing to what an alarming extent those who produce poetry lack such virtues. Art is purveyed for small persecuted colonies, dispersed throughout this continent, and hidden away among its stone walls and steel foundations. They simply do not join in the great funny time that is being had by all. . . . Thus, while the age itself is given to upheaval, our poets, insensibly enough, strike perfectly traditional poses and have nothing to say which would place them in this time rather than in Heine's or Landor's time." Now, in the first place, I should deny that Mrs. Wylie fails to express any contemporary reality. She may not, to be sure, give voice to the emotions of a vaudeville actor, a pugilist or an advertising man; but she does convey something that lies concealed below the lives of many educated Americans— and that is not merely an imitation of the emotions of Heine or Landor, but a feeling which, when it finds vent at all, acquires a peculiar intensity and brilliance from the hardness of the unsympathetic surface that society opposes to it and the severity of the Puritan tradition that has hitherto held it in check. Elinor Wylie is the Edith Wharton of our poets. Her pride, her submerged passion and her museum show-case culture are all characteristically American; her images of glass and bronze and gold and graved flint and crystal lenses have the hardness and exactitude and glitter of the world in which she has lived; they could have been cast in no other society than that of the American East. When I read Mrs. Wylie, I think of high rooms in dustless expensive houses, of old mirrors and silverware kept up to looking gleamingly new, of gilt backs of Congreve and Keats behind the panes of mahogany book-cases. Or rather she is the symbol of the soul which has learned to subject itself to the discipline of these things and which finds itself at last in revolt against them, which feels that stirring within her that would sever its bonds and be off, that would make her to arise and follow after the milk-white hounds of the moon. She is the pang of the heart that is transfixed by the splinter-sharp ice of lack, the woman-cry in its sheerest bell-timbres—snow-silvers, white-golds, copper-blues—

MR. JOSEPHSON. Go on; that is very amusing; but I hope you don't consider it criticism.

MR. ROSENFELD. What do you mean? I thought that Elinor Wylie did express something real and I was trying to explain what it was.

MR. JOSEPHSON. That is precisely the kind of thing that has compelled my colleagues and me to write about you so much and so bitterly. The day for irresponsible rhapsody as a substitute for exact analysis has now long passed. What you publish as critical essays are, of course, merely opium visions: they have no real relation to their subjects. They are simply romantic fantasies exfloreating a century too late. Like all romantics, you are under the delusion that in order to produce literature, the only thing necessary is to let one's feelings go. Now, if you measured your feelings against the fact, you would realize that your outburst just now has nothing to do with Elinor Wylie; it probably expresses some emotion of your own. And if you measured Elinor Wylie against the fact, you would see that she is not important. Neither you nor Elinor Wylie exists in the face of the great American Fact!

MR. ROSENFELD. Well, I may be more or less of a ro·manticist but I understand the value of tradition; and, to return to your review of *Black Armour*, I do not see why Elinor Wylie should not build on Landor and Heine. Every artist invents his own language, and the language of art changes with the changes of civilization. First Beethoven is unintelligible; then Wagner; then Stravinsky; but in the end the world has always to recognize that the language of art is its own. And in the meantime each one of these men has built on his prede·cessors and without him could not have existed. Did not Virgil derive from Homer, and Dante derive from Virgil? Yet all three are completely different: they have written the poems of three different worlds. It is not merely a question of taking over a technique or of reflecting a point of view but of living up to a standard of excellence. Let me remind you how much Joyce's *Ulysses* is ob·viously indebted to Homer, and how devotedly T. S. Eliot has gone tu school to the Elizabethans.

MR. JOSEPHSON. Precisely: and on that account neither one of them is of very much interest to us. You are like all Americans who think themselves modern; you feel the thrill of doing something sensational when you come out for *The Waste Land* or *Ulysses*. But the one is only the last excretion of naturalism as the other is the last gasp of romantic poetry. Joyce tries to brace himself to his dreary task of reporting bar-room conversations by playing a game with the structure of Homer, just as Eliot, shrinking from a world which he cannot embrace and enjoy, flees for refuge to Tourneur and Webster; there is scarcely an original word in *The Waste Land*— there is scarcely a line which is not either a quotation or an echo of someone else. And yet you American critics

have been making an extravagant fuss about it and calling it an authentic interpretation of the world in which
you live, and you have thus joined the party of defeat.
It is the same with Arnold Schoenberg, whom you praise
and a passage from whose *Pierrot Lunaire* you have compared to *Tristan und Isolde:* you are right about that,
of course; but Schoenberg is the death of Wagner, the
dissolution of a romantic corpse; he is the creaking of
the rusty hinges in the ruined palace of Klingsor. Like
Eliot, he has nothing to offer but the whine of a dry complaint. We who have been lately in Germany and France
and who have had the advantage of acquaintance with
some of the more tonic figures of the younger generation,
such as Tzara and the other dadaists, can see clearly that
Eliot and Schoenberg and Joyce are as dead for the
purposes of the present as Shakespeare, Flaubert and
Wagner. The man who would master the gigantic, the
gorgeous, the fantastic world of the twentieth century
must be able to identify himself with it, not cry out
against it as they do, not for ever be wailing over something that is gone and that nothing now can ever bring
back. That is why I have said in the review to which
you take such exception that the time "demands hardier
poets, such as can straddle the language of our people,
or know the genius of this people as well as a vaudeville
comedian or an advertising copy-writer." You do not
understand my position at all if you suppose that you
can prove your case by the example of Eliot or Joyce.
You have, besides, with your romantic inexactitude, mis-
stated my position completely: you assume that Elinor
Wylie, in imitating her predecessors, has created a language of her own, but I do not admit your contention
that she has anything new to express. What I wrote was
that "our poets have nothing to say which would place
them in this time rather than in Heine's or Landor's."

Elinor Wylie translates Greek epigrams just exactly as Landor did; she writes a lyric on a Nocturne of Chopin. Of what use is that to anybody? The Greeks and Landor and Chopin were all very well in their time, but they do not represent *our* reality.

MR. ROSENFELD. The life of feeling is always real. I grant you that its language changes—but man himself does not change so quickly in a mere two thousand years. He suffers the same chagrins; he is roused by the same passions. So long as he is capable of love and pain, he will continue to read Sappho and Catullus, Heine, Mus set and Keats; his emotions will find lyric expression very much as theirs have done. The language of the heart which has already survived from the Greek and Roman worlds to Heine's has not become obsolete in the space of a hundred years!

MR. JOSEPHSON. Your case is even worse than I thought: you have not only failed to adjust yourself to the great revolution that has taken place; you apparently do not even realize that there is any adjustment to be made. You still entertain the delusion that you are living in the early nineteenth century. I am sure that you read Goethe in the subway and sing Schumann and Schubert in the shower. Yet the subway and the shower them- selves are more magnificent poems than anything by Schubert or Goethe. Isn't it marvellous, an obus of steel, loaded with human beings and thundering under the earth through a tunnel a hundred miles long! A marble cell with a gleaming canopy that releases at a touch of the hand a cascade of crystal needles! What does the shower or the subway train have to do with the language of the heart? What did the people who created them care about it? What have Sappho and Catullus and Heine and Schubert and Elinor Wylie to say to the people whose privilege it is to revel in this monstrous poetry, whose lives are all compounded of it, who are themselves the improvisatori of a prodigious mechanical fantasy? Our American engineers, our industrialism, our business and finance themselves, have created this astounding world. To interpret it, you must take it on its own terms. The great processes of manufacture and distribution and organization go on with stupendous and resistless gestures; they are for America today what the conquests and the explorations were for the Renaissance. And today it is the vaudeville comedian or the artist of the comic-strip who truly conveys the excitement of America's hilarious brutality, the gusto of its gargantuan appetite. It is the writer of advertising copy who forges its literature. "Meaty Marrowy Oxtail Joints": there is the beauty of our real world, the satisfaction of producing a savory soup and the uninhibited joy of consuming it! "The velvety clutch responds to the merest pressure . . . the pliant but positive gears engage silently at a touch of the convenient control": there is a cadence from motoring, from the delicacy of a sensuous machinery. People who are employed in washing themselves in silver-fitted snow-dazzling bathrooms, with fragrant non-sinkable soap, in eating such an abundance of different kinds of food as no nation in the world has ever known, in transporting themselves through the air, under the earth or across its surface at a speed hitherto unimagined, and in selling all these marvels to other people who are eager and delighted to buy, such a race has ceased to feel the need for what you call the "language of the heart." They have learned to do without "the heart"; their life is all in appetite and action. You will never be able to interest them in the old kind of literature again. Or music. Or plastic art. What does "literature" amount to now? The last complaints of the dying poets! What is music? You admire Varèse; but what is Varèse at his boldest but the echo of the music of the streets?—and the streets do it better than he. The hawking taxis, the screaming sirens, the joyous yell of the mechanical life, all this we hear every day; it is the rhythm to which we dance, to which the power-drunken city exults. It is an impertinence for a modern composer to think himself a clever fellow for capturing a few of these noises, so glorious and wild in their native state, and clipping them and toning them down to be handled by the instruments of an orchestra and performed at a single little concert to which a few hundred people will listen. And what is painting? What is sculpture? A bad monument to cele-brate a battle, a landscape not much larger than a play-ing-card in a gallery like a mausoleum, which only a handful of people in New York will ever come in to see and which the millions in the rest of the country will not even hear about! How can you set up these trivialities as rivals to the electric sign, which thousands of people see every day—a triumph of ingenuity, of color, of imagi-nation!—which slings its great gold-green-red symbol across the face of the heavens themselves and tells the world that it has made a new Chewing Gum or a Pickle or a Cigarette that will give you a new sensation! I tell you that culture as you understand it is no longer of any value; the human race no longer believes in it. That is why I am giving my support to the campaign for Henry Ford for President! Henry Ford never listens to music nor looks at pictures nor reads poetry; it is, in fact, even a matter of doubt whether he is able to read at all. He has said openly that he would not give ten cents for all the art in the world. But he Gets Things Done; he Gives Us a Laugh; he takes the Whole World for a Ride! He sends tractors to the lumber camps and cuts in half their titanic labor; he charters a ship and sets out for Europe to put an end to the war; he succeeds in making Congress turn over to him the federal water plant at Muscle Shoals on a lease of a hundred years. And these things Henry Ford can do just because he ignores the past, just because the restraints and the pieties that your schooling imposes on you do not exist for him. It is only such a figure as Ford that America really respects and who will eventually be able to rule it. As I have written, "There shall be one great Powerhouse for the entire land, and ultimately a greater one for the whole world. . . . Let Ford be President. Let him assemble us all into his machine. Let us be *properly* assembled. Let us all function unanimously. Let the wheels turn more swiftly."

MR. ROSENFELD. I am afraid that you have come back to America—after living so long abroad—with rather a mistaken idea of what the life here is like. You have been influenced by the notions of America of such people as Léger and Cocteau—

MR. JOSEPHSON. You must not imagine that my point of view has anything in common with Jean Cocteau's! Cocteau is as old-fashioned now as Anatole France or Verlaine. He is merely a belated aesthetic who tries to be up-to-date—he would have been more at home in the eighties. Between Cocteau and myself there is scarcely communication. My affiliations have been with the dadaists, with Tzara, Breton, Soupault—

MR. ROSENFELD. —You have been influenced by the dadaists, then. In any case, my point is this. Your dadaists, like Cocteau, have made a sort of cult of America. The United States looks so exotic to people who have never been here. I have had the same illusion myself when I have been living a long time abroad. The truth is that the French have seen pictures of our skyscrapers and enormous bridges, they have been thrilled by the pace of our movies and excited by our Negro jazz, and, being nowadays the most cautious and balanced, the least precipitate people in the world, they are fascinated by the idea of a country where such excesses are of common occurrence. They have been using America as a war-cry with which to rally against the staleness and banality into which their classical tradition has fallen, never dreaming how much more banal five-eighths of America is than the dirtiest and poorest French town. A European whom I know and who had been much in Paris with the modern composers and writers, came recently for the first time to America and was very much disappointed. "Is this New York?" he exclaimed when he landed. "Why, it is just exactly like Europe!" He had expected to see people riding automobiles up the sides of enormous buildings, as they do in the comic films; impossible elevated railroads running on top of one another in tiers; skyscrapers as high as the Matterhorn, and Heaven knows what else. Now I cannot help feeling a little that you have caught this point of view. When you are back in American life again, I do not know if you will be able to preserve it—I do not know if you will enjoy "the great funny time that is being had by all." You seem to think that the people who compose the ads necessarily believe in the things they write, that their enthusiasm for their products is genuine. But actually, the chances are that the man who writes the paeans to oxtail joints has never seen one in his life and would not care to eat it if he did. The chances are that he is sickened by advertising and everything that reminds him of it. Sherwood Anderson until very lately was a writer of advertising copy; but do you think he found that inspiring? Do you imagine he shared your view that selling manufactured goods was the highest form of creative activity? On the contrary, he devoted all his leisure to working at that kind of literature that you say you regard as futile—to fixing, in his stories, those visions that reveal with a poet's art the limited, the stunted lives of the people of the factories and the farms, the gentleness and the fineness that lie quivering underneath the burden of the cities and the barrenness of the fields, the soul of man so long exiled from its heritage that it scarcely dares recognize itself nor remember to what visitations it once had been opened wide. No: surely, only one point of view is possible at the present time for the writer of good faith in America—or for the artist of any kind—and that is *against* all the forces which you are making an effort to flatter—against the America which would starve us all and exhaust us and grind us under, so that the machine might "function unanimously" and "the wheels turn more swiftly." These artists like Sherwood Anderson, whom you describe as "small persecuted colonies," as if they were cowards or defective people unable to ride the whirlwind and direct the storm, are perhaps now our only real heroes because they have dared to oppose themselves to it and to blurt out one desperate word, in the teeth of routine and vulgarity, for the honor of the human spirit!

MR. JOSEPHSON. The Honor of the Human Spirit . . . the Principles of Justice and Humanity . . . Liberty, Fraternity, Equality . . . the Dawn of a New Day . . . Workers of the world, unite! you have nothing to lose but your chains! . . . E. E. Cummings could make an amusing poem by mixing them all up together and sticking in the Paris urinal and the venereal affiches. My dear fellow, you take it all too seriously. In Europe no one takes those things seriously. Those clichés from the eighteenth century, old campaign cries and catchwords and shibboleths, are as stale and as lifeless now as old newspapers of the war. The world was hysterical then and still babbled a romantic liberalism; but, now that its fever has subsided, it has settled down to give

itself up to the working out of economic forces, and it
finds that that will do very well. They may prove to
have a wisdom of their own. It can even enjoy its own
absurdity and make a lark of its fantastic confusion.
And that is where dada comes in. It was dada that
awakened laughter when humanity had been worrying
too long about the honor of the human spirit and all
those other insipid abstractions. The younger and more
alert minds of the countries involved in the war now
feel free to be gay without shame. The time has now
come to amuse ourselves. We have worked and suffered enough—and for what? For the most colossal farce
of all time! For Mussolini, for the starvation of Russia,
for a war between England and France. Not that I object
to wars, which are among the livelier numbers in the
universal vaudeville; nor that I disapprove of Mussolini,
whom I admire for his buffoonery and his vigor. But
they are certainly not what anybody wanted nor what
anybody thought he was fighting for. The results of the
war are nonsense, superb nonsense! from any point of
view. Think of Wilson taking on the combined prestige
of Lincoln, Cromwell and Christ, assembling thousands
of words on World Peace, day after day, night after
night, marshalling them together, sending them forth,
army upon army of words, besieging an imaginary cita-
del with celestial storm-clouds of words—then finally
choking, collapsing deflated in the great content uncomprehending West and having the gross of green
spectacles that he had brought back with care from
Versailles thrown casually out behind the house by people who had not paid the slightest attention to a syllable he had been saying! What is the next turn?
Landru? D'Annunzio? The Harding administration?
Léon Daudet turning the suicide of his son into a gigantic piece of publicity? Morris Gest turning Reinhardt's

Miracle into a Barnum and Bailey circus? The Oil Scandal? The *Dial* Award? Dada makes the most of them all and turns them all upside down. For dada is the spirit of play, of the fascinating idiocy of things. It shows the lack of connection between everything with a dazzling quickness of mind. And so it is the nonsense comedian like Ed Wynn or Joe Cook, the humorist like Lardner or Benchley, who comes nearest among Americans to the disintegrating laughter of dada and is truest to the spirit of the time. A lady in décolleté steps forward to sing an aria from some popular and saccharine opera, but before she has got further than the opening bars a screen is dropped down in front of her, and Joe Cook appears before it in a burlesque juggling act; then the screen is lifted again and the soprano, who has never stopped singing, complacently completes her aria. Or, in a farce of Ring Lardner's, three men are discovered fishing in boats; from time to time one of them rings a bell and a maid brings them trays of drinks, walking across the water. "Can you imitate birds?" asks one of them, at the end of a long silence. "No," the other replies, "but I can construct a shack suitable for occupancy by six persons." For after all, what is life as we know it but a series of delicious inconsequences? So why not come out frankly for the leaders with the greatest capacity for absurdity? They will provide the greatest amount of fun. That is why we say, "Vote for Henry Ford! the Master Dadaist of the twentieth century!"

MR. ROSENFELD. Yes, I see: that, I suppose, is the real difference between us. For me, it is a serious matter, but for you, it is only a game. I read your manifestos printed upside down, your assertions that *"Oui = Non"* and your plays in which the different acts have nothing to do with each other, and I see the point of their pointlessness; but I cannot quite laugh at the joke. You keep saying that this or that lacks reality or does not represent anything real, but for me the artistic life of Europe, the life of feeling which it makes articulate, is the only authentic reality. When I hear of young musicians killed in the war or starving to death in Russia, of distinguished conductors insulted and great operas banned from the stage, when I see the desolation of a people who, through devotion to such ideals as Henry Ford's, have at last been reduced to a condition in which they live without even such music as the old New England singing societies provided, relegating it to dreary old concert-halls in a few of the largest cities and to the luxury and the banality of the insufferable Metropolitan—I cannot help being saddened. Perhaps I do err through overseriousness; I dare say you are right about that. It may be true that I have been extravagant in expressing my indignation over the later works of Richard Strauss, because I felt that by the surrender to a cheap success he had betrayed the great tradition of German music; and that I ought not to have worried so much about the artistic failure of Mahler. And there are times when my conscience reproaches me for my treatment of poor old Saint-Saëns, whom I accused of selling his soul, when perhaps he had none to sell. One of you younger men could no doubt have done all this much better; you would have been able to snuff out Strauss or Saint-Saëns with a single bizarre sneer. But I shall always be convinced that the thing with which all these men were trying, with however imperfect success, to identify themselves is the only thing in the world from which one can derive any faith to lift one above the nonsense of events. I would save, not the warring states, not the bankers and the politicians, not even the peoples, with their wretched lives, if they had never made anything beautiful, but the fatherland of Goethe and Bach, of

Shakespeare and Wagner and Musorgsky, of the imagination of Europe. It is to citizenship there that I have been bred, and I can understand no other allegiance.

MR. JOSEPHSON. That fatherland has been defeated: America is its defeat.

MR. ROSENFELD. It is a defeat I am ready to share.

MR. JOSEPHSON. What bravado of the romantic spirit that goes on striking noble poses even after it has been abolished! Gestures of that sort, however—though spirited and touching in themselves—can never nowadays seem anything but ridiculous. It is all very well to say that I have lived·too long abroad and that I don't understand America; but there is one thing I can tell you with assurance I appreciate as the Americans appreciate it that you seem to have lived here all your life without ever being aware of at all. You think you are up to the minute in following American music, that you are generously promoting its advance, when you contribute an article to the *Dial* on Leo Ornstein or Roger Sessions. But where are your fanfares for Lopez and Whiteman? for the rich rhythms of the Negro revues? You say that we exist without music at precisely the time when our jazz—a gorgeous and disturbing carnival, one of the most vital expressions of our time—has been making the whole world delirious! And you have not yet, so far as I know, written a word about it. You have no ear for the popular voices. You always refer to vulgarity with loathing. Life for you must be thinned and refined and laid away in an elegant score before you can consent to touch it. You talk about the desolation of a people who have no use for music. But I, all new to the States as I am, see people dancing everywhere to their music, and I throb to the prodigious orgy. There is no desolation in that music—only the drunkenness, the dizziness of life— vulgar life, unrestrained, taut-nerved, hurtling out with its howling trombones in its great gaudy circus parade toward the unknown mechanical future. I have heard that music in the streets, intrepid, cacophonic, triumphant, and I have thrown up my hat for joy! But you have preferred to remain indoors while the parade went by outside. You stagnate in the quietude of the library where Schoenberg and Bach are alike entombed.

MR. ROSENFELD. On the contrary, I have listened to that music, too; and I confess that it has given me pain. I have even had moments of depression when I have fancied that what you say might be true. But make no mistake, my friend: if art is to be defeated, you will be among the victims. You are a poet, like Elinor Wylie; you are a critic, like myself. You can never march with that procession; they have no place for critics or poets. You can only get yourself cut to pieces by prostrating yourself before Juggernaut, in amazement and awe at his might. If you choose to pretend to enjoy it, that is your own affair.

April 9, 1924

II. The Delegate from Great Neck

Mr. F. Scott Fitzgerald and Mr. Van Wyck Brooks

MR. FITZGERALD. How do you do, Mr. Brooks. I'm afraid it's an awful nuisance for you to see me.

MR. BROOKS. Not at all. I'm very glad to. I'm only sorry to have had to put it off. But I've been so frightfully busy with my book that I haven't been able to do anything else.

MR. FITZGERALD. What's that—the James? I suppose you're hurrying to have it out in time to get the benefit of the publicity of the *Dial* award.

MR. BROOKS. Oh, no: it may take me a long time yet. But it's really rather a complicated job, and I don't like to drop a chapter in the middle or I lose all the threads. I've just come to a breathing-space.

MR. FITZGERALD. I should think you'd want to rush it right through and get it out now: it might double your sales.

MR. BROOKS. Oh, I couldn't possibly: I still have a good deal of work to do on it.

MR. FITZGERALD. I suppose you must read hundreds of books, don't you? How many books do you suppose you've read for the James? Two hundred? Five hundred?

MR. BROOKS. Oh, I don't know, I'm sure—everything I could get hold of that threw any light on him.

MR. FITZGERALD. I suppose you must quote on an

average of four or five books on every page of your biographies, don't you?—and you probably refer to four or five others—and you've probably read half a dozen others that you didn't get anything out of. That makes fifteen or sixteen books to a page. Think of it! Reading fifteen or sixteen books just to write a single page! For a book of two hundred and fifty pages that would be—

Mr. Brooks. They're not all different books, you know. One uses the same books again and again.

Mr. Fitzgerald. I know: but even so—it's perfectly amazing! I suppose you must know more about American literature than anybody else in the world, don't you?

Mr. Brooks. Oh, no! not by any means.

Mr. Fitzgerald. Well, you're the greatest writer on the subject, anyway. That's the reason we've sent you this letter. As I told you, I've been delegated by the Younger Generation of American writers to congratulate you on getting the prize. They chose me as really the original member of the Younger Generation. Of course, there were a lot of people writing before *This Side of Paradise*—but the Younger Generation never really became self-conscious till then nor did the public at large become conscious of it. My slogan is that I am the man who made America Younger-Generation-conscious.

Mr. Brooks. I am certainly very much flattered—

Mr. Fitzgerald. Besides, I'm about the only one who still looks really young. Most of the others are getting old and bald and discouraged. So they picked me out to represent them. They thought they ought to send somebody under thirty.—Well, could you stand to have me read you the letter they've written you or would you rather read it yourself?

Mr. Brooks. No: Certainly—read it. Do!

Mr. Fitzgerald (*reading*). "Dear Van Wyck Brooks: We, the undersigned American writers, desire to offer

you our heartiest congratulations on the occasion of your receiving the *Dial* award. If it is a question of critical service to American letters, we believe that there is no one living to whom it might more fitly be given. We soon found, when we first began writing, that your books were among the few that could help us to orient ourselves."
—This first part's pretty heavy—but it gets a little more interesting later on.—I didn't draft the letter myself.

"You yourself had called a caustic roll of the critics whom we found in authority: Professor Irving Babbitt, who, refusing to see in romanticism one of the great creative movements of our time, could do nothing but scold at young writers who derived inspiration from it; Mr. Paul Elmer More, who, for all his sound standards of learning and literary competence—an anti-romantic like Professor Babbitt—had denounced as a form of debauchery what is actually a necessary condition of any artistic activity: the response to irrational impulse, and who thus, if he could have enforced his injunction, would have shut off the arts at their source; and Professor Stuart P. Sherman, who, borrowing the severity of Mr. More's manner without sharing his moral convictions, soon gave out such discordant sounds that he has now been forced to change his tune in the interests of a liberal sweetness. These critics had been preaching restraint to a people bound hand and foot. The country at large may have been suffering, as they thought, from a phase of anarchic expansion; but the failing of our literature was the timidity of the 'genteel tradition.' You were among the first to stand up for the romantic doctrine of 'experience for its own sake' and to insist on the importance of literature as a political and social influence. These ideas are perhaps open to criticism as a definitive aesthetic program; but they have served at least to awaken us to a sense of the drama in which we were playing. Our fathers had been further than our grandfathers from the civilization of Europe, and you goaded us back to our place in the world. You roused us with the cry that the hour had come 'to put away childish things and to walk the stage as poets do.'

"For all this we are forever in your debt, and we have wished to express our gratitude. Do not think us ungracious, we beg, if we accompany it with a plea. You were almost alone, when you first began to write, in taking American literature seriously—in appraising it as rigorously as possible, in comparison with other literatures, and in exhorting us to better our achievements. Yet, in your zeal to confess our deficiencies, you seem sometimes to create the impression that we have so far accomplished nothing. The older generation of critics had fallen down, primarily, as humanists—that is, they had been weak, not in intellect, but in aesthetic sensibility. They had not been able to feel the value of the widely varying forms of beauty which the men of other races and ages had distilled from their varied experience. Can it be that, with more generous intentions than theirs, you, too, with different preconceptions, are tending to fail in appreciation? After all, a good many of the Americans whose inadequacies you have analyzed so damagingly have had each his peculiar sense of life, his particular aspect of America, that he succeeded in getting on paper in some more or less vivid form. Emerson pursuing happy guides through the winey yet fumeless air in his commerce, so blithe and so homely, with the high places of light; Thoreau with his compact prose and his strong and dense colors, like the white of opaque clouds against blue Massachusetts sky, like the clustered green masses of trees around foursquare New England houses—both these men have conveyed to us the beauty of a particular kind of life. We feel in them a freshness and a freedom as of lawns that slope away to fenceless meadows, and we taste a frosty sea-captain sarcasm that seasons ideal and discipline. So Mark Twain has most poignant pages which give us something that we scarcely find in your *Ordeal of Mark Twain*; it is not only the sadness of the Mississippi in the days when life there was poor, but the romance and the humor of the pioneers straying wide across the empty continent; and we recognize in that sadness, that rough romance and that humor, at once genial and cruel, something more than the outlandish product of a particular time and place: we are moved by the troubling compound of life at all times in all places."—

MR. BROOKS. Will you forgive me if I interrupt you a moment? I don't want to find fault so much with your description of the New England writers—though I'm not sure that even there you haven't allowed distance to gild with an imaginary glamor a society that turns out, when we examine it, rather disappointingly barren—but in regard to the West, one is driven, when one comes to look into the subject, to the conclusion that its reputed romance and humor are almost entirely fictitious. The life along the Mississippi that Mark Twain knew in his boyhood was depressing in the extreme—a mere matter of lonely villages scattered along a muddy shore; and such excitement as he afterwards found in Nevada and California was mainly limited to drinking and gambling, with outbursts of violet profanity and occasional outbreaks of murder. The lies and the practical jokes that constituted frontier humor were merely, like those other manifestations, in the nature of hysterical relief from intolerable privations and repressions.

MR. FITZGERALD. Well, I come from the West—the *Middle* West—myself, and of course it's pretty bad in some ways. But don't you think there must have been still a certain romance about it at the time that Mark Twain went there? Don't you imagine even a pilot on the Mississippi, like Mark Twain was in his youth, must have felt a real thrill at knowing that he was personally playing a part in dominating the American continent? And there must have been a marvellous kind of comradeship in the ranches and the mining-camps—when they called each other Captain and Colonel. I always have a feeling of something heroic in the old songs and stories of the West. Think of the men from New York and New England who first dared to build their settlements in the gigantic amphitheaters of Utah, where the great black rock-ranges wall you round like the ramparts of the world! And the red sandstone hills of Nevada! Can you imagine what it must have been like to try to live the white man's life among those fantastic shapes, in the presence of those faceless prehistoric gods? And the first men who went to California, the prospectors of Mark Twain's sixties—they must have been drunk with the sunshine even more than the San Franciscans today—as well as with liquor, of course. I imagine them shaking off their hardships in a tremendous exhilaration when they first found themselves on that golden coast, where no worry from the old world ever comes, where Time itself seems to have been left behind like some tyrannous medieval institution, where man's life seems restored at last to the primeval leisure of Eden, where it is always summertime and always afternoon! Have you ever seen the mountains turning purple at sunset and the purple-fringed sea? Think of the men from the shacks and the diggings looking out on that new horizon, that new ocean that opened to the Orient, and hearing the drums of the surf that beat out the somnolent rhythms of the reefs and white sands of the South Seas! No older generation and no taboos! Big fortunes easy to make! Don't you think that, if ever Americans have really felt free in America, those early Californians must have?

MR. BROOKS. The condition of survival for the pioneer, even in California, was the suppression of all those instincts which might tend to conflict with his adjustment to his rude environment. You assume that a man of Mark Twain's generation would have been capable of the enjoyment of landscape. But we find no evidence that this was the case. The enjoyment of landscape results in an enrichment of the spiritual soil which bears its fruits in artistic creation, and the generation of Mark Twain— who can doubt it?—throttled its impulse to delight in natural beauty as an interference with its concentration upon its immediate material task. The psychology of the Puritan and the pioneer has always, it seems to me, made Americans rather blind to natural beauty. It may, in fact, be seriously questioned whether America has ever had a writer who can be said to have appreciated it properly. Think of the vital relation to natural objects that one finds in a Ruskin or a Jeffries, and then summon the most distinguished examples that our literature is able to show. How meager, how relatively pale, how lacking in genuine significance, the latter must inevitably appear!

MR. FITZGERALD. Well, I really oughtn't to try to talk about it because I don't know the subject the way you do. —I dare say that that part of the letter does lay it on pretty thick, but they wanted a purple passage to show you what they meant about enthusiasm.—Shall I go on reading?

MR. BROOKS. Do.

MR. FITZGERALD. "In the case of Henry James, again, we have been a little disappointed as we have read the published chapters of your forthcoming book about him. What we had hoped for was a definitive study of a novelist of genius who, fortunately for us, happened to be an American; but what we seem to be getting is the tragedy of an American who was rash enough to try to become a novelist. Yet, for all James's partial failures at filling in the outlines of his canvases, he was surely a first-rate artist, one of the few real masters of literature that the United States has produced; and his position as an American expatriate must have given him a peculiar advantage as an international critic of society that made up for whatever he had missed in intimate experience of American life. Must we believe that his social maladjustment as an American of his period had really for his work the disastrous results on which you insist in these chapters? Your first instalment is based on James's own autobiographical volumes; yet what interests us when we read these books is less the record of the provincial background and the writer's relation to it than the wonder and excitement of the artist enchanted by the spectacle of life— life even in the nineteenth century, even in the United States. Do not, we beg you—it is the burden of our plea —lose too much the sense of that wonder!"—

Mr. Brooks. I, beg your pardon: but I really do think you overestimate those autobiographical volumes! To me, there has always seemed to be something rather flaccid and empty about them. Think how much more colorful and spirited is Cellini's autobiography! How much more candid Rousseau's! How infinitely much more alive to the intellectual currents of their time the autobiographies of Renan and Mill! How much richer in psychological interest the memoirs of Marie Bashkirtseff! James wrote in his later years, you know, of "the starved romance of my life." And what I feel in his autobiography is the starvation rather than the romance. What American can fail to recognize the inexorable spiritual blight of which James himself spoke so often? Have we not all run up

against it—an impotence and a blindness of the soul—
like one of those great blank implacable walls that balk
the view in American cities?

MR. FITZGERALD. The Puritan thing, you mean. I suppose you're probably right. I don't know anything about
James myself. I've never read a word of him.—Just let
me finish this letter; there's not very much more.

"We thus deprecate your gloomy verdicts on the value
of the American classics; yet, feeling as we do the force
of your criticism of our general culture, we should never
have thought of complaining, if we had not lately come
to fear that, intent upon the diagnosis of the diseases from
which we have suffered, you have ended by becoming inhibited by an a priori theory which prevents you from
hoping for improvement. You have discovered so many
reasons why artistic achievement should be difficult that
you seem to have become convinced that it must always
remain impossible. When you write of contemporary
literature, it is politely but without conviction: the modern writers who have been most successful in realizing
the ideal you proposed have not received your accolade.
And the effect, in the long run, has been more than a
little discouraging. The other day, one of the youngest
of our number, reading your essay *The Literary Life*,
broke down into a wild fit of weeping and cursed God
for having made him an American."—

MR. BROOKS. Dear me! How distressing! Really—

MR. FITZGERALD. Oh, that's just a silly joke! It didn't
really happen, of course. I made it up myself and had
them put it in. It's the only part I wrote.—I'm sorry: I
suppose it was bad taste!

MR. BROOKS. No—no: not at all! I see! I beg your
pardon. Go ahead.

MR. FITZGERALD. "It is true that our newer critics tend
to err through too easy enthusiasm: it is usually enough

for a book to make pretensions to artistic seriousness for them to hail it as a masterpiece. But their indiscriminate excitement hardly compensates us for your indifference. It is certainly a mistake to behave as if all our contemporary writers were equally successful as artists, but we have the uncomfortable feeling that you may think them all equally deplorable—merely the most recent examples of the various depressing ways in which writers may fail in America—not the beginnings of a literary renascence but fresh waxworks for a Chamber of Horrors; and we wonder whether your disinclination to write anything about your contemporaries may not be due merely to a delicacy that prevents you from cutting up people before they are quite dead.

"Yet the younger generation of writers have been trying to put your precepts into practice. They have not blenched before the boldness of the European masters, as you accuse their fathers of doing: they have tried to follow great examples. They are interested, as you urged them to be, in the life of their own country; and they have opened their souls to experience. For all their pessimistic pronouncements, they are confident, hopeful and gay. But when they have looked for your snow-white banner flying beside their more motley ones, they have found you still brooding the wrongs of an earlier generation, the defeats of an older army. They find you shivering among the archives, and they shiver at the sight of your chill. Meantime, there is life in America—artistic life even—to warm us all. If we reproach you for failing to enjoy it, we are only giving back to you a gospel we have learned from your own books."

And then the names—I won't read the list—but practically everybody, you see.

MR. BROOKS. It was really awfully kind of you to take the trouble to write me like this. I'm very much inter-

ested in what you say.—But I can't reconcile the picture
that you draw of yourselves at the end of your letter with
the account that you gave me yourself when you were
talking about your friends just now. You said, I think,
that the younger generation was "getting old and bald
and discouraged," and that is not a very cheerful picture.
I appreciate your gallant effort to make the best of your
situation; but I am afraid that your admirable spirit has
already been partly broken by the indifference of a commercial society, that your gestures are lost in the void.

MR. FITZGERALD. Oh, I was just kidding about that.
They're not really old and discouraged. I'm the only one
that's discouraged, because I find that I can't live at Great
Neck on anything under thirty-six thousand a year, and
I have to write a lot of rotten stuff that bores me and
makes me depressed.

MR. BROOKS. Couldn't you live more cheaply somewhere else?

MR. FITZGERALD. Nowhere that's any fun.

MR. BROOKS. I can't help thinking it a pity that a
writer as gifted as you should be let in for such heavy
expenses. As you say, it lays you open to exploitation by
the popular magazines; and, though you charge me with
indifference, I can tell you that that is something I regret
very much. I should hate to see your whole generation
fall a victim to that sort of thing. You are "the man," you
told me, you know, at the beginning of our conversation,
"who has made America Younger-Generation-conscious."
Did you realize, when you used that expression, that you
had dropped into the language of advertising? In describing your literary activities, you could not avoid the jargon
of business; and it strikes me that the production of books
by the younger generation has now become an industry
much like another. The first crop of younger writers had
scarcely scored their first successes when a new race of

editors and publishers met them with open arms, eager to commercialize them—not by turning them into hacks of the old sort who would have had to do work of a kind altogether against their conscience but by stimulating them to write much and often rather than responsibly and well, by putting a premium on their second-best; so that, instead of improving on their first attempts, they have often, it seems to me, sunk below them. A half-educated public has created a demand for half-baked work. And I'm not at all sure that you younger writers are very much better off than your predecessors were: in the eighties and nineties, at least, there was a small cultivated public and not much question of pleasing the rest. I will say of the distinguished writers of the day before yesterday, whom you accuse me of undervaluing, that they usually followed their art with a very high sense of its dignity, so that even their journalism sounds like the work of serious men of letters—and this is true of Stephen Crane as much as of Henry James; whereas, in the case of you younger men, one sometimes cannot help feeling that your most ambitious productions are a species of journalism. Is it possible to resist the conclusion that you are succumbing to our capitalist civilization in a way you could never have foreseen?

Mr. Fitzgerald. I knew that what I said about making America Younger-Generation-conscious sounded like advertising. I was just making fun of the way that the advertising people talk.

Mr. Brooks. Let me remind you that Freud has shown us that the things we say in jest are as significant as the things we say in earnest—they may, in fact, be more significant, because they reveal the thoughts that are really at the back of our minds and that we do not care to avow to the world. I was struck, also, by that other joke, which you contributed to the letter—I mean about the man who cursed God for having made him an American. Who can fail to detect in this desperate image an involuntary tragic cry which contradicts everything else you have been straining so hard to affirm? —Another detail that betrays: I notice that when you mention the signatories, who explicitly include yourself, you always speak of them as "they" instead of "we." In doing so, I can't help feeling, you furnish irresistible evidence that the unity you assume in collaborating is more or less artificial, that you are actually, in spirit and point of view, as isolated from one another as it has always seemed that literary men are bound to be in America. In allowing your art to become a business, you have rendered true unity impossible and have given yourselves up to the competitive anarchy of American commercial enterprise. You can at best, I fear, gain nothing but money and big hollow reputations—each man out for himself—and these things for fifty years in America have brought nothing but disillusion.

MR. FITZGERALD. Don't you suppose, though, that the American millionaires must have had a certain amount of fun making and spending their money? Can't you imagine a man like Harriman or Hill feeling a certain creative ecstasy as he piled up all that power? Just think of being able to buy absolutely anything you wanted— houses, railroads, enormous industries!—dinners, automobiles, stunning clothes for your wife, clothes like nobody else in the world could wear!—all the finest paintings in Europe, all the books that had ever been written! Think of what it would be like to give parties that went on for days and days, with everything that anybody could want to drink and a medical staff in attendance and the biggest jazz orchestras in the city alternating night and day! I confess that I get a big kick out of all the glittering expensive things. Why, once, when I'd just arrived in

New York with a lot of money to spend, after being away in the West, and I came back to the Plaza the first night and looked up and saw that great creamy palace all blazing with green and gold lights, and the taxis and the limousines streaming up and down the Avenue—why, I jumped into the Pulitzer fountain just out of sheer joy! And I wasn't boiled either.

MR. BROOKS. Are you sure you weren't a little hysterical?

MR. FITZGERALD. No: I've been hysterical, too. This was exhilaration.—Look: I don't suppose you could possibly be persuaded to come down to Great Neck this weekend. We're having a little party ourselves. Maybe it would bore you to death—but we're asking some people down who ought to be pretty amusing. Gloria Swanson's coming. And Dos Passos and Sherwood Anderson. And Marc Connelly and Dorothy Parker. And Rube Goldberg. And Ring Lardner will be there. You probably think some of those people are lowbrow, but Ring Lardner, for instance, is really a very interesting fellow—he's really not just a popular writer: he's pretty morose about things. I'd like to have you meet him. There'll be some dumb-bell friends of mine from the West, but I don't believe you'd mind them. And then there's going to be a man who sings a song called, *Who'll Bite your Neck When my Teeth are Gone?* Neither my wife nor I knows his name—but this song is one of the funniest things we've ever heard!

MR. BROOKS. Why, thank you ever so much. I'd like ever so much to go—and I'd like to meet all those people. But I'm really afraid that I can't. I'm not nearly done with the James, and I have to devote all my free time to it. And, since you feel that I'm being unfair to him, I must go over my material again and think about it from that point of view.—You know, I appreciate very much your taking the trouble to write me. I'm sorry you find me discouraging: of course, I don't mean to be. On the contrary, I think that your generation is showing a great deal of promise.

MR. FITZGERALD. Well, I'm sorry if I've been a nuisance. It was good of you to listen to the letter.

MR. BROOKS. It was very good of you to write it.

MR. FITZGERALD. Well, I won't bother you any longer. —I'm sorry you can't come down Saturday.

MR. BROOKS. Thank you ever so much. I wish I could!

April 30, 1924

GILBERT SELDES AND THE POPULAR ARTS

I. *The Seven Lively Arts* (1924)

Mr. Seldes has written a valuable and enormously entertaining book on the vulgar arts of vaudeville, jazz music, newspaper satire, the movies, the revue, the circus, and the comic strip. He has tried to do for the field of popular entertainment very much what Mr. Mencken has done for philology in his treatise on the American language; and everybody interested in American culture should pay attention to the results of his researches.

Unfortunately, Mr. Seldes has not to the same degree as Mencken the gift of lucid presentation. He does not seem to realize that the function of his book is primarily one of exposition—the conveying of information, the unfolding of novel ideas—and that in order to do this successfully, you must cultivate patience and order. Mr. Seldes proceeds obliquely by means of metaphysical discussions of theory and elliptical literary allusions, jokes, curses, cries of ecstasy and hysterical revelations—the whole rather bewilderingly distributed among chapters of the normal kind, open letters and imaginary dialogues, which are supplemented by footnotes, appendices and parenthetical interpolations. You have a feeling that the quicksilver ideas are escaping through the interstices of the ill-woven sentences. There are passages in *The Seven*

Lively Arts that I cannot understand at all, and others that I should not understand unless I happened, in the particular case, to possess some independent knowledge of what the author is trying to tell me about. I cite, for example, the footnote on page 336: "I haven't seen The Covered Wagon. Its theme returns to the legendary history of America. There is no reason why it should not have been highly imaginative. But I wonder whether the thousands of prairie schooners one hears about are the film or the image. In the latter case there is no objection." Now what does he mean by this? On the opposite page I find: "By corrupting the action [of novels and plays which were being turned into movies] the producers changed the idea; bad enough in itself, they failed to understand what they were doing and supplied nothing to take the place of what they had destroyed." I can see that a possible sense might be given to this passage by interchanging the semicolon and the comma, but there are so many other passages like it that it is impossible to tell whether this particular one has been misprinted or not. Again: "You [the 'movie magnates'] gave us Marguerite Clark in films no better than the 'whimsy-me' school of stage plays." Now I know what Mr. Seldes means when he refers to the "whimsy-me" school of drama, because I happened to be present on the single night when the Algonquin group of humorists put on the entertainment called *The No-Siree*, and saw their burlesque of A. A. Milne in which an old gentleman said, "Ah, whimsy me!"; but if I had not, I should barely have been able to guess what Mr. Seldes meant by this passage.

Mr. Seldes does succeed, none the less, for all his tendency toward woolly writing, in disengaging some judicious observations. The chapter from which I have just quoted, for example, contains admirable criticism of the movies; and the discussion of the technique of vaude-

ville is, it seems to me, equally sound. And, though his
bons mots do not always come off, he strikes at times—
as in his passage on Christopher Morley—a debonair
vein of wit that has the air of unexpectedly igniting
when he is not trying for it especially. But where he
seems to me most successful is in simply reporting the
things that he has seen. It is then that he writes his best
prose and produces his most persuasive effects. The descriptions of the Chaplin films, the Krazy Kat comic
strip and the antics of the Fratellini clowns really bring
them most vividly before us: we laugh with delight as we
read. Mr. Seldes, I suppose, is surest here because he is
closest to his object. As soon as he stops looking at his
object, he has a way of becoming bedazzled by strange
intellectual fancies, and is almost as likely to come out
with something wildly inappropriate as with something
penetrating and true. How, for example, did he arrive
at the following: "It was odd that in *Vanity Fair's* notori-
ous 'rankings,' Krazy tied with Doctor Johnson, to whom
he owes much of his vocabulary." In what way does
Krazy Kat's vocabulary resemble Doctor Johnson's? The
romantic passages quoted certainly fail to convince one
of this. Mr. Seldes describes Krazy Kat, also, as "a
creature more like Pan than any other creation of our
time"—though it is difficult to see how Krazy Kat is
much more like Pan than he is like Doctor Johnson. And
on what evidence does he prophesy that Ring Lardner
is capable of becoming a second Mr. Dooley? Ring Lardner, so far as I know, has never shown a taste for political
satire; his recent tendencies have been, on the one hand,
toward sheer nonsense and, on the other, in such short
stories as *The Golden Honeymoon*, toward a sort of realistic fiction. Nor is it possible to understand what the
passage about the kittens that Mr. Seldes quotes from
Lardner has to do with the "Black Beauty-Beautiful Joe

style of writing," of which Mr. Seldes says it is a parody. "It may shock Mr. Lardner," says Mr. Seldes, "to know that he has here done in little what Mr. Joyce has done on the grand scale in *Ulysses*." It is not only Mr. Lardner who is likely to be surprised by this statement; and he will not be more surprised than the composers of *I Wonder Who's Kissing Her Now* when they learn from Mr. Seldes's book that they have "skillfully built up a sentimental situation in order to tear it down with two words." These shots go too far or miss, but Mr. Seldes often does hit the mark—as when he says that Mr. Dooley, in respect to the Dreyfus case, was performing the same service for Americans that Anatole France performed for the French. The difference was, as he notes, that a different sort of audience required a different vehicle of satire. What Mr. Dooley had to say was essentially no more genial than what Anatole France had to say, but it was only his good humor and his dialect that made it possible for him to say it at all. So, in our generation, when manners have passed from back-slapping to brutality, we have Mencken using a bludgeon on a society that understands nothing but bludgeons. We have never yet reached the stage when an Anatole France could be influential.

Much of the clouding of Mr. Seldes's judgment in individual cases arises, I fancy, from his feverish approach to his subject as a whole. In his most ecstatic moments, he is given to making extravagant claims—as when he asserts that Charlie Chaplin and George Herriman, the inventor of Krazy Kat, are the only two "great artists" in America, and that Krazy Kat is our "most satisfactory work of art"; then, apparently in reaction from such excesses, he will protest for whole chapters at a time that he is not really trying to compare Herriman with Picasso and Irving Berlin with Stravinsky, but merely backing them against the "faux bon," the "bogus" imitations of the fine arts—thus creating, with an immense amount of pother, what is, so far as I can see, very largely an artificial issue, and one that lands Mr. Seldes in a foolish and inaccurate disparagement of opera and the drama. Why shouldn't it be possible for him simply to go ahead and write a book about the popular arts, without all these protestations? They have been written about before—by Anatole France, for example, who did not think it necessary to denigrate the theater in order to justify the café chantant. Well, there is a real reason, no doubt, why the popular arts should present a slightly more difficult problem in America than they do in a country like France. The French have a culture which diffuses itself more or less through all their social classes and their various fields of activity. The same thing which you find at its highest pitch of purity and intensity in a comedy of Molière appears also in a farce by Guitry, a topical revue by Rip, an illustrated joke in *Le Rire* or even in a conversation between strangers in a railway coach. But in America we have no such homogeneous culture penetrating our whole society. Today a whole race of Americans goes to school and arrives at maturity without more than the sketchiest acquaintance with the classic Anglo-American culture that has been so far our only heritage; and it is inevitable that, among this race, individuals should sometimes appear who, working in some department of popular slapstick humor and with no other language than the common slang, should achieve distinction or brilliance. Such a popular humorist as this may not only go unrecognized as an artist; he may not know that he is one himself. Herriman, I suppose, is such a man; so, perhaps, is Ring Lardner. And Mr. Seldes, in *The Seven Lively Arts*, has performed a feat of some daring in bringing them within the field of criticism. He has overdone it a little, and his case may suffer in consequence; but if he had not been capable of overdoing it, he might never have done it at all.

One thing which, I suspect, has had much to do with making Mr. Seldes self-conscious in his relation to the popular arts is the fact that, unlike most Americans, he has not been brought up on them from boyhood, that he has not learned to take them for granted. He tells us that he had scarcely in his youth ever been either to a circus or to a vaudeville show; and his failure to discuss either the early work of Opper (save for a bare mention of Happy Hooligan) or the burlesque of Weber and Fields, suggests that he may never have known them. This lack of familiarity has the advantage of putting Mr. Seldes in a position to see in the vulgar arts certain qualities of style and imagination which are likely to be missed by people who do not expect anything of them, because they have left them behind with childhood, but it also has the disadvantage of allowing Mr. Seldes to approach them with a sensibility so sophisticated, that, not, for example, having been entertained by a given vaudeville act at the mental age for which it was intended—that is, at the age that Mr. Seldes was about twenty years ago and that the average vaudeville audience is forever—he tends either to reject it angrily as an unsuccessful attempt to do something artistically dignified or to read into it all sorts of profundities that do not have any actual existence.

As a result of this deficient background, we find Mr. Seldes neglecting an interesting aspect of his subject which I should very much like to see discussed: I mean, the revolution in humor that seems to be taking place in New York. In the old days of Weber and Fields, the latter would look down from his bullying height at the former's flowered vest and say, "Aha, now I know vere de

lounge vent!" Nowadays, Joe Cook asks "the Senator,"
his stooge, "How's your uncle?"—and the Senator answers, "I haven't got an uncle." "Fine," says Cook. "How
is he?" The difference is that the Weber and Fields joke
is a "gag": it is fantastic but it makes sense; whereas
Cook's is simply idiotic: you laugh at it, if you do,
because it is perfectly pointless.

I should like to bring to the notice of Mr. Seldes two
of the older vaudeville comedians who seem to have been
transition figures in this change from the smart to the
silly: Charlie Case and James J. Morton. Charlie Case
was a black-face monologist with a Chaplinesque overtone of pathos who used to sing curious unrhymed songs
to a monotonous dirge-like accompaniment. He had developed a vein of his own which was refreshingly unconventional, since it did not depend on gagging, and his
death is said to have been hastened by disappointment at
his failure to establish himself with anything like the
public he deserved. If he had been launched only eight
or ten years ago, he would probably now have a show of
his own—like Frank Tinney who is, to my mind, a much
less gifted performer than Case. As it was, Charlie Case
was the object of a cult on the part of a few fans like F.
P. A., who printed Case's songs in his column at the time
of the latter's death. James J. Morton, the other of these
comics, was a large solemn middle-aged man in an ill-
fitting frock-coat, who gave a schoolboy recitation that
began, "Hark, mother! I hear the sound of footsteps in
the village street," to the accompaniment of deafening
off-stage noises, and told interminable pointless stories
rather in the manner of Ed Wynn. Neither Case nor
Morton had much in common with the typical comedians
of that era: the Jimmy Powerses, the Nat M. Willses, the
McIntyres and Heaths. They were more subtle, more intellectual, more like the comedians in vogue today. One

can see in them the first faint foreshadowings of the Algonquin school of humor—the cult of the flat joke, the irrelevant remark, the sophisticated naïveté.

That this cult has some meaning as a sign of the times and is not merely a local fashion would seem to be indicated by its kinship with the European movement called dadaism. It has always been natural for the people of the English-speaking countries to amuse themselves with what they call nonsense, and, though the nonsense of Joe Cook and Robert Benchley is distinct from that of Carroll and Lear, it is not in itself a phenomenon that has anything abnormal or surprising about it. But that our cultivation of nonsense of this special kind should have been paralleled in France by the development of a similar school of nonsense suggests a common cause. For the French have never been given to nonsense; they have scarcely even understood it. French jokes, unlike English jokes, are usually funny, not because they are silly, but because they reveal some truth. The French, since the war, however, have suddenly discovered nonsense. Jean Cocteau's *Le Potomok* and *Les Mariés de la Tour Eiffel* came close to Carroll and Lear, and the dadaists have gone all the way in the direction of a deliberate lunacy. Though the French have made an issue of their nonsense, an occasion for polemics and riots, as Benchley or Lardner would never do, the non sequiturs and the practical jokes of the French and the American humorists (though the dadaists pretend to grim seriousness) seem the product of similar situations: in France, the collapse of Europe and the intellectual chaos that accompanied it; in America—what is perhaps another aspect of a general crisis: the bewildering confusion of the modern city and the enfeeblement of the faculty of attention. It relieves some anxiety for people to watch acts or listen to stories that are completely inconsecutive and pointless, because that is the way the world is beginning to seem, the way their own minds are beginning to work. They have to think about too many things and the relation between all these things is not in the least clear. It is comforting to hear Joe Cook when he is genially incoherent: our laughter both confesses and dismisses our fears.

In any case, *The Seven Lively Arts* is a genuine contribution to America's new orientation in respect to her artistic life which was inaugurated in 1915 by Brooks's *America's Coming of Age* and two years later more violently promoted by Mencken's *A Book of Prefaces*. Mr. Seldes's view of the arts has perhaps been a little confused by his evidently quite recent discovery that it is possible to appreciate, not only Krazy Kat at the same time as James Joyce, but both Krazy Kat and Joyce at the same time as "the *Medea* of Euripides"; but his book contains a brilliant chronicle of the high spots in our popular entertainment. If not all these forms of entertainment have really quite reached the dignity of arts, Mr. Seldes has succeeded in inventing them as such: it is he who is the artist here. He has precipitated pure crystals of irony from the cheap adulterated compounds in which it is usually sold; he has caught the enchanting echoes of our popular gaiety and melody as they drift in the city air. To read his book is to live again the last ten years of vaudeville and revue, newspapers and moving pictures, but in a purified and concentrated form—tasting nothing but the magic tune, the racy flash of characterization, the moment of mad laughter. As for the trained dogs, the melodramatic playlet and the sentimental soloist, they, too, become entertaining through the wit of our guide's comments. If he were only a little less fanatical about magnifying the importance of the whole affair, he would make the perfect companion.

September, 1924

II. *The Great Audience* (1950)

In 1924, Mr. Gilbert Seldes published a book called *The Seven Lively Arts*, the object of which was to show that the popular arts in America were remarkable for vitality and imagination and that the best they had produced was to be preferred to the "faux bon" of our respectable arts. There were chapters on vaudeville, movies, revues, newspaper humor, the comic strip, ragtime and jazz music, and Mr. Seldes's heroes were Joe Cook, Charlie Chaplin, Florenz Ziegfeld, Ring Lardner, Krazy Kat, Al Jolson and Irving Berlin. That was the epoch, in the United States, of the liquidation of genteel culture, and Mr. Seldes's audacious book marked one of the steps in this process. He had at that time just resigned from the managing editorship of the *Dial*, a literary and artistic monthly that maintained very close relations with everything that was newest in Europe, and *The Seven Lively Arts* had its connections with the more general movement of which the jazz rhythms of Stravinsky and Edith Sitwell, the ballets of Jean Cocteau and the premeditated delirium of the dadaists were among the manifestations. Gilbert Seldes had at that time, in common with these, a touch of that upside-down snobbery of the café chantant and the music hall that probably stemmed from Toulouse-Lautrec. The Fratellini clowns of the Cirque Médrano figured among his favorites, along with Ed Wynn and Joe Jackson.

During the twenty-six years that have elapsed since the appearance of this early book, Mr. Seldes has been up to his neck in the seven lively arts, as well as in a couple of new ones that had not yet arrived at that time. He has not only continued, as a critic, to follow and comment on the various phases of popular entertainment; he has served on the production end of several of them and got to know them from the inside. Between 1937 and 1945, he was head of the Television Program Department of C.B.S., functioning also as producer, director, writer and M.C., and he has also been associated with the radio side of C.B.S. and has intermittently written radio scripts and delivered series of broadcasts. He has collaborated on movie documentaries and he has sweated out his term in Hollywood on the writing staff of Paramount. Through all this, he has steadily worked—as a check on his activities shows—to realize the best possibilities, aesthetic and educational, of these new techniques of mass amusement; and he has now written a large-scale study of television, radio and movies, with a section on comic books, summing up his conclusions about them.

Mr. Seldes's new book, *The Great Audience*, is quite different from *The Seven Lively Arts*, but it is a logical sequel to it, which makes, also, a dramatic contrast. The early book was a series of essays celebrating distinguished artists. The new one has little to say about individual writers and performers; it uses them only as illustrations. It is a solid and sober report, authoritatively documented, of the industries with which it deals: a history of their development, an analysis of their economic and technical problems, a survey of their present condition and an estimate of their probable future. It is also a critical essay, the most comprehensive and searching I know, on mass entertainment in the United States—an essay which draws conclusions that could never have been foreseen by the early Seldes or by anybody else at that stage. These analyses, predictions and conclusions will undoubtedly provoke objection, but they cannot fail to carry weight. This is the first time, so far as I know, that a man of intelligence and taste, with a sound enough education to give him cultural and historical perspective, who has at the same time a practical grasp of the technical and financial aspects of the entertainment business, has set out to attack the whole subject: to describe it, to explain it, to assess it, to assign it to its place in society; and before one goes on to discuss the special questions that Mr. Seldes raises, it should be said that *The Great Audience* seems one of those "definitive" works that, taking advantage of a crucial moment, sum up and deliver judgment on some phase of human activity; that make us understand what has happened, that establish enduring assumptions and that remain indispensable landmarks.

It is not possible to summarize briefly the contents of Mr. Seldes's book, but its main conclusions are these:

The movies, he says, have been losing their public. Between 1947 and 1950, a thirty-percent drop has taken place, and the movie-theater audience is mainly made up of teen-agers; after twenty, people go less often, and after thirty, almost not at all. The films are mostly aimed at the young and, in consequence, have become, at the present time, repetitions of stereotyped myths that have no roots whatever in reality. Mr. Seldes is at his most brilliant in his descriptions of the imaginary worlds presented by the mass entertainments. He shows that the contemporary world of the films is one in which men and women are never allowed to have sexual relations. Extramarital liaisons are barred, and even when people get married, the consummation is infinitely delayed by a series of unfortunate accidents. Later on, when the wives have acquired children by some parthenogenic process, the marriage may be threatened by a bad woman whose badness consists of an interest in sex; but Providence will always arrange that the couple shall be brought together by the injury or illness of a child. In the meantime, the hiatus left by the exclusion of sensual passion that is imposed by the censorship is filled by a strangely uncensored sadistic indulgence in violence. A woman may not be desired but she may be indecently spanked or given a sock in the jaw. And the hero and heroine never work; it is enough for the young man that he should marry the boss's daughter, or, in the case of a composer, that he should write "a great song or symphony in a single blinding flash of inspiration." Only the milkman and such people work, and these workers are invariably good-natured and respectful toward the more fortunate class they serve. The married couples remain immature till the children begin to grow up, whereupon they revert to the springtime of youth and are saved from amorous follies only through the intervention of their bright adolescent children. No one, says Mr. Seldes, ever really grows up in the movies, and that is the reason they do not interest adults.

While the movies, in the thirties and forties, were petrifying into these formulas, the radio had been developing two new kinds of formularized commodity: the news broadcast and the daytime serial. The problems of free speech and good taste that arise in connection with news commentators and the commercial announcements of sponsors have been decided in different instances, the most important of which are recorded by Mr. Seldes, in a variety of different ways; but, with the recent decline in radio, in proportion as television has been taking its place, the barriers against propaganda and the plugging of obnoxious products have been largely broken down. You can now buy time for almost anything: a laxative that is advertised at mealtime or a bigoted religious program. As for the daytime serial, it is a dreary and insipid story that is made to creep on from day to day in such a way that as little as possible will happen in any given instalment and that that little will take as long as possible. The typical situation here is one in which a decisive and self-dependent woman intervenes in the lives of others. She must never meet another character who is vigorous and determined also, because that would precipitate action. Her husband is invariably unready and hesitant; he probably suffers from impotence. She herself is probably frigid. A check on radio audiences has shown that the listeners to these serials are housewives with impoverished lives, themselves lacking competence and resolution. The continual small anxieties created by the situations in the serials correspond to their own anxieties and afford the humble satisfaction of hearing them vicariously resolved. But it is probable, Mr. Seldes believes, that this interminable purveying of anxieties has the effect of keeping up artificially the state of mind it appears to soothe, just as the playing down to immaturity, in the case of the young movie audience, has become perhaps the principal influence that induces it to remain immature.

What, then, about television, with which Mr. Seldes has been involved almost since its commercial inception and to which, though he does not say so, he has contributed his own best efforts with a view to directing its development toward a respectable art of its own? He admits that, at its present stage, TV has produced nothing really new, but he believes that since it has the advantage of letting you both see and hear its performers while their performance is going on, it should encourage a more natural relation between the performer and his audience than either radio or movie does, and he hopes that, in its handling of drama, it will approximate to the regular stage in allowing us to see characters in the round. Unfortunately, the only examples that Mr. Seldes is able at this time to invoke in order to persuade us of these possibilities are such features as Milton Berle and the puppets Kukla, Fran and Ollie, about whose quality he makes it plain that he is not enthusiastic, and he has already chilled the reader's blood by introducing his section on this subject with the heading *Pandora's Box*.

Mr. Seldes has tried to be as hopeful as the conditions will possibly permit; he does not want to accept dead ends. Television, if it only will, can, he says, give us real theater in the living room. The movies can retrieve their slipping public by appealing to an untouched audience—that of mature men and women. He preaches to the public as a whole the need for non-official protests on the part of groups of citizens—though he has noted the discouraging apathy of the people who patronize these mass media. To those who don't listen to radio, who don't look at television, and who rarely go to the movies, he insists that this will not save them. They must live in a common society conditioned by the effect of these things. Might not a man who had never turned on the radio find himself being trampled to death by a panic-stricken mob driven frantic by some such broadcast as Orson Welles's *War of the Worlds*? On the other hand, the remedy proposed for minimizing this kind of hazard seems a heavy price to pay for escape from even such a fate as this. In order to keep informed as to what is going on in these departments, the non-lover of television and radio will be obliged, Mr. Seldes suggests, to "suspend whatever he is doing and look for an hour or two at the best that is now offered." But "if a nation cannot survive half slave and half free, a democracy cannot endure if the forces making for free minds are apathetic and the forces of invincible ignorance are aggressive and brilliantly managed and irresponsible. If it is already inconvenient to attack them, it will be dangerous in five years, and it will be impossible in ten." If no pressure is brought by the public to have the level of these media raised, the result may be simply that the movies will be superseded by television, and that radio will go bankrupt in the attempt to finance its successor before television has had the chance to outgrow its rudimentary stages. This would greatly facilitate the step that is Mr. Seldes's principal bug-bear, as it may well be anyone's: the taking over of the mass media by the government and the use of them, not for more or less legitimate informative and cultural purposes, as the B.B.C. has used them, but for unscrupulous total control of a spineless depersonalized public. The exploiters of mass entertainment, in aiming, for steady and sure returns, at the lowest common denominator, have in some departments been losing their audience, but they have also been stultifying those who share in this lowest common denominator and artificially extending its realm.

We are almost as far here from the Seldes who delighted in the *Ziegfeld Follies* and the vaudeville turns at the Palace as we are from the Toulouse-Lautrec who frequented the Nouveau Cirque or, for that matter, from Toulouse-Lautrec's predecessor, the seventeenth-century Jacques Callot, who amused himself in Italy at the *commedia dell' arte*. This book is about the audience, not about the artists. Mr. Seldes says he cannot take time to pay his compliments to the shows and the actors that have given him particular pleasure, but, after all, the films as we have them could hardly produce a new Chaplin. Mr. Seldes has told briefly here the story of Walt Disney's capitulation, in competition with the comic books and under pressure to pay off his financing, by turning out long features in quantity. He might have added that of Jimmy Durante, surely the greatest comic that has appeared since Mr. Seldes's first book, who has been compelled to descend from the wild poetry of the Parody Club to the routine personality gags of his work on the screen and air. Mr. Seldes mentions in passing that Li'l Abner may perhaps "to a degree" take the place of Krazy Kat; but he is occupied chiefly with the problem of curing the degenerate tendencies of the seven hundred million comic books that are now printed every year.

Mr. Seldes, since he left the *Dial*, has been cultivating certain conceptions that sometimes land him in a false position. He asserts that the more serious American writers have always been contemptuous of "the average man," that they have vilified American life and made no effort to understand America. He even goes to the length of implying that Walt Whitman was deficient in sympathy for ordinary American humanity and indifferent to the Civil War. It is a pity that Mr. Seldes should so long ago have taken up a position that has prevented him from becoming as well-acquainted with the history of American thought as he is with that of our popular arts. Since this question, in his latest book, is raised only incidentally, one need not go into it here any further than to make the point that the better American writers have given expression to a variety of points of view and that these points of view themselves have varied in response to varying epochs. Mr. Seldes's own point of view seems rather to belong to the category of what Frank Moore Colby meant when he called one of his books *Constrained Attitudes*. This attitude is contradicted on almost every page of Mr. Seldes's book by what he thinks and says and is. Such occasional pokes as he takes at his antagonist, the straw-man "intellectual," who is supposed to disdain the popular arts, are quite inconsistent with the bitter complaints of "anti-intellectualism" that he brings against the radio and movies for their habit of representing schoolteachers as invariably either "angular spinsters" or "absent-minded professors," who are treated "the former without sympathy, the latter without respect," and their convention that all studious young people are absurd little prigs and bores.

The truth is, of course, that Mr. Seldes is nothing if not an intellectual himself, and, as *The Great Audience* proves, an exceptionally able one. He has come out of his twenty years of wrestling professionally with the lively arts even less well-disposed toward mediocrity, toward the facile, the false and the trashy, than he was at the time when he was editing the *Dial* and when the floods of that rubbish were not threatening to swamp us. Mr. Seldes's whole appeal to the public is based on the hope —I believe quite justified—that there are still a great many Americans who are also intellectuals, to the degree, at least, of not being satisfied with the goods that the mass media are putting out. His "intellectual" and his "average man" are in reality demagogic devices, taken over from the very agencies against which he now protests; they have never been anything other than masks to mislead the simple. Mr. Seldes shows them up at once when he comes to grips with his subject, as in his section called *Nine P. M. Tuesday*, in which he tells us that "the average man lives at many emotional and intellectual levels," and when he declares, in *The Menace of the Years,* that "the people desperately need arts that are serious." Intellectual that he is, he cannot help expressing a doubt whether, at this point, the people are "capable of accepting" them; and no critic of our post-Civil War period or of the Mencken and Lewis era has ever taken a gloomier view of the results of American commercialism or issued a grimmer warning. The radio and movies, Mr. Seldes says, "are the great engines of democratic entertainment and culture," yet, through their imposition of uniformity, "they are committed to the destruction of democracy."

October 28, 1950

HOUDINI

HOUDINI IS A SHORT strong stocky man with small feet
and a very large head. Seen from the stage, his figure,
with its short legs and its pugilist's proportions, is less
impressive than at close range, where the real dignity
and force of the enormous head appear. Wide-browed
and aquiline-nosed, with a cleanness and fitness almost
military, he suggests one of those enlarged and idealized
busts of Roman consuls or generals. So it is rather the
man himself than the stage personality who is interesting.
Houdini is remarkable among magicians in having so
little of the smart-aleck about him: he is, of course, a
tremendous egoist, like many other very able persons,
but he is not a cabotin. When Houdini performs tricks,
he does it with the directness and simplicity of an expert
giving a demonstration and he talks to his audience in a
quite different way from that of the ordinary conjuror:
straightforwardly, with no patter. The formulas—such as
the "Will wonders never cease?" with which he signalizes
the end of a trick—have a quaint conventional sound, as
if they were perfunctory concessions to the theater. For
preëminently Houdini is the honest craftsman which his
plain speech and German accent suggest—thoroughgoing,
earnest, enthusiastic.

Houdini is in fact a German Jew (Houdini is not his
real name)—born in the state of Wisconsin. In his youth,

he served an apprenticeship to circuses and dime-museums. He mastered the whole repertoire of magic and took his place, with a show of his own, as a magician of the first rank. Houdini has until recently been most celebrated for the specialty known as the "escape." He has succeeded in extricating himself from every conceivable kind of strongbox, straitjacket, handcuffs and chains under every conceivable kind of circumstances; and, though this is a department of trickery which has always seemed to the present writer less artistically interesting than others, it is characteristic of Houdini that, not content with the ingenuities of illusion and the perfection of sleight-of-hand, he should have chosen to excel in that branch of magic which offered the most dangerous challenge and the best chance of performing feats unlikely to be duplicated, and which also took him farthest from the masks of the theater. Lately, however, Houdini has achieved a new kind of celebrity in connection with the investigation of spiritualism. It was formerly the custom to have spiritualistic phenomena authenticated by scientists of various sorts, and, as a result of this method of research, many surprising discoveries were reported—culminating, at the end of the war, in the ectoplasm revelations. When the French magicians, however, of whose committee Houdini had been made a member, challenged the ectoplasm mediums to admit magicians to their séances, they refused to perform under those conditions; and when Houdini was later included in the *Scientific American*'s committee to investigate Mrs. Crandon, the Boston medium, who nearly succeeded in winning the prize offered by that publication for the production of genuine phenomena, he detected her tricks at once and proceeded to construct a cabinet which would make it impossible for her to repeat them. The truth is, of course, that in a committee of scientists on which

Houdini sits, it is Houdini who is the scientist. Doctors, psychologists and physicists are no better qualified to check up on spiritualistic phenomena than lawyers, preachers or poets. They are deceived just as readily by magicians on the stage as anybody else in the audience, and it is equally easy for them to be deceived by magicians as mediums. The problem is whether the "medium" is a real medium or merely a conjuror, and this is something that only a conjuror is really equipped to find out.

Houdini is thus perhaps the first investigator of spirtualism who is competent for the task. He is one of the most accomplished magicians in the world, and— what is rare—he has brought to the study of trickery a true scientific curiosity: he seems now to have become more interested in understanding how effects are pro- duced than in astonishing people with them, and to derive more satisfaction from lecturing on the methods of the mediums than from contriving illusions of his own. He has collected a library of books on trickery, occultism and kindred subjects which is said to be the largest in the world; and he has himself published a book on spiritual- ism called *A Magician Among the Spirits* and a pamphlet setting forth his observations in connection with Mrs. Crandon and with Argamasilla, a Spanish clairvoyant who claimed to be able to read through metal. He has even taken the trouble to attempt a retrospective exposé of Daniel Home's famous levitation of fifty years ago, visiting the London hotel at which Home is supposed to have floated out of the window of a room and in at the window of the room next door and discovering that the passage from one ledge to the other could easily have been made with a rope. As a result of his study of the supernatural, Houdini has come to the following con- clusions. He believes that, so far as the evidence goes, the phenomena of spiritualism are fraudulent, because, in all the cases on record in which experts on magic have been called, their testimony has gone against the mediums; he asserts that telepathy does not exist and that he himself can reproduce by trickery any telepathic phenomena of which he has ever heard; that the miracles of which the legends are always reaching us from the East—the Indian Rope Trick, the stopping of the pulse and the Yogis who survive being buried alive—are either tricks long understood by magicians or travellers' tales which have never been authenticated; and that all other supposed supernatural occurrences are to be put down either to coincidence or to momentary hallucination.

Houdini declares that he has never been duped, that he has never failed to see through a trick, but that he lives in continual terror of someday being outwitted by a telepathist or a medium—in which case his dogmatic denials would be made to look ridiculous. And this has given him a certain edge, a certain nervous excitement, as of a man engaged in a critical fight. Where he once challenged the world to tie him up, he now challenges it to convince him of the supernatural; and, in spite of his apparent self-confidence—sometimes thought excessive—he is very keenly aware of the perils of his position. It may be indeed that Houdini has appeared at a crucial moment in the history of spiritualism and that he is destined to play an important role. For a spectator at one of his Hippodrome performances, it is difficult to understand how a credulous disposition toward mediums can long survive such public exposures. Here one can see Houdini reproduce the classical phenomena of the megaphone that floats, the bells that ring and the ghostly hands that brush one's face, in full sight of the audience, who see how the tricks are done, but to the bewilderment of a blindfolded man who sits with him on an isolated platform. When one has watched Houdini, with his hands and feet both held by his vis-à-vis, get hold of a megaphone by his teeth, one does not find it surprising that the editors of the *Scientific American* should have been fooled by the same trick performed by Mrs. Crandon in a dark room. And when we have heard him, by means of devices that he afterwards gives away, tell members of the audience whom he has never seen before, their names and their addresses and facts about their private affairs, we are prepared to accept any marvels of this kind that the mediums, with their elaborate intelligence service, are reported to be able to accomplish.

The real situation, however, is of course that with the people who frequent séances, the difficulty is not for the mediums to convince them that the phenomena are genuine but for the tricksters to handle things so badly as to make their clients suspicious. A friend of mine was once told by a professional medium of a séance that had gone wrong when he had found that he could not get his hand free; he had tried to represent the spirit by touching the client with his cheek and then in a panic remembered that he had not yet shaved that day; but the lady allayed this fear, as soon as the séance was over, by telling him that the manifestations that day had been certainly their most successful, since the supernatural essence of the spirit had startlingly communicated itself by a sharp electrical pricking. One thinks also of the French savant who, as a result of methodical research, undertaken at the behest of the government, reported his success in establishing that spirits had hair on their heads, that they were warm, that they had beating hearts, that their pulse could be felt in their wrists, and that their breath contained carbon dioxide.

June 24, 1925

POE AT HOME AND ABROAD

THE RECENT REVIVAL of interest in Poe has brought to light a good deal of new information and supplied us for the first time with a serious interpretation of his personal career, but it has so far entirely neglected to explain why we should still want to read him. In respect to such figures as Poe, we Americans are still perhaps almost as provincial as those of their contemporaries who now seem to us ridiculous for having failed to recognize their genius. Today, we take their eminence for granted, but we still cannot help regarding them, not from the point of view of their real contributions to western culture, but primarily as fellow-Americans, whose activities we feel the necessity of explaining in terms of America and the circumstances of whose personal lives we are, as neighbors, in a position to investigate. Thus, at a date when "Edgar Poe" has figured in Europe for the last three-quarters of a century as a writer of the first importance, we in America are still preoccupied—though no longer in moral indignation—with his bad reputation as a citizen. Thus, Dr. J. W. Robertson, who perhaps started off the recent researches, five years ago published a book to show that Poe was a typical alcoholic. Thus, last year we saw the publication of Poe's correspondence with his foster-father. Thus, we are promised the early revelation of Poe's plagiarism of his plots from a hitherto unknown

German source (as James Huneker has pointed out that Poe's later and most celebrated poems must certainly have owed a good deal to an obscure American poet named Thomas Holley Chivers). Thus, a Miss Mary E. Phillips has just published an enormous biography running to sixteen hundred and eighty-five pages—*Edgar Allan Poe, the Man*—a monument of uncritical devotion which it must have taken a lifetime to compile, stuffed with illustrations that include not only photographs of the little Scotch town from which Poe's foster-father came, of the librarian of the University of Virginia at the time when Poe was a student there and of the clock on the mantelpiece of Poe's cottage at Fordham, but also maps of New York, Richmond and Baltimore at the time when Poe lived in those cities; and containing embedded in its pudding-stone prose perhaps more miscellaneous facts about him than have ever before been assembled.

The ablest and the most important of recent American books on Poe, is, however, without any doubt, Mr. Joseph Wood Krutch's *Edgar Allan Poe: A Study in Genius*. Mr. Krutch has made an attempt to go beyond Doctor Robertson in diagnosing Poe's nervous malady, and his conclusions are by this time well known: he believes that Poe was driven in the first instance into seeking a position of literary eminence by a desire to compensate himself for the loss of social position of which his foster-father had deprived him; that, in consequence, perhaps of a "fixation" on his mother, he became sexually impotent and was forced, as a result of his inability to play a part in the normal world, to invent an abnormal world full of horror, repining and doom (the universally recognized concomitants, according to Mr. Krutch, of sexual repression of this sort) in which he could take refuge; that his very intellectual activity, his love of working out cryptograms and crimes, had been primarily stimulated by the desire to prove himself logical when he felt he was going insane; and, finally, that his critical theory was merely a justification of his peculiar artistic practice, which was itself thus, in turn, a symptom of his disease. It must be said, in fairness to Mr. Krutch, that he does not fail to draw, at the end of his book, the conclusions about artists in general which follow from his particular conclusions. Mr. Krutch fully admits that, if what he says about Poe is true, it must also be true of "all imaginative works," which, in that case, should be regarded as the products of "unfulfilled desires" springing from "either idiosyncratic or universally human maladjustments to life." This does not, however, prevent Mr. Krutch from misunderstanding Poe's writings and seriously undervaluing them, nor even from complacently caricaturing them—as the modern school of social-psychological biography, of which Mr. Krutch is a typical representative, seems inevitably to tend to caricature the personalities of its subjects. We are nowadays being edified by the spectacle of some of the principal ornaments of the human race exhibited exclusively in terms of their most ridiculous manias, their most disquieting neuroses and their most humiliating failures. Mr. Krutch has chosen for the frontispiece of what he calls a "study in genius" a daguerreotype of Poe taken in 1849, shortly before his death: it shows a pasty and dilapidated personage with untrimmed untidy hair, an uneven toothbrush mustache and large pouches under the eyes; the eyes themselves have a sad unfocussed stare; one eyelid is drooping; one hand is thrust into the coat-front with an air of feeble pretentiousness. The dignified solemnity of the figure is as ludicrous as a bad old-fashioned actor attempting to play *Hamlet*, and its visible disintegration unpleasantly suggests an alcoholic patient recently admitted to a cure. And something like this is the final impression left by Mr. Krutch's book. Mr. Krutch quotes with disapproval the statement of President Hadley of

Yale, in explaining the refusal of the Hall of Fame to accept Poe among its immortals: "Poe wrote like a drunkard and a man who is not accustomed to pay his debts"; and yet Mr. Krutch himself, so interesting as a psychologist, is almost as unperceptive when he tells us, in effect, that Poe wrote like a dispossessed Southern gentleman and a man with a fixation on his mother.

For the rest, Mr. H. L. Mencken has written with admiration of Poe's destructive reviewing—that is, he has paid a tribute to an earlier practitioner of an art of his own; Mr. Van Wyck Brooks has examined Poe's work for evidences of the harshness and the sterility of a Puritan-pioneer society, and found it unsatisfactory as literature; and Mr. Lewis Mumford, in *The Golden Day*, seems to have taken his cue from Mr. Brooks when he finds in the hardness of Poe's effects the steel of the industrial age. It may, I believe, be said that no recent American critic, with the exception of Mr. Waldo Frank in his article on the Poe-Allan letters, has written with any real appreciation of Poe's absolute artistic importance.

II

One of the most striking features of all this American criticism of Poe is its tendency to regard him as a freak, having his existence somehow apart not merely from contemporary life but even from contemporary literature. "That his life happened to fall," writes Mr. Krutch, "between the years 1809 and 1849 is merely an accident, and he has no more in common with Whittier, Lowell, Longfellow or Emerson than he has with either the eighteenth or nineteenth centuries in England. . . . His works bear no conceivable relation, either external or internal, to the life of any people, and it is impossible to account for them on the basis of any social or intellectual tendencies or as the expression of the spirit of any age."

Worse than this, we are always being told that Poe has no connection with "reality," that he writes exclusively of a "dream world" which has no point of contact with our own. The error of this second assertion immediately becomes apparent when we consider the falsity of the first. So far from having nothing in common with the spirit of the first half of the nineteenth century, Poe is certainly one of its most typical figures; that is to say, he is a thorough romantic, closely akin to his European contemporaries. Thus, his nightmarish vein of fantasy is very much like that of Coleridge; his poetry in its earlier phase derives from Shelley and Keats; his "dream fugues" resemble De Quincey's and his "prose poems," Maurice de Guérin's. His themes—which, as Baudelaire says, are concerned with "the exception in the moral order"—are in the tradition of Chateaubriand and Byron, and of the romantic movement generally. It is, then, in terms of romanticism that we must look for reality in Poe. It shows a lack of historical sense to expect of him the same sort of treatment of life that we find in Dreiser or Sinclair Lewis and the recent preoccupation with which seems so to have misled our critics. From this modern sociological point of view, the European writers whom I have named above had no more connection with their respective countries than had Poe with the United States. Their settings and their dramatis personae, the images by which they rendered their ideas, were as different as those of Poe from the images of modern naturalism, and they used them for a different kind of story-telling which conveyed a different kind of moral.

What, then, are the morals of Poe, the realities he tried to express? The key is to be found in Baudelaire's phrase about "the exception in the moral order." The exception in the moral order was the predominant theme of the romantic movement. It is absurd to complain, as our critics do, of Poe's indifference to the claims of society, as if this indifference were something abnormal: one of the principal features of romanticism was, not merely an indifference to the claims of society, but an exalted revolt against them. The favorite figure of the romantic writers was the sympathetic individual considered from the point of view of his non-amenability to law or convention. And in this, Poe runs absolutely true to type: his heroes are the brothers of Rolla and René; of Childe Harold, Manfred and Cain. Like these latter, they are superior individuals who pursue extravagant fancies, plumb abysses of dissipation or yield to forbidden passions (Poe made one or two experiments with the common romantic theme of incest; but his specialties were a frigid sadism and a curious form of adultery which never took place till the woman whom the hero betrayed was dead). And, as in the case of the other romantic heroes, their drama is the conflict of their impulses with human or divine law. This impulse of the individual does not, however, in Poe, take often, as it does with the other romantics, the form of a too generous passion overflowing the canals of the world; but assumes rather the sinister character of what Poe called the "Imp of the Perverse." Yet this very perversity of Poe, the kind of dizzy terror it engenders, due to whatever nervous instability and whatever unlucky circumstances, have their poetry and their deep pathos—from those lines in one of the finest of his poems in which he tells how the doom of his later life appeared to him even in childhood as he gazed on "the cloud that took the form (When the rest of Heaven was blue) Of a demon in my view," to that terrible picture of the condemned man, "sick—sick unto death with that long agony," when "first [the candles] wore the aspect of charity, and seemed white slender angels who would save me; but then, all at once, there came a most deadly nausea over my spirit, and I felt every fibre in my frame thrill as if I had touched the wire of a galvanic battery, while the angel forms became meaningless specters, with heads of flame, and I saw that from them there would be no help. And then there stole into my fancy, like a rich musical note, the thought of what sweet rest there must be in the grave." And it is the lifelong "agony" of his moral experience that gives to Poe's *William Wilson* its superior sincerity and intensity over Stevenson's *Doctor Jekyll and Mr. Hyde*. In Stevenson, it is the virtuous half of the dual personality that destroys the divided man by exorcising the evil; but, in Poe, it is the evil half that does away with the good and that is even made to tell the whole story from its own point of view. Yet does not *William Wilson* bring home to us the horror of the moral transmutation more convincingly than the melodramatic fable of Doctor Jekyll and Mr. Hyde?

There is one special tragic theme of Poe's which deserves to be noted in this connection. Mr. Krutch says that Poe was impotent, and that, for this reason, though perhaps unconsciously, he chose to marry a girl of thirteen with whom it would be impossible for him to have regular conjugal relations. Mr. Krutch does not offer any proof of this, but we do not have to assume it to be true in order to agree with Mr. Krutch that Poe's marriage with Virginia Clemm was somehow unsatisfactory, and that it plays a strange role in his work. Virginia was Poe's first cousin, and it may be that, on this account, he had scruples about consummating the marriage. In any case, she became tubercular, and, twelve years after their marriage, died; while Poe himself grew neurotic, irritable and at last unbalanced. He was obsessed by desperate fantasies and seems, after her death, to have been almost insane. It is possible to follow Mr. Krutch in admitting that the atrocious sadism of many of Poe's later tales must have been due to some emotional repression. Though he undoubtedly adored Virginia, he seems at the same time to have wished her dead. He is always imagining, in his tales, long before her actual death, that a woman like Virginia has died and that her lover is free to love other women. But even here, the dead woman intervenes: in *Ligeia*, she reincarnates herself in the corpse of her successor, who has also died; in *Morella*, in her own daughter. And it is evidently this conflict of Poe's emotions which inspires, not merely these bizarre fancies, but also the unexplained feelings of remorse that so often haunt his heroes. After Virginia has actually died, the situation he has foreseen in the stories seems to be realized. He conducts flirtations with other women; but they are accompanied by "a wild inexplicable sentiment that resembles nothing so nearly as a consciousness of guilt." "I was never really insane," he writes to Mrs. Clemm just before his miserable death, "except on occasions when my heart was touched. I have been taken to prison once since I came here for getting drunk; but then I was not. It was about Virginia." The story of Poe and Virginia is a painful and rather unpleasant one; but it is perhaps worth discussing to this extent, for we recognize in it the actual relation which, viewed in the light of a romantic problem and transposed into romantic terms, fills Poe's writings with the ominous sense of a deadlock between the rebellious spirit, the individual will, on the one hand, and both its very romantic idealisms and its human bonds, on the other. "The whole realm of moral ideals," says Mr. Krutch, "is excluded [from Poe's work], not merely as morality *per se*, but also as artistic material used for the creation of conflicts and situations." What, then, does he suppose such stories as *Eleanora* and *Ligeia* are about? He goes on to say that horror is the only emotion which is "genuinely Poe's own" and that this "deliberately invents causes for itself," that "it is always a pure emotion without any rational foundation." How, he would no doubt ask, can anything describable as moral interest be found in the *Descent into the Maelström* or the *Case of M. Valdemar*? This question I propose to discuss in a moment.

III

Poe was, then, a typical romantic. But he was also something more. He contained the germs of a further development. By 1847, Baudelaire had begun to read Poe and had "experienced a strange commotion": when he had looked up the rest of Poe's writings in the files of American magazines, he found among them stories and poems which he had "thought vaguely and confusedly" of writing himself, and Poe became an obsession with him. He published in 1856 a volume of translations of Poe's tales; and from then on, the influence of Poe became one of the most important in French literature. M. Louis Seylaz has recently traced this influence in a book called *Edgar Poe et les Premiers Symbolistes Français*, in which he discusses the indebtedness to Poe of the French symbolist movement, from Baudelaire, through Verlaine, Rimbaud, Mallarmé (who translated Poe's poems), Villiers de L'Isle-Adam and Huysmans, to Paul Valéry in our own day (who has just written some interesting pages on Poe in a preface to a new edition of Baudelaire's *Les Fleurs du Mal*).

Let us inquire as to precisely in what this influence of Poe consisted that was felt so profoundly by the French through a whole half-century of their literature, yet which has so completely failed to impress itself upon the literature of Poe's own country that it is still possible for Americans to talk about him as if his principal claim to distinction were his title to be described as the "father of the short story." In the first place, says M. Valéry, Poe brought to the romanticism of the later nineteenth century a new aesthetic discipline. Perhaps more than any other writer, French or English, of the first half of the century, he had thought seriously and written clearly about the methods and aims of literature. He had formulated a critical theory, and he had supplied brilliant specimens of its practice. Even in poetry, by the time that Poe's influence had begun to be felt in France, it had been the ideals of naturalism that the post-romantic generation had tried to bring into play against the extravagance and the looseness of romanticism running to seed. But the American was now to provide them with a new and logical program that would aim to lop the overgrowths of romanticism and yet to achieve effects that can only be called romantic. What *were* these ultra-romantic effects which had first been described by Poe, and by what means did he propose to attain them?

"I *know*," writes Poe, "that indefiniteness is an element of the true music [of poetry]—I mean of the true musical expression . . . a suggestive indefiniteness of meaning with a view of bringing about a definiteness of vague and therefore of spiritual *effect*." This is already the doctrine of symbolism. Poe had exemplified it in his own poems. Poe's poetry is rarely quite successful; but it is, none the less, of first-rate importance. He tells us rather pathetically, in his preface to his poems, apologizing for their imperfections, that "events not to be controlled" have prevented him "from making, at any time, any serious effort in what, under happier circumstances, would have been the field of my choice." The immaturity of his early verse, where he is imitating Shelley and Coleridge, is certainly not redeemed by the deliberate tricks of his later, which he seems to have borrowed from Chivers and which are always a little trashy. Yet all of Poe's poetry is interesting, because more than that of any other romantic (except perhaps Coleridge in *Kubla Khan*), it does approach the indefiniteness of music—that supreme goal of the symbolists. That is to say that, from the ordinary point of view, Poe's poetry is more nonsensical than that of any of the other romantics—and nonsensical in much the same way as, to the ordinary point of view, much of our best modern poetry appears. To note but a single instance: one of the characteristic traits of modern symbolism is a sort of psychological confusion between the impressions of the different senses. This confusion distinctly appears in Poe: thus we find him, in one of his poems, *hearing* the approach of the darkness; and, in the marvellous description in one of his tales of the fusing sensations that follow death, we read that "night arrived; and with its shadows a heavy discomfort. It oppressed my limbs with the oppression of some dull weight, and was palpable. There was also a moaning sound, not unlike the distant reverberation of surf, but more continuous, which, beginning with the first twilight, had grown in strength with the darkness. Suddenly lights were brought into the room . . . and issuing from the flame of each lamp, there flowed unbrokenly into my ears a strain of melodious monotone."

Poe's theory of short-story writing was similar to his theory of verse. "A skilful artist," he writes, "has constructed a tale. If wise, he has not fashioned his thought to accommodate his incidents; but having conceived, with deliberate care, a certain unique or single *effect* to be wrought out, he then invents such incidents—he then combines such events as may best aid him in establishing this preconceived effect." So the real significance of Poe's short stories does not lie in what they purport to relate. Many are confessedly dreams; and, as with dreams, though they seem absurd, their effect on our emotions is serious. And even those that pretend to the logic and the exactitude of actual narratives are, nevertheless, also dreams. The happenings in them differ from the mere macabre surprises and the astonishing adventures and voyages of such imitators of Poe as Conan Doyle. The descent into the maelström is a metaphor for the horror of the moral whirlpool into which, with some justification, Poe had, as we know from more explicit stories, a giddy apprehension of going down; the precariously delayed dissolution of M. Valdemar stands for that horror of living death that figures also in *Premature Burial*, which, arising from whatever blight, haunted Poe through all his later life. No one understood better than Poe that, in fiction and in poetry both, it is not what you say that counts, but what you make the reader feel (he always italicizes the word "effect"); no one understood better than Poe that the deepest psychological truth may be rendered through phantasmagoria. Even the realistic stories of Poe are, in fact, only phantasmagoria of a more circumstantial kind. Any realism of any age which does not convey some such truth is, of course, bound to be unsatisfactory. And today when a revolt is in progress against the literalness and the superficiality of the naturalistic movement that has come between Poe's time and ours, he ought to be of special interest.

"Poe's mentality was a rare synthesis," writes Mr. Padraic Colum. "He had elements in him that corresponded with the indefiniteness of music and the exactitude of mathematics." Is not this what modern literature is tending toward? It was Poe who sent out the bridge from the romanticism of the early nineteenth century to the symbolism of the later; and symbolism, as M. Seylaz points out, though scarcely any of its original exponents survive, now permeates literature. We must not, however, expect that Poe should be admired or understood in his capacity of suspension across this chasm by critics who are hardly aware that either of its banks exists.

December 8, 1926

THE TENNESSEE POETS

I. A Water-Colorist

MR. JOHN CROWE RANSOM is a poet of much charm and a certain amount of originality. The narrative in sonnet sequence which gives its title to his new book—*Two Gentlemen in Bonds*—does not represent him at his best: it is prettily enough done, but all in a vein of rather too mild, too quaint, too sweetly wise irony—an irony somewhat suggestive of Mr. E. A. Robinson, but without the fine and delicately cutting edge which that poet occasionally unsheathes. In general, a cutting edge of some sort is what we chiefly miss in Mr. Ransom. Skillful, agreeable and personal as are the casually broken rhythms of his inveterate iambic pentameter, we come to wish at last that the good-natured iambs, which so easily allow themselves to forfeit the beat of their meter in the interests of a tone of conversation, would decide to set straight their slipped stresses, to vindicate their true accent, and to march, to sound their trumpets or to strike. We have, however, to have had a good deal of Mr. Ransom before we arrive at this state of mind. In the meantime, we can read him with the same sort of pleasure that we get from Edith Sitwell or Wallace Stevens, to whom he is closely akin. Mr. Ransom is not a great poet, but he is a delightful and distinguished one, one of the very few American poets of whom we may be sure that he will never bore us or let us down into banality. His humor and his grace never fail him; and we find in the best of his poetry the light and translucent loveliness—deliciously satisfying and more precious than so much more pretentious work —of a master of water-color:

Go and ask Robin to bring the girls over
To Sweetwater, said my Aunt; and that was why
It was like a dream of ladies sweeping by
The willows, clouds, deep meadowgrass and the river. . . .

Let them alone, dear Aunt, just for one minute
Till I go fishing in the dark of my mind:
Where have I seen before, against the wind,
These bright virgins, robed and bare of bonnet,

Flowing with music of their strange quick tongue
And adventuring with delicate paces by the stream—
Myself a child, old suddenly at the scream
From one of the white throats which it hid among!

February 2, 1927

II. *Fugitives*

This anthology contains a selection from the work of eleven poets who published for four years in Nashville, Tennessee, a magazine called *The Fugitive*. Three of them—John Crowe Ransom, Laura Riding and Donald Davidson—have since brought out books of their own; and others have become better known through the appearance of their poems in New York magazines. But these poets, aside from their individual merits, have a special importance as a group; and this anthology makes it possible to see how much alike they are, how far their ideas and their style have been affected by their close association. It may, I suppose, be said that Mr. Ransom was the leader of the Fugitives; and there is perhaps not one of these poets who does not seem in some way to derive from him. What they all have in common with Mr. Ransom are an intonation of irony, a "metaphysical" turn and a rich English vocabulary. It is true that these are characteristics which they share with many other modern poets; but the strength of their position as a group has enabled them to develop an original vein of imagery and even a rhythm of their own. They have constituted an organism vigorous enough to throw off the influence of T. S. Eliot, to which so many other poets have succumbed but of which relatively few traces are to be found in the work of the Fugitives.

In another respect, also, the Fugitives are interesting in their group aspect. They are one of the many recent manifestations of the creative awakening of the South. We had become accustomed in this quarter to old-fashioned florid oratory and early nineteenth-century romanticism. Not even George W. Cable, a man of first-rate intelligence and considerable literary ability, was altogether unaffected by the decomposition of the Southern style; and James Branch Cabell, in transposing it to the Middle Ages, did not escape its vices. But now, from New Orleans, from Richmond, from Nashville, from South Carolina itself, we are beginning to get a new literature that is as free from the flowers of rhetoric as it is from the formulas of gallantry. It is capable, in fact, as the Fugitives are, of showing itself cruel and astringent. But, although it has sloughed off these demoded trappings, it has kept much of the grace and distinction with which they were formerly worn. By reason of the very slow tempo of the South, its leisured detachment from the industrial world and the persistence of its local tradition, the Southern writer at the present time enjoys certain peculiar advantages; and it is possible that the literary South may eventually come to play, in relation to the great centers of the North and the West, a role in some respects similar to that which eighteenth-century Ireland has played in relation to London.

The standard of the Fugitives is high. Of the poets who have not published books, I have found Mr. Allen Tate and Mr. Robert Penn Warren the most interesting. Mr. Warren, in fact, gives the impression of being one of the most promising young poets who have recently appeared on the scene. His characteristic style is nodulous, tough and tight:

> Of old I know that shore, that dim terrain,
> And know how black and turbulent the blood
> Will beat through iron chambers of the brain.

He is, in fact, we feel, a little *too* tight: we are conscious of the iron chambers rather than of the blood beating through them. We suspect that Mr. Warren suffers from a trouble one often finds in young poets: his mastery of language and his subtlety of mind seem at the moment developed disproportionately to his emotions and his ideas, which are still rather vague and immature. This accounts, I believe, for his frequent obscurity. Some of the poems of Mr. Warren which I most admire—for example, *Croesus in Autumn*—I have read carefully several times, yet I cannot really understand them. Lines and images burn with a life of their own more intense than any life I can feel informing the poem as a whole— "Now green is blown and every gold gone sallow"—

and I suspect that Mr. Warren's real poems still remain to be written.

Mr. Allen Tate, however, is older than Mr. Warren, and his work is quite mature. There is something too much of Eliot in *Causerie II* and an image from Valéry at the end of the *Ode to the Confederate Dead*; but even where Mr. Tate is imitative he possesses a strange originality, a special vein of macabre imagination, a deeply stained color, of his own. What commands our admiration in these two longest of Mr. Tate's poems is his capacity for sustained phrasing—there are no lapses and no blanks, no stop-gaps. But though, line for line, these poems are amazing, they seem, in some way, as wholes, to lack emphasis, to fail of cumulative effect (the *Causerie* especially; the *Ode* somewhat less). In the case of Mr. Tate's shorter poems, however, these objections do not hold. *Mr. Pope, Death of Little Boys* and *Idiot* are like elaborate oriental ornaments which have been produced at an immense expense of materials, patience and cunning skill. We can have them around us and pick them up to examine them again and again, and we find that we do not get tired of them: they are as intricately patterned as cloisonné vases, as heavy as little bronzes (they differ in this from the inveterate lightness, sometimes flimsiness, of John Crowe Ransom). We admire the silver wire embedded in the blue and green enamel and the beautiful polish and glaze; we consider the precious alloy that has gone to make the grotesque image. One could give no idea of these extraordinary poems save by quoting them in their entirety. It is only possible here to include a few striking lines that make their effect by themselves.

Of the urn containing Pope's ashes:

> The urn gets hollow, cobwebs brittle as stones
> Weave to the funeral shell a frivolous rust.

A railroad train:

> Far off, a precise whistle is escheat
> To the dark . . .

A sick child:

the windowpane extends a fear to you
From one peeled aster drenched with the wind all day.

March 7, 1928

THE MUSES OUT OF WORK

WHEN ONE LOOKS back on the American poetry of the season, one is aware of only two events which emerge as of the first interest: *The King's Henchman* by Miss Edna St. Vincent Millay and *White Buildings* by Mr. Hart Crane. Mr. E. A. Robinson's *Tristram* has been extravagantly admired in some quarters; but, though it is undoubtedly more easily readable than his other Arthurian poems, though it contains a better story more energetically told and though it is by no means poor in those flashes of moral vision that make the weaker poems of Robinson more interesting than the strongest of a good many of his contemporaries, it seems to me that these luminosities are too low-burning and evanescent to justify the whole of a long narrative that reads at its worst like a movie scenario and at its best like a novel of adultery of the nineties, full of long well-bred conversations of which the metaphysical archness sounds peculiarly incongruous in the mouths of the heroes of medieval legend. What is admirable about *Tristram* is that now, after so many years during which Mr. Robinson's work has been growing more and more spectral, he should suddenly come to life to write a poem with so much vividness and animation, if not precisely with much poetic reality or much poetic art. But, with all respect for a fine poet and for one of the most honorably won of our contemporary reputations, I would still exchange the whole of Mr. Robinson's Arthurian cycle, with its conventional romantic stage properties of castles and seas and wars and its false starts at passionate expression always foundering in "before we knew what we were yet to see" or "until we saw as far as we should know," for one of his New England elegies. Miss Millay's poetic drama (which in its published form is considerably longer than the libretto used for the opera) has a theme very much like Mr. Robinson's and, though she treats it but little less conventionally, gets out of it better poetry. Miss Millay has an instinct for drama, but not much imagination for character; and, in writing *The King's Henchman*, she seems to have been somewhat hampered by the traditions and the requirements of the opera libretto. Nor do I think her last act so effective as her situation warrants. But the *Henchman*, in point of style, is remarkably well-sustained and quite out of the class of her other plays: the language remains simple without ever ceasing to be personal, terse and, as it were, well-seasoned. And at its high point, in the love scene of the second act, Miss Millay, instead of merely allowing her lovers, as Mr. Robinson does, to debate about their love at length, is able to find for their emotions an equivalent in poetic music.

It is precisely to this mastery of Miss Millay's of the music of English verse that she owes her present pre-eminence (not that Mr. Robinson is not himself sometimes a master of this, but his music is mostly confined to the pathetic or ironic "dying fall"). The imagist movement, it seems to me, has caused to be accepted in America an entirely inadequate ideal of what poetry ought to be: the imagist poets have popularized a sort of surface-poetry, poetry of description, poetry for the eye—the poetry of Amy Lowell, Mr. Sandburg and Mr. Fletcher

—a poetry that is based on the cadences of prose and that is full of flat prose vowels. A few years ago, the writer was discussing English poetry with a number of young men, all of them persons of reading and taste and one of them a distinguished follower of the imagist tradition: it appeared, in the course of the conversation, that none of them had any use for Milton. When one confronted them with particular passages, the reason became quite plain: they were tone-deaf to Milton's effects. Compelled to apprehend *Paradise Lost* through the eye and the intellect alone, they could see nothing in the most splendid passages but the bad taste of mixed mythology, the dreariness of obsolete theology, the clumsiness of an inexact imagination and the affectation of a tortured tongue. Wordsworth fared even worse: they thought Wordsworth about the same thing as Longfellow. They could not *hear* the difference between Wordsworth and Longfellow any more than they could hear the kinship between Wordsworth and Milton. The influence of the imagist school has done much to deprive American poetry, as it were, of the dimension of sound. And the dangerous example of Walt Whitman (himself a very great poet) has, paradoxically, rendered it more prosaic: in borrowing from Whitman, his followers seem never to appropriate anything but the formulas of Whitmanesque rhapsody and, for the most part, to have remained insensible to the extraordinary musical gift which makes the best of his long poems symphonic and which enables him, in rendering bird-song, to hit, not merely upon lyrical rhythms but even upon sound-combinations surprisingly similar to those that Aristophanes had found in *The Birds* to mimic the nightingale.* To look only at the poetry of the pres-

* Compare the passages of bird-song in *Out of the Cradle Endlessly Rocking* with *The Birds*, 676-684.

ent season, the work of Miss Lola Ridge, Mr. James
Rorty, Mr. Virgil Geddes and Mr. Eugene Jolas all, in
one way or another, show evidence of this untuning of
verse. Now, Miss Millay, who is perhaps a little deficient
in visual imagination, writes verse as a pupil of Shakespeare and Bach; and, in the second act of *The King's
Henchman*, as a pupil not unworthy of her masters. In
the exquisite music of the love scene, at once so irregular
and so smoothly running, at once so exact and so free, she
has reached one of the high points of her poetry. It is the
magic strain that strikes our ear, seeming wordlessly—by
the very clear outline of its phrases, the definiteness of its
images—to convey the exaltation of young first love, all
its awkwardness turned to beauty.

As for Mr. Hart Crane, he is a singular case; he, too,
commands a diapason. But it is a diapason of which the
phrases are anything but clearly outlined, the images anything but definite. Mr. Crane has a most remarkable style,
a style that is strikingly original—almost something like
a great style, if there could be such a thing as a great
style which was, not merely not applied to a great subject,
but not, so far as one can see, applied to any subject at
all. Mr. Crane's "corymbulous formations of mechanics—
Who hurried the hill breezes, spouting malice Plangent
over meadows" and his "great wink of eternity, Of rimless
floods, unfettered leewardings, Samite sheeted and pro-
cessioned" remind us a little of the poet Chivers, from
whom Poe borrowed his later style and who wrote of "cat-
aracts of adamant uplifted into mountains" and of "the
rising golden glory of the sun in ministrations, Making
oceans metropolitan of splendor for the dawn." One does
not demand nowadays of poetry that it provide us with
logical metaphors or with an intelligible sequence of
ideas: Rimbaud is inconsecutive, his imagery is sometimes confused. Yet, with Rimbaud, whom Mr. Crane

a little resembles, we experience intense emotional excitement and artistic satisfaction; we are dazzled by the eruption of his images, but we divine what it is he is saying. With Mr. Crane, though he can sometimes move us, the emotion is oddly vague:

> Still fervid covenant, Belle Isle,
> —Unfolding floating daïs before
> Which rainbows twine continual hair—
> Belle Isle, white echo of the oar!

> The imaged Word, it is, that holds
> Hushed willows anchored in its glow.
> It is the unbetrayable reply
> Whose accent no farewell can know.

Lines even so explicit as these are rare with Mr. Crane. His poetry is a *disponible*, as they say about French troops. We are eagerly waiting to see to which part of the front he will move it: just at present, it is killing time in the cafés behind the lines.

This development of language beyond its theme is characteristic of a whole group of contemporary American poets. Among writers who have published volumes in the course of the present season, one may cite Mr. John Crowe Ransom, Mr. Foster Damon, Mr. Maxwell Bodenheim and Mr. Archibald MacLeish. Each of these, in greater or less degree, is an example of distinguished style or inventive language in the service of a soul which, at least at the moment, does not strike us as sufficiently interesting. Mr. Ransom is much the best of these—I have paid my respects to him elsewhere—but for so subtle and brilliant a writer, the impression he makes upon us is singularly mild. Mr. Bodenheim's new volume, *Returning to Emotion*, seems to me to have many ingenious figures, but little more emotion than his previous ones (yet Mr.

Bodenheim is a poet, and, though his books are rather disappointing when we set out to read them through, he appears to excellent advantage in the selection made by Conrad Aiken for the anthology called *Modern American Poetry* in the Modern Library Series). And Mr. MacLeish, though he is polished and lettered where Mr. Crane is careless and wilful, presents also a case of a fine style which has not yet been called to the front. Mr. Mac-Leish simply now writes well as a poet of the age of Eliot where he formerly, when he was first out of Yale, wrote well, if I am not mistaken, as a poet of the age of Masefield. He fails completely, in his present phase, to convince one of the moral necessity of his desperate invocation of the void (he is perhaps at his best in his satires and trifles): it is the literary fashion which has changed and not Mr. MacLeish who has grown, who has found his poetic identity. He writes admirable English verse: his instrument is of the very best make; but, emotionally and intellectually, I fear that a good deal of the time he is talking through his new hat. The influence of T. S. Eliot seems to have its unfortunate side: it is making the young men prematurely senile. It was bad enough for Mr. Eliot to imagine himself Gerontion at thirty, but with him the state of mind was real and the poetry had its poignancy; with his followers, it is largely a pose.

In connection with a good deal of the American poetry of the kind I have discussed above, one gets the impression that, if it is true that the manner of it is often more interesting than the matter, this is perhaps because the poets themselves do not lead very interesting lives. Does it really constitute a career for a man to do nothing but write lyric poetry? Can such a man expect the world to be concerned with what he has to say? In certain cases, such a career may justify itself. But more often, I believe, it fails to. Think of the poets of Johnson's *Lives*—almost all of them clergymen, physicians, ambassadors, statesmen or courtiers. Waller sat in Parliament and engineered a Royalist plot; Milton was Cromwell's Latin secretary and narrowly escaped the scaffold at the time of the Restoration; Prior was ambassador to France and took part in negotiating the Treaty of Utrecht. These three poets, in everything else so different from one another, have it in common that their work is distinguished by an interest in public affairs and a large experience of the world. Even in the case of those poets who, in the Rome of Virgil and Horace as well in the England and France of the seventeenth century, played no active part in the life of their time, they benefited much by their contact with the Court, where the civilization of the age had in some respects been brought to its highest point and where the problems of the day were in the air. It is no doubt partly the fault of the American world that the poet has no share in its affairs: politics is unattractive to people of the quality of intelligence that is needed for the writing of poetry; the specialization and high pressure of the professions make the cultivation of literature difficult; and a central social point of vantage from which all the activities of the time may be more or less surveyed—as from Paris, London or Rome—is for the United States apparently impossible. But the writer, from his experience of poetry and poets, has finally been brought to the conclusion that a young poet in America should not be advised at the outset to give up all for the Muse—to seclude himself in the country, to live from hand to mouth in Greenwich Village or to escape to the Riviera. I should not advise him even to become a magazine editor or to work in a publisher's office. The poet would do better to study a profession, to become a banker or a public official or even to go in for the movies. What is wrong with the younger American poets is that they have no real stake in society. One does not want them to succumb to society; but one *would* like to see them, at least, have some sort of relation to it. If the relation is an uncomfortable or a quarrelsome one, so much, perhaps, the better. As it is, the conflicts of feeling and the criticism of society are left largely to the novelists and the dramatists; and the poets content themselves with expressing the chagrin of sterility. Those who admire Yeats and who have put themselves to school to him would do well to consider how much of his strength is derived from his identification of his own aims with those of his people and party. It is perhaps only the political partisan, like Yeats—or like Dante—who has the right to be disillusioned with politics; as it is perhaps only the man of the world, like Catullus or like Byron, who has the right to be insolent to the great.

One of the ways in which American poets—the poets of the opposite camp from those I have just been discussing—do try to establish themselves in some sort of solidarity with society is by trying to immerse themselves, usually by way of Carl Sandburg and Walt Whitman, in the common life of their time. Mr. James Rorty has tried to do this and, to the writer's mind, has failed: his Canadian and Californian "landscapes" are charming, a really fresh and agreeable poetry of the West; but as a prophet of the *New Masses,* Mr. Rorty will convince nobody. Mr. Rorty is at home, and a poet, in the solitudes of the mountains and the prairies, but not yet among the crowds. Mr. Eugene Jolas, in *Cinema,* approaches the vulgar life of America, not through Sandburg and Whitman, but by way of Guillaume Apollinaire and the other up-to-date French fanciers of American skyscrapers and movies; but, on the whole, for all his bold and pyrotechnic images, he seems to write of American life from the outside, better informed than his European masters, but still preoccupied with the phenomena of the surface. (Mr. Jolas is, however, quite successful in writing about railroad journeys.) I do not, of course, disapprove of the policy these poets have followed. I am merely discussing the degrees of success attained by particular poets. And before passing on from this school, I should like to call attention to the very individual work of Mr. Kenneth Fearing which has been appearing in the *New Masses*. Mr. Fearing seems the most promising hard-boiled poet of the younger generation. He has an original flavor and accent and what seems a true intensity. One hopes that he will soon publish a book.

Two poets of this recent lot deserve a separate mention: Mr. Scudder Middleton, author of *Upper Night*, and Mr. Mark Van Doren, author of *7 P. M.* Though neither has a very wide range, both possess musical instruments: they practise English poetry successfully. Neither one is either an eccentric or a follower of the literary fashion; and both seem to write their poetry "on the side," as a natural function of lives that are well occupied with other matters. These other matters do not in themselves appear to be particularly stimulating: Mr. Van Doren conveys an impression of amiable reflective well-being and Mr. Middleton presents an attitude of slightly frustrated equanimity which are perhaps characteristic, in America, of the milieux in which one finds people at once comfortable and sensitive and cultivated. But this poetry in its kind is authentic. Mr. Middleton's *Children of Blossom* and *Burial* and Mr. Van Doren's *7 P. M.*, *Apple-Hell* and *The Crime* are among the best things of the season.

If it is true, as I have suggested, that some of the most gifted of American poets might become even better worth reading if they did not make the writing of poetry their only serious occupation, it is possible that we have here an explanation of the fact that in the United States the women who are writing poetry seem, in certain ways, more interesting than the men. Merely to be a woman is, as a rule, a career in itself, of which her poetry is bound to be a by-product, but a by-product that may reflect fundamentals. I have spoken above of Miss Edna Millay; Miss Léonie Adams, in the past year, has published in magazines a considerable amount of work brilliantly up to her best; and Miss Louise Bogan, a set of poems which surpass her best previous work. Miss Laura Gottschalk of the Fugitives group has brought out a first volume of verse, metaphysical rather than passionate, but distinguished by a fancy and an irony of a highly personal kind.

The writer has been sometimes accused of overrating the more popular irony of Mrs. Dorothy Parker. It is true that Mrs. Parker's epigrams have the accent of the Hotel Algonquin rather than that of the coffee houses of the eighteenth century. But I believe that, if we admire, as it is fashionable to do, the light verse of Prior and Gay, we should admire Mrs. Parker also. She writes well: her wit is the wit of her particular time and place, but it is often as cleanly economic at the same time that it is as flatly brutal as the wit of the age of Pope; and, within its small scope, it is a criticism of life. It has its roots in contemporary reality, and that is what I am pleading for in poetry.

May 11, 1927

This article, which appeared in the *New Republic*, was not very well received by some of the poets discussed. Hart Crane, when he read it—as later appeared in Philip Horton's biography of him—wrote to Ivor Winters as follows:

"You need a good drubbing for all your recent easy talk about the 'complete man,' the poet and his ethical place in society, etc. . . . Wilson's article was just half-baked enough to make one warm around the collar. It is so damned easy for such as he, born into easy means, graduated from a fashionable university into a critical chair overlooking Washington Square, etc., to sit tight and hatch little squibs of advice to poets not to be so 'professional' as he claims they are, as though all the names he had just mentioned had been as suavely nourished as he —as though four out of five of them hadn't been damned well forced the major part of their lives to grub at *any* kind of work they could manage by hook or crook and the fear of hell to secure! Yes, why not step into the State Department and join the diplomatic corps for a change! Indeed, or some other courtly occupation which would bring you into wide and active contact with world affairs! As a matter of fact, I'm all too ready to concede that there are several other careers more engaging to follow than that of poetry. But the circumstances of one's birth, the conduct of one's parents, the current economic structure of society and a thousand other local factors have as much or more to say about successions to such occupations, the naïve volitions of the poet to the contrary. I agree with you, of course, that the poet should in as large a measure as possible adjust himself to society. But the question always will remain as to how far the conscience is justified in compromising with the age's demands."

Mr. John Crowe Ransom addressed a letter to the *New Republic*, which was published in part, with a reply by me, in the issue of July 22, 1927:

Sir: I address myself not to the editorial godhead in its indivisible oneness, but to the portion incarnated recently by Mr. Edmund Wilson, whose *The Muses Out of Work* appeared in the issue of May 11.

Your taste in poetry seems to me admirable; which means, of course, that your likes and dislikes among the poets of the season are much the same as mine. In fact, I admire your natural taste all the more, since your reasoning, by which you go through the motions of fortifying your judgment, seems to me brutal and absurd. May I review your achievement? It is my thesis that you judge well of poetry without knowing why you judge, and that you invite the world to judge of poetry on grounds which are thoroughly insufficient.

You undertake to review the season's poetry according to a single consideration, which you phrase in several ways: Poetry must "have its roots in contemporary reality"; its theme must be important and contemporary; its tone must indicate that the poet "has a stake in society," leads "an interesting life," and has a successful "career," of which the poetry is strictly the by-product.

Permit me to observe that in hardly a single instance has this principle permitted you to make an aesthetic judgment.

Certainly you do not apply it to Miss Millay's poetry. You prefer to ascribe her preëminence to a very different principle (which seems also to be highly dubious): "precisely to her mastery of the music of English verse." Your liking for her verse was in defiance of your doctrine, which she violated. Personally, I was astonished when I heard that the great American opera had at last come to pass with a libretto that harked clear back to the Anglo-Saxon; you must have been appalled, with your bias in favor of the Hotel Algonquin; but, not sharing your bias, I did not have to share your embarrassment, and could honor *The King's Henchman* without damaging a pet

theory. That you, too, honored it, under the circumstances, shows a magnanimity.

You do not seriously apply it to Mr. Robinson's *Tristram,* which just as plainly is a poet's abnegation of the
contemporary reality.

You are on the point of applying it to Mr. Hart Crane's
White Buildings, but again you save yourself; what you
admire there you do not succeed in saying, but it is despite
the fact that you remark the poet's lack of a satisfactory
contemporary theme.

You seem to apply it with favorable results to Mr. Van
Doren's *7 P. M.,* forgetting that you have just now dis-
qualified him with the stipulation that the "career" you
have in mind for the poet must not include the career of
an editor.

You do not apply it anywhere very thoroughly, and the
fact is to your credit. It is a village schoolmaster's principle, and requires you to be presumptuous every time
you apply it in an unfavorable sense, and you very
decently prefer to be evasive for the most part, and let
the principle go.

In opposition to your principle, I venture to submit a
counter set of related propositions. Poetry is automatically
and inevitably contemporary, and in reflecting the most
actual and important experiences of the poet reflects in-
dubitable contemporary data. Sometimes its comments
upon these data are direct, and sometimes they are by
way of indirection; and the latter case is not the less
significant, though it is the more difficult for the critical
analysis. The prime virtue of poetry as a contemporary
document is not its directness, in which it is greatly
exceeded by prose, but its sincerity, in which it is reputed
to have no equals. There is as much of the poet in a
King's Henchman as in a *Figs from Thistles,* and vice
versa. It is impossible to find in the surface "theme" of a

poem any index to the degree of the poet's emotional excitement, since any theme pursued far enough involves the poet's whole mind and all his experience. The "interest" which attaches to a poet's theme is fundamentally the poet's interest, and the single isolated critic is in no better position than the poet to determine whether this is a universal interest; that question must hang in the balance for the process of time to bring to an answer.

These propositions I cannot here contend for; they seem to me to be very nearly axiomatic for critical theory. The general doctrine might be called a Critical Positivism: it is deeply informed with the conviction that critics must renounce their a priori formulas and their ex cathedra manners. They must prepare themselves to admit that their formulas will never fully explain the poem, and will probably not even fully explain their judgment of the poem. . . .

                                        John Crowe Ransom
Nashville, Tennessee

Mr. Ransom has misunderstood me—perhaps I should have stated my position more explicitly. In the first place, I did not "undertake to review the season's poetry according to a single consideration"—that the poet should "have a stake in society," etc. This—like my remarks on "the music of English verse"—were not definitive critical principles, but merely reflections by the way. I am well aware that no set of critical formulas can ever succeed in explaining a poem, and I do not pretend that my own primary judgments as to what is good poetry or what is not are anything other, in the last analysis, than mysterious emotional responses. In any field of literature, however, it is possible, and perhaps profitable, to speculate as to what makes certain productions more satisfactory than others. As for the question of "a stake in society," I never either made such a statement or went upon such an assumption as Mr. Ransom takes for granted on my part: I quite agree with him that the reality and the intensity of the experience which has gone to make a poem, and the excellence of the poem, are not at all to be measured by the contemporaneity of the subject or the form. I have no a priori objections to any sort of subject or form whatever—not even to the Arthurian legends. My contention was simply that the work of certain poets—among whom I did not include Mr. Robinson or Miss Millay—granting them whatever settings and puppets or whatever veins of imagery were congenial to their various temperaments, did not seem to be drawn from a particularly deep or a particularly interesting experience. If I had meant what Mr. Ransom thinks I meant, I should scarcely have spoken with admiration of Milton: Milton's personal emotional experience and his experience of the contemporary world both play prominent parts in his poetry, but the "surface theme" of *Paradise Lost*, for example, relating as it does to the Garden of Eden, is anything but contemporaneous.   E.W.

UPTON SINCLAIR'S *MAMMONART*

MR. UPTON SINCLAIR, having supplied successively economic interpretations of American journalism, American religion and American education, has undertaken, in his new book *Mammonart: An Essay in Economic Interpretation*, to perform the same service for literature and art. "It is my intention," he writes, "to study these artists from a point of view so far as I know entirely new. . . . The book will present an interpretation of the arts from the point of view of the class struggle." One does not see how Mr. Sinclair, who has been intimately associated for so many years with radical ideas and literature, can imagine that this point of view is new. On the contrary, it has become so familiar that, as soon as we have learned what his book is about, we can predict almost exactly what we shall find in it—even though we may be unprepared for the extreme results in certain cases of the author's application of his point of view. Here, for example, is Mr. Sinclair's economic interpretation of *Kubla Khan*: "Note that every one of these images appeals to reactionary emotions, fear or sensuality. By sensuality the reason is dragged from its throne; while fear destroys all activity of the mind, causing abasement and submission. Moreover—and here is the point essential to our argument—almost every image in this poem turns out on examination to be a lie. There is no such place as Xanadu; and Kubla Khan has nothing to teach us but avoidance. His pleasures were bloody and infamous, and there was nothing 'stately' about his 'pleasure-dome.' There never was a river Alph, and the sacredness of any river is a fiction of a priestly caste, preying on the people. There are no 'caverns measureless to man'; while as for a 'sunless sea,' a few arc-lights would solve the problem. The 'woman wailing for her demon lover' is a savage's nightmare; while as for the 'Abyssinian maid,' she would have her teeth blackened and would stink of rancid palm oil. From the beginning to the end, the poem deals with things which are sensual, cruel and fatal to hope."

It would, however, be unjust to Mr. Sinclair to suggest that he does not appreciate *Kubla Khan*. It is true that he announces his intention of proving that "present-day technique is far and away superior to the technique of any art period preceding" and that he attempts to do so by comparing a sonnet of Milton's to one by Mr. Clement Wood to the disadvantage of the former. But, whatever Mr. Sinclair may say for the good of the socialist cause, he has a real appreciation of literature and this somewhat interferes with his indictment. In *The Brass Check*, his book on journalism, he set out to expose a field of which he had had little inside experience and for which he felt, in consequence, no sympathy; but he is dealing in *Mammonart* with the products of his own craft, and the result, from the doctrinaire point of view, is one of the least effective of his books.

Bernard Shaw, with his more rigorous mind, has made a similar revaluation of literature, but he carried it through more logically. He began by assigning all literary works to either one of two departments, according to whether these works were or were not designed to ameliorate social conditions; and he laid down the uncompromising principle that, artistic merits being equal, the second was inferior to the first. But Upton Sinclair has not based his discussion upon any such clear proposition —which at least keeps the artistic question distinct from the moral one. He has tried to write a treatise on art which should function as a socialist tract by asserting that "all art is propaganda" and then justifying this assertion by assuming that any work of art which implies a philosophy, a point of view or even a sensation or an impulse is a piece of propaganda in favor of it. Since no human work can exist that does not rest on some sort of assumptions on the part of the person who produced it, Mr. Sinclair can make out a case; but his book, as a socialist exposé, is by no means the bombshell he has promised. What he has written is an outline of literature (since he has little to say about the other arts) by an able pamphleteer with a real taste for books but some moral and political prejudices which do not seem to prevent his enjoying certain works that run counter to these prejudices but which at least make him protest that he shouldn't. As such an outline, *Mammonart*—at any rate, the latter part—is not at all bad. Mr. Sinclair's memory occasionally lets him down, as when, evidently confusing Paul of Tarsus with the fourth-century Saint Paulinus, he tells us that Saint Paul was "a renegade Roman gentleman and former official of the empire" and writes scathingly of Thackeray's sentimentalizing over the death of Major Pendennis under the impression that Major Pendennis died the death of Colonel Newcome. But, on the whole, he is quite well-informed as to history and literature and knows how to place the writers with whom he deals in relation to the life of their times. He is particularly interesting in his treatment of the American writers of the last generation. Mr. Sinclair is himself a survivor of the era of Frank Norris and Richard Harding Davis, and his account of this is probably unique in its combination of inside knowledge with unorthodox point of view. On Jack London, whom he knew well, he is especially illuminating. One has seen, in fact, a good many less readable and less intelligent literary histories than this of Upton Sinclair. Intending, in his role of political oracle, a devastating social criticism, what he has given us, in his character of literary man, is a book that stimulates one's interest in the arts of God and Mammon both.

What is vulnerable in *Mammonart* is the thinking of Upton Sinclair rather than his literary taste. If, for example, he had begun by reflecting what *Art for Art's sake* really means, he would not have felt obliged to denounce it from beginning to end of his book. *Art for Art's sake*—an excellent slogan—means simply that the artist has the right to practice his art with a view to the perfection of his own kind of product—that he should not be expected to meet the requirements of specialists of other kinds. If somebody, that is to say, is constructing from the phenomena of experience a satisfactory artistic system, it should not be demanded of him that he construct either a political or a moral system, and the critic should not take him to task if his pattern fails to match the patterns of other people's political and moral systems. The artist has his own technique for formulating his vision of truth, and he cannot be expected to worry about the constructions of other people who are working in different materials. Mr. Sinclair comes quite close to this point of view when he writes in connection with Strindberg: "Let the artist give us truth, and we can always find use for it." And I suppose he would not oppose a program of *Mathematics for Mathematics' sake*. He speaks somewhere with admiration of the achievements of modern physics. Yet if mathematicians had not been permitted to indulge in *Mathematics for Mathematics' sake*, these discoveries would have been impossible.

When Karl Friedrich Gauss worked out his fourth-dimensional coördinates, he was engaged in a speculation which not only was quite devoid of political or moral significance but did not even appear at the time to be susceptible of practical application. Yet it was precisely by the aid of these exercises in pure mathematics and of others in the same direction that Einstein arrived at his new discoveries; and it is in the light of Einstein's discoveries that Mr. Sinclair's physicists in California are conducting their researches into the structure of the atom. A work of pure literature of which Mr. Sinclair disapproves is Gautier's *Émaux et Camées*. I take it that he would like to discourage the writing of any more such books. But how can he be sure that putting an end to writers of the type of Gautier might not mean inflicting on literary culture the same sort of injury that would have been inflicted on mathematical and physical culture if Gauss's experiments had been prevented? One of the first rules of civilization should be freedom for the artist and the scientist, and for every other kind of intellectual creator, to pursue his own researches and produce his own kind of work. If the Socialist Coöperative Commonwealth to which Mr. Sinclair looks forward is going to interfere with this, it is difficult to see how its culture will deserve to be considered superior to our own individualist one.

April 22, 1925

THE PILGRIMAGE OF HENRY JAMES

IT IS BECOMING a commonplace to say of Mr. Van Wyck Brooks that he is really a social historian rather than a literary critic, but one cannot avoid raising the question in connection with his new book. *The Pilgrimage of Henry James*, like *The Ordeal of Mark Twain*, is a page of American social history: in it, Henry James figures as the type of sensitive and imaginative American who, in the later nineteenth century, found the United States too barren and too crude for him and sought a more congenial environment in Europe. Mr. Brooks points out James's original isolation as the son of the elder Henry James, that well-to-do wandering philosopher who travelled back and forth between Boston and New York, between the United States and Europe, without finding himself quite at home anywhere; and he traces James's first saturation with European impressions during the formative years of his teens; his attempt at the beginning of his career to establish himself in America as an American novelist working with native material; his discouragement, his longing for Europe, his experiments with France and Italy and his dissatisfaction with his life there; his decision to live permanently in England and to find a field for his art in the depiction of English society; his failure, after years of living among them, to establish intimate relations with the English and his

217

disillusioned reaction against them; the bankruptcy of his imagination, his homesickness and his visit to the United States; his consternation and despair at the spectacle of modern America, and his final return to England. In short, Henry James's tragedy, according to Mr. Brooks, was that of the literary artist who has lost contact with his own society without having been able to strike roots in any other. And of all this aspect of James's career he has given the most intelligent and the most exhaustive account that we have yet had; in fact, it may be said that James's social significance and the part that his social situation plays in his work have here been properly appreciated for the first time. Mr. Brooks has made a contribution of permanent value toward the criticism of Henry James. He has interpreted the complex subject with all his incomparable instinct for divining the feelings and motives of Americans, for getting under their skins; and he has presented his logical theory with the consummate orderliness, neatness and point that he always brings to making out a case. When, for example, he disentangles James's reasons for turning playwright at one period of his career, he generates a kind of excitement in the process of demonstration that seems almost to be independent of the interest of what is being demonstrated. And he has reduced the whole to an entertaining narrative colored by imagination and written with grace. From the point of view of literary form, Mr. Brooks's *Henry James* is, in fact, probably the best of his books.

Where the book is unsatisfactory is in its failure to recognize the real nature and development of James's art. Mr. Brooks has completely subordinated Henry James the artist to Henry James the social symbol, with the result that James's literary work, instead of being considered in its integrity on its own merits, has undergone a process of lopping and distortion to make it fit the

Procrustes bed of a thesis. According to Mr. Brooks's simplification, Henry James was at first a very good novelist and then, later on, a very bad one. Mr. Brooks admires James's earlier fiction as a Turgenev-like social document and writes a warm appreciation of it—that is, he admires James in direct proportion as James performs the same sort of function as Mr. Brooks himself. But what he says, in effect, is that, after the publication of *The Bostonians* in 1886, James's artistic record is an almost total blank: when James had settled in England and had used up his American impressions, his failure to make anything of his English material was virtually complete. Mr. Brooks here lumps together the work of thirty years and, in the interest of an a priori theory, refuses to admit distinctions among some thirty volumes of fiction of widely differing character and merit. The truth is that the work of James's English residence falls into three distinct periods. During the second of these— after *The Bostonians* and while he is already dealing chiefly with English material—he reaches what seems to me indisputably his completest artistic maturity: he has got over a certain stiffness, a certain naïveté, which characterized his earlier work and he has acquired a new flexibility and a personal idiom. He has come for the first time into the full possession of his language and form, and he has not yet lost any of the vividness of his youthful imagination. He has ten years ahead of him still before that imagination will begin to show signs of flagging in such books as *The Awkward Age*, and longer still before that style runs to seed in the thickets of the later novels. In the meantime, in the fiction of this period—particularly, perhaps, in the shorter novels which were characteristic of it: *What Maisie Knew, The Aspern Papers*, etc.—he is to produce what seems to the present writer his most satisfactory and distinguished work. As for the deterioration which afterwards sets in, it is to be ascribed chiefly to advancing age. An important thing to remember in connection with James's latest novels—which Mr. Brooks treats with such severity—is that *The Ambassadors, The Wings of the Dove* and *The Golden Bowl* were all written when James was in his late fifties. Their abstraction, their comparative dimness and their exaggerated mannerisms are such as not infrequently appear in the work of an artist's later years. George Meredith and Robert Browning, who did not labor under the handicap of being expatriated Americans, developed somewhat similar traits. These later novels of James are, in any case, not as Mr. Brooks asserts, fundamentally unreal and weak. Intellectually, they are perhaps the most vigorous, the most heroically conceived, of his fictions; but they are like tapestries from which, though the design and the figures still remain masterfully outlined, the colors are fading out.

When all this has been said, however, there still confronts us, in connection with James, the question of a lack in his work of direct emotional experience—a lack which is naturally felt more disconcertingly in his later than in his earlier books, since it is less easily comprehensible in a mature than in a callow man. One can agree here with Mr. Brooks that this insufficient experience of personal relations may be partly accounted for by James's isolation among the English. Yet to throw all the emphasis thus on James's social situation, as Mr. Brooks seems to do, is surely to proceed from the wrong direction. James's solitude, his emotional starvation, his inhibitions against entering into life, were evidently the result of his fundamental moral character, not merely an accident of his social maladjustment; and with the problem of that fundamental character Mr. Brooks never adequately deals. "An immortal symbol," he sums James up, "the embodiment of that impossible yearning of which Hawthorne somewhere speaks—the yearning of the American in the Old World" for the past from which he has been separated. But this theory that a man's whole career may hinge on his yearning for the European past is humanly unconvincing.

It is precisely because Mr. Brooks's interest is all social and never moral that he has missed the point of James's art. It is possible for him to find James's work so empty and disappointing only because he insists on comparing it with that of writers with whom James has little in common: Hardy, Dickens, Tolstoy and Balzac. One would be in a position to appreciate James better if one compared him with the dramatists of the seventeenth century—Racine and Molière, whom he resembles in form as well as in point of view, and even Shakespeare, when allowance has been made for the most extreme differences in subject and form. These poets are not, like Dickens and Hardy, writers of melodrama—either humorous or pessimistic, nor secretaries of society like Balzac, nor prophets like Tolstoy: they are occupied simply with the presentation of conflicts of moral character, which they do not concern themselves about softening or averting. They do not indict society for these situations: they regard them as universal and inevitable. They do not even blame God for allowing them: they accept them as the conditions of life. Titus and Bérénice, Alceste and Célimène, Antony and Octavius—these are forces which, once set in motion, are doomed to irreconcilable opposition. The dramatist makes no attempt to decide between competing interests: he is content to understand his characters and to put their behavior before us.

Now, it was James's immense distinction to have brought to contemporary life something of this "classical"

point of view. The conflicts in his early novels are likely
to be presented in terms of European manners and morals
at odds with American ones—with a predisposition in
favor of the latter. But later on, James's contrasts tend to
take on a different aspect: they represent, not merely
national divergences, but antagonisms of ideals and
temperaments of a kind that may occur anywhere. I cannot agree with Mr. Brooks when he says that in James's
later novels "the 'low sneaks' have it all their own way . . .
the subtle are always the prey of the gross . . . the pure
in heart are always at the mercy of those that work
iniquity." On the contrary, the leaning toward melodrama
that allowed James in his earlier novels to play virtuous
Americans off against scoundrelly Europeans has almost
entirely disappeared. *The Ambassadors* is obviously a
sort of attempt to re-do the theme of *The American*, as
The Wings of the Dove is to re-do that of *The Portrait
of a Lady*; but one has only to compare the two pairs of
books to realize that James no longer sees life in terms of
the innocent and the guilty. The Bellegarde family in the
earlier novel are cold-blooded and impenitent villains,
whereas Mme. de Vionnet, who plays a somewhat similar
role in *The Ambassadors*, is shown in as attractive a light
as the American to whom she is morally opposed; in the
same way Gilbert Osmond and his mistress, who make
Isabel Archer miserable, are a good deal more theatrical
than Kate Croy and her lover, who try to exploit Milly
Theale. Mr. Brooks's account of *The Wings of the Dove*
seems almost perversely unintelligent. He melodramat-
ically describes Milly Theale as the "victim of the basest
plot that ever a mind conceived"; yet one of the most
remarkable things about *The Wings of the Dove* is the
way in which, from the very first pages, Henry James
succeeds in making us sympathize with the author of this
unquestionably ignoble plot, in making us feel that what

she does is inevitable. Kate Croy, though hard and crass, is striving for the highest aspirations she is capable of understanding, just as the more fastidious Milly is.

It is thus, in James's later novels, not a case of the pure in heart invariably falling a prey to the guilty, of the low sneaks having it their own way. It is simply a struggle between different kinds of people with different kinds of needs. I do not know what Mr. Brooks means when he writes of "the constant abrogation of James's moral judgment, in these years of an enchanted exile in a museum-world" nor when he says that James "had seen life, in his own way, as all the great novelists have seen it, *sub specie aeternitatis*; he was to see it henceforth, increasingly, *sub specie mundi*." On the contrary, James, in his later works, is just as much concerned with moral problems, and he is able to see all around them as he has not been able to do before. He has come to be occupied here even more than in his earlier work with what seem to him the irremediable antagonisms of interest between people who enjoy themselves without inhibitions, who take all they can get from life, and people who are curbed by scruples of aesthetic taste as well as of morality from following all their impulses and satisfying all their appetites—between the worldly, the selfish, the "splendid," and the dutiful, the sensitive, the humble. This humility, this moral rectitude takes on in Henry James the aspect of a moral beauty which he opposes, as it were, to the worldly kind; both kinds of beauty attract him, he understands the points of view of the devotees of both, but it is one of his deepest convictions that you cannot have both at the same time. The point of *What Maisie Knew*, for example, lies in the contrast between Maisie's other guardians—the vivid, the charming or the bold—who live only for their own pleasure and advantage and refuse to be bothered with her, and Mrs. Wix, the ridiculous old governess, who, by reason of her possession of a "moral sense," is left with the responsibility of Maisie, "to work her fingers to the bone." So, in *The Golden Bowl*, the brilliant figures of Charlotte and the Prince are contrasted with the unselfishness and the comparative dreariness of Maggie Verver and her father. Almost all Henry James's later novels, in one way or another, illustrate this theme. Surely this, and not, as Mr. Brooks suggests, any mere technical pattern, is that "figure in the carpet" that is hinted at in the famous short story; and in this tendency to oppose the idea of a good conscience to the idea of doing what one likes—wearing, as it does so often in James, the aspect of American versus European—there is evidently a Puritan survival that Mr. Brooks, in his capacity as specialist in American habits of thought, might have been expected to treat more prominently. As it is, he only touches upon it by way of a different route.

Of Mr. Brooks's queer use of his documents for the purpose of proving the artistic nullity of the latter half of James's career, many instances might be given. We sometimes get a little the impression that, instead of reading James's novels with a sense of them as artistic wholes, he has been combing them intently for passages that would seem to bear out his thesis even in cases where, taken in context, they clearly have a different meaning. The extreme abuse of this method is to be found in the chapter in which Mr. Brooks attempts to prove the inadmissible assertion that none of James's later novels is "the fruit of an artistic impulse that is at once spontaneous and sustained," that they "are all—given in each case the tenuity of the idea—stories of the 'eight to ten thousand words' blown out to the dimensions of novels." One would ask oneself at once: In what way can the "ideas" of *The Ambassadors* and *The Wings of the Dove* be described as being any more "tenuous" than those of their predecessors? How could either of them conceivably be a short story? They cover as long a period as the early novels, they contain just as many important characters, they deal with themes of just the same nature and they are worked out on just as elaborate a scale. But Mr. Brooks does not even pretend to go to the novels themselves in order to justify his critical conclusions about them: he bases his whole case on three passages which he has found in James's correspondence. When we come to examine these, we discover that two of them are references, respectively, to the "long-windedness" of *The Wings of the Dove* and the "vague verbosity" of *The Golden Bowl*—which certainly does not prove in the least that the author thought their *ideas* tenuous. It is in the third of these references that the phrase about "the tenuity of the idea" occurs, in an entirely different connection. James writes apologetically to Howells in regard to *The Sacred Fount* that it had been "planned, like *The Spoils of Poynton, What Maisie Knew, The Turn of the Screw* and various others, as a story of the 'eight to ten thousand words'" and had then spun itself out much longer. He goes on to explain that he might, perhaps, have "chucked" *The Sacred Fount* in the middle if he had not had a superstition about not finishing things. He does not, however, say that he considers these other novels as unsatisfactory as *The Sacred Fount* nor that he had any impulse to chuck them. In the only part of this passage, moreover, that Mr. Brooks omits to quote, he gives a quite different explanation from Mr. Brooks's one for his practice, at this particular time, of projecting short stories instead of novels: *"The Sacred Fount,"* writes James, "is one of several things of mine, in these last years, that have paid the penalty of having been conceived only as the 'short story' that (alone apparently) I could hope to work off somewhere (which I mainly failed of)." That is, he planned short stories rather than novels, because he thought that short stories were more salable. That, against this intention, he should have found the short stories growing uncontrollably into novels would seem to prove, not, as Mr. Brooks says, that James's "artistic impulse" was not "spontaneous and sustained," but, on the contrary, precisely that it was.

Mr. Brooks's misrepresentation of the obvious sense of this passage, his readiness to found upon such meager evidence so sweeping and damning a case, throws rather an unreassuring light on the spirit of his recent criticism. That spirit is one of intense zeal at the service of intense resentment. What Mr. Brooks resents and desires to protest against is the spiritual poverty of America and our discouragement of the creative artist. But, in preaching this doctrine, Mr. Brooks has finally allowed his bitterness to far overshoot its mark and to castigate the victims of American conditions along with the conditions themselves. In the latter part of *The Pilgrimage of Henry James*, we have the feeling that he has set out to show James up, just as, in his earlier one, he set out to show up Mark Twain. The story of Henry James, like that of Mark Twain, might have excited both our pity and our admiration; but in Mr. Brooks's hands, it gives rise to little but irony. Like Mr. Sinclair Lewis, that other exposer of the spiritual poverty of America, Mr. Brooks has little charity for the poor, and his enthusiasm for creative genius is not today sufficiently generous to prevent him, one is coming to feel, from deriving a certain satisfaction from describing its despair and decay.

There are, however, in any case, two reasons why Henry James is not a very happy subject for Mr. Van Wyck Brooks. In the first place, for all the sobriety of Mr. Brooks's tone, he is in reality a romantic and a preacher, who has little actual sympathy or comprehension for the impersonal and equanimous writer like James. One remembers in this connection a curious passage about Shakespeare in *America's Coming-of-Age*: "Why is it," asked Mr. Brooks, "that Shakespeare is never the master of originating minds? Plato may be, or Dante, or Tolstoy . . . but not Shakespeare . . . certainly anyone who requires a lesson of Shakespeare comes away with nothing but grace and good humor." The truth is that Mr. Brooks cannot help expecting a really great writer to be a stimulating social prophet. He can understand the lessons conveyed by a Plato or a Tolstoy, but he seems not much more responsive to Shakespeare than he is to Henry James. From Shakespeare he comes away with "nothing but grace and good humor," and from James with almost nothing at all. In the second place, Henry James lends himself to Mr. Brooks's treatment a good deal less satisfactorily than, say, Mark Twain, because the latter was admittedly a remarkable figure who wrote a few very fine things but the bulk of whose books, partly hack-work, have very little literary interest. In this case, it may be said that the man is more impressive than his work, and Mr. Brooks is in a position to tell us something important about him which is not to be found in his writings. But, in the case of Henry James, the work he accomplished in his lifetime is infinitely more interesting than the man. Henry James was not an intimidated and sidetracked artist, but a writer who understood both himself and the society in which he was living and who was able to say just what he meant about nations and human beings. It is difficult for Mr. Brooks to tell us anything about Henry James that James has not told us himself. *The Pilgrimage of Henry James*, which is shorter than its predecessor, falls short of it, also, in life and force. The *Mark Twain* was driven along by the author's passion of

discovery and his fury of indignation to a conclusion
which is, I suppose, so far Mr. Brooks's highest point of
eloquence; but it is perhaps, in the later book, a sign
of the critic's failure to be fully possessed by his subject,
of his comparatively feeble reaction to it, that the last
page, instead of leaving us, as its predecessor did, with a
dramatic and significant image, should be evidently an
unconscious imitation of the last page of Lytton Strachey's
Queen Victoria.

May 6, 1925

THE ALL-STAR LITERARY VAUDEVILLE

The writer of this article is a journalist whose professional activities have been chiefly concerned with the American literary movement of the last fifteen years.* He has written reviews of the productions of that movement and worked on magazines which were identified with it; he has lived constantly in its atmosphere. And he feels a certain human sympathy with all of its manifestations, even with those of which, artistically, he disapproves. It is to him a source of deep gratification that literature has been "sold" to the American public, and, on principle, in the face of alien attack, he will stand by even the least intelligent, the least disinterested, of its salesmen: he has served in that army himself. But it has recently occurred to him that, when he comes to take stock and is perfectly honest with himself, he must admit to feeling only the mildest interest in most of the contemporary literary goods which now find so wide a market, and that he is disaffected to the point of disgust with the publicity service which has grown up in connection with them. He has to take account of the fact that it is scarcely possible nowadays to tell the reviews from the advertising: both tend to convey the impression that masterpieces are being manufactured as regularly as new models of motor-cars. In the early days of the present era, the reviews of H. L.

* This essay first appeared anonymously.

Mencken, Francis Hackett, Floyd Dell and Louis Untermeyer set an example of honesty and boldness. Today
these journalist critics, having got the kind of literature
they want, are apparently quite content; and most of the
reviews are now written by people who do not try to go
beyond them. The present writers on American literature
all have interests in one phase or another of it: either the
authors know one another personally or they owe one
another debts of gratitude or they are bound together by
their loyalty to some stimulating common cause. And
almost all forget critical standards in their devotion to the
great common causes: the cause of an American national
literature in independence of English literature, and the
cause of contemporary American ideas as against the
ideas of the last generation. Even Stuart P. Sherman,
once so savage in the opposite camp, has become as benevolent as Carl Van Doren and now occupies what has
perhaps become, from the popular point of view, the central desk of authority, to which each of the performers in
the all-star circus, from Ben Hecht to Ring Lardner,
steps up to receive his endorsement. The present writer
has, therefore, for his own satisfaction, for the appease-
ment of his own conscience, made an attempt to draw
up a balance-sheet of his opinions in regard to his contemporaries, not merely in disparagement of those whom
he considers rather overrated but in justice to those he
admires. If he succeeds in disturbing one editor or reviewer, in an atmosphere where now for some time politeness and complacency have reigned, he will feel that he
has not written in vain.

To begin with the contemporary American novel—
which is commonly assumed to be our principal glory—I
must confess that I have difficulty in reading our novelists. We compare our fiction with English fiction and

conclude that we have been brilliantly successful in this field; but the truth is merely that the English novel is just now at a particularly low ebb. We have no novelist of the first importance, of the importance of James, Joyce or Proust; or of that of Balzac or Dostoevsky. Dreiser commands our respect; but the truth is he writes so badly that it is almost impossible to read him, and, for this reason, I find it hard to believe in his literary permanence. To follow the moral disintegration of Hurstwood in *Sister Carrie* is to suffer all the agonies of being out of work without being rewarded by the aesthetic pleasure which art is supposed to supply. Sinclair Lewis, with a vigorous satiric humor, has brought against certain aspects of American civilization an indictment that has its local importance, but, when one has been through *Main Street* and *Babbitt*, amusing though they certainly are, one is not left with any appetite to read further novels by Lewis: they have beauty neither of style nor of form and they tell us nothing new about life. Joseph Hergesheimer, though he knows how to tell a story, writes nearly as badly in a fancy way as Dreiser does in a crude one: the judgment of him that I most agree with is the remark attributed to Max Beerbohm: "Poor Mr. Hergesheimer, he wants so much to be an artist." Cabell, though a man of real parts, is, at his worst, a case of the same kind: *Beyond Life* I regard as one of the most obnoxiously written books I have ever read. *Jurgen* certainly had its merits: it was well-planned and curiously successful in the artificial evocation of the atmosphere of primitive folklore. But, except at Cabell's moments of highest imaginative intensity, which are neither very frequent nor very intense, he is likely to be simply insipid. His genealogies and maps of Poictesme bore me beyond description, and the whole Poictesme business strikes me as the sort of thing with which ingenious literary schoolboys sometimes amuse themselves. I dislike also Cabell's Southern sentimentality, which leaves him soft when he thinks he is most cynical. One cannot help feeling that, in the impression he gives of living and working in a vacuum, he furnishes a depressing illustration of the decay of the South since the Civil War. Willa Cather is a good craftsman, but she is usually rather dull. In spite of a few distinguished stories, she suffers from an anemia of the imagination and, like that other rather distinguished novelist, Zona Gale, is given to terrible lapses into feminine melodrama. As for Waldo Frank, he writes in a style—to me, never quite satisfactory—that combines James Joyce with the Hebrew prophets. At his best, he touches tragedy and, at his worst, embraces melodrama. He possesses a real poetic sensibility and is refreshing in so far as his vision is different from that of any one else; but, in his novels, where we hope to see him stage a drama, he is usually content to invoke an apocalypse. I consider Jean Toomer's *Cane* rather better in literary quality than Frank's somewhat similar *Holiday*. I feel more interest in John Dos Passos and F. Scott Fitzgerald than in any of the writers mentioned above: they are younger than the others, and one does not feel as yet that one knows exactly what to expect of them. Dos Passos is ridden by adolescent resentments and seems given to documenting life from the outside rather than knowing it by intimate experience; but, though, like Lewis, that other documentator, he is far too much addicted to making out cases against society, he is a better artist than Lewis and has steadily progressed in his art. Scott Fitzgerald, possessing from the first, not merely cleverness, but something of inspired imagination and poetic literary brilliance, has not until recently given the impression of precisely knowing what he was about; but with *The Great Gatsby* and some of his recent short stories, he seems to be entering upon a development in the course of which he may come to equal in mastery of his material those novelists whom he began by surpassing by vividness in investing it with glamor. Besides these, there are the other fabricators of fantasy and the realists, satiric and plain; but the former, so far as I have read them, are either tawdry, like Ben Hecht, or awfully mild, like Carl Van Vechten; and the latter, though both in novel and drama they have learned to apply the formulas of naturalism to almost every phase of American life and have, therefore, a certain interest in the history of American culture, are otherwise especially uninteresting at a time when naturalism has run its course and everywhere except in America is either being transformed or discarded. And we have also had the Wellsian social novel, at various levels of mediocrity.

Sherwood Anderson is a different matter. In his novels, despite excellent pages, I invariably become exasperated, before I have got to the end of them, by the vagueness of the characters and the constant repetitiousness of the form. But his short stories and his symbolist prose-poems have a kind of artistic authenticity that neither Lewis's richer resources nor Miss Cather's technical efforts have been able to win for those writers. Without ever having learned the tricks of his trade, Sherwood Anderson, in the best of his stories, has shown an almost perfect instinct that fashions, from what seems a more intimate stratum of feeling and imagination than our novelists usually explore, visions at once fresh and naïve and of a slightly discomfiting strangeness. He could stand to learn something, however, from the methods both of Miss Cather and of Lewis: too much of his material has evaporated in his hands from his not knowing how to deal with it. It can probably be said that, in general, the newer American writers have so far been distinguishing themselves in the short story rather than the novel. The short stories of Sherwood Anderson, Ernest Hemingway's *In Our Time* and Gertrude Stein's early *Three Lives*, to which should be added the best of Ring Lardner, constitute an impressive group and one quite free from the outworn conventions and the suggestion of second-rate imitation that make many of the novels unsatisfactory. It is interesting to note that all four of these writers have certain characteristics in common, that they may almost be said to form a school, and that, remote though they may seem from one another, there is a fairly close relationship between them. Thus, Anderson has read Gertrude Stein and seems to have been influenced by *Three Lives*; and Hemingway has evidently read and been influenced by all three of the others. Each of these four writers has developed what seems only a special branch of the same simple colloquial language, based directly on the vocabulary and rhythm of ordinary American speech; and, if there can be said to be an American school of writing, aside from American journalese or from the use of American slang in otherwise conventional English prose, these writers would seem to represent it. It is a genre that has already produced one masterpiece in Mark Twain's *Huckleberry Finn*, a work to which Anderson, Hemingway and Lardner are probably all indebted.

As for the dramatists, there is still only O'Neill, who, for all his efforts to break away from naturalism, remains a typical naturalistic dramatist of something under the very first rank. He is a writer of the same school as Hauptmann, with much the same kind of merits; but, where Hauptmann is as steady as Shakespeare, O'Neill is hysterically embittered. He forces his tragic catastrophes and, at the same time, fails to prepare them; and, despite the magnificent eloquence of which he is sometimes capable, especially when handling some form of the vernacular, he has grave deficiencies of literary taste which allow him to leave great areas of his dialogue either banal or bald. John H. Lawson has a wit and a fancy which have found their proper vehicle in the theater; but, even more than his ally, Dos Passos, he is given to adolescent grievances and adolescent enthusiasms.

We come now to literary criticism. In my opinion, H. L. Mencken (who is perhaps a prophet rather than a critic) is ordinarily underrated as a writer of English prose. Belonging himself to the line of Butler and Swift rather than to that of Pater and De Quincey, he cherishes a rustic reverence for the more "aesthetic" branch and is never tired of celebrating the elegances of such provincial fops as Lord Dunsany, Hergesheimer and Cabell, who have announced—it is, I think, Mr. Cabell's phrase—that they aim to "write beautifully about beautiful things." But although it is true that Mencken's style lends itself to excesses and vulgarities, especially in the hands of his imitators, who have taken over the Master's jargon without possessing his admirable literary sense, I believe that his prose is more successful in its way than that of these devotees of beauty usually is in theirs. The ideas themselves behind Mencken's writing are neither many nor subtle and, even in his most serious productions, even in *The American Language*, he overindulges an appetite for paradox. But some strain of the musician and poet has made it possible for Mencken to turn these ideas into literature: it is precisely through the color and rhythm of a highly personal prose that Mencken's opinions have become so infectious. He has now been repeating these opinions with the same pugnacious emphasis for fifteen or twenty years, and one has become rather tired of hearing them; yet he sustains a certain distinction and affords a certain satisfaction. Consider, for example, the leaflet he recently circulated on the adventures of the *American Mercury* with the Boston Watch and Ward Society: this statement, of no literary pretensions, in which he appears without war-paint or feathers, displays most attractive eighteenth-century qualities of lucidity, order and force, for lack of which the youngest of the younger literary generation, who have thrown Mencken overboard, have proved so far rather ineffective.

Paul Rosenfeld is another critic very unpopular with this youngest generation who seems to me an excellent writer. Though he, too, has his faults of style, which include a confusing weakness for writing French and German locutions in English, his command of a rich English vocabulary is one of the things that make him exceptional among recent American writers—who are not infrequently handicapped by not having at their disposal a large enough variety of English words, or, if they have them, by not knowing what they mean. Mr. Rosenfeld, at his worst, is given to overwriting: receiving in his soul the seed of a work by some such writer as Sherwood Anderson, himself one of the tenderer plants, he will cause it to shoot up and exfloreate into an enormous and rather rank "Mystic Cabbage-Rose." On these occasions, his prose seems sometimes rather coarse in quality and his colors a little muddy; but, at his best, Mr. Rosenfeld's writing is certainly among our soundest and his colors are both brilliant and true. He is sensitive, intelligent, well-educated and incorruptibly serious; and he is perhaps the only American critic of the generation since that of James Huneker who has written anything of any real value on the current artistic life of Europe. Van Wyck Brooks, who also writes excellent prose, though of quite a different sort, I propose to discuss in another connection.

George Jean Nathan is a wonderful humorous writer

and a better critic of the theater than A. B. Walkley, in a recent article, gave him credit for being; but his writing, which superficially resembles Mencken's, is usually lacking in the qualities that give Mencken's its durable texture. Willard Huntington Wright, some years ago, gave the impression of being some one important; and Lewis Mumford now gives the impression of some one perhaps about to be. Gilbert Seldes, through his activities as an editor of the *Dial* and his cultivation of the popular arts, has filled a role of considerable importance; but his principal literary quality is a kind of undisciplined wit which figures too often in his writings at the expense of lucidity and taste. He has lately become addicted to aesthetic editorial writing, a department for which his alert and vivid but glancing and volatile mind, is perhaps not very well adapted. In my opinion, he is seen at his best in passages of straight description of some movie or vaudeville act which has aroused his imagination. Burton Rascoe has performed the astonishing and probably unprecedented feat of making literature into news. A master of all the tricks of newspaper journalism, which he has introduced into the Sacred Grove to the horror of some of its high priests, his career has yet been singularly honorable in its disregard of popular values; and the cause of letters has profited more from his activities than the proprietors of popular newspapers who have inevitably discovered in the long run that they would feel more comfortable with a literary editor who did not find books so exciting. Mr. Rascoe has always written respectably and, at his best, with much ease and point. Most of the younger generation of critics either are badly educated or have never learned to write, and many suffer from both disabilities. At best, we have produced no literary critic of the full European stature. The much-abused Paul Elmer More still figures as our

only professional critic whose learning is really considerable and whose efforts are ambitious and serious. His
prose is quite graceless and charmless, but always precise
and clear; his point of view, though the Puritan rationalism of which it is a late product has imposed on it some
rigid limitations, has the force of a deep conviction and
the advantage of a definite formulation. Mr. More, although hopelessly inhibited in the exercise of his aesthetic
sensibility, has become, insofar as is possible without the
free range of this, a real master of ideas.

The new post-war method of biography, based on
Strachey and psychoanalysis, has had many practitioners
in America: Katherine Anthony, Van Wyck Brooks,
Thomas Beer, M. R. Werner and others; but, though it
has turned out a number of agreeable books, I have
not seen any except Brooks's *Mark Twain* that seemed
of first-rate importance. In the special departments of
scholarly and expository writing, the general inferiority
of the level of our culture to that of Great Britain or
France becomes inescapably plain. There are not many
of our college professors who can command the attention
of the reading public. Professor John Dewey writes much
and his influence has been considerable, but he has not
inherited with pragmatism William James's literary gift.
Professor Morris Cohen, who does possess a literary gift,
has so far published nothing but reviews, and not very
many of them. In the classics, Professor Tenney Frank
seems the only representative of a new generation; but
Professor Frank, although competent in a literary way
and bold in interpretation, appears to be rather indifferent
to the literary interest of the classics. Professor Paul
Shorey of Chicago is perhaps the only other scholar who
writes readable books in this field. We have, in short,
no university professor with a literary reputation equal
to that of Garrod, of Gilbert Murray, of Mackail, of A. E.

Housman, or of Whitehead or Bertrand Russell or
Lowes Dickinson. I can remember no recent book by an
American professor which has been widely read on its
literary merits, except Professor Warner Fite's *Moral
Philosophy* and Professor Samuel Morison's *Maritime
History of Massachusetts*. In science, we have some
readable popularizers in the rousing modern manner, but
they are mostly undistinguished writers: Doctor Fish-
bein, Doctor De Kruif and Doctor Dorsey. Edwin Slosson
is rapidly becoming a sort of William Lyon Phelps of
scientific culture. The zoölogist William Beebe writes a
prose that is shamelessly journalistic; but he is a man of
some literary ability, who deserves to be read by writers.
One of his assets is an extraordinary vocabulary, which
blends scientific with literary language in such a way
that his scientific words are imbued with a new life and
color. I doubt, however, whether the cable to the *New
York Times* is a very good school of writing. I am sorry
not to be able to do justice to our recent political writers.
I believe that in this department we are somewhat better
off than elsewhere; but it is the one in which I have
lately read least.

As for poetry, the new movement of twelve years ago
seemed at the time to assume impressive proportions.
But who can believe in its heroes now? Edgar Lee Masters did one creditable thing: *The Spoon River Anthology*; but, except for a single fine poem called *Silence*,
I have seen nothing by him since that I could read.
Vachel Lindsay's best poems, such as his *Bryan*, are
spoiled by the incurable cheapness and looseness which
are rampant in the rest of his work. Carl Sandburg, unlike Masters and Lindsay, has a genuine talent for
language; with a hard-boiled vocabulary and reputation,
he offers what is perhaps the most attractive surface of

any of the men of the group. But, when we come to read him in quantity, we are disappointed to find him less interesting than we had hoped; his ideas seem rather obvious, his emotions rather meager. The work of Amy Lowell is like a great empty cloisonné jar; that of John Gould Fletcher a great wall of hard descriptive prose mistakenly presented as poetry. Conrad Aiken, except in a few of his lyrics, is one of those curious people, like William Vaughn Moody, who can turn out a rich-looking texture of words and who can make at first glance the impression of being true and highly gifted inheritors of the English tradition of the nineteenth century, but who leave us, on closer reading, with a feeling that they have not quite got the "afflatus" that their themes and their style imply. Robert Frost has a thin but authentic vein of poetic sensibility; but I find him excessively dull, and he certainly writes very poor verse. He is, in my opinion, the most generally overrated of all this group of poets. Ezra Pound, who deserves all honor as a champion and pioneer, has worked conscientiously and stubbornly as one who understands very well, and as few of his contemporaries do, in what the highest poetry consists, but who has rarely been able to affect us as the highest poets do. His cantos of a "poem of considerable length," so ambitious and so full of fine passages, passages that, standing by themselves, might lead us to believe them mere ornaments from a masterpiece on the great scale, seem entirely composed of such fragments; a mosaic which fails to reveal a pattern, a monument, in its lack of cohesion, its lack of driving force or a center, to a kind of poetic bankruptcy. The other poets of the literary Left, though, like Pound, they can often write, seem to suffer from a similar sterility. Marianne Moore, for example, is sometimes very fine; but, as she herself has shrewdly noted in choosing a title for her collected verse, the bulk of her work answers better to the description of "Observations," than to that of poetry. From a slag of intellectual processes that has only a viscous flow, there emerge intense and vivid images that seem to have been invested with a sharp emotional meaning but that are rarely precipitated out in such a way as to make the piece a poem. H. D., like Carl Sandburg, writes well; but, like Sandburg, there is not much in her. Wallace Stevens has a fascinating gift of words that is not far from a gift of nonsense, rather like that of Edith Sitwell, and he is a charming decorative artist. Alfred Kreymborg has his dry distinction, but he tends fatally toward insipidity. I think I prefer the oddity of his early work, frankly prosaic and dry, to his later more pretentious sonnets. E. E. Cummings possesses, in some respects, a more remarkable lyric gift than any of the poets reviewed above; his feeling is always spontaneous, and his words run naturally into music. But, as in his rather limp line-drawings, the hand does not seem very firm: all sorts of ideas and images have come streaming into his head, and he doesn't know how to manipulate them to make them artistically effective. W. C. Williams and Maxwell Bodenheim I have tried my best to admire, but I have never been able to believe in them.*

Since these poets made their first reputations, the general appetite for poetry seems to have somewhat abated. Among the younger poets, for example, even those of most brilliant promise are having difficulty in getting their poems printed, not by the publishers only, who have evidently come to the conclusion that poetry

* It was at about this time that Maxwell Bodenheim described me in some such phrase as "a fatuous policeman, menacingly swinging his club." In rereading this essay—in which I have qualified or softened some of the original judgments—I have sometimes been reminded of this.

is bound to be unprofitable, but even by the magazines. The editors of the magazines, who have brought out, since the poetic revival, two or three crops of poets, seem content now to close the canon, and have no place for the poetry of unknown men—even if so obviously gifted as Phelps Putnam or Allen Tate—who cannot be found in Mr. Untermeyer's anthologies or among the original contributors to the *Dial*.

I have left aside the women lyric poets in order to discuss them as a group by themselves. On the average, though less pretentious, I think I find them more rewarding than the men: their emotion is likely to be more genuine and their literary instinct surer. Miss Lizette Woodworth Reese, the dean of the guild, astonishes one by continuing to write, not only with the same fine quality, but almost with the same freshness, as forty years ago. Sara Teasdale, the monotony of whose sobbing note caused her to become rather unfashionable when a more arrogant race of young women appeared, has made definite progress in her art since her earlier books of poems and has recently written some of her most charming lyrics. Miss Edna St. Vincent Millay has now, in turn, grown so popular that she, too, is in danger of becoming unfashionable; but she remains the most important of the group and perhaps one of the most important of our poets. Like Mencken, the prophet of a point of view, she has, like him, become a national figure; nor, as in the case of some other prophets, is her literary reputation undeserved. With little color, meager ornament and images often commonplace, she is yet mistress of deeply moving rhythms, of a music which makes up for the ear what her page seems to lack for the eye; and, above all, she has that singular boldness, which she shares with the greatest poets and which consists in taking just that one step beyond where one's fellows stop that, by making a new contact with moral reality, has the effect of causing other productions to take on an aspect of literary convention. Elinor Wylie, in the best of her verse and in her novel *Jennifer Lorn,* gives expression to a set of emotions quite different from those of Miss Millay, but one which has also its typical interest and its own kind of intensity. Her literary proficiency is immense: she is never at a loss for a clever rhyme, a witty reference or a brilliant image; she can command all the finest fabrics, the choicest works of art, the most luxurious sensations, the most amusing historical allusions and the most delicious things to eat. And, as a consequence, her inferior work is almost as well-written as her best; and her best work has both a style and a splendor of a kind very rare in America—where, even when these qualities do appear together, as they did to some extent in Amy Lowell, they too often remain hollow and metallic from the lack of a heart at the core. Edna Millay's inferior work has no such embroidery to deck it; and, save in her vein of classical austerity, she has for her best but the imagery of the sorrel or mullein stalk of the barren and rocky pastures, the purple wild sweet-pea dragging driftwood across the sand, the dead leaves in the city gutters, the gray snow in the city street, the kettle, the broom, the uncarpeted stairs and the dead father's old clothes—grown strange and disturbing now, to this reader's sense, at least, as the prison cell of Verlaine or Catullus's common crossroads. Louise Bogan plucked one low resounding theme on tensely strung steel strings, but it is now the vibrations of this rather than a further development that are ringing still in the air. Léonie Adams's *Those Not Elect* is a very remarkable book, of which the language, which seems to branch straight from the richest seventeenth-century tradition, strikes music from the calm summer starbreak, the bright-washed night after rain or the blue translucence of evening, where a gull or a pigeon that flies alone, seeking freedom in that space and clarity, is lost in a confusion of cloud and light. An anthology of these women poets should include, besides those named above, the *Cinquains* of the late Adelaide Crapsey and the best of Miss Genevieve Taggard, Miss Babette Deutsch and several others, of whom the younger Laura Gottschalk may turn out to be one of the most interesting and in whose company Dorothy Parker, long known as a humorous writer, has recently, it seems to me, fully proved her right to belong.

I have left to the last the two poets whom, among the men, I admire most: T. S. Eliot and E. A. Robinson. T. S. Eliot, though heavily infected with the Alexandrianism of the Left, has been able to imbue with a personal emotion, not only his inveterate literary allusions and his echoes of other poets, but even the lines that he has borrowed from them. He deserves, both as critic and as poet, his present position of influence. I deplore the fatigued and despondent mood that seems lately to have been drying up both his criticism and his poetry; but I cannot believe that a passion for poetry so serious and so intense can be permanently stifled or numbed. E. A. Robinson is the last and, artistically (leaving the happiest flashes of Emerson aside), the most important of the New England poets. Though he has recently run much into the sands of long and arid blank-verse narratives, I believe that he is one of the poets of our time most likely to survive as an American classic. He and Eliot both, though there are times when they disappoint us by the tendency of their motors to stall and times when they get on our nerves by a kind of hypochondria of the soul, have possessed the poetic gift and the artist's mastery of it.

The subject of Mr. Robinson may lead us to some more general observations. I have said that E. A. Robin-

son is the last of the New England poets, and it is true
that he really belongs to an earlier period than the
present and has little in common with the writers in
whose company the anthologists now place him. (He is
closer to Hawthorne and Henry James.) When we look
back on the literary era which preceded the recent
renascence, we are surprised, after all that has been
written about its paleness, its tameness and its sterility,
to take account of the high standard of excellence to
which its best writers attained. When we consider Henry
James, Stephen Crane and even such novelists of the
second rank as George W. Cable and William Dean
Howells, with such critics as Irving Babbitt, W. C.
Brownell and Paul Elmer More, who belong essentially
to the same era, we are struck with certain superiorities
over our race of writers today. It may be said of these
men, in general, that, though their ideas were less "eman-
cipated," they possessed a sounder culture than we; and
that, though less lively, they were better craftsmen. They
were professional men of letters, and they had thoroughly
learned their trade. Note the intense concentration, the
incapacity for careless writing, of even Stephen Crane,
who passed for a clever newspaper man and an outlaw
to respectable literature, but whose work astonishes us
now by an excellence of quality by no means incomparable—as how much of our present fiction is?—to the
best European work in the same kind.

Another writer who, like Mr. Robinson, is bound
closely, through her craftsmanship and her culture, to
this earlier American tradition, but who, by reason of
her critical point of view, makes a connecting link with
our own, is Edith Wharton. Often described as an
imitator of Henry James, she was really, in her important
novels, a writer of a different kind. Henry James, except
at very rare moments, was never a preacher or a bitter

social satirist; but Mrs. Wharton was perhaps the first
American to write with indignant passion *against* American
values as they had come to present themselves by
the end of the last century. Her recent books, since *The
Age of Innocence*, have been of rather inferior interest;
but, in her prime, she produced what I strongly believe
are the best examples of this kind of fiction that we have
had in the United States. She was soon followed by Van
Wyck Brooks, who represented a similar reaction against
a world either brutal and commercial or moribund and
genteel. One of the prophets of the present generation,
he belongs to the older and more sober tradition and has
never, for better or for worse, learned any of the methods
of the new.

Join these writers with the others I have mentioned
and it will be seen that they make a remarkable
group. They have provided both a picture and a criticism
of one period of American life. The writing of our own
age will hardly, I fear, present so dignified or so firm a
front. We have the illusion of a stronger vitality and of
a greater intellectual freedom, but we are polygot,
parvenu, hysterical and often only semi-literate. When
time shall have weeded out our less important writers,
it is probable that those who remain will give the
impression of a literary vaudeville: H. L. Mencken
hoarse with preaching in his act making fun of preachers;
Edna St. Vincent Millay, the soloist, a contralto with
deep notes of pathos; Sherwood Anderson holding his
audience with naïve but disquieting bedtime stories;
Theodore Dreiser with his newspaper narrative of commonplace
scandals and crimes and obituaries of millionaires,
in which the reporter astonishes the readers by
being rash enough to try to tell the truth; T. S. Eliot
patching from many cultures a dazzling and variegated
disguise for the shrinking and scrupulous soul of a hero

out of Henry James. Let us remember, however, that vaudeville has always been an American specialty; and that the writers we value most highly in the pre-Civil War period have not in general been such as I have mentioned above as typical of the generation just before our own. Emerson, Whitman, Poe; *Walden* and *Moby Dick*: they are all independent one-man turns, and who can say that we may not find their peers among our present bill of comic monologuists, sentimental songsters and performers of one-act melodramas?

June 30, 1926

THE CRITICS: A CONVERSATION

MR. HUDNUT. Who has read Hornblende's latest?

MR. BIRD. Not I! I looked into it, and the first thing my eye lit upon was a letter purporting to be written by a Frenchman in which the date was given 1 Janvier with a capital J. After that, I really couldn't go on with it!

MR. HUDNUT. Of course, I think Hornblende's cosmopolitan pretensions are among the most amusing things in contemporary literature. He has never been abroad in his life, you know, but he gets someone over there to supply him with a lot of continental theater programs and menus, which he memorizes for purposes of conversation.

MR. BIRD. Really! Ha-ha-ha! Marvellous! Marvellous!

A LADY. Well, this last book of his almost makes one wonder what one could have seen in the others. It's so *dull,* and so *sentimental!*

MR. HUDNUT. Oh, Bert has always been sentimental— the most sentimental man in the world! All this great show of brutality and ruthlessness with which he tries to impress his readers is merely a screen to defend himself against his own emotions. You know, he always sends a valentine every year to the first girl he was ever in love with—out in South Dakota somewhere.

THE LADY. Well, I'm very much interested to hear that, because that's what I have always felt about him—

248

that he was essentially a weak man trying to disguise his weakness by bluster. It's as if he were continually calling a spade a spade just to show he's not afraid to.

Mr. Latrobe. And, after all, everything that Hornblende tries to do has already been done so much better by Charles Lavender.

The Lady. Oh, yes: Charles Lavender!

Mr. Hudnut. Who is Lavender, Latrobe? I've never heard of him.

Mr. Latrobe. Charles Lavender was an exquisite artist, though he's hardly known today.

Mr. Hudnut. When did he live?

Mr. Latrobe. All his best work came out in the nineties. He treated the sort of subject that Hornblende tries to deal with—and I think it's quite obvious what Hornblende's subjects really are—but gracefully, poignantly, charmingly!

Mr. Hudnut. How can you get hold of Lavender's books?

Mr. Latrobe. They're almost impossible to find nowadays. I suppose that I am probably the only person in America who has a complete collection.

Mr. Hudnut. I'd like to borrow them some time.

Mr. Latrobe. I'm sorry, but I never lend my books—especially my Lavender firsts.

Mr. Bird. I couldn't resist calling Hornblende's blunder to the attention of Jacques Champfleury!

Mr. Hudnut. Yes—tell us about your controversy with Champfleury. I missed the last *Revue Libre*.

Mr. Bird. Well: to begin at the beginning, in 1895, when the old *Revue de Lutèce* was started, an announcement appeared in the first number to the effect that one of the features of the magazine was to be the cultivation of English literature—with all the usual rot about promoting the interchange of ideas between the two countries—and in the very next number there appeared an article on the English novel spelling Dickens D-i-k-e-n-s. D-i-k-e-n-s! I ventured at the time to point out this little error to the editors and received a polite but insincere reply from Camille Vide, who had written the article— professing his profoundest regret and explaining that a correction would be published—which in due course appeared, also polite but insincere. Five months later, in another article, this time on a French subject, Monsieur Vide informed the world that *Le Kiosque Parfumé* of Tristan Kraus had appeared in 1879. Well: there I had him on his own ground! The first edition of *Le Kiosque Parfumé,* limited to twenty-five copies, was privately printed in 1877—two years earlier than that! I wrote an article in excellent French which I called *Les Erreurs de M. Vide* and sent it to the rival magazine, *La Revue des Deux Rives.* Well: to make a long story short, the *Lutèce* crowd have never forgiven me. They reviewed my bibliography of the Mexican drama in the most perfunctory fashion, garbling the passages they translated—

THE LADY (*talking to Hudnut, while Latrobe listens to Bird*). I'm so relieved to hear you say that you don't think Bertram Hornblende is really such a tremendous figure. That's what I've always felt, but up to this latest book I've never dared to admit it.

MR. HUDNUT. Oh, Hornblende is really afraid of life. He tries to get out of himself but he's hopelessly introverted. That's the real reason he's taken to living in Honduras. The grandeur of the tropical coasts that he goes on about so much has nothing whatever to do with it: what he's looking for is a never-never land, where he can completely get away from reality. His wife keeps house for him and does everything for him, and he lives in a continual daydream.

THE LADY. She's pretty awful, isn't she?

MR. HUDNUT. Oh, I like Edith: Edith's a good sort. Of course, she's not terribly stimulating, but then, for the kind of thing Bert wants, I suppose she's absolutely perfect.—Bert has a physical deformity, you know—one of his legs is shorter than the other—and it has affected his whole point of view. He's morbidly sensitive about it—he always sits with his legs crossed, so that it won't be noticed. And when he's photographed, he always makes a point of having the foot of the longer leg on a step or a stump or something—or he's standing on the side of a mountain. That's the reason he's gone in for mountain-climbing. If Bert can be photographed on the side of a mountain, with an alpenstock and a pretty woman, he's perfectly happy—just like a child!

THE LADY. His wife doesn't make it particularly easy for him to see other women, I understand.

MR. HUDNUT. Yes: but her jealousy of poor old Bert is entirely unnecessary. He couldn't—or wouldn't—do anything even if she gave him a chance.

MR. BIRD (continuing his story). Well, Vide went over to the Revue Libre, which his brother-in-law Champfleury was founding, and the Revue began to boom Hornblende as the foremost American novelist, because Mme. Champfleury had translated his first novel. He has even been taken up by that unutterable sheet Hurrah-Moche, which is published by Lavarnier, who also publishes the Revue Libre. The young pro-American French aesthetes hailed Hornblende as one of the prophets of the literature of big machinery. That was before he had gone to Central America—a good joke on them! I wrote them a letter in French, with a translation of the back-to-the-wilderness outburst that he published just before he left. But they never either printed or replied to it. Perhaps they cannot read correct French. The very

title of their magazine is gibberish! They have taken
the English word "hurrah," which they have picked up
and think very smart, and have affixed to it a French
slang adjective. Together the two words mean nothing.
It is nonsense! It is neither good French nor good English!
An insult to the intelligence!

MR. HOSKINS (*speaking for the first time*). It seems
to me that, in all this discussion of Hornblende, we have
really failed so far to face the aesthetic problem he
raises. I must say I disapprove of this habit, which seems
to be becoming so prevalent, of making personal gossip
do duty for an intellectual approach to literature. Hornblende's real weakness, it seems to me, becomes plain
when we subject him to an aesthetic analysis. I begin
by dividing works of literature into three clearly distinguishable classes, whose nature I can indicate best
by an analogy from mathematics. I identify these three
classes, also, with the three states of higher consciousness
defined by Gundeljeff in his Eurasian yogi system. The
first of these classes includes literary artists who represent
some simple aesthetic entity multiplied by itself to a
higher power—they correspond to the cubes, the
squares and the other powers of algebra. Such writers
are Victor Hugo, Horace, Metastasio, Milton and
Trollope. This is Gundeljeff's ectogenetic state of consciousness: the works of art are given off by the artist
from *the outside*. The third class is that which includes
almost all the greatest figures in literature: it has its
mathematical equivalent in the irrational numbers we
call surds—that is, numbers that are not susceptible
of having rational roots extracted—and its philosophical
equivalent is the engenetic state of Gundeljeff: the work
of art is gestated *within* the artist and never wholly
emerges. Into this class fall Mallarmé, John Donne,
Herman Melville, the author of the *Kalevala*, Oscar Pil-

seck and the best parts of Pindar. It was because we wished to insist upon this fundamental aspect of literature that Pilseck and myself have called our magazine $\sqrt{2}$, and, by resorting to a different technique of analysis from any that has yet been applied, we have been able to extract, to an approximation equivalent to ten places of decimals, the root of the aesthetic blend of elements— susceptible, of course, of a qualitative as well as a quantitative analysis—that, raised to the x power, have resulted in the work of art. Performing the inverse operation, we shall also be able to approximate the production of works of art of the irrational engenetic kind, and our essay in the first issue in reality provides prolegomena to the method of a new body of literature, in which what has hitherto been produced by the freaks and the flukes of individual genius will be forged by the application of a rigorous intellectual discipline. There is, however, a second intermediate class, to which Bertram Hornblende belongs—

The conversation is suddenly terminated by the downfall of Western civilization.

August 5, 1925

POPE AND TENNYSON

Mr. Lytton Strachey, by a recently published paper—*Pope: The Leslie Stephen Lecture for 1925*—seems to have revised a flicker of the old nineteenth-century controversy about the poetic merits of Pope. His defense has already provoked a demurrer from Mr. Conrad Aiken. Mr. Strachey's defense rests, however, on entirely different grounds from the championship of Pope by Byron against the attacks of the romantics. The special issue of that time now means little to us: we pride ourselves indeed today on disregarding all the special issues of literature, of taking up no position that can limit our play of intelligence. We have the illusion of appreciating without prejudice the good writing of the most various schools, applauding in each its peculiar success in what it has attempted to do. And yet, like the romantics and the eighteenth century, we must tend to admire in the past only the qualities we cultivate ourselves. We pick out in the poets we seek to revive precisely those lines that, removed from their context, will make them appear more modern. Certain critics by this method have recently performed some veritable conjuring tricks with Dryden; and Mr. Strachey now perhaps does a little for Pope what he makes fun of Pope for doing for Homer: he makes him look like a poet of our own time.

Assuming, however, the standards by which we judge

poetry today, one is persuaded that Mr. Strachey has made out the strongest possible case for Pope and has appreciated certain aspects of his genius as they have never yet perhaps been appreciated. That there were aspects of Pope which were not much appreciated even in his own century seems to be strikingly proved by Dr. Johnson's comment on a couplet that Mr. Strachey quotes with special enthusiasm:

Lo! where Maeotis sleeps, and hardly flows
The freezing Tanaïs thro' a waste of snows.

Pope is supposed to have considered these lines the most successful he ever wrote; and Johnson could not understand this. But if the story is true, it is evident that Pope must have aimed, in his verse, at something a good deal more artistically interesting than the "rocking-horse" aphorisms for which he was denounced by Wordsworth and for which he is still commonly condemned. These lines, with their self-contained pattern, their frozen coldness and retarded flow, have a perfection of linguistic harmonics and an accurate descriptive brilliance that are typical of Pope at his best, but in which the romantics, except for Keats, did not as a rule excel. Mr. Strachey is also particularly happy in citing to support his case two passages in which his poet pulls out a fuller stop than is usual with him: the "fate of old women in society" and the death of Buckingham. These passages are malicious, to be sure, like almost all the effective things in Pope, but they are also undeniably tragic.

II

It is curious to compare Pope with Tennyson, a poet whom, on one of his sides he resembles.

The silver eel, in shining volumes roll'd,
The yellow carp, in scales bedropp'd with gold.

If it weren't for their metallic weight and ring, which
are characteristic of Pope and which perhaps make the
gold and silver a little more real than the fish, these lines
might have been written by Tennyson; yet they come
from *Windsor Forest*. So much of the description of
Tennyson also represents a triumph of artifice, and it
does not always carry him much further than *Windsor
Forest* carries Pope! Consider even the lyrics in *The
Princess*, always played by admirers of Tennyson as
among their strongest cards. *Blow, Bugle, Blow!* is unquestionably a very fine poem so long as it sticks to
rendering the bugle, but the poet in the last stanza tries
to deepen its music by a moral note:

O love, they [the echoes of the bugle] die in yon rich sky;
    They faint on hill or field or river:
Our echoes roll from soul to soul,
    And grow forever and forever.
Blow, bugle, blow! etc.

Is this kind of deliberate morality, of which Tennyson
and so many of his contemporaries—especially in America—were full, any less artificial than that of Pope? If
Tennyson were able to convince us that he had felt the
reverberations of human relationships in connection with
the sound of the bugle (as Wordsworth felt the fading of
the wonder of life in connection with the countryside of
his childhood), we should accept this as an integral part
of the poem; but we feel that these lines are synthetic. As
for *Come down, O maid, from yonder mountain height*,
it is as sheer a piece of virtuosity as anything in Pope.
Compare the freezing Tanaïs of *The Dunciad* with "the
firths of ice That huddling slant in furrow-cloven falls."
Though this poem fixes so many vivid images, it con-

veys little lyric emotion. With Pope, who seems to make no pretence to be anything but superlatively witty, we are delighted when we find him rising to something like the passion of great poetry; with Tennyson, who pretends to the highest prestige of emotional and moral profundity, we are sometimes disappointed to get only wit. Did not Pope, in his most characteristic vein of eighteenth-century irony, hit off at least one charming lyric?

All hail, once pleasing, once inspiring shade!
   Scene of my youthful loves and happier hours!
Where the kind Muses met me as I stray'd,
   And gently press'd my hand, and said, "Be ours!"—
Take all thou e'er shalt have, a constant Muse:
   At Court thou may'st be liked, but nothing gain:
Stock thou may'st buy and sell, but always lose,
   And love the brightest eyes, but love in vain.

Do we not accept the music and the feeling of this precisely because the poet has not tried to write in the least in the manner of Milton on his blindness? Do we not reject much of Tennyson—and of many of his contemporaries—because we suspect them of exaggerating the dignity of their emotions?

III

It would, of course, be unfair to leave Tennyson at this. I have said that *Come down, O maid, from yonder mountain height* conveys little lyric emotion. What it does convey very successfully is the satisfaction in smooth English lawns and rich "immemorial" trees which, as Mr. Harold Nicolson has pointed out in his admirable biography of Tennyson, became the grave of the real poet. When Tennyson is deeply troubled, as he was by the death of his friend, he writes in a different strain. It is interesting to see what he does with a subject that really moves him in that other famous lyric from *The*

Princess: Tears, Idle Tears. Here he is dealing with an emotion as fleeting, as elusive and as complex as anything in French symbolist poetry—the strange poignancy, at once fresh and desperate, of some unexpected echo from the past. One knows from such a poem as,

Les faux beaux jours ont lui tout le jour, ma pauvre âme,
Et les voici vibrer aux cuivres du couchant.

how Verlaine would have treated this theme. But, instead of resorting to the telescoped metaphors and the medley of images of symbolism, Tennyson reduces his difficult subject to a series of lucid statements almost as precise, antithetical and realistically accurate as Pope's:

Fresh as the first beam glittering on a sail,
That brings our friends up from the underworld,
Sad as the last which reddens over one
That sinks with all we love below the verge.

He summons an elaborate simile, based like Pope's upon observation, which renders exactly what he wants to say:

Ah, sad and strange as in dark summer dawns
The earliest pipe of half-awaken'd birds
To dying ears, when unto dying eyes
The casement slowly grows a glimmering square.

In *Tears, Idle Tears,* Tennyson wrote what is not perhaps merely, as Mr. Nicolson suggests, one of the most successful of his own poems, but one of the best poems of his time. In this vein, the Victorian poet was nearer to the school of Verlaine than it is likely to occur to us to notice. Tennyson's peculiar achievement was to have caught in a classic regularity the exquisite moments of a temperament as sensitive as Verlaine's.

September 16, 1925

A LETTER TO ELINOR WYLIE

DEAR MADAM,

It is now two years since you were so kind as to send me the first of your novels, which the vexation of other business and the exigencies of other studies then prevented me from reading. It has, in the meantime, been your reproach, that, whereas you, a year ago this autumn, were prompt to be present at and eager to applaud my tragedy (a kindness, I must confess, uncommon), I have allowed another year to pass without troubling to open your book; and that, although, on the first publication of your poems, I was among the foremost to commend them, my enthusiasm for your genius has so far abated that I have been willing to neglect in private what I have forborne to notice in publick. Let these complaints now cease: as I have offered in excuse of my protracted delay the constant press and perplexity of my affairs, so now, receiving your second novel in a moment of tranquillity and leisure, I have taken the opportunity to prove my candour by a careful perusal of both.

Of the first, it may now seem too late to say much, since it has already been abundantly praised. It was your habit, at the time when I had not yet read it, to call to my attention the extravagant eulogies which had been lavished upon it by Mr. Van Vechten and Mr. Van Doren; but of these two criticks, the first is of so particular a taste as to render him insensible to the beauties of many works, and those among the greatest; so that whatever falls in with his humour obtains the suffrage of his judgment; and the second, like the sun of tropical latitudes, which sheds its warmth all the year around, diffuses his mild benignance upon the excellent and the unworthy alike, until, by its uniformity, it causes us to long for the asperities of more inclement climates. Posterity must, therefore, be as little persuaded by the eloquent caprice of the one as convinced by the universal patronage of the other; and it should be enlightening to the publick, as it must be gratifying to you, for me to add my commendation to theirs. The merits of *Jennifer Lorn* must command a respect far beyond what we are accustomed to accord to light tales of this species, which, as they are written merely to amuse, do not often move us to admire. We are as much instructed by your knowledge of mankind as delighted by your felicity of invention; and amazed no less by the brilliance exhibited in the splendours of the style than by the vigour displayed in sustaining them. Of the character of Gerald, it may be said that our literature affords no more ingenious, and, at the same time, no more dreadful, illustration of the truth, that the most polished taste and the highest accomplishment may coexist with selfishness and cruelty; and the exercise of great abilities have for accompaniment the contempt of religion. Nor, though you stimulate us at first to admire, do you fail at last to provoke us to despise, when one who has commenced as an Atheist, is finally shewn as a thief.

Your second novel, *The Venetian Glass Nephew,* now remains to be examined; and it will not be surprising if you have not found it possible to repeat so remarkable a success in so short a time. I must say first that your choice of a subject seems less happy than in the case of its predecessor: your ignorance of the Italian language and your lack of acquaintance with the country to which it is native have rendered your scenes, on the whole, less natural and easy than in *Jennifer Lorn*. If you reply that a full third of the earlier tale is supposed to take place in Persia, a country of which you know even less than you do of Italy; I must answer that, as Persia, like Arcadia, is a country of which no one knows anything, we may be free, without fear of reprehension, to write anything of it we please; but that, in the case of Venice, we are certain to have among our readers many persons who have been there, and whom it will displease to find the scenes inappropriate or the manners reported inexactly. I must object further that you have mingled the fictitious with the real in a manner hardly allowable; in as much as, though introducing such actual and known personages as Count Gozzi and Cardinal de Bernis, you have juxtaposed to them an imaginary character whose name is a paraphrase of Casanova's and who, though in some cases spoken of in connexion with names that paraphrase those of the impostor's associates, in others is represented as the hero of Casanova's own exploits, such as the escape from the Leads. If you should plead that, since Casanova has left a history of his own life in which its events are recorded with some fulness, and that it would be incredible to ascribe to him an adventure which is not included in that account; I must reply that the same is true of Gozzi, who nowhere mentions in his memoirs the circumstances you relate.

As for the style, though distinguished by elegance and enlivened by wit, which no production of yours can fail of, I fear that the imagery has here become so copious as somewhat to impede the progress of the action. Where we are bewildered by the profusion of the trees, we become incapable of perceiving the forest. Your story is obscured by a luxuriance of phrases, which seems less suited to a novel than a poem, where exfoliation of this kind is more easily accepted; and we are forced to conclude, when we have reached the end, that the plot has not been very carefully contrived. Our attention is directed first to the Cardinal, but we presently discover that he is not among the chief actors; then we are entertained by a long conversation between the Cardinal, the Chevalier and the Count, which occupies a good third of the book, yet appears to lead nowhither, and to accomplish no purpose which might not have been accomplished better in briefer space. If the style would be more suited to a poem, the same may be asserted of the matter, which, involving so much that is supernatural and whimsical, would not invite in verse the same scrutiny to which it must be subjected in a novel, where we are less content to admit the vagueness of fancy or the abstraction of allegory.

Indignatur item privatis ac prope socco
Dignis carminibus narrari cena Thyestae.
Singula quæque locum teneant sortita decentum.

What is here said of the styles of tragick and comick poetry, must with even greater reason be applied to the more dissimilar styles of poetry and prose.

Of the fable itself, it can only be said that, if it is to be taken literally, it is absurd; and if allegorically, licentious. That a young woman should be converted into porcelain by a ceramical calorification, even with the assistance of the Devil—this is a conception as repugnant to reason as it is monstrous to imagination. But we should prefer the extravagances of childhood to the wantonness of maturity. Remember, Madam, that the progress of age, in which I am so much further advanced than you, should bring, not, as we grow accustomed to the spectacle of vice, a cynical indifference to virtue; but a more scrupulous attention to morality and a constant determination to leave no line which could offend it, as we approach more closely to the awful Judgement Seat before which we must all one day stand. I am, dear Madam,

Your most affectionate humble servant,
Sam. Johnson

October 7, 1925

FIRBANK AND BECKFORD

RONALD FIRBANK, the English novelist, died at Rome on
June 7. His last novel, *Concerning the Eccentricities of
Cardinal Pirelli*, has been published in England, but not
yet in the United States. This is in some ways, I believe,
the best book of Ronald Firbank's I have read—certainly
one of the very best written and one of the freest from
the curious "gagging" with which Firbank has had a
way of shutting off the vividness and charm of his
characters by reducing them to the mere comic names
of a sophisticated funny-paper. Ronald Firbank has
usually been treated as a less important representative of
the fashionable school of ironic romance (Van Vechten,
Aldous Huxley, etc.); but, though at first glance he
looks the most trivial, he seems to me to have felt the
artist's vocation more authentically than many of the
others. These others, in general, are graceful writers;
but Firbank is not really a graceful writer: he works
always in brief discontinuous strokes which appear to
have cost him some pains. Whatever else he may not
take seriously, he is serious about literature. The "painted,
love-tired hands" of the toreador's mistress opening and
closing her fan; the "still deep pools" of the Moorish
water-garden, in which the Cardinal sought "like some
Adept to interpret the mirrored music of the sky"; the
Pope with "the head of an elderly lady's-maid," in his

twentieth-century Vatican, remarking, "It's a bore there being no lift!" as he dismisses the Cardinal with a benediction: these do afford something of the pleasure and surprise that we get from the vision of the original artist.

But Firbank, in some ways so highly developed, is fatally deficient in others. As an artist, he presents the disconcerting spectacle of one of those sea-crabs one sometimes finds on which a claw that has been broken off has not yet had time to grow again, and we are shocked by the disproportion between the formidable normal claw and the helpless rudimentary one. In their subjects themselves, Firbank's novels seem to reflect some fundamental malformation; it is not merely the reader who finds them unsatisfactory, but the author who expresses dissatisfaction. All the heroes and heroines of Firbank—in those books that I have read, at least—have the most unfortunate fates; possessed by a bizarre variety of passions, they are almost invariably frustrated in their efforts to satisfy them. This final novel, indeed, seems a fable for the author's own case: can we fail to recognize in the Cardinal, with his "very great distinction and sweetness," whose ecclesiastical career is blighted by his worldliness and frivolity, by his inveterate excessive indulgence toward the weaknesses and vagaries of his flock, a symbol of the fate of that English novelist, distinguished by some very rare qualities, who never came to anything in the world of letters represented, in another of his books, by a delegation consisting of E. V. Lucas, Robert Hichens and Clutton-Brock?

It is interesting to compare Ronald Firbank with another highly special literary case—William Beckford, the author of *Vathek*. Beckford, like Firbank, was a very rich man of unusual literary ability, who never, however, accomplished as much as his brilliance seemed to warrant—an Englishman who lived much out of England and had a taste for the Mohammedan world (both Firbank and Beckford liked to dwell on the excesses of the pre-Adamite Sultans). They both had luxurious tastes and eccentric curiosities. They both derived from French sources; but Beckford is as different from his master Voltaire, and in very much the same way, as Firbank from his master Anatole France. For the cynicism and irony of Beckford do not imply a criticism of society; they seem merely to satisfy a perverse impulse. And Beckford's fancy has the slightly mad silliness that we also find in Firbank. "In vain did she renew her fumigations," writes Beckford of the Princess Carathis, as she is making her supreme effort to put herself in harmony with the powers of darkness, "and extend herself upon the roof to obtain mystic visions. Nothing more could she see in her dreams than pieces of brocade, nosegays of flowers, and other unmeaning gewgaws." One cannot think of any other English writer up to our own time who would be likely to have written this; but it is the sort of thing one does find in Firbank. The unexpected and tragic force of the burning hearts of the Hall of Eblis is also akin to the incongruous bitterness which sometimes makes itself felt in Firbank. Beckford and Firbank both have a cool and trivial cruelty that we might call cattily feminine if it were not so plainly something else. And in their sensitiveness, their subtle intelligence, their taste for fine and gorgeous things, as well as in their malice, their manias and their incurable tic of silliness, they have both much in common with the uncomfortable character of Proust's M. de Charlus.

September 8, 1926

A PREFACE TO PERSIUS

Maudlin Meditations in a Speakeasy

THE OTHER EVENING I had to dine out alone, and, stopping in on my way at a book store, bought a little eighteenth-century edition of Persius, with notes and a translation. The editor and translator was a man named William Drummond, who had also been a member of Parliament. The attractive duodecimo was bound in green morocco and stamped in gold, and, inside the cover, had gray marbled paper with green and yellow runnings. There was a medallion of Aulus Persius Flaccus, with crisp metallic curls on the title-page, and the whole volume, with the edges of its pages gilded on all three sides and its well-spaced and small clear type, had the aspect of a little casket in which something precious was kept. I went to an Italian restaurant and, while I was waiting for the antipasto, I began to read the preface. "In offering to the public," it ran, "a new English version of Persius, my object has rather been to express his meaning clearly, than either to translate his words literally, or to copy his manner servilely. The sentiments of this satirist are indeed admirable, and deserve to be better known than they are; but his poetry cannot be praised for its elegance, nor his language for its urbanity."

The plate arrived, with a glistening sardine, little purple olives, two pearly leeks, bronze anchovies and bright red pimiento slices that looked like little tongues, all against a lining of pale lettuce. There were also a bottle of yellow wine and a goblet of pale green glass. I wondered what had become of the sort of thing that this editor of Persius represented. In the middle of the room where I sat was a party of men and women, all pink and of huge size, who were uncorking loud sour laughter; across the room was a quite pretty young girl, of an obviously simple nature, who had some sort of keen professional interest in pleasing a rather defective-looking half-aquiline man, whose eyes one couldn't see through his eyeglasses. Craning around behind me, however, I caught sight of E. E. Cummings. Cummings, I reflected, was a cultivated fellow and a good writer and came from Boston, but was not a bit like William Drummond. For a point of view like that of Drummond, who would have reproached the inelegance of Persius's poetry yet applauded his admirable sentiments, one would have to go to our own eighteenth-century literature—to Joel Barlow or Philip Freneau. But Drummond was a fancier of letters and a political figure at the same time—Jefferson might have thought and written so. Some of the logic, some of the elegance, some of the moderate and equable opinion which seemed to be the qualities—here found, as it were, in their pure state—of this preface to an ancient classic had gone to the announcement of our national policies and the construction of our constitution. But new interests had taken over the government; and I had been reading in the paper that day of a typical example of their methods—an assault by the state constabulary on a meeting of Italian miners; men clubbed insensible, children gassed, old people badly beaten, a nursing woman knocked down. With the exception, I reflected, of Cummings, and possibly the Italian waiters, there was probably not a person in that room who would not either approve this action or refuse to believe that it had happened; and Cummings was as powerless to prevent its recurrence as the illiterate waiters would be. Perhaps the only element in sight which had anything in common with Drummond on Persius was the Italian dinner itself, of which a bowl of minestrone, with its cabbage, big brown beans and round noodles, had just reached me as the second course, and in the richness and balance of whose composition I could still see the standards of a civilization based on something more comfortably human than commercial and industrial interests. Yet how few generations of Italians speaking English and competing with the natives would it take for them to forget their cooking and their ideal of a good dinner and to go in, as one already saw them beginning to do, for expensive à la carte restaurants with heterogeneous and uninteresting menus?

"The defects of Persius, considered with respect to composition, cannot perhaps be easily defended. Even Casaubon, his fondest admirer, and most successful interpreter, admits that his style is obscure. If, however, any apology can be made for this first sin against good writing, it is in the case of a satirist, and above all, of a satirist who dared to reprobate the crimes, and to ridicule the follies of a tyrant. If Persius be obscure, let it be remembered, he lived in the time of Nero. But it has been remarked, that this author is not obscure, only when he lashes and exposes the Roman emperor. It was very well, it has been said, to employ hints, and to speak in half sentences, while he censured the vices of a cruel and luxurious despot; but there could be no occasion for enveloping himself in obscurity, while he expounded the doctrines of the Stoics to his friend Cornutus, or expatiated to the poet Bassus on the true use of riches."—I looked up, as the chicken and greens were

being set down before me, and saw Cummings, who
had finished and was leaving. If they had felt that way
about Persius, what would they have thought of Cummings? And what was the use, in the eighteenth century, of the critics' having cultivated those standards, if
Cummings was what the future had in store? He stopped
at my table, and I asked him where he had spent the
summer. "I thought of going to Boston," he ejaculated,
"to see the machine-guns!*—but we've all seen plenty of
machine-guns!—commonest thing in the world!—so I
walked around New York, expecting to be blown up
any moment—be a fine thing to blow the subways up!—
of course, my attitude toward this whole thing—I mean,
it's just unfortunate—it's a bore; like somebody losing
his pants—it's embarrassing, but it oughtn't to be a
surprise to anybody—what surprises me is that they
managed to stay alive for seven years!—why, I've seen
them shoot people first and search them afterwards—
and if they've got any bullets in them, they arrest them
for carrying concealed weapons!" He slipped away with
his spirited crest of hair and his narrow self-regarding
eyes. I addressed myself to the salad. So Persius, in
another age that combined moral anarchy with harsh
repression, had, it seemed, expressed himself confusedly,
inelegantly and obscenely. And it is Persius who is the
writer and not the complacent Drummond, as it is Cummings and not the persons who publish books on
American poetry. Where life is disorderly, the poets will
express themselves in nonsense. I had looked at the
beginning of Persius—"*O curas hominum! O quantum
est in rebus inane!*"—it seemed to me entirely in the
modern spirit.

* Sacco and Vanzetti had been executed in Boston on August
23, 1927, and the demonstrations in protest against this had
alarmed the city authorities to the point of having the State
House guarded with tommy-guns.

I went on reading the preface: "While, therefore, I fully admit the charge against Persius, I cannot allow to it that weight, which it would have in most other cases. Indeed, we may as well complain of the rust on an ancient coin, as of the obscurity of an ancient satire. Nature, it is true, always holds up the same mirror, but prejudice, habit, and education, are continually changing the appearance of the objects seen in it. The objections which have been made to my author in some other respects, are more difficult to answer. His unpolished verses, his coarse comparisons, and his ungraceful transitions from one subject to another, manifest, it is said, either his contempt or his ignorance of elegant composition. It cannot, indeed, be contended, that Persius displays the politeness of Horace, or that he shows himself an adept in the *callida junctura*. His poetry is a strong and rapid torrent, which pours in its infracted course over the rocks and precipices, and which occasionally, like the waters of the Rhone, disappears from view, and loses itself underground." Yes: like Cummings's poetry and conversation. Yet Drummond had his poetry, too: "the rust on an ancient coin," "a strong and rapid torrent, which pours in its infracted course"—and it appeared that he was, after all, sympathetic with the unpolished Persius and had earnestly undertaken to defend him against the taste of the time. That was the paradox of literature: provoked only by the anomalies of reality, by its discord, its chaos, its pain, it attempted, from poetry to metaphysics, to impose on that chaos some order, to find some resolution for that discord, to render that pain acceptable —to strike some permanent mark of the mind on the mysterious flux of experience which escapes beneath our hand. So with Persius, poised, as it were, on the edge of the collapse of the Empire, for whom the criticism of the satirist, the philosophy of the Stoic—at the least, the hexameter itself—were all ways, for even so "inelegant" a poet, of introducing some logic and some meaning into the ceaseless struggles of men to make themselves at home in the universe. Then, as it were, relieving the poet, the critic who studies him, in turn, must stand firm against these miseries and horrors, these disquieting shocks of reality—he must pick up the poet's verses, all twisted where disaster has struck them, and he must carry them further, like Drummond, to where there is tranquillity and leisure enough for him to point out what form and what sense the poet had tried to give them, to supply by his own judicial comments the straightness and the soundness they lack. Yet, even beneath the shelter of that firmament of eighteenth-century order, he, too, has felt the shock of reality—the dullness of a rusted coin, the turbulence of a river. For without the impulse from reality, neither criticism nor poetry nor any other human work can be valid.

I had finished the apple, the Brie cheese and the little black demi-tasse, and I turned to the book again: "I cannot conclude this Preface, without lamenting that an early and untimely death should have prevented the Poet, whom I have translated, from giving a more finished appearance to his works." How extraordinary that William Drummond, almost two thousand years after Christ, should have felt this solidarity with Persius, that, bridging the ruin of Rome, bridging the confusion of the Middle Ages, we should find him lamenting this early death as if it were that of some able young man whom he had known in his time in London, some young man who had been educated at the same institutions and shared with him the same values. The discord and chaos of reality! From the point of view of civilization, the whole of the West had caved in. The geographical void of Europe had been too big for Rome to fill; and then later—to change the metaphor, as my wine made it easy to do—when plantations that had been ploughed under had scattered their seed abroad, and at last there had been bred all through Europe such a race as had formerly flourished only on the Mediterranean, a new race to whom Persius could speak as men of his own education—when this had been achieved, there opened, as it were in another dimension, a new void, the social void, below the class of educated people to which Persius and Drummond belonged, and into that yawning gulf of illiteracy and mean ambitions, even while Drummond wrote—the book was dated 1797—Europe heavily and dully sank, not without some loud crackings of her structure. America, in a sense, was that gulf.

I had finished the bottle of wine, which was certainly better than they had had last year—they were really making an effort, I thought, to improve the quality of their wine. How much, I wondered, was it due to the wine that I now myself felt so warmed by this sense of continuity with the past, with Persius and William Drummond, by this spirit of stubborn endurance? Suppose that the federal agents should succeed in suppressing these restaurants where pretty good wine was still served. These restaurants were run by Italians, and it had lately been against Italians that the machine-guns of the State had been trained and the police incited to butchery. In the meantime, there was nothing to do save to work with the dead for allies, and at odds with the ignorance of most of the living, that that edifice, so many times begun, so discouragingly reduced to ruins, might yet stand as the headquarters of humanity!

I left the restaurant in meditation, and, on my way out, had a collision that jarred me with a couple of those bulky pink people who had stopped laughing and were dancing to the radio.

October 19, 1927

BURLESQUE SHOWS

I. The National Winter Garden

THERE IS A RUMOR that the National Winter Garden Burlesque has fallen a victim to the current purity wave and been obliged to abate the Aristophanic license for which it was formerly celebrated. The management of the National Winter Garden (not the Broadway Winter Garden, of course, but the one at Second Avenue and Houston Street) has been kind enough to supply the *New Republic* with a season pass, and, as the result of a recent visit, the writer of these notes is happy to announce that this report is entirely without foundation and to recommend the Minsky Brothers' Follies as still among the most satisfactory shows in town. The great thing about the National Winter Garden is that, though admittedly as vulgar as possible, it has nothing of the peculiar smartness and hardness one is accustomed to elsewhere in New York. It is refreshing because it lies quite outside the mechanical routine of Broadway. Though more ribald, it is more honest and less self-conscious than the ordinary risqué farce and, though crude, on the whole more attractive than most of the hideous comic-supplement humors of uptown revue and vaudeville. Nor is it to be confounded with the uptown burlesque show of the type of the Columbia, which is now as wholesome and as boring as any expensive musical comedy. The National Winter Garden has a tradition and a vein of its own.

For one thing, the Minsky Brothers go in for a kind of beauty which has long passed out of fashion elsewhere. The National Winter Garden has no use for the slim legs and shallow breasts the modern American taste for which has been so successfully exploited by Ziegfeld and the other uptown producers. Save for their bobbed hair and modern shoes, the chorus at the National Winter Garden might have come out of the pictures of Casino girls in old *Munsey's Magazines* of the nineties. And the humor of the National Winter Garden differs, also, from the humor of other shows. It mainly consists of gags, to be sure, but they are not the gags you are used to. For all their violence, the comic interludes have a certain freshness and wit. In the current version of *Anthony and Cleopatra,* a perennial Minsky classic, Julius Caesar, in a tin helmet and smoking a big cigar, catches Anthony (the Jewish comic) on a divan with Cleopatra (the principal strip-tease girl) and wallops him over the bottom with the flat of an enormous sword. "I'm dying! I'm dying!," groans Anthony, as he staggers around in a circle; and Caesar and Cleopatra, the Roman soldiers and the Egyptian slave-girls break into a rousing shimmy to the refrain of "He's dying! He's dying!" "I hear de voices of de angels!" says Anthony. "What do they say?" asks Caesar. "I don't know: I don't speak Polish." He is groggy; he totters; he faints. "I hear de cockroaches calling me!" he cries; and from the orchestra sounds, acrid and sinister, the cry of the expectant roaches. "Bring me the wassup," says Cleopatra, and her slave-girl, kneeling, presents a box, from which Cleopatra takes a huge property phallus. (At some point in the development of the ancient act, the word *asp* was evidently confused with *wasp*.) It is impossible to report in these pages all the incidents of the scenes that follow. Cleopatra falls prone on her lover's body, and Caesar, with pathetic reverence, places on her posterior a wreath, which he waters with a watering-pot. Charmian and Britannicus, after some play of their own with the wassup, finally fall lifeless, too, the girl as she flops on the soldier exploding a toy balloon which he has been wearing as a false chest. This curious piece of East Side folk-drama has been popular at Minsky's for years, and it is always a little different. Sometimes Caesar makes his entrance on a bicycle, blowing his own bugle; sometimes his entrance is heralded by a flourish of trumpets from the orchestra, as the company lines up and looks out the wings: Caesar enters from the other direction and gooses the last man, so that the whole row fall down like dominoes. There is also a remarkable gallows skit, which begins as an affecting piece of realism and ends as a low joke.

The orchestra at the National Winter Garden is energetic even in summer. The girls are not only robust but take a certain jolly interest in the show and sometimes betray their roles by laughing inappropriately at the jokes. The audience are keenly appreciative, and the house peals with easy thunder more infectious than the punctual crashes uptown. The theater, at the top of an office building, is very well ventilated; and just now you can see through an open exit the foothills of the downtown buildings against a pale lilac-gray sky. After the show, you can walk down the fire-escape.

The most celebrated performer of the National Winter Garden was a Yiddish comedian named Jack Shargel, who has now retired from the stage. To these raw buffooneries he is said to have brought a touch of the wistfulness of a Lew Fields or a Charlie Chaplin. A connoisseur of the theater in its best days* has described to me a scene in which Jack Shargel received a rose from a beautiful lady just going off the stage. He kissed it, he smelt it in ecstasy, then, with a graceful and infinitely tender gesture, he stretched out his hand and tossed it away: it fell with a crash of glass.

July 8, 1925

II. *Peaches—A Humdinger*

The National Winter Garden Burlesque has been subjected to a renovation since I wrote about it last summer. The poets, the artists, and the smart magazines have been making it fashionable; and Mr. Minsky, the manager, feeling perhaps that the shabbiness of the old productions was unworthy of his new clientèle, has provided brighter and more elegant settings and a slenderer bevy of girls, with a fresh repertoire of costumes. At a recent performance I witnessed, one of the actors made a speech in the intermission, in which he said that a critic had written, apropos of some risqué Broadway musical comedy, that if he wanted to hear "dubble entenders," he would rather go to the National Winter Garden, "because here's where you get burlesque as you like it, without any camouflage—sincere dubble entenders." Nevertheless, a restraining taste has been exercised, since I last was there, on the traditional Minsky humor. There is even a rumor that a gifted representative of the non-commercial artistic theater is to write and design a sketch for the National Winter Garden. At this rate,

* This was E. E. Cummings, who loved burlesque and was able to make some use of its methods. See the piece that follows on his play *Him.* He made a drawing of Jack Shargel, which appeared in the *Dial.*

it will presently be hardly distinguishable from the Music Box Revue.

To find burlesque in its primitive form, you must go to the Olympic on Fourteenth Street. The Olympic, with more limited resources than the National Winter Garden, makes no attempt to give its patrons anything beyond the fundamentals—that is, instalments of sidewalk conversation alternating with instalments of girls. As for the former, it is mainly manufactured by three unvarying comedians, who reappear time after time in front of the same prosaic backdrop advertising the Monte Carlo Spaghetti House, the Cabin Dancing Academy, the White Rats Tonsorial Parlors and the D. and S. Pants Shop. (An act like the Anthony and Cleopatra of the National Winter Garden would be quite out of the range of the Olympic.) Of these merry-andrews and kings of fun, the leader is, of course, a spruce young man with a clean-shaven face and a straw hat. But, whereas, at Minsky's in its present phase, this conventional role has been given to a comparatively prepossessing fellow not unlike a musical-comedy hero, the "straight man," as he is called, at the Olympic follows the true burlesque tradition by making us feel that, though his neatly pressed clothes contrast with those of his disreputable companions, he is the greatest rogue of the three. The other two, the low comedians, have the appearance of unhappy monstrosities. One is dwarfish, with a very big head and the toil-toughened, staring and honest face of a German nibelung, and he embarks on his comic adventures invariably with the utmost solemnity; when these end in cruel disaster at the hands of his straw-hatted tormentor or of one of the disdainful cuties with bare legs and a brassière, he apostrophizes the audience in Yiddish on a note of bewildered complaint or rage. The other, more nondescript and stunted still, is dressed in clothes which produce a disconcerting effect, like those of a trained chimpanzee, from his inability to wear them in a human fashion, and his face presents no human expression but a heavy and cretinous mask, of which the closed-up slits of the eyes give the impression of some helpless abortion in which the faculty of sight has been scarcely developed. The dialogue of these three artists suffers sadly from a poverty of invention. Here are a couple of examples. One of the Girls: "I'm in love! I'm in love! I'm gonta jump off the Brooklyn Bridge!" The Man with the Straw Hat: "Don't do that: you'll get the water dirty!" The Man with the Straw Hat, who is trying to play a cornet, addressing the Nibelung: "Say, don't look at me! Don't look at me! I can't play when you look at me! Say, you've got the kind of face that only a mother could love! If I had a dog with a face like that, I'd shootum!"

The main thing, however, is the girls. The Olympic, like Earl Carroll's Vanities, is equipped with a double runway. This runway, though it is studded on the inside edge with a row of pink electric-light bulbs, has the aspect—to which, besides, the general appearance of the theater and the shirt-sleeved audience of men contribute—of some sort of bowling alley; but it figures, none the less, for the spectators, as the principal source of glamor. The leading women, with their sinewy thighs and their muscular abdomens, have learned the rhythmic contortions of the stomach-dance; and the chorus does its best to live up to them with such shaking of hips and breasts as it can clumsily manage. Some, evidently accepted for their beauty rather than for theatrical gifts, are too stolid or untrained to dance at all and, smiling at the audience below, merely parade back and forth on the runway. Some do not even smile. But all have their powerful effect on the clientèle of the house.

What strikes you at first, however, when you are new to this more primitive form of burlesque, is the outward indifference of the spectators. They sit in silence and quite without smiling and with no overt sign of admiration toward the glittering and thick-lashed seductresses who stand on a level with their shoulders and who address them with so personal a heartiness. The audience do not even applaud when the girls have gone back to the stage; and you think that the act has flopped. But as soon as the girls have disappeared behind the scenes and the comedians come on for the next skit, the men begin to clap, on an accent which represents less a tribute of enthusiasm than a diffident conventional summons for the girls to appear again. This is repeated from four to six times for every number in the show. The audience never betray their satisfaction so long as the girls are there; it is only when the performance is finished that they signify their desire to renew it. They have come to the theater, you realize, in order to have their dreams made objective, and they sit there each alone with his dream. They call the girls back again and again, and the number goes on forever. When the leading performer begins to strip, they watch the process in silence, recalling her with timid applause when she vanishes behind the wings. Finally, she shows them her breasts, but her smile is never returned; nor is there any vibration of excitement when she has finally got down to her G-string—merely the same automatic summons, to which this time she does not respond. In one of the numbers, the girls come out with fishing-rods and dangle pretzels under the noses of the spectators; the leading ladies have lemons. The men do not at first reach for them; they remain completely stolid. Then suddenly, when the lures have been played for some minutes, a few begin to grab at the pretzels, like frogs who have finally decided to strike at a piece of red flannel or like cats who, after simulating apathy while watching a cork on a string, at last find the moment to pounce on it. When they catch the pretzels, however, they do not take them off the strings or playfully refuse to release them; they let them go at the first jerk and relapse into their impassivity.

The truth is, I suppose, that this audience are struck by a kind of awe, as if before priestesses of Venus, in presence of these gorgeous creatures. Their decorum is not undermined by this brazenly sexual exhibition: on the contrary, it makes them solemn. They have come for the gratification that they hope to derive from these dances; but this vision of erotic ecstasy, when they see it unveiled before them—though they watch it with fascination—frightens them and renders them mute.

August 18, 1926

E. E. CUMMINGS'S *HIM*

Mr. E. E. Cummings, the poet, has published a play called *Him*, of great length and of the utmost impracticability. It is, in fact, rather a dramatic poem in prose, and ought to be judged as such. As a poet, E. E. Cummings occupies a unique and curious place. He is, perhaps, the writer of the younger group who most widely and vividly interests, and who most profoundly influences, other young people writing poetry. And he has certainly deserved this eminence: he has deserved it by his gift for delicious, if frequently incoherent, song, which he seems to shake out so high-spiritedly while most of his fellow-poets are busy stitching images together; by his audacity, and by his original personality, his personal habit of speech, which, until other people began to imitate him, made his poetry quite unlike that of anyone else. Yet Mr. Cummings has always, so far, seemed as an artist rather unsatisfactory. Spontaneity and naïveté are excellent qualities for lyric poetry, but the poet should have at least the patience to calculate his effects and the expertness to carry them out; whereas Cummings seems self-indulgent, as if he never could restrain himself from an extra trick or a silly joke. One suspects in him an incapacity for putting himself in the place of the person who is going to read him. And *Him*, which comes nearer than Mr. Cummings's poetry to letting us see his mind at full length, confirms this impression of self-indulgence. It is characteristic of Cummings that he seems to understand things instantaneously, that he seems to understand everything, but that he rarely seems to try to systematize the flood of impressions that reaches him. This play is the shimmering scaturience of an intelligence and a sensibility of the very first distinction—but a drama deficient in dramatic logic. The main action of *Him* is evidently an ether-dream in the mind of the heroine; and the climax the revelation of the reason for her being under ether. There reënact themselves within her dream the various phases of the love affair that has brought her to her present pass, intermingled with a phantasmagoria of the imaginings of her lover, who, at the time the affair had been going on, had been engaged in writing a play. But the development of the love affair and the connection with it of the phantasmagoria are obscure even to the reader, and one would think that for a theater audience they must prove completely baffling. One's impression is that Mr. Cummings has never really thought out the problems of his very complicated subject. Though he has tried for a dramatic structure, he has still left his materials rather chaotic.

But when all this has been said on the negative side, the remarkable merits of *Him* remain. In the first place, there are comic ideas which would make Mr. Cummings's fortune, if he would only take more thought to exploit them. The burlesque-show Mussolini with his epicene admirers; the morose American traveller bellyaching over the dreariness of a European city in which the inhabitants are starving; the three Fates who, throughout the action, sit knitting and rocking and talking eerie nonsense—all these are capital conceptions that have moments of brilliant vitality, though the author, with a strange lack of instinct for climax, either lets them go on so long that they lose their hold on our interest or allows his scene to trail off in an ineffective ending. Here is a specimen of the happy vein of the brooding conversation of the Fates:

FIRST. George says he doesn't see why guinea-pigs can't have children if children can have guinea-pigs.
THIRD. A clean tooth never decays.
SECOND. Do children have guinea-pigs?
FIRST. Oh yes, more's the pity. Mine often have it.
THIRD. Your nails show your refinement.
SECOND. Badly?

Mr. Cummings also reveals an astonishing faculty for mimicking and caricaturing the speech of a variety of kinds of people: his soap-box orator, his sideshow barker and his American ladies in Paris are both made lifelike and thrown into relief with something of comic genius.

It is, however, in the scenes between the lovers that Mr. Cummings's genius principally appears. They are, to my mind, more successful than anything in his poetry. Here the blurriness and lack of direction of the mind which does not construct is carried off by the extraordinary sensitiveness which is itself a kind of intelligence. Here Cummings is occupied, as in many of his poems, with the attempt to render shades of feeling so special and so complex that language can scarcely follow them. The effort to seize these feelings and to fix them, not by trying to press them into the mold of an accepted convention, which must falsify unique sensations, but in the flux, in the raw confusion, with which they visit our body and spirit, has always, of course, been a primary cause of the obscurity of Cummings's verse. Now in *Him*, where the poet has imposed upon himself the discipline of dramatic dialogue, he has succeeded, with an original and marvellous eloquence, not merely in letting us hear what the lovers say to one another, but also in making us feel what they feel, experience what they experience. These scenes—and especially the one at the beginning of the third act—seem to me the very best things that Cummings has so far done. They make *Him*, for all its stretches of balderdash and its admixture of puerilities, a book which should be read by all persons who prefer the real thing in literature, no matter how drunk and disorderly, to the well-intentioned imitation, no matter how carefully dressed.

It may be that in the wit, the fantasy and the lyric beauty of *Him* we find the germ of an important dramatic poet. The qualities that have gone to make this play are under notably less efficient control than those that went to make *Peer Gynt*, but the two pieces have something in common. I have said that *Him* is impracticable, and so, in its present form, it is; but why does not someone induce the author to reorganize it and cut it down, and try the experiment of producing it?* Our American expressionist dramas have too often been fatally deficient in precisely those elements of eloquence and genuine imagination in which Cummings's play is so rich: they have commended themselves to our interest on the basis of their artistic merits, and then have turned out to suffer from the primary disadvantage of being written by persons who could not write. E. E. Cummings lacks theatrical craft, but he is equipped with a lively dramatic sense, and—what is rarest of all—with a poet's pen.

November 2, 1927

* *Him* was produced at the Provincetown Theater in Macdougal Street on April 18 of the following year and has twice been revived.

A GREAT MAGICIAN

THE TRUE STORY of Houdini's death is told for the first time, apparently, in a new biography: *Houdini, His Life Story*, by Harold Kellock, from the recollections and documents of Beatrice Houdini. Houdini had broken his ankle in Albany while performing his Chinese Water Torture trick, in which he was suspended by the feet in a small cabinet full of water. He had lately been over-working, even more than was usual with him, and had not been to bed for three nights; he had also been very much worried about Mrs. Houdini, whom he had had to leave ill in Providence. When he arrived in Montreal, his ankle was still so sore that he was obliged to spend most of the time on a couch. In this condition, in his dressing-room, he received three students from McGill University, where he had just delivered a lecture on spiritualism. One of the students asked whether it were true "that Houdini could withstand heavy blows without inconvenience. The magician replied that he could do so, if he had warning to brace himself. He then picked up some letters. The student said something about testing Houdini's ability then and there. Houdini, absorbed in a letter, was not paying attention and gave an absent-minded reply, which the boy interpreted as consent. The next instant, Houdini was startled by receiving a series of sharp blows in the abdomen. At the fourth blow, he stopped the young man with a gesture, just as the two other students jumped up in protest. Acute peritonitis developed, and, after a Herculean struggle, he died in the hospital."

There is in this sudden ending to a career which had its heroic aspect something ironic and tragic. It shocks us that Houdini, not much over fifty and at the most interesting point of his career, should thus have fallen a victim to one of the most trivial of his own challenges, to a blow by a college student, given under a misapprehension, when he was ill and reading his mail.

Houdini was the son of a rabbi. His parents had come from Budapest, and settled in Appleton, Wisconsin. The father knew no English; they were poor. Houdini (whose real name was Ehrich Weiss) went off at the age of eleven to earn his own living. He had already learned to do tricks from the conjurors in circus sideshows, and, while working in a locksmith's shop, had mastered the technique of picking locks: he could already, in fact, open handcuffs. He had from the beginning the magician's vocation. He was by turns a messenger-boy, a necktie-cutter and a Wild Man in a tent of freaks; but his concentration on magic was as fervent and unremitting as Lindbergh's concentration on flying.

Houdini had, thus, in his field, the all-absorbing preoccupation of genius, but he was remarkable also for other qualities, the virtues of his sober, pious and self-respecting German-Jewish family, virtues that he managed to preserve through the humiliations and hardships of his early years. Houdini remained all his life, in spite of considerable egotism, the scrupulous, industrious, loyal and generous son of his parents. It was partly this background of family life—his devotion to his wife and his mother is one of his most striking traits—which gave him his solidity and straightness. When, in Yorkshire once, a former hangman who had retired to run a public-house, attempted to bribe the champion, proposing to bet large sums on his ability to tie him up in such a way that he could not escape and then, when Houdini had "thrown" the contest, to divide the winnings with him, Houdini wrote contemptuously in his diary: "Guess he didn't know how I was brought up."

This magician was also romantic, in an essentially Germanic fashion. The story of his marriage is amazing. Mrs. Houdini was eighteen when he met her: she had been taken by her mother to a show that Houdini was giving at the high school, and, in the course of one of his tricks, the magician upset some acid on her dress. He immediately leapt down from the platform and earnestly apologized. The mother remained indignant; but "I managed to whisper to him," Mrs. Houdini remembers, " 'Don't mind Mother. I think you're wonderful.' 'Do you?' he exclaimed, straightening up, and for a long moment our eyes held, while Mother and the rest of the audience were completely forgotten." He brought her a new dress at her house, and though the mother refused to admit him, the girl slipped away and met him outside. He persuaded her to go with him to Coney Island, and made her marry him then and there. The quality of Houdini's imagination sometimes verged on the Gothic. Mrs. Houdini tells the following incident: "The last night the brothers worked together at the dance hall in Coney Island, I had a bad scare. Houdini asked his brother and me to take a walk with him after the evening's work was over. He led us into the country on a dark lonely bridge spanning some swiftly running black water. It was a weird-looking night, with a split moon that seemed to be dodging in and out behind heavy clouds. In the middle of the bridge he halted us, and there we waited for a time silently, I at least in growing trepidation. Finally a distant bell tolled solemnly twelve times. As soon as the last beat ceased to reverberate, Houdini clasped his brother's hand and mine together, raised them aloft and cried: 'Beatrice, Dash, raise your hands to heaven and swear you will both be true to me. Never betray me in any way, so help you God!' " And even in Houdini's later years, when he wanted to go incognito to a spiritualistic seance, he liked to disguise himself in a fantastic and elaborate make-up, which involved a long white beard and a hump, and at the end of the proceedings snatch off the beard and dramatically declare to the discomfited medium, "I am Houdini!"

But all this was quite natural for him, not a part that he deliberately played. His own life was his drama, and he had otherwise little of the actor about him—so little, that when one reads this biography, one feels that he had difficulty in adapting himself to his role of public entertainer. He was, at first, it seems, so poor a showman that he could not arouse adequate interest in feats that were actually unprecedented; and when one saw him in his last years, it was curious to note that his magician's patter was confined to a few quaint perfunctory phrases. Houdini, in his queer chosen line, was scrupulous and serious-minded; and he tended to slough off the charlatanry, innocent though that is, which is essential to the magician's profession.

Houdini mastered conjuring in all its branches, but was far too adventurous and energetic to be satisfied to be merely a conjuror. He had always been interested in opening locks, and he began to specialize in escapes. Now, aside from the exceptional qualities which Houdini applied to these problems, there is nothing particularly fascinating about getting out of bags and boxes by means of various fakes. Yet the tale of Houdini's achievements is an exciting and somehow an impressive one. He has acquired a skill with locks that is probably unrivalled in the world, and he has made himself both lithe and strong. He challenges the world to challenge him, and no prison appears too formidable. He seems eaten by a veritable passion to test himself more and more severely: he must prove to himself and the world that he is invincible, irrepressible, uneclipsable. Here, as I say, if we forget Houdini, the object becomes ridiculous, yet the story which culminates in his breaking out of an inhuman steel "carette" devised by the Russian police for the transportation of prisoners to Siberia—an exploit which seems for the moment to have made him a popular hero in Russia—this story of Houdini's self-liberations has its dignity like the story of any brave man who pits himself against obstacles and bests them.

But Houdini was by no means content with even his undisputed title of Handcuff King. He had also, during all this period, been occupied with scholarly researches: he had been collecting and reading books on magic with a characteristically tireless voracity, and had taken a good deal of trouble to interview retired magicians and investigate all kinds of wonder-workers. He began himself to write on the subject. And in his last years, he did few escapes and for the first time appeared to the public in something like his true character and at something like his full stature. He had been making of spiritualism and mediums the same kind of exhaustive study that he had made of prisons and locks. And he now challenged any medium to show him supernatural phenomena which he could not expose and reproduce. To the demonstrations and lectures of this period, he brought a perhaps even more ardent enthusiasm than he had to his earlier escapes: the deflation of this higher fakery had a certain intellectual and moral interest, and Houdini's campaign against the mediums turned into a veritable crusade. It may be that his famous encounter with the medium called Margery in Boston, who, if it had not been for his exposure of her, would no doubt have received the prize offered by the *Scientific American* for genuine spiritualistic phenomena, will make a landmark in psychic investigation.

In the years before his death, Houdini had come to occupy a unique position. He certainly knew more about trickery than anyone else in the world. The library he had been accumulating had become one of his chief interests and had now reached such enormous proportions that he was obliged to employ a librarian to catalogue it and keep it in order. One regrets that his campaign against the spiritualists should so soon have been cut short by his death. But it is possible that Houdini, by this time, had already reached the limits of his capacity and exhausted the possibilities of his field. The systematic study of trickery, with its far-reaching implications for religion and other departments, must now be pursued by others from a more scientific point of view. But the student will find that Houdini has supplied him with valuable data and an excellent practical method. And, in the meantime, the story of Houdini's life proves more stimulating than we might have expected, and it makes us think better of humanity than the lives of many other figures of more conventional reputation in more distinguished fields. It is exhilarating, even in a juggler, even in a trapeze performer, to see some human skill or faculty carried to its furthest point, to a point where its feats seem incredible. And Houdini had much more than this to commend him to our admiration: he was an audacious and independent being, whose career showed a rare integrity. To follow his early life among the East Side cabarets and the dime museums is to be stirred as one can always be stirred by the struggle of a superior man to emerge from the commonplaces, the ignominies and the pains of the common life, to make for himself a position and a livelihood among his less able fellows at the same time that he learns to perfect himself in the pursuit of his chosen work.

October 17, 1928

MENCKEN'S DEMOCRATIC MAN

H. L. MENCKEN's *Notes on Democracy* adds nothing that is new to his political philosophy: its basic ideas are precisely those which he has been preaching for many years and which already appear in his book on Nietzsche, published in 1908. The human race, according to Mencken, is composed of "gentlemen" and "boobs"; the gentlemen, by virtue of their superiority, have made themselves masters of the good things of the world; and the peasants, who, by virtue of their ineptitude, remain fettered to the plough and the bench, are embittered by envy of "their betters." It is this envy which supplies all the issues of politics in a democracy: it is the desire on the part of the peasants to rob the superior classes of rewards unattainable by themselves or to restrain them from the enjoyment of activities that they are unable to understand. The superior classes possess a monopoly not merely of property and pleasure but of the higher virtues as well: they embody all the learning, all the taste, all the fortitude, all the intelligence, all the sense of personal honor and all the sense of social obligation. A government by the people, therefore—that is to say, a government by persons characterized by the opposites of these qualities—is sure to be a scandal and a farce. The United States is such a farce and scandal.

Mr. Mencken has here expounded this thesis in greater

detail and in more connections than he ever has done before; and he has invoked more authorities to support it. He thus makes the gesture of discussing systematically the machinery of democratic government; he attempts to find corroboration in behavioristic psychology; and he at last receives into his bosom the conclusions of the Binet tests, which he had previously denounced but which he sees now can serve his turn by apparently demonstrating that the majority of the population possess the mentality of schoolboys. Yet, for all this, his book is not really an inquiry: it is Mencken's same old melodrama, with the gentleman, the man of honor, pitted against the peasant and the boob. We are not told what makes people gentlemen or what makes people boobs, or of how it is that both these species happen to belong to the same human race, or of how it is that we often find them merging or becoming transformed into one another. With his fierce inflexibility of mind, Mr. Mencken is capable neither of the sympathy of the historian, of the detachment of the scientist nor of the subtlety of the philosopher. And his new book is not to be taken as a contribution to political science: it is simply another of his "prejudices," treated on a larger scale than the rest.

Yet although these *Notes on Democracy* are not precisely politics, they are quite remarkable as literature. Poe said of his treatise *Eureka* that it was to be taken as neither science nor philosophy, but as what he called a "prose poem," which was, nevertheless, in its own way, true. The same thing might be said about Mencken's *Notes,* which is a sort of obverse of *Leaves of Grass.* Let us, therefore, accept its assumptions and find out what validity it has. Now, it is plain that a population composed, as Mr. Mencken says ours is, almost exclusively of beings without courage, ability, honor or aspiration could never have settled, however crudely, either the West or the East of the United States or established, let alone maintained, however unenlightened a federal government—could never, in fact, have made the efforts or carried out the calculations that are needed for a single street of shops, could never have preserved the discipline that is needed to run a first-rate office or a theater or factory or bank, let alone train an army, a navy, a medical profession, a church, a bar or the personnel of any of our good universities. But let us accept the world that Mencken imagines as we do the country of the Houyhnhnms or the country of Erewhon, and we shall find that it has its reality as these other imaginary places have.

This world which, as I say, has its reality, is simply an abstraction from *our* world of all those features of American life that fall short of Mr. Mencken's standards. What these standards of Mencken's are I have indicated, and we can accept them as more or less sound. But the point is that Mencken's emotions in connection with the things he admires are rarely of a positive kind: they are negative emotions at missing them, and they take the form of rage and scorn for the people who do not represent them. This animus has never been more effectively—perhaps never so effectively—expressed by Mencken than it is in this latest book. The *Notes* lack the cumulative power of a pamphlet by Swift or Shaw, because they do not have the drive of close reasoning to carry us along to the end; and, as a result, the last of the three sections becomes rather repetitious and disappointing. But, as a whole, the *Notes on Democracy* is unquestionably one of the best-written and most intensely felt of Mr. Mencken's books: with *The American Language* and *A Book of Prefaces*, it constitutes the core of his work, that part of Mr. Mencken's writing that, whatever else of his we may skip, certainly ought to be read. He has been saying the same thing for years, but he has never before succeeded in saying it in so pungent and so terse a language or with a satiric force so nearly tragic.

These emotions of contempt and anger have projected, as everyone knows, a ridiculous but terrifying bugaboo: the great American boob. Some of the items in this latest indictment of the fabulous Menckenian dunce may sound perhaps a little fatuous: "What he knows of histology," we learn, "or protozoölogy, or philology or paleontology is precisely nothing. Such things lie beyond his capacity for learning, and he has no curiosity about them. . . . Even those applied sciences which enter intimately into his everyday existence remain outside his comprehension and interest. Consider, for example, chemistry and biology. The whole life of the inferior man, including especially his so-called thinking, is purely a biochemical process, and exactly comparable to what goes on in a barrel of cider, yet he knows no more about chemistry than a cow and no more about biology than its calf. . . . He is more ignorant of elementary anatomy and physiology than the Egyptian quacks of 4000 B.C. . . . He has never so much as heard of ethnology, pathology or embryology. Greek, to him, is only a jargon spoken by boot-blacks, and Wagner is a retired baseball player. He has never heard of Euripides, of Hippocrates, of Aristotle or of Plato. Or of Vesalius, Newton and Roger Bacon. The fine arts are complete blanks to him. He doesn't know what a Doric column is, or an etching, or a fugue. He is as ignorant of sonnets and the Gothic style as he is of ecclesiastical politics in Abyssinia. Homer, Virgil, Cervantes, Bach, Raphael, Rubens, Beethoven— all such colossal names are empty sounds to him," etc., etc. This all sounds a little like M. Jourdain giving

Mme. Jourdain the benefit of his recent instruction in the pronunciation of the vowels (to say nothing of Mr. Mencken's own notions of the conceptions of modern biology—the barrel of cider, etc.). Nevertheless, the *Notes on Democracy* contain what is up to date the author's most effective description of his "Democratic Man." This character is an ideal monster, exactly like the Yahoo of Swift, and it has almost the same dreadful reality. This "boob" has impressed himself on the imagination of our general public in a way that has not been equalled by any other recent literary creation, with the possible exception of Scott Fitzgerald's flapper. Sinclair Lewis's *Babbitt* and the inhabitants of his *Main Street* must have been at least partly inspired by Mencken, and they present themselves as merely species of the genus *American boob*. In the current *New Masses,* one finds a cartoon with the caption "Immaculate Conception," in which the editor of the *American Mercury* is seen suckling "the American superman," a rudimentary one-hundred-percent American, who has been born with a pair of bone spectacles: and this accurately satirizes the situation. The conception of the national boob has, one realizes, been firmly planted, not only in the minds of our writers, but also in the minds of all those, all the otherwise undistinguished citizens, who are to be seen in every state of the Union with the *Mercury* under their arms. We may not always like the heavy-footed superman, who for Mencken is the positive inference to be drawn from the negative caricature, as we sometimes encounter him in Mencken's pages, and we may like him even less when we run into attempts to live up to him on the part of Mencken's admirers; but we must grant that to have made the Americans feel the menace of this super-boor and repudiate their fellowship with him is an achievement of some importance.

December 15, 1926

WOODROW WILSON AT PRINCETON

THE FIRST TWO VOLUMES of *Woodrow Wilson: Life and Letters*, by Ray Stannard Baker, are now before the public. The first of these deals with Woodrow Wilson's early life up to the time of his going to Princeton as a professor, and the second takes him up to his resignation as president of the University. Mr. Baker has both the vices and the advantages of an official biographer—the vices of a loquacious admiration which cannot refrain from continually exclaiming over the utterances and deeds of his hero instead of allowing them to speak for themselves, and a bias which, from beginning to end, prevents him from permitting his subject to appear for a moment as anything but a perfect gentle knight. The result is that, with the copious documentation of a history, his biography moves in something of the miraculous atmosphere of a saint's legend. You would never find out from this record that Woodrow Wilson was, among other things, a resourceful politician: he is invariably represented as carrying all before him by some divine irresistible authority. But Mr. Baker's advantage lies in the fact that he does have the documents; and it may be said that, allowing for his bias, he seems to use them conscientiously and carefully. His book is not very vivid and not very well-written: it has something of the monotony of vocabulary, the lulling repetitiousness and

298

the dilution of ideas of Woodrow Wilson himself. Thus, after quoting from some one of Wilson's utterances in which the weakness of the latter's thought and style are already sufficiently evident, Mr. Baker will add some such comment as: "The sheer eloquence of the man!" or "The sheer fighting spirit of the man!" or something of the sort, using "sheer" in exactly the way that Wilson was in the habit of doing, with the intention of reënforcing some statement, but with the effect of rendering it feebler. It cannot, therefore, be denied that Mr. Baker has been guilty of some insipidity. On the other hand, the material of his biography has been most scrupulously and clearly arranged: his book is extremely well-ordered. He neglects none of Wilson's activities—political, academic, domestic or recreational—and he tells about everything in its place, proceeding deliberately, step by step, indicating exactly the order of events and patiently going back, when necessary, to fill in some aspect of his subject which, for fear of complicating his main narrative, he has been hitherto obliged to neglect. As a result, we have what is undoubtedly the most valuable work on Wilson which has yet appeared. Mr. Baker has thrust into the shadow some of the angles and colors of his subject, but most of Wilson's character is there: it is quite plain in his acts and in his letters. We do not feel any longer, after reading Mr. Baker's first volume—which deals with that part of his life about which least has been written—that there is anything enigmatical about Wilson.

From the beginning the whole man is before us. We have heard a good deal about Wilson's development and the various phases through which he passed; but we see now that, though he sometimes changed his views, his abilities, his ambitions and his relations with the world remained fundamentally the same. The first fact of importance which emerges in this account of Wilson's early life is the extraordinary homogeneity of his family and his ancestry. All Woodrow Wilson's family, so far back as anything is known about his father's side and for many generations on his mother's, were either Scotch or Scotch-Irish schoolmasters, professors or ministers. Wilson's paternal grandparents were born in the north of Ireland; and his mother was born in Scotland. There were among them a number of men of considerable importance in their home communities. The paternal grandfather appears to have been a highly successful journalist and publisher in the West of the early century: he was a member of the state legislature and was locally known as "Judge." "While Judge Wilson was away in the legislature or in Pittsburgh, where, in 1832, he founded a new tri-weekly paper, the *Pennsylvania Advocate*, the redoubtable Anne Adams [Woodrow Wilson's grandmother] and her sons brought out the Steubenville *Herald*." The maternal grandfather Woodrow, a Scotch Presbyterian minister, after emigrating to America, held pastorates, first at Chillicothe, Ohio, and then at Columbus. One of Woodrow Wilson's uncles studied at Harvard under Agassiz, and at Heidelberg. While a professor at the Theological Seminary of Columbia, South Carolina, he taught his classes evolutionary theories, and, in consequence, was tried for heresy; and, though acquitted, obliged to leave. This did not prevent him, however, from being active in religious work; he published a Presbyterian journal, became a successful business man and the president of a bank, and finally president of South Carolina College. "At one time, after the close of the Civil War, when the state government was at its lowest ebb, he made a bid for the state printing which had been done under the most wasteful of political methods. To the astonishment of everyone at the capital,

he secured it. There was great speculation as to whether
he would run his presses on Sunday, as all the former
printers had been forced to do by the exigencies of
publication connected with the legislature. But the people
were not long to be in doubt. At twelve o'clock on the
first Saturday night, Dr. Woodrow turned out all the
lights in his printing office, and the shop remained closed
until one o'clock Monday morning." Wilson's father was
ordained in Ohio as a Presbyterian minister, taught
chemistry and the natural sciences and rhetoric at small
colleges in Pennsylvania and Virginia, then became
pastor of the First Presbyterian Church at Staunton,
Virginia. He later moved to Augusta, Georgia (when
Woodrow was a year old), and when the regional schism
of the Church occurred as a result of the Civil War, the
first Southern Presbyterian Assembly was held in Dr.
Wilson's church. The Southern Church was organized
there, and Dr. Wilson remained for thirty-seven years
its Permanent Clerk. His influence upon his son seems
to have been profound—perhaps the most important of
Wilson's life. When the boy was only a few months old,
"very plump and fat and remarkably quiet," his maternal
grandfather Woodrow is reported to have said: "That
baby is dignified enough to be Moderator of the General
Assembly!"

The whole of Wilson's early life is thus completely
enclosed by the horizons of the Presbyterian home. He
grows up in the post-war South, and he identifies himself
with its fortunes to the extent that, while a student at
Princeton, he is capable of turning pale with passion
and leaving the room over an argument on the subject
of the war; but, except in certain particulars later to be
noted, he does not exhibit Southern characteristics. He
moves always in the antiseptic atmosphere of Presbyterian
public life—that is, lecturing, editorial writing and

preaching—and Presbyterian domesticity. But this is enough to provide him with a discipline and a whole set of social ideals which completely command his allegiance. In order to understand Wilson's career, we must consider the virtues and the deficiencies of the Presbyterian society that nourished him, the peculiar advantages of which he probably enjoyed at their best.

One of the features, then, of Wilson's forebears is that they were men and women of principle—that is, though by no means naïve in their relations with the material world, they habitually put moral considerations above material ones. They may turn a hand to real estate or banking; but they are consecrated to higher causes, to education and to the Church. Much of Woodrow Wilson's power was derived from the passionate persistency with which he adhered, in later life, to this ideal of acting on principle. He carried the devotion to principle into fields where people had never thought to see it, and those whom he astonished were invariably at first either demoralized or won. I have complained that Mr. Baker represents Wilson as carrying everything before him as if by irresistible authority; but this, if we do not slight other elements, to a limited degree is true. All that language of oratorical idealism—truth, righteousness, service, faith—which the ordinary public speaker makes use of without believing in it and, as it were, without expecting to be believed—all these phrases were in some sense a gospel with Wilson, and it was the realization of this that arrested the attention of the public. This was the language that Wilson had always spoken: you find it in all the family documents which Mr. Baker has published; you find it in the devoted letters between Woodrow and his father. Wilson continued to speak it all his life: he would, indeed, never learn any other; and, in his lifelong inability to master the language of the world even when dealing with worldlings or himself resorting to methods which were nothing if not of the world, he illustrates one of the weaknesses, as he does also so astonishingly the strength, of his heritage of Presbyterian culture. For it was characteristic of Wilson that he could not express himself on any issue or describe any action of his own except in the terms of the pulpit, the vocabulary of a semi-religious idealism. I do not believe that he was ever a hypocrite: he gives the impression of being always convinced that the values of a given situation are such as he represents them. Woodrow Wilson had never relinquished his original religious faith: he declined to debate religious questions; he would "go crazy," he insisted, in later life, if he did not believe in God. When his fiancée reads philosophy and raises religious doubts, he writes her that, "so far as religion is concerned, discussion is adjourned." And the validity of his own moral principles, the infallibility of his judgment in acting on them, seem to have become for him articles of faith of an almost equal authority. In the whole of Mr. Baker's two volumes, I cannot remember a single passage, not merely among Wilson's public utterances, but in his letters and diaries themselves, where he confesses himself for a moment to be influenced by anything other than the highest and purest motives. He never admits a personal resentment or an impulse of ill-humor or frivolity, a spiritual or physical distemper; he never calculates anything for interest; he can barely allow that he is writing a book or delivering a public lecture because he is in need of money. One can, therefore, find no evidence that Wilson was ever consciously hypocritical. Yet this haughty and persistent refusal to be subject to the accidents of our common humanity is the most unsympathetic feature of his character. Why are we a little unpleasantly affected by Wilson's repudiation, in New Jersey, of the bosses who had supported him in his campaign for governor? Grover Cleveland did much the same thing, but it is always invoked as an example of his honesty instead of his bad faith. The fact is that it is the way in which Wilson expresses himself about this that irritates us—it is his moral indignation: it is his self-righteous inability to accept with realistic frankness the fact that he has himself been a practical politician playing the political game. Why, again, are we inevitably more shocked by certain of Wilson's prevarications, by his categorical denial, for example, in his conference with the Senate committee, that he had ever heard of the Treaty of London—than we are by, say, Bismarck's falsification of the Ems telegram? Simply because Bismarck knows what he is doing and accepts the moral consequences; that is the way in which he chooses to deal with the world; he has never pretended otherwise. But Wilson *has* pretended, and does pretend, otherwise; he appears to pretend even to himself.

The great handicap of this Puritan culture was, of course, its limited scope and its isolation from the world. Wilson knew little of the arts; he was neither widely nor profoundly read; he had little real intellectual curiosity; and he was never, as we shall see, able to appreciate or respect the points of view of worldly people. The characteristic mode of self-expression of the society in which Wilson grew up was the Presbyterian sermon; and Wilson became a master of the sermon: he was essentially, to the end of his life, not a philosopher, but a preacher; and he had only so much learning, and did only so much intellectual work, as is necessary for a preacher. He understood very well, however, in what his genius consisted: he worked within his limitations. It is surprising, in reading this biography, to discover how early and how exclusively he is preoccupied with public speaking. By the time he has graduated from Princeton and from the law school of the University of Virginia, by the time he has tried practising law and given it up after a year, though he goes to study politics at Johns Hopkins, he does not think of himself as a scholar or even as a writer: he knows that he is neither of these things, and he rebels against the kind of apprenticeship to which he finds himself committed. Nor does he want to be a practical politician: the politics of the time appal him; they seem to him to belong to the order of a different planet from that on which he lives. His father has hoped he would enter the Church; and, though he confines himself to public affairs, it is as an inspirational speaker that he sets out to perfect himself. In this purpose he is magnificently successful. Making speeches was the thing he did best, the thing, indeed, that he did supremely well. In reading his published addresses, we are irritated by the vagueness of the language and the unctuousness of the rhetoric. But Woodrow Wilson's delivery was more distinguished than his style. Even when his language was bafflingly evasive or floridly insipid, his voice remained quiet, well-mannered and beautifully distinct, with an edge that made his words seem incisive. He had just enough of a Southern accent and a grace and ease learned in the South to make one forget his square face and rather rigidly looming figure; and, save when the subject of a dreaded opponent pressed the stop of some querulous note of the schoolmaster or the parson, a persuasiveness that was almost hypnotic. He gave the impression of deep conviction and burning zeal, under imperturbable control. Maynard Keynes, in his account of the Peace Conference, has given an excellent description of Wilson's qualities: "He had no plan," he says, "no scheme, no constructive ideas whatever for clothing with the flesh of life the commandments which he had thundered from the White

House. He could have preached a sermon on any of them or have addressed a stately prayer to the Almighty for their fulfilment; but he could not frame their concrete application to the actual state of Europe."

One must not, however, make it appear that Wilson—especially in his student days—was nothing better than a facile evangelist. The young man who emerges from the letters and the memoirs of the first volume of this *Life* is an attractive and impressive figure. Stiff, earnest, a little pompous, pursuing his career with a grave concentration that is recognizably Scottish, he is none the less sympathetic by reason of his very seriousness and of the self-dissatisfactions and self-scrutinies of which his letters at this time are full. He already knows his strength, but he is poor and and his opportunities seem limited. He had sworn at Princeton with a classmate to a "solemn covenant" that they should "school all our powers and passions for the work of establishing the principles we held in common; that we would acquire knowledge that we might have power; and that we would drill ourselves in all the arts of persuasion, but especially in oratory, that we might have facility in leading others into our ways of feeling and enlisting them in our purposes." "It was not so long ago," he writes to his fiancée from Johns Hopkins, "but that I can still feel the glow and the pulsations of the hopes and the purposes of that moment." He desperately envies a friend who is studying in Germany; he plans, at one time, to go there himself. He is urged by another friend to take steps to have his name put forward for an assistant secretaryship of state: "the office is not much in demand by politicians, and Mr. Bayard, who likes gentlemanly scholarly associates, is finding it hard to fill. . . . Don't you pity me, with my old political longings thus set throbbing again?" But he knows of no one to recommend him, and he is obliged to give up the hope.

He produces, at twenty-nine and while still a student at Johns Hopkins, the best of all his books, a book, indeed, quite out of the class of his subsequent ones. The young author of *Congressional Government* is, within the limited scope of his field, a decidedly intelligent man and a lucid and polished writer. Though, characteristically, when he made this study, he had never once been in Washington to watch the houses of Congress in action, he had produced an essay in political history which was realistic as well as original, and the immediacy of his success is dramatic. But even this sudden and brilliant success fails to allay his restlessness. He is excessively shy; he has already a reputation as an accomplished public speaker and as a singer in college glee clubs, but it is difficult for him to meet people, and when he does so, one gets the impression that he does not very closely apprehend them. He is lonely, repressed and uneasy.

During his year of law practice, however, Wilson has fallen in love. He has gone, on business of his mother's, to visit an uncle in Rome, Georgia, and he there meets Ellen Axson, the daughter of the minister of the First Presbyterian Church: "her grandfather, the 'great Axson,' was pastor of the famous Independent Presbyterian Church of Savannah." Wilson's own description of this incident, in a letter to Ellen when she had become his wife, is worth quoting at length: it is typical of the social atmosphere that surrounded him in his youth, that gave its color to his whole career and character. "The first time I saw your face to note it was in church one morning during the first of my last spring's visit to Rome—in April, wasn't it? You wore a heavy crêpe veil, and I remember thinking 'what a bright, pretty face; what splendid, mischievous, laughing eyes! I'll lay a wager that this demure little lady has lots of life and fun in her!' And when, after the service (I think it had been a communion service), you spoke to Mrs. Bones, I took another good look at you, and concluded that it would be a very clever plan to inquire your name and seek an introduction. When I learned that this was Miss 'Ellie Lou' Axson, of whom I had heard so often, quite a flood of light was let in on my understanding, and I was conscious of having formed a small resolution. I took an early opportunity of calling on the Rev. Mr. Axson. That dear gentleman received me with unsuspecting cordiality and sat down to entertain me under the impression that I had come to see only him. I *had* gone to see him, for I love and respect him and would have gone to see him with alacrity if he had never had a daughter; but I had not gone to see him *alone*. I had not forgotten that face, and I wanted very much to see it again; so I asked rather pointedly after his daughter's health, and he, in some apparent surprise, summoned you to the parlor. Do you remember?—and do you remember the topic of conversation? how your father made me 'tackle' that question that was so much too big for me, 'Why have night congregations grown so small?' " They go on long walks and boat-rides and picnics together. She talks to him about George Eliot, about Wordsworth and Browning; she paints, and she tells him about painting. He has never occupied himself with these things, and it is as if she has thrown open a new world to him: he has been refreshed from a richer mind and a more sensitive temperament. Six months afterwards, they are engaged, and he has already become greatly dependent on her sympathy and her responsive imagination, as he is to remain till her death. Their own home is, in most respects, just such a home as that in which he has found her, just such a home as that from which he comes. Ellen Wilson, who, outside her household, commanded so little attention, who found herself overwhelmed by the social responsibilities of her position in Princeton and Washington, devoted herself to her husband's career and to a sort of intensive family culture, with all the energy of her girlhood idealism. She is even said to have played the determining role in some of Wilson's political decisions. The Wilson home was always, in fact, an abode of sweetness and light of an old-fashioned and not undistinguished kind; but it was firmly disciplined and strictly bounded. The books, for example, that the young ladies were allowed to read were censored by vigilant parents; and on one occasion at least in Princeton—as the writer has heard at firsthand—one of the Wilson daughters was embarrassed at not being able to return a volume of the poems of the now faded Aubrey de Vere which her mother had sternly destroyed before she knew it was borrowed. Wilson's marriage had meant for him a fledging of wings, a cultural illumination, one of the major events of his life; yet a fledging and an illumination that had taken place within the confines of the Presbyterian world in which he was born.

II

One of the most striking features of Woodrow Wilson's early life, which Mr. Baker's biography has brought to light, is his passion for drawing up programs and framing constitutions. Already, as a boy in Atlanta, he provided a set of rules for a club that met in a hayloft, and at Davidson, at Princeton, at Virginia, at Johns Hopkins and at Wesleyan colleges, he reorganized the debating societies and turned them, in every case, into something of an almost parliamentary impressiveness. This was always the department of college activity which interested Wilson most. He would arrive; in a very short time, he would gravitate to the head of the society; then, with overwhelming energy and enthusiasm, he would proceed to make it over completely. He would frame a new set of rules and aims that would be laid before the other members with all his compelling eloquence and adopted with the utmost eagerness; the society would appear to be entering upon a new phase of importance and popularity; then Wilson would pass on elsewhere. This becomes the type of his activity everywhere, and even as sponsor of the Fourteen Points. He can draw up a fine lucid program and he can get it accepted by a luminous speech. But much beyond this he cannot go. When Wilson has successfully accomplished this, he will not go on to apply himself to the practical machinery and the boring detail, the adjustments with other personalities, that are necessary to put through his proposals. He can only repeat the performance by starting a new movement somewhere else and drawing up a new set of proposals.

One must not, however, again, imply that this purely forensic activity for which Wilson had so much genius was entirely without use or effect. It did not take them long in New Jersey, after Wilson had ceased to be governor, to pull the teeth of the bills he had passed; but at Princeton his policies were vital, and the edifice founded upon them pretty solidly endures to this day. Wilson, indeed, probably deserves most of the credit for rescuing Princeton, at the end of the nineties, from the extreme disorganization and demoralization of the Patton administration: whatever is sound in the college today was established under the presidency of Wilson. As a professor of jurisprudence and politics, he is said to have been a stimulating lecturer, and his courses were certainly popular; but his students did not do much work. He had himself little or no real passion for learning; and his course was known as a "gut," that is, an easy course. But, once he was elected president, he found himself—and for, perhaps, the first time in his life—with an adequate field for his powers. The faculty was at that time directly appointed by the president. Wilson cleared out the dead-wood among the professors with his characteristic combination of radiant enthusiasm and ruthlessness; and even got rid of two trustees who had become involved in an insurance scandal. He then picked out and appointed new professors, with an instinct which today seems brilliant; and got from the trustees an appropriation for fifty younger instructors to be added to the faculty and known as "preceptors," whose function was not to lecture or to hold classes in the ordinary sense, but, by meeting the students semi-formally, to encourage them and supervise their work. He was never, perhaps, more happily inspired than during these early days as president of Princeton. A good many of the professors he brought there are still in the university and among its most distinguished figures. I have been told by men who came as preceptors in the first days of Wilson's administration that they have never at any other time, in the American educational world, seen so much excitement and hope. Wilson was not, however, quite so infallible, quite so triumphantly intelligent, as his biographer represents him. He had his characteristic errors of judgment and mistaken obstinacies. The department of modern languages at Princeton was at that time in a rudimentary state; but Wilson—true, apparently, in this to the Presbyterian tradition—did not much believe in modern languages: he had himself little German and less French, and used to quote with satisfaction a saying of Walter Bagehot to the effect that "a Frenchman can say anything, but has nothing to say."*

* For this information and much else in this essay, I am indebted to the late Christian Gauss, who came to Princeton as a preceptor under Wilson and built up the Modern Language Department (split later into a Romance and a German Department) virtually from scratch. In the early days of the college,

When the department was being reorganized, the President insisted upon dictating—and without allowing any discussion on the part of the instructors themselves—impossible courses of reading. The students, with their inadequate preparation, were unable to cope with these assignments, and the department, in the course of time, was forced quietly to abandon Wilson's program and substitute one of its own. It was characteristic of Wilson at Princeton, as it was in 1919 at the Peace Conference, that he should have shown himself as autocratic in dealing with departments of whose work he knew nothing as with those of which he had had some experience.

What follows is extremely interesting, and anticipates with a curious completeness the pattern of Wilson's successes and failures at Washington. In reading Mr. Baker's biography, we gradually become aware of a feature of Wilson's character which already appears in his early letters and which produces at Princeton its first tragic disaster. Woodrow Wilson is a man of enormous energy, who is always restless when he is not acting and who is capable of only one way of acting—the way indicated above. Once he has secured the adoption of a program, he must immediately pass on to another program. This comes out strikingly in his writings of this period.

French and German had been barred from the curriculum, "because of the atheistic writings in those languages." Charles Godfrey Leland of the class of 1845 says that, for the same reason, French was not taught in his day. My father, of the class of 1885, was drilled in French with more force than finesse by an exiled Polish general, who swore at his students as if they were troops. By the time I came to Princeton, in the class of 1916, the Modern Language Department was one of the best in the country and had become very much the fashion with the more intellectual students. This was one of the results of the Wilson administration, but entirely the creation of Gauss, who had not always found it easy to get Wilson to accept his proposals.

Princeton, he complains, is not yet perfect, it is not yet an ideal university. How could he possibly have expected it to become thus transformed overnight, with the establishment of the preceptorial system, or of any other system? It is quite plain that the true reason for the President's anxiety is to be found in his incapacity to satisfy, to realize himself in any occupation other than his own peculiar kind of statesmanship. Except for politics, he is really not interested in the subjects that universities teach; and in respect to politics, he would rather be an actor than a student. He cannot sit patiently for a time and supervise the life of the college. He looks about him for another constructive proposal, and finds it in the social system. We are here for the first time to encounter a charge that, in the course of his subsequent career, is often to be brought against Wilson—that of reversing a previous position. It is quite true that Wilson reversed his views on many social and political questions, and we may certainly dislike the tone of self-righteous indignation with which he denounces opponents who are merely professing today opinions that he himself professed yesterday. But we should, I believe, be mistaken in supposing that vulgar expediency played anything other than an occasional role among the considerations that moved him. It was rather that Wilson, whose intelligence was not at all far-reaching or subtle, was capable of thinking only about one or two things at a time: when he did think about anything, however, he usually thought in the right direction. He had not so much ideas as divinations, which came forthwith to seem to him self-evident. In this case, it is true that Wilson—Mr. Baker fails to mention this—had contributed a preface to a college handbook in which, with his customary unctuousness, he had written of life in Princeton as incorruptibly democratic. He has, however, come later to see that the undergraduate eating-clubs are a menace: they cultivate social snobbishness, and they break the college up into cliques. He proposes a different system of social units which the university itself should set up and control. This plan was derived from the English colleges and was locally known as the quad system, because the quadrangle around which each of the houses was built would figure as the center of the unit. To each of these houses was to be assigned by the university authorities themselves a group of students and unmarried professors, who would both sleep and eat in the building. Each of these would make a social center, and the clubs were to be abolished.

The writer of the present article is no defender of the Princeton clubs. He believes Wilson's instinct about them to have been fundamentally sound. These eating-clubs are probably the most undesirable of Princeton institutions—not so much because they are snobbish: some sort of snobbishness seems inevitable and perhaps even has its value; but because they are hopelessly dull. Nothing interesting is ever done in them: the students simply eat their meals there and occasionally give house-parties over the weekends. They are not even allowed to live in them, as they are in other colleges in fraternity houses. Movements are put on foot periodically—and on the part of the students themselves—to get rid of them or to do something more sensible with them, for they constitute a force of inertia that has been blocking the development of the university. Yet the buildings are so enormous in bulk and represent such a formidable investment, that it has, so far, been impossible to dissolve the clubs. There is, however, another element to be considered in connection with the problem. In spite of their heaviness and emptiness, the clubs have inevitably become identified with that peculiar idyllic quality which is

one of the endearing features of Princeton. It is difficult
to describe this quality in any very concrete way, but it
has something to do with the view from Prospect Street,
from the comfortable back porches of the clubs, over the
damp dim New Jersey lowlands, and with the singular
feeling of freedom which refreshes the alumnus from an
American city when he goes back to Prospect Street and
realizes that he can lounge, read or drink as he pleases,
go anywhere or dress anyhow without anybody's interfer-
ing with him. Now, it was not Wilson's policy about the
social system which in itself was ill-advised: it was his
methods in carrying it out that were tactless. In the spring
of 1907, he put his proposals before the Princeton faculty,
introducing them with a speech which those who heard
it describe as one of the most eloquent he ever made. The
faculty responded almost unanimously and voted some sort
of resolution of approval. How far this resolution was supposed to go is a subject of controversy, but it is probable
that the professors, for the most part, regarded themselves
as voting merely a general endorsement of the principles
which the President had suggested. He had brought
forward no plausible plan for putting these principles
into practice: he had not discussed the problem of expense. Presumably, they were authorizing him merely to
prepare a more detailed program. Without waiting further, however, he proceeded to compose and send out a
peremptory memorandum to the clubs themselves.

It was commencement, and these institutions were
holding their annual banquets. Wilson caused his memorandum to be read at the banquets. Mr. Baker fails to
show this incident in its full and true significance. His
language about the memorandum suggests that he must
be aware of its having been open to objection, but, quoting from it only a few sentences, he does not make it
possible for his readers to understand its total effect. The

night of these club banquets in June was observed until recently at Princeton as an occasion of peculiar cere- monies and supreme conviviality. The freshmen, who had hitherto been excluded from Prospect Street, were for the first time allowed to invade it. Late in the evening, they would form a parade and, with red fire and Roman can- dles, march down between the rows of clubs. When the older men inside at the banquets heard the sound of their singing and tramping, they would come to the doors with glasses of champagne and offer the freshmen drinks; the more prominent members of the class were toasted. At the same time, the newly elected sophomores felt, for the first time, that they were being officially welcomed: they had entered the haven of content. And the alumni had re- turned with something of that feeling of relief and exhila- ration I have tried to describe above, and no doubt, also, with that touching need for loyalty—a loyalty far in ex- cess of the worthiness or interest of its object—which, in a country with so few institutions that may with dignity command a man's loyalty, must do its best to satisfy itself with the commercial boosting of cities, with lodges and Rotary Clubs. It was this moment that Wilson chose for communicating to the Princeton clubs a note that had the form of an edict—that seemed brusquely to break the news that they were summarily to be disbanded, and that even went so far as to recommend that trustees be ap- pointed at once in whose hands "each club would vest its property," in order that this property might be melted up in the unfamiliar quad system. If Wilson had deliberately sought to discover a strategic move which would render a maximum of alumni opinion immediately antagonistic, he could not have acted otherwise. The proud under- graduates and the jolly alumni—many of them, no doubt, drunk—must have felt as if their delightful houses were being snatched from over their very heads, and that at the moment when they loved them most dearly; that their joyfully renewed goodfellowship, their love of Princeton itself, were receiving a cold affront from the President. In any case, they did not delay to bring pressure to bear on the faculty, and the faculty, astonished and frightened, "reconsidered" their resolution. It is quite probable that, if Woodrow Wilson had gone about the matter more cautiously, and with a sense of the sacred ties of sentiment and conviviality, he would have secured the adoption of his policy. At that time, almost everyone was in favor of it—even those, like Mr. Moses Taylor Pyne, the rich patron of the University, who afterwards came to oppose it. But Wilson had not been able to estimate the lengths to which men will go to preserve for themselves the privilege of an unrestrained freedom and fun such as he had not hesitated to blight—just as many of the persons he offended had no doubt never known the ecstasy of transcendent moral conviction, of the triumph of the personal will which knows also that it "conquers in this sign," of the shaping of God's institutions from the baser habitations, however gilded, of the children of this world.

But the forces antagonized by the President were now to get a spokesman and champion in a figure that Woodrow Wilson would ultimately find it impossible either to persuade or to subdue—the only man, at that time, in Princeton who possessed enough ambition, self-confidence, persistence and independence to put up a formidable resistance. If it had not been for Andrew West, then a professor in the Classics Department, it is probable that Wilson would have won even over the recalcitrance of the alumni. Now, it is possible to entertain only a moderate opinion of West either as scholar or as educator, yet to feel that he, too, derived a certain moral strength from an ideal of education, and that his collision with Woodrow Wilson—a collision fatal to Wilson—was partly, at least, the result of the latter's contemptuous refusal to sympathize with this ideal. For West, also, had the desire to impose a new pattern on Princeton. He was obsessed by a beautiful vision which was based, to some extent at least, on the ideals of classical humanism. He had imagined a super-graduate school, a withdrawn yet luxurious resort for an aristocratic caste of scholars, all complete with "dreaming spires" remembering the Middle Ages as they dominated the Princeton golf-links and with dons in black gowns having dinner on a daïs, under a sumptuous stained-glass window and a magnificent organ-loft; of a college fairly deliquescent with Oxonian Gothic beauty. What was admirable in this vision Woodrow Wilson did not, perhaps, understand; its vices were only too plain to him. And, what was probably more important, he came to resent and to fear another powerful egoism which had got into his sphere of influence. In the first stages of his career as president, he treats West with great respect; he writes a preface to a prospectus for the graduate school, smoothly commending the project; and when West is offered the presidency of the Massachusetts Institute of Technology, Wilson requests him to remain at Princeton, assuring him that, if he will stay, he shall presently have his desire. West remains and supports Wilson's policies. When the quad system is proposed, however, West becomes rather uneasy; and when Wilson, in the matter of the edict to the clubs, appears to be acting beyond his authority, he is apprehensive and angry. If the reforms are put into effect, they are certain to be expensive. And if the trustees undertake to supply the money, how can the graduate school be built? There seems no doubt that, in respect to the graduate school, Andrew West had a just grievance: he felt that he had received a pledge from Wilson, that he had stayed on at Princeton on the strength of that pledge, and that the pledge had not been redeemed. The retired Grover Cleveland, who had come to Princeton to live partly on account of his friendship with West and who had been made a member of the board of trustees, sympathized with his friend. He had, moreover, himself, as he thought, some evidence that Wilson was treacherous. Mr. Baker has made no attempt to state or to study the case against Wilson. This question, which is the crux of the controversy, he manages to keep out of his book. He does tell us that Wilson was accused of "bad faith," but he does not say how or why. The truth was, undoubtedly, that Wilson, who had already found himself and West in bitter opposition to one another, had become so exaltedly preoccupied with his new dispensation for Princeton that it was easy for him to brush aside the small-minded and snobbish West and his archaizing graduate school. He could not believe they were really important; and he was able to convince himself that, in matters of no importance, it was not important to keep one's word.

The conflict now reaches a phase extremely unedifying on either side—a phase which presents serious difficulties for Wilson's devoted biographer. A rich lady, a Mrs. Swann, has left Princeton a bequest for a graduate school, which, according to the terms of her will, is to be built on the campus itself. Mr. Ralph Adams Cram, the supervising architect at Princeton, has designated a site. West, however, has succeeded, to Wilson's alarm, at an early stage of the proceedings, in securing a free hand for the future in everything connected with the graduate school, of which he is himself to be dean. He proposes to make the school completely independent of the University, and even to collect the students' fees through a separate treasurer's office; and he insists now upon having the new college erected at some distance from the campus. It is true that he is balked in this by the terms of Mrs.

Swann's will, but he soon obtains another bequest, granted on the opposite condition. Wilson, without warning, is one day handed a letter from Mr. W. C. Procter, a graduate of Princeton and the manufacturer of Ivory Soap: in this letter, Mr. Procter announces to Andrew West that he is prepared to give half a million dollars for the proposed graduate school, if West can raise half a million more; but that he has examined the site on the campus selected by Mr. Cram and that he does not consider it suitable; his offer is only conditional upon some other site's being chosen. Woodrow Wilson, who, though president of the University, has not been notified by Mr. Procter of the latter's visit to Princeton in connection with the graduate school, not unnaturally resents this action. He holds, however, a very strong card in the terms of Mrs. Swann's will, and he attempts to play this card. He calls upon Procter in New York and proposes to him that, since it seems impossible to arrive at an agreement on the matter, two graduate schools be erected—one, with Mrs. Swann's money, on the campus; the other, with Procter's, on the golf-links. This proposal is, of course, preposterous, and Wilson counts on Procter's capitulating to the terms of Mrs. Swann's will. The manufacturer, however, remains obstinate; and Wilson at once sits down in the Jersey City railroad station and writes out to Moses Taylor Pyne a note in which he announces his resignation as president of Princeton. When the board of trustees meet again at the beginning of the next year (1910), the opposition plays a trick on Wilson. Unsuspectingly Wilson attends a meeting of the graduate school committee and is confronted with a letter from Procter in which the latter pretends to accept Wilson's proposal that two graduate schools be built—a proposal which had never been intended as anything but a *reductio ad absurdum*. Wilson loses his temper, and for the first time blurts out the truth—that the site of the grad-ate school is actually immaterial: "We could make this school a success anywhere in Mercer County!" The trouble is, it plainly appears, that Princeton is not large enough to hold him and Andrew West both. It is char-acteristic of him, however, that, instead of saying merely, "Dean West and I seem to have conflicting ideas that can hardly be reconciled," or something of that sort, he should declare that "Dean West's ideas and ideals are not the ideas and ideals of Princeton!" The controversy is now at its height; the whole community is divided into factions. Dean West, who is a master of money-getting, an irresist-ible charmer of millionaires, soon secures a third bequest: another rich alumnus dies, appointing West his executor and leaving the graduate school a sum then reported as ten million dollars. The trustees accept it with joy; and Wilson resigns with relief. He has already had overtures from the New Jersey Democratic politicians and is pre-paring to pass on to the governorship.

In the course of these Princeton controversies, Wood-row Wilson, from whose point of view, that of a major prophet, everyone who was not with him was against him, who, as was said of him by one of his own Princeton supporters, seemed incapable of understanding that "in-tellectual error is innocent"—had behaved toward his opponents with the harshest bitterness. He had been on fairly intimate terms with Mr. John Grier Hibben, then a professor in the Philosophy Department; but Hibben had voted against the quad system, and Wilson now dropped him and cut him—as, to his damage, he was afterwards to do with so many other allies who ventured to disagree with him. When Wilson was President of the United States and returned to Princeton to vote, Mr. Hibben, then president of the University, went to the station to receive him; but Wilson refused to speak to him, turned his back and walked away. There was in all this a passionate pride: "I am proud and wilful beyond all measure," he writes to his fiancée, while he is still a student at Johns Hopkins, and this pride was at the root of his strength; but Woodrow Wilson presented in an extreme form one of the paradoxes of the Puritan nature: he was, at the same time, obdurate and ruthless, and excessively thin-skinned. He was sensitive to criticism from friends; he was suspicious and vindictive to his opponents; and he was unable to deal with either except by overwhelming the one and overriding the other. As President of the United States, he repeated after the War his whole tragedy as president of Princeton—with Lodge in the role of West, the League of Nations in the place of the quad system, and the Senate in the place of the Princeton trustees. It is possible to observe in certain lives, where conspicuously superior abilities are united with serious deficiencies, not the progress in a career or vocation that carries the talented man to a solid position or a definite goal, but a curve plotted over and over again and always dropping from some flight of achievement to a steep descent into failure. Casanova's is such a life: his memoirs show again and again the same triumph of impudence and cunning as well as of intelligence and imagination, followed soon by the detection of a fraud that discredits and eclipses the whole man, with the result that he is forced to go elsewhere and begin the whole performance again. Woodrow Wilson's career, in its so different fields and terms, presents similar abrupt fluctuations.

If I have dwelt at length on Wilson's weaknesses, it is not for lack of admiration, but in the attempt to correct Mr. Baker's bias, which has obscured some of the elements in Wilson's story. It may, in general, be said that the public enthusiasm for Wilson, which reached, at the time of the war, both at home and abroad, such almost apocalyptic proportions, has ebbed rapidly—the tragic descent of the curve—since his compromise at Versailles and the defeat of the League of Nations, followed by collapse and death, till there are few to praise him today. The professional intelligentsia, especially, are afraid of taking him seriously. Yet, in the bankruptcy of political idealism which has followed his administration, as in the dreary timidity and stodginess toward which our academic life is always dragged by the force of inertia, we may still find it salutary to look back on Woodrow Wilson's career, and we may read many less profitable books than Mr. Baker's *Life*. In any case, we should certainly do ill to fall in with the cowardice and ignorance of American public opinion which, in spite of his errors and faults, idealized Wilson till he broke, then, in spite of his heroic audacity and his genius for leadership, was willing to deride and forget him.

November 30, 1927

It may be interesting to add here to this sketch of Woodrow Wilson's career at Princeton a story told by Norman Thomas in an interview with Tex McCrary and Jinx Falkenberg, which appeared in the New York *Herald Tribune* of February 13, 1950.

"One thing I have learned," Mr. Thomas says, in speaking of his political fights: "Never give up, but don't nurse a grudge in politics. Woodrow Wilson taught me that lesson.

"In Princeton, I took all the courses available under Woodrow Wilson—no, I never heckled him. That was before I became a Socialist. But in my senior year, we were looking around for some normal healthy mischief to do. There was a big ugly picket fence around the president's house on the campus, and that was our target! We organized a big protest meeting, which turned into a parade—Mr. Wilson was away from Princeton at the time—and we marched over and tore down his fence and took it away and hid it in the woods! As I was to learn later, Wilson never liked opposition of any kind. When he got back and found his fence torn down, he was very angry. But he couldn't very well discipline the whole senior class.

"Years later, when I was editor of the Socialist *World Tomorrow*, and we actively opposed United States intervention in Russia after the first World War, President Wilson's Attorney General thought I belonged in jail even more than Eugene Debs did. Wilson didn't go that far, but he did say to me: 'There is such a thing as indecent exposure of private opinion in public.'

"A few years after Mr. Wilson died, I met his daughter at a reception, and as we were being introduced, she froze—and said, 'I believe I have heard a great deal about Mr. Thomas!' I smiled and asked her which of my political sins she was referring to, and she replied, still angry: 'You were in Princeton, Class of 1905, weren't you? Yes—that was the class that was so cruel to father!' A grudge had been passed on to another generation!"

AMERICAN HEROES: FRÉMONT AND FRICK

JOHN CHARLES FRÉMONT—the subject of a biography by
Allan Nevins: *Frémont: The West's Greatest Adventurer*
—was the illegitimate son of a Virginian lady, who had
been married at seventeen to a sixty-year-old husband. She
ran away with a French émigré, and after some years of
wanderings in the South, in the course of which her lover
died, she went to live in Charleston, South Carolina,
where her son came to manhood in the duelling, drinking and racing society of the old South. He distinguished
himself at Charleston College as an enthusiastic classical
scholar: Greek especially, he afterwards wrote, "had a
mysterious charm, as if behind the strange characters belonging to an ancient world I was to find things of wonderful interest"; but he presently fell in love with a beautiful Creole girl, with large dark eyes and blue-black hair,
and thereafter so neglected his studies that he was finally
dismissed from college. Of his escapades with Cecilia,
however, he was afterwards to write that they were
"days of unreflecting life when I lived in the glow of a
passion that now I know extended its refining influence
over my whole life." He was handsome, and at sixteen
already exhibited what were later to prove his dominant
characteristics: "ardor, imagination, ambition, quickness,
endurance and reckless impetuosity."

After a brief period in the Navy, the young Frémont was given an opportunity to participate in a surveying expedition for the route of a projected railroad between Charleston and Cincinnati. "The survey," he said, "was a kind of picnic, with work enough to give it zest, and we were all sorry when it was over." In the course of it, he fell in love again, and made his first acquaintance with the Indians: "He sometimes visited Indian feasts which broke up, when the Cherokees became mad with drink, in furious disorder; he saw them end in bloody frays, the braves slashing each other with knives." Joel R. Poinsett, then Secretary of War, the first describer and the eponym of the poinsettia, was struck with the young man's abilities and had him commissioned in the Topographical Corps and included in an expedition, under the Frenchman Joseph Nicolas Nicollet, to survey the almost unknown region between the upper Mississippi and the Missouri. Here he encountered voyageurs, scouts, fur traders, frontier soldiers, Indians, buffalo, prairie fires and, in the lowlands near Lac qui Parle, an astonishing contrast of purple asters with the yellow of goldenrod, which he was never to forget.

When Frémont returned from this expedition, he went to live in Washington with Nicollet, upon whom he had made a great impression, at the house of the superintendent of the Coast Survey, a distinguished Swiss scientist, who kept a French chef, did a great deal of entertaining and "used to be driven through the streets in what he called the 'ark,' a huge comfortable carriage which he used in visiting his surveying parties, and which was packed with red and white German wines, choice foods and soft bedding." Frémont and Nicollet worked at their maps together and had an astronomical observatory built on the roof. Frémont fell in love with Senator Benton's daughter, who was then not yet sixteen. "There came a glow into my heart," he wrote, "which changed the current and color of daily life, and gave beauty to common things." Jessie Benton was high-spirited and strong-willed, as well as exceptionally well-educated—she had learned French in a convent at St. Louis; between St. Louis, Washington and her grandfather's estate in Virginia, she had acquired a certain knowledge of the world. Benton thought her too young to marry, especially to marry so young and poor a man, and tried to get Frémont out of the way by having him sent on an expedition along the Des Moines River. When he returned, since the parents remained obdurate, he and Jessie were married secretly. When the young couple confronted the Senator, he lived up to his august role with a scene of repudiation in the old-fashioned grand manner; Jessie, clutching Frémont's arm, replied with the words of Ruth, "Whither thou goest," etc. The Senator did not drive her out; Frémont came to live with them, and Benton was presently playing the role of his son-in-law's principal supporter in the career of exploration and fighting that so stimulated the American imagination and made him a national hero.

Henry Clay Frick (to borrow the formula of the Teasing Tom song in *Patience*)—about whom George Harvey has just written a biography, *Henry Clay Frick: The Man*—was born thirty-seven years later than Frémont (in 1849) in Westmoreland County, Pennsylvania. His parents were German and Swiss; his grandfather, a pious Mennonite, was the original manufacturer of that admirable Old Overholt rye whisky which is still bottled in bond by the government. Frick's father was a small farmer, and, as a boy, the son worked on the farm. His education was very meager: he left school at seventeen, and, in the meantime, he worked in an uncle's store, getting nothing in return but his board and the privilege of

sleeping on the counter. He graduated later on to the
store of another uncle, where he is said to have been paid
three dollars a week. On one occasion, when Henry was at
school and the teacher had threatened to whip one of his
little cousins, a girl, the boy became furious and averted
the punishment by threatening to beat the teacher. It was
afterwards recalled of him that he had said, at this time,
that his grandfather had made half a million, and that
he intended, before he died, "to be worth a million."
He also inaugurated the policy which he was to pursue
throughout his career of procuring "the best there is": he
discarded his ill-fitting farmer's-boy clothes and bought a
sixteen-dollar pair of black boots with yellow stitching,
which, at the end of six months, he had kept "as bright
and spotless as when new." He developed, in this early
period, an extraordinary gift for bookkeeping, and later,
when he was making first eight, then twelve dollars a
week at a larger store, he would go to business school
every night, after working from six to eight, to study
accounting and banking.

He was later given a place by his grandfather, at a
thousand dollars a year, as chief bookkeeper of the Overholt whisky distillery. When, in 1870, old Overholt
died, young Henry went into the coke business, with a
cousin who had invested in coal lands. They already
foresaw the rise of the steel industry in Pittsburgh, and
they rightly believed that coke would turn out to be indispensable as fuel for the furnaces. Frick succeeded in
borrowing $10,599 and bought with it more lands, and
he persuaded his father to endorse countless notes upon
which he procured small sums from the farmers of the
countryside, "hitching up at dawn and driving all over
the country and coming back at night with pockets full
of greenbacks." He also preached to the father of Andrew
Mellon, who had opened a bank in Pittsburgh, the glori-

ous future of the coking business and borrowed from him
$10,000 for the purpose of building fifty ovens: "Judge
Mellon was not impulsive; he was notably cautious," but
"that he was favorably impressed by the terse representa-
tions, direct methods and engaging manners of his confident young customer may well be believed." And even
before the first fifty ovens were finished, he was asking
for an additional loan in order to build fifty more. Judge
Mellon sent a representative to investigate Frick & Co.,
and was advised not to make the loan, as the director was
a mere boy, who had to give part of his time to keeping
the books of a large store and whose "half-office and half-
living-room in a clapboard shack" was filled with prints
and sketches. Later on, however, the Judge again made
inquiries and received the following report: "Lands good,
ovens well built, manager on job all day, keeps books evenings, may be a little too enthusiastic about pictures, but
not enough to hurt; knows his business down to the
ground; advise making the loan." The loan was made,
and the business prospered.

But in 1873, the panic fell: iron mills were shut down,
mines abandoned; Pittsburgh was paralyzed, and the
demand for coke began to dwindle. "'It was,' said Mr.
Frick nearly half a century later, 'an awful time.'" But
Frick & Co. persisted. The young Frick became his own
sales agent, and, after rising every morning at six, looking over the ovens and seeing that the work was set
going, would take the train to Pittsburgh, where he
tramped from factory to factory, soliciting orders for
coke. At six he would reach home and "attend to the
details of mining till bed-time." At last, however, he
became inspired to bring off what his biographer describes as "a truly dashing stroke." There was between
Mt. Pleasant and Broadford a small railroad built for
transporting coke, which, as a result of the bad condi-

tions, had almost ceased to operate; the stockholders, foreseeing bankruptcy, were eager to sell their shares, and Frick knew that, if the railroad stopped, he would be forced to close his mines. He therefore borrowed a fast horse and drove round to see the shareholders, whom he easily persuaded to sign options on their stock; he then visited the management of the Baltimore & Ohio and preached again the revelation of the future greatness of the coke industry. He pointed out to them the desirability of purchasing now, at the lowest price, a line which must some day become valuable. The B. & O. bought the options at cost and paid Frick himself a commission of fifty thousand dollars, which enabled him to buy, among other things, the fast gray single-footer with which he had rounded up the shares. Judge Mellon was so favorably impressed by the astuteness of this transaction that he granted his young friend a mortgage-loan which now made it possible for him to purchase fifteen thousand dollars' worth of freight cars for the purpose of shipping coke over the road he had just sold and to obtain "a line of discount not exceeding twenty-five thousand dollars."

From this time, the business prospered. By 1897, Henry C. Frick was employing nearly a thousand men and shipping nearly a hundred carloads of coke a day. The price of coke had risen from ninety cents to five dollars a ton. "When springtime came, the various factors of mining, manufacture, transportation and selling had been welded into a smoothly working machine, whose essential attributes required only expansion to assure the ultimate success of the gigantic steel corporation, and the originator of the marvellous system saw his way clear to take his first holiday." This holiday was a trip to Europe with the Judge's young son, Andrew Mellon. Frick proposed two other companions, one a popular young man of their acquaintance, who wrote poems, sang songs and told stories; Henry and Andrew agreed that, being so little lively themselves, it would be a very useful thing for them to have "someone along to do the talking." The other man, however, was notoriously dull, and Mellon demurred a little; Frick explained that there was a "special reason" that he should like to have him of the party. And, in fact, when the excursion was finished and Mellon and Frick had to return home, it was found that the unexplained companion had acquired such an appetite for travel that he was eager to go on around the world and, in order to gratify this desire, consented to sell to Frick, at what was from the latter's point of view a very advantageous price, certain coal lands which he owned in the Connellsville region. When Henry Frick returned to Pittsburgh, he picked out at once, at a "reception attended by all the élite," a young woman just out of her teens, whom he described as "the handsomest girl in the room," and, three months after, had married her. As a climax to their honeymoon, the young husband brought his wife to New York and took her to dinner with Andrew Carnegie and his mother at the Windsor Hotel. A surprise had been reserved for the end: after dinner, Carnegie announced that he and Frick had gone into partnership. Mrs. Carnegie, who had not been warned of this, remarked drily, in the presence of the guests: "Surely, Andrew, that will be a fine thing for Mr. Frick, but what will be the gain to us?"

Such were the lives of these two remarkable Americans up to the time of their marriages, and up to the thresholds of their greatest successes. The most astonishing adventures and the most important achievements of both men were still, at this point, to come, and no brief condensation would do them justice. If the differences between the explorer of the early half of the century and the

capitalist of the latter half seem striking to the point of
melodrama, it may partly be due to the unequal value
and the differing temperaments of their respective biographers. Professor Nevins has produced an attractive
book—well-written, accurate, consecutive, beautifully
proportioned and disciplined by a detachment as far from
the silly irony that has lately become the fashion as it is
from the injudicious impulse to magnify or rehabilitate
of the fanatical enthusiast; and he, also, persuades us the
more easily for the reason that, though he possesses a
sense of the dramatic, he refrains from the obvious
romantic treatment, the overindulgence in the picturesque, that his subject so temptingly invites, and depends for his effectiveness entirely on the quiet arrangement of facts. Colonel Harvey, on the other hand, brings
to his task only that shrewdness of the small Vermont
shopkeeper which enables him to appreciate, en connoisseur, the shrewdness of the shopkeeper in Frick, in Carnegie and in Rockefeller: he has no literary ability and
little imagination, and there is something about his nature
profoundly ungracious and sordid, which makes us feel
that, though he seems to have tried to present his subject
in a favorable light and limited though Frick himself unquestionably was, the collector of Vermeers and Rem-
brandts may yet not have lacked distinction to quite the
ghastly degree that his biographer's pages do.

Yet a contrast comes out of these books that is real
and extremely significant. Frémont had serious weaknesses, and he made a good many mistakes which Mr.
Nevins does not try to disguise: he was sometimes incau-
tious, tactless, egoistic, visionary, vain. His conquest of
California ended in failure; his career as a general during
the Civil War laid him open to damaging criticism; and
he was so poor a business man that he allowed his California estate, valued at $10,000,000, to be wrecked by an

unscruplous speculator, and then lost the little that was left in a badly managed railroad enterprise, so that he died, at sixty, an impoverished man, in a New York boarding-house. Frémont's blunders seem mainly to have been due to an incurable lack of prudence: on his return from his first expedition, he insisted upon running, in an elastic boat, the rapids of an impossible canyon on the Platte River, and succeeded in wrecking the whole party; and his almost lunatic passion for crossing the Sierras in mid-winter, though, the first time, it brought him at last to the beauty and abundance of the Sacramento Valley, ended, the second, in horror and disaster. Yet, when we finish the story of Frémont's life, we are ready to say to ourselves: Who would not die in poverty to have won the satisfaction of such a life? and we are willing to agree with the poet that "only the wasteful virtues earn the sun"—as, with Frick, so much of whose strength lay precisely in his impregnable caution, in his incapacity for taking chances with that soundly invested fortune that he had worked so single-mindedly to amass, we wonder at last, as we read of him in his final years, in the solitude of that museum in which he had managed to entomb some of the glories of other ages and places that had known how to live with more joy than the grim Pennsylvania of his boyhood where his love of his few cheap prints had been badly regarded by Judge Mellon's spy— even among his pictures, to which, his biographer tells us, he liked to go late at night, we cannot refrain from asking what is the good of all this prudence and persistency which can only bring a man, late in life and at the expense of millions of dollars, such enjoyment at secondhand of the subtleties of the spirit and the colors of the world as may be bought with the works of art created by other men. The goldenrod and asters of Frémont, the blue-black hair of Cecilia, were an essential part of his life: they were one of the elements that fed it.

It is all too easy, perhaps, to handle this contrast of Frémont with Frick in such a way as to give the former all the aesthetic best of it—to set Frémont's comments on his own adventures, his statement in his memoirs, for example, that he had, on his first expedition, lived "with the fine Greek joy in existence, in the gladness of living," beside the meager memoranda dictated by Frick to his secretary to commemorate incidents of special interest, memoranda in which he himself is referred to in the third person:

"At Sherry's [in 1912] Mr. Grier bet $50,000 to $400 that if Roosevelt gets both Republican and Progressive nominations, he will be elected.

"In Pittsburgh [in 1916] attended Chamber of Commerce dinner, met Senator Warren Harding of Ohio; he looks like fine Presidential timber.

"Movies taken of Mr. F. playing cards. Very life-like.

"Had ten young farmers from Montana on their way to the war at Thanksgiving Dinner. Splendid chaps.

"Hereafter, when I purchase anything from [naming a certain picture dealer] it will be entered in this diary on the day I buy it. If no memo is entered, it is understood that everything is left on approval.

"Dr. Prichett lunched with others and showed up Wilson's character. Mr. F. drew out others but did not express opinion.

"Stopped at Baltimore and saw the Walters Collection.

"Will Hays called. Contribution.

"Mr. F. left Pride's for New York with Mr. Grier. He had refused to take an overcoat, but found one in the car and threw it out of the window to tease his daughter."

It is all too easy to speculate as to whether that fellow-traveller of Frick's and young Andrew Mellon's who exchanged his coal lands, in a bad bargain, for the expenses of a trip around the world did not perhaps, after all, get the better of the deal. Yet Henry Clay Frick makes, in some respects, a by no means contemptible showing beside the explorer and pioneer. For Frick did have his own sort of heroism, his own courage and independence, his own dignity and even honesty. His battle with his employees, for example, over the terrible Homestead strike required boldness as well as obstinacy. We may dislike the narrowness of his mind, the obduracy of his attitude toward organized labor, his stupidity about so many matters in which we should like to see our rich men interested; yet, in his fashion, Frick makes an impressive figure. He is seen perhaps at his best on the occasion, just after the defeat of the strike which had come so near to proving revolutionary, when the anarchist Alexander Berkman attempted to assassinate him in his office. Though Berkman had shot him twice and stabbed him three times, Frick succeeded in pinioning him to the floor. When a deputy sheriff rushed in and was about to shoot the assassin, "Don't shoot!" commanded Frick, "leave him to the law. But raise his head and let me see his face." When this was done, Frick pointed out that Berkman's jaw was moving, and the sheriff extracted from his mouth a capsule of fulminite of mercury sufficient to blow up the whole office. The wounded millionaire was again trying to prevent any violence to Berkman when he grew faint and had to be carried out. While the doctors were treating his wounds, he was arranging that his wife and his mother should be notified in such a way as not to alarm them; and when they came to extract the bullets, he refused to take an anesthetic, suggesting that he might help the doctors in locating them—which he did. He then had himself propped up at his desk and went on with his day's work, "specifying the final terms of a loan which he had been negotiating." Before he left in an ambulance, he dictated the following statement: "This incident will not change the attitude of the Carnegie Steel Company toward the Amalgamated Association. I do not think I shall die, but whether I do or not, the Company will pursue the same policy, and it will win." He would not have a bodyguard after this, but continued to go to and from his office without any kind of protection. He had made himself a rigid agent of that overwhelming power of the steel mills which dominates and drives the lives of employers and workmen alike: he had come to embody in his person its almost extra-human discipline.

While Frick had lain dazed from the assassin's attack, he had imagined that a little daughter who had died the year before at six and for whom he had grieved ever since, was alive and had come to see him; and at a time when he was still swathed in bandages but directing every move in the resistance, not quite yet at an end, of the now partly scab-manned mills, he was obliged to look on at the death of a son who had been born only four weeks before. We may be touched by the curious cohabitation of the feelings that are tenderest in men with the will that is implacably callous; but we remember, also, Frémont's return after the first of his great expeditions and his spreading upon the bed of the daughter who had been born during his absence the ragged American flag which he had been the first to raise from the highest peak of the Rockies. And beside the iron figure of the Bismarck of Homestead, whose first thought, after the attempt on his life, was to reassure his wife and mother, there arises the shade of the flighty explorer, returning from the long Californian trip on which he had lost touch with his family and was reported to have disappeared, landing late at night on the levee at St. Louis, throwing pebbles at the windows of his own house, told by the

Negro coachman that his wife had gone to spend the night at the house of a sick cousin, and, after first setting out for the cousin's house, sitting down to wait till morning on a bench in front of a hotel, because he feared that the shock of his arrival might be harmful to the tubercular relative.

John Frémont found the road to the West and "from the ashes of his campfires have sprung cities." H. C. Frick produced the coke that made the steel with which were built the railroads that spanned the continent— those railroads in which Frémont invested and lost; and Frick's race, too, was one of giants. They are all here in his biography, these giants—Carnegie, Gary, Schwab, Morgan, the Rockefellers, and they inevitably strike us as comic: for all their immense power, they impress us, in their great transactions, as rather surprisingly clownish, since—aside from the mere size of their projects— they are seen to have no dignified aims and, except in a debased sense, no honor. Trying continually to cheat one another, whether as rivals or friendly associates, they are the performers of a colossal rogues' comedy. We have heard, and still hear, a good deal about the romance of big business, and Americans, whatever we may say, live much in awe of the rich. Yet the narrative of Colonel Harvey, read immediately after that of Professor Nevins, is almost enough to convince one that Nietzsche was right when he said that there are only three kinds of real creator: the scientist, the artist and the sportsman— because they alone play the game for its own sake, because they alone can be free from the appetite for money or power, or for the vulgar good opinion of their neighbors. Frémont, in his early and most brilliant phase, was a scientist and a sportsman; Nicollet and his associates were scientists; Kit Carson and the other frontiersmen whom Frémont knew in the old wild West were sportsmen. That West which they ranged and studied now no longer exists; we live in the world of Rockefeller, Carnegie, Morgan and Frick; and what leadership or revelation may Americans be sanguine enough still to await either from them or from their agents in the government? The great public have already given evidence of their longing for a different sort of hero in their acclaiming those audacious sportsmen, Charles Lindbergh and Commander Byrd. And what new kind of American in what new field may our country now be ready to breed to provide us with heroes and leaders?

April 4, 1928

THE SPORTSMAN'S TRAGEDY

THE REPUTATION OF Ernest Hemingway has, in a very short time, assumed such proportions that it has already become fashionable to disparage him. Yet it seems to me that he has received in America very little intelligent criticism. One finds Mr. Lee Wilson Dodd, for example, in the *Saturday Review of Literature*, with his usual gentle trepidation in the presence of contemporary vitality, deciding with a sigh of relief that, after all, Mr. Hemingway (a young man who has published only three books) is not really Tolstoy or Shakespeare, and describing his subjects as follows: "The people he observes with fascinated fixation and then makes live before us are . . . all very much alike: bull-fighters, bruisers, touts, gunmen, professional soldiers, prostitutes, hard drinkers, dope-fiends. . . . For what they may or may not be intellectually, aesthetically, or morally worth, he makes his facts ours." In the *Nation*, Mr. Joseph Wood Krutch, whose review is more sympathetic than Mr. Dodd's, describes Mr. Hemingway as follows: "Spiritually the distinguishing mark of Mr. Hemingway's work is a weariness too great to be aware of anything but sensations. . . . Mr. Hemingway tells us, both by his choice of subject and by the method which he employs, that life is an affair of mean tragedies. . . . In his hands the subject-matter of literature becomes sordid little catastrophes

in the lives of very vulgar people." I do not know whether
these critics of *Men without Women* have never read
Mr. Hemingway's other two books or whether they have
simply forgotten them. Do the stories in *In Our Time*
and *The Sun Also Rises* actually answer to these descriptions? Does *Men without Women* answer to them?
The hero of *In Our Time*, who appears once or twice in
this new volume of stories, and the hero of *The Sun Also
Rises* are both highly civilized persons of rather complex
temperament and extreme sensibility. In what way can
they be said to be "very vulgar people"? And can the
adventures of even the old bull-fighter in such a piece as
The Undefeated correctly be called a "sordid little
catastrophe"?

One of the stories in *Men without Women* also appeared in the *American Caravan*, and was thus twice
exposed to the reviewers; yet in all the reviews I have
read I cannot remember one which seemed to me to give
an accurate account of it. *An Alpine Idyl* has usually
been mentioned as a simple tale of horror or a tale
of brutality, or something of the sort. Let us examine
this story a moment. Two young men have been skiing
in the Alps. It is spring and the sun is terrifically strong;
but in the shade, the sweat freezes in their underclothes.
They have begun to find this oppressive and are glad to
get down to an inn. On their way, they have passed a
funeral, and at the inn they hear the story behind it.
The woman who is dead was a peasant's wife who had
died during the winter, but the house had been snow-
bound, and the husband had not been able to bring her
out till spring. The man had put the body in the wood-
shed, laying it on a pile of logs; but when he had had to
use the wood, he had stood the corpse up in a corner, and
had later got into the habit of hanging the lantern in its
mouth. Why, we ask ourselves now for a moment, have

we been told about the skiing expedition? Then, immediately, we realize that Hemingway, with his masterly relevance in indirection, has, by telling us of the tourists' oppression, supplied us with the explanation of the brutalization of the peasant. But it is not the mere fact of this brutalization that makes the point of the story. We do not see the point till the end. The peasant comes on to the inn, but he refuses to drink with them there and goes on to another inn. " 'He didn't want to drink with me,' said the sexton. 'He didn't want to drink with me, after he knew about his wife,' said the innkeeper." In a similar way, it is true that *A Pursuit Race* is, as Mr. Dodd would say, a story about a dope-fiend; but what is much more important, it is also a story of a man who has just lost a desperate moral struggle. It is given its point by the final paragraph, in which the manager of the burlesque show, understanding that the struggle has been lost and pitying his recreant advance man, goes away without waking him up. So, in *A Simple Inquiry*—a glimpse of one aspect of army life: that strange demoralization that may bring with it a kind of stoicism—the significance of the incident lies in the fact that the major refrains from dismissing the boy who has just refused his advances.

It would appear, then, that Hemingway's world is not quite so rudimentary as Mr. Krutch or Mr. Dodd represents it. Even when he is dealing with primitive types— as he by no means always is—his drama almost always turns on some principle of courage, of pity, of honor—in short, of sportsmanship, in its largest human sense— which he is able to bring to light in them. I do not say that the world that Mr. Hemingway depicts is not, on the whole, a bad world; it *is* a bad world, and a world where much is suffered. Mr. Hemingway's feelings about this world, his criticism of what goes on in it, are, for all his misleadingly simple and matter-of-fact style, rather subtle and complicated; but he has, it seems to me, made it plain enough what sort of ideas and emotions he is trying to communicate. His first book was called *In Our Time*, and it was a sequence of short stories about a sensitive and healthy boy in the American Northwest. We were, I take it, to contrast these two series. When Mr. Hemingway gave them this title, he meant to tell us that life was barbarous even in the twentieth century; and that the man who sees the cabinet ministers shot and who finds himself potting the Germans from behind the "absolutely topping" barricade has had to come a long way from the boy who, with the fresh responses of youth, so much enjoyed the three days' fishing trip at Big Two-Hearted River. Yet *has* he really come so far? Is not the principle of life itself essentially ruthless and cruel? What is the difference between the gusto of the soldier shooting down his fellow humans and the gusto of the young fisherman hooking grasshoppers to catch trout? Ernest Hemingway is primarily preoccupied with these problems of natural cruelty and its inevitable obverse of suffering.

The barbarity of the world since the war is also the theme of his next book, *The Sun Also Rises*. By his title and by the quotations which he prefixes to this novel, he makes it plain what moral judgment we are to pass on the events he describes: "You are all a lost generation." What gives the book its profound unity and its disquieting effectiveness is the intimate relation established between the Spanish fiesta, with its revelry, its bull-fighting and its processions, and the atrocious behavior of the group of holiday-making British and Americans who have come down from Paris to enjoy it. In the heartlessness of these people, in their treatment of one another, do we not find the same principle at work as in the pagan orgy of the festival? Is not the brutal persecution of the Jew as much a natural casualty as the fate of the man who is gored by the bull on his way to visit the bull-ring? The whole interest of *The Sun Also Rises* lies in the attempts of the hero and the heroine to disengage themselves from this world, or rather to arrive at some method of living in it in such a way as to satisfy some code of their own. The real story is that of their attempts to do this—attempts by which, in such a world, they are always bound to lose out in everything except honor. I do not agree, as has sometimes been said, that the behavior of the people in *The Sun Also Rises* is typical of only a small special class of American and British expatriates. I believe that it is more or less typical of certain phases of the whole western world today; and the title *In Our Time* could have been applied to it with as much appropriateness as it was to its predecessor.

Ernest Hemingway's attitude, however, toward the cruelties and treacheries he describes is quite different from anything else that one remembers in a similar connection. He has nothing of the liberating impulse involved in the romantic's indignation:* he does not, like Byron, identifying himself with the Prisoner of Chillon, bid the stones of any earthly cell "appeal from tyranny to God"; nor, like Shelley, invite the winds to "wail for the world's wrong." Nor has he even that grim and repressed, but still generous, still passionate feeling which we find in the pessimist-realists—in Thomas Hardy's *Tess*, in Maupassant's *Boule de Suif*, even in those infrequent scenes of Flaubert by which one's resentment is kindled at the spectacle of an old farm servant or of a young working-class girl at the mercy of the bourgeoisie. In his treatment of the war, for example, Mr. Hemingway is as far as possible from John Dos Passos or Henri Barbusse. His point of view, his state of mind, is a curious

* This liberating impulse, however, was later to be brought out in Hemingway by the Spanish Civil War.

one, and one typical, I think, of "our time"; he seems so broken in to the human agonies, and, though even against his will, so impassively, so hopelessly, resigned to them, that the only protest of which he is capable is, as it were, the grin and the curse of the sportsman who loses the game. Nor are we always quite sure on which side Mr. Hemingway is betting. We do sometimes feel a suspicion that the conflict we are witnessing is a set-up, with the manager backing the barbarian. Yet to speak in these terms of Mr. Hemingway is really to misrepresent him. He is not, of course, a moralist staging a melodrama, but an artist exhibiting situations the values of which are not simple. Mr. Hemingway enjoys bull-fighting, as he enjoys skiing, racing and prize-fights; and he is unremittingly conscious of the fact that, from the point of view of life as a sport, all that seems most painful in it is somehow very closely bound up with what he finds to be most enjoyable. The peculiar conflicts of feeling which arise in a temperament of this kind are the subject of Mr. Hemingway's fiction. The most remarkable effects of this fiction, effects unlike those of anyone else, are those, as in the fishing-trip in *The Sun Also Rises*, by which we are made to feel, behind the appetite for the physical world, the tragedy or the falsity of a moral relation. The inescapable consciousness of this does not arouse Hemingway to passionate violence; but it poisons him and makes him sick, and thus invests with a sinister quality—a quality perhaps new in fiction—the sunlight and the green summer landscapes of *The Sun Also Rises*. Thus, if Hemingway is oppressive, as Mr. Dodd complains, it is because he himself is oppressed. And we may find in him—in the clairvoyant's crystal of a polished incomparable art—the image of the common oppression.

December 14, 1927

A POET OF THE PACIFIC*

THE NEW SELECTION, made by herself, of Genevieve Taggard's poems—*Traveling Standing Still*—brings her literary personality before us as none of her previous volumes did. She has here chosen from these three earlier volumes twenty-eight poems; and she has exercised, in dealing with her own work, the same excellent critical judgment which has distinguished her literary reviews. One had always been aware before of this distinction of Genevieve Taggard's and of the integrity of her art; but one had never seen her outline so clearly as that of certain of her sister-poets. One had been aware of her originality but would have found it a little difficult to say precisely in what that originality consisted. She has never stood out so vividly in the literary garden—a plant of unique variety, bringing forth flowers of a certain shape and color—as, say, Elinor Wylie or Louise Bogan or Léonie Adams. But in this book she has so stripped her work down, has so rigorously reduced her writing to a residuum of what is most authentic, that it has, at least for a casual reader, for the first time become possible to recognize her art as something distinct and solid. She seems deliberately to have brought herself to focus.

The impression of Miss Taggard that one gets from this is a little unexpected. If one had tended vaguely to

* Written in Santa Barbara, California.

confuse her with a familiar school of women poets—the school which one of their number has recently herself described as the "Oh-God-the-Pain Girls"—Miss Taggard has excluded from this book anything that might encourage it. What we find is a kind of poetry which, however else it may move us, is not in the least "poignant"; and we see that Miss Taggard's point of view, her temperament and her intention must somehow differ from those of the poets with whom, as I say, we tend to class her. She seems, in fact, to differ from her sisters in certain fundamental respects, and I believe that they in some ways are more like one another than Genevieve Taggard is like any of them.

It is probably rather important to remember that Genevieve Taggard was born in the state of Washington and taken as a baby to Honolulu, where her parents were American missionaries; and that she grew up and spent all her early years (she was educated at Berkeley) in Hawaii or on the Pacific coast. Now, we do not, as a rule, in America, get our poets from the other side of the continent. Most of Miss Taggard's most brilliant sisters were born on the Eastern coast. And when we come to reflect upon it, we may even be led to ask ourselves whether the moods and the emotions of lyric poetry are not, to a considerable degree, the products of varying weather. In countries where the seasons change, our feelings also run to extremes: the intensity of our works of art is the result of acute contrasts of feeling, and these contrasts seem to correspond with the contrasts of climatic conditions. In our autumns, with the death of vegetation and the darkening of the skies, we are reminded of the passing of love, the brevity of human life; in our winters, we turn in upon and fortify ourselves: as our bodies redouble their calories to cope with the chill of the winds, so our spirits must generate fire to set off the desolation

of the landscape; and in spring, we feel so much relieved
at the revival of vegetation and the restoration of warmth
that our hearts become hysterically gay. Also, poverty
among us is worse; privation deprives us of more. And
where life is barren or hard, we make character to meet
our conditions—people who are rugged without and
generous-hearted within, or people who are cold on the
surface and passionate in the spirit. But those who have
lived all their lives on our lower Pacific coast have hardly
been subjected to such heatings and coolings. There the
weather is equable and bright; the sea calm, the scenery
gentle; the flowers bloom all the year round, and there is
more fruit than people can eat. The natives have months
of unbroken sun, and they are comfortable, amiable and
healthy. In Southern California, for example, one is surprised even to come upon a graveyard: one had forgotten
that people died; and the mild and dry earth itself seems
to bear its graves lightly.

Now, in the poetry of Genevieve Taggard, we become
aware of this Pacific sun. If most of the lyric poetry we
know owes its vividness, its pathos, its fierceness, to the
coldness, the stoniness, the bleakness, the meagerness, the
illness, the death, with which the poets see themselves
surrounded—so Genevieve Taggard's is the wisdom of
the Western spaces and suns; and it is something quite
other than the wisdom of our keen Eastern winds and
constricted streets. The most striking feature of Miss
Taggard's temperament, in contrast to the writers of the
East, is the fact that her poetry is so rarely the result of
a sharp reaction from one extreme to the other: a girl from
the Pacific islands does not react against nature, as so
many of our New England writers have done, for she
has never been led to indulge in those moral and intellectual overdevelopments which make of nature an
enemy; and, on the other hand, she does not rebound

from the strain of such ascetic states of mind in the direction of nature again, for she has always taken nature for granted and has never divorced herself from it. She is simply and spontaneously physical; she is sensuous as a matter of course. And in the case of many Californians, this means that, since they lack the stimulus of moral dislocation or difficult living to prod them into thought, they do not seem to do any thinking: the problems that perplex, excite and torment the less fortunate parts of the world seem to have no existence for them. One remembers the young Californian girl who, when shown in a Spanish mission a painting of the agony of Santa Clara holding before her her severed breasts on a plate, asked innocently whether they were peaches. Now, Genevieve Taggard is in some respects (and I don't mean to be invidious) rather more like the girl who asked the question than she is like Santa Clara; but she differs from many Californians in the fact that she brings to her sensuous experience a shrewd and a subtle mind—a point of view even rather "metaphysical." And the peculiar interest of her poetry lies in the rare opportunity it gives us for observing such a mind and such a temperament in contact with both West and East.

For Genevieve Taggard, like many gifted Westerners, came early to live in the East. The first effect on her imagination of one of our Eastern winters is to be found in the elaborate *Ice Age*. This remarkable poem is a fantasy by one who has never been frozen-up about people deprived of sunlight. Now, ice has been made terrible in literature as a symbol of the atrophy of human feeling, from the traitors in Dante's Hell, immobilized in the nethermost pit, to the Brand of Ibsen's play, crushed by the avalanche; but Genevieve Taggard's *Ice Age*, vividly imagined though it is, does not bring us to the tragic climax which the poet has led us to expect from her shuddering and effective crescendo. In the end, we are obliged to recognize that the vision has had no moral meaning. Miss Taggard has not written of the cold as a New England writer would. She has merely had a taste of a winter that is colder than the climate she is used to, and it has made her extremely uncomfortable. Just as the dwellers in lands damp and chilly sometimes dream—as the English romantics did—of the languors of tropical climates, so Miss Taggard has been stimulated by New England to imagine a world grown completely cold. With all its sustained brilliance, the poem is a tour de force. Yet Miss Taggard, in coming away from the West, does seem to have quite lost Hawaii: her poems on Hawaiian sun-myths, which are the natural antithesis of the Ice Age, are less, perhaps, rather than more successful. Her memories have only sufficed—in such pieces as *Thirst* and *The Tourist*—for a few little poems of full flavor.

What we finally get is a poet of our common human experience who, despite her fastidious and busy mind, which embroiders it sometimes like lace, stitching it in and out, is singularly close to the ground. Whatever she may say in her bitterer moments—expressing herself in the admirable verses of *The Quiet Woman* and *Dissonance Then Silence*—she accepts what life brings her as natural and right. It is this that has made it possible for her to write, in the piece called *With Child*, the only respectable poem on child-bearing that I remember ever to have seen. The point is that the poet here does not, as is so often the case, repudiate or war with the woman. And even in *B. C.*, where the note is tragic, in warning the mother of Jesus that he will have to face "only agony and another loss of your being" in order to bring forth "an angelic shadow," her tone is not itself agonized, but rather one of sympathetic comprehension and resignation to the common lot. I believe that she is most enjoyable when, as in *Spring Touch* or *Talking Water*, she is most simply sensuous, least anxious.

Yet Miss Taggard has learned the habit of anxiety from her sisters of the East Coast. In a symposium of "statements of belief" that has recently appeared in the *Bookman*, she has told us that, in her early school days, when she had to sing in four-part songs, she always "sat with the altos and sang the dark humming parts." At last, a singing teacher came and identified her as a soprano. The young Genevieve announced her intention of continuing to sing alto. "Very well, and ruin your voice," said the teacher. "You have a real soprano, and you might sing solos." If Miss Taggard does not seem yet, in her poetry, quite to have found her true voice, if she seems sometimes to sing alto with effort, I am inclined to believe that this is not merely due, as she implies, to some anomaly of temperament, but to a certain maladjustment in her relations to West and East. With her eager intellectual appetite, she has devoured our ideas and techniques but she has scarcely been touched by the megrims, the nausea-fits, the moods of sterility that nowadays so often go with them. One looks forward to seeing her take her place as a self-dependent poetic personality, in some ways essentially different from any that we already know.

December 12, 1928

ART YOUNG

Art Young, in *On My Way*, has composed the least pretentious of autobiographies. In fact, the book scarcely pretends to be even an autobiography. He has merely kept a diary for six months, writing down in it every day some reflection, observation or memory. The result is like a series of conversations with a talented but retired and quite unpretentious neighbor, who has seen a good deal of the world and thought a good deal about it and upon whom one might agreeably drop in of an evening in the country.

He talks, as the occasion suggests, of his boyhood long ago in Wisconsin, of the cranks in his home-town who interested him; of his opinion that capitalism is doomed and that socialism will presently supplant it; and he speaks with loyal appreciation of his old master, Bouguereau, and tells how Bouguereau reprimanded him for making a brutal-looking model look too brutal; he says that the trouble with modern New York is that you can see nothing but brick out the windows; he tells about the early days in Greenwich Village: he was present at the celebrated picnic held on top of Washington Arch, when the Village declared itself an independent republic—when people came out the next morning, they all stopped and stared at the balloons flying from the top of the Arch. He used to know Eugene Field, also Jack

Reed and Jack London; he tells about his cat, which has had kittens and was disturbed by the men fixing the furnace, so that it carried all the kittens to the attic; he talks about the change in American humor from the days of Bill Nye and Josh Billings; he mimics an old-fashioned Southern Senator whom he used to hear years ago when he was reporting Congress in Washington; he talks about his neighbors in the country; he remarks that if Frank Harris had known all the famous people he said he had, he would have had to be two hundred years old; he explains that Gustave Doré was the great admiration of his youth; he tells you how he used to campaign for municipal ownership, and how he once ran for the legislature on a Socialist ticket, but that he discovered too late that his speeches had all been made outside his own district—perhaps if his constituents had heard him, they would have given him fewer votes; he ruminates on his career as an artist and wonders whether his unpopular political views have really had much to do with the fact that he has never made money.

But as we gradually acquire, with such a neighbor, a tolerably solid idea of his tastes, his disposition, his views, his work and his associations—so with this book of Art Young's, little of it though there is and casual though it sounds, we feel, by the time we have finished it, that, balancing his inconsecutive notes and making them set off one another, he has succeeded in sketching in a rounded picture of his own personality—of the man who has made that long series of drawings that for the last thirty or forty years have been among the least well-advertized but the most distinguished features of American satiric art.

These drawings of Art Young's themselves are not here very well represented. What one would like to have is an album with a selection, well reproduced, of specimens from all the various phases of the artist's long career, but especially from the period of his connection with the old *Masses,* when his talent had its freest scope and he was able to amaze even those who had admired him for years in *Life,* by his wit, his imagination and his sure and incisive line. The drawings in *On My Way* have been usually chosen to supplement the text. There are, for example, many sketches of celebrities which, although they have their own kind of interest—especially those of Mark Twain, in his old age, walking up Fifth Avenue in a silk hat and P. T. Barnum attending divine service—do not represent Art Young at his best. As he tells us himself, he is not a good caricaturist: he is rather a cartoonist than a caricaturist; and he is rather a straight ironic artist of the type of Steinlen and Forain (in whose country he would probably long ago have occupied a position of acknowledged importance) than a cartoonist of the type of Nast. Yet some of his fine things are here. One finds several of the best of his drawings in wash: the Dantesque "world of creepers," anxiously watching their neighbors, stopping their mouths so they may not speak, holding their hats in their hands, all afraid to lift their heads in a wilderness where there is nothing to fear but themselves; and the workman's kitchen, with its heavy human masses and its hands like catchers' mitts, in which the wife is saying to the husband: "There you go! You're tired! Here I be a-standin' over a hot stove all day, an' you workin' in a nice cool sewer!" There is the admirable line-drawing of the self-possessed old farmer that came out first in the *Dial* with the title *American Peasant* (did Art Young supply that title or the *Dial*?). And there are a number of remarkable little drawings which have evidently been made for the book and which recall those plates of Callot in which the human beings are seen on the scale of tiny tin soldiers, set up as a distant set of

ten-pins for some general or prince to knock over. As one
studies these delicate drawings, one feels that Art
Young himself should perhaps have been an engraver.
The slender figures of *New York Shadows* have been
cut out as clearly in the sunlight (the New York sunlight of yesterday) as their sharp silhouettes on the pave-
ment; and the tree-trunks of *A Speech in the Woods*—
through a rift in which a little human figure is seen
holding forth to a friend—have been given a palpability
of metal. One of the very best things in the book is Art
Young's sketch of himself—*Art Young on Trial for His
Life*—asleep at the *Masses* trial, when he and the
editors, at the time of the war, were being prosecuted for
conspiracy against the government: in a few hasty strokes
he has caught all that strange non-human moroseness,
that engulfing preoccupation, more earnest than any
anxiety, that comes over the faces of people who have
utterly succumbed to sleep.

The text of *On My Way*, necessarily, lacks the relief
of Art Young's drawings; but there is a good deal of insight and wisdom in the lightly delivered opinions: "I
have been reading another book by just another philosopher on the problem of adjusting one's self to this life
with a view to harmony. This time it is Keyserling. All
of these books, which are becoming more and more frequent, could be summed up as: speculations on how to
be happy by ignoring the economic equation in the
forming of conduct, health and happiness; or, how to
live comfortably in the realm of the spirit while living
at the same time in a hard materialistic world. These
philosophers are wild-goose-riders. It may not be wilful
quackery, but it is quackery of a sort." And though his
sketches of celebrities he has known seem sometimes a
little perfunctory, they have in other cases a weight of
underemphasis. Of Arthur Brisbane, under whom he

had worked on the *Journal* and who had said to him, when the *Masses* was started, "You boys are talking to yourselves!," he tells the following anecdote: "Once, after a political campaign meeting, we adjourned to Allaire's, and behind those mugs of ale—such as they served in days gone by—Brisbane talked, mostly about cartoons. When I would express an opinion, he had a beautiful way of saying, 'Do you think so?' Finally he said, 'Young, you ought to be making at least $15,000 a year.'

"Then I said, 'Do you think so?'

"In a few days I went down to Brisbane's office with some cartoons embodying ideas that we had talked over at Allaire's. I felt a little as if I were starting on the high-road to making $15,000 a year, with Brisbane's help. Brisbane looked over the cartoons and said, 'How much do you want for this one?' I named a sum about equal to my unpaid rent and a laundry bill—I think it was seventy-five dollars. Brisbane didn't want to pay that much. He told me the advantages of having my work circulated by the millions in the Hearst papers, and that years hence my cartoons might be worth that, but not now, and besides, he said, 'We can get a boy in the art department to draw the same idea—for thirty dollars a week.' When he got through with me, I felt I was in luck to have my cartoons accepted at all.

"I cite this to show that Brisbane, besides being the highest-salaried editor in the world (even at that time, he told me, he was making as much money as the President of the United States), was also a business man —close on figures. His towering Ritz apartments had not been built then, but he was investing in real estate throughout New York, and had a few seasonal homes. It all added to my wonderment as to how one man could crowd so much responsibility into the span of a lifetime, and why."

Such a story makes Brisbane's career, with all its great profits and its great publicity, seem hollower and more dismal than ever. The personality of such a man, in spite of his air of Olympian power, his ability to operate at a distance, to have himself read in millions of homes, has seemed actually to have been destroyed at some early stage of his life. When you met him, you felt the continual strain, the frustration and even the bewilderment, of one who had irrevocably surrendered to forces outside himself. Such a man does not really control the power he is supposed to represent; he has not made it serve as his weapon: he has himself been absorbed and dissolved. And, beside such a nullity, Art Young is seeen to have accomplished a feat which, in modern America, is difficult and rare: at the cost of popular success, and even of regular employment, he has managed to keep the shape of his personality and the quality of his intelligence. A man of Art Young's durability, however little we may publicly acknowledge it, performs an invaluable service in a society such as ours: he provides us with one of the touchstones of which we unconsciously make use in testing the soundness of character.

January 9, 1929

GREENWICH VILLAGE AT THE END OF THE TWENTIES*

I. 15 Beech Street

AMONG THE EMPTY streets of Greenwich Village, I could catch the rank saline smell of the river. It was as if, now that the people I knew had gone away to Provincetown or Woodstock, now that their world was shut up for the summer, the docks had closed in on our sanctuary. It made me feel rather desolate, and, in the humid dark, through the tangled streets, I drifted to 15 Beech Street. The light in the vestibule there was so dim that I could not see the names on the letter-boxes, so I did not attempt to ring the bell. I opened the heavy double doors and walked into the cavernous hall, with its waste of black-and-white linoleum, its steep and balustraded staircase, its gaunt square-topped radiator and its absolutely grisly hat-rack, of which the varnished ebon antlers and tentacles seemed to have been lopped in such a way as to give it the appearance of the still writhing skeleton of some unidentifiable creature and which was framed in an anomalous niche of imitation and putty-colored marble, the setting, at some prehistoric period, for some unimaginable vase or statue.

I climbed the forbidding stairs and tramped through

* The first of these pieces is fiction; the second, fact.

357

the vast corridors of several floors—of which even the unexpected sproutings and the mysterious interior windows (closely blinded from the inside with dusty cast-off cloths) seemed inhuman and inexpressive. I had come to see Jane Gooch, but I lingered at other doors. Some had strange cards or no cards, and the names that I knew did not answer. Those high halls, with their dismal lights, with their expanses of stale yellow plaster, with their flat odor of unventilated bathrooms and their monotonous trickle of defective toilets, closed me round with a void of abandonment even more formidable than that of the streets. Well, at least, I thought, here was one house which had not changed since I first came to the Village, which had not been demolished overnight to make room for a cliff of apartments, with electric refrigerators, meals "prepared by imported chefs" and, on the street level, smart new drug stores, uptown florists' shops and restaurants with current copies of *The Spur* and *Town and Country* to look at while one waited for a table.

I finally arrived at Jane Gooch's door and made out that her name was still there, and knocked. I waited. She was in: I heard movements at last, sounding ominous and seeming to draw near from a distance. Then she opened the door. She had just been going to bed and received me in a black kimono. The couch had been stripped of its cover and the bed-clothes underneath turned back. It was pleasant and reassuring, after the blank and empty grandeur of the hallways, to find a being so spare and distinguished—as it were, of so clear a significance. Jane Gooch had the straight back, the lankiness, the hatchet profile and the frank direct gaze of the ranches from which she had come: her eyes were very dark, and her smooth black hair, only a little gray, was parted straight in the middle; her gestures with her cigarette had a certain austere elegance.

I asked her if she knew Ralph Davis's address. She had at one time given him asylum in the room adjoining hers, as people often did in the Village and entirely without scandal. "Yes," she said, "he's somewhere out West, you know. I don't hear from him much nowadays, but I have a letter from him somewhere." She got up and began going through the drawers of an old mahogany desk. I looked about the room. Though she did all her cleaning herself, it showed the stamp of her sharp out-line and her neatness. On the white walls, above the row of bookshelves, were brass candlesticks with red candles in them, an oval daguerreotype of a rugged Wyoming grandfather, a black bowl of red holly-berries, an Alaskan illustration that Rockwell Kent had given her and two portraits of herself—one a charcoal drawing and the other a painting that presented her with green skin and half-shut eyes and made her look like a corpse. There were also photographs of Joe Livingston, with whom Jane had been in love and who had died of typhoid in Russia; of George Keppel, the Greenwich Village prophet and metaphysical poet, who had developed a Messianic delusion and had finally been put in jail for robbing Seventh Avenue fur stores (he gave all the furs to the poor, and Jane had worked with tireless zeal to get his sentence commuted); and of Linda Fyfe, that fascinat-ing girl painter, who was seen in the misty chiaroscu-resque picture with her wild bobbed head thrown back and her long lovely throat revealed: Ralph Davis had once lived with her, and she had gone in for male models —first the pretty young drunken poets, then the waiters from the Italian restaurants—and had almost driven him mad with jealousy.

I asked Jane what she heard from Linda, and she told me that she seemed very happy with the elderly banker she had married. I asked also what had become of the couple who had formerly lived across the hall. I had been rather in love with the girl at one time and had gone there a good deal, lured on by the possibility one always felt in the Village that the ménage might break up overnight: the elements were so unstable, and new combinations formed so quickly. Ross and Peggy had indeed broken up, Jane told me, and both were married now—she to the man who kept the Greenwich Village Rendezvous and made enough money to live uptown by selling bad whiskey and gin to people who came from uptown to drink it, and he to a charming little actress (*he* thought she was charming, Jane said) from a very respectable family in Cleveland, who had made her first appearance on Broadway as the ingénue in some play of Molnar's. Ross had a job now on one of the tabloids, and he had had his old Sullivan Street apartment, formerly one of the "mad-houses" of the Village, made over for his well-brought-up bride. "It's just like what you read about in the old novels," said Jane, "making a 'nest' for the bride! First nest I ever saw down here! All I ever knew them to do at most was have the bed made the night they got married. And they used to be ashamed of getting married!"

I saw that Jane looked tired. "Oh, don't bother any more," I said. She was going through great packets of old letters which she had excavated from the desk. "I'm sorry I've come so late and kept you up." "Oh, I don't mind at all," she said. "I'm glad to see you, in fact. Usually I spend the whole evening alone." "I thought you saw a lot of people," I said, "in connection with *Vortex* and the Hole-and-Corner Players." "I do, but very few of the old crowd." She was ransacking the lower bookshelves now and had struck the files of the *Worker,* which had been dislodged amid a cloud of dust. "How is the *New Worker* doing?" I asked. "Not so well, I guess," she replied. "They haven't got the spirit to make it go. When there were Dick Otis and Fred Bullard and Joe, that was different— because they had a Faith. But now nobody has much faith in the Revolution—I haven't myself. I see that Fritz Binney has grown a great big black beard to make him look like a Bolshevik—but it's more like the Bearded Lady. 'Two owls and a hen, Four larks and a wren, Have all built their nests in my beard!' And so they have—his boy friends that help him with the paper."

I inquired about *Vortex,* the little magazine that she published herself. "Well, we're planning a big hydraulic number," she said (she always said "we," though her original collaborators had long ago ceased to be active), "as soon as we can raise enough money." (It came out at irregular intervals and in widely varying sizes and shapes.) "Hydraulic?" "Yes: pipes and oil pumps and plumbing fixtures—and all those things. We've got some photographs of bathrooms by Leo Kleist that are the most marvellous things you ever saw. There's a series —of wash-basins at different angles—that looks just like the tomb of the Medicis. And then there are some paint- ings by Jacques Ducran of oil stations out on the Coast— bright red and orange and bright blue and gold—they look like something Chinese.—Look at this!" She showed me a still-life in rich brown and yellow, with a back- ground of dazzling white. "Isn't that luscious? That's a rubber bath-sponge and a cake of kitchen soap. Of course, people will laugh at us, but we're used to that— and if anything is going to be done to bring the American public to a real appreciation of art—to a realization of the beauty, of the possibilities for beauty, of these things that they use every day—it will have to be done in the teeth of the hoots and the howls and the jeers of all the kept art critics of the bourgeois magazines. I believe that

if we can only raise money enough to have color repro-
ductions made, we'll be able to put over something big.
I saw Max Beaumont yesterday, and he promised me half
of what it would cost, if I could raise the other half. If
I could only get the bills for the last number paid!" (The
last *Vortex* had appeared eighteen months before.) "The
printers are threatening to sue me. I'll have to give them
my salary from the theater this month. And my own bill
collectors wake me up at half-past seven every morning!"
She laughed. "Oh, here it is!" she said, taking a letter
out of its envelope. "Oh, that's fine," I went on to explain: "I'm editing a series of poets, and I wanted to
try to get something from Ralph. I always thought he
was awfully good and that he ought to have published a
book. He had that real disequilibrium of the nerves that
seems to make the best poets. The world really looked to
Ralph just as wild as the deliriums he describes in his
poetry. It made him a little bit difficult personally, because he was always either frightened and suspicious, or
full of delusions of grandeur—especially when he was
drunk. But life must have been an even worse strain
for him than he made it for other people—and when
you thought of what wonderful things he wrote, you
were willing to put up with anything." "Here's a picture
that he sent me," said Jane, taking a photograph out of
the letter, "of him and his wife and their cow. Puzzle:
find the cow. It was taken to illustrate that article, you
know, that he wrote for the *Cosmopolitan*: *I Have Tried
Free Love and Now I Own a Cow*—or something like
that, it was called." "Does it tell his address?" I asked.
"Yes," she dictated it to me. "Care of the *Weekly Fal-
coner,* Falcon Motors, 1192 Penobscot Boulevard, Detroit."

June 29, 1927

II. Hans Stengel

HANS STENGEL, who committed suicide in New York the night of January 28, was a man of considerable gifts who had never found his proper field. His parents were German and at the time that I first met him, he had just come over from Germany, where he had been associated, in Munich, with the group that produced *Simplicissimus*. He had begun by studying painting, but had developed a knack for caricature, which he hoped to turn to account; and, soon after he arrived in New York, he brought his caricatures to the office of *Vanity Fair*, with which I was then connected. They were vigorous and effective drawings of the modern German school, harsh, mordant, sometimes monstrous, sometimes gruesome. But they were, I knew, a kind of thing for which there was little demand. The prevailing taste at that time was for the agreeable triviality and the thin distinction of line of French or English drawing: and Hans Stengel was not merely too harsh, but also, in a sense, too serious. There was then, I believe, in New York, not a single editor of a magazine who would have looked at Stengel's work a second time. The *Liberator*, I think, had already gone out of business; and he could never have made a living by contributing to it. I remember feeling rather ashamed that I could not be more encouraging, that a man of evident talent, who had studied in a sound school, should be met by such a meager prospect of marketing his work in New York. Thereafter, when one encountered his drawings in the magazines and Sunday papers to which, by dint of persistence, he sometimes succeeded in selling them, one saw that he was being cramped by an effort to keep within the limits of what seemed to him the timid and complacent, the

unimaginative American taste. He occupied at one time
the position of principal caricaturist for the Sunday
Herald Tribune, and his best work in the United States
was probably done for this paper; but, as a German with
a strong accent, he had against him both prejudice and
fashion; and during the last year before his death he had
been reduced to turning out a series for a cheap evening
paper, a silly daily "feature" from which he had been
obliged to eliminate everything that made his work
original and which he refused to sign.

It is always difficult, in a given case, to estimate how
far a good artist may have been discouraged from doing
his best by a lack of demand for his work. It is possible
that a caricaturist of the very first rank might have been
able to force New York to accept him. But one cannot
doubt, in Stengel's case, that the talent he had was stifled.
One felt always that there was a great deal in him that
had no field for artistic expression. He was intelligent;
he knew a good deal of the world; he talked extremely
well. There was more imagination and wit in his ordinary
conversation than in anything he drew or wrote (for he
sometimes tried his hand at writing). He was the son of
a German actor, the director of the municipal theater at
Lübeck, and he had cultivated a special instinct, which
must have been theatrical in origin, for building up his
monologues to cumulative effect and exploiting his personality. He was well-equipped to dominate an audience:
he was more than six feet tall; he had served during the
war in the German army and he cultivated the shaved
head and something of the imperious manner (he had
early discarded the monocle) of the traditional Prussian
officer. He was therefore to be seen at his best advantage
when he was holding the attention of a group of people,
at dinner or at one of his Saturday nights; and he had
become, with little money to entertain, one of the

most popular hosts of Greenwich Village. Mencken, Dreiser and Robert Chanler were among his friends in New York; and at a period when the Village had lost most of its old romance with the most remarkable of its old leaders, he stood out as one of the only personalities capable of attracting about him a regular company of friends and admirers. He displayed, on these occasions, a vein of ironic commentary, fantastic but also acute, which, as I say, surpassed anything in his journalism. He was also, for all his Prussian pose, capable of generosity and a certain sensitive feeling; and he loved to live in the grand style. He was able to succeed, to an extraordinary degree, in interesting people in his personal fate and, in spite of furious quarrellings and fallings-out, in commanding their continued loyalty.

For such a man to wait upon editors and do hackwork for the American newspapers was, of course, peculiarly difficult. He was proud, and when his pride was in question, he would immediately resign his job; and though his incapacity for adjusting himself undoubtedly depressed him more and more, one was always struck, when one saw him after one of these ruptures had occurred, by the unmistakable relief of an independent spirit which would not for a time have to strain any more to conform to the requirements of men less intelligent and bold than he. His career since he had come to New York, in spite of his ups and downs, had always enabled him to live pretty well and would have been thought by many people not unenviable; but for Stengel, it was deeply unsatisfactory. He always seemed to regard caricature itself as rather beneath his dignity; and when, last winter, the proprietor of a night club offered him a large salary to act as master of ceremonies—a position for which his gift of holding the attention of an audience unquestionably fitted him well—he refused to consider it except as a joke. During the last few months of his life, he had set himself to write a novel—a novel in which, apparently, a simple sentimental German boy was to contrast with a cynical and arrogant Junker. Perhaps the most striking feature of Hans Stengel's character was his capacity for passionate feeling: he astounded even the inhabitants of Greenwich Village—by no means free, despite their reputation, from the pervasive indifference and tepidity of contemporary American life—by the violence of his despairs and exhilarations. Just as, in spite of the fact that Stengel spoke excellent English, and the English of a man with a literary ear, he spoke it always with German consonants and with many German locutions, so in New York he remained always a foreigner, who was fascinating to people partly because he represented something exotic, and who was never assimilated. It is natural to put down a failure to survive in one's own community—where we ourselves have no difficulty in prospering—to the deficiencies of the person who fails; but it is sometimes a good idea to inquire into the deficiencies of one's civilization from the point of view of what it destroys. Hans Stengel, in the course of the last year, had talked often of returning to Berlin; but New York had, after all, become his home at the same time that his existence here had come to seem to him hopeless. At one of his evening parties—unknown to the guests, but always with a sense of his audience—he shut himself into the coat-closet, tied a rope to his neck and the door-knob and, pulling against it, strangled himself. He was missed by his guests, and they found him there. His body has been cremated, and his ashes are to be scattered to the waters of that city to which he came so few years ago, a young man with his portfolio of drawings.

February 23, 1928

THE CRITIC WHO DOES NOT EXIST

IN PAUL VALÉRY'S address to the Académie Française on the occasion of his succeeding Anatole France, there is a passage in which he describes the literary situation in Paris as he found it in his youth. There were, he says, a number of different parties, each with its own definite set of policies and each with an eminent writer, or group of eminent writers, at its head. There were Zola and the naturalists; Leconte de Lisle and the Parnassians; Renan and Taine and the *"idéologues"*; Mallarmé and the symbolists. These parties stated their programs and defended them against each other: they played roles in a literary politics equally exciting and equally important with politics of the other sort. When five of Zola's followers seceded from his party over the publication of *La Terre*, the event was profoundly significant: it was the first attack in a great campaign. When Valéry, received by the Academy, reasserts the claims of symbolism, at one time a literary minority, in a speech on the career of his predecessor, one of the leaders of a different camp—that is, again, an historic event and marks the success of a revolution. The French writers whom we read most today—France, Gourmont, Proust, Valéry, Gide—all came to intellectual maturity in this atmosphere of debate; and this gives them a kind of interest—the interest of the intelligence fully awakened to the implications of

what the artist is doing, that is to say, to his responsibility
—very rare in the literature of English-speaking countries, and nowadays perhaps nowhere to be found in any
very intense degree save, on a smaller scale, in Dublin.
For there is one language which all French writers, no
matter how divergent their aims, always possess in common: the language of criticism.

When we come to survey the literary landscape of contemporary America, it seems to us at first that nothing
could resemble less the clear political alignments that are
nearly always to be found in France. But then, as we
examine the prospect more closely, we are surprised to
become aware of the presence both of able leaders and
of powerful parties, each professing more or less explicitly
a point of view and acting more or less consistently on a
set of principles. There is, in the first place, H. L.
Mencken, with his satellite George Jean Nathan, his disciple Sinclair Lewis, and his literary nursery, the *Mercury*. Then there is T. S. Eliot, who, despite the fact
that he lives in England and has recently become a British
subject, exerts a tremendous influence in America and
is always regarded by his American readers as still an
American writer. It may be said that Mencken and Eliot
between them rule the students of the Eastern universities: when the college magazines do not sound like
Mencken's *Mercury*, they sound like Eliot's *Criterion*.
Then there is the group of writers—it is a group that
does not have any unity and is almost entirely without
critical self-consciousness—of what may be called the
neo-romantics, of which Edna Millay and Scott Fitzgerald, with their respective imitators and followers, are
the leaders in the present generation, and which had for
precursors such writers as Sara Teasdale, Joseph Hergesheimer and perhaps also James Branch Cabell. Then
there is the more or less organized and highly self-

conscious group of the social revolutionary writers: John Dos Passos, John Howard Lawson, Michael Gold, etc. Their organs are the *New Masses* and the Playwright's Theater. One should mention also—though they constitute a school rather than a group—the psychologico-sociological critics: Van Wyck Brooks, Lewis Mumford (whom I take to be a disciple of Brooks), Joseph Wood Krutch and a number of others.

What we lack, then, in the United States, is not writers or even literary parties, but simply serious literary criticism (the school of critics I have mentioned last, though they set forth their own ideas, do not occupy themselves much with the art or ideas of the writers with whom they deal). Each of these groups does produce, to be sure, a certain amount of criticism to justify or explain what it is doing, but it may, I believe, be said in general that they do not communicate with one another; their opinions do not really circulate. It is astonishing to observe, in America, in spite of our floods of literary journalism, to what extent the literary atmosphere is a non-conductor of criticism. What actually happens, in our literary world, is that each leader or group of leaders is allowed to intimidate his disciples, either ignoring all the other leaders or taking cognizance of their existence only by distant and contemptuous sneers. H. L. Mencken and T. S. Eliot present themselves, as I have said, from the critical point of view, as the most formidable figures on the scene; yet Mencken's discussion of his principal rival has, so far as my memory goes, been confined to an inclusion of the latter's works among the items of one of those lists of idiotic current crazes in which the editor of the *Mercury* usually includes also the recall of judges and paper-bag cookery. And Eliot, established in London, does not, of course, consider himself under the necessity of dealing with

Mencken at all. Similarly, George Jean Nathan scoffs at the plays of Lawson and has never been willing to take seriously the movement he represents; and the *New Masses* has never gone further than an occasional gibe at Mencken. Van Wyck Brooks, in spite of considerable baiting, has never been induced to defend his position (though Krutch has recently taken up some challenges). And the romantics have been belabored by the spokesmen of several different camps without making any attempt to strike back. It, furthermore, seems unfortunate that some of our most important writers—Sherwood Anderson and Eugene O'Neill, for example—should work, as they apparently do, in almost complete intellectual isolation, receiving from the outside but little intelligent criticism and developing, in their solitary labors, little capacity for supplying it themselves.

Now, it is no doubt impossible for an English-speaking country to hope for a literary criticism comparable to that of the French: like cookery, it is one of their specialties. But when one considers the number of reviews, the immense amount of literary journalism that is now being published in New York, one asks oneself how it is possible for our reviewing to remain so puerile. Works on history are commonly reviewed by historians, and books on physics by physicists; but when a new book of American poetry or a novel or other work of belles lettres appears, one gets the impression that it is simply given to almost any well-intentioned (and not even necessarily literate) person who happens to present himself; and this person then describes in a review his emotions upon reading the book. How many works of general literature are ever officially discussed in New York by people with any special knowledge of the subjects on which they are invited to write? Since the death of Stuart P. Sherman, who was second-rate at best, there

has not been a single American critic who regularly
occupied himself in any authoritative way with contemporary literature. Yet what might not have been the
effect on Sinclair Lewis, for example, and on the great
army of Mencken's younger followers, if Mencken had
been systematically and periodically overhauled by a
critic of equal vigor? What might not have been the
effect on all that new crop of poets who have been made
prematurely senile by imitating Eliot's *Gerontion,* if a
critic as intelligent as the people who ridiculed *The
Waste Land* were stupid had, while doing full justice to
Eliot, made fun of this tendency in time? Do not the
champions of proletarian literature deserve the hard-
hitting polemics which their appetite for controversy invites? And might not a critic who enjoyed Lawson's wit
and valued his technical inventions have been of some
service in discouraging his bathos and his bad rhetoric?
And those scattered contemporary romantics who, since
the war, have been repeating over here all the poses, the
philosophy and the methods of the Europe of 1830—instead of finding themselves stalled, bewildered, out of
date almost as soon as they were famous, if their situation
had in time been a little cleared up by a competent
criticism, might they not have already readjusted themselves and applied their brilliant abilities to the production of something more durable? Finally, with the advent
of a new generation, there has emerged from our literature of the past a number of important names, a number
of writers whom we are all agreed in regarding as of first-
rate quality: Emerson, Hawthorne, Thoreau, Whitman,
Melville, Poe, Stephen Crane, Henry James. Yet so far
the studies by American hands which have dealt with
these American classics have been almost exclusively
biographical. We have been eager to expose the weaknesses and curious to probe the neuroses of these ranking

American writers, but have found little to say that was interesting as to why we should consider them so. Have we not been unfortunate in the lack of a criticism which should have undertaken, for example, to show how Hawthorne, Melville and Poe, besides becoming excessively eccentric persons, anticipated, in the middle of the last century, the temperament of our own day and invented methods for rendering it?

I do not of course mean to assert that, except on the lower levels, any criticism, however able, could make or unmake artists. A work of art is not a set of ideas or an exercise of technique, or even a combination of both. But I am strongly disposed to believe that our contemporary writing would benefit by a genuine literary criticism that should deal expertly with ideas and art, not merely tell us whether the reviewer "let out a whoop" for the book or threw it out the window. In a sense, it can probably be said that no such creature exists as a full-time literary critic—that is, a writer who is at once first-rate and nothing but a literary critic: there are writers of poetry, drama or fiction who also write criticism, like most of the French writers mentioned above and like Coleridge, Dryden, Poe and Henry James; and there are historians like Renan, Taine, Saint-Beuve, Leslie Stephen and Brandes whose literary criticism is a part of their history. In America, neither kind of criticism has been very highly developed; and I fear that we must take this as a sign of the rudimentary condition of our literature in general. The poets, the dramatists and the novelists too often lack the learning and the cultivated intelligence to give us in works of art the full benefit of the promising material supplied by experience and imagination; and it may in general be said that where our writers of biography and history fail is precisely in their inability to deal adequately with works of literature.

February 1, 1928

A WEEKEND AT ELLERSLIE

In February, 1928, I had from Scott Fitzgerald a letter, headed "Ellerslie," Edgemoor, Delaware, which—although it may not at once be clear—was an invitation to visit him:

. . . All is prepared for February 25th. The stomach pumps are polished and set out in rows, stale old enthusiasms are being burnished with that zeal peculiar only to the British Tommy. My God, how we felt when the long slaughter of Paschendale had begun. Why were the generals all so old? Why were the Fabian society discriminated against when positions on the general staff went to dukes and sons of profiteers? Agitators were actually hooted at in Hyde Park and Anglican divines actually didn't become humanitarian internationalists over night. What is Briton coming to—where is Milton, Cromwell, Oates, Monk? Where are Shaftsbury, Athelstane, Thomas à Becket, Margot Asquith, Iris March? Where are Blackstone, Touchstone, Clapham-Hopewellton, Stoke-Poges? Somewhere back at G.H.Q. handsome men with grey whiskers murmured "We will charge them with the cavalry" and meanwhile boys from Bovril and the black country sat shivering in the lagoons at Ypres writing memoirs for liberal novels about the war. What about the tanks? Why did not Douglas Haig or Sir John French (the big smarties) (Look what they did to General Mer-

373

cer) invent tanks the day the war broke out, like Sir Philip Gibbs the weeping baronet, did or would, had he thought of it?

This is just a *sample* of what you will get on the 25th of Feb. There will be small but select company, coals, blankets, "something for the inner man."

Please don't say you can't come the 25th but would like to come the 29th. We never receive people the 29th. It is the anniversary of the 2nd Council of Nicaea when our Blessed Lord, Our Blessed Lord, our Blessed Lord, our Blessed Lord—

It always gets stuck in that place. Put on *Old Man River* or something of Louis Bromfield's.

Pray gravity to move your bowels. It's little we get done for us in this world. Answer.

Scott

Enjoyed your Wilson article enormously. Not so Thompson affair.

An invidious salutation, which I here omit; the parody in the first paragraph of what Scott evidently imagined to be the attitude of the liberal weekly on which I was then working (I could not make out why the war should be uppermost in his mind); and the reference to my having been obliged to decline an earlier invitation—all combined to produce the effect of a slightly hostile overtone. The Wilson article mentioned in the postscript was the one that appears in this volume under the title *Woodrow Wilson at Princeton*. The "Thompson affair" was an article called *Vanzetti's Last Statement*, an account by Mr. W. G. Thompson, counsel for Sacco and Vanzetti, of his last interview with his clients the day before their execution, which the *New Republic* had reprinted from the *Atlantic Monthly* and a copy of which I had sent to Scott along with the Wilson piece. I gathered that he

meant to indicate that he did not necessarily range himself on my side of an issue that had, the summer before,
given rise to a split of opinion almost as bitter as that
created by the Dreyfus case. I had seen very little of
Scott since he had taken his family to Europe in 1924,
and I was aware that our personal relations had suffered
a certain chill. It was partly that, from college days, when
I had been a year ahead of him and the editor of the
magazine, he had come to regard himself as somehow
accountable to me for his literary career, and that he had
been struggling unsatisfactorily with his most ambitious
project to date, a novel of matricide, which he had started
in 1925. He had learned very fast as a writer; his ideals
for his art had gone rapidly up. Each of his three novels,
from the point of view of form and conception, had been
a startling improvement on the one before. He had now
gone on to tackle a subject that might well have taxed
Dostoevsky, and he was eventually to find it beyond him.
It must have been a psychological "block" as well as the
invincible compulsion to live like a millionaire that led
him even more than usual to interrupt his serious work
and turn out stories for the commercial magazines. At any
rate, *Tender Is the Night* did not appear till 1934, when
his original subject—the mother theme dropped—was
seen to have modulated into something quite different.
In the meantime, I had always felt that he was expecting
me to point a finger at him and say, "What has become
of that novel?" It was his own artistic conscience that
accused him, but this was beginning to make our meetings uncomfortable, for any inquiry about his work was
likely to bring a sharp retort. But he evidently wanted to
see me, so I went.

I had never yet visited the Fitzgeralds in the house just
outside Wilmington that they had taken on their return

from Europe at the end of 1927, but rumors had reached me of festivities on a more elaborate scale than their old weekends at Westport or Great Neck. Dos Passos had attended a party that Scott had given for his thirtieth birthday, which he described to me as "a regular wake"— Scott had been lamenting the passing of youth ever since his twenty-first birthday, and he had apparently commemorated his twenties with veritable funeral games. I had certainly never seen Scott and Zelda in such a magnificent setting. Ellerslie, Edgemoor, turned out to be a handsome old big square white house, with Greek columns and high-ceilinged rooms. It had been built in the early eighteen-forties and had always up to then been occupied by the managers of the Edgemoor Iron Company. I arrived there with Thornton Wilder, whom I had not known before and whose books I had not read. Scott had had us met at the station, and, in the course of the drive to Ellerslie, we had talked about Marcel Proust. I had just read the final instalment of A la Recherche du Temps Perdu, which had reached New York not long before, and was about to describe it to Wilder. There are few things I enjoy so much as talking to people about books which I have read but they haven't, and making them wish they had—preferably a book that is hard to get or in a language that they do not know. But in this case my expectation was disappointed, for it turned out that Wilder had been following Proust just as attentively as I had and had read Le Temps Retrouvé as promptly. I had had the impression that his novels were rather on the fragile and precious side, and was surprised to find him a person of such positive and even peppery opinions. He had his doubts about Le Temps Retrouvé; he declared that too many of the characters turned out to be homosexual. Charlus was all right, he said; but in the case of Saint-Loup, for example, some further explanation was needed: there was a psychological problem there that Proust had simply shirked. I called his attention to the fact that the novel ended with the phrase "*dans le temps*," as it had begun with the key sentence, "*Longtemps, je me suis couché de bonne heure*," and he said he had noticed this.

Scott met his guests at the door and, the moment their hats and coats were off, took them for a tour of the house, of which he was extremely proud and which he was doing his best to live up to. He would stop in one of the corridors and say mysteriously, "Don't you hear something? Don't you hear something strange?—It's the old Ellerslie ghost." He had posted the butler behind a door to groan and rattle a chain. But at a time when the whole house was buzzing with life and everybody looking forward to cocktails, these sounds did not even attract attention, and the clanking of a chain would, in any case, hardly have meant anything to anyone not fresh from a Gothic novel. We were next taken into a room, where we were given, for our entertainment, a choice of listening to records— which were still a novelty then—of *Le Sacre du Printemps* or of looking at an album of photographs of horribly mutilated soldiers. Scott had discovered the war, and this explained the antiquated allusions of his letter, as well as his just having pointed out to me, hanging on the wall of his study, the trench-helmet which, not having been sent overseas, he had never worn in action. At the time when he had been in the army, he must have been exclusively occupied with the first version of *This Side of Paradise* and his romance with Zelda in Alabama, for it was as if the unpleasant events of 1914-18 were now touching his imagination for the first time. They must have been brought to his notice by his friend Ernest Hemingway, of whom he had seen a good deal in Europe and who was then writing *A Farewell to Arms*. Preliminary drinks were served, but we had not got far with Stravinsky before we were taken outside and involved in a chaotic interlude, of which I can remember—on the darkening lawn—only playing diabolo while carrying on a conversation about Ford Madox Ford.

The crescendo of the evening was well under way when we had our pre-dinner drinks in a large and splendid salon. Gilbert and "Amanda" Seldes were there, and Esther Strachey, the sister of Scott's great friend Gerald Murphy. In a conversation with Seldes and me, Scott somehow got around to inviting us frankly to criticize his character. Gilbert told him that if he had a fault, it was making life seem rather dull; and this quite put him out of countenance till we both began to laugh. John and Anna Biggs arrived. John Biggs was an old friend of Scott's and mine, who had roomed with Scott in college. He practised law in Wilmington—though he was just about to publish his second novel—and it was he who had got Scott established at Ellerslie. I had not seen John since his marriage, and Scott explained Anna to me: "She was one of the famous Rupert girls—don't you remember the beautiful Rupert sisters that were such a sensation at the proms?" In the atmosphere of exhilaration that the Fitzgeralds always generated on these occasions, I was called upon to give them an act that I had sometimes performed years before—after the summer of 1916 at Plattsburg—at convivial college gatherings. This was an impersonation of a Regular Army officer giving a hoarse-voiced lecture on Scouting and Patrolling. Major Waldron, red-faced and bespectacled, standing with his heels together and his arms held stiff at his sides, would bark out, without a gesture or a flicker of expression, such instructions as: "Places of concealment: trees and roofs of houses. If you climb on roof of house, be sure to keep on side that's hidden—side that's away from enemy. Don't get on side exposed to enemy. Scout that gets on side exposed to enemy can be seen by enemy and shot. Scout must keep from getting shot. Scout's no good if he's dead." I had completely forgotten this, but John Biggs fed it back to me, and I did my best to oblige, though I was really not up to it any more. At some point either just before or just after this, Scott took me aside in another room and told me that he had been harboring a grievance against me. It was something that had happened a long time before—he felt that I had behaved with him and Zelda in a way that he ought to resent. I thought it was all nonsense—especially as coming from him; but since Scott, like Dr. Johnson, considered himself an authority on manners, I tried to explain my offense away, and something like our old good relations seemed to be reëstablished.

Then a drove of new people arrived. A play of Zoë Akins'—*The Furies*—was being tried out in Wilmington, and the Fitzgeralds had invited her to dinner, with the designer of the sets and costumes and three or four other men who were also involved in the production. At dinner, we were floating divinely on good wine and gay conversation, in which I noted, however, that Wilder, though extremely responsive, remained sharply and firmly non-soluble. He was talking with Esther Strachey about Colette, and saying that there were some of the Claudine books that he thought were pretty good. I sat next to Zelda, who was at her iridescent best. Some of Scott's friends were irritated, others were enchanted, by her. I was one of the ones who were charmed. She had the waywardness of a Southern belle and the lack of inhibitions of a child. She talked with so spontaneous a color and wit—almost exactly in the way she wrote—that I very soon ceased to be troubled by the fact that the conversation was in the nature of a "free association" of ideas and one could never follow up anything. I have rarely known a woman who expressed herself so delightfully and so freshly: she had no readymade phrases on the one hand and made no straining for effect on the other. It evaporated easily, however, and I remember only one thing she said that night: that the writing of Galsworthy was a shade of blue for which she did not care. But as the dinner went on, Miss Akins began to dominate the conversation. She was herself an accomplished performer in a more grandiose tradition than that of the unceremonious twenties, and she was presently holding the table with resounding speeches from Shakespeare. This rather threw out the Fitzgeralds, who were used to the center of the stage and preferred a more playful tone, and when Miss Akins and her companions had left in order to get to the theater, Scott, who had been charming at the beginning of dinner, now grumbled: "All that memorized Shakespeare!" This was followed by a complete anticlimax. Scarcely had we left the table when the Fitzgeralds announced they were going to bed and left the guests to shift for themselves. I soon went to bed myself.

But this, though I saw nothing more, was by no means the end of the evening. The party from Miss Akins' play had been invited to come back when the performance was over, and, with the exception of Miss Akins herself, they did. Zelda, having had her sleep, decided to emerge again, and, coming into one of the spacious rooms, discovered the little designer, alone, leaning moodily on the marble mantel. "Please go away," he said. "I'm thinking, and I don't want to be disturbed." "Oh, you're not really thinking," said Zelda, for whom, as for all Southern women, any highhanded tone on the part of a man stimulated immediate insolence. "You're just homogeneous!" This could hardly have been due to ignorance: it must have been a species of euphemism intended to soften the remark; but, in any case, its effect was terrible. The young man stalked out of the room and complained to his companions of an insult, and, demanding the Fitzgeralds' car, they all huffily left.

I do not think that Scott, who had slept all night, heard anything about this incident till Zelda got up late the next morning. I remember his sitting around in his bathrobe and reading to Gilbert Seldes and me what must have been one of the early Riviera chapters from his novel then in progress, which was to turn into *Tender Is the Night*. There was especially one dazzling passage with which he had evidently taken much pains and on which he must have counted to stun us. It presented a group of attractive girls—on a beach or in a room, I can't remember—but in any case floating and glowing in richest Fitzgerald glamor. "What do you think of that description?" he asked. We told him we thought it was splendid. "I read this chapter to Dos Passos, when he was here," he said, "and afterwards he said that he liked it 'all except that part,' he said, 'that's so wonderful.' I asked him what he meant, and he said, 'Oh, you know: that part that's so wonderful—that part that's so perfectly marvellous.'" This may have led him to leave it out, or he may have had to scrap it with his original subject, for I cannot now find this passage, in any form I can recognize, in *Tender Is the Night*. Thornton Wilder, who had left early that morning, was, I found, Scott's most recent enthusiasm. He told me that *The Cabala* was the very best thing that had come out, I think, since Hemingway —he did not care so much for *The Bridge of San Luis Rey*. I must absolutely read it—he would send it to me.

But the news of the incident of the night before, when Scott heard of it, profoundly disturbed him. It had been a breach of hospitality, and he must do what he could to repair it. He would look up the offended guests and try to smooth the incident over. He set out in his car after lunch, taking along Esther Strachey and me to talk to him and support his morale. On the way, he questioned the driver—of whom he seemed to have made a trusted familiar—as to what the guests had said while he was taking them home. "Why, the little fellow said, 'Fitzgerald thinks he's got a swell place there, but an uncle of mine's got a house that makes that house look like a dump!' " This visibly depressed Scott, and Esther and I tried to dissuade him from pursuing the matter further; but, "It's only very seldom," he insisted, "that you get a real opportunity to hear what people say about you behind your back.—Didn't anybody," he turned to the driver, "have anything good to say about me?" "There was one that tried to speak up for you," the man replied, "but they had him down on the bottom, with their feet on him." Scott found out in Wilmington that the theater people were not all at the hotel with Miss Akin, and since it looked as if it might take him some time to run them down and to deal with the problem properly, he sent us back to the house. He wanted to make them come back, so that Zelda and he could be nice to them.

The aftermath of a Fitzgerald evening was notoriously a painful experience. I suddenly became terribly irritable and said something sarcastic to Esther about what seemed to me certain chi-chi attitudes that she had recently picked up in Paris. She replied—with great moderation in view of what must have been on my part a very disagreeable tone: "You have an intellectual arrogance that is sometimes very trying." I was somewhat piqued by this—let me say that my friendship of many years with this brilliant and most amiable woman has otherwise been quite unclouded—and I made up my mind that I would leave late in the afternoon. I did not want to see the theater people again; I could not face another evening. It seemed to me the party was slipping, and I knew that when these parties of the Fitzgeralds slipped they were likely to end in disaster. I knew that if I stayed through another night, I should be no good Monday. I was getting too old for this kind of thing. I found that I did not, however, have money for the railroad fare, so I asked Scott, when he came back, to cash a check. He had no money either and tried to persuade me to stay. When I insisted, he went away with the check and then came back to let me know that Esther Strachey was the only person in the house who had ten dollars to spare. This was very embarrassing to me, but Esther was neither embarrassed nor embittered, and the whole thing became a joke.

I later heard that Scott had waked up in the night and decided that he had not done justice to the possibilities of the Ellerslie ghost. He put a sheet over his head and invaded the Seldeses' room. Standing beside their bed, he began to groan in a way that he hoped was an improvement on the butler. But Gilbert started up from his sleep and gave a swipe with his arm at the sheet, which caught fire from a cigarette that the ghost was smoking inside his shroud. In the turmoil, something else caught fire, and everybody was rather alarmed.

Scott sent me a copy of *The Cabala*, which I read with much admiration; and that summer I wrote for the *New Republic* the article on Wilder that follows. In rereading it, this Wilmington weekend has come back into my mind so vividly that, in view of the recent interest in the Fitzgeralds and the twenties generally, I have thought it might be worth while to put on record here this specimen of the literary life of a period in which nonsense and inspiration, reckless idealism and childish irresponsibility, were mingled in so queer a way.

1952

THORNTON WILDER

Now that Mr. Thornton Wilder has become both a best-seller and a Pulitzer prize-winner, he is in an unfortunate situation. On the one hand, the literary columnists have accepted him as a Reputation and gossip about him with respect but without intelligence; and, on the other, the literary snobs have been driven by his tremendous popularity, by the obsequious gossips themselves, into talking as if they took it for granted that there must be something meretricious about him. Mr. Wilder remains, however, a remarkably interesting writer, with a good deal to be said about him which no one, so far as I know, has said.

One of the things about Mr. Wilder that I do not think has yet been said is that he seems to be the first American novelist who has been influenced deeply by Proust. In devoting some attention to this subject, I do not at all mean to imply a lack of originality on Mr. Wilder's part: on the contrary, it is quite extraordinary that a novelist so young should display, from the first page of his very first book, so accomplished a mastery of a form and a point of view so much his own. The Proust influence seems simply the influence of a first-rate senior writer on a first-rate junior one. And what Mr. Wilder has learned from Proust is not merely Proust's complex impressionism: the side of Proust that Sacheverell Sitwell imitated in *All*

Summer in a Day does not figure in Mr. Wilder at all.
He has listened to Proust's very heart, and his own has
been timed to its beat. It is not so much a formula of
style that Thornton Wilder has taken, though there are
echoes of Proust's style, too, but a formula of emotion,
of the criticism of life. And in order to estimate his work,
we should try to discover which part of it represents the
poet Wilder himself, from whom quite un-Proustian
things may eventually be expected, and which part is
mere repetition of cadences caught from the asthmatic
master.

One of Proust's favorite formulas, then—which we
find in almost every situation of *A la Recherche du
Temps Perdu*—is that of an abject and agonizing love on
the part of a superior for an inferior person, or at least
on the part of a gentle person for a person who behaves
toward him with cruelty. Mr. Wilder seems infatuated
with this, and he leans on it a little too heavily. It figures
less conspicuously in *The Cabala* than in *The Bridge of
San Luis Rey*; but the episode of Alix in the former book,
which seems to me also the episode that carries the least
conviction, is simply a reversal of the Proustian relationship in which we are shown a charming and sensitive
man breaking his heart for an unworthy woman: the part
played for Swann by Odette, for Saint-Loup by Rachel
and for Proust's hero by Albertine, is played for Alix by
Blair. One finds, also, everywhere in *The Cabala* unmistakable Proustian turns of phrase; the author has even
taken over a favorite expression of Proust's—a sort of
proverbial phrase in French, which I have never seen
before in English: he likes to talk about somebody or
other "making the fair weather" of somebody else, as
Swann made *"la pluie et le beau temps"* of the Duchesse
de Guermantes. And one finds in *The Cabala*, also, one
passage where the typical Proustian note of hypochon-

driacal melancholy is brought almost to the point of burlesque: a Helen Darrell, a famous beauty, enters the story suddenly like one of those unannounced characters in Proust's social scenes. We are not told precisely what is wrong with her, but, like so many of the characters in *A la Recherche*, she is ill and very soon to die; none of her dearest friends dares to kiss her: they feel that she is blighted and doomed. "She was like a statue in solitude. She presuffered her death." Yet the unfortunate Alix envies her: "He would have loved me," she breathes in the hero's ear, "if I had looked like that. . . . She is beautiful. She is beautiful," he hears her mutter. "The world is hers. She will never have to suffer as I must." The dying beauty asks, before she goes, to be taken to say good-by to a saintly old French poet, who is also about to die. "One wonders what they said to one another as she knelt beside his chair: as he said later, they loved one another because they were ill." I have cited this passage at length because it shows Thornton Wilder when he has slipped into writing pure Proust and when, as it seems to me, he is least successful. Proust's characters are always ill, and Proust thinks that a languishing illness is the most pathetic thing on earth—but he has in French the special advantage of words made for him: *malade* and *maladie*, which he is able to introduce with a mournful and ominous accent that prevents us from becoming impatient with his eternal incurable invalids. Now, the words *ill* and *sick* hardly lend themselves to any such mournful magic: when, in English, you hear that someone is ill, you at once ask what treatment he is taking.

In *The Bridge of San Luis Rey*, the Proustian spirit pervades the book. The Marquesa de Montemayor is made to distil marvellous literature from her love for her selfish daughter, just as Vinteuil in Proust is made to distil marvellous music from his insulted love for his.

The Marquesa, furthermore, is evidently a transposition from Mme. de Sévigné, who plays herself such an important role in Proust. The bad feature here, however, is that Mr. Wilder has followed Proust in exaggerating the cruelty of the beloved to the lover. This is sometimes hard to swallow in Proust himself, but then there is in Proust a bitterness that seems derived from hard experience; whereas with Mr. Wilder we feel that this violence is merely an effective device. I cannot quite believe, for example, in the harrowing scene in which Esteban is dressing Manuel's wound while Manuel abuses him so harshly, and I cannot believe at all in the scene where La Périchole refuses, after twenty years, to allow Uncle Pio to address her by her first name. Isn't there, also, something rather forced about the pining of Captain Alvarados for his daughter? Isn't it one case of hopeless love too many? At one point, Mr. Wilder allows himself to be carried into rewriting the death of Bergotte (by a natural attraction, certainly: no doubt, like Strachey's death of Victoria, it is destined to be imitated many times): "We come from a world where we have known incredible standards of excellence, and we dimly remember beauties which we have not seized again, and we go back to that world." (*"Toutes ces obligations qui n'ont pas leur sanction dans la vie présente semblent appartenir à un monde différent, fondé sur la bonté, le scruple, le sacrifice, un monde entièrement différent de celui-ci, et dont nous sortons pour naître à cette terre, avant peut-être d'y retourner. . . ."*)

This is not, I must repeat, that Proust has been anything other for Wilder than the inevitable elder master that every young writer must cling to before he can stand on his own feet. Since I have cited so many passages in which Mr. Wilder has filled in with Proust, I must quote at least one in a similar key which Proust would never have written and which, in Mr. Wilder's own work, has a quite distinct ring of artistic authenticity: "He regarded love as a sort of cruel malady through which the elect are required to pass in their late youth and from which they emerge, pale and wrung, but ready for the business of living. There were (he believed) a great repertory of errors mercifully impossible to human beings who had recovered from this illness. Unfortunately there remained to them a host of failings, but at least (from among many illustrations) they never mistook a protracted amiability for the whole conduct of life, they never again regarded any human being, from a prince to a servant, as a mechanical object."

The effect of Thornton Wilder is, in any case, not at all like the effect of Proust, or like the effect of anyone else one remembers. From what one hears about him, one may get the impression that he is one of those contemporary writers who seem still to date from the nineties—that he is simply another "stylist," another devotee of "beauty"—that one will find him merely a pretty or a precious writer; but Mr. Wilder, when one comes to read him, turns out to be something quite different from this. He possesses that quality of "delightfulness" of which George Saintsbury has said that Balzac did not possess it but that Gérard de Nerval did. But he has, also, a hardness, a sharpness, that sets him quite apart from our Cabells, our Dunsanys, our Van Vechtens and our George Moores. He has an edge that is peculiar to himself, an edge that is never incompatible with the attainment of a consummate felicity. This felicity, which has nothing of the pose, of the self-conscious effort to "write beautifully," of the professional beautiful writer, is felt through the whole of his work and as much in the conception of the characters and the development of the situations as in the structure of the sentences themselves. It is the felicity of a true poet—not merely the contrived "style" of a literary man with a yearning for old unhappy fancy far-off things—and it makes possible for Thornton Wilder a good many remarkable feats that we should not have expected to see brought off. Mr. Wilder, for example, I understand, has never been in Peru, and ordinarily there are few things more deadly than the dream-country of the twentieth-century novelist. Yet the author of *The Bridge of San Luis Rey* has been able to give us a Peru that is solid, incandescent, distinct. Here is the Marquesa's pilgrimage to Cluxambuqua: "a tranquil town, slow-moving and slow-smiling; a city of crystal air, cold as the springs that fed its many fountains; a city of bells, soft and musical and tuned to carry on with one another the happiest quarrels. If anything turned out for disappointment in the town of Cluxambuqua the grief was some-how assimilated by the overwhelming immanence of the Andes and by the weather of quiet joy that flowed in and about the side-streets. No sooner did the Marquesa see from a distance the white walls of this town perched on the knees of the highest peaks than her fingers ceased turning the beads and the busy prayers of her fright were cut short on her lips." Then the church, the hawks, the llama. . . . It is the city of a fairy-tale, of course; but it is almost of the same quality as *Kubla Khan*. It is not without its preciosity; but this preciosity of Thornton Wilder's is at least as sound as that of *Vathek*.

Mr. Wilder has also a form of his own, which is highly individual and which seems to me to promise more than he has hitherto been able to accomplish. In *The Cabala*, the several heroes of the several episodes seem at first to have nothing in common save the accident of all being observed by the American who is telling the story; then we learn that they are the ancient gods fallen on evil times, and we realize that there is also a significance in their relations with the young American. In *The Bridge of San Luis Rey*, the different characters appear to have in common merely the fact that they were killed by the fall of the bridge; then gradually we are made to understand that their deaths at that moment had meaning, and that there is a meaning in the relations of the people who fell to the people who were left alive. *The Bridge of San Luis Rey* is more ingenious than *The Cabala*, and more completely worked out; but I do not find it completely satisfying. God works in too obvious a way. It is hard to believe that the author believes in the God of his book. The real higher power at work here is the author's aesthetic ideal, which is struggling to incarnate itself.

One ought to say something more about *The Cabala*, which has received less attention than *The Bridge* but which seems to me, in some ways, more interesting. The circle of clever people in Rome turn out to be the gods grown old; Christianity and modern society have finally proved too much for them. The Puritanism of the young American gives Pan (or Priapus?) such a feeling of guilt that he is driven to suicide; and Aphrodite breaks her heart for an American Adonis who pays no attention to her. A brilliant peasant Cardinal, who has spent most of his life as a missionary to China, robs Artemis—if, as I suppose, Astrée-Luce is Artemis—of her pagan religious faith. These are the gods of Europe contending with the influences of alien races. In the end, the young American goes to call on the Cardinal, whom he finds with *Appearance and Reality*, Spengler, *The Golden Bough, Ulysses*, Proust and Freud on the table beside him. In the course of the conversation, the Cardinal pushes them all to the floor: "Yes, I could write a book," he says, "better than this ordure that your age has offered us. But a Montaigne, a Machiavelli . . . a . . . a . . . Swift, I will never be."

The moment after, as the visitor is going, the Cardinal remarks that he would like for his birthday a small Chinese rug. The young American departs for the States: "Why was I not more reluctant at leaving Europe? How could I lie there repeating the *Aeneid* and longing for the shelf of Manhattan?" The shade of Virgil appears to him. "Know, importunate barbarian," says the poet, "that I spent my whole lifetime under a great delusion—that Rome and the house of Augustus were eternal. Nothing is eternal save Heaven. Romes existed before Rome and when Rome will be a waste there will be Romes after her. Seek out some city that is young. The secret is to make a city, not to rest in it." . . . "The shimmering ghost faded before the stars, and the engines beneath me pounded eagerly towards the new world and the last and greatest of all cities."

Mr. Wilder himself, however, next turns up in Peru. I have already praised this fairy-tale country. I am told that it owes part of its vividness to its grasp of the Spanish character. Thornton Wilder's feeling for national temperaments—French, Italian and American—had already appeared in *The Cabala* as one of his most striking gifts. But I wish, for our sakes, and perhaps for his own, that he would now follow Virgil's advice and return for a time to New York. I wish that he would study the diverse elements that go to make the United States, and give us *their* national portraits. Mr. Wilder already knows Europe, and he also knows something of the Orient; and now we need him at home. I believe that this player on plaintive stops has more than one tune in his flute.

August 8, 1928

THE DEATH OF ELINOR WYLIE

ELINOR WYLIE died on the night of December 16, 1928. The account of this given me by her husband, William Rose Benét, was somewhat fuller than that which appears in the memoir of her sister, Miss Nancy Hoyt (*Elinor Wylie: The Portrait of an Unknown Lady*). It had been Sunday, and, after a good deal of going out, they had decided to stay at home for the evening. The day before, Elinor had put in order the manuscript of her last book of poems, *Angels and Earthly Creatures*, which was to go to the publisher on Monday. She had picked up her own novel *Jennifer Lorn* and had read in it for a while; then had closed it in her definite way, saying, "Yes: *Jennifer Lorn is* better than *The Venetian Glass Nephew!*" and had gone to the kitchen to get them some supper. In a moment, her husband heard her call, and went in and found her fainting. She asked for a glass of water and when he gave it to her—I learn from Miss Hoyt—said, "Is that all it is?" He carried her to her bedroom, where she died.

The sense of loss expressed in the following article was felt by a good many people. Elinor Wylie had meant to us more than we had always been aware of at the time she was living. With her fine bindings, her formal furniture, her old-fashioned dining-room still-life and her old-fashioned literary culture that made one remember that her godfather had been Horace Howard Furness, the

Philadelphia scholar who made the great Variorum Edition of Shakespeare, and her talk that had both style and wit, she occupied a unique position in the region below Fourteenth Street, where, as Frank Crowninshield wrote about her later, she "liked to pretend that she was a Bohemian, but the sham was at all times apparent." Yet it was not this shell that she carried about that gave her her peculiar prestige: it was the fact that, living inside it, she managed to remain a free spirit as few Bohemians are. I was trying to convey this; and the eloquent tone of my article is also explained by the fact that Elinor was the first to die of my close literary friends, the commemoration of whose passing is a recurrent and, I fear, rather depressing feature of this chronicle and its successor.

The death of Elinor Wylie hardly yet seems a real event. When people whom we know die, we have usually been prepared for their deaths by some weakening or decay of personality. But in Elinor Wylie's case, a personality still vigorous and vivid suddenly went out of being. A mind alive with thoughts and images, at what seemed its point of fullest activity, was annihilated at a stroke. In a letter she wrote me from England, just before her return in December, she told me that she had never been so happy, had never loved life so much: she had written forty poems, she said—an unusual rate of production for her. I was out on the West Coast at the time of her death, and I found that, even after the news had reached me, I kept unconsciously looking forward to seeing her in New York again. A part of my mind still kept turning toward her—for she had left New York with no farewell, but, on the contrary, with salutations and with the promise that I should see her soon.

It was true that, of recent years, she had been suffering

severely from high blood-pressure, and had been warned by the doctors of the danger of a stroke such as that which actually ended her life. She had been told that, if she wished to escape it, she must diet, abstain from coffee and alcohol, be careful not to overtax herself, etc. But she paid little heed to these admonitions, and, as year followed year, used to laugh at her defiance of medical advice and her obstinate survival in spite of it.

In these latest doomed years of her life, her energy seemed actually to increase. When I first knew her, only five years ago, Elinor Wylie was a brilliant amateur, who had produced a few striking poems and started a novel or two, but who had never worked with much application. Yet by the time *Jennifer Lorn* was published, she had become one of the most steadily industrious and most productive writers of my acquaintance. She had always first composed her poems in her head and then simply written them down (in many cases, she never afterwards changed a word); but she now sat at her typewriter day after day, and turned out novel after novel, as well as a good deal of miscellaneous journalism. With a mind that seemed never to flag, she continued up to the last to go out night after night and to meet and talk to all sorts of people. In the meantime, she read insatiably. All her fiction was more or less historical and required special research. For her novel about Shelley, she collected and mastered a whole library. Her labor, in this case, was double, for she had to get up the American West in the pioneering days as well as the English nineteenth-century background. She had authority even for her landscapes, which she would prettily rework in her own colored silks from the narratives of old books of travel. And she seemed to find time, besides, to get through all the poetry and fiction of any distinction or interest that appeared in either England or America.

It was, no doubt, partly her very abnormal condition that so sped up her energy and imagination. Her vitality, during the years after she had come to live in New York, triumphed and flourished at the cost of desperate nervous strain. Though she had sometimes enjoyed fairly long periods of tranquillity, comfort and leisure, her life had been broken up by a series of displacements and emotional dislocations which might have destroyed a weaker nature. In Elinor Wylie's case, it had left her like one of those victims of the war who recover from critical operations and are sent out into life again, but whose condition is a little precarious. Irritation of the old wounds would at once cloud her mind with distress and terror; and one had to remember where they were. Yet in that still scarred and shaken being, who had had to live so long at the mercy of fate and under the domination of others, exasperated inescapably by the recurrent necessity to struggle, there came to birth, in these later years, what seemed to be a new and more powerful personality.

It was like the possession of a poor human life by some strong and non-human spirit, passionate but detached, all-worldly-wise and yet unworldly, generous without devotion, ruthless without spite, laughing with unbiassed intelligence over the disasters of the hurt creature it inhabited, and the mistress of a wonderful language, in which accuracy, vigor and splendor seemed to require no study and no effort and in which it spoke sometimes simply of its own divine estate, sometimes fled to bright and cooling visions for forgetfulness of its human exile, and sometimes tried to entertain by inventing the kind of tales, lending itself to the kind of sentiments, that maudlin human beings enjoy.

Such a spirit, among human beings, can nowhere find itself at home. Received in the conventional world with aversion, suspicion and fear, it creates in that other world where people avowedly live by their wits and their imaginations, an embarrassment almost equally uncomfortable. Yet the inhabitants of both worlds stand in awe of it, for they know that they must look to it for the values which they attach to the things of their worlds, for their very opinions of themselves and for their hopes of life itself. And the presence of such a spirit makes illness and death seem unreal. There are beings—and sometimes among the noblest—who pass their lives in the shadow of death. Putting all faith in the ecstasy of the senses, they cannot but fear the moment when the senses must fade: when the body fails, for them, the world ends. But for a spirit like Elinor Wylie's, death can never quite seem serious. The doctors can never dismay it. And when such a spirit drops its abode, we do not feel in its departure any pathos. Yet in its absence, we find ourselves blank: its vanishing has thrown us out more than we might have expected. It is almost as if the intellect that orders, the imagination that creates—those abstractions which have come to seem to us to have some sort of existence of their own, independent of any individual—had themselves been suddenly cut off. We are here among doubtful human creatures, all quarrelling or herding together, knowing little and thinking less, vague, pig-headed, purblind and violent. We come almost to wonder at last whether that spirit has really been among us—whether it may not have been merely, like the others, a blind, violent and crippled human life. Then we remember that harsh unflurried, that harsh unembittered laughter, and we look up the lovely lines in the book; and we know that in this sea without harbors, our compass must still be set by such magnets as the jest and the verse.

February 6, 1929

BURTON RASCOE

A Bookman's Daybook contains a selection of passages from Burton Rascoe's diary, which used to appear with that heading in the Sunday literary section of the New York *Herald Tribune.* On the jacket appears a slender and languid young man, who lies reading in the shade of a tree, surrounded by a flowery mead, while above him the swallows circle. Inside we find something quite different: the literary life of New York in the early years of this decade when there was little fresh air and little leisure. The Bookman who figures in the book is not at all like the young man on the cover; it is the Burton Rascoe we knew in those years—alert, nervous, always in a hurry, always going to so many places and seeing so many people that we can hardly imagine him relaxed or alone. Here is his own description of his impressions on rereading his diary:

"I was struck particularly," he writes, "with the sanguine enthusiasm of this Burton Rascoe of five or six years ago and with his rather breath-taking anxiety to get glimpses of his contemporaries, records of what they were talking about, ideas they were expressing and impressions of his own down on paper, for all the world as though he imagined that a cataclysm might destroy that world he lived in at any moment and that he was making light the labors of some future archeologists and his-

torians. This impression I have of him as taking his
mission seriously permits me to understand the fellow's
audacity."

Rascoe did take his mission seriously—he did make a
desperate effort to get the literary life of New York down
on paper, and that he succeeded to a considerable degree
is proved by this volume of selections, which in some
ways makes a better impression than the original diary
did. It has been edited by Mr. Hartley Grattan, who has
been able to throw out all the padding, all those long
conversations and ruminations that Mr. Rascoe used
sometimes to reel out, late at night in the *Herald Tribune*
office, when hard-pressed to fill his space and over-
keyed-up with coffee. Here we find a great many things
which posterity may well be glad to read about: the conversation of Mencken and Nathan and their methods of
amusing themselves; the arrival of Joseph Conrad in New
York; the controversies over *Ulysses* and *The Waste
Land*, which split up dinner tables and divided families;
an example of Cummings's top-speed monologues, so
difficult to catch and reproduce, but, in their way, as
remarkable as his poetry. It is true that we find, also,
other matters of a good deal less dignity and interest—
glimpses, for example, of the writer of this article, now
performing conjuring tricks, now talking about Whitehead through his hat. But all these things serve Rascoe's
purpose—all contribute to establishing an atmosphere. I
will not say that this atmosphere is a rarefied one. The
literary life of New York, as we recognize it in Rascoe's
Daybook, remains undisguisably a babel of tongues, a
round of disorderly parties, an exchange of malicious
gossip and a blather of half-baked opinions. But it does
have its exhilarating qualities of ready response and
variety. It was amusing, if nothing else; and Burton
Rascoe was just the man to write about it.

The Rascoe of *A Bookman's Daybook* is a young man just arrived from the West. In Chicago, he has performed the astonishing feat of making good literature exciting to the readers of a great Western paper. True, the spirit of the time has been with him; and he has had, in Chicago, for friends and allies, such writers as Carl Sandburg, Ben Hecht and Sherwood Anderson. But the awakening of a new generation at which he has been assisting has been mostly taking place at a distance; and he has had to develop senses of preternatural keenness. He has had to become almost telepathically aware—at a time when few people were aware at all—of what Mencken was doing in Baltimore, Hergesheimer in Philadelphia, Cabell in Richmond, Conrad Aiken in Boston, of what everybody, in fact, was doing everywhere. Certainly no other American critic at that time, with the exception of Mencken himself, had so prompt and comprehensive an intelligence of what was being written in the United States.

But, scattered though our writers are, the literary center is always New York, and Burton Rascoe decides to shift his base to the East. He arrives full of excitement and high expectations; eagerly he gets to know everybody who is writing, as he already knows everything they have written. He rushes about from one group to another. He attends all the literary teas, the publishers' luncheons, the theatrical openings, the miscellaneous drinking-parties. And he brings to it all his shrewdness, his audacity, his humor, his extraordinary memory and his undiscourageable enthusiasm for literature. He makes us feel, as we read this record, that there is something really important in the air, that the work of all these people is interesting, that their opinions deserve attention.

Nor was this all an invention of Rascoe's. There *was* something going on in those days. One did feel that great books were being written, that decisive battles were being fought. The New York journalists who were young at that time are still bound by a common consciousness of having taken part in some sort of movement. One has no longer this consciousness today. Excellent books, to be sure, are being produced; but, for the most part, the people who write them and the people who write about them do not see very much of one another. There are no clear ideas in the air, and no new discoveries looming. The world of teas, dinners and parties, which appears when we look back on it now, as we read about it in Burton Rascoe, to have been a good deal of fun, has come now to be dominated by Book-of-the-Month Clubs and Literary Guilds, and organized and exploited by publishers. No sane person of adult years would go today to a literary luncheon, unless he had to make a living by reporting such matters; and the first-rate novelists, dramatists and poets mostly avoid New York like the plague.

It is partly the character of the city itself that inevitably makes impossible any close and really profitable exchange between different kinds of literary people. New York is too expensive for most writers, and even when they do manage to live here, the distances are usually too great for them to be able to see much of each other. And the spirit of artistic and intellectual adventure has, as I say, been deadened by the pressure of the commercial book clubs, which, however discriminating the tastes of the individual members may be, are bound to illustrate the same principle that is always being brought forward as an apology for the mediocrity of the movies, since their choices must always represent a compromise between their personal preferences and the preferences of their vast public in the provinces. New York, it turned out, had no place for Burton Rascoe in his original role of popular journalist who persisted in taking literature seriously. The *Herald Tribune* book supplement today is an interesting and attractive survey—it is probably better edited than when Burton Rascoe ran it. But it no longer contains any feature as remarkable as the writing of Rascoe. What one misses is an independent mind surveying the literary world; and one is forced to the conclusion that, in this department, there is really no room on a large New York paper for independent points of view. The result has been that Burton Rascoe has practically given up journalism. He has become, precisely, one of the directors of one of the big book-distributing companies. And aside from this, he plays the stock market, to which he now devotes that special faculty for divining what is likely to become valuable that he formerly displayed in the literary field.

Like most writing people today who still hope to accomplish something, Mr. Rascoe no longer lives in New York. Though he has given up literary journalism, he has not given up literature; he has, he intimates in his foreword, turned to writing novels. And it is reassuring to learn that the irreverent wit, the sure hand at prose and the swift intelligence of the *Bookman's Daybook,* though they have vanished from Manhattan journalism, are still being exercised elsewhere. After all, we reflect, that jacket with the young man reading in the shade of a tree is perhaps more appropriate to Rascoe's book than we had realized when it first met our eye. Burton Rascoe is not only not a product of New York—he is not even a product of Chicago. He was not bred by the city at all. He is a Kentuckian who spent most of his boyhood in the countryside of Oklahoma; and all that he has brought that is soundest to the literary life of the cities has been the fruit of solitude and rural peace—all that is toughest and most vigorous has come out of a provincial country-life perhaps fifty years behind the times, as one thinks of the times in New York. What Rascoe brought with him from the South and the Southwest is invaluable and indestructible. The surest proof of its value—in spite of his inaccuracies, his mistakes of judgment, his occasional faults of taste (some of them perpetuated in this book) —is the difficulty he has encountered in making it survive in New York. He offered us a dramatization of the world of art and ideas; and though his show, at the time it was running, attracted a certain attention, it has been allowed to go off the boards. I have heard Burton Rascoe accused of cheapening the material with which he dealt. But, as I reread the *Bookman's Daybook,* I feel strongly that it has been we who have let him down, and not he us. At any rate, he has now been driven to confining his activities in the city to a lucrative attention to the stock market and retreating to the country for serious work—and who will not approve his policy and wish him success at both?

May 29, 1929

SIGNS OF LIFE: *LADY CHATTERLEY'S LOVER*

THIS FINE NOVEL of D. H. Lawrence's has been privately printed in Florence, and it is difficult and expensive to buy. This is a pity, because it may very well be one of the author's best books. About the erotic aspect of *Lady Chatterley's Lover*, which has prevented it from being circulated except in this subterranean fashion, I shall have something to say in a moment. But one ought tc begin by explaining that the novel is something more than the story of a love affair: it is a parable of post-war England.

Lady Chatterley is the daughter of a Scotch R. A., a robust and intelligent girl, who has married an English landowner from the Midlands coal-mining country. Sir Clifford is crippled in the war, and returns to his family estate, where he lives amid the unemployment of the decaying industrial towns. He occupies himself at first with writing, sees the literary people in London and publishes some short stories, "clever, rather spiteful, and yet, in some mysterious way, meaningless"; then later he applies himself feverishly to an attempt to retrieve his coal-mines by working them with modern methods: "Once you started a sort of research in the field of coal-mining, a study of methods and means, a study of by-products and the chemical possibilities of coal, it was

astounding the ingenuity and the almost uncanny cleverness of the modern technical mind, as if really the devil
himself had lent a fiend's wits to the technical scientists of
industry. It was far more interesting than art, than literature, poor emotional half-witted stuff, was this technical
science of industry."

But Sir Clifford, semi-paralytic, is in the same unhappy
situation as the hero of *The Sun Also Rises*; and his
attractive wife, in the meantime, has been carrying on
an affair with the gamekeeper—himself a child of the
collieries, but nevertheless an educated man, who has
risen to a lieutenancy during the war, and then, through
inertia and disillusion, relapsed into his former status.
There has been an understanding between Sir Clifford
and his wife Connie, that, since he cannot give her a
child himself, he will accept an illegitimate child as his
heir. But Connie has finally reached a point where she
feels that she can no longer stand Sir Clifford, with his
invalidism, his arid intelligence and his obstinate class-
consciousness. She has fallen in love with the gamekeeper; and when she finally discovers that she is going to
have a child, she leaves her husband and demands a
divorce. We are left with the prospect of the lady and
her lover going away to Canada together.

Now, Lawrence's treatment of this subject is not without its aspects of melodrama. It is not entirely free from
his ill-mannered habit of nagging and jeering at those of
his characters who arouse his contempt or resentment.
Poor Sir Clifford, whom his shrill creator cannot refrain
from baiting, was, after all, however disagreeable, a man
in a pathetic situation for which he was in no way to
blame. And, on the other hand, Mellors, the gamekeeper,
has his moments of romantic bathos. Yet the characters
do, in general, maintain a certain heroic dignity, a certain
symbolical importance, which enable them to carry off

all this. D. H. Lawrence's theme is a high one: the self-affirmation and the triumph of life in the teeth of all the sterilizing and demoralizing forces—industrialism, physical depletion, dissipation, careerism and cynicism—of modern English society; and the drama he has set in motion against the double contrasting background of the collieries and the English forests has both solid reality and poetic grandeur. It is the most inspiriting book from England that I have seen in a long time; and—in spite of Lawrence's occasional repetitiousness and his sometimes rather overdone slapdash tone—one of the best written. D. H. Lawrence is indestructible: censored, exiled, denounced, snubbed, he still possesses more vitality than almost anyone else. And this one of his books which has been published under the most discouraging conditions and which must have been written in full knowledge of its fate—which can, indeed, hardly yet be said to have seen the light at all—is one of his most vigorous and brilliant.

D. H. Lawrence, in *Lady Chatterley's Lover*, has thrown over the Anglo-Saxon conventions and, in dealing with sexual experience, has decided to call things by their common names. The effect of this, on the whole, is happy. I will not say that the unlimited freedom which Lawrence for the first time enjoys does not occasionally go to his head: the poetic sincerity of the gamekeeper does not quite always save his amorous rhapsodies over certain plain old English terms from being funny at the wrong time; and one finds it a little difficult to share the author's exaltation over a scene in which the lovers are made to decorate one another with forget-me-nots in places where flowers are rarely worn. But, on the other hand, he has greatly benefited from being able, in dealing with these matters, to dispense with circumlocutions and sym-

bols. It gets rid of a good deal of the verbosity, the
apocalyptic grandiloquence, into which this subject has
so often led him, and it keeps the love scenes human. It
may, in fact, probably be said that these scenes in *Lady
Chatterley's Lover* contain the best descriptions of sexual
experience that have yet been written in English. It is
certainly not true, as is sometimes asserted, that erotic
sensations either cannot or ought not to be written about.
D. H. Lawrence has demonstrated here how interesting
and how varied they are, and how important to the
comprehension of emotional situations in which they
play a part.

The truth is simply, of course, that in English we have
had, since the eighteenth century, no technique, no
vocabulary even, for presenting such scenes in a novel.
The French have been writing directly about sex, in
works of the highest dignity, ever since they discarded
the proprieties of the age of Louis XIV. For this purpose
they have adopted a vocabulary which is conventional
and classically abstract; and they have even, for a long
time, in their realistic fiction, been printing the vulgar
language of the farmyard, the street and the bar. But
James Joyce and D. H. Lawrence are the first modern
English-speaking writers to put this language into serious
books; and the effect, in the case of *Ulysses*, at least, has
been shocking to English readers to an extent that must
seem very strange to a French literary generation who
read Zola, Octave Mirbeau and Huysmans in their youth.
But, aside from this question of coarseness in faithfully
reporting colloquial speech, we have in English, as I have
said, the problem of dealing with sexual matters at all.
We have not evolved any equivalent for the literary
vocabulary of the French. We have only, on the one
hand, colloquial words that will deeply offend some
people and no doubt be unintelligible to others, and, on

the other hand, the technical words used in works on biology and medicine. Neither kind goes particularly well in a love scene intended to generate an illusion of charm or romance.

This is the problem that Lawrence has tried to solve in *Lady Chatterley's Lover*, and, on the whole, he has been successful. He deserves a special medal from the Republic of Letters for his courage in facing the obloquy to which his experiment was sure to expose him, to say nothing of the other kinds of losses he must take for it—for he cannot have had printed in Italy many copies of the original edition or have made very much money by selling them, and he can claim no rights in the pirated edition that is being printed and sold over here. But there can be no advance in this prohibited direction without somebody's taking losses; and no writer of first-rate merit has done so since Joyce's *Ulysses*, in which it was a question rather of allowing the characters to use certain words than of genuine pioneering in the description of sexual intercourse. All serious writers in the English-speaking countries are much in Lawrence's debt, for even the limited circulation of *Lady Chatterley's Lover* cannot fail to make it easier in future to disregard the ridiculous taboo that the nineteenth century imposed on sex.

July 3, 1929

DOSTOEVSKY ABROAD

A TRANSLATION has just appeared—*The Diary of Dostoevsky's Wife*—of the journal of Dostoevsky's second wife during the spring and summer of 1867, when Dostoevsky had been forced to leave Russia to escape from his own and his brother's creditors. From this account, it would appear that the Dostoevskys spent most of their time in Germany quarrelling with waiters over tips, quarrelling and making up with each other, and pawning their belongings to pay the bills when Dostoevsky had lost his money gambling. Anna Grigorevna is simple and touching; Dostoevsky's own complicated character here appears to its worst advantage: he is selfish, disagreeable and silly. It was the range of Dostoevsky's intelligence and the brilliance of his conversation which made people forgive him these qualities. When, for example, we read Baron Wrangel's account of his talks with Dostoevsky in Siberia, or the description of him by Sonia Kovalevsky, the woman mathematician, with whose sister Dostoevsky was in love, we have a vision of a quite different person. Anna Grigorevna, though she frequently speaks of long conversations with her husband, and notes exactly how much everything costs, almost never puts down his opinions. Yet from Dostoevsky's letters of this time, we know that he was already preoccupied with the ideas with which he was afterwards so profoundly to impress himself on Russian thought.

Perhaps the nearest that Mme. Dostoevsky comes to touching on these ideas is in her record of the already famous quarrel between Dostoevsky and Turgenev. Here is her report of the former's account of the visit he paid the latter in Baden-Baden:

"According to him, he is very embittered, even to the point of being venomous and talks the whole time about his new novel, which Fyodr never even so much as mentioned. Turgenev is furious over the notices in the papers, saying he has been most fearfully cut up in *Golos* and *Vaterländischen Nachrichten,* as well as in other publications. He also said that the Russian aristocracy, at the instigation of Philip (?) Tolstoy, had done their best to exclude him from their society, but that none the less nothing had come of it. He added, moreover: 'If you only knew how delighted I should have been!' Fyodr, as usual, treated him none too gently, telling him to procure himself a telescope, for, since he always lived in Paris, he couldn't otherwise expect to know what was happening in Russia, let alone understand it. Turgenev declared he was a realist, and Fyodr said he only thought he was. When Fyodr declared he found the Germans extremely stupid and very apt to be dishonest, Turgenev promptly took offense, assuring Fyodr he had irreparably insulted him, for he himself had now become, not a Russian any more, but a German. Fyodr said that he hadn't known that and greatly deplored the fact. Fyodr said that for the most part he had spoken in a facetious tone of voice, which had obviously annoyed Turgenev considerably, and that he had quite openly told him that his novel had met with no success. But on the whole they parted friends, and Turgenev promised to give him the book. Of all the curious men—how could he possibly be proud of being a German instead of a Russian? I should have thought that no Russian writer on earth would want to repudiate his country and least of all to declare himself a German! What, when all's said and done, has he got to be grateful to Germany for, seeing that he has grown up in Russia, which has supported him and done its very utmost to encourage his talent. And now he breaks right away from it and declares that if Russia were to go under, the world would not be the loser! Of all the appalling things for a Russian to say! Enough of the whole matter—but I know that this conversation with Turgenev has excited Fyodr beyond words, and that he always gets beside himself when people repudiate their fatherland."

It is clear from the first part of this account that Turgenev on this occasion had special reasons for being irritable; and it is equally true that Dostoevsky had special reasons for resenting Turgenev: Dostoevsky had borrowed two years before fifty thalers from the richer man and had never paid them back. Yet there was something more important and interesting than appears from Mme. Dostoevsky's description at the bottom of the quarrel between the two writers, who were contemporaries in age and who had had, as young men in St. Petersburg, their first successes at the same time. Dostoevsky belonged, like Turgenev, to the Russian educated class; but his imprisonment in Siberia had modified his point of view profoundly. The Russian governing classes spoke French, and they looked habitually toward Western Europe for culture and ideas; they regarded Russians as barbarians, and could not sometimes, according to Dostoevsky, even write their own language correctly. Their liberal aspirations, when they had them, were derived from Republican France. Dostoevsky had had himself this sort of education and had at one time shared these ideas. He had belonged to a political and literary club composed of Russian intellectuals of this type, and, as a member of this club, he had been convicted of conspiracy against the Tsar and sent for four years to prison. He had found there that, as an educated man, he was regarded by the ordinary Russians with hatred and suspicion. It had seemed to him then that the gulf between the educated class and the people was so deep as to make it impossible for even the most sympathetic artists, for even the reformers themselves, to contribute anything really valuable to the development of the national life. Russian novelists wrote about Russia, as he himself in his early fiction had done, from a Western European point of view, from a point of view derived from writers who had been dealing with societies quite unlike the Russian; and Russian reformers behaved as if a solid and enlightened bourgeoisie, such as had engineered the French Revolution, could be counted on to take over in Russia. Neither knew Russian life at firsthand; both, by their very education, were unfitted to understand it; and both inhabited worlds of illusion. Contemptuous or despairing of the antiquated social system and the semi-savage population from which they themselves had sprung, they had removed, either actually or spiritually, to the other end of Europe; and, even when intelligent and benevolent, had persistently succeeded in evading the realities of the national life. The correspondence of Dostoevsky, during these years of his own enforced exile, is full of hunger for Russia: he devours the Russian newspapers; he complains again and again that a novelist cannot create in exile. For him, Turgenev was a gifted Russian who had run away from Russia, who had too easily given up as hopeless a world that he feared to face, and who patronized the fellow-countrymen whom he had made his reputation by writing about.

When we read Dostoevsky on this problem, we come to realize that a good deal of what he says applies equally to expatriate Americans in Europe. We feel that the

difficult position of the artist or intellectual who turns his
back on a provincial country with which he cannot make
any wide contact has never—not even by Brooks in *The
Pilgrimage of Henry James*—been studied more profoundly than by Dostoevsky. There is, in many respects,
a striking analogy between the situation of Russia in
respect to Western Europe and the situation of the
United States; and it is of special interest to Americans
to see how Dostoevsky deals with it.

The course recommended by Dostoevsky was for educated Russians, as far as possible, to clear their minds of
preconceived ideas from abroad and, from a firsthand
realistic examination of their country and its institutions,
to try to understand the Russian character and the
Russian point of view. Now, the conditions of Russian
life are, and were, very different from our own; but
they resemble our own in this: that both are fundamentally different from the conditions of Western
Europe. Like the Russians of Dostoevsky's day, we have
been used to looking to Europe for ideas; and the ideas
with which we have been supplied have, as in Dostoevsky's Russia, been imperfectly suited to our needs. This
has always been the problem in America: simultaneously
to adapt European culture to the alien conditions of
American life and to cultivate from our own peculiar and
un-European resources an original culture of our own.
But our situation, since the war, has, in some respects,
become more serious. Since the war, we have been importing from Europe the emotions and the points of view
appropriate to bankruptcy and exhaustion—resignation,
futility and despair—into a country full of money and
health; while Europe seems herself to be looking to us,
as she never has done before: the very books that she
sends us denouncing us seem to suggest that she has been
disappointed. Yet what America sends Europe, in her

famine, are still principally scientific researches uninspired by creative theory and works of art, often illiterate
and usually secondhand, imitated from European models.
The principal philosophy, so far as one can see, that
America has exported abroad during the period since the
war, has been Watson's behaviorism—the invention of
an experimental psychologist who is certainly not a
great thinker and who has since, as a matter of fact, gone
into the advertising business.

If, however, we pursue the conclusions to which Dostoevsky's position led him, we come upon a further
analogy between the Russian situation and our own.
When Dostoevsky had set his face away from Western
Europe to direct his attention toward Russian institutions,
he found himself confronted by the Tsardom, the feudal
system of landowning and the Greek Orthodox Church;
and there is something both heroic and embarrassing in
the spectacle of one of the most intelligent men of his
time making the effort to swallow all these. Thus, in a
somewhat similar way, an American who would turn for
sustenance to contemporary American institutions will
find himself confronted by elements not easy to assimilate.
He will find the Chamber of Commerce, the Rotary
Club, the American political machine, all apparently the
willing instruments of the nationwide commercial solidarity which harasses American communities with company
spies and informers and dragoons them on occasion with
strong-arm men; which persecutes without justice or
mercy Sacco and Vanzetti and how many others!; and the
upholders of which it sufficed for an honest municipal
servant like Al Smith to speak out with a moderate common sense and a by no means unhampered frankness to
strike with panic and fire with resentment.

Yet Dostoevsky's instinct was sound: the fact that the
American problem seems a particularly formidable one

is no excuse for fleeing or evading it. We must, of course, take European ways of thinking along with our language, our alphabet; but we must try to stick close to the realities of our contemporary American life, so new, and so different perhaps from anything that has ever been known, that, if we cannot find out for ourselves what we want and where we are going, it is improbable, with Europe declining, that anybody else can tell us. Of all this, more presently.

January 30, 1929

CITIZEN OF THE UNION

THE PUBLICATION of *George W. Cable: His Life and Letters* by his daughter, Lucy Leffingwell Cable Bikle, reminds us how completely this once-popular novelist has now passed into eclipse. Few people read Cable today; and the critics never discuss him. Yet in the eighties and the nineties he was enormously read both at home and abroad; and he deserved the high standing he was given. The decline of Cable's reputation is, I believe, mainly due to the general lack of interest, on the part of the critics of the new generation, in the American literature of the period just behind them. We are rediscovering Irving Babbitt and Paul Elmer More, but we have not yet discovered John Jay Chapman; we leave Stephen Crane in half-shadow, and George Cable in complete eclipse.

The prevalent notion of Cable today seems to be that he was a romantic novelist, of a species now obsolete, who made a good thing of exploiting the sentiment and charm, the quaintness and picturesqueness, of a New Orleans long gone to decay. This idea seems, indeed, to some extent, to have been shared by the public who read Cable, that public for whom taste and intellect were represented by Richard Watson Gilder, the editor of the *Century Magazine*. When George Cable was presented with an honorary degree of Master of Arts by Yale, it was "with the desire of recognizing publicly the eminent success which you have achieved in embalming in literature a unique phase of American social life which is rapidly passing away." Yet Cable himself had no idea that he was engaged in embalming anything: he supposed himself to be dealing with the realities of contemporary life—and, in the work of his best years, this was true.

The New Orleans of George Cable's time—and even the New Orleans of today—is a laboratory where certain American situations present themselves, if not in a form necessarily more acute than elsewhere, at least in more vivid colors. Louisiana, originally French, was transferred in 1762 to Spain, with the result of arousing extreme hostility between the French and the Spanish inhabitants. At the beginning of the nineteenth century, it was transferred back from Spain to France, and then sold by Napoleon to the United States, with the result of provoking a new kind of hostility, this time between the original Latin Americans, Spanish and French, on the one hand, and the Anglo-Saxon Americans who had come in to take possession, on the other. At the same time, the mingling of the whites with the large Negro element of the population had resulted in a class of mulattoes who constituted a special problem. Thus, one found in New Orleans simultaneously in a concentrated field and in intensified form, the conflict of European nationalities, as between the Spanish and the French; the conflict of the Latins and the Anglo-Saxons; and the conflict of two totally different races, as between the Negroes and the whites. Add to this the sectional conflict at the time of the Civil War, of the American South with the North, a conflict felt so much more painfully and for so much longer a time after the war by the South than by the North. The whole American problem of diversity and unity was here, and no writer ever studied it more thoroughly or thought about it more intelligently than George Washington Cable did.

For Cable was essentially a sociologist. He was not in the least a fancier of lavender and old lace. He was a good deal closer to Upton Sinclair than he was to Myrtle Reed. He had a real sense of beauty, but there was too much of the Puritan in him—his mother had been a New Englander, and it was only comparatively late in life that Cable was able to make up his mind that the theater was not immoral—to allow him much to cultivate his sensibility. Though his books have their own sort of atmosphere, which seems to have enchanted his readers, it is certainly not the atmosphere of Cable's novels which appears most successful today. Compare one of Cable's Louisiana descriptions with a description of the same region by Lafcadio Hearn. The lush background that Hearn is so good at investing with color and glamor has a way of turning flat in Cable. Beneath the floridity of the Southerner and his courteous and affable manner, we catch a glimpse of William Wetmore Story and his statue of Cleopatra. And so, though Cable had a most remarkable, an almost unexcelled ear for human speech, though he reported it with the most scrupulous accuracy, he did little to make it attractive. Just as he listened with attention to the songs of birds and transcribed them into musical notation, so he studied the different varieties of the French, Spanish and Negro Creole dialects and the language of the Acadians, both English and French, with a scholarly exactitude that must be as valuable to the phonetician as it is forbidding to the ordinary reader. This rendering, with pitiless apostrophes, of these special pronunciations was complained of even in the period of Cable's greatest popularity, and it constitutes a formidable obstacle to appreciating him today.

Cable's own conception of his craft comes out plainly in certain of the letters included in this biography. Of *The Grandissimes*, he writes that the editors of *Scribner's*, in which it first appeared, did not know "that the work I should by and by send them was going to have any political character. But that was well-nigh inevitable. It was impossible that a novel written by me then should escape being a study in the fierce struggle going on around me, regarded in the light of that past history—those beginnings—which had so differentiated Louisiana civilization from the American scheme of public society. I meant to make *The Grandissimes* as truly a political work as it has ever been called. . . . My friends and kindred looked on with disapproval and dismay, and said all they could to restrain me. 'Why wantonly offend thousands of your own people?' But I did not intend to offend. I wrote as near to truth and justice as I knew how, upon questions that I saw must be settled by calm debate and cannot be settled by force or silence."

The Grandissimes was the first full-length instalment of Cable's anatomy of Southern society. He prepared at about the same time for the United States Census of 1880 a report on the "social statistics" of New Orleans which was specially commended by the authorities; and it was this blending of what may perhaps be taken as a New England respect for facts with a humanism quite alien to New England which left Louisiana, in Cable's writings, perhaps the most satisfactorily studied of nineteenth-century American communities. For Cable, who had never been in France, had read and spoken French al'. his life and who, brought up as a Presbyterian, had come to manhood in a Catholic community, could penetrate Louisiana in every layer and all directions.

In *The Grandissimes* Cable incorporated a story that he had never been able to sell to the "family" magazines of the period and that had consequently not been included in the popular *Old Creole Days*. The reason for rejecting this manuscript that had been given by George Parsons Lathrop, writing for William Dean Howells, then editor of the *Atlantic Monthly*, was "the unmitigatedly distressful effect of the story." This was the *Story of Bras-Coupé*, the adventures of an African king sold into slavery in the United States. When Bras-Coupé is brought to Louisiana and taken into the fields, and he first comes to understand that it is intended for him to work with common Negroes, he hits the foreman over the head with his hoe, picks up one of the other slaves and bites him in the leg and throws him away, and raises havoc till the overseer shoots him down. A woman slave, who speaks his language, is brought to interpret to him, and he instantly falls in love with her and allows himself to be ruled through her. He demands to marry her; and, on the night of his wedding, gets drunk and forgets his status; he knocks down his master, who has already resented being treated by him as king to king. He is brutally hunted to death. As a study of what man can make of man, of the deformation of human relations by unnatural social institutions, the story of Bras-Coupé is as powerful in its smaller scope as *Uncle Tom's Cabin* itself. With the story of Mme. Lalauré in *Strange True Stories of Louisiana* and some other detached episodes, it almost puts Cable in the class of the great Russian chroniclers of serfdom.

For it is not the love stories in Cable's fiction that really interest Cable: it is the social and political situations. It is human life throttled in the web of society that arouses all his emotion, at the same time that he can trace with nicety every one of the tangled strands and explain the necessities that have strung it. One of the features of this biography is a hitherto unpublished account by Cable of the development of his political ideas. He had fought in the Confederate Army, but had afterwards come to unorthodox conclusions in regard to the Negro question and the relations of the North and the South. About the time that he began to give public expression to his opinions on these subjects, he moved his family from New Orleans to New England. The real occasion for this change of residence was the ill-health of Cable's wife; but, in spite of the fact that he made it a rule never to publish an opinion in the North which he had not first put forward in person from a public platform in the South, returning there expressly for the purpose, there can be no doubt that Cable's native city was no longer very comfortable for him. He was one of the clearest-minded Americans of his time, and in the South, after the Civil War, so detached and realistic an intelligence was uncommon and unwelcome. It was not common or welcome anywhere. Cable understood both South and North; the American and the European; the white man and the Negro; and he would not become the partisan of any of them. What he believed in were democratic principles of the kind that he understood the American Republic to have been founded to put into practice; and he devoted all his study and art to the attempt to impress their importance on a public that were occupied for the most part—during our period of industrial development after the Civil War—with aims that ran counter to these. The moral of Cable's stories is always that distinctions between human beings on social or national or racial grounds must be regarded as merely provisory; that there can never be a true equilibrium, that there can only be conflict and agony, where such discriminations are used as pretexts for unequal privilege.

February 13, 1929

VIRGINIA WOOLF AND THE AMERICAN
LANGUAGE

AN ARTICLE BY Virginia Woolf in the *New Republic* of February 13, 1929, started a controversy that went on for months, in the correspondence columns of that magazine, about the differences between British and American English. The first three of these letters appeared in the issue of April 24 of the same year:

Sir: In her article *On Not Knowing French*, Virginia Woolf says, "Thus a foreigner with what is called a perfect command of English may write grammatical English and musical English—he will, indeed, like Henry James, often write a more elaborate English than the native—but never such unconscious English that we feel the past of the word in it, its associations and attachments."

Just as a matter of curiosity, I am interested to know what she considers the native language of Henry James—Choctaw, perchance!—since he came from the wilds of Boston.

I am quite familiar with that "certain condescension" which the English display towards us poor benighted Americans, but it is a surprise to learn that we are looked upon as newcomers to the English language.

Harriot T. Cooke

Cannes, France

To this Mrs. Woolf replied:

Sir: I hasten to submit to your correspondent's correction and to retract my opinion that because Henry James was born in Boston he therefore did not write English like a native. I will do my best to believe that the language of Tennyson and the language of Whitman are one and the same. But may I explain that the responsibility for my error rests with Walt Whitman himself, with Mr. Ring Lardner, Mr. Sherwood Anderson, and Mr. Sinclair Lewis? I had been reading these writers and thinking how magnificent a language American is, how materially it differs from English, and how much I envy it the power to create new words and new phrases of the utmost vividness. I had even gone so far as to shape a theory that the American genius is an original genius and that it has borne and is bearing fruit unlike any that grows over here. But in deference to your correspondent I hasten to cancel these views and will note for future use that there is no difference between England and America; climate and custom have produced no change of any sort; America is merely a larger England across the Atlantic; and the language is so precisely similar that when I come upon words like *boob, graft, stine, busher, doose, hobo, shoe-pack, hiking, cinch* and many others, the fact that I do not know what they mean must be attributed to the negligence of those who did not teach me what is apparently my native tongue.

Having thus admitted my error, may I "just as a matter of curiosity" ask to be enlightened on another point? Why, I wonder, when I say that Henry James did not write English like a native, is it assumed that I intend an insult? Why does your correspondent at once infer that I accuse the Bostonians of talking Choctaw? Why does he allude to "condescension" and refer to "us poor benighted Americans" and suppose that I look upon them as "newcomers to the English language" when I have said nothing of the sort? What have I done to make him angry? Lowell's essay *On a Certain Condescension in Foreigners* (for such he apparently thought the English) should, I think, have for pendant *On a Certain Touchiness in*—dare I say it?—*Americans*. But may I implore you, Sir, if I use that word, not to infer that I thereby imply that you wear a pigtail and paint your forehead red? If I speak of "Americans" it is merely because our common ancestors some centuries ago agreed, for reasons best known to themselves, to differ.

Virginia Woolf

London, England

I had been told by Elinor Wylie, after one of her trips to London, of a meeting with Virginia Woolf which—though Elinor may have distorted a little—had sounded rather disagreeable. Mrs. Woolf, she declared, had asked her why she tried to write literary English; she had told Elinor that it would be much more interesting if she let herself go in her native American and tried something in the line of Ring Lardner. I was goaded to the following intervention:

Sir: I deplore the tone of this controversy. It is true that Mr. Cooke is touchy, but it is also true that Mrs. Woolf takes rather a perverse view. No one will dispute that English is spoken and written differently in England and in the United States, but English English and American English are not so different as Mrs. Woolf—and as certain American writers themselves—would like to have us believe. If they were as different as all that, the *New Republic* would never be able to publish Mrs. Woolf's articles. As a matter of fact, American writers do write as "unconsciously" as English ones (does Mrs. Woolf suppose that Walt Whitman learned the language he wrote in like Latin?)—and one does "feel the past of the word . . . its associations and attachments" in what they write. The difference is simply that, in the case of American writing, the attachments and associations are partly those which, during the past two or three hundred years, have been acquired in North America instead of in the British Isles. Behind both English and American English lies the much longer past of English literature and speech which Americans and Englishmen have in common. Thus, for example, though there is so much that is Yankee in the accent and vocabulary of Emerson, there is at least as much of the Elizabethan poets whom he seems to have been always reading; and even Mr. H. L. Mencken, our most conspicuous champion of an "American language," owes a good deal of his peculiar flavor and humor to his combination with American slang of a curious literary vocabulary that sounds as if it had been derived from Restoration comedies and eighteenth-century novels.

What is the use of pretending that the English spoken by Englishmen and the English spoken by Americans are actually two different languages? There are quite enough different languages already, and they have caused quite enough trouble. The so-called American language is partly American slang (a good deal of which is taken over by the English, as we take over a good deal of theirs), and partly illiterate English written in the United States. Ring Lardner, for example, is merely an expert in different kinds of American illiteracy and slang, and in his stories about New York actors, Western baseball players, etc., he is doing exactly the same sort of thing that Kipling has done in those stories of his which are supposed to be told by Irish soldiers or Scotch engineers. I do not know whether Mrs. Woolf supposes that all the different characters and authors of all the different American books that she reads are speaking the same picturesque tongue, and that this is "American." But I can assure her that, in the United States as elsewhere, there is a good deal of difference between North and South, East and West, rich and poor, town and country, etc., and that the speech of one kind of American may often seem as strange to another as Burns or William Barnes must to a Londoner. In the meantime, there is a standard English intelligible all over the United States, and intelligible also, apparently, to English people —so that it is possible for Mrs. Woolf and Mr. Cooke to carry on a correspondence without referring to a grammar or a dictionary. (Incidentally, Henry James was born, not in Boston, but in New York, and bitterly resented being taken for a New Englander.)

Mrs. Woolf's only comment on this, in a letter not intended for publication, was that for her what Whitman wrote was American and that she was content to let the controversy rest.

From the several letters that followed, I add one by Professor George E. G. Catlin that appeared in the issue of May 8, because it makes a point that I omitted, in calling attention to the fact that the differences between British and American English were due precisely to the fact that "the past of the word," whether for better or worse, has in many instances been longer preserved in the United States than in England:

Sir: As an Englishman resident during part of each year in America, will you permit me to comment on Mrs. Virginia Woolf's thesis that the English and American languages are different tongues and that the Americans must suffer from an inferiority complex if they are not proud of that fact?

Except in the case of slang, the meaning of which is frequently unknown to many of my American friends themselves, but the origin of which is often to be found in the English sporting papers of the last century, I have never found that I failed to understand what was said to me in America. The use of "guess" may sound novel until I recall Chaucer; of "some" until I recall Aubrey; of "candy" until I recall the "candie shoulder" of James I; of "sure" until I recall Milton; of "gotten" until I recall the Bible. In Yorkshire, on the other hand, I only sometimes understand what is said to me; in Ayrshire, I seldom understand; while nowhere are my ears assailed by such debased English as in London. There are more differences to be found between the popular speech of two English counties than between the speech of the literate in Oxford and Harvard or in Ely and Seattle.

These things are, of course, commonplace knowledge to Mrs. Woolf. Were her thesis correct, there would be, not only an American but a Canadian and an Australian language. There are, however, many British subjects in the European section of the Empire who are desperately anxious to take out a patent for the English language. The cause of their evident annoyance when the patent is infringed, I leave to those psychoanalysts to discover who are curious about the significance of "correct speech" as a symbol. But I do not doubt that it is very vexatious to a literary group when the living flood of popular speech sweeps over the deadening breakwaters of purism.

I heartily agree with Mr. Wilson that there are more than enough languages already; they do not need to be multiplied inside the English-speaking world. It may be that the place of honour ("honor," wrote King James) in that world is now on this side of the Atlantic; I do not know. Kant (an old-fashioned liberal) said that diversity of language was one cause of war: whether that be true

I do not know. But I do suggest (with all respect to a fascinating and distinguished writer) that Mrs. Virginia Woolf should reflect whether her view is not untenable in literature, pernicious in politics and evil in its cultural consequences.

George E. G. Catlin

Cornell University,
Ithaca, New York

But this correspondence left untouched the large problems of the future of English in the English-speaking countries. The situation of English in the United States was at that time and afterwards in a continual state of crisis. We did not have, and we do not have now, any generally accepted standards of vocabulary, grammar or spelling for the language in which we write. Every American writer has had to decide for himself how much he would try to retain of academic traditional English and how far he would allow himself to exploit this or that form of the American vernacular. The English, in the meantime, were drawing up, for the first time in the history of their literature, a set of rules for correct usage. Their great authority, the Fowlers' *Modern English Usage,* could hardly have been conceived by Ben Jonson, the author of the first English grammar, who, in spite of his preoccupation with the inflected classical languages, wrote habitually, like other Elizabethans, such phrases as "between you and I"—a misuse condemned as an Americanism in an English article quoted by one of the *New Republic* correspondents; and, in his section on the inflection of pronouns, fails even to mention this question. The result of this process in England (though not in the case of Virginia Woolf) was to weaken and impoverish the language by assuming as an ideal for good prose a mere linking of accredited formulas.

Some later discussions of this subject will be found under *Talking United States*. Neither Professor Catlin nor I tackled squarely the question of American usages that are neither illiterate nor slang and that have since been compiled on an enormous scale in the *Dictionary of American English* and the *Dictionary of Americanisms*, both published by the University of Chicago.

DOS PASSOS AND THE SOCIAL
REVOLUTION

JOHN DOS PASSOS'S *Airways, Inc.*, was produced in March
as the last play of the second season of the New Playwrights' Theater, and almost entirely failed to attract
attention. This was due, principally, I believe, to the
fact that by that time the critics had become rather discouraged with the revolutionary drama of Grove Street
and that the New Playwrights themselves were so low
in funds that they could not afford proper publicity.
None the less, *Airways, Inc.*, was a remarkable play,
perhaps the best that the New Playwrights have done;
and though this is not the place to speak of the merits of
the Grove Street production, which I thought were
considerable, the published text of the play demands
attention as a work of literature.

Airways is, like the group's other plays, a social-
political-economic fable; but Dos Passos is more intelligent than most of his associates—he is able to enter into
more points of view—and he is a much better artist. His
play is neither a naturalistic study nor a vaudeville in the
manner of John Howard Lawson, though it has some
of the elements of both; it is rather a sort of dramatic
poem of contemporary America. With great ingenuity,
Dos Passos had assembled on a single suburban street-
corner representatives of most of the classes and groups

that go to make up our society. We concentrate upon the life of a single middle-class household, but this is submerged in a larger world: its fate is inextricably bound up with a current real-estate boom; a strike that eventually gives rise to a Sacco-Vanzetti incident; and the promotion of a commercial aviation company. Nor, as is likely to be the case in this kind of play, are the social types merely abstractions which never persuade the imagination. Dos Passos has succeeded in producing the illusion that behind the little suburban street-corner of the Turners lies all the life of a great American city— all the confusion of America itself; and *Airways* made the meager stage of the bleak little Grove Street Theater seem as big as any stage I have ever seen. Dos Passos has also given the household of the Turners an extension in time as well as in space: he has provided a chorus of two old men, an American inventor and a Hungarian revolutionist, whose role is to relate what we see to what has gone before in history and to what may be expected to come after.

It is in the construction of this sort of sociological fable that Dos Passos particularly excels. The strength of his novel, *Manhattan Transfer*, lay in the thoroughness and the steady hand with which he executed a similar anatomy on the city of New York as a whole. As a dramatist he is less expert; and *Airways* suffers in certain ways from comparison with *Manhattan Transfer*. Dos Passos sometimes interrupts his action with long passages of monologue, which, though they might go down easily in a novel, discourage our attention in the theater; and his last act, though the two separate scenes are excellent in themselves, fails to draw the different strands together as we expect a third act to do. But, on the other hand, *Airways,* at its best, has an eloquence and a spirit that *Manhattan Transfer* largely lacked. It is one of the best-written things that Dos Passos has so far done—perhaps freer than any other of his productions both from rhetoric doing duty for feeling and from descriptions too relentlessly piled up. Dos Passos is probably only now arriving at his mature prose style.

So much for the purely artistic aspect of *Airways*. It is impossible to discuss it further without taking into account Dos Passos's political philosophy. Dos Passos is, one gathers from his work, a social revolutionist: he believes that, in the United States as elsewhere, the present capitalistic regime is destined to be overthrown by a class-conscious proletariat. And his disapproval of capitalist society seems to imply a distaste for all the beings who go to compose it. In *Manhattan Transfer*, it was not merely New York, but humanity that came off badly. Dos Passos, in exposing the diseased organism, had the effect, though not, I believe, the intention, of condemning the sufferers along with the disease; and even when he seemed to desire to make certain of his characters sympathetic, he had a way of putting them down.

Now, in *Airways*, there are several characters whom Dos Passos has succeeded in making either admirable or attractive, but these are, in every case, either radicals or their sympathizers. His bias against the economic system is so strong that it extends beyond its official representatives to all those human beings whose only fault is to have been born where such a system prevails and to be so lacking in courage or perspicacity as not to have allied themselves with the forces that are trying to fight it. In Dos Passos, not only must the policeman not fail to steal the money with which the street-kids have been playing craps; but even the young people of *Airways* who, however irresponsible and immoral, might be expected to exhibit something of the charm of youth—become uglier and uglier as the play proceeds, till they finally go com-

pletely to pieces in a drunken restaurant scene which
is one of Dos Passos's masterpieces of corrosive vulgarity.
It is especially curious to note the treatment which the
American aviators receive at the hands of both Dos Passos
and Lawson. The aviator is one of the authentic heroes
that our American civilization now produces. But for
Lawson or Dos Passos, an aviator cannot be an authentic
hero, or even, apparently, a genius, because he is not on
the side of the revolution. The truth is, of course, that the
aviator of the type of Lindbergh or Byrd never troubles
himself with these questions at all and, even when, as in
the case of Lindbergh, he is exploited for a time by the
government, he exists and performs his achievements in
a world independent of politics. But to a Lawson or a
Dos Passos, he is suspect: they cannot let him get away
with anything, and eventually, in what they write, they
succeed in destroying or degrading him. In Lawson's
play, *The International*, another New Playwrights production, the Lindbergh character appears as a drunken
taxi-driver—or perhaps as a drunken bum in a taxi—
amid the débâcle of the capitalist state; and in *Airways*,
the young aviator is sent up by the agents of his capitalist
employers to scatter leaflets on a strikers' meeting. He is
drunk, and falls and breaks his back.

Now, the life of middle-class America, even under
capitalism and even in a city like New York, is not so
unattractive as Dos Passos makes it—no human life under
any conditions can ever have been so unattractive. Under
however an unequal distribution of wealth, human beings
are still capable of enjoyment, affection and enthusiasm—
even of integrity and courage. Nor are these qualities and
emotions entirely confined to class-conscious workers and
their leaders. There are moments in reading a novel or
seeing a play by Dos Passos when one finds oneself ready
to rush to the defense of even the American bathroom,

even the Ford car—which, after all, one begins to reflect, have perhaps done as much to rescue us from helplessness, ignorance and squalor as the prophets of revolution. We may begin to reflect upon the relation, in Dos
Passos, of political opinions to artistic effects. Might it
not, we ask ourselves, be possible—have we not, in fact,
seen it occur—for a writer to hold Dos Passos's political
opinions and yet not depict our middle-class republic as
a place where no birds sing, no flowers bloom and where
the very air is almost unbreathable? For, in the novels
and plays of Dos Passos, everybody loses out: if he is on
the right side of the social question, he has to suffer, if
he is not snuffed out; if he is on the oppressors' side, his
pleasures are made repulsive. When a man as intelligent
as Dos Passos—that is, a man a good deal more intelligent
than, say, Michael Gold or Upton Sinclair, who hold
similar political views—when so intelligent a man and
so good an artist allows his bias so to falsify his picture
of life that, in spite of all the accurate observation and
all the imaginative insight, its values are partly those of
melodrama—we begin to guess some stubborn senti-
mentalism at the bottom of the whole thing, some deeply
buried streak of hysteria of which his misapplied resentments represent the aggressive side. And from the moment we suspect the processes by which he has arrived
at his political ideas, the ideas themselves become suspect.

In the meantime, whatever diagnosis we may make of
Dos Passos's infatuation with the social revolution, he
remains one of the few first-rate figures among our writers
of his generation, and the only one of these who has
made a systematic effort to study all the aspects of
America and to take account of all its elements, to
compose them into a picture which makes some general
sense. Most of the first-rate men of Dos Passos's age—
Hemingway, Wilder, Fitzgerald—cultivate their own

little corners and do not confront the situation as a whole. Only Dos Passos has tried to take hold of it. In the fine last speech of *Airways,* he allows the moral of his play to rise very close to the surface. The spinster sister of the Turner household has just received the news that the strike leader, with whom she has been in love and who has been made the victim of a frame-up, has finally been electrocuted: "Now I'm beginning to feel it," she says, "the house without Walter, the street without him, the city without him, the future that we lived in instead of a honeymoon without him, everything stark without him. Street where I've lived all these years shut up in a matchwood house full of bitterness. City where I've lived walled up in old dead fear. America, where I've scurried from store to subway to church to home, America that I've never known. World where I've lived without knowing. What can I do now that he is gone and that he has left me full of scalding wants, what can I do with the lack of him inside me like a cold stone? The house I lived in wrecked, the people I loved wrecked, around me there's nothing but words stinging like wasps. Where can I go down the dark street, where can I find a lover in the sleeping city? At what speed of the wind can I fly away, to escape these words that burn and sting, to escape the lack that is in me like a stone?"

It is true that the lack of real leadership is felt by us today as a stone. It is Dos Passos's recognition of this—his relentless reiteration of his conviction that there is something lacking, something wrong, in America—as well as his insistence on the importance of America— that gives his work its validity and power. It is equally true, of course, of H. L. Mencken that he finds something lacking and something wrong; but the effect of Mencken on his admirers is to make them wash their hands of social questions. Mencken has made it the fashion to speak of politics as an obscene farce. And Dos Passos is now almost alone among the writers of his generation in continuing to take the social organism seriously.

April 17, 1929

T. S. ELIOT AND THE CHURCH OF
ENGLAND

For Lancelot Andrewes by T. S. Eliot contains essays on Lancelot Andrewes and John Bramhall, two seventeenth-century English divines, and on Machiavelli, F. H. Bradley, Baudelaire, Thomas Middleton, Crashaw and Irving Babbitt. They all display the author's unique combination of subtle and original thinking with simple and precise statement, and will be read by everybody interested in literature. T. S. Eliot has now become perhaps the most important literary critic in the English-speaking world. His writings have been brief and few, and it is almost incredible that they should have been enough to establish him as an intellectual leader; but when one tries to trace the causes of the change from the point of view of the English criticism of the period before the war to the point of view of our own day, one can find no figure of comparable authority. And we must recognize that Eliot's opinions, so cool and even casual in appearance, yet sped with the force of so intense a seriousness and weighted with so wide a learning, have stuck oftener and sunk deeper in the minds of the post-war generation of both England and the United States than those of any other critic.

For Lancelot Andrewes, however, is not, like *The Sacred Wood*, a book merely of literary criticism. The essays which it contains have been selected by Eliot for the purpose of indicating a general position in literature, politics and religion. This position, he tells us in his preface, "may be described as classicist in literature, royalist in politics, and Anglo-Catholic in religion"; and it is further to be expounded in "three small books," called respectively *The School of Donne, The Outline of Royalism* and *The Principles of Modern Heresy.*

Mr. Eliot's ideas, in *For Lancelot Andrewes,* appear chiefly by implication; and we run the risk of misrepresenting them in attempting to discuss them on the basis of this book. Still, Eliot has invited us to read this slender collection of essays as a prelude to the trilogy mentioned above, and it is difficult to know how else to deal with it. The clearest and most explicit statement on the subject of religion I can find is the following from the essay in which Eliot points out the deficiencies of Irving Babbitt's humanism: "Unless by civilization you mean material progress, cleanliness, etc. . . . if you mean a spiritual and intellectual coördination on a high level, then it is doubtful whether civilization can endure without religion, and religion without a church." One recognizes a point of view which is by way of becoming fashionable among certain sorts of literary people, yet this usually presents itself merely as a sentiment that it would be a good thing to believe rather than as a real and living belief. And, though Eliot lets us know that he does believe, his faith, in so far as we find it expressed in these essays and in his recent poems, seems entirely uninspired by hope, entirely unequipped with force—a faith which, to quote his own epigraph, is merely "ready to die."

Now, no one will dispute that, at the present time, our society is in need of the kind of ideals which the churches were once able to supply; but the objection to Eliot's position is simply that the churches are now out of the question as a solution to our present difficulties, because it is so difficult to get educated people to accept their fundamental doctrines—and that, even if a few first-rate ones can convince themselves that they do, one does not see how they can possibly hope for a revival general enough to make religion intellectually important again. I agree that, without a church, you cannot have a real religion; and I sympathize with Mr. Eliot's criticism of certain substitute religions, like that of H. G. Wells, which try to retain the benefits of faith while doing away with the necessity of believing. You cannot have real Christianity without a cult of Jesus as the son of God. But since it has plainly become anachronistic to accept the prophet Jesus in this role, it seems that we must reconcile ourselves to doing without both the churches and religion. The answer to Mr. Eliot's assertion that "it is doubtful whether civilization can endure without religion" is that we have got to make it endure. Nobody will pretend that this is going to be easy; but it can hardly be any more difficult than persuading oneself that the leadership of the future will be supplied by the Church of England or by the Roman Catholic Church or by any church whatsoever.

Nothing seems to me more sadly symptomatic of the feeble intellectual condition of a good many literary people, of their unwillingness or incapacity to come to terms with the world they live in, than the movement back to Thomas Aquinas—or, in Eliot's case, back to Bishop Andrewes. It is not, of course, a question of the wisdom or the spiritual authority of Aquinas or Andrewes in his own day, when it was still possible for a first-rate mind to accept the supernatural basis of religion. But to argue, as in the literary world one sometimes finds people doing, that, because our society at the present time is badly off without religion, we should make an heroic effort to swallow medieval theology, seems to me utterly futile as well as fundamentally dishonest. If the salvation of our civilization depends on such religious fervor as our writers are capable of kindling—if it depends on the edifying example of the conversion of Jean Cocteau and the low blue flame of the later Eliot—then I fear that we must give up hope.

I was writing last week of John Dos Passos and his mirage of a social revolution. It seems to me that T. S. Eliot is a case of much the same kind: Eliot, like Dos Passos, is a highly cultivated American who does not care for contemporary America; but, instead of escaping from the American situation by way of Greenwich Village radicalism and the myth of a serious-minded and clear-eyed proletariat, as Dos Passos attempts to do, Eliot has gone to England and evolved for himself an aristocratic myth out of English literature and history. Eliot's classicism, royalism and Anglo-Catholicism, from the notion I get of them in his recent writings, seem to me as much academic attitudes, as much lacking in plausibility, as Dos Passos's cult of the class-conscious proletariat: it is as hard to imagine royalty and the Church becoming more instead of less important, even in England, as it is to imagine the American employees becoming less instead of more middle-class. Most Americans of the type of Dos Passos and Eliot—that is, sensitive and widely read literary people—have some such agreeable fantasy in which they can allow their minds to take refuge from the perplexities and oppressions about them. In the case of H. L. Mencken, it is a sort of German university town, where people drink a great deal of beer and devour a great many books, and where they respect the local nobility—if only the Germany of the Empire had not been destroyed by the war! In the case of certain American writers from the top layer of the old South, it is the old-fashioned Southern plantation, where men are high-spirited and punctilious and women gracious and lovely, where affectionate and loyal Negroes are happy to keep in their place—if only the feudal South had not perished in 1865! With Ezra Pound, it is a medieval Provence, where poor but accomplished troubadours enjoy the favors of noble ladies—if only the troubadours were not deader than Provençal! With Dos Passos, it is an army of workers, disinterested, industrious and sturdy, but full of the good-fellowship and gaiety in which the Webster Hall balls nowadays are usually so dismally lacking—if only the American workers were not pre-occupied with buying Ford cars and radios, instead of organizing themselves to overthrow the civilization of the bourgeoisie! And in T. S. Eliot's case, it is a world of seventeenth-century churchmen, who combine the most scrupulous conscience with the ability to write good prose—if it were only not so difficult nowadays for men who are capable of becoming good writers to accept the Apostolic Succession!

Among these, the writers like Dos Passos and Mencken stay at home and denounce America, while the writers like Eliot and Pound go abroad and try to forget it. It is peculiarly hard for such men to get an intellectual foothold in our world: New York, in particular, just now, is like the great glass mountain of the *Arabian Nights*, against which the barques of young writers are continually coming to grief. And this is true not merely of the United States, but more or less of the whole Western world. Industrially, politically and socially, Europe itself is becoming more and more like America every day; and the catastrophe of the war has demoralized America, too. It is up to American writers to try to make some sense of their American world—for their world is now everybody's world, and, if they fail to find a way to make possible in it what T. S. Eliot desiderates: "a spiritual and intellectual coördination on a high level," it is improbable that any one else will be able to do it for them. That world is a world with a number of religions, but not amenable to the leadership of a single church—and it is a world in which, whatever reorganization one may prophesy for the democratic state, the restoration of the monarchic principle seems improbable to the last degree. It is a world in which Eliot's program would not appear very helpful. We shall certainly not be able to lean upon the authority of either Church or King, and we shall have to depend for our new ideals on a study of contemporary reality and the power of our own imaginations.

April 24, 1929

DAHLBERG, DOS PASSOS AND WILDER

In *The Woman of Andros*, Thornton Wilder has turned Terence's *Andria* into a fable of the world without Christianity. At some indeterminate date before the birth of Christ, the son of a well-to-do merchant on the Greek island of Brynos falls in love with the sister of an hetaira and gets her with child. But it has been arranged for him by his family to marry a girl of his own class, and he is in doubt as to what to do about his mistress. The intelligent and sympathetic father leaves it up to the young man, who seeks enlightenment in a religious fast and vigil. In the meantime, however, the hetaira's household —the hetaira herself having died—has been sold to a visiting pimp, and by the time the father has succeeded in buying Glycerium back and the son has returned from the temple with his mind firmly made up to marry her, the poor girl has been overcome by the strain of her situation, and both she and her baby die.

Thornton Wilder has achieved his effect with accomplished technical skill: he has induced us to follow his story with sympathy and suspense, but he has kept us from understanding the full significance of the incidents we have been witnessing until we read the final sentence of the book, which is repeated from the first paragraph, where it has seemed to have only a casual interest, but which now retrospectively illuminates all that has come between: "But behind the thick beds of clouds the moon soared radiantly bright, shining upon Italy and its smoking mountains. And in the East the stars shone tranquilly down upon the land that was soon to be called Holy and that even then was preparing its precious burden." Looking back, we now understand that we have been watching a world in half-darkness: these people have been groping and perplexed—they have as yet known no revelation, they can depend upon no authority, to justify their impulses toward charity, toward putting the instinct of brotherhood before those of convention and interest. We see now that the cultivated hetaira—who, in conformity with the tradition of Wilder's novels, is secretly and hopelessly in love with the boy—in her acceptance of disappointment and death, and her final philosophical reflections: "I want to say to someone . . . that I have known the worst that the world can do to me, and that nevertheless I praise the world and all living. All that is, is well. Remember some day, remember me as one who loved all things and accepted from the gods all things, the bright and the dark"—we see that Chrysis is supposed to represent the highest culture and moral wisdom which, before the coming of Christ, the pagan world could attain, and that she has already, in making her house an asylum for simpleton, pauper and cripple, anticipated a new and deeper morality. We see that the ascetism of the priest of Apollo anticipates that of the Christian priesthood, that the merchant and his son are groping for principles that only the gospel of Christ can supply, and that the dead mother and child are a symbol for the death of the pagan world, which another mother and child, in "the land soon to be called Holy," are to waken to another life.

This moment before the advent of Christianity has already been exploited as a theme for fiction; it has even been a favorite theme. Its popularity has been due, I suppose, partly to the influence of Renan, who, in his *Origines du Christianisme*, subtly creates the impression that the Graeco-Roman culture was itself tending independently toward all that was best in Christianity, and that it had, also, virtues of its own that were more attractive than most of the Christian ones. Pater's *Marius the Epicurean* seems to have taken its subject and mood from the final volume of the series, which describes the reign of Marcus Aurelius; but Pater slightly shifted the emphasis: he gave Christianity a certain advantage. The Gospel is with Pater, as with Wilder, the word for which humanity has been waiting, the only thing needful that the ancient world has lacked. Anatole France followed Renan, also, but, with a livelier malice than Renan's, he tipped the scales against Christianity, and delighted, in *Sur la Pierre Blanche*, in showing how Paul before Gallio at Corinth had not really, as Renan had said, represented in his unprepossessing person the imminent future of Europe, of which the cultivated Roman had no suspicion, but had been merely the fanatical product of a semi-barbarous interlude—since, when Europe should have recovered from the Middle Ages, she was to aim, in her civilization, at Gallio's ideals, not Paul's.

Now, Wilder has picked up this pagan-Christian theme and, tipping the balance, as Pater did, in favor of Christ again, has written a book which belongs to the period of Pater and Anatole France. *The Woman of Andros*, though it is very well done, strikes me as being a kind of thing that there is no longer much point in doing. I am sure that, in revisiting the ancient world, the author has intended to tell us, as every writer must do, something interesting about our own. We gather from Wilder's play *The Angel That Troubled the Waters* that he himself is a believer in the Christian creed, and I assume that in *The Woman of Andros* he is trying to show us the sorrows and doubts that we ourselves must experience if we live without the Christian religion. There is behind many a page of this book a broken-hearted Proustian sob which has welled up, all too unmistakably, from the peculiar sentimentality of our own time and not from any state of mind that one can associate with the Greeks; and there are also some admirable passages that speak to us directly of ourselves: "From time to time she peered into her mind," Wilder writes of the dying hetaira, "to ascertain what her beliefs were in regard to life after death, its judgments or its felicities; but the most exhausting of all our adventures is that journey down the long corridors of the mind to the last halls where belief is enshrined." But the further Thornton Wilder withdraws into the past, the more imitative he becomes. This ought not necessarily to be true; but the fact is that, ever since the romantic revival set the fashion of recreating the past, the writers have been ringing the changes on the Christian-pagan theme, loading the dice for one or the other, and that dealing with the past, for Wilder, means not merely going back to Greece, not merely going back to Terence, but going back to the Paris of yesterday. His new book, for all the charm of its style, the grace of narrative and the spare firm outline which Wilder never fails of, as it is paler than his other books, comes closer to seeming mawkish. Wilder announced, or made his hero announce, at the conclusion of *The Cabala* that he was returning with high hopes to New York. But he was next heard from in Cluxambuqua, and he now hails us with rather a far faint voice from a Greek island of some vague date B.C. One always reads with pleasure and edification anything that Thornton Wilder writes—but just because he is evidently a first-rate man, one would like to see him more at home.

Edward Dahlberg, the author of *Bottom Dogs*, is, on the other hand, very close to us—he is closer to us, indeed, than we quite care to have literature be. *Bottom Dogs* is the back-streets of all our American cities and towns. Mr. Dahlberg, as a writer, has nothing in common with the consummate sophistication of Thornton Wilder, and his narrative is sometimes dull; but what he has brought in from the obscurer sections of Los Angeles, Cleveland, Kansas City is something more than an interesting document—it is a work of literature that has the stamp of a real and original gift. The prose of *Bottom Dogs* is partly derived from the language of the streets itself, but to say this may give a misleading impression: Dahlberg's prose is primarily a literary medium, hard, vivid, exact and racy, and with an odd kind of street-lighted glamor. I do not agree with D. H. Lawrence, who has written for this sordid story a curious and suggestive introduction, that the dominating feeling of the book is repulsion. It would be easy for a writer of another kind to make Dahlberg's kind of experience repulsive, but I do not feel that Dahlberg has done so: the temperament through which he has strained his orphan homes, his barber shops and bakeries, his dance-halls and Y.M.C.A.'s, though he is always realistically observant, seems a gentle and unassertive, and, consequently, an unembittered one. We read the book, at any rate, with wonder to see how the rawest, the cheapest, the most commonplace American material may be transmuted by a man of talent, so submerged in it that he can only speak its language, yet acting upon it so strongly, so imbuing it with his own tone and color and texture, that he can make it yield a work of distinction.

Now, John Dos Passos, in *The 42nd Parallel*, has consciously and deliberately worked out a medium similar to

Dahlberg's. *The 42nd Parallel*—which it seems to me Dos Passos's publishers have made a serious mistake in not announcing for what it is: the first section of a large-scale novel—is to deal with the role of the United States in relation to the rest of the world during the early years of the present century; but though it is written from the point of view of an unusually internationally minded American of unusually wide culture, the author has been able to immerse himself in the minds and the lives of his middle-class characters, to identify himself with them, to a degree that must astonish any reader of Dos Passos's other novels. In this respect, *The 42nd Parallel* is quite different from *Manhattan Transfer* and marks a striking advance beyond it. *Manhattan Transfer*, after all, might almost have been written by a very intelligent and very well-documented foreigner: the characters are seen from the outside and do not always seem organically human. But in this new work of fiction, Dos Passos has abandoned the literary baggage that encumbered his exploration of New York. Here one finds no elaborate backdrops and no Joycean prose-poems. For the method of *The 42nd Parallel*, Dos Passos has perhaps gone to school to Ring Lardner and Anita Loos; he is, at any rate, the first of our writers—with the possible exception of Mark Twain—who has successfully used colloquial American for a novel of the highest artistic seriousness. This has enabled him to keep us close to the characters as we never were in *Manhattan Transfer*. He still has moments of allowing his people to contract into two-dimensional caricatures of qualities or forces he hates; but, in general, we live their lives, we look at the world through their eyes.

These characters of *The 42nd Parallel* belong mostly to the white-collar class. Almost all of them begin as obscure and more or less mediocre-appearing people, who, from the ordinary American point of view, are anxious to improve their condition. Neither the gentle spinster stenographer from Washington, the amiable publicity director from Wilmington nor the sharp woman interior decorator from Chicago, has an intimation of any other values than those of the American business office, of the American advertising game, of the American luxury trade, out of which they make their salaries and in terms of which they conceive their ambitions. Only the nephew of the radical Irish printer reacts against the habits of the white-collar class and tends to identify his interests with those of a proletariat. The author introduces separately each one of his five principal characters —we have of each a continuous history from childhood. For this, he has invented a narrative method which enables him to cover a great deal of ground with astonishing rapidity and ease, yet to give us the illusion of finding out all about his people's lives: their friends and the members of their families, their amusements and their periods of stagnation, the places where they work and how much they get, the meals they eat, the beds they sleep in. And without any explicit commentary, each of these sequences of data and incident is made to create a character. Eleanor Stoddard's cold-blooded shrewdness and passionate appetite for refinement or J. Ward Moorhouse's unconscious charlatanry is presented entirely in terms of *things*. And when these commonplace individuals, who have first been presented to the reader independently of one another, are finally brought together, they take on a further significance—we realize that what we have been witnessing is the making of our contemporary society. And as Dos Passos can indicate in masterly fashion the shift from one city to another, so that we understand, without having been overtly told, the difference between the way people behave and feel in Chicago and the way they behave and feel in New York, in Washington, Minneapolis, Pittsburgh or Mexico City; so—also, apparently, without being told—we at last seem to understand the national character of America. The author has sandwiched in, between the sections of the life-histories of his characters, what he labels as "news-reels"—-that is, medleys of newspaper-clippings—that give us a picture of the public consciousness running parallel with the private events of the lives that are nar-rated in detail; as well as a series of brief biographies (very well done) of eminent contemporary Americans, all shown as hampered, stunted or perverted by that same commercial society in which the characters of the novel are submerged. And at the end of this first instalment, with the entrance of the United States into the war and the appearance of the last of the characters, a young garage man from North Dakota, who in his wanderings has fallen in with a rich and drunken cracker from Okeechobee City and been persuaded by him that he ought to go over and get a load of the fun in Europe "before the whole thing goes belly-up"—Dos Passos, in the perfectly aimed final paragraphs, reveals this character suddenly as a symbol for the American people, adven-turous and well-intentioned but provincial and immature, voyaging out from its enormous country into a world of which it knows nothing.

This novel, when it has been completed, may well turn out to be the most important that has yet been produced by any American of Dos Passos's generation. Dos Passos seems the only one of the novelists of this generation who is concerned with the large questions of politics and so-ciety; and he has succeeded in this book in bridging the gap, which is wider in America than anywhere else and which constitutes a perpetual problem in American litera-ture and thought, between the special concerns of the intellectual and the general pursuits and ideas of the peo-

ple. The task of the intellectual is not merely to study the
common life but to make his thoughts and symbols *seem*
relevant to it—that is, to express them in terms of the
actual American world without either cheapening them
or rendering them vapid. Dos Passos, who has read as
much and traveled as widely as Wilder, does not always
avoid spinning literature—especially in the first section,
which has a flavor of *Huckleberry Finn*; and, in consequence, he is sometimes flimsy, where Dahlberg, in dealing with a similar subject, would be authentic and dense.
But, though in neither intensity nor skill is Dos Passos
superior to Hemingway, *The 42nd Parallel* seems to me,
from the point of view of its literary originality and its
intellectual interest, by far the most remarkable, the most
encouraging American novel that I have read since the
end of the war.

March 26, 1930

NOTES ON BABBITT AND MORE

THE FOLLOWING NOTES deal with the essays by Irving Babbitt and Paul Elmer More which appeared in the humanist symposium called *Humanism and America*.

Humanism: An Essay at Definition

By Irving Babbitt

(1) *The law of measure on which it [humanism] depends becomes meaningless unless it can be shown to be one of the "laws unwritten in the heavens" of which Antigone had the immediate perception, laws that are "not of to-day or yesterday," that transcend in short the temporal process.*

This seems to me a grotesque misapplication of the famous speech from Sophocles. Let me point out, in the first place, that what Antigone says is "ἄγραπτα κἀσφαλῆ θεῶν νόμιμα"—"unwritten and unfailing laws of the gods"—and that Professor Babbitt, in changing "gods" to "heavens" (which is particularly inappropriate in this case, since Antigone has just specified the gods of the underworld), is following the Victorian tradition of Jebb and Jowett, who, by substituting such Christian words as "God" and "heaven" for the pre-Christian conceptions of the Greeks, almost succeeded in giving Sophocles and Plato the aspect of pious English dons. But Babbitt has

turned Sophocles into something worse and even more
alien to his true nature: he has turned him into a Harvard
humanist. In the scene in question, Antigone is not talking about the law of measure or anything remotely re-
sembling it—she has disobeyed Creon's edict by performing funeral rites for her brother and she is justifying herself for her insubordinate conduct. There is no self-
control about Antigone's behavior: she has committed an
act of passionate personal loyalty, regarded as excessively
rash and wrong-headed by everybody else in the play, including her own sister, whose "inner check" is more
highly developed than Antigone's. When Creon demands
how Antigone has dared to break the law, she answers
fiercely that such a law as his edict is contrary to the laws
of the gods.

The romantic might, in fact, turn this scene against
the humanist with more appropriateness than the humanist can use it against the romantic. Antigone has the
same hasty insolent intemperate nature as her father
Oedipus—we are told so explicitly in the play—and she
is asserting her individual will in defiance of law and
expediency—she is making an impulsive and desperate
gesture. Aristotle—"a true humanist," according to Babbitt—says of this passage, in showing the distinction
between conventional and natural law, that Antigone
vindicates the latter in asserting "ὅτι δίκαιον, ἀπειρημένον,
θάψαι τὸν Πολυνείκη, ὡς φύσει ὂν τοῦτο δίκαιον,"—that her
act, though it violated the prohibition, had the sanction
of natural right, was "right according to nature." Now
Antigone, of course, is not a nineteenth-century romantic,
and Aristotle does not mean by "nature" quite the same
thing that Rousseau does. But what Rousseau means does
have something in common with what Aristotle means
that Antigone means, whereas what Antigone means can't
by any possible stretch be associated with Babbitt's "law

of measure." Babbitt grossly misrepresents Sophocles when he applies Antigone's speech in this way: "The laws unwritten in the heavens" is one of Babbitt's favorite quotations: he has used it again and again in order to give us the impression that Sophocles has endorsed the humanist "will to refrain." Yet, as I say, if it is a question of slinging classical texts, the old-fashioned romantic who is Babbitt's bugbear—if there be any such still alive— might turn Antigone's outburst against Babbitt—and, relapsing into the truculence of the age of Bentley, which the manners of the humanists invite, might add, as Antigone does:

σοὶ δ' εἰ δοκῶ νῦν μῶρα δρῶσα τυγχάνειν,
σχεδόν τι μώρῳ μωρίαν ὀφλισκάνω.

Babbitt elsewhere in this essay says that Sophocles "ranks high among occidental humanists," though he admits—making reservations in regard to the opinion of Matthew Arnold—that "perfect poise is no doubt impossible; not even Sophocles succeeded in seeing life steadily and seeing it whole." I don't know in precisely what respect Professor Babbitt considers Sophocles to have fallen short of perfect poise; but it is certainly true that Sophocles' characters are usually remarkable for anything but poise—they are as violent and as harsh as the people in the plays of Eugene O'Neill. Where the "law of measure" comes in is certainly not in connection with the conduct of Sophocles' people—the hot-headed overconfident Oedipus; the "fierce child of a fierce father," Antigone; the relentless and morbid Electra, etc. —but in Sophocles' handling of his material—the firmness of his intellectual grasp, the sureness of his sense of form, the range of psychological insight which enables him to put before us the rages, the ambitions, the loyalties, of so many passionate persons, that spend themselves against one another and expire in the clear air, leaving only with the echo of their tirades the vibration of the taut verse. In a world dominated by the law of measure, there would, however, be no humanist masterpieces such as the tragedies of Sophocles—since Babbitt claims them, with reservations, as humanist masterpieces—because there would be no violent passions to write about. This might be a good thing—perhaps we ought to be glad to do without the Sophocleses if we could get rid of the unruly passions. But, on the other hand, we ought perhaps to think twice before letting ourselves in for a world where the sole masterpieces were humanist symposia.

(2) *It would not be easy to argue with any plausibility that the typical modernist is greatly concerned with the law of measure; his interest, as a glance at our newspapers should suffice to show, is rather in the doing of stunts and the breaking of records, in "prodigies, feats of strength and crime," the very topics that, according to the traditional report, Confucius banished from his conversation.*

In this respect, our age is no worse than any other. What is done today for the people by the newspapers was done formerly by the composers of ballads, and ballad literature has always been occupied with prodigies, feats of strength and crime. The *Iliad* itself was presumably made out of ballads—and, in any case, there can be no question that it deals with prodigies, feats of strength and crime. The Greek dramatists, including Sophocles, got their themes from Homer or similar sources. It is true that the genuine poet is able to do with such stories something that the simple reporter is not usually able to do, but the material that he deals with is the same. And the general run of the ballads of any age has been as crude as newspaper stories. The sages of our own time—Professor Babbitt, for example—are, I should say, as little preoccu-

pied with the prodigies and crimes of the newspapers as
Confucius was with the common gossip.

(3) *In the case of such encroachments [of naturalism
upon the domains of humanism or religion] there is not
only a quarrel between the naturalist and the humanist,
but a quarrel of first principles. When first principles are
involved the law of measure is no longer applicable. One
should not be moderate in dealing with error.*

It has apparently never occurred to Professor Babbitt
that one's moderation ought to extend to not being too
sure that one is absolutely right and that others are absolutely wrong—though Mr. More, in his companion
essay, quotes from Whitehead, against the dogmatists of
Darwinism, Cromwell's, "My brethren, by the bowels of
Christ I beseech you, bethink you that you may be mistaken!" We might have thought that if the law of measure were valuable anywhere, it would be valuable in the
domain of ideas, where the failure sufficiently to respect
it has notoriously bred war and oppression since the
beginning of the world. Babbitt surely did not learn from
Plato, whom he invokes in the next paragraph, that we
should feel so sure of our own opinions that we need not
be moderate with other people who happen to have
different ones. The hero of Plato's novel of ideas is, of
course, Socrates, but Plato's dialogues are a novel, none
the less, and the impression, I think, that most people get
from them, though they may be persuaded by Socrates'
opinions, is that the world has a good many aspects and
that there is a good deal to be said on all sides. The people
in Plato who follow Babbitt's precept that we "should
not be moderate in dealing with error" are the judges of
Socrates. I doubt whether even Aristotle was so sure that
he was right as Babbitt. If Mr. Babbitt wants to find a
tradition for his policy in dealing with error, he must

look not to the Academy and the Lyceum, but to the councils of the Inquisition, the revolutionary tribunal of the Terror and—to come closer to Professor Babbitt's home—Dedham Courthouse and Boston State House.*

(4) *Positively one may define it [the higher will] as the higher immediacy that is known in its relation to the lower immediacy—the merely temperamental man with his impressions and emotions and expansive desires —as a power of vital control* (frein vital).

So Paul Elmer More asserts (in *Aristocracy and Justice*) that if a man "retires into himself and examines his own motives and the courses of his self-approval and discontent . . . he will discover that there is a happiness of the soul which is not the same as the pleasure of fulfilled desires, whether these be for good or for ill, a happiness which is not dependent upon the results of this or that choice among our desires, but upon the very act itself of choice and self-control."

Now, why on earth is virtue, with the humanists, always made to reside exclusively in what Babbitt calls the "will to refrain"? "Humanism," says Professor Babbitt, in making a distinction between humanism and religion, "is not primarily enthusiastic." So far as I can see, it is not enthusiastic at all. Professor Babbitt goes on to say that the humanist, though he "cannot afford to be an enthusiast in Rousseau's sense, on the other hand should not neglect the truth of Rousseau's saying that 'cold reason has never done anything illustrious.'" But the writings of the humanists strike us with a chill even more mortal than that of reason. And how can one be seriously impressed by a philosophy which enjoins nothing but negative behavior?—as if humanity were not, now as always, as much in need of being exhorted against cold-

* This refers to the Sacco-Vanzetti case.

ness and indifference and routine as against irresponsible
exuberance—especially Anglo-Saxon humanity. As if it
were not obvious that Boston and New York, Manchester
and London, were not suffering rather from a lack of
normal human fellowship and normal human hope and
joy than from any demoralizing effects of unbridled
"humanitarian" sympathies, indiscriminate emotional
"expansiveness" or universal orgiastic dissipation—as if
our clerks, our factory workers and our respectable professional and business classes were all in danger of falling
victims to the rhapsodical enthusiasm and the lawless
individualism of romanticism! If it is merely a question of
refraining, these people are all good humanists: they have
either been compelled by society to refrain from most of
the enjoyments, from the exercise of most of the faculties,
that make the amenity of human life, or they refrain
because their education has been too limited to enable
them to conceive their own aesthetic and emotional possibilities, or because their natures are too poor to have
any.

As a matter of fact, however, Professor Babbitt, as I
have noted above, has managed to exempt his own professional activities from the law of measure, the duty to
refrain. He makes it plain that, in "dealing with error,"
we are no longer obliged to be moderate; and as Professor
Babbitt, in his writings, hardly ever deals with anything
but error, he is rarely obliged to be moderate. Professor
Babbitt—and the other humanists—are permittted to
drop their ideal of decorum the moment they put pen to
paper. It is not decorous to look for nothing but mistakes
in the writings of your contemporaries; it is not decorous
always to call attention to these mistakes with a sneer; it
is not decorous to take a word like humanism, which has
formerly been applied to the great scholars, philosophers,
satirists and poets of the Renaissance, and to insist that

it ought to be regarded as the property of a small sect of schoolmasters so fatuous that they do not hesitate to assign schoolmasters' A's, B's and C's in humanism to "Homer, Phidias, Plato, Aristotle, Confucius, Buddha, Jesus, Paul, Virgil, Horace, Dante, Shakespeare, Milton, Goethe, Matthew Arnold, Emerson and Lowell" (I quote a list of their preferred great figures); it is not decorous to assume that you yourselves are the only persons who have taken seriously the vices and woes of your own time and that everybody except yourselves is engaged either perversely or stupidly in trying to make them worse. The exercise of decorum by the humanists is evidently confined to their private lives, where the public cannot benefit by it.

(5) *This movement has, from the eighteenth century and in some respects from the Renaissance, been marked by a growing discredit of the will to refrain. The very word renunciation has been rarely pronounced by those who have entered into the movement. The chief exception that occurs to one is Goethe (echoed at times by Carlyle). Any one who thinks of the series of Goethe's love affairs, prolonged into the seventies, is scarcely likely to maintain that his* Entsagung *was of a very austere character even for a man of the world, not to speak of a saint.*

It seems to me that assumptions are here being made in regard to sexual morality which require a good deal of proving on Professor Babbitt's part. He goes on to say, a little further, that "the real humanist consents, like Aristotle, to limit his desires only in so far as this limitation can be shown to make for his own happiness." If one disapproves of Goethe's love affairs, but if the end to be achieved is happiness, one would have to show first that these love affairs failed to make Goethe happy. It seems

NOTES ON BABBITT AND MORE 459

to me that Mr. Babbitt should shoulder this burden of proof and argue that it did not do Goethe good at the same time that it did the ladies no harm for him to fall in love after he was seventy. But these are questions which Babbitt and More will never consent to argue, as to which they simply make assumptions—just as they assume that virtue is identical with the will to refrain— for the reason that these opinions are not really conclusions from evidence, but the mere unexamined prejudices of a bigoted Puritan heritage which these gentlemen—for all their voyaging through the varied realms of the mind—have never succeeded in sloughing off, and which they persist in mistaking for eternal and universal laws, because—they have put this forward as an overwhelming justification—when they look into their own natures, they find them there.

The Humility of Common Sense

By Paul Elmer More

(1) *It is a nice question to ask whether belief in the absolute irresponsibility of the artistic temperament has engendered the modern ideal of absolute art, or the contrary. . . . The point I would make is the falseness and futility of the logical deduction that art can . . . dispense with the stuff of humanity or nature, or can weigh anchor and sail off into a shoreless sea of unreality.*

In the first part of Mr. More's essay, marked by his usual intellectual arrogance, which he incongruously entitles *The Humility of Common Sense,* he is occupied with the old "art for art's sake" doctrine as it has recently been formulated by some of its champions. Now, one may agree with Mr. More that the artist should not be irresponsible and that he cannot dispense with humanity and nature—one may even agree that "art for art's sake" has given rise to a good deal of nonsense, as indeed what doctrine has not? But it is obvious that Mr. More fails to see how this point of view is the natural and inevitable product of a particular situation. Art is, of course, a profession like medicine, law or banking, a trade like market-gardening or carpentry, that supplies certain human needs; it is one of our human devices for adjusting ourselves to the world and for mastering it in a way that the other animals cannot do. It is preposterous, certainly, for artists to talk as if they were able to work *in vacuo* or as if it were possible for them to remain indifferent to the effects of their work on human life. But in the course of the nineteenth century, they were goaded into talking in this way, into making a cult of art for its own sake, by the progress of the industrial revolution and the rise of the middle class. It was one of the fatal defects of industrial-commercial society that it neglected or discouraged the appetites for which the artists had formerly provided; and as the market value of art depreciated to the point where its practitioners found themselves pushed almost into the role of outlaws, they became embittered and desperate. They swore, if they had any spirit, that they were going to work at their craft even though nobody wanted their wares, and they thus arrived at the slogan that has irritated so many people. The fact that they should have felt the necessity for asserting the value of what they were doing was a sign of their maladjustment, of the abnormality of their situation; but, given this situation, the very faith in aesthetic values, the dogged devotion to art, not infrequently called forth qualities of heroic endurance and self-denial. It was to some extent true,

of course—especially toward the end of the century—
that the isolation of the artist, his consciousness of
swimming against the current, had sometimes the effect
of deforming his work. But what student of literature
who is not content naïvely to praise or blame while
referring works from different periods to the same ideal
standards, what critic aware of art in its relation to the
other forces of the society in which it is practised, will
assert that even the poet of the fin de siècle could or
should have done otherwise? In the generation of the
middle century, even so great a man as Flaubert had
found it possible to save his soul only through the cult
of art. Yet the notion that the cynical Flaubert and the
diabolistic Baudelaire could have exercised, in their novels
and poems, the most exacting kind of self-discipline,
exerted, in dealing with the materials supplied them by
their imaginations, a rigorous will to refrain; that their
work might thus fortify their readers as well as entertain
them—this is something Mr. Paul Elmer More seems
incapable of conceiving. He apparently believes that the
only way in which it is possible for a reader or a writer
to school himself in these bad days is to read or write
literary criticism of the type of his own and Babbitt's,
which, though based on thorough reading and distinguished by sound writing, has obviously not required
a discipline a tenth as difficult as that which has gone
to produce some of the works it so loftily castigates.

Even aside, however, from its meaning in this special
situation, the slogan of "art for art's sake" has a meaning
which would still remain valid even in an age which
did not, as our own does, freeze out the artists and make
them defiant. From this point of view, Mr. More's attitude is open to the same sort of criticism as that of the
not insensitive but rather unintelligent socialist of the
type of Upton Sinclair. Upton Sinclair disapproves of

works of art which do not point explicitly a socialist
moral, as Paul Elmer More disapproves of works of art
which do not point explicitly the moral of self-control.
Each insists on denouncing as irresponsible and evil or
futile all the writers in which it is impossible for him to
find his own particular moral stated in his own particular
terms. Now, aside from the fact that reality presents a
variety of aspects and may be expected to suggest more
than one kind of moral, and aside from the fact that
fine workmanship itself always contains an implicit
moral, it should further be borne in mind that in the
arts as in the sciences a certain freedom for experimentation is necessary: one must allow a good deal of apparently gratuitous, and even empty or ridiculous work, if
one wants to get masterpieces. Gregor Mendel was
dead eighteen years before anyone had even suspected
that his hobby of interbreeding green peas was anything
other than a harmless monastic diversion; Gauss's non-
Euclidean geometry, which he had been too timid to
publish, as well as Ricci and Levi-Civita's calculus, had
seemed the idlest of mathematical exercises till Einstein
found them just the tools he needed, ready to his hand.
But, in general, the gratuitous experimentation of the
scientific world is known only inside its own laboratories,
whereas the corresponding work of the literary world is
likely to be circulated more widely. When it happens to
fall under the eye of an Upton Sinclair or a Paul Elmer
More, he is infuriated by what seems to him its fatuity:
he demands at once to know what these writers imagine
they are good for. Well, they may not be good for anything, but, on the other hand, they may be valuable—
one has to wait and see what comes of them, what other
writers may get out of them. Virgil, a poet in high repute
with Mr. More and the other humanists, had laid under
contribution not merely Homer but also the romantic

rebel Apollonius Rhodius, whose innovations, in Alexandria, had had no important results; but from whom, two and a half centuries later, Virgil was partly to derive his misty and subtle feeling for nature and human life. The Alexandrians—as, for different reasons, the poets of the end of the century—were denied participation in the life of a great society, and they cultivated art for art's sake. In view of their having kept alive the poetic tradition of Greece as well as having made contributions to the later poetry of Rome, will Paul Elmer More contend today that the work of these writers was futile?

(2) *They ["a few restless souls" among the "radical writers of to-day"] hold deliberation to be the foe of liberation. Hence the later theory, exemplified in English by James Joyce, that art shall not reproduce a picture of life as the humanist sees it, or even from the point of view of the realist, but for its subject matter shall descend to what they call the pure "stream of consciousness." The hero of fiction shall have no will, no purpose, no inhibition, no power of choice whether for good or evil, but shall be merely a medium through which passes an endless, unchecked, meaningless flux of sensations and memories and emotions and impulses.*

But Joyce does not exemplify anything of the sort: his characters are all going about their business like the characters of any other novelist. Bloom, Dedalus, Mrs. Bloom and the others do have their wills, their purposes, their inhibitions, and they make their moral decisions—indeed, these moral decisions are the crucial events of *Ulysses*. What has probably misled Mr. More is Joyce's method of dealing with the human mind, not by telling us what it does, but by trying to present it directly in the terms in which it is aware of itself from hour to hour, from moment to moment. The minds of the people

in Joyce are sometimes relaxed or confused, at other times
intent and lucid: it depends on the character and the
situation. The principal way in which *Ulysses* differs
from the kind of novel to which Mr. More is accustomed is not in Joyce's depriving his characters of moral
sense or will, but simply in his showing us their conscious-
nesses as if they were beehives under glass, and of making
us watch them through the whole of a day—it is a
difference of technique, and of pace and scale. But I
cannot suppose, as a matter of fact—from the extreme
inappropriateness of Mr. More's remarks about Joyce—
that he has ever done anything more than look into him,
and I will venture to say that this high-handed habit on
the part of the humanist critics of attempting to dispose
of contemporary writers whom they obviously haven't
read by supercilious classroom jeers is an even more
serious scandal to their cause than their misrepresentation
of the ancients, whom they have at least carefully studied.
So Mr. More, in *The Demon of the Absolute,* has described Dos Passos's *Manhattan Transfer* as "an ex-
plosion in a cesspool" without apparently the faintest
suspicion that Dos Passos intends his novel as an indictment of the same social conditions of which Mr. More
himself has always taken so gloomy a view. But not
only is Mr. More unable to recognize in *Manhattan
Transfer* the work of a man who, like himself, has
been "deafened," as he once wrote of his own state of
mind, "by the 'indistinguishable roar' of the streets" and
can "make no sense of the noisy jargon of the market
place," and who finally causes his hero to escape from the
modern American city with as much relief as ever Mr.
More did when he went into his celebrated retreat at
Shelburne; he has not even succeeded in informing
himself from any other sources than this novel as to Dos
Passos's general point of view. If Dos Passos had been a

second-rate eighteenth-century essayist, Mr. More would know everything about him, including his political opinions—if he had been the most obscure New England poet (of the seventeenth century, that is), Mr. More would have read him through.

(3) *"The only way of mitigating mechanism,"* he [A. N. Whitehead] says, *"is by discovery that it is not mechanism." And so, instead of admitting humbly that mechanism is mechanism while beside it there exists something of a totally different nature, and that the ultimate nexus between these two fields of experience surpasses our comprehension, he must demonstrate mechanism out of the world altogether.*

But why *should* Whitehead admit humbly that mechanism is mechanism and that humanity exists beside it as something of a totally different nature? Why *should* he assume that the ultimate nexus between these two fields of experience surpasses our comprehension? I do not feel with Mr. More that the effect of Whitehead's metaphysics is to "make a travesty of the inorganic world," that it threatens "to deprive humanity of what is distinctly human." Why should Mr. More take for granted that to change our idea of humanity necessarily means to degrade it? There can be no advances in philosophy without the altering of old conceptions. And I cannot, for the life of me, see that Mr. More has any other real objection to Whitehead's ideas than that they would, as he believes—and I am not sure that he is right even here—tend to discredit the distinction between "man" and "thing" upon which his own humanistic philosophy is based. He makes no attempt to show that Whitehead's speculations are not justified, that his arguments are not sound; he makes no effort whatever to discuss the scientific findings—the conception of the "event," for ex-

ample, as the ultimate unit of both the organic and the
inorganic worlds—upon which Whitehead has based his
metaphysics and which he did not himself invent. He
merely asserts that Whitehead should never have undertaken at all to account for the relations between the
organic and the inorganic worlds. He says that he "admits" this "humbly," but one gathers from his tone that
he would, if he could, get out an injunction against all
wanton metaphysics directed to this end, just as he
would, if he could, get out an injunction against all experimentation in the arts. Yet it is plain that if the philosophers of the past had been content to accept so in-
curiously the apparent paradoxes of experience, we
should not have any philosophy at all, and Mr. More
would have no Plato and no Platonists to beguile his
academic retirement. One cannot avoid the conclusion
that the primary difficulty for Mr. More is to admit that
it is possible for anyone, either in art or in science, to find
out anything new, and I cannot explain this state of mind
except on the hypothesis that Mr. More is really an old-
fashioned Puritan who has lost the Puritan theology
without having lost the Puritan dogmatism. Mr. More is
more certainly than Professor Babbitt a man of some
imagination; he is able, up to a point, to follow the
thought of the modern world, as appears from his not
unintelligent and often sensitive expositions of the ideas
of other writers (if they are not absolutely contemporaries); but some iron inhibition seems inevitably to
come into play to restrain Mr. More from agreeing with
anything in modern philosophy or from accepting anything in modern art. Everything he encounters here seems
to have the effect of alarming him, even when, as in the
case of Whitehead, one would think he ought to find it
reassuring. One law for man and another law for thing
is the whole of philosophy for More, as the will to re-

frain is the whole of morals. Outside these—anywhere, that is, except among the brave little band of humanists —he sees only perdition, chaos. It is as if Mr. More, on one of his sides, were capable of meeting on his own ground the great modern philosopher or poet, but as if some other element in his nature—which he tries to foist upon us, too, as the universal law of the "inner check"—had operated to make him shy away from philosophy and poetry themselves, so that, in spite of his vigorous intellect and his genuine sensibility, he is unable to allow himself to profit by any book not written sufficiently long ago to have acquired an academic sanction almost equivalent to a religious one.

A certain passage from Whitehead's *Science and the Modern World* is quoted by Mr. More as follows: "When Darwin or Einstein proclaim[s] theories which modify our ideas, it is a triumph for science." Mr. More is going on to criticize this passage, but in the meantime he has observed that Whitehead has been so indiscreet as to write "proclaim" as a plural verb after two subjects connected by "or," and where any ordinary critic would either have left Whitehead's sentence as he wrote it or have made him a present of the singular ending without calling the reader's attention to it, Mr. More has put it in brackets, as who should comment scornfully "[sic!]." Mr. More may not be able, or may not dare, to imagine, as Whitehead has done, a metaphysical explanation of the relations between the organic and the inorganic worlds, but he can, and, by Heaven, he will, correct this philosopher's grammar!

March 19, 1930

SOPHOCLES, BABBITT AND FREUD

MR. SEWARD COLLINS has taken me to task in the October number of the *Bookman* for my remarks on Irving Babbitt and Sophocles published in the *New Republic* of March 19, and I see that Mr. Gorham B. Munson also considers me unsound on this point. I had objected to Professor Babbitt's advertising his "law of measure" as one of the authentic "unwritten laws of the gods" to which Antigone appeals in the scene where she defies Creon. It is plain that Professor Babbitt has never, in the name of his law of measure, attempted to induce anyone to defy any written law whatever; but Mr. Collins asserts that he is justified in his allusion to Sophocles' heroine, because Babbitt, like Antigone, is appealing to conscience. They are both vindicating moral principles that are not prescribed by the letter of the law, but that are matters, primarily, of individual insight. He refers me to a passage in *Oedipus Rex,* where the laws of the gods are also invoked. I have looked this passage up, and I find that the divine laws are mentioned here in quite a different connection. The chorus are frightened and worried, because things are looking bad for Oepidus: they are doing the Greek equivalent of crossing themselves, they hope that they may be kept pure in word and deed. If Babbitt wanted a tag from Sophocles, this passage would have been more to his purpose, but the fact is that he always uses *Antigone*. I also found in Jebb's text a note that referred to a passage in Book VII of Plato's *Laws,* and I looked this up, too. There the phrase is much closer to *Antigone* than the phrase in *Oedipus Rex*—ἄγραπτα νόμιμα, Sophocles; ἄγραφα νόμιμα, Plato—but it turned out that the "unwritten laws" in question were not the higher insights of conscience, but the ancient uncodified customs—in connection with education and the care of children— "commonly called unwritten laws." "Unwritten laws," then, was a common phrase used by Antigone for her own particular purpose. If it means to her what it means to Plato, she is referring merely to the traditional custom of sprinkling earth on the bodies of the dead, in which case it has obviously nothing in common with the moral revelations of Babbitt. And if it is taken as a justification of her own moral revelations, it still seems to me that there is a grotesque discrepancy between Antigone standing up to Creon and Babbitt and Mr. Collins making themselves disagreeable over humanism. It still seems to me that Irving Babbitt is very far from understanding Antigone.

But of course Mr. Collins thinks that it is I who do not understand Antigone. He believes that, by describing her as "passionate" and "fierce," I have made her into "a Greenwich Village heroine." Well, first of all, I hadn't supposed that anybody denied that Antigone was fiery and insubordinate—Jebb certainly doesn't: see his introduction. Mr. Collins says that when I call her "fierce," I have only one word to go upon and that that represents in the text a momentary and erroneous opinion on the part of the troubled chorus; but actually the chorus again and again apply to Antigone such terms as "passionate" and "fierce," and the line that I quoted, "fierce child of a fierce father," indicates—what is otherwise plain from the way in which she behaves—that Sophocles intended Antigone to have inherited certain qualities from Oedipus. I suppose that even the humanists will not dispute that Oedipus was hasty and insolent—his deplorable ὕβρις is an academic cliché. The dramatist, as a matter of fact, represents the whole family of Oedipus, with the single exception of Ismene, as exceedingly bad-tempered and rash (see the brawl between Oedipus and his father, the quarrel between the brothers, and the cursing of his son by Oedipus). Bad-tempered people are Sophocles' specialty; his characters, as I said, resemble in this respect—and I said that they resembled in this respect only—the characters of Eugene O'Neill.

Granted, however, that Antigone is naturally impetuous and wilful, why does she make such an issue of performing the funeral rites for her brother, Polyneices? According to Mr. Collins, her insistence is merely a matter of "family piety and religious duty." Again, I did not know that anyone disputed that Antigone's motive was a special affection for her brother. But this raises an interesting question, which must be my excuse for prolonging this controversy. In the *Antigone* as it stands in the manuscripts, and as Sophocles presumably wrote it, one of the striking features of the heroine's behavior is the fact that, though she is engaged to be married, she never mentions this fact or her fiancé. In her anxiety for her dead brother, no thought of her living lover comes to make her hesitate a moment in her resolve to sacrifice herself. She does not even go to Haemon to complain about the edict, as a woman in love would be sure to do— especially since Haemon is Creon's son and it would have been natural for her to try to get him to intercede with his father. We, in fact, hardly hear about Haemon at all till he comes to intercede on his own account. When Antigone is about to be led away, she laments that she must die unmarried, but only in a general way and still without mentioning Haemon, who a little while before has rushed off in fury and desperation and who will kill himself after a vain effort to save her. She does, however, apostrophize Polyneices: she tells him that what she has done for him she would never have done for a child or a husband—for one can always get another child or husband, whereas a brother is irreplaceable.

This, as I say, is what happens in the *Antigone* as Sophocles presumably wrote it. But Richard Jebb, following certain other scholars, has found this version unintelligible and has proceeded to alter the text in such a way, from his own point of view, to make Antigone more winning than human. His first intervention occurs in a scene in which Antigone's sister, the gentler and more conventional Ismene, remonstrates with her uncle Creon for robbing his son of a bride. Antigone is standing by, but, as is normal with Sophocles, only two persons speak in the dialogue. Now Jebb, with no textual justification, takes away one of Ismene's lines, in which she exclaims "O beloved Haemon, how thy father wrongs thee!" and assigns it to Antigone, and avoids making the dialogue more complicated still by attributing the next line to the chorus, who are immediately to take up the theme. Thus Antigone is given, as he says, a "solitary reference to her love" which "heightens in a wonderful degree our sense of her unselfish devotion to a sacred duty." Jebb's only attempt to make this tampering acceptable by adducing internal evidence consists of a single objection on the basis of a phrase in the line that follows, an objection that he himself invalidates by quoting from Sophocles' *Electra* an example of a similar phrase used precisely in the sense that he wants to discredit. And when he comes to the sixteen-line passage about dying for a brother rather than a husband, he rejects it altogether as spurious, in spite of the fact that Aristotle had it and that Jebb himself is forced to confess that he can hardly discover a shadow of a linguistic reason against it. The principal argument is that certain of these lines have a close resemblance to a passage in Herodotus; but may this not be merely a case of a common ancient saying which both Herodotus and Sophocles had heard and which Sophocles makes his heroine press into service naïvely to explain and defend her behavior, just as he makes her resort to the phrase about the "unwritten laws of the gods"? I am told by an English friend of a similar saying in England, which he heard as a child from his nurse, about the unique value of brothers as compared with lovers. Jebb, however, finds the scene incomprehensible, and he is able to invoke the authority of Goethe, who told Eckermann that this speech of Antigone's vitiated the whole play by assigning to the heroine an "unworthy" motive after she had "given the most admirable reasons for her conduct" and "shown the noble courage of a stainless soul." But this objection had never occurred to Aristotle, and can we suppose that it would have occurred to Goethe if he had lived late enough to have read Freud?

For it is not, I believe, due entirely to the accident of Sophocles' having written a play involving an incestuous relation that the Oedipus complex has been named after his hero. Mr. Collins has reproached me for showing myself "about as near to the true spirit of Sophocles as an Oedipus complex"; but if he will read the passage in *Oedipus Rex* in which Jocasta tries to reassure her son-husband by telling him that men often dream of sexual relations with their mothers, he will see that there is more in common between Sophocles and Freud than he supposes. And it seems to me plain that, in Antigone, the poet was consciously presenting a case of what we should call nowadays a brother-fixation. Sophocles did not call it that, and he did not consider it from our clinical point of view; but his comprehension of human motives was profound and realistic, and it seems to me impossible not to conclude that he emphasized deliberately for his dramatic purpose the difference between Antigone's attitude toward Haemon and her attitude toward Polyneices.

When we compare Antigone with Electra, our suspicions are further confirmed. Antigone and Electra are in certain ways very different: Electra is ingrown and virulent whereas Antigone is candid and appealing. But they are in other ways much alike: both are self-willed and ruthless, and both are contrasted with weaker, more "feminine" sisters: Electra's scenes with Chrysothemis are obvious counterparts to Antigone's scenes with Ismene. Jebb himself notes the closeness of this parallel. Furthermore, both Electra and Antigone are passionately attached to brothers. The first things that we learn about Electra are that she bitterly hates her mother and broods continually on the wrong done her father; she is morbid, vituperative, harsh: we tend at first to find her unsympathetic. It is only when she is told that her brother is dead and given the urn that is supposed to contain his ashes that we really come to understand her. She breaks down over the urn, and it is revealed to us for the first time how much tenderness, affection, devotion has for years been subdued and perverted by a life vowed entirely to vengeance. It has been only the memory of Orestes, her brother whom she has nursed as a child, as dear to her as to his mother, whom she had not allowed to be cared for by the servants and who had called her alone among his sisters "Sister"—it has been only the memory of Orestes and the hope of his eventual return that have kept her alive in the hated household (Euripides' Electra is married, but Sophocles' is not). Now Orestes appears and reveals himself—the brother and sister are reunited for the first time in ten years: the avengers drop their masks, and the most moving scene in the tragedy occurs. Then Orestes, with the connivance of Electra, goes in and kills Clytaemnestra.

Now, Seward Collins asserts that Antigone "is impelled primarily by religious conviction" and accuses me of being incapable of admitting that "the heroine of a Greek drama might have acted from noble motives." But Electra also, for that matter, is acting with a religious sanction. Has not Apollo himself told Orestes to kill his mother? And how do the humanists stand in regard to the nobility of matricide and in regard to all the other outrageous things for which the characters in Greek tragedies claim a divine sanction? The chorus in *Electra* too, invokes the unwritten laws, in connection with her duty to her murdered father—and how can you get any humanism out of *Electra*? The moral philosophy that the humanists profess to derive from Sophocles seems to me pure boloney. Sophocles is essentially a dramatist, a presenter of character in conflict. If he happened to be a modern, a single blast of the black bitter pessimism of the choruses of *Oedipus Coloneus* would have been enough to scare them off this poet for life. And his Freudian situations would have caused them to shudder with horror.

Apropos of these latter, has nobody ever written about the Freudian aspect of Antigone, in connection with this controverted passage? If the scholars have not yet done so, the analysts surely must have.

December 3, 1930

This article attracted the attention of Professor Walter R. Agard of the University of Wisconsin, who had been working on the problem of the controverted lines in the *Antigone,* and he later sent me a paper on the subject— *Antigone* 904-20, in the issue of *Classical Philology* of July, 1937—which defends the authenticity of this passage, analyzing the motives of Antigone and corroborating my view of her character:

"This rationalization [of her concern for her brother]," Mr. Agard writes, "admittedly unconvincing to any sober-minded person, is in keeping with the character of Antigone. She is not sober-minded. Not only in this play and in the *Oedipus at Colonus* of Sophocles, but also in the *Seven against Thebes* of Aeschylus and Euripides' *Phoenician Women,* Antigone is pictured as an emotionally high-strung girl, devoted above all else to her ill-fated father and brothers, with whom she closely identifies herself. Feeling rather than reason controls her actions, as the Chorus is frank in saying (383, 'captured in folly'; 471-72, 'passionate child of a passionate father, she does not know how to yield to misfortune'). Toward Polyneices this feeling is directed with special intensity. It is obviously more than religious duty that impels her to bury his body. She loves him passionately (Antigone 48, 'my own'; 73, 'I shall lie in death beloved, with him, my dear one'; 81, 'my dearest brother'; 503, 'my own brother')."

But it is probably unnecessary at this late date to insist that Antigone was not a humanist.

"H. C."*

ONE'S FIRST ENCOUNTERS with Herbert Croly were likely to be rather baffling. It was never very easy for him to deal with people, and if the visitor himself were at all diffident, he would be likely to find the conversation petering out in a discontinuous series of remarks offered more and more haltingly by the visitor, to which Croly would mutter responses more and more fragmentary and more and more imperfectly audible. Eventually the visitor would lose heart and stop, and a terrible silence would fall: the atmosphere would become taut with panic. Croly would sit absolutely motionless, his eyes dropped on his hands, which would be clasped in his lap; his face was rather sallow, and to the visitor appeared hostile or morose. As the silence went on longer and longer and became more and more unbearable, the visitor would finally be driven to break it at any price by some absurd or irrelevant opening, to which Croly would be likely to return some equally wild reply; and the visitor, uncomfortable and puzzled, would conclude that the interview was over and that, brief and inconclusive though it might have been, he had already stayed too long. He would awkwardly take his leave and

* This was written for an issue of the *New Republic* devoted to memoirs and appreciations of its late editor-in-chief, Herbert Croly, who had died on May 17, 1930.

go away more mystified than ever as to the personality of
the editor of the *New Republic,* who seemed to play
so important a role in American political journalism
without one's ever having been able to discover precisely
what sort of man he was.

But on some other occasion, if one continued to see
him, a contact would eventually be made. Something
said would reach below the level on which ordinary
conversation is conducted—a level at which it was almost
impossible for Croly to carry on conversation at all—and
he would respond with an earnestness which, with a
minimum of emphasis, carried a maximum of conviction.
He would lift his gaze and meet you directly: his eyes
were clear, firm and green, and his look was one of the
straightest I have ever known. One felt that one had
looked into the eyes of an absolutely candid and honest
person—that the public affairs of which one had been
talking were things that mattered to Croly as deeply as
our private affairs do to the rest of us. When he stood up,
one became aware that his figure—he was an excellent
tennis-player—was slender and erect. And as one had
been surprised by the clear straight green gaze from those
dim and meditative, those brooding eyes, so when thereafter one read his editorials, one had the sense of, behind
their anonymity and their sometimes forbidding style, the
absolute sincerity and seriousness which made him in
the intellectual life of his time a figure so much more
important and so much more interesting than many more
brilliant writers and more picturesque personalities, even
when they had succeeded in learning what Croly had to
teach and had expressed it more strikingly than he could.
Political journalism is, after all, even among radicals and
liberals, much of the time merely a job like another, and
may as easily become a matter of routine as a job of any
other kind. But this it never became for Croly: a distant

war, a scoundrel returned to office, which for most of us would be merely a subject for a disapproving editorial, would be for Croly events which touched his life, which, when he spoke of them, obviously gave him pain.

But one might be aware of all this and yet at first have no idea of the sensitivity, the intelligence and the intensity which his constraint so often masked. If he seemed impassive—and he sometimes impressed people as being as impassive as a Chinaman—it was not because he remained impervious to the things that went on around him, but because he felt them too much. He was, for example, extraordinarily perceptive of people's personal qualities and behavior, and he could see at once what most people were up to. This was one of the principal reasons for his value as a political critic: he was usually able with remarkable accuracy to calculate what sort of abilities any figure in public life would develop and how he would be likely to act. He was sometimes accused of serious mistakes, in politics as well as in journalism, in attributing his own integrity, his own liberal idealism, to persons who had nothing in common with him; but in cases of this sort, I usually felt that Croly had not so much been blind to the dubious aspects of the man in question as merely giving him the benefit of the doubt. He had, also, though he was sometimes criticized for a lack of aesthetic appreciation and though he believed himself deaf to music and incapable of enjoying poetry, something certainly of the sensibility that goes to make the artist. His imagination was easily touched, and he responded to atmospheres and scenes as readily as anyone I have ever known. I have heard him describe a Mexican landscape—the combination of dryness and vibrancy in the light and air of the high plateau and the strange exhilaration which had thrilled him with an unexpected sense of renewal and revelation—with the subtlety and the precision of one of those French novelists who specialize in *paysages*. And you would finally understand—what you might never, when you first knew him, have suspected—that he was one of those rare persons whom we prize because we can touch them at any time, in any mood, on any subject, and be sure of an instant and true response. The contrast between his real accessibility, his real range of intelligence and feeling, and his apparent lack of warmth, was one of the curious paradoxes of his character. If one had assumed, as one was likely to do, that he was inarticulate and indirect, he surprised one by openness and frankness; if one had supposed that he was withdrawn and introspective, he shocked one by clairvoyance and realism; and for all his inhibiting shyness, his almost excessive sensitiveness in both his public and his private relations, he could if necessary, be formidable and final.*

A similar contrast appeared in his writing. He once rather surprised me by telling me that he considered his culture mainly French—for, in spite of his years of study in Paris and his addiction to French political philosophy, it seemed to me at the time that nothing could be less French than his habitual long heavy sentences, than the Latin derivatives and vague abstract phrases, only occasionally relieved by some pungent American colloquialism, which tended to blur his thought. Yet when I came to read him more carefully, I found that a paragraph in

* Jane Addams of Hull House once told me later that she had known Herbert's mother, Jane Croly—who had an active career as a journalist and as one of the original organizers of the American women's clubs—and had sometimes gone to her house. Herbert, then a little boy, would get behind the curtains of the drawing-room and attract the attention of the company by bulging and flapping them about without allowing himself to be seen. She said that she had always thought of this as characteristic of him.

this plodding vein would often be picked up at last by some brief, clear and happy sentence which put the whole thing with a certain wit. I saw that it might be true that his mind was in some respects closer to the French than to the Anglo-Saxon, and when he told me that his father had been Irish, I understood whence these qualities had come. He was most sensible to qualities of style in other writers, though, in his editorial capacity, if an article came in which was badly written, he could never suggest how to improve it. Yet clumsiness, pretentiousness, vulgarity, in writing as in everything else, seemed actually to make him suffer. I remember meeting him once between the acts at the first night of Eugene O'Neill's *Welded*—that baldest of O'Neill's poorer plays —and feeling that I had never seen distress so nakedly displayed by a human face. He spoke of O'Neill's dialogue as if it had been a terrible accident that had happened to one of his friends—as indeed it actually was, for Stark Young had directed the production.

But as one came to know Croly better, one learned to pay less attention to these superficial aspects of his personality and to value the spirit they partly veiled: one could put it to oneself more clearly in what precisely consisted his peculiar superiority, his peculiar originality. I came to the conclusion that Croly was not primarily a political philosopher, that he had become an editor and journalist only, as it were, by accident. The last sentence of the last paragraph of his most important book, *The Promise of American Life,* reads as follows: "The common citizen can become something of a saint and something of a hero, not by growing to heroic proportions in his own person, but by the sincere and enthusiastic imitation of heroes and saints, and whether or not he will ever come to such imitation will depend upon the ability of his exceptional fellow-countrymen to offer him acceptable examples of heroism and saintliness." Now, it seems strange that a writer on politics should estimate the promise of American life from its possible capacity for producing saints; yet it was natural for Herbert Croly, because he himself was a kind of saint, and it is not at all difficult to imagine him becoming, in some other period, not a writer on public affairs, but, say, the founder of a religious order. Not that, meeting him in New York, one would have recognized him as a type of ascetic. On one of his sides, he was a man of the world. He loved the city and was never long happy away from it—he loved London and Paris; he liked the theater, liked going to lively places, enjoyed meeting clever people. He not infrequently went in for gay waistcoats, and always carried and smoked his own cigars. And in spite of the fact that considerable trouble had been taken over the lunches at the *New Republic,* the cuisine at last came so to bore him that it was difficult to induce him to eat there except on the two crucial days of the editorial week—though the smile with which he used to confess this had a shade of that sadness which would cloud his spirit at the general failure even of things connected with idealistic causes to live up to a high level of distinction. He had also a strong taste for gambling and was addicted to both poker and bridge, for which his face, with its effect of drawn blinds, must especially have qualified him.

Yet, essentially, he was one of the most unworldly men that I have ever known. It may have been partly due to his parents having been born in Europe and their having been deeply imbued with the ideas of the eighteenth-century Enlightenment in the forms in which it had persisted into the nineteenth century, that, looking out upon the beginning of the American twentieth, it had troubled him to be forced to recognize that our very American democratic ideal of unhampered individual enterprise had resulted, with the rise of industrialism, in a society where the richest men were generally regarded as the most admirable and their money and their ways of getting it as not to be criticized or tampered with, no matter what bankruptcy and degradation this involved for other sections of the population or what corruption and stultification for themselves. It may be, as I say, that this tendency had been partly derived from his parents, both professional British "intellectuals" who had come to the United States (the elder Croly, to whom Herbert dedicated *The Promise of American Life,* had himself written a book called *Glimpses of the Future*). Yet one came to feel that Herbert was the kind of man who in any civilization at any time would have found himself dissatisfied with society. From *The Promise of American Life,* which Theodore Roosevelt had laid under contribution, to the signing of the Treaty of Versailles, he had— for all his skepticism and shrewdness about practical politicians—fixed his hopes on political programs. He had had the *New Republic* back Wilson when he took us into the war, in the expectation that Wilson would justify this by the peace he would be able to make. After the peace conference, the *New Republic* was obliged to disavow the peace treaty; it maintained its sedate and self-confident tone, and continued as a political journal; but for Croly, with his scrupulous nature, his sense of personal responsibility, the outcome of the war was a source of actual anguish and humiliation. During those days, he despaired of politics and really never quite took them seriously again; and from the moment he turned away from politics, he gravitated toward religion. Herbert's parents had been followers of Auguste Comte— he had been the first child in the United States to be

christened in the Positivist faith, that dryest, least se-
ductive or inspiring of all the de-supernaturalized sects—
and his whole training had been rationalistic. He seemed
now to be making an effort to reconcile with this incul-
cated rationalism some profound mystic feeling that was
natural to him.

It was this, I think, that had given him, from the
beginning, his peculiar spiritual authority. I never knew
Herbert Croly intimately, except in so far as any contact
with such a man is more intimate, because it touches us
at a deeper level, than many close associations with
ordinary people; and I can write only a series of impressions which to those who knew him better may
appear misleading. Yet I feel that Croly's personality was
of a kind that must present a certain mystery even to
those who knew him best. We learn to recognize, as we
grow older, the same elements and motives in others
with which we have become all too familiar in our experience with ourselves; but in men like Herbert Croly
there seems to emerge in a pure and intensified form a
virtue that arrests our attention and that is ultimately
able to command us because we cannot understand it,
cannot analyze it or explain it away. And I believe that
Croly's later writings represented an attempt on his own
part to explain to his rational intelligence this well-
spring of spiritual power. He was attempting to assign
it somehow to a God of more vitality and majesty than
Comte's Supreme Being, to a more acceptable version
of that Deity in whom he had been taught not to believe.
To a friend and associate even less a believer than he, it
did not seem that he was ever successful. But to such an
associate, of a younger generation, and so at a further
remove from the God of the ancient faith, it was plain—
and especially of late, at a time, during the period of his
illness, when one could see him only rarely and briefly—

that he was one of those who make it possible for us to maintain that faith in life itself which, in the United States of our day, the brutalized, the comfortable, the timid, the hopeless and pleasure-drugged, the fatigued and machinery-driven, seem pressing on every hand, and within ourselves, to destroy. He was one of those who, quite without dogmatism and though he seemed all his life to be seeking truth in collaboration with others rather than telling people what to think, somehow manage to establish the enduring values which argument in itself is impotent to prove or disprove; and, aside from one's personal affection for him, his death may disturb one, for a time at first, as if it were a blow at those values themselves—as if we found ourselves more at the mercy of the blindness and confusion of life.

July 16, 1930

THE NIETZSCHEAN LINE

NORMAN DOUGLAS has been aroused by *Mother India* to write an attack on Western civilization called *Good-bye to Western Culture: Some Footnotes on East and West* (the English title is *How about Europe?*). His notes on the tyrannies and manias of European as contrasted with Hindu life make an entertaining book; but they represent a line of criticism which is no longer so impressive as it once was.

The oppression of our laws, in the West, says Douglas, is much worse than that of an oriental despot. The latter "is uncertain," (he is here quoting another writer) "and leaves to the oppressed chances and hopes of escaping it; it varies with the individual; and those who suffer, if not benefited, are, at least, consoled by the vengeance that, sooner or later, overtakes the guilty. The tyranny of law is a dead and immovable weight, that compresses at once the activity of the limb and the energy of the mind; leaves no hope of redress, no chance of escape; is liable to no responsibility for its acts or vengeance for its crimes." And in Europe, "an air of pointless preoccupation hangs about like influenza, infecting the sanest and most self-possessed of us. You encounter it in every walk of life and every grade of society: complications and glumness, with feverish streaks in between; in a word, fluster. There is as much grace and dignity in a European existence just now as there is in a fat bourgeoise running after an omnibus. The Americanization of life on this continent may have contributed its share; it has infused a note of impermanence. Gregarious and homeless, fearing solitude as never before, our European is losing his idiosyncrasy. Hustle is his opiate, his refuge from self. . . . Hindus are not afflicted with the fidgets. . . . They do not imagine, like Europeans, that they are driving a machine because they happen to be tangled up in its works." "Why," he finally demands, "does one belong to such a race, so sad and yet so ferocious?"

So far we may heartily agree; but Norman Douglas's farewell to Europe is like Clive Bell's book on "Civilization" and the tirades of H. L. Mencken (both of whom Mr. Douglas invokes). We ask, What then?—and we get no answer. What does Mr. Douglas want to do with Western society? How does he propose to bring it back to those virtues which it has abandoned and which he is still able to admire in the East. Mr. Douglas would reply, I suppose, that he does not propose to do anything: he is content to live in Capri and keep away from it all. He is content to occupy himself with the animals and the birds of the Greek anthology, about which he has written a learned book. So Clive Bell merely wants to be let alone to enjoy beautiful pictures and fine wines; and so Mencken asks for nothing but his Brahms, his beer and his books, and the hilarious spectacle of his neighbors. When we look for a central point of view in Douglas, we find much the same thing that we do in Mencken: a diluted and inconsistent Nietzscheanism (he has a good deal to say about Nietzsche, and his book is dedicated to Oscar Levy, Nietzsche's English translator). Like Mencken, Norman Douglas believes that the illiterate should be left illiterate; that the poor should be left poor; that the socially inferior should be kept in their places. The caste system is one of the things that he most approves of in India; and, like Mencken, he has a good deal to say about the scarcity in Europe of "gentlemen." (Mencken, of course, as an American, thinks that Europe is full of gentlemen, but Norman Douglas, being a European, thinks the gentlemen are all in the East.) For Mr. Douglas, one of the great merits of the caste system seems to be that it unfailingly provides for European gentlemen travelling in the East devoted, efficient and handsome servants.

Here are Douglas's final conclusions as to what is wrong with the Western world: "I become more and more convinced, with increasing years, that the roots of the mischief lie far back, in the Roman point of view. The shoddiness of our ideals—the shoddiness of all our ideals, social and political—is a heritage from those unimaginative Roundheads, with their ingrained vulgarity, their imperialism, their pernicious doctrine of the *raison d'état*, and the welcome they gave, as vulgarians naturally would give, to imported pinchbeck like Christianity." The religious wars and the Spanish Inquisition have "consumed our mental fiber to this day, and blunted our apperception of finer issues"; and Christianity has led to "our cult of those fetid 'masses' whom, in accordance with New Testamentary injunctions, we are now breeding as carefully as if they were Pekingese spaniels, and who, in return, have imposed on us by law their own fatuous and degrading aspirations." The pernicious political results of Rome are, first, that "that tiresome standardizing mania of theirs [has] destroyed the more delicate tissues in the national character of people subject—however superior intellectually—to themselves"; and second, that "the state idolatry of the Romans, their toga tomfoolery, has converted European races into a pack of mongrels snarling at each other."

It will be seen that the vein is a familiar one. Norman Douglas, who writes so clearly, does not think any more clearly than any other dilettante of epicurean tastes who desires to figure as a champion of all the moral and aesthetic values without being willing to deal with the problem of how these values are created or lost. The passages I have quoted are full of such words and phrases as "shoddiness," "ingrained vulgarity," "vulgarians," "pinchbeck," "coarsened our mental fiber," "our apperception of finer issues," "those fetid 'masses'," "destroyed the more delicate tissues,"—phrases which are calculated to convince us of Norman Douglas's "ingrained" refinement and to establish between him and us—Mencken and Clive Bell do the same thing—a genial understanding that he and we belong to a rare superior order of beings; that we are, in fact, "aristocratic," and that the other people don't matter. The way in which writers of this kind persuade us to accept their opinions is precisely similar to the methods by which "quality" advertising is conducted—by which a picture, for example, of a smart-looking woman eating paté de foie gras and a smart-looking man with a monocle, with some smartly printed text about "these charming people" who are "always so casually yet successfully pioneering in the realm of enjoyment," is used as a bait to make people spend their money on "menthol-cooled cigarettes." If the reader can be induced to imagine himself one of these charming people, he may not even know whether or not he enjoys cigarettes that are flavored with menthol, just as the reader of Norman Douglas may fail to notice that vulgarity and delicacy, fetidness and refinement, are treated as if they were God-given qualities, independent of other factors—as if they had no relation to questions of money and education. But what makes people "vulgar" or "fine?" And in

a civilization like our present one—the creation of a
single class, the middle class, of that eighteenth-century
society whose passing Mr. Douglas laments, in the course
of the exploitation of a single human aptitude, mechanical invention, for the purpose of getting rich—in a
civilization like our own, how can you tell whether they
are fine or not? From the island of Capri, it may not be
possible to see them very clearly; and from the point of
view of one engrossed in the birds and the beasts of the
Greek anthology, it may not be easy to appreciate the
peculiar sort of refinement—refinement in the various
mechanical and scientific techniques—that our industrial
society has certainly achieved.

The Nietzschean of Norman Douglas's type is moreover always trying to have it both ways: he always attempts to combine a ruthless and contemptuous attitude
toward those aspects of ordinary humanity that happen
to be distasteful to him with a sympathetic and even
sentimental one toward those aspects that happen to
appeal to him. Mr. Douglas, for example, is all against
our cult of "those fetid 'masses' whom," in accordance
with New Testamentary injunctions, he alleges we are
now "breeding as carefully as if they were Pekingese
spaniels." Very well: should he not, as a Nietzschean,
be willing to let them die? Yet in an earlier part of the
book, he made a point of wringing our hearts with an
account of the wretched children in English and French
reformatories. These children do not, as a rule, belong
to Mr. Douglas's class: they belong to "those fetid
'masses'." So why should Mr. Douglas worry about them?
If it is true that the "filthy and damp walls exude misery
and vice," this is a condition appropriate to the fetid. If
it is true that young girls are put in straitjackets and made
to lap up their food from the floor, a punishment from
which they sometimes suffocate—this certainly does not

err in the direction of breeding them like Pekingese. Why on earth should Mr. Douglas care whether the reformatories are cleaned up or not? If it is true, as he says, that there are six thousand French convicts "rotting in French Guiana" and that "the whole [penal] system is riddled with cruelties and abuses and absurdities," what should that matter to a resolute Nietzschean, who elsewhere refers to the unemployed as "scum" and objects to paying taxes for poor relief?

The few constructive suggestions that are offered by Mr. Douglas, with a great air of realism and common sense, appear to me more or less frivolous. "In England we build 165,000 new houses every year, and yet, in London alone, there are said to be 130,000 persons living in insanitary dens. An ex-Mayor of Manchester has lately written a book on *How to Abolish the Slums.* I have not read it, but can suggest a solution of the problem that would cost not a half-penny: stop this breeding. And the point to notice is this, that the breeding would stop automatically were it not officially encouraged." What makes Mr. Douglas so sure of this? "They manage these things better, out East," he declares. You think that he is going on to tell us that in India they exterminate the poor; but it turns out that he is thinking of the fact that the East is full of beggars and that begging is there a recognized profession. But how can you make English working people beg even when they are out of work? And do they deserve, for their reluctance to do so, to be described by Mr. Douglas as "dregs," inferior to the beggars of the East?

In spite of Mr. Douglas's denunciations of the meddlesomeness and absurdity of law-making, it is curious to note that, the moment it is a question of anything that he himself has an interest in seeing done or not done, he is as prompt to appeal to legislation as any other modern European. He protests against some English by-law which makes it necessary to get a license for a dog-kennel, but later on he becomes equally indignant over the lax enforcement of another by-law which makes "the fouling of footways by dogs" an offense liable to a fine. Only eight people, it seems, have so far been convicted. "When eighty thousand have been fined," says Douglas, "that downcast look of the cockney will begin to disappear." This is a matter about which he feels strongly, so call in the police by all means.

I have considerable respect for Norman Douglas. His career has been an honorably independent one. He has lived in a variety of countries and is not easily intimidated by the conventions of his own place and time. But the kind of social criticism represented by *Good-bye to Western Culture*—and, as I say, we have had a good deal of it—seems to me essentially trivial.

October 22, 1930

THE LITERARY CONSEQUENCES OF
THE CRASH

A CHANGE OF TONE and of point of view will be noted in my articles of the early thirties.

Even before the stock market crash of October, 1929, a kind of nervous dissatisfaction and apprehension had begun to manifest itself in American intellectual life. The liberating movement of the twenties had by that time accomplished its work of discrediting the gentility and Puritanism of the later nineteenth century; the orgy of spending of the Boom was becoming more and more grotesque, and the Jazz Age was ending in hysteria. The principal points of view of this period I tried, after the crash, to sum up in an article of March 23, 1932:

The attitudes of the decade that followed the war, before the depression set in, already seem a long way off:

The attitude of the Menckenian gentleman, ironic, beer-loving and "civilized," living principally on the satisfaction of feeling superior to the broker and enjoying the debauchment of American life as a burlesque show or three-ring circus; the attitude of old-American-stock smugness, with its drawing aloof from the rabble in the name of old Uncle Gilead Pilcher who was Governor of Connecticut or Grandfather Timothy Merrymount who was killed in the Civil War—though the parvenus kept crashing the gate so fast, while the prosperity boom was on, that it was becoming harder and harder to get one's aloofness properly recognized; the liberal attitude that American capitalism was going to show a new wonder to the world by gradually and comfortably socializing itself and that we should just have to respect it in the meantime, taking a great interest in Dwight W. Morrow and Owen D. Young; the attitude of trying to get a kick out of the sheer size and energy of American enterprises, irrespective of what they were aiming at; the attitude of proudly withdrawing and cultivating a refined sensibility or of losing oneself completely in abstruse intellectual pursuits—scholastic philosophy, symbolic logic or metaphysical physics; the attitude of letting oneself be carried along by the mad hilarity and heartbreak of jazz, living only for the excitement of the evening; the attitude of keeping one's mind and morals impregnably disinfected with the feeble fascism-classicism of humanism.

I have in one mood or another myself felt some sympathy with all of these different attitudes—with the single exception of humanism; and they have all, no doubt, had their validity for certain people, for special situations. Yet today they all look rather queer: they are no use in our present predicament, and we can see how superficial they were. We can see now that they all represented attempts on the part of the more thoughtful Americans to reconcile themselves to a world dominated by salesmen and brokers—and that they all involved compromises with the salesman and the broker. Mencken and Nathan laughed at the broker, but they justified the system which produced him and they got along with him very well, provided he enjoyed George Moore and had pretensions to a taste in liquor; the jazz-age romantics spent the broker's money as speedily and wildly as possible and tried to laugh off the office and the factory with boyish and girlish jokes; the old-American-stockers sniffed at him, but though they salved their consciences thus, they were usually glad to get in on any of his good things that were going; the liberals, who had been vaguely unhappy, later became vaguely resigned and could never bring themselves to the point of serious quarrelling with him; the poets and philosophers hid from him—and the physicists grew more and more mystical in the laboratories subsidized mainly by the profits from industrial investments; the humanists, in volume after volume, endeavored by sheer hollow thunder to induce people to find in the stock exchange the harmony and dignity of the Parthenon.

I did not include in this catalogue a cult that was spreading in New York and that had converts in and around the *New Republic:* that of the Russo-Greek charlatan Gurdjieff, who undertook to renovate the personalities of discontented well-to-do persons. He combined making his clients uncomfortable in various gratuitous ways—such as waking them up in the middle of the night and training them to perform grotesque dances—with reducing them to a condition of complete docility, in which they would hold, at a signal, any position, however awkward, that they happened to be in at the moment, They were promised, if they proved themselves worthy of it, an ultimate initiation into the mysteries of an esoteric doctrine. Gurdjieff's apostle in the United States was the English ex-journalist A. R. Orage, a funereal and to me a distasteful person, who drilled his pupils, not in dancing, but in a kind of dialectic and who acquired at one time a considerable influence over the mind of Herbert Croly, whose inhibited personality and unsatisfied religious instincts laid him open to the lures of a cult that pretended to liberate the mind and to put one in touch with some higher power. But Croly was a fastidious man, and in the long run he found Orage grating. I was myself the object of several attempts to recruit me to the Orage group, but the only interchange of influence that took place between Orage and me consisted of my once persuading him to go to the National Winter Garden (described under *Burlesque Shows* above); when I next saw him, he told me with a severity that suggested a sense of outrage that he had not enjoyed it at all. Gurdjieff, however, whom I never met, had apparently a rogue's sense of humor. A young man in the office, a bishop's son who had lost his faith and was groping for something to take its place, told me of the banquets of roast sheep or goat, served in great pots in the Caucasian style and eaten with the fingers, to which Gurdjieff would invite his disciples and at which he would have read aloud to them a book he had written called *A Criticism of the Life of Man: Beëlzebub's Tale to His Grandson.* "It sounds as if it had been written," said this neophyte, "just on purpose to bore you to death. Everybody listens in silence, but every now and then Gurdjieff will suddenly burst out laughing—just roaring —nobody knows about what."

I did not read *Beëlzebub's Tale,* but I did read *Das Kapital.* Not that I want to compare the two works, but there *was* a certain similarity in the way in which people then approached them; and I was surprised to find that an apparently social evening that would turn out to be a conspiracy to involve one in some Communist organization resembled a dinner I had once attended at which I was chilled to discover that the springes of Orage had been laid for me—and these both recalled to me an earlier occasion on which a literary conversation, in the rooms of the proselytizing rector of the Episcopal Church at Princeton, had been prodded by amusing remarks in the direction of the Christian faith. People did want faiths and churches badly, and though I am good at resisting churches, I caught a wave from the impulsion of the Marxist faith.

The stock market crash was to count for us almost like a rending of the earth in preparation for the Day of Judgment. In my articles of the months just before it, I had often urged writers to acquaint themselves with "the realities of our contemporary life," to apply themselves to "the study of contemporary reality," etc. I myself had not exercised enough insight to realize that American "prosperity" was an inflation that was due to burst. I had, however, become aware that we liberals of the *New Republic* were not taking certain recent happenings so seriously as we should. The execution of Sacco and Vanzetti in August, 1927, had made liberals lose their bearings. During the months while the case was working up to its climax, Herbert Croly had been away in Honolulu attending a conference called by the Institute of Pacific Relations. When he returned, I was surprised to learn that he did not entirely approve of the way in which we had handled the case. Croly's method of commenting on current events was impersonal and very abstract; and, in his absence, we had given way to the impulse to print certain articles which were certainly, for the *New Republic*, unusually concrete and militant. I first became aware of a serious divergence between my own point of view and Croly's when I was talking with him one day about a leader called *A Nation of Foreigners* that I wrote for the paper in October. He did approve of this editorial, but for reasons that put me in a false position. My article had dealt with the futility of attempting to identify "Americanism" with the interests and ideas of the Anglo-Saxon element in the United States, pointing out that, in this case, the Irish, who had been snubbed by the

Anglo-Saxon Bostonians, had combined with them in the most wolfish way to persecute the immigrant Italians; and I discovered that Croly was pleased at my treating the subject from this angle rather than from that of class animosities. This class aspect he wanted to deny; it was one of the assumptions of his political thinking— I had not then read *The Promise of American Life*— that the class struggle should not, and in its true form did not, occur in the United States.

I had been running the literary department, and this was my first excursion on the political side of the paper, which Croly had kept strictly in line with his own very definite ideas. Sometime in the later months of 1928, he had the first of several strokes, and was never able again to perform his full functions as editor-in-chief. When he died in May, 1930, the paper was carried on by the editors as a group, with no one in Croly's position, and we had—rather difficult with men of conflicting opinions and temperaments, with nobody to make final decisions —to work out a policy of our own. I had been troubled by another incident that took place in the autumn of 1929. The bitter and violent Gastonia strike of the textile workers in North Carolina had been going on ever since spring. It was the first major labor battle conducted by a Communist union. Sixteen union members, including three women, were being tried for the murder of a chief of police, who had invaded without a warrant the tent-colony in which the strikers had been living; and the death penalty was being asked for all of them except the women. Feeling on both sides had been roused to the point of ferocity—we were not then familiar with the Communists' habit of manufacturing martyrs—and, after the execution of Sacco and Vanzetti, one was apprehensive of another judicial lynching. John Dos Passos and Mary Heaton Vorse both asked the *New Republic* to send them to report on Gastonia, but both were thought to be too far to the Left to be reliable from our point of view. "The liberals," Dos Passos said to me, "are all so neurotic about Communists!" This was perfectly true; and the pressure on us to do something about Gastonia had at the time almost no effect. The young man who had been hooked by Orage—who had had no experience of labor disputes—was going down to a fashionable wedding at Asheville, not far from Gastonia, and he was asked to drop in at the seat of trouble. When he came back, this young man reported that there was nothing of interest going on. I do not know whom he could have talked to. He had been in Gastonia on the very day, September 14, when the hostilities were coming to a climax. In an attempt to prevent a union meeting, an armed mob had fired on unarmed strikers and had killed a woman named Ella May Wiggins, a widow with five children, who had written songs for the strikers and was extremely popular among them. Her death gave the Communists a battle-cry and the strikers an unforgettable grievance. It was obvious that the *New Republic,* which was supposed to cover labor sympathetically, was falling down on this part of its program.

The next month the slump began, and, as conditions grew worse and worse and President Hoover, unable to grasp what had happened, made no effort to deal with the breakdown, a darkness seemed to descend. Yet, to the writers and artists of my generation who had grown up in the Big Business era and had always resented its barbarism, its crowding-out of everything they cared about, these years were not depressing but stimulating. One couldn't help being exhilarated at the sudden un-expected collapse of that stupid gigantic fraud. It gave us a new sense of freedom; and it gave us a new sense of power to find ourselves still carrying on while the bank-

ers, for a change, were taking a beating. With a business-
man's president in the White House, who kept telling
us, when he told us anything, that the system was perfectly sound, who sent General Douglas MacArthur to
burn the camp of the unemployed war veterans who had
come to appeal to Washington, we wondered about the
survival of republican American institutions; and we became more and more impressed by the achievements of
the Soviet Union, which could boast that its industrial
and financial problems were carefully studied by the
government, and that it was able to avert such crises. We
overdid both these tendencies; but the slump was like
a flood or an earthquake, and it was long before many
things righted themselves.

THE ECONOMIC INTERPRETATION
OF WILDER*

PERHAPS NO OTHER literary article published in the *New Republic* has ever aroused so much controversy as Michael Gold's on Thornton Wilder in the issue of October 22. We have received, and are still receiving, dozens of letters about it, and most of these letters are earnest protests.

Now, this magazine has, of course, no prejudice against Thornton Wilder—his books have been often enough praised in its pages to invalidate this charge. But, on the other hand, it considers Michael Gold also an important writer whose critical opinions have a special interest, since he is one of the only American critics of any literary ability who writes about books from the Marxist point of view. Most of our critics, like most other Americans, have no central point of view—they are in the habit of merely sampling different kinds of books and writing down the various thoughts that come into their heads. Does not the very outcry which Mr. Gold has provoked show up the insipidity and pointlessness of most of our criticism?

For the harsh and scurrilous things that Mr. Gold says about Mr. Wilder can hardly account in themselves for the disturbance his review has created. Criticisms

* This appeared in the *New Republic* as an unsigned editorial.

equally scurrilous have been printed about other writers: witness Hemingway's satire on Sherwood Anderson in his burlesque novel *The Torrents of Spring* or the amenities of the humanist controversy. Yet, so far as we know, no article, review or editorial on a literary subject has ever recently aroused such an uproar as Gold's economic analysis of Wilder; and it seems to us, in spite of the possible objections which might be made to the manner of Mr. Gold's essay, that he has raised a fundamental issue and that there is a good deal to be said on his side.

First, however, for what is to be said against it. The Marxist critic of the type of Michael Gold must assume that the character of the literature produced during any period is determined by the economic position of the class for whom it is written. That economic and social factors do play a much larger part in molding people's ideals, and consequently in coloring their literature, than most people are willing to admit, we are perfectly ready to agree. Yet there are groups which cut through the social classes, and these tend to have an independent existence. The writers make a group of their own; the painters make a group of their own; the scientists make a group. And each of these groups has its own tradition, its own craft and body of doctrine which has been brought down to the present by practitioners that have come from a variety of classes through a variety of different societies. In dealing with a work of literature, we must consider it not only from the point of view of its significance in the social system, but also from the point of view of its craft. A Communist critic who, in reviewing a book, ignores the author's status as a craftsman is really, for purposes of propaganda, denying the dignity of human work.

A typical example of this is to be found in Upton Sinclair's *Mammonart*: in this book, he appraises the literature of the world with the social-economic touch-stone, but then goes on to glorify without reserve the physicists in the California laboratories. Yet if the people exploring the atom should be regarded as disinterested intellectuals, why may not the poets be? And if the works of the poets are influenced by feudal patrons and bour-geois audiences, why may not the discoveries of the physicists be conditioned—as they probably are—by the outlook of the capitalist society which has supplied them with the money for their laboratories? Has not the artist as good a chance as the scientist of living up to an imper-sonal ideal! Mr. Sinclair and Mr. Gold ought to think about this. The author of *Jews Without Money*, espe-cially, ought to recognize and confess how much he has in common with the author of *The Bridge of San Luis Rey*—sensitiveness to human contacts, a love of pic-turesque detail, a gift for molding firm prose into short comprehensive units, and even a touch of sentimentality.

Not, however, that the author or scientist—except, rarely, at some extreme limit—can ever be *completely* dis-interested, can ever detach his mind from the social community, the organism, to which his body belongs, to function as if in a vacuum. The various guilds of the arts and sciences do *tend* to become independent, but they never can quite succeed; and it is true that a social situation is implied in every product of human thought, no matter how remote from society its propositions or images may be or how impersonal the technique that presents them. Now, the furious protest raised by Michael Gold's attack on Wilder suggests that there is some-what more point to the Marxist objection to that writer than one had before suspected. It has already been pointed out in these pages that Thornton Wilder owes a good deal to Proust—in fact, without being aware of it and though he is a writer of real originality, he has in a sense been a popularizer of Proust. He has tapped the main of Proust's rich, luxurious, intoxicating sentimentality and brought a pipe-line to every American home. For Proust is surely the writer who, more even than any of the romantics, has made heartbreak a protracted pleasure: the romantics' hearts broke against desolate backgrounds but Proust's heart breaks at the Ritz. Now, Wilder in *The Cabala* is also at the Ritz, and he sticks, in his subsequent books, to a decorative Parisian antiquity that amounts to the same thing. The malaise, the frustration, the misery, with which he and Proust both deal are the illnesses of the cultivated people in a capitalistic society, which neither the luxuries of the Ritz nor the up-to-date fragments of the past—which Anatole France was always collecting—to be found in the fascinating antique shops and galleries can do more than deaden a little. The pathos in Proust, after all, is merely the more presentable side of the impotence, the creeping corruption, the lack of the will to live. And so in Wilder the pathos and the beauty derived from exotic lands of the imagination may be, as Michael Gold suggests, a sedative for sick Americans. The sedative and the demand for it are both products of the same situation: a people disposed to idealism, but deprived of their original ideals and now making themselves neurotic in the attempt to introduce idealism into the occupations— organizing, financing, manufacturing, advertising, salesmanship—of a precarious economic system the condition for whose success is that they must profit by swindling their customers and cutting one another's throats.

November 26, 1930

SCHNITZLER AND PHILIP BARRY

A FRAIL, SENSITIVE and lovely woman in a Middle Western town is married to a good and dull young man, who breeds horses and loves college reunions, but who cannot give her a child. There arrives in town on a lecture tour a brilliant psychologist: he stays with them and makes love to the wife. Then he goes, and the woman has a child by him without the husband's suspecting that it is not his own. But the mother unintentionally antagonizes the boy against his supposed father, who, in spite of the child's fear of horses, insists upon making him ride. The boy has a bad fall and sinks into a neurotic stupor, from which it is impossible to rouse him. At this moment the voice of the lover is heard on the radio lecturing in Chicago. The mother flies to the phone and summons him, and the doctor, alone in the room with the child, finds a lever to lift the psychological obstruction and bring him back to normal consciousness. The doctor's first impulse is to put an end to the whole distressing situation by taking both the child and his mother away; but the situation has gone on too long—the blow would be too hard for the husband. And, besides, the psychologist is a congenital bachelor; he has been dependent for years on the support of an adoring assistant, who jealously looks after him and keeps him out of trouble. He takes his leave again. The doctor is a man of genius, who is able to illuminate the woman's life, give her a gifted child and, by exercising his professional art, liberate the child's mind, but he is also a relentless egoist, absorbed in his own career as an inspired scientific spellbinder and with the weaknesses of such a man. He could never take, as the husband does, the lifelong responsibility for either the child or the mother—he can only come and go; and it is the husband who, in the end, has the care of both woman and child, while the psychologist must return to his eternally maladjusted life, leaving the woman as much as ever in love with him. "Not changed. Complete!" she exclaims about him almost joyfully, as she watches him from the window.

If this is the story that Mr. Philip Barry means to tell in his new play *Tomorrow and Tomorrow*—and I am not quite sure that it is, so uncertain is Mr. Barry's touch —he has, I think, started out with a promising theme, out of which a first-rate comedy might have been made. The best parts of *Tomorrow and Tomorrow* are, in fact, very good comedy—for example, the relations between the silver-tongued doctor and his devoted but hard-boiled secretary. This secretary, Gillespie, played perfectly by Osgood Perkins, is the only person in the play through whom Mr. Barry allows himself to exercise his skill at the American humorous "line." The psychologist and his secretary have just been making the inevitable social rounds in the university town.

"HAY. Bring a chair, Gillespie.

"GILLESPIE. Not me. I ate Mrs. William A. Plant's chicken salad and drank her cocoa.

"HAY. I was wiser.

"EVE. I think you behaved beautifully, both of you.

"GILLESPIE. Why's she called 'Mrs. William A. Plant'? Is there another Mrs. Plant? A William H.? Or Willy K.—?

"EVE. Not that I know of.

"GILLESPIE (*thoughtfully*).—And still always Mrs. William A. Plant. H'm.—Oh, well, why not?

"*He goes out again into the library, with the books, sweater, hat and brief-case.*"

The best scene in the play, it seems to me, is that in which the psychologist says good-by for the last time: he pulls out his watch to see how near it is to train time and finds that the crystal has come out again. It has been coming out for years, he says—he is always hoping that it will break so that he can get a new crystal, but all it does is come out. Why? asks Eve. Because it doesn't fit. She asks him for the first time how he lives and, speaking for the first time matter-of-factly, he tells her that he lives in hotels, that he works almost all day and that he doesn't sleep at night. Then he and Gillespie catch the train.

The greater part of *Tomorrow and Tomorrow* is, however, unfortunately, not like this. Mr. Barry has here set out to do a bang-up serious play, and he is acutely conscious of the fact. He has aimed at austerity and brevity, and the effect is extremely unnatural. For example, it is not very long after Gillespie has gone out of the room and left Eve and the doctor together in the scene from which I have quoted above that Eve remarks to the doctor: "I have been at such pains about this little supper." This might be a bad translation of Ibsen or Strindberg—some of Eugene O'Neill sounds like this, too, and it may be by way of O'Neill that Philip Barry has caught this way of talking; but it is not what an American woman like Eve would be likely to say about a little supper. Most of the dialogue is in this vein. Even admitting that Doctor Hay is supposed to have an element of ham, the scenes between him and Eve—finely played though they are by Herbert Marshall and Zita Johann—are romantic in a banal way that makes it impossible to take them seriously at the same time that none of the lines is ever clearly underlined as comic: "HAY. It [the wine] tastes of sun and rain and earth. EVE. Good things to taste of." —"Is the laurel in bloom, Eve." etc.

It is curious to see Arthur Schnitzler's *The Affairs of Anatol* after *Tomorrow and Tomorrow*. The Austrian is always perfectly sure of the effect he will produce with his characters: he knows how to make them ridiculous and sympathetic at the same time, and the one sentimental scene is sentimental to just the right degree, so that it does not jar with the rest. One speculates as to what Schnitzler might have done with Eve and Dr. Hay; one can imagine how he would have made us laugh at the lecturer's easy poetry and his weakness and at Eve's naïveté without losing either the romance of their meetings or the pathos of their farewells. Yet the trouble is not simply that Philip Barry is an inferior dramatist to Schnitzler: Schnitzler himself is, after all, no giant; but he does have the considerable advantage of a sounder culture behind him. It is precisely in this department of high comedy deriving from character—or lightly handled tragedy—that the Americans show up worst. The case of Philip Barry is strikingly like that of Clyde Fitch: Clyde Fitch's straight comedy was excellent—original and authentically American; but as soon as he set out to be serious, he was stilted, commonplace, insupportable. He suffered evidently from a deep-seated assumption that being serious and being comic were two entirely different things; he was unable to realize that comedy does not have to be mere refined horseplay, that it may be serious in itself, and that, if it isn't, no amount of stage rhetoric, no injections of sentimentality, can ever make it so. The plays of Philip Barry, like certain other products of New

York—like the songs of Cole Porter, like a good deal of the *New Yorker* magazine—have the deftness and a glimmering of the comic sense that are cultivated in a high civilization, but, like other things of the kind in New York, they remain imperfect, uncertain, rather unsatis· factory, because they have no stable social system behind them and consequently no fixed code of manners or definite point of view. They flicker and float on the surface of the shifting heterogeneous city; are at their best when they reflect its queer mixtures and its disconcerting surprises. But to write a really first-rate comedy, you ought to have a set of standards, even if those of a small class or group, to refer people's behavior to. Eugene O'Neill, for all his faults, has these for the whole of humanity; Arthur Schnitzler has them for the sophisti-cated pre-war Viennese. But Philip Barry, who writes for a sophisticated class with little social tradition and little real education—this play has no more to do with the Indiana town in which it is laid than Cole Porter's new musical show—has a very hard time getting hold of any-thing that will enable him to take a clear line in regard to all the curious things that he sees going on about him.

February 4, 1931

JOSEPH DE MAISTRE

When literary people, hard pressed by the threat of democratic reforms, feel the need for a reactionary authority, they are likely to resort to Joseph de Maistre.

De Maistre was one of the few really distinguished writers who spoke for the Catholic reaction in the period after the French Revolution; and he has always been especially useful to conservative-minded intellectuals, because, in reading or remembering him, they are able to tell themselves that in that era all the brilliant brains were not on the subversive side. I have so often had de Maistre thrown at my head as an antidote to modern radicalism that I recently decided to look into him; and my report is that the "prophet of reaction" is by no means so formidable a thinker as he has sometimes been represented.

There was of course after the French Revolution a role for a critic like de Maistre. By the time the Revolution had run its course, it was not difficult to perceive the extravagance of the eighteenth-century doctrines which had led up to it. Rousseau had said that people were naturally good and that it was only institutions which had perverted them. Well, Robespierre had been Rousseau's disciple, and by the time the Republic had foundered in the blood of its quarrelling leaders and given way to the Emperor Napoleon, it did not look as if the people were so naturally good or so amenable to the reforms of the Goddess of Reason as the Rousseaus and Condorcets had asserted.

De Maistre wrote, in his *Essai sur le Principe Générateur des Constitutions Politiques*: "One of the great errors of a century that confessed all the errors was the belief that a political constitution could be written and created a priori, when reason and experience agree in showing that a constitution is a divine production and that precisely the most fundamental and most essentially constitutional part of a nation's laws is something that can never be written." It was impossible, de Maistre insisted, that the work of the Revolution should last: the new system was a purely theoretical one which had been artificially imposed by cranks. De Maistre makes merry over the efforts of the cranks to dignify their work with classic names. It is use and use alone, he says, that can dignify and fill with meaning the names of places and buildings—the Tuileries, for example—that were originally commonplace. And you cannot prop up something ephemeral by giving it a grandiose name. The Odéon, for example: for all the pretentious Greek label, it couldn't last! And then, the Olympic Games, so presumptuously inaugurated, of which an enthusiastic contemporary had asserted that "the day would come when they would attract the whole of Europe to the Champ de Mars"—how preposterous that was! De Maistre's instances were not well-chosen, and his arguments do not sound so good today as they may have done in 1809. There is something in what he says: you cannot invent a new social system and get people to accept it overnight. But that did not mean that in France the old régime had been preferable or that the new, in spite of Napoleon, had not taken a very strong hold—which were the conclusions de Maistre drew.

Joseph de Maistre was a petty noble—very proud of his connections with the French aristocracy—from a family of Savoyard magistrates. He had had his first education at the hands of the Jesuits and then had gone to study law at the University of Turin. He worked hard at mastering French, but he never allowed himself to read any book without first writing home for permission from his parents. He sat afterwards in the Savoyard senate, of which his father was president.

De Maistre in his early phase entertained somewhat liberal views. He even belonged for a time to a Reform Lodge and was considered by the authorities a dangerous character. But when the French Revolution was threatening, he was delegated by his fellow-members to report to the King of Sardinia that the lodge had been dissolved. When the armies of the Republic invaded Savoy, de Maistre fled with his family. He could have saved his property from confiscation, after Savoy had been annexed by the French, by taking the oath of allegiance to the new government; but he had brothers on the other side, and he refused to contribute to the support of the revolutionary army. After some years of knocking about rather miserably—at one time he and his wife were reduced to their last pieces of silver plate—he was finally, in 1803, sent to St. Petersburg, as envoy extraordinary and minister plenipotentiary to the King of Sardinia. Separated from his wife and children, he remained there for fifteen years. By this time he was an embittered reactionary, and he occupied the long days of his exile by writing books to expound his position.

What is impressive about Joseph de Maistre is what is impressive about most sincere reactionaries from Dr. Johnson to Dostoevsky: his vision of human sin.

The great radical is likely to be one who either is free from a sense of guilt or has evolved a psychological mechanism which enables him to turn moral judgments against himself into moral judgments against society. A

man like Kropotkin is himself so guileless, so benevolently
disposed toward his fellow-men, that it is impossible for
him to imagine that other people, if left to themselves,
may not all be as pure as he. A Rousseau, with the elements much more mixed, was able, at the moment of his
revelation, to put off all the humiliating experiences
which had hindered him and rankled with him on an
iniquitous social system, quite alien to the natural man,
from which he could dissociate himself.

The reactionary, on the other hand, is likely to start
from a profound conviction of the evil of the natural
man. Instead of worrying because people do not get
enough freedom, he is obsessed by the need for police—
authority, discipline, order. How else can you keep the
Devil under control? Dr. Johnson, who would not let
Garrick take him behind the scenes of his theater for fear
of the demoralizing effect on him of the bare necks and
arms of the actresses, was all for Church and King;
Dostoevsky, who, when the peasants had murdered his
father, felt a kind of common guilt with the murderers
and who behaved as if he were expiating in Siberia
crimes with which he had never been charged, came back
full of loyalty to Church and Tsar. De Maistre, who was
able to justify the apparent injustice of the days when he
and his wife and children had been exiled, homeless and
starving, by the sins he knew his soul must answer for
before the tribunal of God, defended the divine right of
kings and the infallibility of the Pope; and he thus most
commands our respect when he is insisting on the evil of
life as something which cannot be avoided, which reason
can never abolish or rhetoric conjure away. Injustices,
from our human point of view, do certainly occur,
he says (in *Les Soirées de Saint-Pétersbourg*); people
suffer for crimes that they never committed. But if you
take mankind in the gross, as God does, you will see that

we all share in human sin. This sin is our common inheritance, our common debt; not one of us is free from it; and we must all of us contribute to paying it. De Maistre repudiates, he tells us, the snobbish point of view of that queen who was supposed to have said, "You may be sure that God thinks twice about damning our sort of people!" No: not one of us is innocent! That Elizabeth of France, the King's sister, should have had to die by the guillotine just as the monster Robespierre did, does not prove that God is unjust: "Every man, in his quality of man, is subject to all the ills of humanity." We are subject to unjust executions just as we are to apoplexy. But if we look at things in the large, we shall see "that the greatest mass of happiness, even temporal happiness, goes, not to the virtuous man, but to virtue." Because, if this were not true, the whole moral order would be wrong—which is absurd.

This leads de Maistre to one of his most famous performances. The whole moral order is *not* wrong, and in reality our human justice is acting in behalf of the divine. The executioner, therefore, in spite of the fact that all the world avoids him, is a man appointed by God, "created like a world" and set apart. How else is it possible to account for him?—how else is it possible to explain that a man can be found to accept the job? Yet the executioner does exist and carries out his terrible orders. De Maistre tells you about it:

"A somber signal is given: an abject minister of justice comes to knock at his [the executioner's] door and let him know that he is needed. He sets out; he arrives at the public square, which is crowded with an eager excited throng. A prisoner or a murderer or a blasphemer is given over to him. He seizes him and stretches and ties him on a horizontal cross; he lifts his arm and a horrible silence falls. Nothing is heard but the cry of the bones

cracking under the heavy rod and the howlings of the
victim. Then he unties him and carries him to the wheel;
the shattered limbs get twisted in the spokes; the head
hangs; the hair stands out; and from the mouth, gaping
open like a stove, come only now a few bloody words
which at intervals beg for death. Now the executioner
has finished: his heart beats, but it is for joy; he applauds
himself, he says in his heart: 'Nobody is better at the
wheel than I!' He comes down and holds out his blood-
stained hand, and the Law throws into it from a distance
some gold pieces which he carries away with him through
a double hedge of people, who draw away in horror. He
sits down to table and eats; then he gets into bed and
goes to sleep. When he wakes up the next day, he begins
to think about something quite different from the work
he has been doing the day before. Is he a man? Yes: God
receives him into his temples and allows him to pray. The
executioner is not a criminal; yet no tongue is willing to
say, for example, that he is 'virtuous,' that he is 'a good
fellow,' that he is 'estimable,' etc. No moral commendation
fits him, because any such commendation assumes some
sort of bond with mankind, and the executioner has none.

"And yet all grandeur, all power, all discipline are
founded on the executioner. He is the horror of the
human association and the tie that holds it together. Take
out of the world this incomprehensible agent, and at that
instant will order give way to chaos, thrones fall and
society vanish. God, who is the source of all sover-
eignty, is, therefore, the source of all punishment, too."

It has been objected to de Maistre that he is hard. The
truth is that he is not hard enough. As he says, a professional executioner is incomprehensible to him. In his
earlier days, as a matter of fact, he had resigned from the
senate of Savoy, which had judiciary functions, precisely
because he could not bring himself to sentence people to

death. And, although he was willing to face the fact that everything he valued in the world depended on that horrible wheel, he evaded this uncomfortable situation as much as he possibly could. If, according to the divine arrangement, the virtuous must sometimes suffer, then the innocent must sometimes get tortured. What about Jean Calas, the Protestant merchant who had been persecuted by a Catholic mob for a crime he had perhaps never committed and who had been broken on the wheel?—Calas, whom Voltaire had defended and whose name he had made a symbol for the savagery of religious intolerance? Well, the truth is, de Maistre replies, that Calas was probably guilty. The chief thing that makes de Maistre think so is the flippancy displayed by Voltaire while he was agitating in Calas' defense—this flippancy having been exemplified by a remark in one of Voltaire's letters: "You find my memoir too hot, but I am working on another one for you which is going to be a scorcher." Nothing can be more probable than that God Himself, in a case like this, makes a point of helping the police so that they won't fail to get the right person; and, besides, there is always the chance that, even if a man is executed for a crime which he did not commit, he may deserve to be punished for something else. And yet, even where the victim is certainly guilty, an execution like that of Calas, by "torture ordinary and extraordinary" and by breaking alive on the wheel, is unquestionably a distasteful affair. Even when we can reconcile ourselves to contemplating the agonies of the wicked, how can we contemplate the state of mind imposed on the executioner? We can get around this haunting difficulty by no less heroic a piece of sophistry than excluding the executioner from the human race! De Maistre has to invent for this man a character as frankly inhuman as that of a goblin or a djinn in a fairy-tale. (One is not even convinced by de Maistre's description that he has ever actually witnessed an execution.) He is obliged to tell himself that Jack Ketch is *not* really a man like himself, that he is a different kind of being altogether from the fellow whose humane sensibilities compelled him to resign from the Senate.

I know of no more striking example of the lengths to which an intelligent man can go to escape the disagreeable implications of a position he has an interest in maintaining. The Boston lawyers who steadily maintained that, though Sacco and Vanzetti might well be innocent, it was necessary to have them executed, in order to uphold the authority of the Massachusetts courts, though they are less sympathetic than Joseph de Maistre, were really arguing more soundly than he, as they were arguing more soundly than the thousands of their respectable and kindly fellow-townsmen who, like de Maistre, did their best to convince themselves that, in spite of the dubious evidence, the accused were very likely guilty, or that, if they didn't deserve death for murder, they did for political heresy.

You find this wanting to have it both ways all through *Les Soirées de Saint-Pétersbourg.* So with those other earthly evils—cancer and war. After describing with some vividness their horrors, he tries to show us they are, after all, not so horrible; religion and self-discipline are stimulated in time of war; and as for cancer, there is a girl in St. Petersburg whom cancer has gradually converted into a model of pious devotion. Even in regard to the Revolution, de Maistre is not really so uncompromising as he is sometimes assumed to be. He could not extirpate his early liberalism, and this weakened his royalist position. He was too serious and too intelligent not to realize and deplore the corruption and incompetence of the old régime. But the Revolution was "a great and terrible sermon which Providence has preached to men—a sermon with two morals. Revolutions are made by abuses: this is the first moral, and it is addressed to sovereigns. Nevertheless, it is infinitely better to have abuses than revolutions: this is the second moral, and it is addressed to peoples." And he accepted the French Republic in so far as he believed it the only thing which could hold France together against her enemies.

Not a very satisfactory position. Knowing well that on that quarrelsome continent, where the nations were well engaged in the path that was to lead to 1914, no sovereign could ever bring unity, he advocated setting up a body which should derive its authority from the Pope and keep peace by imposing its decisions. The truth was that Joseph de Maistre had himself been irremediably influenced by the rationalism and humanitarianism of the bourgeois philosophers he patronized. His class bias was, of course, very strong; we see it even in his attempts at justice. The worst crime that de Maistre could imagine was the guillotining of the King's sister. Calas was far from mattering so much. But why, then, should he have mattered at all? From de Maistre's point of view, he was a heretic in any case. Voltaire, against whom, from the St. Petersburg of Alexander I, de Maistre is always railing, has got him worried about Calas after all. And why bother about the fates of common soldiers? A thoroughly hard-boiled aristocrat ought to have taken all that for granted. But Joseph de Maistre's attitude is never really hard-boiled and realistic, but, on the contrary, sophistical and literary. It is an affair of ingenious reasoning and elegiac rumination in a limbo between two worlds. When de Maistre died, Talleyrand said of him: "The prophet of the past has fallen asleep in the bosom of eternity, with his memories which he takes for premonitions."

August 24, 1932

AN APPEAL TO PROGRESSIVES

THE FOLLOWING ARTICLE appeared in the *New Republic* of January 14, 1931. It was announced as "the first of a series . . . discussing the position of the contemporary progressive, . . . the outcome of conversations among the editors, which have been occurring for several months." The editor-in-chief, Herbert Croly, had died on May 17, 1930.

It seems to me that the time has come for liberals seriously to reconsider their position. The liberalism which the *New Republic* has represented in the past was derived primarily from Herbert Croly's book *The Promise of American Life*, written more than twenty years ago. This book was an original interpretation of American political and social history, which in its field set a new standard of realism. In the earliest days of the Republic, the strong centralization policy of Hamilton had been established for the protection of the propertied classes, and the reaction led by Jefferson was intended as a democratic antidote. But Mr. Croly showed that when the Jeffersonians got into power, they took over the Hamiltonian structure practically intact, though at the same time they refused to abandon their democratic pretensions, thus, as he says, beginning "that career of intellectual lethargy, superficiality and insincerity which

ever since has been characteristic of official American
political thought." The American democratic ideal was
thus more or less disingenuous from the beginning: the
actual purpose of the government was one thing and the
rhetoric of politics was another. It got to be stock procedure to claim as a democratic "right" the freedom to
pursue any course that happened to promote one's own
interests. The institution of slavery, for example, was
guaranteed by the Constitution, though it violated in the
most shocking manner the spirit of the Declaration of
Independence: the Southerners claimed their legal
"rights," and the Abolitionists claimed natural "rights."
The contradictions involved in our government and the
ideals associated with it gave rise to a double rebellion—
the rebellion of the South against the government and
the rebellion of the North against the Constitution.
The Civil War ensued, and, as a result, both the Constitution and the social structure of the South became
altered in important respects. The machine and the ideal
were now repaired and started on their way again.

Herbert Croly goes on, however, to show that the
industrial development of the country had then produced
a second critical situation as serious as that which had
brought on the war. Our society transformed itself: the
masters of industry and commerce came rapidly to constitute a special and supremely powerful class; the lawyers, who had formerly run the government, were turned
into another special class that prospered by keeping the
bankers and business men out of trouble; politics was
left to a third specialized class, the bosses and professional
office-holders—the labor unions grew up as a fourth, engaged (at first) in fighting the other three. The old
machine and ideal, even in their amended form, failed
to meet the needs of the new American world by as much
as the Bethlehem steel works, the Grand Central Station

and the Singer Building were unlike Mount Vernon, Monticello or the log cabin where Lincoln was born. A readjustment as drastic was required as that which had cost us the Civil War. "The time may come," Croly wrote, "when the fulfilment of a justifiable democratic purpose may demand the limitation of certain rights, to which the Constitution affords such absolute guarantees; and, in that case, the American democracy might be forced to seek by revolutionary means the accomplishment of a result which should be attainable under the law." Croly did, however, still believe that this result might be attained under the law—that the wholesale corruption of politics, the shameless exploitation of labor, the ruthless wrecking by competitive business of thousands of honorable careers and the general degradation of the national standards in everything except technical skill might be dealt with at a not too distant date by our machinery of representative government. He conceived this new democratic goal as a return to Hamiltonian centralization, but in the interests not merely of the propertied class but of the American people as a whole—a new machinery and a new objective which he says he is not afraid to have called "socialism." Everyone, in the United States, had again been claiming as some sort of "right" the freedom to do whatever he pleased—the business men, the lawyers, the politicians and the labor organizers. What was needed was a frank confession that, if we were to save the democratic ideal, we must discard the illusion of unlimited freedom and work out a systematic curtailment of the rights of everyone in the interests of all.

Yet Croly still believed that this result might eventually be accomplished by an orderly series of reforms. In spite of his unsparing criticism of our official political ideals and even of our political reformers, he still had faith in American politics—or rather, perhaps, in an American democratic spirit able to control life through politics, a spirit embodied for him by Lincoln, the man who had changed the state and preserved it, too. Herbert Croly differed from the out-and-out socialist of his time by encouraging the idea of nationalism—not the imperialistic nationalism of Great Britain and of the late German Empire, but a nationalism which did impel him to support the entrance of the United States into the European War. He expressly repudiated the notion of an international working-class movement dedicated to fighting international capitalism. It was still possible for Herbert Croly to feel that the United States was a kind of mystical entity—something isolated, self-contained and self-perpetuating—that could be counted on to solve its own problems and eliminate its own diseases. And to the extent that he believed in the United States, he thus believed not only in nationalism but in capitalism as well. He thought that the American spirit would be strong enough to compel American capitalism to restrain and reform itself.

That Herbert Croly came to lose hope as time went on—though he never abandoned his original position—is proved by his acute distress over the failure of Woodrow Wilson at Paris and by his increasing skepticism about politics. It seems to me impossible today for people of Herbert Croly's general aims and convictions to continue to believe in the salvation of our society by the gradual and natural approximation to socialism which he himself called progressivism, but which has more generally come to be known as liberalism. That benevolent and intelligent capitalism on which liberals have always counted has not merely not materialized to the extent of accepting socialism—it has not even been able to prevent a national economic disaster of proportions which neither capitalists nor liberals foresaw and which they both now profess themselves unable to explain. There are today in the United States, according to the census director, something like nine million men out of work; our cities are scenes of privation and misery on a scale which sickens the imagination; our agricultural life is bankrupt; our industry, in shifting to the South, has reverted almost to the horrible conditions, before the Factory Acts, of the England of a hundred years ago, and the fight of the unions there for recognition is all to begin again; so many banks are failing that the newspapers do not dare to print the truth about them. And when we look to South America or to the European countries west of Russia, we see only the same economic chaos, the same lack of capacity or will to deal with it, and the same resultant suffering. May we not well fear that what has broken down, in the course of one catastrophic year, is not simply the machinery of representative government but the capitalist system itself?—and that, even with the best intentions, it may be henceforward impossible for capitalism to guarantee not merely social justice but even security and order? May we not fear lest our American society, in spite of its apparently greater homogeneity, be liable, through sheer inefficiency, the heritage of political corruption, to collapse in the long run as ignominiously as the feudal regimes of old France and Russia?

The capitalist Americans of the twentieth century are certainly more kindly and democratic than the landlords of the feudal age; but, on the other hand, the capitalist system makes it very much easier for people not to realize what they are doing, not to know about the danger and the hardship, the despair and the humiliation, that their way of life implies for others. The feudal lord might flog or kill his serfs, but he was dealing directly with the human realities as the stockholder or the banker is not. The feudal master might be arrogant and cruel, but his arrogance and cruelty were open, accepted as necessities imposed or enjoyed as privileges conferred by superior social position. But the chivalrous Southerner whose interest is mounting up in the bank that lends money to the textile mill is no more conscious that he has helped pull the trigger that murdered Ella May Wiggins* than the cultivated Bostonian knows that the money that reaches his pocket from the shares in the South Braintree shoe company in which his broker has recommended his investing has on its way helped turn on the switch that electrocuted Sacco and Vanzetti. Mr. Lawrence Dennis, late of Seligman, has recently written in this magazine of the queer and unenviable lot of the bond salesmen, who, taking over their bonds on trust from the bankers and selling them to customers who take them on trust, do not assume any professional responsibility and never touch at any point the realities of the things with which they are dealing. Not only are the people in a capitalist society very often completely ignorant as to what their incomes come from; it is actually sometimes impossible or very difficult for them to find this out. And as long as a fair proportion of the bankers, the manufacturers, the middle men, the merchants and the workers whom their capital and machines keep busy are able to make a little more money than before, no matter how unscrupulously or short-sightedly, we are able, as a nation, to maintain our belief in our prosperity and even in our happiness.

That is what has been happening in the period which has just now come to a close. The liberal Stuart Chase tried to make us see this situation in his little book called *Prosperity: Fact or Myth?* published in 1929, on the eve of the stock-market crash. Between 1922 and 1928, he tells us, the average income in the United States was increased twenty percent, but this left the average annual

* See page 498.

wage in 1929 "well below $1,500." Through this whole
period the coal, textile, shoe, leather, shipbuilding and
railroad-equipment industries were all doing more or less
badly and the people employed in them were hanging on
to the bare edge of subsistence; the farmers became more
and more impoverished; the mergers and the new machinery were throwing more and more people out of work;
and the radio and motor industries, on which the illusion
of prosperity depended, were prospering at the expense
of selling these articles to many people who didn't need
them. The salesmen and advertisers had had to begin to
break down the "sales resistance" of their public: it was
no longer a question merely of persuading people of the
attractiveness of one's wares but of combating a positive
antagonism to them. The sales departments resorted to
both inspirational and scientific methods, but when the
public began to come to from the industrial opium-dream,
the motor-car industry was suddenly sunk and the rest of
American business went with it. May we not ask ourselves whether it is possible, in the conditions of our
capitalist society, for any further spectacular appearance
of revival to be anything more than a spurt depending
on the overinflation, equally senseless and mischievous,
of some other inessential industry?—an inflation just as
sure to end in another abject disaster?

In any case, American optimism has taken a serious
beating; the national morale is weak. The energy and
the faith for a fresh start seem now not to be forthcoming: a dreadful apathy, unsureness and discouragement is felt to have fallen upon us. It is as if we were
afraid to go on with what we were doing before or as if
we had no longer the heart for it. I want to suggest that
the present depression may be nothing less than one of
the turning-points in our history, our first real crisis since

the Civil War. The Americans at the present time seem to be experiencing not merely an economic breakdown but a distinct psychological change. From the time of the Civil War on, all our enthusiasm and creative energy went into the development of our tremendous resources. This development had two aspects: one was the exploration of the continent and the engineering feats involved in reclaiming it; the other the amassing of gigantic fortunes. Today the discoveries have all been made: we no longer look toward the West, as the Europeans once looked to America, as to a world of untold treasures and wonders—and the excitement of mastering new seacoasts, new rivers, forests, prairies and mountains seems now completely spent. This was already true at the time of the European War (when, incidentally, we were running into a business depression), but the war gave us a new objective—new discoveries, the discovery of Europe; new heroic stunts of engineering, the transportation of our army to France. Since the end of the war, however, we have, as a people, had nothing to carry us along except the momentum of money-making. We have been trying still to find in it the exhilaration of the money-making of our earlier period, which had been largely the exhilaration of the wildness and size of the continent—the breaking it in to the harness of the railroads, the stumbling upon sudden riches. But during these last years our hope and our faith have all been put behind the speed of mass production, behind stupendous campaigns of advertising, behind cyclones of salesmanship. Our buoyancy had been becoming hysterical. And the reaction from an hysterical exhilaration is a slump into despondency and inertia. What we have lost is, it may be, not merely our way in the economic labyrinth but our conviction of the value of what we were doing. Money-making and the kind of advantages which a money-making society provides for money to buy are not enough to satisfy humanity—neither is a system like ours in which everyone is out for himself and devil take the hindmost, with no common purpose and little common culture to give life stability and sense. Our idolization of our aviators—our extravagant excitement over Lindbergh and our romantic admiration (now beginning to cool off) for Byrd—has been like a last desperate burst of American idealism, a last impulse to dissociate our national soul from a precipitate progress that was taking us from automobiles and radios straight through electric refrigerators to Tom Thumb golf-courses.

The old American ideal and legend of the poor boy who gets to be a millionaire, which gradually came to take the place of the poor boy who got to be President, has today lost almost all its glamor. Not only do people not hope to be Hoover—they do not even hope so often as they did to be Carnegie or Henry Ford. The romance of the legend of the poor boy was the romance of the old democratic chance, of the career open to the talents— but the realities of a millionaire society have turned out to be the monstrosities of capitalism: the children of the successful poor boy get lazy and sick on their father's money, and the poor boys who afterwards arrive on the scene discover that—with the crippling of the grain market, the elimination of the factory worker by the development of the machine and the decimation of the white-collar class, even though sometimes apparently well on their way to getting in on the big money themselves, by enormous business mergers—the career is no longer open to the extent that had originally been hoped. What began as the libertarian adventure of eighteenth-century middle-class democracy seems to have ended in the cul de sac of an antiquated economic system. And capitalist-minded as the Americans have now become, they seem to feel they are in a cul de sac. It is as if they did not dare to go on. In spite of the fundamental absurdity of so much of what we have lately been doing, we are considerably better educated and more intelligent than we once were, and since the war we have been closer to Europe. The Buicks and Cadillacs, the bad gin and Scotch, the radio concerts interrupted by advertizing talks, the golf and bridge of the suburban household, which the bond salesman can get for his money, can hardly compensate him for daily work of a kind in which it is utterly impossible to imagine a normal human being taking satisfaction or pride—and the bond salesman is the type of the whole urban office class. The brokers and bankers who are shooting themselves and jumping out of windows have been disheartened by the precariousness of their profession—but would they be killing themselves if they loved it? Who today, in fact, in the United States, can really love our meaningless life, where the manufacturer raises the workers' wages only in order to create a demand for the gadgets which for better or worse he happens to have an interest in selling them, while agriculture goes hang, and science and art are left to be exploited by the commercial laboratories, the market for commercial art illustration and the New York publishers' racket, or to be fed in a haphazard way by a dole from the fortunes of rich men who have been conscience-stricken or simply overpowered at finding themselves at the end of their careers with enough money on their hands to buy out an old-fashioned empire?

We liberals have professed not to love it, yet we have tried to believe in it, none the less. In a country where money changes hands so often and social position fluctuates so easily, where the minds of the working class have seemed largely to have been absorbed into the psychology of the middle class, we have been unable to believe in the Marxist doctrine that capitalism must eventually give rise to class warfare, and we have perhaps never taken sufficiently seriously Karl Marx's prediction that for many years to come the stupid automatic acquisitive instinct of humanity would still be so far ahead of its capacity for intelligent and disinterested behavior that the system of private enterprise would never even be able to run itself with foresight enough to avoid a wreck. It used to be pointed out that in America our support of this system was indestructible, since the stock market made it possible for anybody who had been able to save a little money to become a capitalist himself, with interests presumably identical with those of J. P. Morgan and Charlie Schwab. But can we expect that to be true in the future?—and even if people persist in aspiring to be stock-market capitalists, should they be encouraged in this or even left to their luck? Should they not rather be shown that their interests are incompatible with capitalism itself?

Yet the truth is that we liberals and progressives have been betting on capitalism—and that most of our heroes and allies: heterodox professors like Dewey and Beard, survivors of the old republican tradition like Woodrow Wilson and Justice Holmes, able and well-educated labor organizers like the officers of the Amalgamated, intelligent journalists like Lippmann and Chase, though all sincere and outspoken democrats, have been betting on capitalism, too. And now, in the abyss of starvation and bankruptcy into which the country has fallen, with no sign of any political leadership which will be able to pull us out, our liberalism seems to have little to offer beyond a discreet recommendation of public ownership of water power and certain other public utilities, a cordial feeling that labor ought to organize in a non-social-revolutionary way and a protest, invariably ineffective, against a few of the more obviously atrocious of the jailings, beatings-up and murders with which the industrialists have been trying to keep the working class docile.

Doesn't this program today seem rather inadequate? We liberals have always insisted on the desirability of a planned society—the phrase "social control" has been our blessed Mesopotamian word. If this means anything, does it not mean socialism? And should we not do well to make this plain? It may be said that at the present time it is utopian in America to talk about socialism; but with the kind of administrations that the country has lately been getting, do not all our progressive proposals, however reasonable or modest, seem utopian? Is it not obvious, as was lately made plain by an article in this magazine, that a government like our present one is incapable of acting in good faith in even the simple matter of preserving the water power which is supposed to be operated for the general benefit from being exploited by private profiteers? Our society has finally produced in its specialized professional politicians one of the most useless and obnoxious groups which has perhaps ever disgraced human history—a group that seems unique among governing classes in having managed to be corrupt, uncultivated and incompetent all at once. We know that we are not even able to depend on them today to protect us against the frankly disreputable race of blackmailers, thieves and assassins who dominate our municipal life. We know that we cannot even complain that the racketeers are breaking the laws which are supposed to be guaranteed by the government, because the government differs little from the racketeers. How can we expect them, then, to check the relatively respectable scoundrels who merely rob us of the public utilities by more or less legalistic means?

Yet, as I say, it may be true that, with the present breakdown, we have come to the end of something, and that we are ready to start on a different tack. If we look back through the depressions of the last fifty years, we see that through every one of them there always remained something for which the Americans could still legitimately feel ambition or enthusiasm, something to challenge the national spirit and appeal to the national imagination. After 1885, there were still the West and the consolidation of the railroads; after the prolonged depression of the nineties, the final consolidation of great industries such as United States Steel as well as the crusade led by Theodore Roosevelt against these great corporations in the interests of the dangerously increasing number of those who were being injured by the process of consolidation, and the robustious Rooseveltian imperialism; after the slump of the early years of the European War, our entrance into the war; and after the slump that followed the war, the period of the glorification of the automobile and the airplane. Today the further consolidation of the big business units is ruining more people even than in Roosevelt's time, and there is no sign of a Roosevelt or a Wilson to revive our political vision and to persuade the people who are out of luck that something is about to be done for them. It may be that the whole money-making and -spending psychology has definitely played itself out, and that the Americans would be willing, for the first time now, to put their traditional idealism and their genius for organization behind a radical social experiment. The future is as blank in the United States today as the situation is desperate: the President seems so inhibited by dread of encouraging subversive forces and by faith in the capacity of the capitalist system to right itself and survive that it is impossible for him to act, and when he tries to, he is deadlocked by Congress; nor have the industrialists or the financiers come forward with any constructive proposal.

But this very blindness of the outlook may mean that we are looking in the wrong direction and that help may be coming from some other quarter. In the meantime, one gets the impression that the people who don't deal in ideas are doing more thinking at the present time than the professional ideologues.

The minds of the general public have, furthermore, been more affected by the example of Soviet Russia than is easily grasped by anyone who has been in the habit of assuming that it is only the radical or liberal who understands what Russia is up to, and that the ordinary American citizen is bound to be stupidly prejudiced against the Soviet system. During the NEP period in Russia, the capitalist powers were relieved to feel that the Russians had been forced to recognize the impracticability of Communism and were quietly returning to laissez faire. But with the inauguration of the Five-Year Plan to eliminate capitalist business in Russia, the aspect of things changed. The apparent success of the plan has had its effect on all classes in all the rest of the world—on the Americans, surely, not least. In the course of this winter of our capitalist quandary, the Soviets have been emerging from the back pages of the New York newspapers and are now given much and prominent space—even to interviews with Stalin's mother; and behind what one reads on the subject in even the reactionary papers, one feels as much admiration as resentment. After all, the great Communist project is distinguished by almost all the features that Americans have been taught to glorify—the extreme of efficiency and economy combined with the ideal of a herculean program—like a Liberty Loan drive—to be put over by concerted action to the tune of impassioned boosting. The Russians, furthermore, on their own side, have been studying American methods: they have imported a thousand American engineers and

put them at the head of enormous enterprises with practically a free hand, and one would not be at all surprised
to hear that Mr. Edward L. Bernays had been in Moscow
at the time of the recent trial. We have already, in spite
of the Treasury regulation, been doing a good deal of
trading with Russia, and an important New York bank
was at one time on the point of advancing to the Soviets
the loan that has been advocated by this magazine.

The Communists in the United States assume that,
by their very nature, neither our government nor our
business is capable of learning anything from or of asso-
ciating itself with the Soviets. They believe that a war
against Russia is inevitable. They believe, moreover,
that they themselves constitute a trained compact minority which, at the moment when American capitalism
shall have finally broken down completely and been left
helpless in its ignorance and anarchic selfishness, will
be able to step in and man the works. To liberals, this
idea has always sounded absurd, but who will say that it
is entirely fantastic today when the machine is so badly
in need of repairs, and one can see no political group in
any position of power that has either a sensible plan or
even good intentions? I believe that if the American
radicals and progressives who repudiate the Marxist
dogma and the strategy of the Communist Party still
hope to accomplish anything valuable, they must take
Communism away from the Communists, and take it
without ambiguities, asserting that their ultimate goal is
the ownership by the government of the means of production. If we want to prove the Communists wrong,
if we want to demonstrate that the virtue has not gone
out of American democracy, if we want to confute the
Marxist cynicism implied by "economic laws" the
catastrophic outcome of which is, after all, predicted only
on an assumption of the incurable swinishness and inertia
of human nature—if we seriously want to do this, an

American opposition must not be afraid to dynamite the old conceptions and shibboleths and to substitute new ones as shocking as necessary. Who knows but they may seem less shocking to the ordinary suffering public than to us shibboleth-experts ourselves? When John Dos Passos proposed last summer that what was really needed in the United States was a publicity expert like Ivy Lee to familiarize the public with the idea of Communism and induce people at least to remain neutral toward Communist agitation instead of clapping all the Communists in jail, the suggestion, to some, sounded comic. Yet Dos Passos at once had a letter from a publicity man in San Francisco, who said that the same idea had recently occurred to him and that he would like nothing better than a chance to carry it out. There are some signs that the liberals are having ideas as well as the publicity men: Stuart Chase has said lately that the past year may represent "the end of an epoch" and has offered a set of suggestions for rescuing the economic structure, and John Dewey has just proposed to Senator Norris that he lead a new political party. The extreme illiberalism of the post-Wilsonian period has had the effect of discouraging liberals. We have gone on complaining and recommending, but with a vigor that has tended to diminish in proportion as we came to be conscious that people were not listening to us. Who knows but, if we spoke out now with confidence and boldness, we might find our public at last? January 14, 1931

From the fall of 1930 to the spring of 1934, I spent a good deal of time reporting political and industrial events, and thereafter, till 1940, writing a study of Marxism and the Russian Revolution, so that I did not give the literary events of these years as much attention as I had given to those of the twenties or as I was afterwards to give to those of the forties.

THE LITERARY CLASS WAR

In the fall of 1930, a year after the stock-market crash, there appeared in the *New Republic* an attack by Michael Gold on Thornton Wilder. Michael Gold is, of course, a Communist, and his article was an attempt to arraign Mr. Wilder at the bar of the Communist ideology. He declared that Mr. Wilder's writings were the poetry "of a small sophisticated class that has recently arisen in America—our genteel bourgeoisie" and on a plane with "luxury hotels, golf, old furniture and *Vanity Fair* sophistication." *The Cabala* and *The Bridge of San Luis Rey* were among the things that helped this "parvenu class to forget its lowly origins in American industrialism"—providing them with "a short cut to the aristocratic emotions," disguising "the barbaric sources of their income, the billions wrung from American workers and foreign peasants and coolies" and encouraging them to "feel spiritually worthy of that income." Mr. Wilder's Christianity was merely "that newly fashionable literary religion that centers around Jesus Christ the First British Gentleman"; and his style a "neat tailormade rhetoric," whose serenity was "that of a corpse" and which, when pricked, would "bleed violet ink and *apéritif*." How, he asked, could "this discreet French drawing-room hold all the blood, horror and hope of the world's new empire? . . . Where are the modern streets of New York, Chicago and New Orleans? . . .

Where are the cotton mills, and the murder of Ella May and her songs?* Where are the child slaves of the beet fields? Where are the stockbroker suicides, the labor racketeers or the passion and death of the coal miners?"

This assault provoked one of the most violent controversies which the literary world has lately known. The writer of the present article had felt, when he first read Gold's article, that the latter had overshot his mark and had read into Wilder's popularity a Marxist moral that it did not have. But as the letters began to shower in and kept up for months without abatement, he was finally forced to the conclusion that there *was* a class issue involved in the dispute. For equally severe attacks on other equally popular authors had never brought forth anything like this. The people who applauded Gold seemed to be moved by a savage animus; those who defended Wilder protested or pleaded in the tone of persons who had been shocked by the desecration of a dearly beloved thing. Strange cries from the depths arose, illiterate and hardly articulate.

The editors of the *New Republic* decided at last that the controversy called for some sort of official comment on the part of the magazine; and the writer produced a leader in which he justified Gold's attack—pointing out that Thornton Wilder obviously owed a good deal to Proust; that the pinings and dissatisfactions that were the dominant emotions in Proust represented the illness of the cultivated classes in a capitalistic society; and that Wilder, without intending it and though a writer of genuine merit, had popularized Proust for American readers.

The author of this leader was not in a position to take other writers to task too severely for coming under the influence of Proust, since he himself had not long before

* See page 498.

contributed to the same magazine a long and sympathetic essay on *A la Recherche du Temps Perdu* and had also published a novel not unflavored by the fumes of the cork-lined chamber. His editorial on the Gold-Wilder controversy had been written from the bourgeois point of view, as Michael Gold's article had been from the proletarian one. Yet it turned out to be too Marxist for many *New Republic* readers, who at once, in a revival of the controversy, transferred their indignation from Mr. Gold to myself, and so deluged us with letters that the editors were obliged to put an end to the discussion.

The situation was made more complicated by the fact that Mr. Gold, on his side, was under criticism from his own Marxist camp. He had just published and had been having considerable success with his book about the New York East Side, *Jews Without Money*, and the Communist critics were scolding him for having made this a volume of personal memories that centered around an individual, the official theory being that, in a Communist work of art, there ought not to be a protagonist, since the subject should be always the group. One of these critics, Mr. Melvin Levy, in an otherwise appreciative review— which also appeared in the *New Republic*—had insisted that *Jews Without Money* was "written without reference to the mass"; that "labor organizations and strikes" were "not mentioned," though they were "probably more a part of the life of this group than any other in America"; that the big shirtwaist makers' strike and the Triangle fire, for example, though they had taken place during the period with which *Jews Without Money* dealt, received no attention in it; and that the characters were not proletarians at all, but "merely poor people" whose sorrows and strivings were not the inevitable products of a class situation, but individual accidents: if they had not happened to have hard luck, they might have

turned into contented petty bourgeois. Yet it was evident
that Mr. Melvin Levy had not always been so clear himself about the duty of the revolutionary writer: he had
published not long before a novel about Greenwich Village, which, I believe, did not deal at all with the struggles
of the proletariat; and, in a review of an earlier book by
Mr. Gold, he had complained that some of the stories had
been "tailored to meet a pattern of 'proletarian literature'
and propaganda." "It is not merely," wrote Mr. Levy,
"that they sacrifice artistic excellence for propaganda: if
they did that successfully, they would be justified. But
they have not the veracity and conviction that make good
propaganda. They are distant and unreal: unmoving."

To the first of these reviews, Mr. Gold made an eloquent reply:

"I think Comrade Levy [he wrote] is too dogmatic in
his application of the proletarian canon. There is nothing
finished or dogmatic in proletarian thought and literature. We cannot afford it. We are pioneers. . . . It would
be fatal for us to have fixed minds. Proletarian literature
is taking many forms. There is not a standard model
which all writers must imitate, or even a standard set of
thoughts. There are no precedents. Each writer has to
find his own way. All that unites us, and all we have for
a guide, is the revolutionary spirit. . . .

"To my mind, it is the task of each proletarian writer
to describe that portion of proletarian life with which he
is most saturated. . . . Comrade Levy . . . is disappointed
because I . . . did not include the Triangle fire and the
great garment strikes. Yet I could do nothing else honestly and emotionally at the time. I could only describe
what I had seen with my own eyes. I did not want to
falsify the emotional values and bring in material that I
did not feel. I do not believe any good writing can come
out of this mechanical application of the spirit of proletar-

ian literature. In America, where everything is confused, we must begin humbly with the things we know best."

He then went on to make an interesting plea:

"It is difficult to write proletarian literature in this country, because all the critics are bourgeois. If a Thornton Wilder writes books in praise of the Catholic theology or if a Robinson Jeffers preaches universal pessimism and mass-suicide, that is art. But if a revolutionary writer, even by implication, shows the social ideals that are stirring in the heart of the working class, he is called a propagandist. This taunt which one meets on every side creates a powerful psychic force which proletarian writers will have to ignore. I will admit it had set up inhibitions in my own mind that I have not yet overcome. Perhaps Levy has perceived this in *Jews Without Money*, but I assure him that it is hard to overcome in a first book. It will take other books; it will take a group literature and collective experimentation before we can feel as easy in our proletarian world as every bourgeois writer feels in his. Meanwhile, let us not fear to be crude or propagandistic. We are going somewhere; the rest of literature is sinking into the arms of Catholicism, and death."

This whole controversy, in short, took place in an atmosphere of intellectual confusion—an atmosphere which has not yet cleared up. The results seem to have been that Michael Gold has taken to writing for the *New Masses* little Communist Sunday-school stories, in which the role of a proletarian hero is subordinated with effort and imperfect success to the conflicts of a social group; while Thornton Wilder, not unmoved, apparently, by the reproach of neglecting America, has brought out a volume of little plays several of which—and they are quite good—deal with American subjects, one of them transferring the Christian motif so obnoxious to his Marxist critics from the Greek island of *The Woman of Andros* to Trenton, New Jersey, and another presenting a Pullman car with a technique based, as Mr. Wilder explains, on the Japanese Noh plays, but with an effect faintly reminiscent of Dos Passos and John Howard Lawson in their New Playwrights' Theater days. He is said to have stated a belief that every enormously popular book has concealed in it some sentimentality.

There is no question that the Gold-Wilder case marks definitely the eruption of the Marxist issues out of the literary circles of the radicals into the field of general criticism. It has now become plain that the economic crisis is to be accompanied by a literary one.

May 4, 1932

C. L. DODGSON: THE POET LOGICIAN

IF THE LEWIS CARROLL centenary has produced anything of special interest, I have failed to see it. C. L.
Dodgson was a most interesting man and deserves better
of his admirers, who revel in his delightfulness and cute-
ness but do not give him any serious attention. "Frankly
this is to be the book of Lewis Carroll," wrote John
Francis McDermott in his introduction to Dodgson's
collected verse, published three years ago, "and I have no
intention here of allowing Charles Lutwidge Dodgson,
a dull and uninteresting person, to intrude in it any more
than is absolutely necessary." Richard Herrick, the editor
of *The Lewis Carroll Book,* is so determined that we shall
see in Dodgson nothing but an exponent of pure nonsense that he does not hesitate to mutilate his work. He
reprints, out of *Rhyme? and Reason?,* only the poems
that happen to please him; he suppresses, with the exception of a few stanzas, the long and elaborate *Phantas-*
magoria, for the extraordinary reason that he believes it
to have been spoiled by "Carroll's serious interest in
psychic matters"; and he lops off the charming and significant epilogue to *Through the Looking Glass,* without
which the book is incomplete:

> Still she haunts me, phantomwise,
> Alice moving under skies
> Never seen by waking eyes.

On the other hand, he includes some very amusing letters and a mathematical fantasia called *A Tangled Tale*. The whole book seems thrown together as a hasty publisher's job—there is not even a table of contents—and is typical of the careless handling that Lewis Carroll ordinarily gets.

The truth is that, if Dodgson and his work were shown as an organic whole, his "nonsense" would not seem the anomaly which it is usually represented as being. It is true that on one of his sides he was a pompous and priggish don. He used to write letters to friends the next morning after he had been having dinner with them and beg them never again in his presence to speak so irreverently of Our Lord as they had the evening before, because it gave him infinite pain; and he wrote to the papers in a tone of indignation worthy of Mr. Podsnap protesting against the impiety of W. S. Gilbert in being whimsical about curates on the stage. But even this side of Dodgson should not be kept out of the picture: the *Alice in Wonderland* side has an intimate relation with it. Under the crust of the pious professor was a mind both rebellious and skeptical. The mathematician who invented Alice was one of those semi-monastic types—like Walter Pater and A. E. Housman—that the English universities breed: vowed to an academic discipline but cherishing an intense originality, painfully repressed and incomplete but in the narrow field of their art somehow both sound and bold. A good deal of the piquancy of the Alice books is due to their merciless irreverence: in Alice's dreaming mind, the bottoms dismayingly drop out of the didactic little poems by Dr. Watts and Jane Taylor which Victorian children were made to learn, and their simple and trite images are replaced by grotesque and silly ones, which have rushed in like goblins to take possession. And in the White Knight's song about the aged man a-sitting on a gate, a parody of Wordsworth's *Leech-Gatherer*, Lewis Carroll, in his subterranean fashion, ridiculed the stuffed-shirt side of Wordsworth as savagely as Byron had ever done. Wordsworth was a great admiration of Dodgson's; yet as soon as he enters his world of dreams, Lewis Carroll is moved to stick pins in him. This poem in its original form, before it had been rewritten to adapt it to Alice's dream, had been even more subversive of Victorian conventions:

> I met an aged, aged man
>   Upon the lonely moor:
> I knew I was a gentleman,
>   And he was but a boor.
> So I stopped and roughly questioned him,
>   "Come, tell me how you live!"
> But his word impressed my ear no more
>   Than if it were a sieve.

It is curious what ordination as a clergyman of the Church of England can do to an original mind. The case of Dodgson is somewhat similar to those of Donne and Swift—though Dodgson was shy and stammered and never took priest's orders; and he was closer, perhaps, to Swift and Donne than to the merely whimsical writer like Barrie or A. A. Milne, for Dodgson had a first-rate mind of a very unusual sort: he was a logician who was also a poet.

The poetry and the logic in Dodgson were closely bound up together. It has often been pointed out that only a mind primarily logical could have invented the jokes of the Alice books, of which the author is always conscious that they are examples of faulty syllogisms. But it also worked the other way: his eccentric imagination invaded his scholarly work. His *Symbolic Logic* (which had nothing to do with the subject called by the same name of which A. N. Whitehead and Bertrand Russell laid the foundation in their *Principia Mathematica*) contains syllogisms with terms as absurd as any in the Alice books:

> A prudent man shuns hyenas;
> No banker is imprudent.
> No banker fails to shun hyenas.

Dodgson's *Euclid and His Modern Rivals* had nothing to do with non-Euclidean geometry, but in the section called *A New Theory of Parallels* of his *Curiosa Mathematica* he grazed one of the conceptions of relativist theory; and is there not a touch of Einstein in the scenes in which the Red Queen has to keep running in order to remain in the same place and in which the White Queen gives a scream of pain before she has pricked her finger?

In literature, Lewis Carroll went deeper than his contemporaries realized and than he usually gets credit for even today. As studies in dream psychology, the Alice books are most remarkable: they do not suffer by comparison with the best serious performances in this field—with Strindberg or Joyce or Flaubert's *Tentation de Saint Antoine*. One of Alice's recent editors says that the heroine's personality is kept simple in order to throw into relief the eccentrics and monsters she meets. But the creatures that she meets, the whole dream, *are* Alice's personality and her waking life. They are the world of teachers, family and pets, as it appears to a little girl, and also the little girl who is looking at this world. The creatures are always snapping at her and chiding her, saying brusque and rude and blighting things (as if their creator himself were snapping back at the authorities and pieties he served); and she in turn has a child's primitive cruelty: she cannot help mentioning cats when she is swimming around with the mouse, and later on, with the birds all around her, she comes out, as if naïvely, with, "Dinah's our cat. And she's such a capital one for catching mice, you can't think! And oh, I wish you could see her after the birds! Why, she'll eat a little bird as soon as look at it!" But though Alice is sometimes brutal, she is always well-bred; and, though she wanders in a world full of mysteries and of sometimes disagreeable surprises, she is always a sensible and self-possessed little upper-class English girl, who never fails in the last resort to face down the outlandish creatures that plague her: she can always bring the dream to an end by telling the King and Queen and the Court that they're nothing but a pack of cards or by picking up the Red Queen and shaking her. She can also be sympathetic and sometimes —for example, with the White Knight—exhibits a maternal instinct, but always in a sensible and practical way. Lewis Carroll is never sentimental about Alice, though he is later on to become so, in the messiest Victorian way, in the Sylvie and Bruno books. Yet *Sylvie and Bruno*, too, has considerable psychological interest, with its alternations of dream and reality and the elusive relationships between them. The opening railway journey, in which the narrator is dozing and mixes with the images of his dream his awareness of the lady sitting opposite him, is of an almost Joycean complexity and quite inappropriate for reading to children.

I do not, however, agree with Mr. Herrick, in the case of the Alice books, that the Alice that grown-ups read is really a different work from the Alice that is read by children. The grown-ups understand it better, but the prime source of the interest is the same. Why is it that very young children listen so attentively to Alice, remember it all so well and ask to hear it again, when many other stories seem to leave little impression? It is surely the psychological truth of these books that lays its hold on us all. Lewis Carroll is in touch with the real mind of childhood and hence with the more primitive elements of the mind of maturity, too—unlike certain other writers who merely exploit for grown-ups an artificial child-mind of convention which is in reality neither child-like nor adult. The shiftings and the transformations, the mishaps and the triumphs of Alice's dream, the mysteries and the riddles, the gibberish that conveys unmistakable meanings, are all based upon relationships that contradict the assumptions of our conscious lives but that are lurking not far behind them. In the "straight" parts of *Sylvie and Bruno*, Lewis Carroll was mawkishly Victorian to the point of unintentional parody (having produced in *The Two Voices* a masterpiece of intentional parody!), but in the Alice books he quite got away from the upholstery and the gloomy institutions of the nineteenth-century world. I believe that they are likely to survive when a good deal of the more monumental work of that world—the productions of the Carlyles and the Ruskins, the Spencers and the George Eliots—shall have sunk with the middle-class ideals of which they were the champions as well as the critics. Charles Dodgson who, in morals and religion, in his attitude toward social institutions, was professedly and as he himself believed, more conventional than any of these, had over them the curious advantage of working at once with the abstract materials of mathematical and logical conceptions and with the irrationalities of dreams. His art has a purity that is almost unique in a period so cluttered and cumbered, in which even the preachers of doom to the reign of materialism bore the stamp and the stain of the industrial system in the hard insistence of their sentences and in the turbidity of their belchings of rhetoric. They have shrunk now, but Alice still stands.

I suggest to the Nonesuch Press that it would do well to get out a definitive and comprehensive one-volume edition of Dodgson, like their admirable editions of Blake and Donne. The trouble about such collections as that which Mr. Herrick has edited is that they are intended primarily for children. There is no Charles Lutwidge Dodgson for grown-ups. *Sylvie and Bruno,* which is never reprinted, ought to be made available; and there ought to be at least as many readers for the *Curiosa Mathematica* and the *Dynamics of a Parti-cle* as for Donne's sermons or Blake's prophetic books. Dodgson's letters should be included, his articles on local events at Oxford and his journal of his trip to Russia; and there ought to be a good memoir. The only biography of Dodgson is a conventional life by a relative published in 1899. No writer, so far as I know, has ever done a serious portrait of him or made a real study of his work.

May 18, 1932

The needs pointed out in this article were very promptly supplied. In 1935, Mr. J. F. McDermott brought out a volume of the miscellaneous writings of Dodgson: *The Russian Journal and Other Selections from the Works of Lewis Carroll;* and in 1937 the Nonesuch Press did publish, as I had suggested, a well-produced omnibus volume, *The Complete Works of Lewis Carroll,* containing almost everything of Dodgson's (the Russian Journal is not included) that a non-scholarly person could read. *Some Aspects of Pastoral* by William Empson (American edition called *English Pastoral Poetry*), published in 1935, includes an interesting study of the Alice books, which treats the cataclysmic finale of the dinner at the end of *Through the Looking-Glass* as the eruption of a repressed don, exasperated by dining with his colleagues.

The first full-length biography since *The Life and Letters of Lewis Carroll* by his nephew S. D. Collingwood appeared in 1945: *Victoria Through the Looking-Glass: The Life of Lewis Carroll*, by Florence Becker Lennon. This book has its unsatisfactory features. Mrs. Lennon presents her material in rather an untidy way: she nowhere, so far as I can find, for example, gives the date of Dodgson's birth—certainly not in the proper place; and the filling-in of the background, done from this side of the Atlantic, is synthetic and not easily assimilable. But this study is, nevertheless, the best thing that has yet been written about Lewis Carroll. The literary criticism is excellent; the psychological insight sometimes brilliant; and Mrs. Lennon has brought together, from the most scattered and various sources, a good deal of information. The impression that she actually conveys of what Dodgson's existence was like is more convincing than some of her theories. Mrs. Lennon believes that Charles Dodgson was intimidated by his clergyman father, so that he felt himself obliged to take orders and never dared question the creed of the Church. She seems to believe that he might otherwise have developed as an important original thinker. She also worries about what she regards as his frustrated sexual life: if he had only, she sighs, been capable of a mature attachment for a woman which would have freed him from his passion for little girls! (a penchant with which his position as elder brother of seven motherless sisters as well as the strong feminine streak in him noted by Mrs. Lennon must have had a good deal to do). What she does not understand, I think, is that Dodgson, in terms of his age and place, was remarkably "well-adjusted." His enjoyment of the Oxford "Studentship," with its relatively agreeable work and exceptionally comfortable quarters, which he won on his graduation was dependent on his acceptance of celibacy; and there is nothing to show that this irked him much. His admiration and affection for his father seem to have been complete; the rectory in which he grew up was obviously as little as possible like that described by Samuel Butler in *The Way of All Flesh*; and with the Dodgsons the church tradition was strong: Charles's father and mother, who were cousins, had had the same Archbishop for a grandfather. Since reading this biography and Collingwood's memoir, I am less disposed than I was when I wrote the above article to assume that Charles Dodgson was seriously cramped by his role. Mrs. Lennon insists that, in his photographs, he has the look of one "crucified," but she does not produce any evidence that he actually suffered much. There is mockery of course in Alice, who finds herself at odds with the "creatures"; there are, as both Mrs. Lennon and Mr. Empson suggest, outbreaks of contemptuous violence at the ends of the Alice books and *Sylvie and Bruno;* but the forces of benevolence and common sense always triumph in what is not merely the conventional Victorian happy ending, as they certainly did in Dodgson's life. The conditions of teaching in an English university in the middle of the nineteenth century may seem to us today unnatural, but all social and professional situations involve their special disabilities, and in the position that Dodgson had chosen he seems to have functioned well. If a part of his intelligence lived underground, if a part of his personality was screened, it is plain that—Mrs. Lennon admits this—Alice would never have gone down the rabbit-hole, would never have walked through the mirror, if this had not been the case. Dodgson's work in mathematics and logic was somewhat eccentric, too, and he sometimes, we are told, proposed problems, just as his stories do, that probed into the depths of their subjects; but in these scientific fields as in fiction he seems to have given the world all that he was capable of. The author of *Sylvie and Bruno* was trying already for more than he could manage. Mrs. Lennon, has, I believe, been the first to point out the exact and complicated parallels between the dreams and the actualities that make this book psychologically interesting (my own references to these above have been added for the sake of completeness since the article was first written), but the novel for grown-ups is otherwise childish; and in mathematics and logic, according to the expert opinions cited by Mrs. Lennon, he either ignored or had never discovered the more advanced work in these fields, and did not perhaps get even so far as in his exploration of dreams.

It is one of the pioneering merits of *Victoria Through the Looking-Glass* that Mrs. Lennon has looked up these authoritative estimates of Dodgson's mathematical and logical work; and, a poet, she is able herself to provide an expert opinion on his poetry. The only aspect of his varied activity to which she does not seem quite to do justice is his achievement as an artist-photographer; but this subject has been dealt with since in a book called *Lewis Carroll Photographer* by Helmut Gernsheim (1950). Mr. Gernsheim considers Dodgson "the most outstanding photographer of children of the nineteenth century" and, after Julia Margaret Cameron, "probably the most distinguished amateur portraitist of the mid-Victorian era." In this field he was eccentric and perfectionist as he was in everything else. He showed the real reckless artist's passion in his pursuit of his two favorite kinds of subjects: celebrities and little girls. The former he besieged unabashedly, undaunted by occasional snubs and not afraid to arrive before breakfast, with all his apparatus in a cab, so that his prospects would not have a chance to escape. In his search for attractive little girls, he attended such incongruous func-

tions as archery meetings and Freemason's fêtes, and
spent part of his vacations at the seaside, supplied always
with safety-pins in case he should find "a little girl
hesitating to paddle in the sea for fear of spoiling her
frock." His trophies repaid him for his risks and ordeals.
A few of his portraits were reproduced in the Collingwood *Life and Letters,* but these do not give an adequate
idea of the interest and scope of these plates. There was,
it seems, an enormous body of work, of which twelve
albums are known to survive. The sixty-four plates from
three of them that Mr. Gernsheim includes in his book
show a dramatic sense of personality—in the posing, the
arrangement of the backgrounds and the feeling for
facial expression—that one would not have suspected in
Dodgson from his letters and his literary work and that
reminds one of his love of the theater (which, in taking
Holy Orders at Oxford, he made sure that he would not
be expected to renounce). Here, humanly appealing and
vivid, you have the troubled Elizabethanism of Tennyson;
the jaunty, almost rakish bohemianism of Tom Taylor,
the editor of *Punch;* the contemptuous independence of
Rossetti; the serious and challenging young-womanhood
of the eighteen-year-old Ellen Terry; the healthy Victorian attractiveness of Alexander Munro and his wife;
and the morbid Victorian intensity of "Mrs. Franklin
and her daughter Rose." There is a liveliness and a
humor in these pictures that sometimes suggest Max
Beerbohm. It is, one supposes, unlikely that Max could
have seen these albums at the time he did his drawings
of *Rossetti and His Circle,* but the photographs of the
Millais's and the Rossettis seem to anticipate these. As
for the pictures of children, they, too, are extremely
varied and provide a new revelation of Lewis Carroll's
special genius for depicting little English girls that is as
brilliant in its way as Alice.

LYTTON STRACHEY

IT IS SOMETIMES the case with first-rate people that their lives seem to come to an end—sometimes very suddenly—just when they have finished performing their function. This was the case with Lytton Strachey. Lytton Strachey's chief mission, of course, was to take down once for all the pretensions of the Victorian Age to moral superiority. His declaration in the preface to *Eminent Victorians,* "Je n'impose rien; je ne propose rien: j'expose," was certainly not justified by the book that followed. His irony here was so acid that it partly dehumanized his subjects. The essays on Manning and Dr. Arnold, though the technique gives an effect of detachment, have a force of suppressed invective; and the essays on Florence Nightingale and Gordon, written with the same metallic accent, make the subjects less sympathetic than they probably deserve to be. In attempting to destroy, for example, the sentimental reputation that had been created for Florence Nightingale, he emphasized her hardness to such a degree as to slight her moral seriousness and the deep feeling for suffering that drove her. Only at moments does he let these appear: "O Father," he quotes her as writing, "Thou knowest that through all these horrible twenty years, I have been supported by the belief that I was working with Thee who wast bringing everyone, even our poor nurses, to perfection";

and "How inefficient I was in the Crimea, yet He raised up from it trained nursing." Such a woman must have been more than the mere demon of energy that Lytton Strachey tried to make her appear.

But from *Eminent Victorians* on, the ferocity of Strachey abates. Queen Victoria is already a different matter. In this book, both Victoria and Albert become human and not unattractive figures. He is said to have approached them originally in the mood of *Eminent Victorians* and then found himself relenting. Victoria is not caricatured as Florence Nightingale is: she is presented simply as a woman, living, for all her exalted position and her public responsibility, a woman's limited life. To Strachey's Victoria, the role of queen is a woman's personal experience, a matter of likes and dislikes, of living up to social obligations. This is the force of the famous deathbed scene, which has been imitated so often by people who have tried to reproduce the cadences without understanding the point: that Victoria has lived through the Victorian Age, has stood at the center of its forces, without knowing what it was all about.

But in Strachey's next biography, *Elizabeth and Essex,* he produces a somewhat similar effect without the same ironic intention. *Elizabeth and Essex* seems to me the least satisfactory of Strachey's books. His art, so tight and so calculated, so much influenced by the French, was ill-suited to the Elizabethan Age. His Elizabeth, though a fine piece of workmanship like everything he did, is worse than metallic, it is wooden. It concentrates so narrowly on the personal relation between the Queen and her favorite that we wonder, glancing back to the earlier book, whether it really was Victoria who lacked interest in the politics and thought of her time, whether it was not perhaps Strachey himself. Certainly Elizabeth lived in a larger intellectual world than Victoria, yet we get almost none of it in Strachey. In general, we do not feel that the individual fates of the characters are involved with the larger affairs of history. The personal story is told with insight, but then, after all, Michelet tells a thousand such stories, taking them in his stride. And we here, for the first time with Strachey, become disagreeably aware of the high-voiced old Bloomsbury gossip gloating over the scandals of the past as he ferrets them out in his library. Lytton Strachey's curious catty malice, his enjoyment of the discomfiture of his characters, is most unpleasantly in evidence in *Elizabeth and Essex*. His attitude toward women—Florence Nightingale, Mme. du Deffand, Queen Victoria or Queen Elizabeth—was peculiar in this, that he was fascinated by their psychology without feeling any of their attraction, and rather took pleasure in seeing them humiliated. The feminine subjects he chose were certainly lacking in feminine charm, and he seemed to do everything possible to make them unappetizing. His study of Queen Elizabeth in the light of modern psychology brings her character into sharper focus, but the effect of it is slightly disgusting; it marks so definitely the final surrender of Elizabethan to Bloomsbury England.

The revolt against Victorian pretences thus ends in faintly scabrous psychology; and in his next book Lytton Strachey recapitulates his view of history—a view with which Flaubert and Anatole France, Henry Adams and T. S. Eliot have already made us familiar and which assumes that modern society, in relation to the societies of the past, represents some sort of absolute deterioration. In *Portraits in Miniature*, which seems to me one of Strachey's real triumphs, he gives glimpses, through a series of thumb-nail sketches of for the most part minor historical and literary personages, of the evolution of modern society from the Elizabethan to the Victorian

Age. These personages, by very reason of their special interest or small capacity, supply cultures particularly clear of the social and intellectual bacteria at work during the periods in which they lived. The first specimen is Sir John Harrington, the Elizabethan inventor of the water-closet; then we are shown some seventeenth-century types: an amateur scientist, a truculent classical scholar, an ambitious university don, the leader of an uncouth Protestant sect, and a few eighteenth-century types: a French abbé who consorted with the philosophers, a French magistrate and country gentleman who insisted on his rights, a lady of sensibility; and we end with Mme. de Lieven, whose liaison with the bourgeois Guizot marks for Strachey the final surrender of the splendid aristocratic qualities he had admired in Queen Elizabeth. A second series of miniatures reviews the British historians from the eighteenth-century Hume to the Victorian Bishop Creighton, and suggests a similar moral. The industrial, democratic, Protestant, middle-class world is a come-down, says Strachey by implication, from Queen Elizabeth, from Racine, from even Voltaire (these last two are favorites of Strachey's, on whom he has written more than once). When one considers the great souls of the past, the present seems dreary and vulgar—the Victorian Age in particular, for all its extraordinary energy, was a disgrace to the human spirit. This is the whole of the message of Strachey; and when he had said it as pointedly as possible in the fewest possible words, he died.

But not only did Strachey in his writings point an historical moral: he illustrated one himself. In his gallery of English historians, he himself should fill out the series. Certainly one of the best English writers of his period, he makes us feel sharply the contrast between

Shakespeare's England and his. Shakespeare is expansive and untidy and close to the spoken language. Lytton Strachey, whose first-published book was a history of French literature, is so far from being any of these things that one of his chief feats consists in having managed to achieve in English some of the effects of French. His biographical method, though novel in England, was already an old story in France. Sainte-Beuve was the great master of it, and Strachey's ironic tone has something in common with his. The weaknesses as well as the virtues of Strachey's style are the result of his imitation of French models. He is lucid and cool and precise, but he is terribly given to clichés. The penalty of trying to reproduce in English the chaste and abstract vocabulary of French is finding one's language become pale and banal. No wonder the age of Shakespeare turned rigid and dry in Strachey's hand. And by the time he had reached *Portraits in Miniature,* he was importing belatedly to England a point of view that since the middle nineteenth century had become a commonplace in France.

The real force and audacity of Lytton Strachey are therefore seen best, as I have indicated, at the beginning of his career. In *Eminent Victorians,* which was published just at the end of the war, he stripped forever of their solemn upholstery the religion, the education, the statesmanship and the philanthropy of the society which had brought it about. The effect in the English-speaking countries was immediate and swiftly pervasive. The biographers turned at once to the easy game of exposing accepted celebrities, and this soon became a bore and a nuisance. The harshness of *Eminent Victorians* without Strachey's wide learning and bitter feeling, the intimate method of *Queen Victoria* without his insight into character, had the effect of cheapening history, something

Strachey never did—for, though he was venomous about the Victorians, he did not make them any the less formidable. He had none of the modern vice of cockiness; he maintained a rare attitude of humility, of astonishment and admiration, before the unpredictable spectacle of life, which he was always finding "amazing" and "incredible." But neither the Americans nor the English have ever, since *Eminent Victorians* appeared, been able to feel quite the same about the legends that had dominated their pasts. Something had been punctured for good.

September 21, 1932

THE SATIRE OF SAMUEL BUTLER*

THE GENIUS OF Samuel Butler was a livid intense flash. It brought out the black darkness around it, then itself rather quickly dimmed out.

The child of a provincial English rectory, he grew up in the narrowest, the most snobbish, the most bigoted and the most ungracious atmosphere which the Protestant nineteenth century produced. He rebelled against it and broke away from it, and he damned it forever in his masterpiece, *The Way of All Flesh,* which is likely to survive as one of the classical accounts of how hateful life could become when the successful British middle class mixed avarice with religion. "I had to steal my own birthright," says Butler. "I stole it and was bitterly punished. But I saved my soul alive." The punishment had affected him more permanently than he knew. He had blasted Langar Rectory to eternity, but it had left upon him its blight. His soul was alive; but, as Bernard Shaw says, he had been maimed by his early training. Having begun as the bad boy of a pious family, he was never to outgrow his original reactions. The dread of his father's bullying rage and his mother's harrowing prayers could still inhibit his mental processes; and up to the day of his death he could never assert himself without something of the sulkiness of the adolescent child who

* Written as an introduction to *Erewhon.*

blurts out that he doesn't believe the Bible, betraying by his excessive pugnacity the delusion that the world, like his family, was conspiring to keep him down.

The Freudian would be able to show how, even after Butler had escaped from the domination of his father, he was still forced to keep putting in his father's place other persons of high authority and, identifying himself with some lesser person, to insist on the latter's superior claims. Dante, Virgil, Bach, Beethoven and Darwin had all to play the role of old Butler, while Handel, Giovanni Bellini, Tabachetti and Guadenzio Ferrari were one by one put forward as the snubbed young man. When he did admire accepted reputations, as in the case of Shakespeare and Homer, he had to work up heretical theories that flew in the face of authority as to who they had really been and what they had really meant. And though in *Erewhon* and *The Way of All Flesh* his revolt against his father had inspired him to what is certainly his most brilliant work, his controversies with substitute fathers became less and less interesting as Butler grew older, and he himself ended as a kind of crank. The shadows of the rectory were closing on him. His wit had attracted attention when *Erewhon* had first come out, but his work was not to be accepted as a part of the general culture of the time till after Butler's death, when *The Way of All Flesh* was published, and Bernard Shaw, the great popularizer, introduced him to a larger public. Shaw points out that, though Butler had revolted against the intolerance of his parents and though he yearned all his life toward a world in which opinions were playful and manners easy, he became as intolerant about Darwin as his father had been about himself; and the elder Yeats has put on record that, if one happened to meet Butler on a railway journey, his aspect could be so forbidding that one did not dare to speak to him first.

Erewhon, however, which was written in Butler's late twenties and early thirties, has the freshness and the bravado of his first defiance of the rectory and of his escape from his father and from England; and it is consequently his most attractive though not perhaps his greatest book. While the young Samuel Butler, just up from Cambridge, had been preparing for ordination in London, his religious faith had been shaken by his discovery that, among the poor boys in a class he was teaching, the ones who had not been baptized were by no means, so far as he could see, morally inferior to the ones who had; and, to the tune of lamentation and fury on the part of his father and mother, he had decided that the Church was not for him. He had persuaded his father to send him to New Zealand; and there in less than five years' time he had nearly doubled the £4,400 with which his father had grudgingly equipped him. The adventures amid wild and beautiful landscapes which finally bring Butler's hero to *Erewhon* are simply Butler's own travels in New Zealand; and his satire has here the clear-headedness and the high spirits of freedom of a young man on his own a long way from home. When he comes back to England, his father will not fail to cloud this clearness by insisting that the publication of *Erewhon* has caused Samuel's mother's death; and when in later years he travels in Sicily, he will receive no more vital revelation than that of his unprovable theory of the feminine authorship of the *Odyssey.* But he enjoys, in his *Erewhon* period, something of true intellectual liberation. (Two of the best of his later books—*The Way of All Flesh* and *Life and Habit*—followed closely on *Erewhon.*) He comes into contact here more intimately than ever afterwards with that ideal race of healthy and natural beings, gay, good-mannered and with comfortable consciences, whom he had imagined as the antithesis of the rectory and who were to haunt him and make him wistful all his life. (It will still be the legend of such a race which will delight him so much in Homer; and the "authoress of the *Odyssey*" herself seems a fantasy of such an ideal mate as he might have hoped to find among them.) Here even the eternal antagonism that Butler felt toward his father loses some of its bitterness and strain. In the chapter on *The World of the Unborn*, there is a magnanimous, an almost tender, insight of a kind very rare in Butler. For the moment he is free not to hate; he can understand that parents have not chosen their children any more than their children have chosen them, and that the plight in which the situation places us may be equally cruel for both.

Butler's *Erewhon*, therefore, is not a production that can be compared with *Candide* or *Gulliver's Travels*. The book is not a definite expression of a satirical point of view based on mature experience: it is the brilliant first fling of an able and gifted young man. It does not pretend to either the logic of Swift or the singleness of intention of Voltaire. The narrative is simply a device for uniting an assortment of satirical notions—in some cases, reductions to absurdity of English conceptions and institutions; in other cases, whimsical suggestions for improving them by their own methods; in still others, flights of fantastic reasoning whose application is rather uncertain.

Of this last kind, *The Book of Machines* is a curious and interesting example. Here there seem to be several intentions involved. One recognizes at once a burlesque of the methods of theological controversy. Samuel Butler had been brought up on theology, and its sophistries had affected his habits of thought in such a way that, when he sets out to write mock apologetics in a later book, *The Fair Haven*, attempting to discredit the Resurrection by inventing a simple-minded churchman who defends it with fallacious arguments, he misses fire through working on too large a scale and sounding too much in earnest, whereas the arguments of *The Authoress of the Odyssey*, which he means to be taken seriously, coming after his insidious satires, only put us on our guard against his theory. *The Book of the Machines*, he asserted as first, was a parody of the famous *Analogy* of that Butler (unrelated to himself) who had tried to defend revealed religion against the attacks of the Deists by demonstrating that their objections could equally well be urged against the known constitution of Nature. In a discussion of *Erewhon* in a letter, not long after its publication, Butler says of what he calls his "obviously absurd theory that they [the machines] are about to supplant the human race and be developed into a higher kind of life": "When I first got hold of the idea, I developed it for mere fun and because it amused me and I thought would amuse others, but without a particle of serious meaning; but I developed it and introduced it into *Erewhon* with the intention of implying: 'See how easy it is to be plausible, and what absurd propositions can be defended by a little ingenuity and distortion and departure from strictly scientific methods,' and I had Butler's *Analogy* in my head as the book at which it should be aimed, but preferred to conceal my aim."

But he had also another book in mind. This disquisition, when it had first appeared as an article in a New Zealand paper, had been called *Darwin Among the Machines*; and though Butler denied in his preface that he had intended to make fun of Darwin's theory, he acknowledged later on that he *had* intended to criticize it. "With *Erewhon*," Butler declared in a letter of 1902, "Charles Darwin smelt danger from afar. . . . He knew very well that the machine chapters in *Erewhon* would not end there." The *Book of the Machines* is thus, also, the first thrust in the battle with Darwinism that Butler was fighting all his life. If man and the other animals could develop through natural selection, why could not machines do so likewise? Had not Darwin, in assuming that the animals were mechanical, made it unthinkable that life should be purposive? Had he not "banished mind from the universe"? Samuel Butler has put himself in the queer situation—which would be interesting to analyze—of attacking on moral grounds the man who had supplied the most damaging weapons to the assault on that orthodox religion against which Butler himself was a rebel. For Samuel Butler was a moral philosopher, to use the old-fashioned term: he never became a modern scientist. He stuck halfway in an anomalous position between science and traditional theology. It was again the shell of the rectory which Samuel the rebel could never shed—and perhaps he felt some envy of Darwin, who had been a pupil of his grandfather's, the Bishop Butler who had been head of Shrewsbury School. Yet, working in his cramped intellectual space, he was able to drive home his Lamarckian point with intensity and telling effect.

There is, of course, however, in the fantasy of the machines another satiric theme and one much more obvious to us today, though evidently not so obvious to Butler: the appalling possibilities of the enslavement of man by the machine. "Man's very soul," Butler writes, "is due to the machines; it is a machine-made thing; he thinks as he thinks, and feels as he feels, through the work that machines have wrought upon him, and their existence is quite as much a *sine qua non* for his, as his for theirs." Nor does he fail to note the relation between the development of machinery and the competitive industrial system: "It is for neglecting them [the machines]

that he [man] incurs their wrath, or for using inferior
machines, or for not making sufficient exertions to invent
new ones, or for destroying them without replacing
them. . . . The machines, being of themselves unable to
struggle, have got man to do their struggling for them:
as long as he fulfills this function duly, all goes well with
him—at least he thinks so; but the moment he fails to
do his best for the advancement of machinery by encouraging the good and destroying the bad, he is left
behind in the race of competition; and this means that
he will be made uncomfortable in a variety of ways,
and perhaps die."

How did Butler, five years after *Das Kapital*, eighteen
years after Dickens' *Hard Times*, fail to satirize the
profit-motive, which was turning the machine into a
tyrant? He was far from approving the kind of civilization that the middle class had brought with it in its
rise. He envied, on the one hand, the civilized primitives
of the world of the Homeric poems (who lived before
the machines) and of Erewhon (where they had destroyed them); and, on the other hand, the worldly upper
class as represented by Townley in *The Way of All
Flesh*. When he makes Ernest in *The Way of All Flesh*
turn shopkeeper and marry the housemaid whom his
mother has turned away and send his children to be
brought up by simple people such as his own great-
grandfather had been, Butler is criticizing the evolution
of his own family. The Butlers, taking flight from the
linen-draper who had been the father of Bishop Butler,
had accumulated in two generations the education, the
religion and the snobbery which they had unloaded on
the unhappy Samuel. He understood very well the preoccupation of the Victorians with money; and in his use
of money as a comic motivation he ran true to the satiric
school of his time. For the Elizabethan dramatists, the

Barabases and the Volpones were still more or less exceptional monsters. But for Dickens, the Jonas Chuzzlewits, the Bounderbys, the Smallweeds and the Grides were common types of the dominant class. And with such comedies of Gilbert's as *Engaged* and the plays of the Marxist Shaw, money comes to play a similar role to that of gallantry in Wycherley and Congreve. Samuel Butler could not even write a classical oratorio on the idyllic theme of Narcissus without yielding to an impulse to ridicule it with such program notes as the following:

> An aged lady taken ill
> Desires to reconstruct her will;
> I see the servants hurrying for
> The family solicitor;
> Posthaste he comes and with him brings
> The usual necessary things.
> With common form and driving quill
> He draws the first part of the will,
> The more sonorous solemn sounds
> Denote a hundred thousand pounds, etc.

It is the entanglement of quarrels about money with disputes about religion that makes the conflict between Ernest and his father in *The Way of All Flesh* so comic and so ignoble.

Yet Butler, though he could be most amusing about people's mercenary motives, was too much a middle-class man himself to analyze the social system, in which, for all his financial difficulties, he occupied a privileged position. As soon as he got back from New Zealand, he invested all the money he had made there in a group of new joint stock companies, which a banker friend of his had financed and in which he was induced to become a director. These companies were manufacturing steam-engines, patent gas-meters, tanning extracts and other commodities produced by the menacing machines. The companies all failed, and Butler lost most of his money. He had felt bound in honor to buy back the shares of friends who had invested in them at his advice. Then, almost as badly off as before he had gone to New Zealand, he threatened to make certain claims against an interest in a family estate to which he believed his father had induced him, while still a minor, to sign away his rights—the case of the youth in *Erewhon* who "was charged with having been swindled out of a large property by his guardian"—and compelled the old man to make him an allowance. "If in my books," wrote Butler late in life, "from *Erewhon* to *Luck or Cunning?* there is something behind the written words which the reader can feel but not grasp—and I fancy that this must be so— it is due, I believe, to the sense of wrong which was omnipresent with me, not only in regard to Pauli, the Darwins and my father, but also in regard to my ever-present anxiety about money."

When the elder Butler died, however, Samuel inherited his interest in the estate and lived comfortably the rest of his life. For all his satiric insight, he had basically the psychology of the *rentier*. One of the things that had nagged him most all his life was the fact that he had not had the family income to which he thought himself entitled; and when he did finally get it, he promptly sat down to write the Life and Letters of his grandfather, Bishop Butler, whom he had satirized in *The Way of All Flesh*. Later he described himself, in the preface to his last book, *Erewhon Revisited*, as "a member of the more advanced wing of the English Broad Church."

May 24, 1933

ANDRÉ MALRAUX

NOBODY ON OUR SIDE of the Atlantic has yet written anything, so far as I know, about André Malraux, the French novelist; and, though I have read only two of his half-dozen books and am unable to deal with his work in any thoroughgoing fashion, I want to bring this fascinating and profitable writer to the attention of American readers. If the recent apotheosis of André Gide has been tending to discourage you with French literature, you will be glad to see the French genius cropping up again in a field where you would least expect it. A fault of much French writing lately has been that it has all seemed to be steeped in the atmosphere of the literary world of Paris, with its smug and self-conscious dependence on the French literary tradition. But M. André Malraux turns up a long way from Paris, and he nowhere—at any rate, in either of the books I have read—pays his pious respects to Racine.

M. Malraux first visited the orient at the age of twenty-three as head of an archeological expedition to Indo-China; but he presently dropped the cultural problems of ancient Cambodia for the political problems of the present. The orient that Malraux writes about is not the orient of *Madame Butterfly*. He published in 1928 a novel called *Les Conquérants*, which dealt with the events of the Chinese revolution in 1925. The reader who picked up this book was dazzled by an unhoped-for searchlight into a region which had previously seemed distant and dim. Here was a picture, based evidently on intimate knowledge, of the conflict of forces in modern China, with every figure, oriental or European, thrown into brilliant relief, every Chinese water-front or street—junks and steamers, pagodas, bars and banks—made distinctly and solidly visible. And here was something even more remarkable—something one had not yet found in contemporary fiction to the same degree: the psychological atmosphere of stress, with its own peculiar passions and moralities, its tense and sustained attitudes, which is coming to be felt throughout the world.

A translation of *Les Conquérants* (*The Conquerors*)—made, I am told, at Aldous Huxley's suggestion—has been brought out in England, but seems to have had no success at all. I do not know whether the odious role that is played in the book by the British has had anything to do with this. The novel has done no better here. Harcourt, Brace brought over sheets and sold only eight hundred copies. Yet I urge American and English publishers —especially now that reviewers are beginning to take Jules Romains as solemnly as he takes himself—to consider bringing out a translation of Malraux's new and even more important novel, *La Condition Humaine*.

I have spoken of Malraux's achievement in conveying the sense of strain produced by the antagonisms of modern society. The publication of *Les Conquérants* was followed, in *La Nouvelle Revue Française*, by a controversy between Malraux and Trotsky. (Trotsky's two papers are included in his *Problems of the Chinese Revolution*.) It was Trotsky's complaint that Malraux, though he had chosen a revolutionist for hero, had "introduced into his observations a small note of blasé superiority, seeming to

excuse himself for his transient contact with the insurrection of the Chinese people, as much perhaps to himself
as to the academic mandarins in France and the traffickers
in spiritual opium." This is putting it a little too strongly;
but it is true that Malraux's hero, Garin, has a certain
alloy of old-fashioned romanticism. There are moments
when he gives the impression of being simply another
René or Manfred, somber, tortured, terrifying, a solitary
savage rebel, seeking in the revolution what René had
sought in the American forests, grasping at his bureau of
propaganda with the same sort of desperation that Byron
had brought to Greece. Part Swiss and part Russian, formerly an anarchist, Garin hates the bourgeoisie without
real fellow-feeling for the masses: " 'I don't love humanity. I don't love even the poor, the people—those, in fact,
for whom I am fighting.' 'But you like them better than
the others.' . . . 'I like them better, but only because
they're beaten. Yes: on the whole, they have more feeling, more humanity, than the others—they have the
virtues of the beaten. What's absolutely certain, however, is that I have nothing but hatred and disgust for the
bourgeoisie from which I come. But as for the others, I
know very well that they'd become quite abject as soon
as we'd conquered together. We have our struggle in
common—that's clear, at any rate.' " His dominant passion, he admits, is for power, and in the final scenes of
the story, worn out with his work and dying of malaria
and dysentery, he declares in his delirium that he now
regrets having chosen to serve the Communists instead of
England, since it is England that commands the real
power. Yet in spite of his doubt and his egoism, he sticks
by the revolution and is receiving, on the final page, the
dispatches that bring the news of victory. Trotsky has
expressed the opinion that what Garin needed was "a
good inoculation of Marxism." Malraux retorted to this

that there was something of Garin in Trotsky—pointing out that when you read in Trotsky's autobiography "the moving account of his fall, you forget that he is a Marxist, and perhaps he forgets it himself." He also protested that *La Condition Humaine* was not—what Trotsky had called it—a "novelized chronicle" of the Chinese revolution. "The principal emphasis," he says, "is on the relation between individuals and a collective action, not in the collective action alone." "The book," he explains, "is first of all a presentation of the human situation (*une accusation de la condition humaine*)."

André Malraux's new novel has this phrase for its title, *La Condition Humaine*, and it develops in a more explicit way the ideas implicit in *Les Conquérants*. *La Condition Humaine* is a much more ambitious and a more remarkable book than *Les Conquérants*. In the latter, Garin pretty well holds the spotlight, and there is an "I" who plays the role of Dr. Watson, deeply agitated by his hero's every utterance and standing by, indefatigably wide-eyed, while Garin receives portentous telegrams. He also plays the role of Conrad's Marlow. He is, in fact, our old friend the fictional observer who, from a more or less conventional point of view, looks on at a mystery or a moral problem. In this new book, however, the novelist gets rid of his European observer and, meeting Trotsky's challenge, attacks the revolution directly. Dealing with cultures the most diverse, moral systems the most irreconcilable, he establishes a position outside them which enables him to dispense with the formulas alike of the "academic mandarins" and of the orthodox Communists. I do not know of any modern book which dramatizes so successfully such varied national and social types. Beside it, even E. M. Forster's admirable *A Passage to India* appears a little provincial; you even—what rarely happens nowadays to the reader of a French novel—forget that the author is French. You see juxtaposed the old Buddhist China and its half-Europeanized children; the vaporing imagination of ruined aristocratic Europe and the single-minded will to money of the European business king; the American Calvinist missionary unwittingly building the character of the young Chinese terrorist; and—growing up under all the rest like the elm that splits the pave-ment—the new world of the revolutionary Marxist which is reorienting all the moralities. Nor is this handled in the manner of the journalist, as Paul Morand might have done it. The personalities of Malraux's characters are organically created and thoroughly explored. We not only witness their acts and see them in relation to the forces of the social-political scene: we share their most intimate sensations.

The handling of this huge and complicated subject must have given the author a good deal of trouble. He evidently sat down like an engineer to the problem of designing a structure that would meet a new set of con-ditions; and an occasional clumsiness of mechanics ap-pears. The device of presenting in dramatic scenes the exposition of political events, to which we owe Garin and his eternal dispatches, here appears as a series of con-versations so exhaustive and so perfectly to the point in their function of political analysis as—in spite of the author's efforts to particularize the characters—occasion-ally to lack plausibility. And we are sometimes thrown off the track when a thesis that deals with psychology comes butting into a paragraph devoted to explaining the "ob-jective conditions" or when a description that had seemed as external as a colored picture postcard of Shanghai takes a sudden subjective turn.

Yet, on the whole, the author has met these problems with amazing originality and skill. He has a genius for effects of contrast. The opening of *La Condition Hu-*

maine, which follows the activities of a Communist group —a Chinese, a half-breed Jap, a Belgian and a Russian— the night before the insurrection, is a masterly dramatization. The initial inability of Tchen to bring himself to murder the man from whom he must steal the orders for the guns and his immediate realization afterwards of his terrorist's vocation; Baron Clappique's romances in the night club and his subsequent revelation of his ignoble trade; the confession of Kyo's wife that, on the eve of the insurrection, she has been unfaithful to him, and its repercussions on revolutionary solidarity; Tchen's report of what he has done and felt to his Buddhist-sociologist master, Gisors, and Gisors' prompt liquidation of his own anxiety and horror in an opium dream, in which the ripples from a boat on a lake full of water-lilies spread out to sweep all horror and anxiety into the purity and peace of the Divine—followed immediately by the spectacle of the real boat putting out in the Shanghai harbor to steal the guns for the insurrection: each one of these shocks is a flash that illuminates the conflicts and anomalies of the tense international city.

I have spoken of Malraux's success in avoiding conventional formulas. Where, however, is his own center? What is his frame of reference? What he wants to show us, he says, is the human situation. What is his view of the human situation? What every human being wants, he makes his philosopher Gisors explain, is not the object of his ambition itself, but to escape from the conditions of life, to give oneself the illusion of being God. Gisors attains this through opium; Tchen through assassination —an act in which he immolates himself, is the destroyed as well as the destroyer; Ferral, the French business man, tries to reach it through his sexual relations, in which he imagines himself in the roles of both possessed and possessor; even the rickety Baron Clappique finds it at the

THE SHORES OF LIGHT

gambling table, where he identifies himself with the roulette ball, the master of both gain and loss; Kyo, the Japanese, rises above life when, for the sake of the revolution, he commits hara-kiri with cyanide; and Katov, the Russian Communist, gives his cyanide to brother Communists whose morale is weaker than his, when they have all been condemned to be burnt in the furnace of a locomotive. Tchen, Malraux lets us know, has saved his soul; Kyo has saved his, and more nobly; and Katov most nobly of all, because he can only fulfil himself by sacrificing himself to others.

There is, then, something else in the book besides the mere theme of escape from the human situation. The events described in *La Condition Humaine*, which occurred in 1927, must still have been going on while *Les Conquérants* was being written. At the end of the earlier novel, the Chinese revolution—there presented as the work of Garin as well as of Chiang Kai-shek—is assumed to be already victorious; in the later, the Communists fail, sold out by Chiang Kai-shek to the interests of Western capital and paralyzed by the faulty policy of the Comintern itself. Malraux seems, in line with Trotsky's advice, to have made some progress in Marxism. His interpretation of recent events seems now essentially Marxist—though he never, as I have said, slips into the facile formulas; and though the criticism his characters make of the line of the Comintern is more or less that of Trotsky, he maintains in relation to Trotsky, too, an attitude of independence. Marxism, Gisors observes, is not a doctrine but a will; and it is simply that, in Malraux's world, the only men he respects are animated by the Marxist will. *La Condition Humaine* ends with Gisors, who has lost his son Kyo, sinking back into the culture of the East and lighting up the opium pipe, while May, Kyo's widow, sets out for Moscow.

August 9, 1933

M. Malraux, on reading this article, wrote me the following letter:

n.r.f.   Le 2 oct.

Monsieur—Je trouve à mon retour à Paris l'article que vous voulez bien me consacrer.

Comme je vous réponds en suivant cet article permettez-moi d'abord quelques précisions. Je n'ai publié, en plus des livres que vous avez lus, qu'un livre et une plaquette (que je vous envoie)—le reste est très court et sans importance. D'autre part, mon père n'était pas fonctionnaire en Indochine.* Je suis allé en Asie à 23 ans, comme chargé de mission archéologique. J'ai alors abandonné l'archéologie, organisé le mouvement Jeune-Annam, puis suis devenu commissaire du Kuomintang en Indochine et enfin à Canton.

Il y a du vrai dans ce que dit Trotsky de Garine, et dans ce que vous en dites vous-même. Peut-être faudrait-il pourtant tenir compte d'une certaine objectivité. Que ce personnage soit marxiste, certes non. Peut-être a-t-il tort, mais c'était ainsi. Il y avait à Canton en 1927 (ce fut très différent en 1927) singulièrement plus d'aventuriers révolutionnaires que de marxistes. Et lorsque Borodine discutait avec Sun-Yat-Sen, il n'était jamais question de lutte de classes.—Je ne voudrais pas faire de cela un argument, mais une nuance. Car il est fort vrai que le rôle joué dans mes livres par l'objectivité n'est pas de premier plan, et que *Les Conquérants* sont un roman "Expressioniste" comme, toutes proportions gardées, *Wuthering Heights* ou les *Karamazoff*.

Vous dites très justement que *La Condition humaine* développe certaines idées implicites dans *Les Conquérants*. Et aussi que le livre est meilleur (à la verite, du

* This corrects an erroneous statement that I had made in the original version of my article.

moins, c'est le seul que j'aime). Ma construction, en effet, ne pourrait rejoindre celle d'un écrivain comme Morand: ses types reposent sur l'observation ironique, le mien sur le besoin de traduire à travers des personnages un certain ordre de valeurs éthiques.

Ne voyez en ce semblant de discussion qu'un moyen de remercier plus longuement le premier critique, en Amérique, qui s'intéresse à ce que j'écris et croyez, je vous prie, Monsieur, à ma sympathie artistique, car je suis depuis longtemps l'effort de la *New Republic*.

André Malraux

GERTRUDE STEIN OLD AND YOUNG

I. 27, rue de Fleurus

GERTRUDE STEIN has written her memoirs. But she has attributed them to her friend and companion of twenty-five years and has called them *The Autobiography of Alice B. Toklas*. Her book is thus something rather different from the ordinary volume of memoirs. It is Gertrude Stein's imaginative projection of how she and her life and her circle must look to Alice B. Toklas. Miss Toklas is presented as the enthusiastic admirer and the obedient shadow of Miss Stein; she turns toward her as the sunflower toward the sun. Yet Miss Toklas's personality is by no means indistinguishable from Miss Stein's: Miss Stein has created her as an individual. And *The Autobiography of Alice B. Toklas* has something of the character and charm of a novel—a novel of which the subject is the life that Miss Stein and Miss Toklas have made for themselves in Paris, the salon over which they have presided, the whole complex of ideas and events of which they became the center: a social-artistic-intellectual organism.

It is an instructive and most entertaining book. The chapters which deal with the period before the European War are perhaps the most interesting part: here Miss Stein tells about her discovery of Picasso and Matisse,

what they were like in their early phases, the gradual
taking-shape as a movement of the tendencies of isolated
artists, the development of her own literary methods.
There is a good deal of wisdom about art and artists,
literature and writers: "As Picasso once remarked, when
you make a thing, it is so complicated making it that it is
bound to be ugly, but those that do it after you they
don't have to worry about making it and they can make
it pretty, and so everybody can like it when the others
make it." All this part of the book has the excitement of
artistic adventure, which Gertrude Stein skillfully points
up by making the narrator, Miss Toklas, come into the
Stein world from the outside without knowing at first
what it is all about. These chapters, with their stories of
Matisse's insulted portrait, Gertrude Stein's posing for
Picasso, Braque's assault on the picture expert and the
dinner for the douanier Rousseau, are moving in their
quiet understatement. It was what Jean Cocteau called
"the heroic age," and Gertrude Stein's account of it evokes
a nostalgia for the days when the independent shows and
the little magazines were matters of prime importance,
when everybody was serious about art and it was possible for American spinsters in Paris to coöperate in perfect understanding with revolutionary poets and painters.
At the banquet for the douanier Rousseau, Marie
Laurencin "sang in a thin voice some charming old norman songs"; Rousseau, "blissful and gentle, played the
violin" and talked about his memories of Mexico; and
Guillaume Apollinaire invited Miss Stein and Miss
Toklas "to sing some of the native songs of the red
indians" (to follow Miss Stein's usage). André Salmon
got drunk and chewed up Miss Toklas's new hat; but she
did not resent it long, as he "woke up very charming and
very polite" and it was all by way of homage to the
douanier.

The high heart of this period, however, was shaken by the death in the war of Guillaume Apollinaire; the movement had collided with historical events. The later chapters of the book are less exciting. The painters have all arrived; the writers are all arriving. Everybody, as Gertrude Stein intimates, is bent on his own career. Miss Stein and Miss Toklas become more waspish. "Gertrude Stein liked him [Ezra Pound] but did not find him amusing. She said he was a village explainer, excellent if you were a village, but if you were not, not." "There was also Glenway Wescott but Glenway Wescott at no time interested Gertrude Stein. He has a certain syrup but it does not pour." And they are pretty hard on Ernest Hemingway: "Gertrude Stein and Sherwood Anderson are very funny on the subject of Hemingway. The last time that Sherwood was in Paris they often talked about him. Hemingway had been formed by the two of them and they were both a little proud and a little ashamed of the work of their minds. . . . And then they both agreed that they have a weakness for Hemingway because he is such a good pupil. He is a rotten pupil, I protested. You don't understand, they both said, it is so flattering to have a pupil who does it without understanding it, in other words he takes training and anybody who takes training is a favorite pupil. They both admit it to be a weakness. Gertrude Stein added further, you see he is like Derain. You remember Monsieur de Tuille said, when I did not understand why Derain was having the success he was having that it was because he looks like a modern and smells of the museums."

It is true that, as one reads this book, one is more forcibly struck than ever by Hemingway's debt to Gertrude Stein. Such passages as the following suggest that he has been influenced by her conversational as well as by her literary style (I hardly dare suggest that the writing of Miss Stein may in turn have been somewhat affected by the conversations of Hemingway's characters): "It was about this time that the futurists, the Italian futurists, had their big show in Paris and it made a great deal of noise. Everybody was excited and this show being given in a very well known gallery everybody went. Jacques-Emile Blanche was terribly upset by it. We found him wandering tremblingly in the garden of the Tuileries and he said, it looks alright but is it. No it isn't, said Gertrude Stein. You do me good, said Jacques-Emile Blanche." Or: "He and I always say that he and I will be the last people of our generation to remember the war. I am afraid we both of us have already forgotten it a little. Only the other day though Elmer announced that he had had a great triumph, he had made Captain Peter and Captain Peter is a breton admit that it was a nice war. Up to this time when he had said to Captain Peter, it was a nice war, Captain Peter had not answered, but this time when Elmer said, it was a nice war, Captain Peter said, yes Elmer, it was a nice war."

Yet one feels that Miss Stein, in her criticism of certain of her friends and disciples, as expressed at any rate in this book, is affected by two unavowed considerations which tend to bias her judgment. In the first place, she is the ruler of a salon: there is something of Mme. Verdurin about her. You get the impression that when her protégés go elsewhere or cease to need her, she can no longer believe in them quite so strongly. She seems, for example, to hint that the virtue began to pass out of Matisse as soon as he became popular and prosperous and, moving away from Paris, no longer could come to her dinners. In the second place, she is a writer who has herself had some difficulty in getting published and who has not yet received the recognition to which she considers herself entitled. Her only references to Joyce in this book are (1) a mention of a project to bring him to see her that never came to anything and (2) the report of a derogatory remark that Picasso made about his work. Herself Miss Stein describes as "in english literature in her time . . . the only one." Success, for her, seems to imply some imposture or deterioration. Yet it is hard to tell how much deliberate irony there may be in the presentation of all this through the medium of Alice B. Toklas. There is evidently a certain amount of pure mischief in her treatment of Hemingway, as to whom a distinct difference is indicated between Miss Stein's and Miss Toklas's opinions. And it is hardly imaginable that the creator of Miss Furr and Miss Skeene can be insensible to the humors of Miss Toklas and Miss Stein. A cool and pervasive irony has always been one of the characteristics of Gertrude Stein's writing; and there is certainly, in this portrait of two ladies, more artistic impersonality than most of the comments I have heard will allow. When you have read it, you take away an impression of Miss Stein and Miss Toklas in Paris that is not in the least like anything you get from the memoirs, say, of Margot Asquith or of Isadora Duncan, but, rather, like your recollection of one of the households of Jane Austen.

The Autobiography of Alice B. Toklas, though not Gertrude Stein's most important book, is likely to prove her most popular. It is the only thing she has published since *Three Lives* which, from the ordinary point of view, is very easily readable. And she explains here, or makes Alice B. Toklas explain, in simpler language than heretofore, what she has subsequently been trying to do in the experiments that, beginning with *Tender Buttons,* have stimulated and troubled the literary world.

Let us hope that the *Autobiography,* with its wisdom, its distinction and its charm, may persuade the general public to recognize Gertrude Stein for what she is: one of the remarkable women of her time and, if not "in english literature the only one," at least one of the original ones. Hitherto, though her influence has always been felt at the sources of literature and art, her direct communications with this public have been intermittent and blurred, and, on the whole, neither the readers of modern books nor the collectors of modern painting have realized how much they owe her. When she was lecturing at Oxford and was asked by her hecklers why she "thought she was right in doing the kind of writing she did," she replied "that it was not a question of what anyone thought but after all she had been doing as she did for about twenty years and now they wanted to hear her lecture. This did not mean of course that they were coming to think that her way was a possible way it proved nothing, but on the other hand it did possibly indicate something." The interest in the publication of these memoirs from quarters in which she has been scoffed at or ignored is a tribute of the same kind.

October 11, 1933

II. *Things As They Are*

THE Banyan Press of Pawlet, Vermont, has published, in an edition of five hundred and sixteen copies, a very early manuscript of Gertrude Stein's: a short novel, to which the author had given the title *Quod Erat Demonstrandum* but which the editor, making use of a phrase from the story, has retitled *Things As They Are*. The manuscript is dated October 24, 1903, when the author was twenty-nine, and it must have been written before *Three Lives*, the first of her published books, which came out in 1909. Like *Three Lives*, it is quite comprehensible, and it does not even show any tendency toward the Steinian repetitiousness that already appears in *Three Lives*. It is a production of some literary merit and of much psychological interest. The reviewer had occasion some years ago to go through Miss Stein's work chronologically, and he came to the conclusion at that time that the vagueness that began to blur it from about 1910 on and the masking by unexplained metaphors that later made it seem opaque, though partly the result of an effort to emulate modern painting, were partly also due to a need imposed by the problem of writing about relationships between women of a kind that the standards of that era would not have allowed her to describe more explicitly. It seemed obvious that her queer little portraits and her mischievously baffling prose-poems did often deal with subjects of this sort. Now the publication of *Things As They Are* comes to confirm this theory. It is a story of the tangled relations of three Lesbian American girls of the early nineteen-hundreds, told with complete candor and an astonishing lack of self-consciousness.

When one says that it is told with candor, one does not mean that it has much in common with those case-histories of Havelock Ellis that, published in his *Studies in the Psychology of Sex* between 1897 and 1910, did a good deal to clear the air. In this document of Gertrude Stein's, there is nothing in the least scandalous (unless the subject itself be considered so), and the whole thing is done with a sobriety, even an abstractness of language, that recalls the French classical novels of the type of *Adolphe* and *La Princesse de Clèves*. (The author's geometrical title was, in fact, so perfectly appropriate that one wonders why the editor should have wanted to change it.) Yet this study has behind it something of the modern scientific temper and brings us back to the brilliant young woman who, at Radcliffe, took psychology with William

James and was called by him his best woman pupil, and who went through—though she did not graduate—five years of medical school at Johns Hopkins.

Gertrude Stein went to Europe in 1903, after she had dropped her medical work, and the heroine of *Things As They Are*, a college graduate named Adele, is first seen on a ship bound for Europe. She has given herself up in her steamer chair "to a sense of physical weariness and to the disillusionship [sic] of recent failures" when she is approached by a handsome girl, well-to-do and college-bred like herself, whose obvious interest in her has the result of suddenly awakening her from a "long emotional apathy." This girl, whose name is Helen, tactfully pays her court, and Adele, though with a certain passivity, more or less responds to her attentions. But Helen has another friend, Sophie, an intimate of long standing, who is also a friend of Adele's and who later explains to Adele, when they are back in the United States, the nature of her (Sophie's) relations with Helen. Adele is at first filled with horror but, goaded by Helen's challenge, eventually herself succumbs. This gives rise to something in the nature of the heterosexual ménage à trois, but with differences that come out distinctly in the report of an observant woman who is not much disturbed by emotion. The homogeneity of sex seems in some ways a stabilizing influence, yet the intrusion of a masculine element on the part of the women themselves and the difficulty they have in keeping it up are uncertain and upsetting factors. Adele will assert of Sophie that "it was not that she had the manners of a perfect hostess but the more obtrusive good manners of a gentleman," and will try to assure herself that, in her attitude toward the trusting and deceived Sophie, she has not behaved like "a cad"; but at other moments strained relations collapse into feminine cattiness and lead to bitter altercations that seem almost to reach the hair-pulling stage. This inevitably becomes faintly comic, as if one were witnessing a triangle between three mislaid empty gloves, all intended for the left hand, and one cannot be sure that Gertrude Stein is not already treating the situation with irony. One does feel some personal animus on the part of the author toward Sophie, and the triangle results in an impasse that is painful for all three of the ladies—since Helen, of whom her family disapprove and who is kept by them on short rations, is obliged to do her travelling at Sophie's expense (Europe is a necessity for all of them), and Adele, realizing at last that she cannot break up the pair, finds it too much for her pride always to be following Helen and stealing moments from her intimacy with Sophie. Yet the smiling detached Gertrude Stein is already emerging in *Things As They Are* from the perplexities and the trying adjustments of the young woman intellectual who insists that she is loyal to the middle-class virtues. You are reminded in certain passages of the comedy of Miss Furr and Miss Skeene, that touching pair of left-hand gloves who are the heroines of another story.

This latter detachment of Gertrude Stein's is seen in its beginnings in *Things As They Are*, not only in the author's tone but also in the character of Adele. Adele is self-centered and rather inert; she does not readily give herself; she likes to be alone and ruminate, to feel that she is "her own man." Helen and Sophie, with their passions and reproaches, stimulate but also annoy her; her involvement with them hampers her movements. "Much as I wanted you," she says to Helen, "I was not eager [to see you again] for after all you meant to me a turgid and complex world, difficult yet necessary to understand, and for the moment I wanted to escape all that, I longed only for obvious, superficial, clean simplicity." Her impulse, when she is faced with a problem, is not to see it through,

for which Helen sometimes scolds her, but simply to drop
it and go away and turn her attention to something else—
as the young Gertrude Stein had declined to take William James's examination, explaining that she was very
sorry but did not feel like an examination that morning.
James gave her an A just the same, but she fared worse at
Johns Hopkins, where her peculiar insouciance had to
contend with hostile instructors who had not been convinced, in that era, that women should be admitted to
medical schools. One feels, in *Things As They Are*, that
Adele might have bucked Sophie if she had not so
determinedly insisted on deserting the "strapped" Helen
and going abroad again by herself. The mature Gertrude
Stein later on—in her literary personality—went up on a
high mountain, where she could dwell, when she chose,
in a cloud. The already well-marked egoism of her heroine
Adele is brought out by the comments of Adele's companions. It had grown, by the time of *Three Lives*, to
that of the egoism of "Miss Mathilda," about whom re-
volve like satellites the three respectful maids, the Good
Anna, Melanctha and the Gentle Lena, who give their
names to the stories; and it had swollen to monstrous proportions by the time of *The Autobiography of Alice B.
Toklas*, in which Miss Mathilda of Bridgepoint becomes
frankly Miss Stein of Paris, an Olympian known only remotely through the impressions of an admiring high
priestess.

The frustration of the young Adele, at the end of
Things As They Are, is a matter, one feels, less of tragic
loss than of failure of domination. Gertrude Stein, in her
subsequent career, did partially succeed in dominating,
through her salon, her collection, her wide reputation,
her influence on certain writers; and in so far as she failed
to carry off her pretentious claims, she seems to have concealed this—to add a third suggestion to the two I have

already made to explain her later impenetrability—by putting herself, once for all, out of the reach of uncomfortable criticism. This reviewer met Miss Stein only once, but he received, in the course of that interview, an agreeable first impression of a quick and original intelligence dealing readily from the surface of the mind with the surfaces presented by life—the responses so direct and natural, the surfaces seen so unconventionally, that one did not at first feel anything wrong; but a chilling second impression of (to resort to an overworked metaphor) a great iceberg of megalomania that lay beneath this surface and on which, if one did not skirt around it, conversations and personal relations might easily crash and be wrecked. This iceberg—heavy and hard as the stone that her name brings to mind—must have been forming in an emotional solitude, and it now held her two-thirds submerged. I doubt whether the obscurity that hid it—the function of which seems to me quite different from that of Joyce or Virginia Woolf—will interest future readers as much as the limpidity of *Things As They Are*.

In any case, we must not leave *Things As They Are* without a glance at the attractive figure of the young independent girl in the costume of 1900, "the cut of whose shirt-waist alone betrayed her American origin" and of whom her friends, meeting her in Rome, exclaimed that she "looked as brown and white and clean as if [she] had just sprung out of the sea"; who liked to sit "in the court of the Alhambra watching the swallows fly in and out of the crevices of the walls, bathing in the soft air filled with the fragrance of myrtle and oleander and letting the hot sun burn her face and the palms of her hands" and who enjoyed making friends with a young Spanish girl whose language she could not speak and from whom she parted "as quiet friends part," turning again and again and "signing a gentle farewell" as long as they could see one another; who came back to "the white snow line of New York harbor," from the damp of a London winter, delighted to see the American flag, "the clean sky and the white snow and the straight plain ungainly buildings all in a cold and brilliant air without spot or stain," and who wandered for days about the Boston streets, "rejoicing in the passionless intelligence of the faces." She would be able, she must already have begun to feel, eventually to do without passion.

September 15, 1951

I may have exaggerated in this review the Lesbian aspect of Gertrude Stein's obscurity. At any rate, the first volume of her unpublished writings in the Yale University Library—brought out since this article was written— which consists of prose portraits composed in the years 1908-1912, does not seem to bear out my theory. One feels rather that the ruminative dimness is the result of an increasing remoteness in her personal relationships.

MR. WILDER IN THE MIDDLE WEST

A FEW YEARS AGO, Thornton Wilder was the center of a controversy on Marxism and literature. He was challenged by Michael Gold and others to come away from his first-century Greek islands and his imaginary eighteenth-century Perus and turn his attention to the United States. Mr. Wilder seems to have taken up this challenge in his new novel called *Heaven's My Destination,* and though, in the course of the polemical battle, he was sometimes unfairly treated, the episode should not be regretted if it is true, as has been reported, that it stimulated Mr. Wilder to attack this American subject.

Heaven's My Destination seems to me much Mr. Wilder's best book. It is as brilliant and sharp as *The Woman of Andros,* which seems to me his weakest novel, was comparatively mawkish and pale. The effect, in fact, on Mr. Wilder of taking his opponents' advice—if that is really what happened—has been so vividly to bring him to life that they are likely to experience a shock. In the first place, he has applied to the smoking-cars, the summer camps and the boarding-houses of the Middle West that gift for social observation that he exercised in *The Cabala* on an aristocratic international society, but on which in his intervening novels he has not had much occasion to call; and Oklahoma City, Kansas City and Ozarksville become much more entertaining places than even his Roman drawing-rooms. Besides this, Mr. Wilder has created in his central character, George Brush, a religious textbook salesman, a more complete and living person than any in his other books. And the pathetic Proustian cadences, here, have vanished from Mr. Wilder's style; his sentimentality is nowhere in evidence. The tone is always comic or matter-of-fact—with the result that Mr. Wilder's vision of an imperfect and suffering humanity comes through a good deal more tellingly than in any of his earlier novels. Finally—what makes *Heaven's My Destination* unique in its Middle Western field—he has handled his Sinclair Lewis material with his characteristic elegance of form and felicity of detail, his Mozartian combination of lightness and grace with seriousness. (The Keatsian and Mozartian affinities of Wilder were what his opponents in the Michael Gold controversy tended to leave out of account; but he is probably the only contemporary American whom it is possible to mention in connection with such names.)

George Brush, Mr. Wilder's hero, though professionally a textbook salesman, is by vocation a saint. "Of all the forms of genius," Mr. Wilder quotes on the title-page from *The Woman of Andros*, "goodness has the longest awkward age." When we first encounter George Brush, he is attempting to save souls in the smoking-car and annoying hotel managers by writing Bible texts on the blotters. He comes from a farm in Michigan, he has graduated from Shiloh Baptist College, where he has been converted by a child evangelist, hopped up with morphine. But he has thought out his own principles of righteousness, and he has become many kinds of a crank. He is unworthy, he believes, to go into the church, on account of having once fornicated with a farmer's daughter at a farm where he was spending the night. He has been looking for her ever since to marry her. He is always getting arrested, as a result of his unconventional behavior in his attempts to live up to his principles. He insists upon riding in a Jim Crow car, because he believes in the equality of the races; draws all his money out of the bank and tries to give the bank the interest, because he believes in "voluntary poverty"; and makes a point of allowing a hold-up man to collect from him more money than he needs to, in order to show the thief that "he's really a beggar at heart." In the course of his twenty-fourth year, the period covered by the story, he makes himself absurd and obnoxious in an extraordinary variety of ways. In the course of his adventures as a travelling salesman, he encounters a variety of human types: the conscientious and desperate man, the cynical and desperate man (the story takes place during the depression), the intelligent man caught in a routine, the brilliant man embittered by pride, the professional prostitute and the professional minister of the Gospel, the criminal and the policeman. They reason with George Brush, remonstrate with him, play jokes on him, insult him, rob him, beat him up, jail him; but, in a sense, they are all powerless against him, because he is a genuinely virtuous man, sustained by the knowledge that he wants to do right. Although his program for edifying people is almost completely wrong, he manages to do them good in ways that he has not planned simply by being what he is: a man who takes his obligations to the rest of humanity so seriously that he never thinks at all of his own interest.

At last he succeeds in finding the girl whom he feels he is bound to marry. She is more or less unattractive and doesn't in the least want to marry him; but he finally induces her to do so. For her, the marriage is not a success. He has to go out on the road again, and she lets him know that she wants to leave him. (This marriage is the only part of the story that seems to me incomplete and a

little unconvincing. Why did Roberta, when George
Brush turned up again, find him so completely distasteful? Why, when they were married, did he not proceed
with his program of producing the half dozen children
that he considered essential to an American home?) He
loses his faith on the road and falls ill. He is desolated by
the idea that his life has been all a failure, that everything he has done has been stupid and that everybody has
come to hate him.

But an incident now occurs that, slight though it may
seem in itself, has strangely important results. There has
been living in Kansas City a Polish priest named Father
Pasziewski. We have heard almost nothing about him except that he has been at death's door with gallstones, that
he has then recovered and gone on with his work, that he
is "an awful disappointed man" because the boys and girls
of his parish—"the Knights of St. Ludowick" and
"Mary's Flowers"—to whom he has devoted himself, have
been turning into gangsters and dance-hall girls. He and
George Brush have never met, but each has always inquired about the other: each has recognized the other's
vocation. George Brush has been deeply moved by the
news that Father Pasziewski was praying for him on Fri-
days. Now Father Pasziewski has died, and he has sent
George one of his silver spoons (is this a symbol of
apostolic succession?). George Brush recovers from his illness, and goes on trying to do people good and getting
into new kinds of trouble.

Mr. Wilder has told this story with great skill and has
made it on the surface extremely funny. A gift of humor
one might not have suspected is another of Mr. Wilder's
resources that has suddenly emerged in this book. But his
real theme is George Brush's development, the education
he derives from his misfortunes; and the remarkable feat

Mr. Wilder performs is to make us end by liking and respecting his hero.

I do not see any reason that the radical reviewers who have been nagging at Thornton Wilder to write about his native country should not find *Heaven's My Destination* acceptable. Mr. Wilder, through Father Pasziewski, has tied up George Brush with the Church. But the act of divine intervention—I suppose that Mr. Wilder intends it as such—the arrival of the silver spoon, is not in itself, like the well-timed collapse of the Bridge of San Luis Rey, implausible to the non-believer. And in the meantime we have been given something more than a brilliant and veracious picture of an American variety of religious experience. George Brush, as I have said, is the type of saint, and he is therefore a universal character. The saint is a very special kind of person, but he turns up in other fields besides the religious one. The radical movement, too, has its saints, and they are people fundamentally akin to George Brush. Upton Sinclair in his early phases resembled him in some ways quite closely and committed some of the same sort of absurdities.

The radical's real objection to *Heaven's My Destination* would be that George Brush's creator never allows him to encounter a radical. What about the next generation of Father Pasziewskis? I happen to know the child of a family of Polish priests who has become an energetic Communist. And what about George Brush in ten years? We leave him at twenty-four: what is to be the rest of his education? He has evidently already discarded the fundamentalism that he affirmed at twenty-three. We are apparently intended to understand that he has finally investigated Darwin and no longer accepts the Garden of Eden. But is he not almost sure to go farther in the rationalistic criticism of his beliefs? What is to prevent him, with his pacifist principles, from discovering, as did A.

J. Muste, that other religious pacifist, with whom, also, George Brush has something in common, that the causes of war are involved with the social-economic system—and becoming a labor organizer?

From the tenor of Mr. Wilder's other work, I assume that, when George Brush gets well and goes on trying to live up to his principles, he has recovered his faith in God. But this is actually left rather ambiguous, and perhaps Mr. Wilder ought to be challenged once more to make it clear just what George Brush's point of view is when he goes out on the road again.

January 6, 1934

THE LITERARY WORKER'S POLONIUS

A Brief Guide for Authors and Editors

Nature of Magazines and Editors

THE PRIMARY FACT to be grasped about editors is that they are not independent agents, but function as parts of the larger organisms known as magazines. Magazines, like other living organisms, develop according to certain laws and pass through regular life-cycles. These cycles may vary in length from a few to many years; but they all complete the same cycle (unless they meet untimely ends); they have a youth, a maturity and an old age. In its earliest years, a magazine may seem spontaneous, novel and daring; but by the time it has reached its maturity it has, as the French say, "taken its fold," and it succumbs to a force of inertia against which the youngest and freshest editor is as powerless as the oldest and stalest. Thereafter, it grows old, declines and dies.

Magazines derive their principle of being from a relation between some part of the mind of the editor and some part of the mind of the public. They rarely represent the whole of the editor or the editor at his best; and they do not usually give the public all it wants. But the relationship, once established, apparently cannot be altered. Both editor and reader may be bored by the contents of the magazine; but at this point it will be impossible to introduce any real novelty or to make any serious new departure. To his readers as well as to his contributors, the editor may seem timid, pedantic, unimaginative, obsessed by formulas. But anyone who has had anything to do with magazine offices knows that there is always a Higher Power which decides all important issues: the magazine as an entity in itself. And this entity takes on eventually a purely metaphysical character: it has nothing to do with commercial considerations. It can often be demonstrated that a drastic change in policy would increase the circulation of the magazine; but such a change is no more possible to effect than the transformation, by grafting on wings or claws, of one kind of animal into another.

Magazines cannot be born again. The most that can be done with a magazine is to subject it to a sort of face-lifting process, which, though it may improve its look at long distance, only exposes it, on closer examination, in a more hideous state of senility. Or, as in the case of the old *Dial,* a magazine can be deliberately killed off, and the name taken over for a new one. But, otherwise, the most that can be hoped is that a magazine may pass its old age in something like comfort and peace without lapsing from its original standards. All too often it must linger on in a dotage or a cheapened form which disgusts its former readers.

Duties of the Editor to the Contributor

The scope within which it is possible for the editor to exercise independent volition is thus seen to be narrowly circumscribed. It is limited, in fact, to the purely business aspects of his dealings with his contributors. The selection of material is determined by the higher will of the magazine; but the editor can be more or less prompt in registering and conveying to the contributor the decisions thus arrived at. And the prompt communication of decisions is one of the editor's prime duties to his writers. The editor has a regular job; the writer very often has not, and he may even depend for the necessities of life on selling what he has written. He usually wants an immediate decision even though it may be adverse; such a decision would at least make it possible for him to send his manuscript elsewhere.

Some editors are efficient about this: Mencken and Nathan, for example, were remarkable for the definiteness and promptness of their decisions. But many editors are either the victims of badly organized offices or lack consideration for writers, and cause by their negligence or irresolute stalling an immense amount of depression, exasperation and sometimes even actual privation.

A piece of writing, once accepted, should be paid for on the nail (if the finances of the paper permit it); and, once accepted, it should be printed. In the first connection, the ideal method is that of one of the New York weeklies, which sends the check with the letter of acceptance. In the matter of printing, it ought to be said that there are sometimes extenuating circumstances, which the writer should understand and allow for. One of the editors may have pressed a decision in favor of accepting a manuscript which one or more of the other editors may afterwards consciously or unconsciously sabotage; or an editor may sabotage a manuscript which he has been responsible for accepting himself. Allowing, however, a certain small margin for sincere doubts and differences on the part of editors, it must be asserted, as a general thing, that the writer has just cause for complaint when an editor accepts his manuscript and then suppresses it by leaving it in the "barrel."

Connected with this is another matter which has probably caused between the editor and the writer more mis-

understanding and bitterness than any other aspect of
their relations, and which has often for the writer, and
sometimes for the editor, resulted in serious loss. This
is the question of ordering things in advance. The problem of making these decisions clear and afterwards keeping them straight is entirely in the hands of the editor,
and it is sometimes not the least difficult of his problems,
since the writer, through his eagerness for the order, will
sometimes unconsciously do his best to mistake an expression of possible interest for a commitment to buy
what he writes; but any editor with a primary grasp of
the duties of his position will school himself never to
leave any doubt as to whether or not an article is ordered
and to stick by his engagement, once it has been made.
If the manuscript turns out too badly, he is not absolutely
bound to print it; but he is certainly bound to pay for it
and to give it back to the writer, so that the latter may
have a chance of publishing it elsewhere.

Duties of the Writer to the Editor

On the other hand, the writer should allow the editor
a reasonable length of time in which to decide and
should not pester him with letters and telephone calls till
a maximum of, say, two weeks has elapsed.

The writer should always have his manuscript typed,
and he should never send it in to the magazine accompanied by a long letter, or, unless he knows one of the
editors, by any letter at all. In the first place, these letters
are rarely read; and, in the second place, they usually
have the effect of prejudicing the editor against the
piece instead of stimulating his interest in it. This prejudice may sometimes result in unfairness on the part of
the editor, if the writer is inexperienced and has thought
it the natural thing to address himself directly to the
editor—since he is used to being addressed by the editor,
in the editorial department of the magazine, in a friendly

and even confidential manner. But such writers should be warned that manuscript-reading is one of the most trying of an editor's tasks and that the notion of reading long letters in addition is one that he rejects with impatience. Manuscripts must speak for themselves; letters can never help them. If the writer should happen to know one of the editors, who he imagines may be sympathetically disposed toward him, he may address his manuscript to this editor (though some magazines have tried to bar this): he may possibly get prompter consideration. But he should never write more than a line.

Nature of Authors

The relations between authors and reviewers are a constant source of anxiety to authors. To understand why this should be so, we must first examine the nature of authors.

Authors in the main are persons who are preoccupied with constructing and peopling individual intellectual worlds. They may be roughly divided into three classes:

1. *Fiction-Writers.* Novelists and short-story writers are writers who make up fantasies about imaginary people. Such writers may in certain instances be on fairly good terms with one another, but the imaginary worlds they inhabit tend to be mutually exclusive. As a result, they seem ungenerous to one another, and it is sometimes superficially concluded that they are exceptionally vain and envious people. This is, however, not always the case. The pure type of fiction-writer who merely reacts to the stimuli of life with no broad philosophical or historical interest will feel naturally that the work of another such writer, especially if he is dealing with the same material, is a monstrous misrepresentation or even a deliberate imposture.

2. *Poets.* Poets are today imaginative writers who use

the technique of verse. This technique, though employed by the ancients for almost every form of utterance and record, from songs to dramas and epics, from legal codes to medical treatises, has come to be confined in our epoch to functions of a specialized kind. Where the novelist deals in character, adventure and situation, the poet is usually limited to the expression of emotion and mood or to the simple description of people and objects. As a consequence, being a poet is rarely a full-time job, and the poet has large spaces in his life which are not filled by his literary activity proper and in which he is likely to occupy himself with a kind of professional politics. Poets form into groups, which in their combinations, disruptions and recombinations, their debates, practical jokes and fierce battles, tend to keep them in a state of excitement. In this group instinct they somewhat resemble painters—though painters, by reason of the fact that they practise a genuine handicraft instead of a purely intellectual métier, have a certain amount of physical work to tire them and are not so erinaceous as poets. The reactions of groups of poets toward one another may be said to correspond more or less to the reactions of individual novelists.

3. *Scientific, philosophical and critical writers.* This class includes all those writers who are occupied with the attempt to present or to interpret known events, or to investigate the nature of reality. They are sometimes capable of a kind of collaboration hardly known among novelists and poets, for the reason that, where the materials are facts themselves, it usually requires more than one person to ascertain what the facts are and to organize them, and where the field is that of mathematical or metaphysical theory, a staff of several persons may be enlisted to develop the ramifications of a subject. But though it is possible for a number of experts to work

together on some special subject, it not infrequently happens that monopolies are attempted by the groups themselves or by powerful authorities in some department, and these may lead to stupendous combats like the brawlings of Leviathan and Behemoth. It should be added that literary critics may develop the worst characteristics of any of these other classes of writers.

(It may be suggested that the writers of fictionized biography and history constitute a fourth class, which should be listed between classes 1 and 2; but the truth is that producers of books of this type are not genuine writers at all, but merely a kind of chimera believed in during the Boom by publishers.)

It will be seen, then that all classes of authors tend to assume that their personally created worlds have some kind of general validity, and that they are likely to be disturbed when an attempt is made by anyone else to question or upset this assumption.

The author is most often upset in this way by the people who review his books. For an author, the reading of his reviews, whether favorable or unfavorable, is one of the most disappointing experiences in life. He has been laboring for months or for years to focus some comprehensive vision or to make out some compelling case, and then finds his book discussed by persons who not only have not understood it, but do not even in some instances appear to have read it. In twenty-two reviews out of two dozen, either the reviewer has attempted nothing more than to give a description of the contents of the book, not even doing this correctly (and these reviews are often copied word for word from one another), or his comments, either praise or blame, seem to the author to have little or no relevance to the book he believes he has written. The reading of his reviews, indeed, is so likely to let the author down after the excitement and satisfaction of finishing his book that there is a good deal to be said for the practice of those writers who go off on trips to remote parts of the world as soon as their last proofs have been corrected.

In order to understand why the reviewer thus disappoints the author, we must inquire as to who reviewers are and under what circumstances they do their work.

Nature of Reviewers
Reviewers may be classified under five heads:

1. *People who want work.* Every magazine office is a clearing-house for people who need money or jobs: the waiting-rooms are always full of college graduates, indigent radicals, escaped débutantes and wives, young boys who have just bummed their way from the Coast, and many other types of persons who want to write or to associate themselves with writing, as well as personal friends of the editors in difficulties. These people should be given considerate attention, if only because it sometimes turns out that there is a really good writer among them; and it is customary on magazines with literary sections to try them out on writing book reviews. These book reviews are often very bad and not far, if at all, removed from school exercises. But the editor will want to pay for them if he knows that the writer needs money, and when he has paid for them, he will feel that he ought to print them if by any means they can be made presentable. The best solution to this problem is probably that adopted by one of the New York weeklies. This magazine sells the extra books which come into the office for review and provides a permanent fund for the relief of needy writers, thus rendering it unnecessary to purchase from them reviews which may turn out to be either unpriptable or

printable only at the expense of a great deal of drudgery on the part of the editor.

To the groups mentioned above should be added the impoverished novelist or poet who, though gifted and expert in his own field, may have no aptitude for or practice in reviewing.

2. *Literary columnists.* The writer of a newspaper literary column has to read and talk about one or more books a day for five or six days of the week. To go through all these books conscientiously and comment upon them thoughtfully is a task beyond human capacity; and, in consequence, it is not to be expected of these writers that they should give us much serious criticism. Not all of them are interested in books: some are literary columnists merely by accident; others may be well-equipped persons who have to write so much and so fast that they are not able to do themselves justice. But in any case one should judge these writers, not as essayists or critical authorities, but as chroniclers of the literary news, who are managing more or less sensibly and more or less entertainingly to give, by a selection of excerpts or a swift résumé of a book's contents, a more or less adequate idea of the events of the publishing season.

Where the newspaper reviewer is most likely to go wrong is in explaining the purport or the significance of a book. A short and concentrated piece of writing such as one of Ernest Hemingway's short stories is very quickly read (these reviewers are naturally delighted when they strike something easy to get through), and the chances are that the reviewer will miss many things that the author has worked hard to make implicit in it, that he will, in fact, miss the point. And in the case of a long book, he is likely to be forced to skip through it, and so not only mistake the author's intention, but make blunders as to what has been said. When André Malraux's *Man's Fate* came out in English, for example, the newspaper accounts of the characters and the story seemed to me so different from what I remembered from reading it in French that I was driven to look up the translation. But the translator had in general been accurate: it was the reviewers who had sometimes been confused from having had to deal hurriedly and briefly with so crowded and complex a work. Yet it is also true that even in the case of Thornton Wilder's *Heaven's My Destination*, one of the newspaper reviewers managed to mix up the characters. It may perhaps be demanded of the newspaper reviewer that he avoid this sort of literal inaccuracy, but even that is demanding a good deal and the most, probably, that one should expect.

3. *People who want to write about something else.* Book-reviewing is frequently exploited, especially by the young, as a pretext for writing an essay of one's own on the subject dealt with by the book or for neglecting the book altogether and writing an essay on some other subject. Such reviews are often bitterly resented both by authors and by conscientious critics; but anyone who has ever been an editor must regard them, if they are interesting in themselves, with a certain amount of leniency: it is so relatively rare for an editor to get really interesting articles of any kind that he cannot afford to discourage them even on those occasions when they displace proper reviews. The author may console himself with the thought that the review he might otherwise have had would probably have been as poor as most reviews.

We may also treat under this head the problem of young people in general. Should a brilliant but inexperienced young writer be allowed to treat a mature writer unfairly in a brilliant but uncomprehending review? The young must be given a chance, and their point of view is sometimes important, even when what they say is entirely aside from the mark. Older writers have sometimes to resign themselves to being mistreated by youth. And there are also, of course, the embittered old who are irked at being driven to write reviews and who take it out in putting the young in their places and in undermining their more prosperous contemporaries.

4. *Reviewer experts.* The so often unsatisfactory results of having books of poetry reviewed by persons who have never written verse, works of philosophy by persons with no philosophical training, and so forth, have led editors to try to get poets to write about poets, philosophers to write about philosophers. The trouble with this, however, is that the philosopher or the poet is likely to belong either to the same school or to some opposing school, so that in either case the review may be biased and produce for the outside reader a misleading impression of the book.

5. *Reviewer critics.* These are extremely rare. Most people who are capable of first-rate criticism do not want to interrupt their other work for jobs as unremunerative as book reviews. Exceptional cases were Van Wyck Brooks and H. L. Mencken; but the former was rather narrowly specialized, and the latter has always tended to use book-reviewing as a way of putting over his own personality and his opinions on all sorts of subjects. The only American writer who has tried recently to do this kind of thing the way, ideally, it ought to be done was a second-rate man, Stuart P. Sherman. Such a reviewer should be more or less familiar, or be ready to familiarize himself, with the past work of every important writer he deals with and be able to write about an author's new book in the light of his general development and intention. He should also be able to see the author in relation to the national literature as a whole and the national literature in relation to other literatures. But this means a

great deal of work, and it presupposes a certain amount of training. Sainte-Beuve had to work all week—hardly taking time out for lunch—for each of his *Causeries du Lundi*. But Sainte-Beuve was perhaps a unique case. Has there ever been another example of a man of Sainte-Beuve's abilities devoting so large a part of his life to weekly articles on miscellaneous subjects?

I want to suggest, however, that it might be a profitable idea for some editor to get a really able writer on literature and make it worth his while to do a weekly article. For a man who should combine a sound education with intelligence and literary ability he would probably best go to the universities, where the *Herald Tribune* got Stuart Sherman and the *New Masses* Granville Hicks. Let him take, say, a Newton Arvin or a Haakon Chevalier, impose upon him no duties that would impede his weekly articles—Burton Rascoe's articles evidently suffered, when he ran the *Herald Tribune* book section, from his having too much to do—and pay him enough to live on. He should not be expected to cover what is published, but to write each week of a man or a book. I believe that such a feature would prove valuable to the magazine that installed it and an excellent thing for the literary world in general.

Attitude of the Author toward the Reviewer

It will thus be seen that the author has no justification for expecting serious criticism from reviewers, and that, in becoming elated or indignant over anything that is written about his books, he is wasting his nervous energy.

His reviews, if he knows how to read them, may have for the author a certain interest; but he will not be able to find out from them very much about the value of his work. For this he will have to depend on other sources, such as remarks made in casual conversation and evidences of his effect on other writers—always bearing in mind, however, that the true excellence or badness of what he has written may never really be grasped during his lifetime—a hazard for which we must all be prepared. And in the meantime he should read his reviews, not as the verdict of a Supreme Court of critics, but as a collection of opinions by persons of various degrees of intelligence who have happened to have some contact with his book. Considered from this point of view, there is occasionally something to be learned from them.

Special Psychology of Reviewers

The reviewer, like other kinds of writers, has his ego; and, since he is continually occupied with other people's books, it is somewhat peculiarly difficult for this ego to assert itself. One of the best ways in which a reviewer can give himself a vicarious sense of creation is by encouraging and presenting new writers who have previously been unknown; but when a writer is already known, the reviewer may procure the sensation of power by making the gesture of putting him down. This psychology must always be reckoned with. In the literary world in the last few years, one has seen a number of writers cried up at the time when they were still obscure, by the more discerning critics, and then afterwards disparaged by them. This has happened in turn to Eugene O'Neill, Edna St. Vincent Millay, Ernest Hemingway and Thorton Wilder. It is the rarest thing in the world at the present time to find a word of intelligent critical comment on any of these important writers. And the unfortunate Mr. Saroyan has been put through the cycle in record time. He was first discovered by the editors of *Story* and acquired a reputation among its readers. Then, when his book was published, he got some prompt enthusiastic reviews. But he had now been triumphantly brought out, and after this there was nothing left for the later reviewers of his books but to try to make him ashamed of himself.

Duties of the Reviewer to the Author

On the other side, however, the reviewer has certain obligations in relation to the author.

I have recommended lenience toward reviewers who use the books they are supposed to be reviewing as pretexts for expressing themselves; but only in cases where their articles—what happens comparatively rarely—are interesting in themselves. There is no excuse at all for an uninteresting review that tells nothing about the book. The reviewer, at the very least, should be expected to supply information. The retelling of the story of a novel, the summary of an historical or philosophical book, the selection of representative passages and the attempt to communicate the quality of a poet, is the most boring part of the reviewer's business, but it is an absolutely essential part. The reader should be given a chance to judge whether or not he would be interested in the book, irrespective of what the reviewer may think of it; and it is an indispensable discipline for the reviewer, or any critic, to give the gist of the book in his own words. The reviewer, when he sets about this task, is quite likely to find that there is more in the book, or less in it, or something different in it, than he imagined when he first went through it. If the author is incoherent or woolly, the critic will be able to detect it. If the reviewer is incompetent, his incompetence will be evident to his more acute readers when they find out he cannot tell them what is in the book.

The failure to follow this procedure is one of the factors responsible for those opaque pretentious essays, aesthetic, metaphysical or social, that, especially in the highbrow reviews, are sometimes hung on the titles of books. The reader has no means of knowing, if he has not himself read the books, whether they prove the critic's points or not: the titles play the role of counters to which, from the reader's point of view, no value has been assigned. It is as vitally important for the critic to establish definite identities for the books that he discusses in an essay as it is for the novelist to establish them for the characters who figure in his story.

Attitude of the Author toward His Public

Another class of persons toward whom the poised author should adopt an unemotional attitude are the people who write him letters. Most of these fall into the following categories:

1. *Insane people and cranks.* The author should be able to spot these and should remember that people in abnormal states of mind are likely to be set off by anything.

2. *Lonely women and persons in provincial isolation.* Of these, even when they are sane, very much the same thing may be said: the fact that they write authors letters shows merely that they need to communicate with somebody and does not necessarily imply any interest or merit in the author's books.

3. *Young people who want the author to read their manuscripts.*

4. *People who want the author's autograph.* These, for the most part, either want it for a collection, and have no interest in the author's books, or want it in order to sell it.

Along with a good many of these, the author will receive a few letters from people who are interested in what he has written and have something to say to him

THE SHORES OF LIGHT

about it. But, in general, it may be assumed that the letters written to authors mean nothing. No writer who has been an editor can ever take letters so seriously as is often done by writers who have had no such experience. Every editor has seen almost incredible evidence that one cannot publish anything in a magazine so bad that some reader will not write in to say that it has changed his life, or so good that it will not cause someone to cancel his subscription.

Duty of the Public toward the Author

One should never send manuscripts to authors. They have enough to do writing their books. If authors read the manuscripts sent them, they would never be able to do anything else. The author of a manuscript who desires advice should send it to a publisher or editor: they pay people for this kind of work.

Duty of Authors to Other People

The author should not make a practice of sending out to his friends, or to persons whom he admires but does not know, large quantities of his books, inscribed. In the first place, he will be out of pocket if he exceeds the publisher's quota of free copies. In the second place, inscribed books from authors are likely to prove a nuisance: the person to whom the book has been sent is likely to feel that he ought to read it and yet at the moment may not be able to; he will go around having it on his conscience that he ought to have written to the author. And when he does get around to reading it, he may feel that the flattering or affectionate inscription obliges him, whether he likes it or not, to say something nice about it. Such a present is really a bribe that is likely to prevent the reader from coming out with the candid opinion which the author imagines he values.

Duty of the Novelist to the Public and the Profession

The novelist should never put at the end of his novel a date of the following kind:

Boulogne-sur-Mer-Hoboken
December 1934-January 1935

This kind of thing has been in fashion ever since Joyce dated *Ulysses*:

Trieste-Zurich-Paris 1914-1921

but it is rarely justified. In Joyce's case, the book took seven years, and the date has a special point, for Stephen Dedalus in 1904 is made to tell the Dubliners of the novel that he will produce something important in ten years' time. But it is usually a mistake for other writers to imitate this, for the reasons that, in the first place, it is dangerous to suggest a comparison with Joyce; and, in the second place, that such dates are irrelevant. In the case of a poem, date and place may in certain instances be in order if they add something that helps in understanding it and that cannot be conveniently put into the poem. But if a novelist is really successful, he will have interested us in characters and happenings that are supposed to have nothing to do with himself; he will have induced us to accept their reality, and it is therefore an impertinence to his own creation to remind us of himself and where he has worked. If the novelist has been unsuccessful, the reader, when he has got through the book, will not care to be reminded of the author and his sojourn at Boulogne-sur-Mer.

June, 1935

THE CLASSICS ON THE SOVIET STAGE

In 1935, I spent five months in the Soviet Union. While there, I was invited to contribute an article to an English-language paper published in Russia, the Moscow *Daily News*. I settled upon the only subject in the contemporary cultural field in Russia upon which it would be possible for me to write without saying anything unacceptable: the current productions of classical plays (I did not want to discuss the new Soviet plays). This was approved at first; but then my dossier was no doubt consulted, and it was discovered that I had, in New York, been associated with Max Eastman, at one time an admirer of Trotsky and a critic of the Soviet Union, on the advisory board of the *Modern Monthly*, a non-Stalinist magazine. There was a tradition in Russian Communism—inaugurated, I fear, by Lenin—of making people who had come over to Bolshevism denounce publicly their previous non-Bolshevik connections. When D. S. Mirsky had returned to Russia to pursue a Soviet literary career, he had been forced to publish a book, *The Intelligentsia of Great Britain*, unmasking, as it was then called, the English writers among whom he had been living in exile. I was now called upon to write for the *Daily News* a formal repudiation of Max Eastman.

This I refused to do, and I induced them to accept the following article.

We used to hear a good deal in America about Soviet suppression of the classics. We were told that whenever a pre-revolutionary play was produced on the Soviet stage, it was caricatured out of all recognition. It is true, I believe, that in a recent production of *Hamlet,* some startling innovations were made to bring it into line with Marxist ideology. But one of the things that have most struck me since I have been here has been, not only the excellence of the theater, but in respect to the drama and music of the past, the freedom and scope of its range.

I had expected something rather different. My attitude when I first arrived may be indicated by the experience of an American friend of mine who attempted soon after her arrival to see Meyerhold's production of *Camille.* She had heard much of this brilliant director who did daring and original things with the classics, and she had understood that everything on the Russian stage was given a strong revolutionary emphasis. When, therefore, before the curtain went up, two sailors came out and shook hands, she was not in the least surprised. And then afterwards when, instead of a Paris salon, she was confronted with the deck of a ship and when it turned out that Camille was a sort of woman sailor and that, instead of having but two or three serious admirers, she was evidently worshipped by the whole crew, my friend continued to set it all down to the new proletarian interpretation of the bourgeois Dumas *fils.* Nor was she seriously troubled at the end, when the lady of the gardenias was shot down on deck with her shoes on instead of dying of "consumption" in bed. It was only as she was leaving the theater that my friend found out that what she had been witnessing was not Meyerhold's production of *Camille,* but Taïrov's production of *The Optimistic Tragedy,* a play of the Civil Wars, which dealt with the Baltic fleet and had a brave woman commissar for heroine.

In a somewhat similar state of mind, the night of my own arrival in Russia, I went to hear Verdi's *Otello* and was surprised to find simply an admirable but, it seemed to me, quite traditional operatic production. Later, I saw Meyerhold's version of the Pushkin-Chaikovsky opera *The Queen of Spades,* and felt afterwards that I understood better both the pre-Soviet Russian soul and the romantic nineteenth century. I could not see that the story had been used to point a revolutionary moral. *The Cherry Orchard* seemed the same as ever, aristocratic nostalgia and all. And *The Pickwick Club* at the Second Art Theater gave the impression of being actually too gay and mild. I thought that it had failed rather regrettably to make the most of certain opportunities for "propaganda" that Dickens himself had supplied. After seeing Ostrovsky's *Talents and Admirers,* I did, to be sure, learn that the original ending had been changed; but I confess that the new one—in which the poor young student, abandoned by the ambitious actress, justifies himself and his work in a more or less revolutionary speech instead of committing suicide as Ostrovsky had intended him to do seemed to me the best scene in the play.

Of course, it is true that the Soviet point of view does pervade in one way or another the whole of the Russian theater. I can see, looking back on the Dickens play, that not only is Sam Weller made to figure as the real hero (as he actually becomes in the novel), but that he is also made to emerge from the devoted subordination to his master which allowed the Victorian audience to approve of him in spite of his audacities, and to assert himself with more force and rudeness. And I suppose that Verdi's *Otello* may partly owe its present popularity to the Soviet attitude toward race problems. But the theater of every place and age has been stamped by the interests and purposes of the society which has paid to see its shows; and I cannot see that the Soviets at the present time can be accused of mistreating the classics. Take even a case—the only one I have seen—where the handling of an old play had obviously been strongly affected by the special preoccupations of the moment: the production of *Romeo and Juliet* by the Theater of the Revolution. This was plainly a *Romeo and Juliet* inspired by and designed for the Komsomol. Lots of energy —sometimes rather self-conscious, sometimes misapplied, as when Romeo and Juliet and the Nurse were continually throwing themselves around and rushing up and down steps and ladders. And it surely does some violence to Shakespeare's intention to play the balcony scene in such a way as to make the audience laugh—in order, I was told, to fall in with the unromantic attitude toward love of the younger generation. Yet when I compared this Soviet production, with its seriousness, its large scope and its elaborate attention to detail, with a production of *Romeo and Juliet* which I had seen in New York last winter, it must be admitted that the Soviets had still very much the best of it. Shakespeare, in the Soviet production, whatever liberties had been taken with him, had the Komsomol to bring him to life. In New York, he had nobody at all. I remembered that the actress who played Juliet in New York had been so dreary in the scene in the bedroom in which she drinks the sleeping potion that, responding to the idea of the narcotic rather than to the terror and passion that the poet had tried to convey, I had actually myself gone sound asleep—an accident of which I was not in danger at the Theater of the Revolution, though the production lasted five hours.

We English-speaking audiences should look ridiculous complaining of the damage done to Shakespeare by the Soviet productions of his plays when we have ourselves been tolerating for two centuries all sorts of arrangements and adaptations, which bowdlerize him, sentimentalize him and make hash of him—until we have finally even come to believe that the gags that Colley Cibber wrote into *Richard III* are Shakespearean masterstrokes. In nothing more conspicuously, in fact, does the vitality, the imagination and the significance of the Soviets' own great role appear than in this power to make real and to throw into relief the symbolic fables of the stage. Today, when the cultural tradition of Russia, interrupted for a time by the Revolution, has been resumed, and resumed with fresh interest, keener scrutiny and bolder enthusiasm, the Soviet theater takes its place as, I suppose, the most brilliant in the world: one of the few real artistic glories of these artistically barren years.

July 2, 1935

It was true, at the time I was there, that the Soviet theater was splendid. Though this was after the murder of Kirov and the political purges had already begun, the cultural life of the Soviet Union was still in its relatively liberal phase, when the "directive" was that artists should not hesitate to learn from the art of the feudal past and from the bourgeois art of the present. The great theatrical producers were still very important figures, with whom it was difficult to interfere, and their theaters, whose personnel enjoyed more personal freedom and a higher standard of living than perhaps any other group, came as near as had ever been possible for any institution under the Soviet system to functioning in an autonomous way. This privileged domain of the theater has recently been described, in a book called *Taming the Arts,* by a Russian violinist, Mr. Juri Jelagin, now in the United States. He tells, also, how, the year after my visit, the terror caught up with the arts, and the government began breaking up these theaters and censoring productions of the classics. The cultural tyranny of Stalin ended by imposing everywhere a type of propaganda drama that dealt only in idealized characters so different from anything that actually existed that, in order to make the actors believe in them, it was necessary, says Mr. Jelagin, artificially to create for them living conditions that approximated to those represented on the stage. Meyerhold's theater was closed, and he was charged with the crime of "formalism"; when he protested against the new policy, he was arrested and disappeared. His wife, an actress, was killed in her apartment, and found, Mr. Jelagin says, with seventeen knife-wounds in her body.

LETTER TO THE RUSSIANS ABOUT
HEMINGWAY

WHEN I VISITED the Soviet Union, I was assigned as a
guide and advisor by the cultural liaison organization
VOKS Sergei Tretyakov, then a well-known literary
figure. I knew him already as the author of an effective
melodrama, which had been done in New York under
the title *Roar, China!* He was tall, very sober and a little
rigid; he wore spectacles and had shaved his gray hair;
and he rather resembled, as was sometimes said of him, a
professor or a Protestant pastor. But in literature he was
earnestly Leftist. He was a great participator in groups.
He had passed through futurism and the group called
LEF, in both of which—he was very proud of this—he
had been associated with Mayakovsky. He was at that
time one of the great champions of "fact literature" as
distinguished from "plot literature"; he declared that the
Soviet newspaper was the *War and Peace* of the present,
and he was engaged in writing a novel about the collective farms, which was a matter of pure documentation
that took him into the country on fact-gathering excur-
sions. Though Tretyakov was theoretically one of the
most intransigent of Soviet writers, who had declared his
scorn of fellow-travellers, I found him both mild and
polite. He did his best to be helpful to me, and I ate
some good dinners in his apartment, where he would

show me the old files of the LEF magazines. On one
occasion, he prepared me for meeting his father by saying, "He's a real peasant!," but when I was presented to
the elder Tretyakov, he seemed to me a well-bred old
gentleman, whose mustaches and small Van Dyke beard
must always have been carefully tended.

I wanted to buy books. There was some difficulty about
this, due to restrictions and my lack of money; and Tretyakov suggested that I contribute an article to the Russian edition of *International Literature* and have the
Writers' Union pay me in books. There was a considerable excitement about Hemingway in the Soviet Union
then, and it was agreed that I should write about his
latest book, which had not yet been translated. Just before
I left Moscow, Tretyakov took me to a bookseller in the
ancient Tverskaya, now rechristened Ulitsa Gorkovo,
who dealt in pre-Soviet books. To enter it was something
of a shock, for one seemed to step out of the new Russia
and land in a pocket of the past. The proprietor, with his
skull-cap, his ivory pallor, his tarnished green velvet
jacket, his archaic fringe of red beard that ran under
his chin from ear to ear, might have been a contemporary
of Gogol's. These old books, especially in good editions,
were rather rare in the Soviet Union, and it was forbidden to take them out of the country, unless one bought
them for valuta at Intourist emporiums and could show
a certificate for them; but the amiable Tretyakov, with
his slightly complacent official air, promised to arrange
all this. I chose a set of Turgenev that was rather expensive and several other things, and I left with the
bookseller some books that I had already acquired elsewhere and that I wanted to have sent with the others,
including a large-paper two-volume edition of Taine's
Théorie de l'Intelligence, which had been given me by
a friend in Leningrad. Few of these I ever saw again,

either my old books or the new purchases. When a package finally reached me in America, I found, instead of the set of Turgenev, one very badly battered volume of a Soviet edition on cheap paper: Volume XII, the last, which contained a miscellaneous collection of Turgenev's reviews and speeches. The only thing I had ordered that they sent me was a volume of Mayakovsky's drawings. The Taine had disappeared. So not only have I never been paid for the article that follows by the Soviet periodical that ordered and ran it, but I was robbed of my Taine on account of it. Poor Tretyakov vanished in the purge, along with almost everyone else who represented the Leninist tradition of socialist idealism. His obstinate loyalty to it may well have seemed to his inquisitors stupid. He had staked his whole career on the iconoclasm—which was bound to be for Tretyakov not an uproarious but a solemn matter—of his brilliant ally Mayakovsky; he had sworn on Marx and Lenin a lifelong devotion to the doctrine that an up-to-date report on industrial work in progress was the highest form of literature. I felt very badly about him. It outrages one's sense of justice that a man should be encouraged by the government to maintain an official attitude and then punished for doing so when this attitude is repudiated by the government. Such people as Tretyakov, industrious, pious and a little absurd, have been among the most pathetic victims of Stalin's soul-destroying reign.

Letter to the Russians about Hemingway

I have been very much disappointed by the new book by Ernest Hemingway. *Green Hills of Africa* is certainly far and away his weakest book—in fact (leaving out of consideration the burlesque *Torrents of Spring*), the only really weak book he has written.

Green Hills of Africa is a narrative of an actual hunting expedition, in which "the writer has attempted," as Hemingway says, "to write an absolutely true book to see whether the shape of a country and the pattern of a month's action can, if truly presented, compete with a work of the imagination." In my opinion, he has not succeeded. The sophisticated technique of the fiction-writer comes to look artificial when it is applied to a series of real happenings; and the necessity for sticking to what really happened prevents the writer from supplying the ideal characters and incidents which give meaning to a work of fiction. The book is thus an instructive experiment: it brings out very clearly the difference between actual experience and the imaginary experience of fiction, but it is a warning of reefs to steer clear of.

Aside from this—or perhaps for the very reason that he has chosen to treat his material in the wrong way— the literary personality of Hemingway here appears in a slightly absurd light. He delivers a self-confident lecture on the high possibilities of prose-writing, with the implication that he himself, Hemingway, has realized or hopes to realize these possibilities; and then produces what are certainly, from the point of view of prose, the very worst pages of his life. There is one passage which is hardly even intelligible—the most serious fault for a writer who is always insisting on the supreme importance of lucidity. He inveighs with much scorn against the literary life and the professional literary men of the cities; and then manages to give the impression that he himself is a professional literary man of the most touchy and self-conscious kind. As a newspaper reviewer has said of Hemingway, he went all the way to Africa to hunt, and then when he thought he had found a rhinoc-

eros, it turned out to be Gertrude Stein—an old friend
and admiration of Hemingway's, who wrote of him dis-
paragingly in her recent autobiography and upon whom,
in *Green Hills of Africa,* he has taken the opportunity
to revenge himself. He affirms in accents of defiance his
perfect satisfaction with the hunter's life and his passionate enthusiasm for Africa; and then turns out the only
book I have seen that makes Africa and its animals seem
dull.

When the Soviet critic, I. Kashkin, who has contributed to the English edition of *International Literature*
a very able essay on Hemingway—what is, in fact, perhaps so far the only serious full-length study of him
that has yet been made—when Kashkin comes to read
Green Hills of Africa, he will no doubt find much confirmation for his theory that the author of *In Our Time*
has been becoming more sterile in proportion as he has
become more detached from the great social issues of the
day. And it is true that one of the things which strikes
us most and which depresses us as we read *Green Hills
of Africa* is the apparent drying-up in Hemingway of his
interest in his fellow-beings. Wild animals can, of course,
be made extremely interesting; but the animals in this
book are not interesting. We do not learn very much
more about them than that Hemingway wants to kill
them. Nor do we learn much about the natives: there is,
to be sure, one fine description of a tribe of marvellous
runners, but the principal impression we carry away is
that the Africans were simple people who enormously
admired Hemingway. Nor do we learn much more about
his hunting companion than that the latter had better
luck than Hemingway and inspired Hemingway with
envy; nor much more about Mrs. Hemingway than that
she is fond of Hemingway. Nor does the author seem,
in any really serious way, even to take very much in-

terest in himself; the self-dramatized Hemingway we get
has the look of having been inspired by some idea of
what his public must expect after reading his rubbishy
articles in the men's-wear magazine, *Esquire*.

Yet I am not by any means sure that—as Kashkin perhaps would conclude—it is Hemingway's material which
is here at fault. It is not the fact that, in *Green Hills of
Africa,* he is dealing with an African hunting expedition
instead of with the American class struggle that is really
at the bottom of its failure; but rather the technical
approach of the writer to his subject, and the psychological attitude that follows from it. One can imagine the
material of *Green Hills of Africa* being handled quite
successfully in short stories or as a background to one of
Hemingway's novels. But for reasons which I cannot
attempt to explain, something dreadful seems to happen
to Hemingway as soon as he begins to write in the first
person. In his fiction, the conflicting elements of his
nature, the emotional situations which obsess him, are
externalized and objectified; and the result is an impersonal art that is severe and intense, deeply serious. But
as soon as he speaks in his own person, he seems to lose
all his capacity for self-criticism and is likely to become
fatuous or maudlin. The artist's ideas about life, or rather
his sense of what happens and the way in which it happens, is 'in his stories kept deep below the surface and
conveyed not by argument or preaching but by directly
transmitted emotion: it is turned into something as hard
as a crystal and as disturbing as a great lyric. When he
expounds this sense of life, however, in his own character of Ernest Hemingway, the Old Master of Key
West, he has a way of making himself ridiculous. It may
be that he himself is imposed on by the American publicity legend which has been created about him and

which, as Kashkin has pointed out, has very little to do with what one actually finds in his stories. But, in any case, among his creations, he is certainly his own worst-drawn character, and he is his own worst commentator. His very prose style goes to pot—or rather, he writes a different prose style from the one he has perfected in his fiction, which seems to me to be without question one of the finest we have had in America and one of the finest in the world today.

This vein of Hemingway maudlin, this vein of unconscious burlesque, had already broken out in the personal interludes of *Death in the Afternoon*, his book on the Spanish bull-fight, but in that book there was so much objective writing, so much solid information, that these monologues could not spoil it. *Green Hills of Africa* is almost all such an interlude—and I doubt whether it is anything more than an interlude in Hemingway's work as a whole. His latest collection of stories, *Winner Take Nothing*, showed certainly a further development rather than any degeneration of his art. One of them, a simple anecdote of a man who goes out to plunder a wreck and finds that he cannot even crack open the porthole—this short story, with its implications of the irreducible hazards and pains of life and of the private code of honor that one has to evolve to live among them, is worth the whole of the *Green Hills of Africa*.

These moral implications of Hemingway, as one finds them in this story, for example, it seems to me that Kashkin underestimates. The Marxist must no doubt maintain that no hazards and pains are irreducible. But these will not be eliminated next year, nor even five years from now, nor even after five years more. And in the meantime, if Hemingway were to address himself to writing about the social conflict, there is no reason to believe that his stories would not continue to illustrate the same personal tragic sense of the way in which things happen. We can get some idea of what we might expect from the introductory note he has written to the exhibition of drawings by the Spanish revolutionary painter, Luis Quintanilla. He has an acute sense of the cost and the danger involved in doing anything worth doing, including revolution; and he knows that people do not always live to get the benefit of what they pay for. "The world breaks everyone and afterward many are strong in the broken places. But those that will not break it kills. It kills the very good and the very gentle and the very brave impartially. If you are none of those you can be sure that it will kill you too but there will be no special hurry" —says the hero of *A Farewell to Arms*. This is not in the least the same thing as saying that there is no use in being good or brave. The truth is that, though, as Kashkin says, Hemingway is very much given to writing about the end of things, the effect of what he writes is bracing rather than dispiriting. His short story, *The Undefeated*, which describes the humiliating death of a superannuated bull-fighter, is, as its title indicates, not really a tale of defeat. The old man's courage in itself constitutes a victory. It is true that Hemingway writes about decadence, but there is always something else that is pitted against the decadence. It is true that he writes about death, but in order to write tellingly about death, you have to have the principle of life in you.

Can it not be said that on the highest plane of imaginative literature, the plane on which Hemingway must be considered, what is written about an old bull-fighter is written, also, about other kinds of men? Is not real genius of moral insight a motor that will start any engine? The non-Marxist who reads a banal Marxist fable, written without real insight or feeling, does not feel or imagine anything. The Marxist who reads a story presenting a dramatic conflict, though the conflict may be as far from the class struggle as the battle between a man and a bull, will surely, if the story is written with sympathy, passion and skill, identify himself with the hero. Do we not translate what moves us in literature into terms of whatever we do in our lives?

But that, Kashkin might reply, is an extremely dangerous doctrine. Suppose the hero of the story in question is frankly a counter-revolutionary. How can we be sure that the reader will translate counter-revolutionary courage into terms of revolutionary activity? How do we know that he will not be persuaded to admire the counter-revolution? We cannot know this, of course. But we may be assured that wherever the main current of human hope and progress runs, the readers will get out of all kinds of literature the kind of inspiration they need for their own particular activities, the kind of consolation they require for their own particular defeats. That the Soviets assume this to be true is indicated by the fact that they are at present translating wholesale the classics both of antiquity and of the modern world and republishing their own classics with pious care. I observed, when I was recently in Russia, that even the novels of the counter-revolutionary Dostoevsky were still of interest to Soviet readers and that the government was bringing out his note-books. And surely there is something more to the increasing popularity of Shakespeare in Russia than a desire on the part of the Soviet audiences to study the failures of feudal princes. Individuals in Russia still fail; they still suffer their griefs and frustrations; and people still go to the theater to have their souls purged through pity and terror.

I feel that Soviet critics, as well as many Marxist critics elsewhere, sometimes underestimate the positive qualities of the modern non-Marxist masters. A writer like Kashkin might answer that today the only positive forces are those which are working for the destruction of the rotten old capitalist world and for the liberation through socialism of stunted and cramped human powers. I can only adduce, as an example of the law of moral interchangeability which I would invoke on behalf of Hemingway, that on my recent visit to Russia the passage from contemporary literature that I found came most often to mind, that seemed to me to express most eloquently the effect of the Revolution on all kinds and conditions of people in the Soviet Union, was from the writings of that arch-bourgeois, arch-snob, arch-aesthete and arch-decadent, Marcel Proust. It is that passage at the end of the section describing the death of the novelist Bergotte in which Proust speaks of the moral obligations that make themselves felt in spite of everything, and that seem to have reached humanity from some source outside its own wretched self—obligations "invisible only to fools—and are they really even to them?" Proust was speaking here of the artist's obligations—for him, in his world of dissolving values, art was the only element which seemed to keep its validity and last. But when I was travelling in the Soviet Union, these words would come back into my mind, and I would find that the obligations involved in the ideal of the Leninist tradition, permeating even those parts of society, motivating even those individuals, by whom at first sight it seemed least to be felt, had substituted themselves for the obligations involved in Marcel Proust's ideal of art. "Invisible only to fools—and are they really even to them?"

December 11, 1935

This article, which came out in the *New Republic* on the date given above, appeared later in Russian in issue No. 2 for 1936 of *Internatsionalnaya Literatura* (the two texts are slightly different). It was accompanied by an editorial rejoinder, which I here translate (the italics are the writer's):

We are glad to print the interesting article by Edmund Wilson written by him especially for Soviet readers. Wilson is one of the most considerable critics who have appeared in the post-war generation of American literature. He has of recent years taken an active part in the Left movement of the intelligentsia, and though he has not arrived in the camp of revolutionary literature, stopping halfway, he has nevertheless accomplished a significant evolution toward the Left. The article written by E. Wilson, after a visit (last summer) to the Soviet Union, constitutes a new link in the development of Soviet-American literary relations.

It would be out of place here to attempt a general discussion with Wilson on the fundamental problems of Marxist criticism, especially since, in formally replying to the article on Hemingway by I. Kashkin, Wilson is actually arguing against very primitive theses that he has picked up somewhere or other and that sound rather like a *parody* of Marxist criticism. Over these theses E. Wilson is able to score an easy enough victory.

What interests us more is the positive part of E. Wilson's article. In connection with this we shall allow ourselves to make two observations.

Hemingway's book before the last, *Winner Take Nothing*, was met with fixed bayonets by the American bourgeois critics. Hemingway, they said, was "repeating himself," and this fact annoyed them extremely. When *Green Hills of Africa* came out, a book that was really bad, a regular Witches' Sabbath took place in the literary departments of the newspapers and magazines. The critics, frothing at the mouth, demonstrated that Hemingway was "finished." They could not have been more anxious about this if they had been the hired agents of publishing houses who were competing with Hemingway's publisher.

The article by E. Wilson does not belong to this *vulgarly commercial* type of criticism. On the contrary, it is obvious that Wilson likes and esteems Hemingway and that he is saddened by his creative collapse. All the more striking, then, is *the shirking of the task of analysis of the contradictions in Hemingway's work* which constitutes, as it were, the invisible axis of Wilson's article.

That Hemingway has lost the ability to embody the contradictions by which he is torn in harmonious artistic form, has unmistakably been shown by Wilson. Wilson cannot be suggesting seriously that the central problem by which Hemingway is confronted is the recovery of his lost artistic quality on the basis of his former contradictions. Now, come: is this really possible? Has E. Wilson read Hemingway's article on the veterans,* in which the writer speaks in the first person, as he does in *Green Hills of Africa,* and is no less "intense and severe" than in the best of his artistic productions.

Not to speak out about these questions amounts to a betrayal of the fact that one takes even less interest in Hemingway's fate than the malice-breathing newspaper critics. To limit oneself to a consideration of the "aesthetic factors" means to alienate oneself from the living processes of literature, to dissociate oneself from political and moral responsibility for the artist's fate in the disintegrating bourgeois world. An article by Granville Hicks which we read in the *New Masses* not long ago on the same subject as Wilson's article expressed a deep

* An article by Hemingway called *Who Killed the War-Veterans in Florida?* which appeared in *Internatsionalnaya Literatura,* No. 12, 1935.

concern for the artist and did its best to discover ways by which Hemingway might escape from his creative blind alley. Here you may see at once the advantage of Marxist criticism over the passively contemplative kind.

And now, one more observation.

The attempt to judge artistic questions *sub specie aeternitatis* has the defect that, even when accompanied by good intentions about dealing with the facts, it must lead to excessive generalizing. Thus Wilson is correct in pointing out that *courage* is one of the elements in Hemingway's "moral code." But his further discussion of the role of Hemingway's creative activity under conditions of socialist culture is definitely not correct. The courage of Hemingway's heroes is the *courage of despair.* It may inspire the respect, even the admiration, of the Soviet reader, but it is powerless to awaken in him any valid social and psychological conceptions, because it is entirely lacking in the *dynamic optimism* that constitutes the *fundamental characteristic of the courage of the socialist world-view in life and in art.*

The "over-all" theory of the psychology of the mechanism of response to art which is involved in Wilson's idea that the reader identifies himself passively with *any* fully realized character in an artistic production, independently of this character's intellectual content, is *absolutely false.*

In the response to works of art, as in the creation of works of art, there is always an intellectual and moral element; the Marxist reader, in his approach to bourgeois literature, pits himself against it, actively selecting the feelings and ideas that he recognizes as close to his own, and rejecting the alien and hostile ones.

This does not mean that the Soviet publishers bring out the works of Hemingway or Proust for the sole purpose of demonstrating "bourgeois decay." Every genuine work of art—and such are the productions of Hemingway and Proust—enriches the reader's knowledge of life and heightens his artistic sensibility and his emotional culture—in a word, it figures in the broad sense, as a factor of educational value. Liberated socialist humanity inherits all that is beautiful, elevating and sustaining in the culture of previous ages. Such are the laws of historical development.

———

I do not know which now seems more touching: my conviction that the Leninist idealism was sure to command universal respect in the Soviet Union of the thirties or my critic's belief that their "liberated humanity" would be allowed to help itself freely to the cultural treasures of the past.

TALKING UNITED STATES

THE ARTICLES RAZZING the New Deal which have been appearing in the *American Mercury* over the name of H. L. Mencken have been sounding so much like the compositions supposed to be transmitted from the other world by the spirits of Mark Twain and William James that it is reassuring to have at last from Mencken's authentic living hand a new edition of *The American Language*.

This fourth edition of Mr. Mencken's *Inquiry into the Development of English in the United States* is more than twice as long as the *Preliminary Inquiry* of 1919. In this new version, little survives of the original tentative essay: the work has been brought to maturity—re-organized, filled out and deepened, and it presents itself in its present form as one of the few recent books of which it is possible to say that it ought to be in every American library and that it ought to be read by every foreigner who wants to understand the United States. What is most remarkable about it is that a work which covers so much ground and which illustrates with copious examples so many philological phenomena should remain for eight hundred pages so uniformly entertaining. It is rarely that a student of language is also a literary artist: Mr. Mencken has collected his American-isms and exhibits them in the pages of this book with

the loving appreciation of a naturalist mounting butterflies or ticketing new fishes. Yet even this image is too
pedantic. One is made to feel throughout *The American
Language* the movement and the pressure of the American people, vindicating their independence, filling out
their enormous country, attracting and consolidating with
themselves the peoples of older nations, inseminating
that older world itself with their habits of thought and
their speech. We listen to their voices here, as they
change the intonations of English, develop a new vocabulary, break the language into a new syntax—from
the accents of Noah Webster, sedulously carrying
through, in the department of spelling and punctuation,
the recent revolution against England, to those of the
latest arrivals in the back streets of the "foreign" sections
of cities, where old tongues lose their primitive inflections
under the influence of the easy new speech, yet, in the
process of deliquescence, shoot their particles into the
air around.

There are certain significant differences to be noted
between this latest edition and the earlier editions of
Mr. Mencken's study. Seventeen years ago, Mr. Mencken
was still uncertain as to whether American usage would
come eventually to dominate English or whether the
two dialects would simply drift apart. But today he seems
to have no doubt that English is destined "to become, on
some not too remote tomorrow, a kind of dialect of American, just as the language spoken by the American was
once a dialect of English." At the end of the first edition,
he ventured the following prophecy: "Given the poet,
there may suddenly come a day when our *theirns* and
would'a hads will take on the barbaric stateliness of
the peasant locutions of Old Maurya in *Riders to the
Sea*. They seem grotesque and absurd today because the
folks who use them seem grotesque and absurd. But that

is a too facile logic and under it is a false assumption. In all human beings, if only understanding be brought to the business, dignity will be found, and that dignity cannot fail to reveal itself, soon or late, in the words and phrases with which they make known their high hopes and aspirations and cry out against the intolerable meaninglessness of life." This passage has now been omitted. The prophecy is already coming true. Since the first *American Language* of 1919, we have had Sinclair Lewis and Eugene O'Neill, Sherwood Anderson and Carl Sandburg, Hemingway and Dos Passos, Ring Lardner and Mencken himself in his more colloquial works.

Looking back today, we can see that this first edition of *The American Language* marked a stage in the development of our literature. It marked the moment when the living tide of American had mounted so high along the sands of "correct English" that some formal recognition was necessary. Six years later, in 1925, the review *American Speech* was started, and Sir William Craigie, one of the compilers of the big Oxford dictionary, sailed for the United States to begin work on a dictionary of American. To many readers of Mencken's first edition, the chapter on the syntax of "the common speech," in which he was bold enough to suggest that we should eventually conjugate the past indicative of the verb *to be* with *was* for all persons and numbers, must have seemed entirely frivolous. Today it makes more impression; we are not so sure of the grammar of the future; and, in any case, we must give Mencken credit for one of the really valuable services performed in our own day by American criticism for American writing. For the period of literary activity which reached its height just after the war, two critics of importance stand out: Mencken and Van Wyck Brooks. Brooks exposed the negative aspects of our literary tradition and urged us to get away from our governesses.

Mencken showed the positive value of our vulgar or colloquial heritage; and he did more than anyone else in his field to bring about that "coming of age" for which Brooks had sounded the hour. The publication of Mencken's *Book of Prefaces* in 1917, with its remarkable essay on Dreiser and its assault on "Puritanism as a Literary Force," was one of the cardinal events for the new American literature. Mencken did not discover Dreiser, but he was the first critic to focus him clearly as a figure to be taken seriously, because he was able to appreciate, and to stimulate in us a certain appetite for, the Americanism of Dreiser in all its rawness. This *positive* treatment of Dreiser—so different from the negative attitude with which even sympathetic critics had so often in the past approached Mark Twain—was really the weight that tipped the scales; and the appearance of *The American Language* gave Mencken's position a scholarly base which the academically minded—a group to which most of our critics belonged—did not find it easy to brush aside.

Mr. Mencken has invited corrections and suggestions, so I will mention the following points:

It seems to me that Mr. Mencken has underestimated the recent influence of fashionable English slang on the smart patter of the United States. There exists a kind of blended Anglo-American jargon in the insouciant British tradition, which I believe to be mainly the creation of the Englishman P. G. Wodehouse, who lived for years in the United States and whose American musical comedies, written with Jerome Kern, have been as popular as his English novels. This patter has not been confined, as Mr. Mencken thinks such things are, to "consciously elegant circles," but has seeped down through middle-class youth in general to an extent

hitherto unknown for any slang tinged with Briticism. . . .
In his discussion of English and American "honorifics,"
I think that Mr. Mencken should mention the difference
between the English usage, which prefers a single
Christian name or, if there is a middle name, two simple
initials (C. K. Ogden, H. G. Wells), and the usage
in the United States, where we go in for family middle
names (Harriet Beecher Stowe, Richard Grant White—
I pick them at random from Mencken's pages). This
habit represents no doubt a desire to store up and transmit distinction in a society where titles are impossible,
an attempt to weave a net of prestige, to establish a
solidarity, for the property-owning classes, among
kaleidoscopic mixtures of stock and across the gaps of
enormous spaces.

Mr. Mencken describes Henry James as "a violent
Anglophile" and quotes criticisms of American habits of
speech uttered by him late in life when he had long been
living in England. The truth is, however, that the early
Henry James who wanted to be the American Balzac,
was well aware of the possibilities of American. I quote
the following from *An Animated Conversation* (included
in *Essays in London,* but first published in 1889). The
imaginary dialogue is taking place between English
people and Americans:

OSWALD *(to Clifford).* What do you mean by my
language?

CLIFFORD. I mean American.

OSWALD. Haven't we a right to have a language of
our own?

DARCY. It is inevitable.

CLIFFORD *(to Oswald).* I don't understand you.

BELINDA. Already?

CLIFFORD. I mean that Oswald seems at once to
resent the imputation that you have a national tongue

and to wish to insist on the fact that you have it. His position is not clear.

DARCY. That is partly because our tongue itself is not clear as yet. We must hope that it will be clearer. Oswald needn't resent anything, for the evolution was inevitable. A body of English people crossed the Atlantic and sat down in a new climate on a new soil, amid new circumstances. It was a new heaven and a new earth. They invented new institutions, they encountered different needs. They developed a particular physique, as people do in a particular medium, and they began to speak in a new voice. They went in for democracy, and that alone would affect—it *has* affected—the tone immensely. *C'est bien le moins* (do you follow?) that that tone should have had its range and that the language they brought over with them should have become different to express different things. A language is a very sensitive organism. It must be convenient—it must be handy. It serves, it obeys, it accommodates itself. . . .

BELINDA. . . . I listen to Darcy with a certain surprise . . . for I am bound to say I have heard him criticize the American idiom.

DARCY. You have heard me criticize it as neglected, as unstudied: you have never heard me criticize it as American. The fault I find with it is that it's irresponsible —it isn't American enough. . . .

BELWOOD. You have the drawback (and I think it a great disadvantage) that you come so late, that you have not fallen on a language-making age. The people who first started our vocabularies were very *naïfs*. . . . New signs are crude, and you, in this matter, are in the crude, the vulgar stage.

DARCY. That no doubt is our misfortune. . . . But we have always the resource of English. We have lots of opportunity to practise it.

CLIFFORD. As a foreign tongue, yes.

DARCY. To speak it as the Russians speak French.

CLIFFORD. The Russians are giving up French.

DARCY. Yes, but *they've* got the language of Tolstoy.
. . . Our great writers have written in English. That's
what I mean by American having been neglected.

Lastly, I wish that Mr. Mencken would add a chapter,
or even write a companion volume, on the development
of style in America. How have the different rhythm
and tempo of American speech, how have the different
values given the English vowels, affected the writing of
poetry? And how is it that the prose-styles of writers so
different from one another as, say, Mark Twain, Henry
James and Dreiser are all, in their several ways, modes
of expression characteristically American which could
never have been produced by the English? Two things,
certainly, would be plain from such a study. First, that
at a time when prose-style in England was growing more
and more ornate or elaborate (Ruskin, Carlyle, Meredith: even Dickens suffers badly from the upholstery
of the period, except when his characters are talking),
American prose was reverting to something more like
the colloquial directness of the writing of the seventeenth
century. If it is not true, as Ernest Hemingway has
said, that "all modern American literature comes from
Huckleberry Finn," it is certain that one stream of it
does. It would be impossible to bring the language of
literature any closer to the language of ordinary talk than
has been done by Mark Twain and his successors. Some
of the best of American fiction has been written as a
series of simple statements connected only by *and*.

Another feature of our literature has been its comparative neglect of the English heritage proper and its
readiness to resort to other sources. The influence of
French culture in America, which goes back to the

Francophile Jefferson and Franklin, has certainly been very much greater than it has, during the same period, in England (setting aside the Irishmen George Moore and James Joyce, and the Pole Joseph Conrad). The American fiction of the last generation was profoundly affected by the French novel—from the influence of Flaubert and his school on Henry James and Edith Wharton to the influence of Zola on Frank Norris; and the poetry of our own generation has been pretty well permeated by French symbolism. Our culture is polyglot in its elements: in spite of the English basis of our language, we are culturally almost as close to the other European countries as to England. The stray French and Spanish words which fluttered into Whitman's poems were harbingers of more sweeping migrations. Mencken's burlesque denunciations certainly come straight from the German as do Dreiser's long doleful and laboring sentences. And lately the patterns of our fiction have been shaken by reverberations from Russia.

One wishes that Mr. Mencken would bring out, also, with specimens and commentary, a study of American writing.

July 15, 1936

In reviewing, on August 25, 1945, the first volume of Mencken's *Supplement to The American Language,* I noted that he promised for the second volume an appendix on American prose-style (for which, however, he was not to find space); and I discussed this subject again:

Every American writer, more than ever today, has to struggle with a problem of language in choosing between current American and traditional literary English. Henry James, in his own time so much under suspicion of infatuation with England, actually mixed Americanisms with Anglicisms—along with a sprinkling of colloquial French—to produce an international style. Relatively uneducated writers like Ring Lardner and Mark Twain have had so poor a literary vocabulary that they were likely to seem bald or thin when they attempted straight English prose, and they could only express themselves adequately by having their story told by a character who spoke some form of illiterate dialect or special slang. Dos Passos, in *U.S.A.*, met the problem by using the third person for the life-stories of several characters but telling each in the special idiom of his locality, occupation and stratum, and interweaving them in such a way as to achieve, through parallel and contrast, a larger drama and a symphonic effect. Writers like Fitzgerald and Faulkner, whose prose has a basis in lyric verse and who have needed the vocabulary of literature, have suffered sometimes, in weaving their spells, from unintentionally setting the teeth on edge by their imprecise use of words. A writer like Elinor Wylie, whose mastery of literary English was accurate, complete and brilliant, suffers a little, on the other hand, from the effect of artificiality that we are likely to feel in America in the presence of any collection of precious objets d'art from abroad. Mr. Mencken himself, in his early writings, invented a bold combination of literate traditional English with alive-and-kicking native slang and the robustious tone of German polemics. The first edition of *The American Language* was written, however, in a more sober style. One remembers a British reviewer's pointing out that, in arguing for American, Mr. Mencken was content to write mainly in orthodox British English. That reproach can no longer be made. In this supplement, Mr. Mencken has succeeded in adapting the American idiom to the requirements of philological exposition.

The truth is that, since 1919, when Mr. Mencken merely ventured to suggest that the vernacular might someday be accepted as a medium for serious writing, the American form of English has been rapidly coming into its empire—absorbing, for the purposes of literature, more and more of the idiom of daily life, redeeming it from its comic and plebeian connotations, blending it with the language of books, and pouring it into well-rounded molds for work that may prove enduring.

It will be noted that, though there is no basic contradiction between the opinions expressed in these articles and my views of 1929 that are to be found under *Virginia Woolf and the American Language*, there is a definite shift of emphasis. In the earlier letters to the *New Republic,* the other correspondents and I were arguing against Mrs. Woolf for the historical right of Americans to claim as their own the English language; later on, I was defending our right to do with it what we liked.

AMERICAN CRITICS, LEFT AND RIGHT

I. Communist Criticism

I QUOTE THE FOLLOWING from Maurice Baring's *Outline of Russian Literature,* written before the Russian Revolution:

"The didactic stamp which he [Belinsky] gave to Russian aesthetic and literary criticism has remained on it ever since, and differentiates it from the literary and aesthetic criticism of the rest of Europe, not only from that school of criticism which wrote and writes exclusively under the banner of 'Art for Art's sake,' but from those Western critics who championed the importance of moral ideas in literature, just as ardently as he did himself, and who depreciated the theory of Art for Art's sake just as strongly. Thus it is that, from the beginning of Russian criticism down to the present day, a truly objective criticism becomes a political weapon. 'Are you in my camp?' If so, you are a good writer. 'Are you in my opponent's camp?' Then your god-gifted genius is mere dross.

"The reason of this has been luminously stated by Professor Bruckner: 'To the intelligent Russian, without a free press, without the liberty of assembly, without the right to free expression of opinion, literature became the last refuge of freedom of thought, the only means of propagating higher ideas. He expected of his country's literature not merely aesthetic recreation; he placed it at the service of his aspirations. . . . Hence the striking partiality, nay unfairness, displayed by the Russians toward the most perfect works of their own literature, when they did not respond to the aims or expectations of their party or their day. . . .'

"Herein lies the great difference between the Russian and Western critics, between Sainte-Beuve and Belinsky; between Matthew Arnold and his Russian contemporaries. Matthew Arnold defined the highest poetry as being a criticism of life; but that would not have prevented him from doing justice either to a poet so polemical as Byron, or to a poet so completely unpolitical, so sheerly aesthetic as Keats; to Lord Beaconsfield as a novelist, to Mr. Morley or Lord Acton as historians, because their 'tendency' or their 'politics' were different from his own. The most biassed of English or French critics is broadminded compared to a Russian critic. Had Keats been a Russian poet, Belinsky would have swept him away with contempt; Wordsworth would have been condemned as reactionary; and Swinburne's politics alone would have been taken into consideration. At the present day, almost ten years after Professor Bruckner wrote his *History of Russian Literature,* now that the press is more or less free, save for occasional pin-pricks, now that literary output is in any case unfettered, and the stage freer than it is in England, the same criticism still applies. Russian criticism is still journalistic. There are and there always have been brilliant exceptions . . . but as a rule the political camp to which the writer belongs is the all-important question; and I know cases of Russian politicians who have been known to refuse to write, even in foreign reviews, because they disapproved of the 'tendency' of those reviews, the tendency being non-existent—as is generally the case with English reviews—and the review harboring opinions of every shade and tendency. You would think that narrow-mindedness could no further go than to refuse to let your work appear in an impartial organ, lest in that same organ an opinion opposed to your own might appear also. But the cause of this is the same now as it used to be, namely that, in spite of there being a greater measure of freedom in Russia, political liberty does not yet exist; liberty of conscience only partially exists; the press is annoyed and hampered by restrictions; and the great majority of Russian writers are still engaged in fighting for these things, and therefore still ready to sacrifice fairness for the greater end—the achievement of political freedom."

Russian literary criticism, then, runs to party politics, just as French criticism runs to ideas; and this tendency has probably been intensified since the Marxist revolution. At any rate, it has penetrated through the Communist movement to the criticism of other countries. We have been suffering in America for a long time, in the critical writing of the Left, from a virulent infection with it. It is not merely a question of criticism written from a social point of view, or even of Marxist criticism; but of criticism dominated by the quarrels of Russian factional politics.

And, due to the turn which Stalinism has been taking, this has now become a serious nuisance. As Stalin has been rousing against him more formidable political enemies and has been resorting to more violent methods of silencing them, the literary criticism of the Stalinist press has become, not more perhaps, but more conspicuously, diverted from its proper objects to playing the role of special pleader for Stalin. There was a time when literary Communists were few and when they were the spokesmen for a most important point of view which had hardly got into the liberal weeklies, let alone the old family monthlies. One could count on Michael Gold, for example, to stand outside the bourgeois literary world and to give its illusions no quarter. But today, when half that world has turned Leftist, the Communist point of view is no longer a rarity, and we have a right to call its exponents to account.

One of the worst drawbacks of being a Stalinist at the present time is that you have to defend so many falsehoods. Not only has the whole role of Trotsky been travestied or suppressed to suit Stalin's purpose, but, on account of Lenin's relations with Trotsky and his criticism of and conflicts with Stalin, it has even been made impossible to write a real biography of Lenin or even to publish his later correspondence. The great Marxist scholar D. Rzyanov, the head of the Marx-Engels Institute and the collector and editor of the complete Marx and Engels, whose only sin in the field of Marxist research had been a too zealous desire to justify Marx against any possible kind of criticism, was never allowed to finish his work but sent to die in prison, on political charges of which one of the most serious seems to have been his failure to feature Stalin sufficiently in his commentary. The trials which have followed the assassination of Kirov have thrown up a nightmare structure of accusations and imputations—including the assertion, rather strange on the part of a socialist government, that the defendants had "lost the characteristics of human beings"—in which it is difficult to separate the true from the false but of which a good deal must certainly be false; and the condemnation of Zinoviev and Kamenev has involved the authorities in the further rewriting of Bolshevik history at their expense. The death of Gorky and the recent imprisonment of Radek, already himself

badly compromised by his compliance under pressure
with the official myths, were like the extinction of the
final sparks of intellectual light connected with the
Stalinist dictatorship.

This is not to disparage the executive abilities of Stalin
or the practical achievements of the Soviets, but a
political group which adopts as a policy the suppression
of opinion and the falsification of history on the scale
and with the unscrupulousness of the Stalinists is hardly
a beneficent influence for the production of literature or
ideas. I cannot see that the new United Front is making
a bit of difference. This change in the Communist tactics
has coincided with a period of bitter struggle between
Stalin and his political opponents and with a tightening
of the terror; and, from behind the anxious affability of
the Communist literati toward writers who do not seem
likely to offend because they do not yet know anything
about Communism, there appears, at any suggestion of
criticism, the nervousness, which now seems verging on
panic, of the satellites of a jealous boss who does not
brook the least doubt or disrespect. One is shocked to
find writers whom one has known before as sober and
conscientious reviewers quoting passages out of their
context in such a way as to give them a different meaning, inventing passages which do not exist, trumping up
counter-revolutionary charges and misrepresenting the
author's plain drift in a way that implies not, perhaps,
necessarily a deliberately dishonest intent but rather, due
to the influence of fixed ideas, an actual misreading of
the text. The Stalinist intelligentsia at the present time
are like chickens that have been mesmerized by a chalk-
line drawn from their beaks: they stand paralyzed with
their beaks on the line, they cannot look away from the
line, and at the end of the line there is nothing.

One can feel, at this stage, very little hope that any

intellectual health will ever come out of Stalinist Communism. It is the old problem of gathering figs from thistles—and what is that saying of Krylov's, in the fable of the peasants and the river, that the young will never be corrected where the old are committing the same sins? How can you expect the pupils to report reliably on the books they review when the masters are corrupting whole libraries? Stalinist criticism, then, is doubly suspect: in being Stalinist and in being Russian. As for the Trotskyists, they are often more intelligent, and they are freer to think and to say what they think. But they suffer, also, from the Russian defects in being the obverse of the Stalinist coin. They, too, tend to turn everything into a factional issue and are likely to proceed to a literary discussion with all the polemics of a party unmasking. The whole thing reached a high pitch of comedy when a writer in the *New Masses* the other day, on the evidence of an editorial in the *Nation* on the subject of the Zinoviev trials and the signature of two *Nation* editors to a petition intended to procure for Trotsky the right to defend himself, made an effort to force the *Nation* to acknowledge itself a Trotskyist journal, "the organ of a band of counter-revolutionary conspirators and assassins"; while at the very same moment an attempt was made by a writer in the *Modern Monthly* to represent the *New Republic* as Stalinist. From the point of view of the Communist groups, the whole world of the political Left is divided into Stalinist, Trotskyist and Lovestonite, and it seems absolutely inconceivable to them that it is possible for anyone not to belong to one or another of these factions.

Now, all this is straight Russian, and it would make no sense in the United States, even if the politics involved were not those of the Soviet Union. Mr. Baring, in the passage I have quoted, does no doubt exaggerate a little in speaking of English reviews which have no political tendency; yet it is certain that such tendencies as they and the *Nation* and the *New Republic* represent are of a general non-factional kind. In respect to literary criticism, we have never developed the fierce partisanship of the Russians because we have never, except locally or briefly, found ourselves in the same situation as they. We can afford to leave party politics out of our literary discussion, and even out of our political discussion, because we are free to express ourselves in speeches and editorials as the Russians have never been able to do. The great English critics like Johnson and Coleridge have been men of wide range and independent judgment. They had strong political opinions; and Johnson has been accused of allowing his—in the case of Milton, for example—to bias his literary judgment. But Johnson on Milton seems magnanimous if we compare it with, say, Joseph Freeman on Trotsky's *History of the Russian Revolution* or on the murals that Diego Rivera has been painting since he associated himself with Lovestone. And even the American critics, Van Wyck Brooks and Vernon L. Parrington, whose work has social implications, are never partisan in the Russian sense. It is absurd for Communist literary men to play, in the United States, at living in a world of veiled propaganda and conspiratorial movements—or in a world in which their group has seized power and can excommunicate and suppress. (For the Russian revolutionaries persisted, even after their victory, in regarding literature and the other arts as branches of party politics. Hence the efforts of repressive groups like RAPP to invest themselves with official authority, and the continual meddling of the government, as in the Shostakovich incident, with the natural development of the arts. A new revolutionary dictatorship, not yet sure of its position, can hardly be expected to countenance direct counter-revolutionary propaganda; but the relation at the present time between the Soviet government and Soviet literature is something specifically Russian which would be quite abnormal elsewhere. In all the fuss we have been hearing lately about the right and the wrong party-line in literature, it never seems to have occurred to anybody to say: "Party-lines in literature are nonsense! Literature will get along quite well without the interference or guidance of even the most brilliant politicians. Even a socialist government will have concerned itself quite enough with these matters when it has secured for the public interest the profits of the publishing business." The contrary policy in Russia has resulted in a situation where not only are the writers and artists forbidden to criticize the administration, but they are always in danger of being suddenly pilloried and told, as in the case of poor Shostakovich, that they will have to change their style of writing, since they are not supplying tunes that can be easily hummed by the head of the government.)

This tendency is also quite alien to the practice of Marx and Engels, who in general enjoyed art for what it was worth and pursued their political-economic analysis, even when applied to art, as something belonging to a different department. Even Lenin, who was troubled by the exaltation that he felt in listening to Beethoven, because it made him forget the crimes of society, manifested in his contacts with literature no such pettiness of party solicitude—see his attitude toward Gorky, for example—as the Communist intellectuals that speak in his name.

The real problem has been brought out into the open in an article in *Partisan Review* by Mr. Louis Kronenberger:

"There is really no fundamental dilemma," he says.

"It is more necessary for us to interest ourselves in an important subject treated without much merit than in an unimportant subject treated with considerable merit. *Culture herself* demands that we put the right social values ahead of the right literary values; and whenever we encounter people who want to keep art dustproof, who bewail the collapse of 'aesthetic values,' it is our duty to ascertain just how far their indignation is a screen for reactionary and unsocial thinking.

"The obverse of this—which is the cultural coarsening inevitable to a period of stress—is on the other hand a very serious problem for the critic. As men of thought tend increasingly to approximate the psychology of men of action, as the business of saving civilization increasingly ousts from their minds the idea of enriching it, there must follow all along the line a relaxation of standards, both ethical and aesthetic. The amenities decline, the non-utilitarian aspects of culture decrease, tolerance ceases to be feasible, and reason to be altogether sufficient. It is less important that the search for truth should survive than that the cancers of society should be cut out; but it is important enough. The critic therefore must act with a full sense of authority and responsibility toward what, when the crisis is over, we shall want to come back to; culture of that kind is like a cathedral where, just now, we cannot often pray but which we must preserve from bombardment. And culture of that kind has its uses in any program of protest. It must not stop men from fighting to restore order to the world, but it may give them a sense of what order signifies and stands for."

Mr. Kronenberger has attacked this subject with a good deal more seriousness and candor than it usually gets in that quarter (I take it that *Partisan Review* is edited by Stalinist Communists); but it seems to me that he still leaves things somewhat unclear. What course would you follow, precisely, in order to maintain the attitude recommended by Mr. Kronenberger? Mr. Kronenberger himself works on *Fortune,* writes book reviews for the *Nation,* translates La Rochefoucauld and edits anthologies of light verse and of English eighteenth-century literature. Does this fill the bill?—or what? What precisely is involved in the "relaxation of standards, both ethical and aesthetic"? At what point does the "search for truth," which is "important enough," become less important than "that the cancers of society should be cut out"? Does this mean that it is all right to assert on the word of the Stalin administration that Trotsky is a species of Fascist, who has been working in conspiracy with the Nazis to assassinate the Soviet leaders? Or does it mean that one can go merely so far as to misrepresent the contents of a book which contains some criticism of Stalin? Or does it mean merely that we may "put the right social values ahead of the right literary values"? And does this mean that, in your role of book-reviewer, you ought to caricature a good novel by Hemingway or Wilder and glorify an indifferent one about a textile strike? Or merely that you ought to neglect the one and respectfully notice the other. The root of the difficulty here may be seen, in the passage I have just quoted, in Mr. Kronenberger's use of the word "right." What he really ought to arrive at is a point of view from which it would be possible for him to say that, for himself, certain things are right and certain other things wrong. But he is only able to get so far as to assert that culture herself demands that social values be put ahead of literary values, and yet at the same time to talk about them both as "right." Right for whom, doing what? How can you take part in the civil war and at the same time preserve the cathedral?

The times, it is true, are confusing. It is not always

easy to know what to do. But one thing that is certainly
not worth doing is formulating theoretical positions. One
has to make up one's mind in what capacity one is going
to function. And from the moment one is not trying to
function as an organizer or an active politician (and agi-
tational literature is politics), one must work in good
faith in one's own field. A conviction that is genuine will
always come through—that is, if one's work is sound.
You may say, This is no time for art or science: the
enemy is at the gate! But in that case you should be at
the gate: in the Spanish International Brigade, for example, rather than engaged in literary work. There is
no sense in pursuing a literary career under the impression that one is operating a bombing-plane. On the one
hand, imaginary bombs kill no actual enemies; and, on
the other, the development of a war psychology prevents
one's real work from having value. When you "relax the
aesthetic and ethical standards," you abandon the discipline itself of your craft.

January 20, 1937

II. Bernard De Voto

As FOR THE literary Right, it hardly exists any more.
Irving Babbitt is dead, and Paul Elmer More writes
little. It is unfortunate that there is nobody nowadays
to uphold the conservative point of view. The academic
background of the older critics had certain decided advantages. They had the scholarly habit, for one thing,
of doing a thorough and careful job, and could never
have adapted themselves to the kind of miscellaneous
monthly reviewing that even the better-grade critics—
such as Mary M. Colum in the *Forum* and John Cham-

berlain in *Scribner's*—have recently been reduced to: a kind that can have little weight because it imposes the necessity of grouping together a number of books that may have nothing whatever in common except simultaneity of publication. The featured reviewer who dealt regularly, from a definite point of view, with subjects of serious interest seemed to have become extinct.

Then a conspicuous exception appeared in the shape of Mr. Bernard De Voto, the new editor of the *Saturday Review of Literature*.

Mr. De Voto is evidently something new, and he deserves our respectful attention. First of all, it must be said that it is pleasant to find regular weekly reviewing done by a man who can write, who ranges widely and observes acutely, who studies an author's whole work and attempts to sum it up, and who is truculently independent. Mr. De Voto has already succeeded in making the *Saturday Review* quite interesting. The whole magazine is coming to bear the stamp of the new editor's ideas and special interests, and it gets from them a force and an accent that it never has had before. Mr. De Voto is a Westerner who has been trained at Harvard but who has never repudiated the West. On the contrary, he has stuck to it stubbornly, making use of the lessons he has learned from it in dealing with the rest of the world, and championing its cultural importance. He has written some interesting papers on Mormonism (Utah is his native state); and in his book on *Mark Twain's America,* he has thrown some new light on the life of the frontier and on Mark Twain's literary sources. Among the literary phenomena of his own time, he has maintained a toughness of mind that has become more and more uncommon. No popular reputation passes current with him till he has attempted to assay its worth for himself; and he seems to shed fashionable shibboleths as easily as a really good rain-coat sheds water. Furthermore, he has the academic training which has enabled him, for example, to clean up without remorse on the psychoanalytical biographers who have been aping Lytton Strachey. We must, therefore, be thankful for Mr. De Voto. He is trying to do something in the *Saturday Review* that nobody else has been doing, and he has qualifications for doing it well.

Yet precisely because Mr. De Voto has undertaken this kind of responsible criticism, we expect of him more than he has given us yet. We expect of him an intelligible basis of taste and an intelligible general point of view. He *sounds* as if he were being discriminating in his discussion of the relative merits of books, yet the standards by which he judges them remain obscure; he *sounds* as if his strictures on other people's doctrines were based on some solid philosophy of which he was very certain; and yet, though we keep on reading him in the interested expectation of being told what that philosophy is, its outlines never appear. On the surface, Mr. De Voto is positive and plainspoken, but when we try to go below the surface, we find ideas that seem confused and erratic.

Mr. De Voto as a critic may be examined most satisfactorily in his book on *Mark Twain's America,* which is the most elaborate of his literary studies and typical of his methods and habits of mind. This "essay in the correction of ideas" somewhat labors under the disadvantage of being one of those books that have been written, not primarily to present the author's own view, but to combat somebody else's. This is characteristic of Mr. De Voto, who always seems to approach his subjects with a chip on his shoulder. In this case, the writer with whom Mr. De Voto is trying to pick a quarrel is Mr. Van Wyck

Brooks, the author of *The Ordeal of Mark Twain*. Now, it is true that Mr. De Voto is able to correct some minor errors on the part of Mr. Brooks, and at least one serious one: the assumption that, in the last century, when the country was full of communities organized by socialist and religious groups, Americans had taken no part in the movements represented, as Mr. Brooks says, by "the Tolstoys and the Marxes, the Nietzsches and the Renans, the Ruskins and the Morrises." And he is able to correct the lugubrious picture that Mr. Brooks painted of the old Far West by filling in the more cheerful aspects. But one ends by deciding that Mr. Brooks is a kind of King Charles's head for Mr. De Voto: an obsession which is not altogether rational.

For, after all, by the time Mr. De Voto is done, he seems to have supplied evidence himself for most of Mr. Brooks's points: that the life of the frontier was savage and taxed the pioneer's endurance and that Mark Twain's humor (as a consequence of this, according to Mr. Brooks —Mr. De Voto deplores the phenomenon but he does not attempt to explain it) tends to run to the disgusting and the horrible; that the genteel tradition of the East had an emasculating influence on letters and that, for Mark Twain, this influence, as represented by Boston and Hartford and Olivia Clemens, imposed an ordeal of another sort. Where Mr. De Voto attempts to ignore Van Wyck Brooks's findings, he obviously exposes himself. He is, for example, quite ready to throw out all the literary deadwood that is the basis of Brooks's contention that Mark Twain did not mature as an artist; but he hardly touches at all on the rankling indignation at institutions which is Brooks's very striking evidence that there was an undeveloped social prophet in Mark Twain. And, though Brooks's psychoanalytic interpretations may sometimes seem a little far-fetched, he does at least try to establish a relation between Mark Twain's choice of subjects and his methods of treating them and his character and social background; whereas De Voto is content to exclaim that Mark Twain was a great artist and a fine old boy, and, aside from tracing some of his sources, to leave his relation to his work unexplained.

It may possibly be true that Mr. Brooks has attached too much importance to the incident related by Mark Twain's biographer, in which the young Sam, much given to mischief, is made to swear by his mother at his father's deathbed that he will always thereafter be a good boy. But the duality that Mr. Brooks attributes to Mark Twain is there in his work as plain as day—in the antagonism, for example, represented for Huckleberry Finn by Miss Watson and her world, on the one hand—to which Tom Sawyer is more or less committed—and the Nigger Jim and the raft, on the other; and this duality does account, as Mr. De Voto scarcely attempts to do, and scoffs, in fact, at the notion of doing, for the dualities of *Pudd'nhead Wilson* and the Siamese twins in *Those Extraordinary Twins*.

What is more serious is that Mr. De Voto completely evades the central question which Mr. Brooks is most impressive in illuminating: the question of Mark Twain's pessimism. Mr. De Voto's explanation of this pessimism is simply that Mark Twain had seen a good deal of life and that, being no fool, it had made him gloomy. But so had Dickens and Dostoevsky and a great many other people, who did not, nevertheless, become pessimists. The pessimism of Mark Twain is surely one of the blackest cases on record. Such documents as his thoughts on the death of his daughter, which Mr. De Voto does not mention, are rare in the history of Western civilization. We know that there were special causes for the pessimism of a Swift or a Leopardi; and Mr. Brooks is certainly well advised in looking for a special cause for the pessimism of Mark Twain. He is perfectly convincing, it seems to me, in finding it in causes similar to those that evidently operated in the cases of Leopardi and Swift: in a crippling insurmountable frustration. Involved with all this is Mr. De Voto's failure to give an adequate account of *Huckleberry Finn*. Mr. Brooks may have praised that book too scantily, but he did put his finger on its meaning; whereas, if you believe Mr. De Voto, it is simply a marvellous story about floating down the Mississippi. Mr. De Voto devotes eleven pages to *Huckleberry Finn* and yet manages never to mention the theme which gives the book its emotional force and makes it something more impressive than a mere picaresque novel: the contrast between Huck's natural instincts and the distortions of civilization.

The truth is that Mark Twain's books, though funny, are in general, sad—just as that other great Westerner, Lincoln, who was also funny, was sad; and Mr. De Voto never explains or even faces this fact. Of course, the Far West of the sixties and seventies was more hilarious and more exciting than Mr. Brooks, in his earlier and dolorous phase, was able to represent it, and Mr. De Voto's correction is in order; but the kind of whooping it up for the good old days that Mr. De Voto attempts in his chapter called *Washoe* is just as emotional and just as "literary," that is to say, just as poetic, as Mr. Brooks's bitterness. In one of the essays in his collection called *Forays and Rebuttals*, Mr. De Voto denounces literary "fantasy," which he opposes to historic "fact": "The fantasies of the literary historian are frequently beautiful and nearly always praiseworthy, but they are a form of protection or of wishful thinking, a form of illusion and even of delusion," etc. Yet in what sense is Mr. De Voto's vision of a mining-town in Mark Twain's day "fact" that would make Mr. Brooks's vision "fantasy"? Mr. De Voto's book is full of rhetoric—the "incandescence" of the West, for example, which is always being brought in to do duty for more exact description. Parts of it sound, in fact, as if they had been written for declamation. There are moments when it suggests a Hollywood picture made from a novel by Fannie Hurst. Mr. De Voto is even capable of throwing out Mark Twain's own testimony (page 124) when it does not fall in with his own conception; and at one point he seems to be wanting us to accept bear-and-badger-baiting as evidence that the life of the pioneer was not devoid of gaiety and charm. (Observe, also, that in the above quotation, he is trying to psychoanalyze somebody—though one of his great objections to Brooks is that Brooks tried to psychoanalyze Mark Twain.)

As for Mr. De Voto's main grievance, it seems to me largely unfounded. He complains that American criticism has written down Mark Twain as a failure and insufficiently appreciated his work; whereas the fact surely is that the period he complains of has been that in which Mark Twain has been appreciated most. The older critics tended to exclude him from serious literature; but, beginning with William Lyon Phelps's essay and going on through John Macy and Mencken, the respect for Mark Twain has been growing. Stuart P. Sherman's chapter on him in *The Cambridge History of American Literature,* published in 1921, though rather uninspired, certainly takes Mark Twain seriously. Even Brooks does not belittle Mark Twain: he dignifies him by making him tragic; and the negative influence of Brooks and those who have followed his line has been negligible in comparison with the influence of Mark Twain's writings themselves. Ernest Hemingway and Sherwood Anderson have amply acknowledged their debt to Mark

Twain; and the main stream of American humor has followed the channel he deepened. It is certainly not true in general that the Croly-Brooks view of the frontier has dominated in the writing of our period. On the contrary, the folklore and romance of the West have, if anything, been overdone. Haven't we all heard enough by this time about Sutter and Paul Bunyan and Billy the Kid? The Wild Bill Hickoks and Calamity Janes are now the heroes and heroines of Hollywood; and the demand for American folk humor has actually now reached a point where the author of *Caleb Catlum's America* has found it profitable to produce it synthetically.

What, then, is Mr. De Voto's real grievance? This indignation at other people's errors which seems to prevent him from stating his own case, this continual boiling-up about other people's wild statements which takes a form not merely wild but hysterical, have been characteristic of all his criticism.

Well, this may be partly due to the Westerner's grudge against the Easterner; and I should say that a certain amount of it was due to the peevishness of the literary professor against the writer outside the academic enclosure. Stuart Sherman behaved in very much the same way till he himself came to work in New York. It is a combination of disapproval, often on sound enough grounds, of what seems to them cheap and superficial in the work of writers ignorant of the classics and with no training in the standards of scholarship, and of envy of the freedom of the non-academic. The critic who is or has been a teacher cannot seem to help adopting toward his readers the tone he has acquired in the classroom. That Bernard De Voto has been somewhat conditioned by the academic environment is indicated, I think, by the fact that, in his essays on education, where he is dealing with a world in which he has lived, whose difficulties and hopes he has shared and whose victories he has helped to win—even in criticizing that world severely—he gives out both heat and light; but that whenever he encounters, for example, the graduates or denizens of Greenwich Village, which has also had its hopes and its hardships, its ignominies and its victories, he stiffens with the distrust of a stranger.

Yet De Voto, I should say, fundamentally, has nothing of the supercilious professor. There is evidently some other reason for his attitude toward his contemporaries; but the difficulty is to imagine from what point of view it is possible to charge them all with a common guilt. In his review of Carl Van Doren's *Three Worlds,* he seemed to sweep them all together and accuse them of "misrepresenting" America; he seemed to ascribe to each one all the opinions of all the others. He must have mastered some precious secret which the rest of us badly need if he is not to be included himself in this general potpourri (he belongs to the same generation as the writers of the twenties he denounces, and he has been publishing novels for years)— if he can claim the privilege of standing apart and knowing that he is saved, while he looks on at the plunge of the Gadarene swine.

But what *is* this point of view, this secret? Mr. De Voto never lets us know. He only hints, and on the basis of his hints one is unable to construct anything that hangs together. One gathers that he is definitely opposed to certain tendencies that he regards as prevalent and which he characterizes variously as "progressive," "Utopian" and "religious." These tendencies evidently have to do with the desire to see the economic system modified in such a way as to safeguard human society against the social inequalities, depressions and wars which, visibly in Europe, as Mr. De Voto writes, are destroying civilization itself. Mr. De Voto's antagonism to Mr. Brooks seems, in fact, to have been primarily inspired by the latter's concern about these problems. Well, of the people that Mr. De Voto lumps together, some are no doubt Utopians; but others are Marxists, and Marx and Engels exploded Utopian socialism almost a century ago.* Yet all of them, one gathers from Mr. De Voto, have in some way been untrue to America. And not only the ones who want to get rid of capitalism—equally those who, like Sinclair Lewis, simply stayed at home and criticized. All the works of this period, apparently— Lewis's caricatures, Hemingway's idyls, Brooks's diagnoses, O'Neill's tragedies, Dos Passos's social webs, Fitzgerald's drinking-parties, Sherwood Anderson's waking dreams, Edna Millay's lyrics—had it in common that they betrayed America.

But in the interests of what is Mr. De Voto speaking? Who or what has been betrayed? A group, so far as one can gather, that Mr. De Voto calls the middle class. These middle-class people, it seems, have been going about their business, taking care of the country's essential work and maintaining its moral soundness, while our writers of the twenties and thirties have been jeering at them and leaving them in the lurch and attempting to bemuse them with Utopian visions. It is hard to understand why this solid middle class should have bought and read so many copies of the books of the above-

* I have had to let this statement stand in order not to be in the position of suppressing my own past errors while perpetuating Mr. De Voto's. I was later to discover that in this connection Mr. De Voto could have made out a very good case, and that the scientific pretenses of Marxism smuggled in a Utopian element which has made possible, in the Soviet Union, one of the hugest impostures of history. See *Marxism at the End of the Thirties.*

named writers, who have blasphemed their American heritage.

What then? All is dim after that. Fitful chinks in the clouds of words show principles leaning at unexpected angles, which seem to change between the chinks. For example: "Revolutions are always struggles between special groups; only propaganda tries to make them seem the will of the people in action. The people remain mostly unharried by them, neither willing nor acting, and in the end pay tribute to the old group, victorious, or to the new one which has cast it out. Even agrarian revolt has little to do with the agrarians in a mass." Then another barrage against the intellectuals, under cover of which no troops seem to advance. Then a vision—very vivid and convincing, this one—of the rise of the Mormon community in Utah: we are shown how, beginning with something that was in some ways very similar to communism, it developed a privileged hierarchy and succumbed, in the long run, to the financial and industrial interests. From this, some kind of moral seems supposed to be drawn. But what is it? Something about dictatorship and how all dictatorships must take the same course? Something about the enslaving effects of capitalism? Does he mean to suggest that Salt Lake City exhausts the possibilities of human society? One would think that the absorption of the communism of the Mormons in the expansion of the capitalist system precisely proved the Marxists' case. There are any number of questions that we should like to put to Mr. De Voto. Since we do not understand his premises, it is difficult to know how to debate with him. He seems content to tear his hair and, lumping us all together like one of those composite pictures that does not resemble anybody, pretend he is arguing with us.

I am sure that I am being unfair to Mr. De Voto, but I have written in the hope of smoking him out. He has been influenced by the Italian sociologist Vilfredo Pareto, and, since I have not myself read Pareto, I haven't this key to his system. I *have* read the number of the *Saturday Review* that Mr. De Voto devoted to Pareto, but the articles, including his own, threw very little light on the subject. I gather that the discipline of Pareto enables you to detach yourself from social groups and to study them objectively and dispassionately. Is that what Mr. De Voto is trying to do when he becomes so madly excited about the life of the American frontier?

Let him stand and unfold himself. What does he want? If he does not believe in the improvement of society, to what does he look forward, then?—and where do the values of literature come in? Let him not merely refer us to Pareto. Let him not merely tell us we are Easterners (especially since a good many of us are Westerners) who will never understand the frontier. It is a long time since anybody new in this field has really had anything to say to us; and if Mr. De Voto has something to say, he may be sure of an attentive audience.

February 3, 1937

IT'S TERRIBLE! IT'S GHASTLY! IT STINKS!

I HAVE LAUGHED a good deal in reading a new book—
The Great Goldwyn by Alva Johnston—about Sam
Goldwyn, the Hollywood producer. It is fun to hear how
Mr. Goldwyn, when told that a script was "too caustic,"
said: "To hell with the cost! We'll make it anyway!";
and how he brought Maeterlinck to Hollywood in a
private car and then, after seeing his first script, rushed
out of the room screaming: "My God, the hero is a bee!"
Alva Johnston, who is an adept at this kind of personal
sketch, has handled his subject with deftness. He has
turned out a good piece of light reading, through which
the Goldwyn gags are sprinkled in such a way as to give
the whole story a certain comic sparkle.

And yet this book makes one slightly sick. It has the
slave-brand of Hollywood upon it. Instead of being able
to present Sam Goldwyn as the rich humorous character
he undoubtedly is, with whatever credit for energy and
enterprise he deserves, Mr. Johnston seems to feel forced
to flatter him. Mr. Johnston does not, to be sure, offer
up his homage to Goldwyn with quite the piety of a
denizen of the studios. He is used to writing "profiles"
for the *New Yorker,* and he makes a point of turning his
paeans off with quick winks and light changes of tone.
But the flattery is there just the same. One gets very
definitely the impression that Mr. Johnston has written

his sketch in such a way that Mr. Goldwyn will be able to read it or to have certain selected passages read to him and imagine that he has been apotheosized by Mr. Johnston, while at the same time Mr. Johnston will be let out with his friends in New York by the delicate irony which he has aimed in their direction but which may not be perceptible to Mr. Goldwyn. Or it may be all a special kind of publicity designed to give more serious weight to Mr. Goldwyn by scaling down his colossal vanity and ignorance, and what sounds from Mr. Johnston's account like a lack of ordinary sportsmanship and decency, to the proportions of amusing foibles which only endear him the more to his friends.

I will quote only two examples—the whole book is written in the same way. "It has been said," says Mr. Johnston, "that if Shakespeare were alive today, Goldwyn would have him. It is an interesting notion; some of the bad plays, like *Cymbeline, Troilus and Cressida* and *Pericles,* might have been tightened up into great dramas if the playwright had had a producer over him to tell him, 'It stinks, Wagspeare. It's lousy. It's terrible. It's ghastly. You're ruining me, Wagstaff.' " Very funny about Goldwyn talking to Shakespeare; but what is Mr. Johnston's object in asserting that the defective plays of Shakespeare could have been converted by Mr. Goldwyn into "great dramas"? Mr. Johnston must know as well as anybody that Mr. Goldwyn would not be able to do anything for the least of Shakespeare's plays except turn it into something different and worse. And here is the conclusion of *The Great Goldwyn*: "Last year was Sam's twenty-third in the movie business; his press department at that time spotted him two years and celebrated the completion of his quarter-century in the business. Next year is Sam's real silver jubilee. It is something for everybody to feel patriotic about. The

U.S.A. leads the world by a wider margin in pictures than anything else, and one of the chief reasons is the Great Goldwyn."

Well, I for one will be damned if I will feel patriotic about Sam Goldwyn's silver jubilee, which his agents have been unable to restrain themselves from celebrating two years too early. In what sense does the United States lead the world in moving pictures? We make more of them than any other country and are, I suppose, more proficient technically, but have we ever turned out anything that was comparable artistically to the best German or Russian films? I can think of nothing except Charlie Chaplin, who is his own producer and produces simply himself. There was a time—up to, say, 1930—when our pictures seemed to be improving. There were new actors brought in from Europe and from the speaking stage in New York; there was mechanical experimentation and an aesthetic attention to photography; intelligent directors were given their chance.

But then the depression fell; the producers were frightened and forced to retrench; and the whole movie business seemed to harden into something immovably banal. It nailed down its favorite formulas in all their vulgarity and falsity, and almost entirely abandoned any attempt to make the old situations seem lifelike or to point them up with novel direction. The actors who were brought to Hollywood were handled with extreme stupidity, and, if they stayed there, almost invariably ruined. A lot of talent has been fed into the studios, and what have our pictures to show for it? How shall we ever know now, for example, whether Katharine Hepburn—or, for that matter, Greta Garbo—ever really had anything in her? They set the talented Emil Jannings to performing over and over again wretched parodies of his German masterpieces, with everything that had given them reality and made them human and moving bleached out by the insipid Hollywood sun, until he could stand it no longer and departed. Charles Laughton has also escaped and has returned to England and the Old Vic. Marlene Dietrich, who must have had some ability at least as a night club singer, because she has made marvellous phonograph records in German, has been turned into something in the nature of one of those loose-jointed dolls designed to be propped up against the pillows in boudoirs with sateen bedspreads, and has been made to appear in pictures so foolish, so unsightly and of such horrible taste that the most beautiful woman in the world could not play in them without looking ridiculous. But the only mirrors, apparently, in which film actors can look at themselves are the magazines that exploit the glamor of the trade and are edited for adolescent schoolgirls. That able Soviet actress Anna Sten the Great Goldwyn was unable to use at all; and I see that she is now making for another producer pictures with such titles as *Love Me Again, Gorgeous* and *Orchid Girl*. Mae West, whose peculiar attraction was that she worked up her own material and created a legendary world of her own, now has to have savorless imitations written for her by Hollywood hacks, who have quickly converted her fantasies into run-of-the-mill goods. The vultures of the Coast get them all. A director like King Vidor who has serious aspirations ends by turning out the worst kind of monstrosity: the bad serious picture. The shimmering polish of Lubitsch ends as a veneer on the awful old formulas. We have actually got to a point where features like Tarzan and Charlie Chan are the most satisfactory things one can go to. They are absurd, they are fairy tales; but they do have a certain independent existence.

The other day, after long abstinence from the movies, the result of having seen nothing but bad films for a

year, I went to one for the first time in months. I had
assumed that the Marx brothers were indestructible.
True, I had been reading the publicity stories about their
new picture, *A Day at the Races*: how it had first been
taken all over the country in the form of a stage entertainment, with a view to weeding out every gag that
could not be immediately appreciated by the audience
of the average town of over two or three thousand inhabitants. (This was partly, apparently, the work of Mr.
George S. Kaufman, who, years ago, after his first experience of Hollywood, wrote *Once in a Lifetime* as a
satire on it but later went back to learn the trade.) But
I hadn't foreseen that the result of this would be to
deprive the Marx brothers of all their natural vitality
and spontaneity. As if even popular comic art, if this
is really to capture the public, were not more a matter
of putting over on an audience (as Charlie Chaplin and
Walt Disney have) something from one's own imagination than of finding an infallible formula to provoke its
automatic reactions! The idea of establishing and exploiting the lowest common denominator of audiences has
finally killed the movies. They are absolutely sterile
and static. And even the Marx brothers are no longer
the Marx brothers. Their corporate élan has been deadened by unnatural selection of their dullest gags; and
they now fall asunder helpless. It would be amusing if
A Day at the Races, after all the special trouble taken
with it, should turn out to be a total flop.

And the writers. Before the vultures have picked the
bones of theatrical talent, the big white worms of the
studios have grown fat on the decaying flesh. But the
vultures get the worms, too. Have we not all had needy
friends who have gone West with a smile on their lips
and who have never returned again?—from whom we
have ceased to hear and whose names we no longer men-

tion, whom we remember as young people of promise, wondering what they have found to do and never thinking to connect them with the processed stuff we hear croaked out, between kisses and pistol-shots, by the smooth-faced gigantic phantoms, when we are foolish enough to go to the movies? It is true, as Mr. Johnston tells us, that Sam Goldwyn always wants the best writers; and there they are out on the Golden Coast, cooped up in their little cells, like school children in study-hour. Teacher is the supervisor, and one hopes to be teacher's favorite. There they are, blowing in their money on goofy Los Angeles houses and on ostentatious cocktail parties, at which they talk about their salaries and their options and always speak of their superiors with admiration, while they submit to being spied upon and having their correspondence opened. Those who do not care to admit surrender pretend to be uncompromising Leftists, getting together in little groups to give three discreet cheers for Stalin and to shed a tear for Republican Spain. But when the Writers' Guild was organized, it took only one woof from Schulberg to send them running like prairie-dogs— leaving the job to the technicians and the actors. And now the blacklisted leaders are creeping back, having become so profoundly habituated to high salaries for low work that, no matter how radical they claim to be, they don't know how to get along without them.

I remember only one American critic who has seemed to me to do full justice to this subject of the Hollywood producers: Mr. George Jean Nathan in the *Smart Set*. Mr. Nathan had the rich and reckless language for it; I am sorry that my own powers are relatively feeble. That was ten years or more ago; but it is plain that to-day's producers, including the Great Goldwyn and the late lamented Irving Thalberg, are the same megalomaniac cloak-and-suit dealers that their predecessors were

You have only to look at their products. You have only to look at their staffs. From the servant you may know the master. Mr. Johnston can have had only a brief submergence, and look at the book he has written.

July 21, 1937

1961. When this article first appeared in the *New Republic,* Mr. George S. Kaufman wrote in to complain of its inaccuracy in regard to himself. I had forgotten about his letter when I reprinted the piece in this book, but I came upon it later and I now want to make the correction. "In my entire life," Mr. Kaufman wrote, "I have spent something like three months writing for the movies; I did not write *A Day at the Races,* with which Mr. Wilson so gleefully credits me, and it is untrue that I 'went back for more' after *Once in a Lifetime,* because up to that time I had never seen the place, and neither had Moss Hart."

THE OXFORD BOYS BECALMED

ı CONFESS TO feeling somewhat less enthusiasm than usual for the two new books of W. H. Auden: *On This Island,* a volume of poems, and *The Ascent of F-6,* a play written with Christopher Isherwood. It looks as if the group to which Auden belongs—the school of young Oxford poets which includes C. Day Lewis, Stephen Spender and Louis MacNeice—had lapsed, after their first lift of enthusiasm for the clean sweep that communism promises, the first exhilaration of repudiating the world to which they belonged, into a period of relaxation, of cooling down and marking time.

Mr. Auden himself has presented the curious case of a poet who writes an original poetic language in the most robust English tradition, but who seems to have been arrested at the mentality of an adolescent schoolboy. His technique has seemed to mature, but he has otherwise not grown up. His mind has always been haunted, as the minds of boys at prep school still are, by parents and uncles and aunts. His love poems seem unreal and ambiguous as if they were the products of adolescent flirtations and prep-school homosexuality. His talk about "the enemy" and "their side" and "our side" and "spying" and "lying in ambush" sounds less like anything connected with the psychology of an underground revolutionary movement than like the dissimulated resentments and snootiness of the schoolboy with advanced ideas going back to his family for the holidays. When this brilliant and engaging young student first came out for the class struggle so strongly, it seemed an audacious step; but then he simply remained under the roof of his nice family and in the classroom with his stuffy professors; and the seizure of power he dreams of is an insurrection in the schoolroom: "I should like to see you make a beginning before I go, now, here. Draw up a list of rotters and slackers, of proscribed persons under headings like this. Committees for municipal or racial improvement—the headmaster. Disbelievers in the occult—the school chaplain. The bogusly cheerful—the games master—the really disgusted—the teacher of modern languages. All these have got to die without issue. Unless my memory fails me there's a stoke hole under the floor of this hall. The Black Hole we called it in my day. New boys were always put in it. Ah, I see I am right. Well look to it. Quick, guard that door. Stop that man. Good. Now boys hustle them, ready, steady—go."

With all this—and at times out of all proportion to the interest of what he has had to say—Mr. Auden's imagery and language have been remarkable for an energy, a felicity, a richness, a resource, a nerve, which have made him a conspicuous figure. He certainly has more of what it takes to become a first-class poet than anybody else of his generation in England or, so far as I can think, in the United States. And in one department Mr. Auden is entirely and brilliantly successful: he has invented a new satire for the times. The most satisfactory part of his work seems to me that which includes such skits as *The Dance of Death*, with its cheap and weary rhythms; the satiric-elegiac choruses of *The Dog Beneath the Skin*; and such poems as the one, in this new collection, in which he describes the Cambridge intellectuals,

THE OXFORD BOYS BECALMED

Who show the poor by mathematics
    In their defense
That wealth and poverty are merely
Mental pictures, so that clearly
Every tramp's a landlord really
    In mind-events.

He is especially good at calling the roll of the lonely, the neurotic, the futile—of all the queer kinds of individuals who make up the English upper classes. No one else has given us just this sense, at once pathetic and insipid, of the slackening of the social organism and the falling apart of its cells.

But, once having taken their stand, once having put themselves on record, we get the impression that Mr. Auden and his associates are at a loss as to what to do next. In some ways they appear to be retrograding. Thus the idiom of Auden in this latest book seems to me to be actually less personal than it was in his earlier poetry. He had revived in that earlier work the great idiom of English poetry at its most vigorous, its liveliest and freest, telescoping the whole tradition, from the emphatic alliteration of Anglo-Saxon through the variety and ease of the Elizabethans to the irony and bizarre imagination of the generation just before his own. But in *On This Island* it seems to me that the rhythms of the lyrical and reflective poems let one down by approximating too closely to the deliberate looseness of the satirical ones; and the off-rhymes begin to get on one's nerves. (Near-rhymes and negligent rhythms are, I suppose, a symptom of blurred emotions. There are moments when Louis MacNeice sounds like a serious Ogden Nash.)

It has come to be a depressing feature of the literary scene at the present time—noticeable also in this country —that writers who had hitherto seemed able to stand on

their own feet have begun flopping over on one another
and imitating one another's idiom—without there necessarily being any question of the normal attraction of the
weaker toward the stronger. Thus Auden, whose voice
we have known and liked, disconcerts us by suddenly
falling into the accents of Housman or Yeats or the palest
of the later Eliot. Thus Louis MacNeice, who seems to
me perhaps (except Auden himself) the most gifted of
the Auden group, the master of a lyric impressionism that
differs from the work of the rest, appears, in a recent
number of the English magazine *New Verse*, to have
toppled over on Auden and to have become almost indistinguishable from him.

The second of the Auden and Isherwood plays, *The
Ascent of F-6*, is certainly very much inferior to *The Dog
Beneath the Skin*. *The Dog Beneath the Skin* had its
shortcomings: a good deal of its satire was banal—it
sounded as if the clever schoolboys had just discovered
some of the stalest jokes of Marxism and worked them up
for a school entertainment. But the first part, at any rate,
was very funny; and the choruses, as I have said, were
certainly of Auden's best. *The Ascent of F-6* suffers even
more from the flimsiness of amateur theatricals; and here
Marxism has been forgotten for a relapse into Freudian-
ism. The theme is a sort of psychoanalytic version of a
career like that of Colonel Lawrence. This piece has the
annoying defect of appearing to be padded in a tiresome
way and yet at the same time to be too short and not to
exploit the possibilities of its subject.

Not, however, that Auden and his group are any worse
off than other Left intellectuals. They have, in fact, an
advantage over most of them in having been able to give
expression to their plight and their time more brilliantly
and with fewer false attitudes. The combination of communism with homosexuality, of an England suburban-

ized and Americanized in the peculiarly dreary English way with an English university culture as rich as the richest fruitcake, is something quite new in literature, which it took some courage and genius to manage. MacNeice and Auden are only thirty; C. Day Lewis is thirty-two; Stephen Spender is twenty-eight. They are remarkable, at that age, in having been able to say so well something that had not yet been said at all:

So in this hour of crisis and dismay,
What better than your strict and adult pen
Can warn us from the colors and the consolations,
The showy arid works, reveal
The squalid shadow of academy and garden,
Make action urgent and its nature clear?
Who give us nearer insight to resist
The expanding fear, the savaging disaster?

This then my birthday wish for you, as now
From the narrow window of my fourth-floor room
I smoke into the night, and watch reflections
Stretch in the harbor. In the houses
The little pianos are closed, and a clock strikes.
And all sway forward on the dangerous flood
Of history, that never sleeps or dies,
And, held one moment, burns the hand.

February 24, 1937

PRIZE-WINNING BLANK VERSE

THERE IS PERHAPS not much point, at this time and in this place, of writing a depreciation, merely for the sake of a depreciation, of the plays of Mr. Maxwell Anderson. Mr. Anderson is by no means pretentious about his work. It is the donors of the Pulitzer Prize, who gave a prize to *Both Your Houses*, and the members of the Drama Critics' Circle, who have twice in succession chosen plays of his for their award, that have made his work appear pretentious. And Mr. Stark Young has already discussed in these pages the various productions of Mr. Anderson's plays and dealt admirably with their literary as well as with their theatrical qualities. I see, moreover, that Mr. V. F. Calverton and Mr. George Jean Nathan have chosen this moment to light into him. There are, however, certain things to be said about Maxwell Anderson's general aims that none of these critics has said, so I shall lay on with the rest.

Toward the end of the season last year, when *Winterset* had been covering itself with glory, I went around to see what I understood from the reports of it I had heard to be a great American poetic drama on the theme of Sacco and Vanzetti. What I was actually confronted with was a belated disembodied shadow of the productions, so unpopular in their day—universally neglected by the critics—of the old New Playwrights' Theater in Grove

Street. There were the Jews out of Em Jo Basshe's *The Centuries*; the street scene, with its agitators and policemen, out of Dos Passos's *Airways, Inc.*; and a general influence of the stagecraft—the set that accommodates a variety of scenes—of John H. Lawson. During the first act, I became quite interested, for it seemed to me that the writers of the New Playwrights might have founded a school, after all, and I was hoping that Mr. Anderson might have succeeded in improving on his originals. But as the play went on, I was baffled at discovering that the New Playwrights' characters were expressing themselves in blank verse of an hypnotic monotony and imagery of a dismal banality. The revolutionary social content had been extracted from the New Playwrights entirely. *Winterset* was indeed that wonderful coffee which enables you to sleep like a child. I did, in fact, fall asleep in the course of the last act and only woke up again when somebody fired a gun. All the characters were now being killed in an ending which was Elizabethan at least in its wholesale slaughter; but I was left quite unmoved by the fate of stage fictions who talked Mr. Anderson's blank verse.

I afterwards made a point of reading the text of *Winterset* in order to find out what I had missed. But the play seemed to me even feebler than it had when I had seen it on the stage. The production and the acting had invested some of the scenes with something like imagination; but in the text I could not discover anything that seemed to me in the least authentic as emotion, idea or characterization. Mr. Anderson is dealing with the aftereffects of such a tragedy as the execution of Sacco and Vanzetti. He makes the son of an anarchist father, executed for another's crime, fall in love with the sister of the real criminal, whom he has devoted his life to pursuing. The young man gives up his revenge, sparing the girl's brother and allowing himself to fall into the hands of the gang. Miriamne has come to represent for him "all hope and beauty and brightness drawn Across what's black and mean"; he wishes to emerge from "this everglades of old revenge" and "forget to hate," perhaps at last to forgive. But it is too late. The gangsters kill them both. The Talmudic old Jewish father closes the play by announcing the "masterless might" of the universe, and declaring that only the human "cry toward something dim In distance, which is higher than I am" makes man the "emperor of the endless dark even in seeking."

> this is the glory of earth-born men and women,
> not to cringe, never to yield, but standing,
> take defeat implacable and defiant,
> die unsubmitting.

But what is the point of this? Mr. Anderson's hero, Mio, has just given up his life's purpose. In what sense is his defeat "implacable and defiant"? He is supposed to be the son of an anarchist, a class-conscious victim of the class war, and such a man would scarcely have regarded the exposure of the real culprit and the vindication of his father's innocence as merely a matter of private revenge. Yet Mr. Anderson makes him succumb to his interest in a little girl whose supposed sweetness of character is made to manifest itself in speeches that sound as if they had been written under the influence of a favorite English teacher and published in the school magazine by a young daughter of the bourgeoisie; and then gives him a funeral speech—of a kind, by the way, not especially appropriate to the mentality of a Talmudic Jew—which suggests some Promethean champion of the human mind and will.

I have also read—not having seen them—*The Masque of Kings* and *High Tor*, and they make upon me the same impression of pointlessness and mediocrity. The protagonist of *The Masque of Kings* gives up his revolutionary purpose just as Mio gives up his revenge; the protagonist of *High Tor* gives up the noble stand he has taken against the vandalism of industrial development. Mr. Anderson's heroes are always retiring: they become disillusioned with their own designs before instead of after they have realized them, and this makes his dramas rather disappointing. There is never any real fight. When everything is over, some sententious character gives expression to the thought "*Sic transit gloria mundi!*" in more or less hackneyed terms, and Mr. Anderson's performance is finished.

For the rest, Mr. Stark Young has analyzed these plays as much as it is profitable to do, and he has even, I feel, sometimes been led by skillful production or acting to give them a little more credit than they deserve. He is quite kindly about *High Tor*, which seems to me—among plays that make any claim to serious consideration—one of the silliest I have ever read. I agree with Mr. Young when he says that some of the bursts of Mr. Anderson's poetic eloquence "sound like a Stephen Phillips version of an Arthur Symons translation of a decadent German versifying of a lax translation of Euripides."

Yet Maxwell Anderson's writing is not all so bad as that. The point is that in his blank verse he is seen at his worst. The prose parts of his plays are much better. And in the days when he wrote prose altogether—in *What Price Glory?* and in the hobo play that he made from Jim Tully's *Beggars of Life*—he showed a gift for vernacular dialogue much richer and more original than anything that has appeared in his verse.

Mr. Anderson has, however, a positive conviction that plays should be written in verse. He has explained in his preface to *Winterset*. "Those," he says, "who have read their literary history carefully know that now is the time for our native amusements to be transformed into a national art of power and beauty. It needs the touch of a great poet to make the transformation, a poet comparable to Aeschylus in Greece and Marlowe in England. Without at least one such we shall never have a great theater in this country, and he must come soon, for these chances don't endure forever. I must add, lest I be misunderstood, that I have not mistaken myself for this impending phenomenon. I have made my living as teacher, journalist and playwright and have only that skill as a poet which may come from long practice of an art I have loved and studied and cannot let alone."

This assumption of Mr. Anderson's seems to me quite mistaken. It is true that verse has been passing out as a technique for writing plays; but is it true that it is really needed? After all, verse-technique has also passed out in all sorts of other departments of literature to which no one would now think of restoring it. In the last century, it was still used for novels; in the eighteenth century, for essays. Before that, in the ancient world, it was used for prophecies, laws, science, history and manuals of agriculture. Whatever the reasons for its falling into disuse, it is undeniable today that pure verse-technique has come to be employed—and is almost never otherwise effectively employed—in a narrow and specialized field: that of lyric poetry. The modern writers who come closest to the great writers of epics and the great dramatic poets of the past—the Flauberts and Tolstoys and Ibsens and Shaws and Prousts—have almost invariably written prose. At most, there is a blending with prose of something of the technique of verse: in certain writers one can see the transition quite clearly. For example, the long poems of Robinson Jeffers show a tendency to disintegrate into prose; and the prose novels of James Joyce contain vestiges of the rhythms of verse. Isn't it true that if Synge and O'Neill, of whom Mr. Anderson speaks, had lived in Otway's time, they would have still been writing their tragedies in verse? And is Mr. Maxwell Anderson prepared to assert that the plays of Molière, for example, which, through an accident purely chronological, happen partly to have been written in verse, would be the worse for having been written in prose? The mere literary technique itself is not the issue here: the technique is determined by the rhythms of speech, and it changes with these rhythms, which in turn are determined by the pace of life and, basically, by man's relation to his environment, which changes from age to age. One sees this very plainly in Ibsen, who began by writing plays in verse, of which his countrymen say he was one of their great masters, but who, outgrowing the influence of the romantic era, became later a master of prose. Does Maxwell Anderson consider that *The Wild Duck* and *Hedda Gabler* are less successful than *Brand* and *Peer Gynt,* and can he imagine them written in verse? And what could be more synthetic than the costume-dramas of Rostand, the chief practitioner of modern poetic drama?

Mr. Anderson, it seems to me, in his own plays, has presented the most striking example of the obsolescence of verse-technique. He is capable of writing well—in prose, and when he is close to American speech. But in these recent verse-plays he writes badly—not, I think, because he is technically incompetent, but rather because English blank verse has no longer any relation to the tempo or tongue of our lives, and so can provide no vehicle for his genuine gift of dialogue: the old rhythms can inspire him to nothing but a flavorless conventional imagery that was already growing trite in our grandfathers' time. When Mr. Anderson makes an effort to combine blank verse with the language of everyday speech, he gets something, as in *Winterset*, which is neither, and dreadful. (It is true that T. S. Eliot, in *Murder in the Cathedral*, has done better with the verse-drama than Maxwell Anderson; but, to my mind, the best scenes in this play are the prose ones: the sermon and the speech of the assassins.)

I am inclined to believe, furthermore, that it is Maxwell Anderson's infatuation with blank verse that has aborted his talents all around. Along with the rhythm goes not only the imagery, but the attitude, the point of view. Instead of any sentiments that any real people might conceivably feel today in connection with the events he depicts, the commentators in Mr. Anderson's plays can only proffer the dimmest echoes of the sentiments of the Elizabethans in connection with events of quite a different character. A technique ought to grow out of the material; but Mr. Anderson is trying to impose on his a technique that has nothing to do with it. Instead of getting deeper into reality as he progresses in his artistic career, he is carried by his blank verse farther away.

June 23, 1937

"GIVE THAT BEAT AGAIN"

THE NEW BOOK by Miss Edna St. Vincent Millay I have found a little disappointing. For the first twenty-five pages or so, *Conversation at Midnight* is stimulating. Seven men of different kinds are brought together and made to talk about love, religion, communism, fascism, war and other subjects of current interest—with interludes on hunting, fishing, racing and mushroom-collecting. The poet is plunging with her ready intelligence into the confusion of cross-currents of the time, and the reader is put on the qui vive: he is expecting a revelation. But the discussion doesn't come to much. It covers familiar ground, and the people—the stockbroker, the Communist, the liberal, the Roman Catholic, the artist, the sensualist, the advertising man—say many of the clever things that people usually say without arriving at very many of the illuminating things which people do not usually say but which the poet ought to make them say. We expect the conversation to gather momentum, but in the latter part it rather bogs down. At the very end, it mounts to a climax with an increasingly acrimonious altercation between the stockbroker and the Communist—each of whom accuses the other of submitting slavishly to regimentation—to which the liberal host puts an end by offering both parties a drink.

But the dialogue is rarely allowed to penetrate to the

fundamentals of the problems on which it touches. There are insights of considerable vividness—the picture of secularized man howling at night over the grave of God, the picture of the atheistic Communist rejecting the advances of Faith when he confronts it in its familiar form only to yield to it when it comes in a different guise; but the really great forces that are upsetting the world somehow do not get squarely on the stage. What is really involved, for example, in such an argument as that between the radical and the stockbroker is the conflict between the classless and the class ideal, and Miss Millay has sidestepped this by making the pretenses of both parties ridiculous.

It may be that this part of the discussion has been blurred as a result of the accidental burning of Miss Millay's first manuscript and of her having had to write the poem over. The worst developments of the Stalin dictatorship in Russia, with the new phase of the Stalin-Trotsky quarrel, which figure in this second version, had not yet taken place when the first was written; and it may be that Miss Millay has been goaded by this to make her imaginary Communist more fanatical and less convincing in his desire to see his fellows happy and free than he had been in the original version. In one of her most revealing flashes, she makes the liberal address the Communist as follows:

Russia under Lenin is so many light-years away,
Its noble beam approaches you but now;
You stand transfigured in the golden light today
Of a star that, even while you bask in its bright ray,
Blackens, and disappears.
We must allow,
Perhaps another nineteen years,
Before you see what's happening in Russia now.

The debate in *Conversation at Midnight* cannot have failed to be confused by all this. Yet there are larger issues involved in these questions of religion and socialism, fascism and democratic ideals, which go deeper than the passing events of politics, as they go deeper than the prejudices and emotions of such persons as Miss Millay presents; and one cannot see that Miss Millay has kept these issues in sight. For her, the whole upshot of the matter seems to be that both the stockbroker and the radical hanker only after the status of obedient cogs in a smoothly running machine. But is this what they are fighting about in Spain? Miss Millay probably does not really think so, since she has lately contributed to a volume of translations of Spanish poems, for the benefit of the Loyalist cause; but you would never find this out from *Conversation at Midnight*. Nor, failing to dramatize the issue of the democratic versus the capitalist society, does she focus the various opinions and types from any other clear point of view.

I believe that the fundamental trouble here is that Miss Millay is rather lacking in the dramatic imagination —that is, that it is not quite natural for her to identify herself with imaginary characters. Of her plays, *Aria da Capo* was an eclogue, highly charged and deeply disturbing, like all her best work of that time; but the characters—as was suitable—were pure abstractions. *The King's Henchman*, which had some beautiful poetry in it, was a dramatic poem rather than a play, as the plays of Yeats are poems. But in *Conversation at Midnight*, Miss Millay has tried to animate and keep distinct a number of different people, with their characteristic points of view; and her own point of view, so personal, so strongly created in her other poetry, turns out not to lend itself easily to this kind of dissociation. She is attempting a sort

of thing not unlike some of Bernard Shaw's plays and
very much like G. Lowes Dickinson's *A Modern Symposium*; but, failing their expertness in the analysis of
ideas, she ought to, and tends to, get out of such a subject effects of emotional conflict of a kind quite alien to
Dickinson or Shaw. Yet these chemical emotional reactions do not, to my mind, quite occur. What does happen is that, on the one hand, Miss Millay is either satiriz-
ing her characters' banalities or commenting on them
from a long way off, while, on the other hand, her own
peculiar pessimism, with its noble magnanimity and
bitterness, is always trying to rise to the surface but is
never allowed to emerge. We keep listening instinctively
through the chatter and chaff for the voice we are accustomed to hear, and now and then we think it is speaking:

> Ricardo said, "Whatever the case for God, the
>   splendor of Man
> Cannot be questioned."
> This Music, this proud edifice erected
> Out of reach of the tide
> By drowning hands,
> This deathless, this impeccable, projected
> By peccant men, who even as they labored sank
>   and died,
> Irrefutable witness to that splendor stands.
> It speaks more loud
> Than the waves that batter
> The wild bluff:
> There is no God.
> But it does not matter.
> Man is enough.

But compare this to Miss Millay's sonnet, *On Hearing
a Symphony of Beethoven*. For anyone capable of that,
this was hardly worth doing at all. And in the meantime,

the dramatized points of view of Miss Millay's fictitious personalities never give rise to any conflict half so real as the conflicts within the poet herself, as she has expressed them directly in her own person:

> Pity me that the heart is slow to learn
> What the swift mind beholds at every turn.

A good deal of the interchange of *Conversation at Midnight* falls into a vein of banter, worldly and witty and sometimes cute, which has not been exploited by Miss Millay since her prose sketches and dialogues of about fifteen years ago, published under the pseudonym of Nancy Boyd. To handle this kind of badinage in verse, she has developed a new semi-verse medium which is something like a combination of Ogden Nash and Robinson Jeffers, but which, in her hands, is much more flexible, as it follows a play of the intelligence that is quicker and subtler than either of theirs. *Conversation at Midnight is* really very witty; and the imagery, as is usual with Edna Millay, provides an element of excitement and surprise through its power to intensify realistic observation presented with a daring baldness:

Corruption, too, is a kind of development—it depends on
    the viewpoint. . . .
To the buzzard under his shabby wings appraising the
    beach from above, the whip-ray
Till he be stranded and the land soldier-crabs have taken
    his eyes out
Has not achieved maturity.

But Nancy Boyd is not Edna Millay; and this group of ventriloquial figures does not bring her much closer to being so. Not, of course, that Nancy Boyd isn't good in her way; not that this book isn't more or less brilliant. But the best of the impersonal poems in the volume called

The Buck in the Snow are more truly philosophical than the whole of this long symposium.

As for the verse, this reviewer has been prophesying for years about the obsolescence of verse-technique and the gradual victory of prose; but now he finds himself a little dismayed at the rapidity with which the process is going forward. Little did we think in our youth, when the Miltonic line seemed irrefrangible and when, in our innocence, we used to laugh, as the poet intended us to do, at W. S. Gilbert's rhymed but meterless Bab Ballad of *The Lost Mr. Blake*, that we should live to see the day when its interminable lines that look and sound like paragraphs of prose would be the type of much serious poetry. The old strong beat of English verse has by this time been so broken, sprung, muted, loosened, that it might almost as well be abandoned altogether. Compare Mac-Neice and Auden with Yeats and Housman; Robinson Jeffers with John Masefield; Eliot's *Murder in the Cathedral* with his earlier work; Ogden Nash with Franklin P. Adams. And now Edna St. Vincent Millay, one of the sole surviving masters of English verse, seems to be going to pieces, too. She was beginning to indulge a loose hand with her metrics in the volume called *The Buck in the Snow*—quite successfully in some of the lyrics; and she went even further in this direction in a later book, *Wine from These Grapes*. But it was not till her translations from Baudelaire that the ravages of the mischief became alarming. Instead of rendering Baudelaire's alexandrines in English meters equally ringing, she fell into what seemed a fallacy entirely uncharacteristic in assuming that the effect of the French could be conveyed by slurring over the English stress and producing a line completely fluid. But the result was not a bit like Baudelaire: it was merely inferior verse for Edna St. Vincent Millay.

Now in *Conversation at Midnight*, you see metrics in full dissolution. The stress is largely neglected; the lines run on for paragraphs; sometimes the rhymes fade out. Occasionally poor little sonnets, like souls from the Platonic overworld that want to be born again, flutter in and are carried along by the all-liquefying flux, filling up quickly with its varied content, to which their form has no special appropriateness, in which it is difficult for them to crystallize a pattern. This is all something quite distinct from the *vers libre* of the early nineteen-hundreds, which, though proselike, was often redeemed by a lapidary sharpness and precision or had the rhythms of the Whitmanesque chant. But the rhythms are weary now. They and the near-rhymes, as Mr. Max Eastman has said, almost amount to a joke on disciplined writing itself.

I do not complain of this state of affairs: I know that it is all on the cards. And *Conversation at Midnight* is, in any case, a highly entertaining interlude in Miss Edna Millay's work. Miss Millay at her most relaxed is livelier than most of our poets at their brightest. Yet I miss her old imperial line.

July 28, 1937

DREAM POETRY

THE OTHER NIGHT I made up a poem in my sleep and remembered it after I woke up, and it has set me thinking
about dream poetry.

The outstanding examples of imitation dream poetry
are, of course, those of Lewis Carroll and James Joyce.
Everybody knows the dream gibberish of *Jabberwocky*
and the familiar classics gone wrong of *You are old,
Father William* and *Sitting on a Gate*. And James Joyce's
new book,* which is all a dream, contains some equally
amusing examples. At one point the sleeping hero
imagines himself coming out of a public house with a
party of convivial companions. They insist on somebody's singing a ballad, which turns out, however, when
it is finally heard, to be a pitiless exposé of the hero (a
man named H. C. Earwicker, who has a tendency, in
inferior-feeling moments, to associate himself with
earwigs):

Have you heard of one Humpty Dumpty
How he fell with a roll and a rumble
And curled up like Lord Olaga Crumple

* *Finnegans Wake* had not come out in book form and did
not as yet have a name. The ballad was quoted from one of the
instalments that appeared in the magazine *transition*, in the
form in which it there appeared. Its final form was somewhat
different.

By the butt of the Magazine Wall,
Of the Magazine Wall,
Hump, helmet and all.

He was one time our King of the Castle
Now he's kicked about like a rotten old parsnip.
And from Green Street he'll be sent by order of
    His Worship
To the penal jail of Mountjoy
To the jail of Mountjoy!
Jail him and joy.

He was father of all schemes for to bother us
Slow coaches and immaculate contraceptives for
    the populace,
Mare's milk for the sick, seven dry Sundays a week,
Openair love and religion's reform,
And religious reform,
Hideous in form . . .

'Tis sore pity for his innocent poor children
But look out for his missus legitimate!
When that frew gets a grip of old Earwicker
Won't there be earwigs on the green?
Big earwigs on the green,
The largest ever you seen, etc.

These are, however, the creations of comic art. Before
going on to true dream composition, one may note that
there exists, also, a sort of unintentional pseudo-dream
poetry. T. S. Eliot suggests that the poetry of Swinburne
really belongs in this category:

> Before the beginning of years
>   There came to the making of man
> Time with a gift of tears:
>   Grief with a glass than ran . . .

"This is not merely 'music,'" says Eliot. "It is effective because it appears to be a tremendous statement, like statements made in our dreams; when we wake up, we find that the 'glass that ran' would do better for time than for grief, and that the gift of tears would be as appropriately bestowed by grief as by time." But the poetry of Swinburne seems to me to be alcoholic, rather than dream, poetry; and alcoholic poetry is a distinct department. A better example of involuntary dream poetry is the verse of the late George Russell, who signed himself AE. I remember coming home very tired one night and picking up what I thought was a volume of Yeats, with the intention of reading myself to sleep. I had an experience that gave me the creeps for a moment. Something strange seemed to have happened to the familiar poems. They sounded like Yeats all right, but were suffused with an uncanny iridescence which made everything insubstantial, somehow slightly unpleasant and, so far as I could see, meaningless. The poems were not Yeats's but AE's, which had been brought out by the same publisher in a format almost identical with the collected Yeats. It was a copy sent for review that I had put in my bookcase and forgotten about. I had never looked into it before, and it had given me for a few moments the illusion that I was dreaming.

But these are not the real thing. There is perhaps only one great classic of well-authenticated dream poetry: Coleridge's *Kubla Khan*, which was begun in an opium trance and interrupted by somebody's knocking at the door, so that the poet, with his waking mind, was never able to finish it. Here the opium must have intensified the vision and speeded up intellectual activity. A more normal example is the well-known set of verses called *Dominus Illuminatio Mea*, which the novelist R. D.

Blackmore, the author of *Lorna Doone*, is said to have composed in a dream:

In the hour of death, after this life's whim,
When the heart beats low, and the eyes grow dim,
And pain has exhausted every limb—
    The lover of the Lord shall trust in Him. . . .

This piece seems to have been a great favorite with Sir Arthur Quiller-Couch, who included it in two of the Oxford anthologies; but, interesting though it is as a specimen of what can be done by the sleeping mind, I have never been able to feel any enthusiasm for it. It is characteristic of dream poetry, as Eliot says, that it never means as much as it seems to.

A distinguished American poet* once told me that he had dreamt of composing a poem which had seemed to him in his dream the consummation of his whole career, if not the highest triumph of literature—a work of supreme beauty which also gave utterance to the profoundest thought ever compassed by a poet's mind. When he woke up, he still knew the poem, which turned out to run as follows:

It's white to be snow,
    It's cold to be ice,
It's windy to blow,
    And it's nice to be nice.

My own verses were of this gnomic character. I had dreamed that I was taking a cruise along the west coast of Italy. The principal stops were Cologne, Brescia, Rome and Santiago. We were playing a game like bouts rimés with very peculiar conditions, of which one was

* The late Ridgely Torrence.

that the words "the mandrake shrieks" were to appear in every poem. With enormous labor, but, as it seemed to me, great brilliance, I produced the following stanza; then decided to leave the ship and go back to Paris, because I was afraid I should fall down in the contest by not having time enough to supply another stanza equally remarkable:

> The human heart is full of leaks;
>> The human head is full of vapors.
> The crows disband; the mandrake shrieks;
>> The scandal was in all the papers.

Some crows were actually making a racket and had evidently penetrated my dream without being able to wake me.

But the most remarkable specimen of dream poetry which I have ever personally encountered was composed by a lady of my acquaintance.* The curious thing is that the other verse of hers I have seen, written during her waking hours, is distinctly inferior to this dream poem, which seems to me quite delightful and a little in the vein of *Kubla Khan*.

> And you, my love, and you, my sweet,
> The beauty of the morning greet,
>> For me it's end of day.
> Unclosed my eyes, unclosed the night;
> I saw star-clusters reel and right
> And nothing was that was the same
> As it had been ere this night came:
>> The moon knelt down to pray.
> I went back through the hidden door
> Where no sane man had gone before;

* Mrs. William McFee.

I saw the beauties, touched the dross;
I drank the wine and kissed the cross
      And gave your love to pay,
That I might touch eternity
A moment's space, now you are free,
      Long gone, long lost, away.

It is true, of course, that one of the main currents of modern poetry has been tending toward something like a condition of dream since Mallarmé, and even since Poe. Modern life seems to have had the effect of driving the old kind of lyric feeling, which used to embrace the world, into the depths of the private consciousness; and the deliberate formulas and attitudes derived from the study of external reality which the younger poets are trying to impose on their poetry have a way of yielding nothing but rhetoric. Who knows but we may not, in the long run, have to depend on our dreams for lyrics?

July 31, 1937

This article brought me several letters with specimens of poetry written in dreams.

Mr. George V. Lockard, writing from Lancaster, Pennsylvania, sent me the following verses:

The evening ends in noise and folly,
Speeches beneath the one bright star
Changing to sleepers on the trolley,
Electric jolting of the car.

Who seemed an Artemis on background green
Mantling the darkness in Virgilian airs
Decides to let her wit be seen,
Dwindles to Millamant and public stares.

Mr. George W. Lyon, writing from Pittsburgh, sent me a copy of a letter published in the New York *Times Saturday Review of Books* of March 19, 1910, in which he told of composing a poem in a dream and gave the text of the poem, with a gloss which he had later added:

Two Voices

Out of the atoms of earth we come,
Back to the atoms of earth we go;
Out of the dark of earth to light,
Back to the dark of earth and night.
Life is a problem and death is its sum—
Out of the atoms of earth we come,
Back to the atoms of earth we go.

> This is the Voice of abysmal gloom and utter hopelessness.

Out of the clod is sped the soul,
Back to the Giver of Life to go;
Out of the shade of earth and night,
Back to the glow of realms in light.
Free is the wine from the clay of the bowl—
Out of the clod is sped the soul,
Back to the Giver of Life to go.

> This is the Voice of triumphant hope and regeneration.

Mrs. Marjorie Bell, writing from New York, sent me the following poem, with an explanation of the circumstances under which it had been composed: "My father went to bed one night woozy with the high temperature of an oncoming cold, for which he had dosed himself with aconite. He always credited the verses to this combination of circumstances. He woke suddenly with an exalted sense of creative achievement, and managed to write down the lines word for word as he dreamed them, before they eluded him." The title, she says, "came with the poem, but doesn't quite fit."

The Jealousy of Taurus

A mighty ox with trenchant horn
Thrust at the earth when it was born
He made a gash both deep and wide—
"By Jove," he cried, "'tis red inside!"

And since that day, that mighty gash
With fire and smoke and lightning flash
Pours forth a flood of liquid flame—
And thus it was Mount Etna came.

Mr. John Chamberlain tells me that he once composed a sonnet in a dream, from which, when he awoke, he was able to remember the first two lines of the sestet:

And even though the tall giraffes were tough,
And even though the tough giraffes were tall ...

Mr. E. M. Forster, in an essay called *An Outsider in Poetry* in his book *Two Cheers for Democracy*, says that he composed in a dream his only two lines of "modern poetry":

I will put down Hastings, you shall see
Companion to India as a boat gnawed.

He calls these lines modern, he says, "because they are obscure and minatory."

"COUSIN SWIFT, YOU WILL NEVER BE A POET"

SWIFT'S VERSE has for some years been out of print. The last edition was that of William Ernst Browning, published in 1910, which was neither very adequately annotated nor very well arranged. Mr. Harold Williams has now prepared and the Oxford Press produced a scholarly and handsome edition—*The Poems of Jonathan Swift*—in three volumes. There seems, however, to hang a sort of curse over the indexes to editions of Swift's poetry, which prevents one's being able to use them. The Browning edition had indexes in the fronts of the volumes which listed the poems in their printed order, but no alphabetical index and no index of first lines. The Williams edition includes, at the beginning of each volume, an index of the three volumes that lists the poems in groups of "political," "personal," etc., but no index by titles of all the pieces, and an alphabetical index that covers all three of the volumes, but proves to be a nuisance in a different way, due to the fact that the three are consecutively paged and it is usually difficult to know in which volume to look for a given poem. One of the good features of the Williams edition is three facsimiles of manuscripts of Swift's in his firm and clear and beautiful hand.

It is to be hoped that the Oxford Press will eventually bring this edition out in a single volume at a lower price.

I hasten to express this hope, yet I fear that even a cheap edition would fail to do very much to make the poetry of Swift more popular. His cousin John Dryden told him, on seeing one of his early pindaric odes, that he would never become a poet; and many people will not admit that he ever did. Yet the question of whether or not Swift is a "poet" comes down, as Leslie Stephen said in his English Men of Letters volume, to "a question of classification." "Swift's originality appears in the very fact that he requires a new class to be made for him." Leslie Stephen, it seems to me, is even too niggardly in the space that he devotes to Swift's verse. My own conviction is that it is almost as remarkable as his prose, and that a good deal of his very best writing is to be found among these five hundred or so pieces. This writing is not merely a versification of the prose of his satires and pamphlets. For there is a strong sensuous side to Swift—though, like Huysmans, he is sensitive mainly to ugly or disagreeable impressions. This comes through in the realistic similes which give a good deal of their flavor to his prose writings, and when he is dealing with certain congenial subjects such as the coins of the *Drapier's Letters*, which we seem to see and hear and handle. Swift had always a feeling for money: it stimulated his imagination, and he raised to a kind of poetry his tracts on financial questions.

But there is much more of this in his verse, and it makes him a poet of a special kind. He is inferior to Dryden and Pope in variety of color and delicacy of ear. He was too great a master of prose to be able to command entirely, though he was able to do so partly, the resources of the other technique. The sobriety and restraint which give his prose its distinction seem sometimes to impoverish his verse; his habit of hitting the nail on the head that makes the arguments of a pamphlet compelling, may produce a monotonous emphasis that deadens a development in verse.

This granted, we must recognize that Swift does successfully work in his poetry a vein hardly touched in his prose. He is here one of the most vivid portrayers of the life of the eighteenth-century city. *Morning* and *A City Shower*—of the latter of which he was rightly proud—the terrible panels of *The Progress of Virtue, The Progress of Beauty*, etc., which only Swift's strong drawing and his classic severity make tolerable—these are the products of a sharp observation hardly found in the novelists of the period. They are closer to Hogarth's engravings. Later on, he was to do Ireland superbly. *Helter Skelter*, the circuit ride of the attorneys, is a masterpiece of social caricature; so is *The Grand Question Debated*, with its picture of country-house life; so are even the *Verses Made for Women Who Cry Apples, etc.*, with Swift's feeling, sad and comic, for the lives of the women and his savoring of the wares they sell. Swift had, like Huysmans, an actual appetite for homely or sordid detail. When he is obliged to wait for the boat at Holyhead, he sits down to describe his bad accommodations, the "muddy ale and moldy bread"; when Stella is about to return from a visit, he describes to her, as if with relish, how the shabby surroundings of her home must take the place of the luxuries of the gentry:

> But now arrives the dismal day:
> She must return to *Ormond Key*:
> The coachman stopt, she lookt, and swore
> The Rascal had mistook the Door:
> At coming in you saw her stoop;
> The Entry brushed against her Hoop:
> Each Moment rising in her Airs,
> She curst the narrow winding stairs:

THE POETRY OF SWIFT

> Began a Thousand Faults to spy;
> The Ceiling hardly six Foot high;
> The smutty Wainscot full of Cracks,
> And half the Chairs with broken Backs ...

Yet all through Swift's life there reëchoes a chagrin that had preyed upon him in the poverty of his youth. The great spirit subjected to indignity will dignify that indignity itself. And so, condemned to his deanship in Dublin, he gives the misery of the Irish a kind of grandeur. The poems that he wrote in Ireland supplement his political writings: they illustrate his economic arguments with a picture of the physical degradation of the people.

Besides this, there are flights of a macabre fantasy— *Death and Daphne* and *On Cutting Down an Old Thorn* —to which he does not give scope in the matter-of-fact extravagances of his prose. And there are many pieces, always interesting and sometimes very moving, that deal directly with his personal life. Swift's self-dramatization in his poems is really one of his most brilliant achievements—whether in the pièce de résistance on the reception of the news of his death and the well-known verses on Stella and Vanessa or in the less well-known Market Hill poems and the imitations of Horace, in which he writes of his relations with Harley. The best of these poems sometimes rise to the kind of tragic irony that one finds in his prose but which has here a special personal accent: the joke that is only a joke but of which the effect is crushing:

> Deaf, giddy, helpless, left alone,
> To all my Friends a Burthen grown,
> No more I hear my Church's Bell,
> Than if it rang out for my Knell:
> At Thunder now no more I start,

Than at the Rumbling of a Cart:
Nay, what's incredible, alack!
I hardly hear a Woman's Clack.

There is nothing else quite like this in literature. The curses and sneers of Swift created a new kind of lyric.

December 8, 1937

PEGGY BACON: POET WITH PICTURES

IN NO FIELD have fashions and cliques come to play a more important role than in that of verse-reviewing. A writer who belongs to no group and has no connection with any current trend is likely not to get much noticed, let alone given a place in the anthologies. It would not be true to say that Peggy Bacon has not been appreciated and praised: her caricatures, her prints and her children's books have brought her a considerable reputation; but her volumes of pictures and verse, which contain some of the best of her work, have received almost no attention.

Miss Bacon has published two of these collections: *Animosities* and *Cat-Calls*. Here the verses help the drawings out, and we feel that we are getting her essence, as with her prints, her pastels and her paintings, we do not always do. The best of her prints and her bigger drawings are of course incomparable: she is, I suppose, the first woman artist successfully to invade the field of Hogarth, Goya and Daumier. But she sometimes attempts elaborate subjects that stagger a very feminine talent: where Hogarth is able to organize a complicated crowded print about a center of point and light that throws the whole picture into perspective, the larger groups of Peggy Bacon sometimes seem to get beyond her control and to coalesce in dark indistinctness; and in those of her larger productions where only a few figures are framed, she sometimes leaves great spaces of baldness that overbalance the wit of the rest. But these small drawings which illustrate her verses seem to me almost always quite perfect. They are as compact as medals of Pisanello, as clear as tiny plates by Callot.

Her verses have not always quite this sharpness. They are sometimes a little amateurish. But they are original both in accent and in pattern. They possess the immense distinction of not having been produced synthetically, as so much contemporary poetry is. And the work in her second volume shows an improvement over that of the first: in *Cat-Calls* there begin to appear, among the epigrams and ironic sketches, short lyrics—*Autumn Burden* and *Illusion*—which, in spite of some inexpert passages that a little more care would correct, find new words for personal moods. All the work in these books of Miss Bacon's has the mark of the authentic artist in that it does not derive from the desire to produce an impression for its own sake but pursues as its primary object what the writer really feels and thinks.

At first glance, these pictures and verses may seem waspish and a little morose. But, reëxamining them, one comes to appreciate their marvellous delicacy and fancy, their dryness, their elegance, their point—till they have become permanent sources of pleasure. This is the poetry of the ugly, the inadequate, the sordid, the ridiculous, the sad, but all distilled to a new felicity; it is the poetry of the pastoral suburban, the middle-class domestic and the human and animal young, but never kewpified or jollified or arch. The children are untidy and tend to be bad; the pets are dogs and cats, nothing more: they are not complicated by human attributes, but nobody has ever been more sensitive than Peggy Bacon is in catching the various phases of real cat and dog nature. Mamma and Poppa are none too handsome and none too smartly dressed, and the sitting-room where they read in the evenings is furnished in none too good taste. At the evening party, the women get rather silly, and the men are rather wistful old stuffed shirt-fronts. In the city, the houses are dingy, the kids dirty and the cats thin; an old horse has his nose in a feed-bag while the sparrows pick up the crumbs. In the towns, there are timid young ladies who peek out through the slits in the shutters and disdainful old parties in antiquated mansions who think nobody else lives on their street. In the country, the sun is rising on people asleep in their houses, who, on waking, will be rather astonished to find themselves confronted with one another and will make an effort to refocus their sight. In the fields, an old stump, an old shack falling down, a scarecrow with a woman's old dress and hat that seems to attract the crows. A tumbler and pills on a sick person's table; abandoned blocks and dolls on the floor; a pet bird that has turned up its toes and that will have to be buried in a candy-box. The old deformed and rundown shoes on the shelf in the cobbler's shop; the bald tailor, intent in his basement, driving his needle into somebody else's coat:

> The blackmailer
> slew the jailer
> —some distress
> and a scrap of crêpe—
> there is no jailer
> to watch the tailor,
> but nevertheless
> he can't escape.

In the midst of all this, one finds posted, as a beacon of a sort, here and there, some simple and wholesome object: a fine little glass of red wine in the center of a scalloped doily; a narrow old-fashioned clock with slender

mahogany columns; a good plate of meat, peas and pota-
toes, with the heel of a loaf of white bread, a napkin and
a mug of milk; a toy top, tipping but fixed, spinning on
a point like an etcher's tool; and a hand with long craftsman's fingers, deliberately threading a needle or holding
a spiky shell. Against all that is imperfect and dismal,
such symbols of soundness stand: the symbols of food
and work, of steadiness opposed to the flux of time, to
the futile fatigue of movement.

This is what the life of art ought to be. What it ought
not to be is rhetoric, personal or aesthetic. The trifles of
Peggy Bacon, like the fables of La Fontaine, wear well
and come to mean more the longer we know them.

April 27, 1938

TWILIGHT OF THE EXPATRIATES

The Tropic of Cancer, by Henry Miller, was published in Paris four years ago, but nobody, so far as I know, has ever reviewed it in the United States, and it seems to me to deserve some notice.

Every phase of literary opinion is responsible for its critical injustices. During the twenties, this book would have been discussed in the *Little Review,* the *Dial* and *Broom.* Today the conventional critics are evidently too much shocked by it to be able to bring themselves to deal with it—though their neglect of it cannot wholly have been determined by the reflex reactions of squeamishness. A book bound in paper and published in Paris has no chance against a book bound in cloth and brought out by a New York publisher, who will buy space to announce its appearance. The conservative literary reviews have not been so easily outraged that they would not give respectful attention to John O'Hara's *Butterfield 8* or squander space on the inferior Hemingway of *To Have and Have Not.* As for the Left-Wingers, they have ignored *The Tropic of Cancer* on the ground that it is merely a product of the decadent expatriate culture and can be of no interest to the socially minded and forward-looking present.

Expatriate Mr. Miller certainly is: he is the spokesman, par excellence, for the Left Bank; but he has produced the most remarkable book which, as far as my reading goes, has come from it in many years. *The Tropic of Cancer* is a good piece of writing; and it has also a sort of historical importance. It is the epitaph for the whole generation of American writers and artists that migrated to Paris after the war. The theme of *The Tropic of Cancer* is the lives of a group of Americans who have all more or less come to Paris with the intention of occupying themselves with literature but who have actually subsided easily into an existence almost exclusively preoccupied with drinking and fornication, varied occasionally by the reading of a book or a visit to a picture exhibition—an existence for which they muster the resources by such expedients as pimping for travellers, playing gigolo to rich old ladies and sponging on one another. The tone of the book is undoubtedly low; *The Tropic of Cancer*, in fact, from the point of view both of its happenings and of the language in which they are conveyed, is the lowest book of any real literary merit that I ever remember to have read; it makes Defoe's Newgate Calendar look like Plutarch. But if you can stand it, it is sometimes quite funny; for Mr. Miller has discovered and exploits a new field of the picaresque.

The disreputable adventures of Mr. Miller's rogues are varied from time to time with phosphorescent flights of reverie devoted to the ecstasies of art or the doom of European civilization. These passages, though old-fashioned and rhetorical in a vein of late romantic fantasy reminiscent of *Les Chants de Maldoror,* have a youthful and even ingenuous sound in queer contrast to the cynicism of the story. And there is a strange amenity of temper and style which bathes the whole composition even when it is disgusting or tiresome. It has frequently been characteristic of the American writers in Paris that they have treated pretentious subjects with incompetent style and sordid feeling. Mr. Miller has done the opposite: he has treated an ignoble subject with a sure hand at color and rhythm. He is not self-conscious and not amateurish. And he has somehow managed to be low without being really sordid.

The last episode of *The Tropic of Cancer* has a deadly ironic value. A friend of the narrator called Fillmore, who is unique among these cadgers and spongers in enjoying a small regular income, becomes entangled in an affair with a French girl, who is pregnant and declares him responsible. Poor Fillmore first drinks himself into an insane asylum; then, emerging, falls straight into the clutches of the girl and her peasant family. They reduce him to utter abjection: he is to marry her, set her father up in business. The girl quarrels with him every night over dinner. The narrator suggests to Fillmore that he run away and go back home. For the latter, the glamor is all off Paris: he has been up against the French as they really are (in general these émigrés see nobody but one another); he realizes at last that the French regard Americans as romantic idiots; and he is weepily homesick for America. He allows himself to be sent off on a train, leaving the narrator a sum of money to provide for the girl's accouchement.

But as soon as Fillmore is gone, the helpful hero, left to himself, with the money for the girl in his pocket, decides that good old Paris, after all, is a wonderful place to be. "Certainly never before," he thinks, "had I had so much in my fist at one time. It was a treat to break a thousand-franc note. I held it up to the light to look at the beautiful watermark. Beautiful money! One of the few things the French make on a grand scale. Artistically done, too, as if they cherished a deep affection even for the symbol." Ginette need never know about it; and, after all, suppose her pregnancy was all a bluff.

He goes for a drive in the Bois. Does he want to take the money, he asks himself, and return to America too? It is the first opportunity he has had. No: a great peace comes over him now. He knows that for half an hour he has money to throw away. He buys himself an excellent dinner and muses on the Seine in the setting sun. He feels it flowing quietly through him: "its past, its ancient soil, the changing climate." It is only when they are looked at close-to that human beings repel one by their ugliness; they become negligible when one can put them at a distance. A deep feeling of well-being fills him.

In retelling this incident from *The Tropic of Cancer*, have I made it more comic than it is meant to be? Perhaps: because Mr. Miller evidently attaches some importance to the vaporings of his hero on the banks of the Seine. But he presents him as he really lives, and not merely in his vaporings or his poses. He gives us the genuine American bum come to lead the beautiful life in Paris; and he lays him away forever in his dope of Pernod and dreams.

March 9, 1938

Mr. Miller, in reply to this review, wrote the *New Republic* the following letter, which appeared in the issue of May 18. I regret that I am unable to restore a passage cut by the editors.

Sir: There are several inaccuracies in Mr. Wilson's review of *Tropic of Cancer* . . .

First of all, I should like it to be known that the book has been reviewed before, by Professor Herbert West. It has been mentioned numerous times in a sensational manner by so-called reputable magazines in America. . . . The theme of the book, moreover, is not at all what Mr. Wilson describes: the theme is myself, and the narrator, or the hero, as your critic puts it, is also myself. I am not clear whether, in the last paragraph of his review, Mr. Wilson meant to imply that Fillmore is the genuine American bum, or myself. If he means the narrator, then it is me, because I have painstakingly indicated throughout the book that the hero is myself. I don't use "heroes," incidentally, nor do I write novels. I am the hero, and the book is myself. . . .

Perhaps the worst mistake which the eminent critic makes in his review is to say that because a book is bound in paper and published in Paris, it has no chance against a book bound in cloth and sold in New York. This is the very contrary of the truth. Without any hocus-pocus of the American publicity agents, almost entirely by word-of-mouth recommendations, *Tropic of Cancer* has already gone into several editions at a price which for Europe is prohibitive. It is now being translated into three languages. It may be procured at leading book-stores in practically every important city of the world excepting those of America, England, Germany and Russia. It has been reviewed enthusiastically by some of the foremost critics of Europe. If it has not yet brought me riches, it has at any rate brought me fame and recognition. And, whether it is given notice by American reviewers or not, Americans coming to Europe buy it, as they once bought *Ulysses* and *Lady Chatterley's Lover*.

A conspiracy of silence, like censorship, can defeat its own ends. Sometimes it pays *not* to advertise. Sometimes the most effective, realistic thing to do is to be impractical, to fly in the face of the wind. The Obelisk Press took my book on faith, against all commercial wisdom. The results have been gratifying in every way. I should like to add that the Obelisk Press will publish any book of quality which the ordinary commercial publisher refuses, for one reason or another, to handle. Any writer with guts who is unable to get a hearing in America might do well to look to Paris. And damn all the critics anyway! The best publicity for a man who has anything to say is silence.

Henry Miller

Paris, France

THE PLEASURES OF LITERATURE

By a Book Lover

WITH HOW SURE an expectation of solace, amid the turmoil and perplexities of our time, do I turn, when the
fires of evening are lit, to my silent companions of the
library! Here the din of the city dies away; here the
feverish antagonisms of men reveal themselves *sub specie
aeternitatis*. Here may I be rapt as by a magic carpet to
those miraculous isles of Greece—"lily on lily, that o'er-
lace the sea"; or to journey with the returning Ulysses
among the enchantments and terrors of Homer's golden
day; or I may bid imagination run riot with Shakespeare
and his carnival fellows of the spacious days of great
Elizabeth, assuming the motley of their bawdy humors,
the purple of their splendid passions, the mourning of
their fantastic revenges; or I may prowl with Dickens or
Balzac among the mysteries of the dark modern cities or
lurch with George Borrow along the hedgerows; or I
may revel in the thousand and one tales, more enthralling
than the *Arabian Nights,* of Voragine's *Golden Legend,*
Vasari's *Lives of the Painters* or Havelock Ellis's *Psychology of Sex.*

What a sovereign remedy is a book for the distempers
both of the mind and of the body! How it protects us
against sordidness and boredom! Shall I ever forget the

exquisite delights of my first perusal of Congreve's plays, as I rode back and forth on the elevated, the subway or the electric car, in my days as a "cub reporter" on one of our great metropolitan dailies—an exercise which, I like to believe, had the effect of tempering my style against the pressures of newspaper writing? Or the ecstasy of my discovery at college, and at almost the same moment, of Dante, the greatest poet, and Plato, the greatest proseman, of all time?—how, cycling alone in the Princeton lanes, leafy and fragrant with May, I would declaim the ringing tercets of the former!—how, to the fluttering of the pages of my lexicon, the paragraphs of the *Symposium* or the *Phaedo* would commence to grow incandescent with a radiance that seemed steadily to glow more brightly till the radiance of morning itself made luminous the Jersey murk!

With what relish—nay, what famished appetite!—did I consume in my rare leisure moments the only book I read at Plattsburg in the summer of 1916, Anatole France's *Thaïs*—the enjoyment of which and the bottles of milk that we drank after our parching perspiring marches, as well as of my conversations with the Eli-bred Charles R. Walker, then at the peak of his early brilliance and his eye, as his comrades were wont to say, "in a fine frenzy rolling," are my only agreeable memories of an experience which could but convince me that, though I might perhaps do something with literature, I should never make an acceptable soldier. How Michelet's *History of France* later peopled the hills and the fields of Lorraine with the armies of Charles the Bold as I plodded among them in khaki—making them seem so eroded and worn, so patinated and yet so blighted, by that history of traditional quarrels which was still going on at the time and in which I found myself involved that I felt, with how poignant a pull!, the advantages of my own America, where we were not oppressed so much by history. Did I not shoulder the thick volumes of Renan in my burdensome blanket-roll and lug them to German Trier, considerably hampering my movements, but maintaining uninterrupted my access to an admirable spirit, international and humanistic, at a time when such qualities were by no means in evidence either among his countrymen or in the nation he had more or less regarded as his intellectual fatherland?

O indispensable books! O comforting alternative worlds, where all discords are finally resolved, if not by philosophy, then by art—how without you should we reconcile ourselves to this troublesome actual world? How right is Mary M. Colum when she tells us that one of the most terrible wounds that have been dealt to the human spirit by the hand of dictatorship is its constriction of the dream-life of humanity! For how should the palaces of statesmanship flourish where the cathedrals of thought are forbidden?

At least that is the way I am getting to feel as I read, in the more serious-minded reviews, the current discussions of literature. They are driving me right back into the arms of Charles Lamb and Walter Pater and John Addington Symonds: old bookworms whom a diet of belles-lettres had rendered a little bit boozy, but who did promote the appreciation of literature.

In my youth, we used to read James Huneker, who, chaotic and careless though he was, made you ravenous to devour his favorite writers. Later on, we read T. S. Eliot, who, though as sober as Huneker was boisterous, still stimulated the appetite for poetry and made the poets seem full of exciting surprises. But Eliot's criticism was completely non-historical. He seemed to behold the writing of the ages abstracted from time and space and spread before him in one great exhibition, of which, with imperturbable poise, he conducted a comparative appraisal. This was of course an intellectual triumph, and his essays had their very great value; but it was a feat that could only be performed at the cost of detaching books from all the other affairs of human life; and the author of this complaint used at that time to try to encourage the practitioners of literature to interest themselves in the development of society and in the larger events of the world —as most great literature, after all, has done. Even the non-moral and non-doctrinal Shakespeare, whose detachment seems so bafflingly consummate, presents issues— as Orson Welles's *Julius Caesar* has recently emphasized —of which, if you had read only Eliot on Shakespeare, you could never have had any notion. The economic disasters of the thirties have had, therefore, a useful effect in compelling attention to the "social significance" of novels, poems and plays. But the trouble is that social significance has now become an obsession. Today one is confronted by the spectacle of a philosophico-social criticism of a character purely analytic, which almost invariably comes to negative conclusions, and a politico-social criticism which, without making even the attempt of the other to ascertain the position of the writer in the bigger historical frame, is content to give him a high or low grade corresponding to the degree of his readiness to subscribe to the mechanical slogans of this or that political faction.

The young, usually subject to exaggerated enthusiasms, are today not enthusiastic—not enthusiastic, that is, about books: they merely approve or disapprove when a book does or does not suit their politics. But, seriously, I think it a pity that they do not learn to read for pleasure. They may presently find that an acquaintance with the great works of art and thought is the only real insurance possible against the barbarism of the time.

So back, I say, to the Renaissance, with its hunger and thirst for books! Back to Matthew Arnold and the "best that has been thought and felt in the world"! Back to John Keats first looking into Chapman's Homer! Back to Karl Marx reading Aeschylus through every year!

Edmund Wilson (not Christopher Morley)

January 29, 1938

COLD WATER ON BAKUNIN

Mr. E. H. Carr is an odd phenomenon—perhaps a symptom of the decay of Great Britain. A former member of the English diplomatic service, with an unusual equipment of languages, he now uses his knowledge of Europe to write the biographies of nineteenth-century revolutionists. These biographies have certain indisputable merits, to which I shall revert in a moment; but what is odd is that Mr. Carr should choose to write them. He has obviously had no first-hand experience of revolutionary movements or revolutionaries, and he seems to feel very little sympathy with them. Yet, on the other hand, he does not condemn them; he seems merely to regard them as futile. But, even in depicting them as wrongheaded and ineffective, he does not seem, even by implication, to be criticizing their revolutionary theories from any contrasting point of view—even one of universal irony. There is, to be sure, a slight accent of irony discernible in his treatment of his subjects, but the tone is mainly one of amused condescension. We wonder sometimes why Mr. Carr should have gone to the trouble of exploring these inaccessible materials and getting up these complicated subjects—he has written books on Marx, Bakunin and Herzen, as well as one on Dostoevsky —merely in order to lift the eyebrow over them; and we ask ourselves whether Mr. Carr may not be simply a Foreign Office Englishman who has been led more or less accidentally, through his knowledge of German and Russian, to do some work in an historical field hitherto not much worked in English.

In his new book, *Michael Bakunin*, Mr. Carr has written the best of his biographies. It has the faults of his other books—the dependence on colorless clichés, which makes impossible any vividness of evocation; the never intermitting British chill, which is always putting Bakunin in his place and which gets on one's nerves with its characterization of all Bakunin's projects as "interesting," all his ideas as "remarkable": "On the day of Bakunin's arrival in Lyons, municipal elections were held, and the short-lived and rather ridiculous Committee of Public Safety abdicated in favor of the new municipal council." . . . "Bakunin decided on the creation of a new revolutionary organ which was called, with singular inappropriateness, the Committee for the Saving of France." . . . "One other decision of the Bâle Congress had a certain piquant interest." . . . "The stalwarts of Le Locle had recently begun to publish a fortnightly journal entitled *Progrès,* devoted to the propagation of the aims of the International." . . . "The defunct Committee of Public Safety had, in a moment of enthusiasm, followed the famous though short-lived precedent of 1848 and turned the local factories into national workshops. The Municipal Council inherited this blessing from the Committee." Bakunin did sometimes conceive designs which might be characterized as "singularly inappropriate"; and revolutionary organizations do certainly have their humors. But why should it be assumed that there is something intrinsically absurd about the movement for national workshops, the decisions of the International or the agitation in favor of that body carried on by the Jura watchmakers?

Here, as in his book on Marx, Mr. Carr tells us everything about his subject except what it is all about. If one had no independent knowledge of Marx and Bakunin, one might almost wonder, after reading these biographies, why Mr. Carr had thought the subjects important enough to write about. Even when he indicates their importance, he does nothing to make us understand it; for he has accomplished the singular feat of telling the stories of the leaders of working-class movements without dealing with those conditions of working-class life under pressure of which they came into existence. For Mr. Carr, the labor movements of the nineteenth century tend to present themselves merely in terms of a more or less inept parliamentary politics. Nor does he really understand the psychology of these men who have chosen the working-class side, who have rejected the whole complex of organized society yet who have to continue to live in it when they no longer want to be of it; who must work underground, who spend decades in exile, always in danger of prison and wasting their emotions and their energies in sterile political quarrels and the bickerings of émigré life.

Yet this writer, it must be said, through his very detachment from the struggle, is in a position to perform certain services which biographers who are socialists or anarchists themselves are not always able to get around to. For one thing, he is careful and impartial in checking up on matters of evidence. Old party traditions and loyalties mean nothing to him. And for another thing, he devotes to the personal aspects of the careers of his revolutionists an attention that they do not usually get at the hands of the narrowly political biographer, who is interested only in the movement and systematically disregards the family life and the love affairs of his hero. Mr. Carr has brought out facts about Bakunin which are important and unfamiliar. He is at his best in the first part of this book, in which he is dealing with Bakunin's life in Russia. Mr. Carr has a special knowledge of Russia, and he is here occupied with a milieu not alien to him: the country life of a landowner's family. The story of the Bakunin household, with their susceptibility to tender emotion and to mad intoxication by ideas, sounds much like Tolstoy or Turgenev. Mr. Carr seems to have established incontrovertibly that the "behavior-pattern" of all Bakunin's life was fixed by his family relationships. Michael Bakunin was the oldest boy of a family of ten boys and girls: he dominated his brothers through his age and his sisters by reason of his sex. He was, on his own confession, in love with one of his sisters, and he seems to have been jealous of them all. He was always inciting the children to rebellion against their father. When his sisters began to have admirers and marry, Michael would exert himself to spoil their relations with their suitors and husbands. Later in life, he did the same thing with other women; but he never became any woman's lover. He was apparently impotent all his life. In Siberia, when he was forty-four, he married an eighteen-year-old girl, who eventually, while still living with Bakunin, had two children by another man.

One cannot tell whether Mr. Carr is aware of the obvious connection between Bakunin's incurable impotence and his orgiastic passion for destruction, though he does see that Bakunin's hatred of the State was a prolongation of his quarrel with his father, and seems to suggest that his playing at conspiracies which did not exist outside his imagination was carried over from the plots of his childhood, as his pathological borrowing was a survival of infantile dependence. I am not sure, however, that Mr. Carr really explains Bakunin's conversion to the cause of revolution. Bakunin, during his youth in Russia, had been a loyal subject of the Tsar; when he had left it for western Europe it had been simply to see the world; he seems to have been nearly thirty before he began moving toward the Left with the Young Hegelian movement in Germany; he did not declare himself an atheist till he was fifty; and he did not come to believe in the revolutionary role of the working class or to formulate the creed of anarchism until 1866, when he was fifty-two. It may be that Bakunin was driven by the logic of politics and ideas to take each of the later steps of this progress: the last of them followed on his disillusion, as the result of the defeat of the Poles, with insurgent nationalism as a democratic revolutionary force. But what were really the determining factors in his taking that first step which counts? At what moment, so relatively late in life, was the attitude formed in the household at home transferred to contemporary society?

With the comic aspects of Michael Bakunin's career Mr. Carr is appreciative and skillful. How Bakunin unwittingly enrolled as an ally the Tsar's principal agent in Switzerland and sent him to Russia to report for him on revolutionary activities and to intercede with Bakunin's family in his efforts to induce them to surrender to him his share of the family estate, and how he finally compelled this agent, who was masquerading as a retired Russian general, to help him out with a considerable sum of money, which the man actually obtained from the Tsar as expenditure in the line of duty; how Bakunin persuaded one of his Italian followers, who had just inherited a fortune from his father, to allow him to blow it in, with no calculation of means or costs, on a magnificent house and estate designed to be a home for Bakunin and an asylum for revolutionists, how Bakunin wrote his wife to join him, as he was now in a position to keep her in comfort, how the money was all swallowed up before the place was finished, how the young Italian was horrorstruck and indignantly repudiated Bakunin, how, when poor Antonia arrived, Bakunin could not bear to tell her that the place was not really his and that the owner did not want them to live in it, and how he finally ran away rather than face this—these are enchanting and fabulous stories, which Mr. Carr has handled well.

Yet even here one a little resents the tone. After all, there must have been something in Bakunin—something great-visioned and noble—which enabled him to command such sympathy, to excite people with such extravagant dreams. As Mr. Carr does not show us the need which goaded the proletariat to go to Bakunin for leadership, so, though he calls Bakunin a "genius" and "great," he never gives us a sense of the power which he was able to devote to their service. The anarchist movement, after all, has long survived its prophet; and if it owes its founder Bakunin something of its lack of common sense, it owes him, also, something of its energy, its audacity and its humanity. Even such imprudent bravery as that of Bakunin in the Dresden revolution, hopeless, inconsistent politically and paid for by long and terrible years of prison, has had a value for the human spirit in its struggle against the timid self-interest perpetuated in human institutions. This exploit of Bakunin's was the kind of mistake that Marx would never have made; but it was prompted by a kind of exuberance, an irrepressible magnanimity, that gave Bakunin, in this one respect, a real superiority over Marx.

December 7, 1938

SHUT UP THAT RUSSIAN NOVEL

The Soviet Union is an immense expanse of territory, including the extremes of geographical contrast and inhabited by some hundred and seventy-five million people of varying races, social antecedents and degrees of education. These people, like people elsewhere, are compelled to make considerable exertions in order to survive in their environment; and when they are not eating, drinking or starving, quarrelling or copulating, idling or amusing themselves, they devote a certain amount of attention to organizing representative bodies for the purpose of safeguarding their social groups and to elaborating disciplines and devices to make possible their higher development.

These statements seem obvious enough; but if all that you knew about Russia were derived from our political press, you would hardly have gained any inkling of them. The name of the Soviet Union, for all the millions of souls it comprises, has ceased to signify a real section of the earth. It has become a battle-cry, a term of abuse, a counter in a political game. All this is because in this area an attempt has been lately going forward to vary the forms of social organization in such a way as to make it possible for the whole population to share in the facilities for higher human development instead of allowing these facilities to be controlled by certain specialized members of the community who enjoy them at the expense of the rest.

During the period just after the Russian Revolution, the USSR was a bugbear: all the hundred and forty million Russians were supposed to be what were called Communists—that is, greedy and murderous barbarians who wanted to take people's Ford cars away from them. Then gradually the Soviet Union came to mean for the American Left intellectuals the realization of the ideal modern community: American democracy and technical efficiency plus socialist elimination of unearned profits. For a great many Jews, it has figured the fulfillment of their millennial hopes; for the Stalinists, it has come to be the war-cry of a kind of international patriotism with which they have deafened themselves; for the Trotskyists, a lost fatherland, which would be wonderful if Trotsky were only there; for the Communists in general, a slogan in the struggle against the capitalist world; for the Marxists in general, the keystone of a thesis—that is, of an intellectual construction which enables one to feel safe and smug without studying contemporary realities or involving oneself in them in any way. More recently it has come more and more, on the part of dissatisfied middle-class persons, to be a pretext for making oneself disagreeable, for feeling comfortably superior to one's neighbors or for enjoying a vicarious sadism. For the liberals, it has always been a piece in a game as simple as checkers—a game which takes place in the liberals' minds. The checkers in this game are either white or black—that is, either desirable or undesirable. In the case of the Soviet Union, it has at times been a little bit difficult to make sure whether the checker representing it should be assigned to the liberals' side or to that of the liberals' opponents. At first, it was supposed to be definitely black; but later it was thought to be definitely white. Just now it is causing trouble by becoming more and more unmanageable for the appropriate moves of a white checker: some continue to try to play the game on the assumption that the piece is still white; others have decided to call it black. And in the meantime the one hundred and seventy-five million people, who know as well as you or I that they are people and not a bogey, a utopia, a millennium, a slogan, a thesis, a neurosis or a checker either black of white, are experiencing the same sensations that make other human beings contented or wretched and taking part in a social drama of immense importance and interest.

For what has been happening in Russia *is* important and interesting; but it is a pity that so very few people really exert themselves to look into it. There are, it is true, certain difficulties in the way; but it is possible to find out a good deal more than you might gather from reading the political journals. The truth is that most of the people who like to talk about Russia would much rather cherish their myths than give attention to such reports as are available and try to draw from them objective conclusions.

We have lately had a number of adverse reports—by Fred Beal, Eugene Lyons and Victor Serge—which have been valuable because they contained a certain amount of new information, but which, taken without reference to anything else, have simply produced a fresh myth: the myth of the False Revolution. The writer of the present article has even been taken to task by Mr. Lyons in the *Saturday Review of Literature* for describing a statue of Lenin in the lobby of an opera-house in Leningrad as having "a look both piercing and genial, at once as if he were giving back to labor what it had made and inviting it to share for the first time in its heritage of human culture, and as if he were opening out to humanity as a whole a future of which for the first time they were to recognize themselves the masters, with the power to create without fear whatever they had minds to imagine." These ideas, asserts Mr. Lyons, are certainly not "Mr. Lenin's" but "Mr. Wilson's." Yet these ideas *were* certainly Lenin's: he was expounding them all his life. And the statue for its purpose was a good one, in which the sculptor had succeeded in expressing some such feeling as I put into words.

What, then, is now causing Mr. Lyons to talk as if this Lenin had never existed, as if the Bolshevik Revolution had never seemed to offer anything that the world might have been glad to have? If the Bolsheviks had not announced, from the moment of their coming to power, the aims that I have imputed to Lenin, Mr. Lyons would never have gone, as he did, to live in the Soviet Union, would never, as he so earnestly did, have propagandized in its behalf. His reaction now from one-hundred-percent loyalty takes the form of one-hundred-percent disapproval. His attitude seems to be that he has simply made a dreadful mistake. In other words, he is as biassed as before. His recent book, *Assignment in Utopia,* interesting though it is, is a monody of complaint. There is very little attempt—and this is true of Mr. W. H. Chamberlin, too—really to understand the Russians, to explain in terms of Russian character and wider historical analogy the development of the Bolshevik Revolution. Mr. Lyons is disappointed and angry and won't play with the Russians any more. He does not care to make any effort to form a realistic opinion. It will take centuries, he tells us (I quote him from memory), for humanity to digest such an event. Well, that may be true for the long-view historian; but for the rest of us at the present time, the Soviet Union is part of our lives, one of the phenomena of the world in which we find ourselves; and we must not only be as well-informed as possible about it, we must try to judge it as coolly as possible.

One enlightening piece of evidence on recent conditions in Russia is a book called *Un Mineur Français Chez les Russes* by a French trade unionist named Kléber Legay, who visited the Soviet Union in the autumn of 1936. M. Legay is a militant labor leader, who is not, however, a Communist and who had been critical of the so-called Stakhanovist methods adopted for increasing production in Russia. He was induced by his Communist colleagues to go and see for himself, and he was promised full freedom to travel where he pleased and to talk personally with the Russian miners. But the moment Legay arrived, he was taken in hand by a guide, and he was kept for eight days in Moscow and compelled, very much against his wish, to march in a parade reviewed by Stalin. The French delegates, however, asserted their independence by refusing either to sing or to keep in step. He was allowed to visit some factories, where he discovered that the accounts of rates of pay which had been given him by the guides and officials were invariably contradicted by the testimony of the workers; and that, as soon as the authorities became aware of the persistency with which he was checking, they put an end to his investigations.

At last he was taken, as had been agreed, on a tour of the Don Basin; but when he had got there, he was not allowed to leave the train on which he lived and slept, except under the usual escort. The same discrepancy between fact and publicity appeared. Contrary to what he had been told by his guide, he found women at the bottom of the mines engaged in the heaviest kind of work. This underground work by women has been forbidden, he tells us, in all other, including the fascist, countries. At the mouth of the mine, young men with guns were standing guard over these women and over men of sixty; in the depths were more men with guns, who were squatting in the darkness of a corner and seemed to be trying to conceal themselves from the visitors. A mine worker's home which he insisted upon exploring revealed an appallingly low standard of living. The family told him that they earned more money but lived considerably worse than before the Revolution; and one of the officials put a stop to this by glaring fiercely and speaking sharply to the husband. Later, Legay's guides explained that the man had been drunk, though he had not observed any signs of it. As for the Stakhanovists, they had been raised out of the rank and file and had been given, like Ford service men, the pro-management point of view of employees on the fringes of the governing groups. They were the equivalent of our "loyal workers." M. Legay was at pains to ascertain how wages and programs of work were determined. He discovered, he says, that the mine administration makes out a budget for each mine and that if the workers find in practice that the fraction allotted them does not amount to a living wage, their only redress is to prove to the management that money can be saved from other expenses—in which case they may take the difference. If they cannot establish this to the mine administration's satisfaction, they must simply go to work at the wages prescribed. They have, of course, no right to strike; and the young men with guns are there to prevent them from attempting to do so. In the matter of planning production, the Party officials and the union officials are apparently all-powerful and final; they are themselves controlled by the Party. The engineers have little to say; but they are made entirely responsible for the carrying out of the program. If the program proves impossible of execution, they are charged with sabotage and shot.

Before he had been allowed to visit the mines, M. Legay had been subjected to a good deal of determined pressure in an effort to extract from him a general endorsement of the achievements of the Soviet Union. But he refused to give out statements or make speeches, and even insisted, at banquets, on drinking his toasts in water.

Yet even here, where we do have unquestionably an expert foreign opinion on workers' conditions in Russia, M. Legay—like Mr. Chamberlin and Mr. Lyons—tends to judge what he saw in the Soviet Union on the basis of the standards of the more advanced countries plus an ideal of socialist society. In France, he declares, whole departments which had been devastated during the war were reconstructed under the capitalist system in less than ten years' time, whereas in Russia the roads were still bad, the houses crude and the people dirty, after twenty years of what was supposed to be socialism. The point is that complaints of this kind are out of order in connection with Russia. This tone is natural enough in view of the Soviet pretensions, but one ought to get past one's impatience. One ought to take into account what Russia was like before the Revolution. The roads were always bad; the people were always dirty. They had no standards to restore like the French. And so with the new social structure of Russia, which turns out, for people like Kléber Legay, to present so different an aspect from that which he had been led to expect. It is quite obvious that the Soviet Union has developed a new class-stratification; but this phenomenon should be studied, not denounced. Why was such a development inevitable? What conclusions should we draw from it about Marxist theory?

Marx and Lenin predicted correctly that the old class-stratifications would carry over into socialist society in the shape of inequality of privilege and the varying rates of pay which it would not be easy to eliminate in view of the varying abilities and habits of people who had been bred under the old system. In other words, the socialist rulers would find that they could not persuade, say, a physician or the director of a theater to contribute to the creation of the communist humanity if they fed him and lodged him like a peasant. Karl Marx had given most of his thought to the future of the Western countries, in which bourgeois democracy and industry had already run their full course. In his last years, he was making special efforts to study the case of Russia, at the instigation of Russian revolutionists who had asked him whether a mainly feudal country like theirs might not skip some of the stages of Marxist development, and go straight from Russian village communism to socialist collectivism. Later on, Lenin did try to skip them, but was soon forced, with bitter laments over the short-comings of his countrymen, to allow capitalist commerce some further scope through the measures of the New Economic Period. Yet he never seems to have foreseen the danger that, in a society just struggling out of feudal-ism and only beginning to master machinery and to claim the career open to the talents, a natural tendency to re-produce the history of the bourgeois countries might prove stronger than socialist principles. In the Soviet Union today, twenty years after the Bolshevik Revolu-tion, they seem to have ended by evolving, much as we have done in the United States, a system of government by political bosses and an industrial and financial ex-ploitation of those who have only muscle by those who have clever wits, and to have subsided to the low general level of intelligence in regard to public affairs which is inevitable for a community in which most of the people have only recently learned to read and write and have never had a chance to own anything.

One ought not to be indignant about this. One should look, not for villains, but for natural causes. Evasion of responsibility is one of the Russian vices: the Russians so dread making decisions that they usually pass them on, if possible, to the authorities higher up; they thus create their own despots. And closely involved with this habit is the national tendency to lie, which verges upon and merges into the oriental. The difficulty that they seem always to have had in meeting a situation squarely, in responding with a straight answer to a straight question, even in trusting their own constancy of purpose, has greatly complicated both their industry and their politics. The shifting moods and susceptible imaginations which have enabled them to produce their great novelists and poets, their great composers and actors, have not fitted them for statesmanship or organization. This gives rise to brutality in the governing groups; but those groups —though our critics of the Soviet Union no longer mention the fact—have always had their heroic element: the public spirit of those more conscientious, more constructive or more energetic persons who have tried to make themselves responsible for seeing to it that things do sometimes get done. How such persons are faring at the present time in relation to the racketeers of the Revolution, it is impossible for a foreigner to know; but one must not forget that such people have played a great role in Russia and that even the purges of Stalin can hardly have made them extinct.

One must also remember that the Soviet Union has suffered terribly for her socialist principles; and that her political ills have been aggravated by the ostracism or suspicion on the part of the rest of the world that the announcement of those principles has incurred. Here the Russian imagination has been playing a role of a kind which might perhaps have been impossible for a more prosaic or practical people: if the Soviets have been bogging down, at this very bad moment for all the world, through Russian executive incompetence and mechanical ineptitude, if they have been betrayed by Russian bureaucratism and their habit of passing the buck, they have at least been the first to introduce into the domain of actual statesmanship, to impress ineffaceably on the mind of the world, the ideal of the classless society. But it has, of course, been partly the fault of this very imagination that we have made the Soviet Union a myth. We have fallen under the spell of the often brilliant Soviet publicity just as we used to do under that of the Russian novel. Yet what we need at the present time is to try to see the Soviets realistically. We should not, for example, be drawn into supporting a war against Japan in order to defend a myth called "the Workers' Fatherland" any more than we should spend our energy fighting a mythical monster called "Stalin." The Russians, after taking as many losses in the interests of ideal revolutionary ends as any people can be expected to do, have, it seems, settled down for the present to a new kind of stratified society dominated by a new kind of governing class. The situation deserves sympathetic but soberly sociological attention. So long as we persist in imagining those one hundred and seventy-five million people as either a nightmare or a New Jerusalem, we shall never be able to deal with them. Let us shut up that Russian novel.

April 6, 1938

MARXISM AT THE END OF THE THIRTIES

MARXISM IS IN relative eclipse. An era in its history has ended. It may be worth while at this moment to look back and try to see what has happened.

Let us begin by asking ourselves what we mean, whether we really mean anything definite and fixed, when we casually use the word "Marxism."

The Marxism of Karl Marx himself was, in its original form, a mixture of old-fashioned Judaism, eighteenth-century Rousseauism and early nineteenth-century utopianism. Marx assumed that capitalist society had corrupted the human race by compelling it to abandon spiritual values for the satisfactions of owning things: he believed that the day would arrive when the spirit would come back into its own, when humanity would destroy its false idols and the sheep be set off from the goats: this could only be accomplished by communism—i.e. the common ownership of the means of production which would make possible a society without classes.

Friedrich Engels, the son of a Rhineland manufacturer, who had worked in the Manchester branch of the family textile business and been horrified by the misery of the working class, turned Marx's attention to political economy and supplied him with data on the industrial system. They had both come to the conclusion that the economic factor was of fundamental importance in the development of human society; and, taking over from the philosophy of Hegel his principle of revolutionary change, they evolved a picture of history in which the machinery of progress was represented as a process of continual class conflict. Every important change in the methods providing the necessaries of life gave rise to new social-economic classes, which had to struggle with the obsolete classes in order to get control of the machine. The bourgeoisie had contended with and disposed of the feudal system, which was obstructing the freedom of the merchant to trade and the freedom of the worker to hire himself that were necessary for the successful functioning of the early competitive phases of capitalism; and the industrial proletariat would, in turn, do the same thing to the capitalist system, when this, in its later phases, should prove obstructive to the logical development of large-scale industry and financial monopoly into the single centralized system which could only be run by the state.

Marx and Engels, therefore, did what they could to promote the success of labor organizations which aimed at the enfranchisement of the working class or at procuring better pay or conditions: the English Chartist movement and the Communist League of the forties, the Workers' International of the sixties and seventies; and they tried to convince the members of these movements that they, the representatives of the working class, were enacting leading roles in the Marxist drama of history.

This drama, as imagined by Marx on the eve of the revolution of 1848, was to move swiftly to a catastrophic climax which would be followed by something in the nature of a millennium. Engels was envisaging the future in terms of the French Revolution plus the Apocalypse. But when, later, parliamentary machinery was set up in that feudal Germany which had made the background for the thought of both men, the German socialists who had been trained on Marx but who were now able to get themselves elected to the Reichstag began to decide that there was nothing inevitable about the social-economic impasse and the class-war Armageddon which Marx had been predicting. Since the pressure of the working class had been effective in securing certain reforms, there was perhaps, after all, no reason to believe that the socialist aims might not be accomplished by orderly and gradual legislation. And Marx himself in his later years began to concede that in democratic countries such as England, the United States and Holland, the socialist revolution might be effected through peaceful parliamentary methods—though he thought this would be likely to stimulate a revolt of the outvoted reactionaries.

Karl Marx sometimes praised the achievements of the democratic countries, as when he backed the cause of the North during the American Civil War; but more often —it represents the bent of his own somber and savage personality—he talks in terms of Armageddon, and Armageddon is what he leads us to expect. He even applauded the Commune, when the workers and soldiers of Paris rose against the bourgeois government and held the city two months—though the procedure of the Commune was a good deal more drastic than that which he had contemplated. He had never believed in the possibility of simply abolishing bourgeois institutions and setting up socialist ones in their place, which was what the Communards had attempted, but had expected that the proletarian dictatorship would begin by taking over the machinery of the existing bourgeois state.

It ought, also, to be noted here that one can find in the whole immense work of Marx and Engels a considerable variety of attitudes toward the main problems with which they were concerned. In the first place, there are two personalities involved, and their emphasis is somewhat different. Engels left to himself, as he was after Marx's death, was more tolerant and flexible politically, and insisted somewhat less on the materialistic side of what they called their Dialectical Materialism; and Karl Marx had within his own nature tendencies so strongly divergent that his formidable machinery of logic never succeeded in making them consistent: he was at the same time a moralist and prophet, who wanted to blast a generation of vipers, and a scientific student of history, who aimed at an objective analysis of economic processes. Add to this that the points of view of Marx and Engels, both, varied in relation to the apparent imminence or the apparent improbability of a revolutionary working-class movement in which they could take an active part; and that the young fighters of '48, who saw the industrial worker on one side of the barricades and the capitalist exploiter on the other, never quite came to terms with the elderly observers of the years of their exile in England, who were forced now to take account of the unexpected situations to which the capitalist system gave rise in its later and more complicated phases.

The writings of Marx and Engels thus lend themselves to being exploited, very much as the Scriptures have been, to furnish texts for a variety of doctrines; and there have even been different Marxist canons prepared by the different creeds. The German Social Democrats did not hesitate to tamper with the texts themselves; and the Russians of the Marx-Engels Institute, in publishing these texts as they were written, were at pains to provide a commentary which supplied the "correct" interpretation.

II

Marxism first reached Russia as early as 1868, when a translation of *Das Kapital* was published there, and it began to take hold in the eighties, after the Terrorist movement had culminated in the assassination of Alexander II. But as the Germans had made Marxism respectable, academic and parliamentarian, so in Russia, of necessity an outlawed movement, it became, in its most effective form, narrow, concentrated, grim and cruel. In Russia, the first problem of the radical was to get rid of a feudal autocracy which would not even hear of a constitution and which excluded the bourgeois liberals from its institutions of learning.

Vladimir Ulyanov, who called himself Lenin, belonged to a section of the professional classes which had been hard hit in the eighties. His father, the director of schools for the province of Simbirsk on the Volga, had made his own career, an energetic and honorable one, which had earned him a patent of nobility, during the period of the educational reforms inspired by Alexander II, and had been prematurely retired from his post and forced to see his work undone when the reaction of Alexander III came to punish the murder of his predecessor. Lenin's elder brother, a student at the University of St. Petersburg, became involved in a plot to carry on the work of the Terrorists by assassinating Alexander III, but was caught by the police and hanged. The older Ulyanov had just died of a stroke, perhaps partly as a result of chagrin, and Vladimir was now head of the family. He profoundly admired his mother, who found herself everywhere ostracized as a result of her son's execution; and the succession of family misfortunes caused the iron to enter his soul. During his first eager years of young manhood, he was to find his own progress brutally blocked. As the result of a student demonstration in which he had played no important part, he was dismissed from the University of Kazan on suspicion as the brother of the Terrorist; and he was forbidden to study a profession either at home or abroad. In this period of frustration, he read Marx.

The harshness of the Tsarist autocracy inevitably called forth harshness on the part of the groups who were fighting it; and Russian Marxism took on some of the characteristics of the Terrorist movement of the seventies. The band of trained and dedicated revolutionists projected by Lenin in *What Is To Be Done?*, his pamphlet of 1902, and afterwards realized by him in the Bolshevik and Communist parties is a conception not to be found in Marx, who had never got much further as an organizer than drafting programs and presiding at meetings for the Communist League and the Workers' International. Lenin, confronted with the ignorance of the illiterate Russian masses, had frankly to propose that they should be directed by a nucleus of revolutionary intellectuals; and, confronted with the ineffectual loquacity of the common run of Russian intelligentsia, he had to insist that these upper-class leaders of the proletarian movement should not be merely talkers or even thinkers, but persons who would work actively for the Party and who would be ready to take real responsibility. The springs of Lenin's own activity were profound, irresistible, instinctive. His prime motivations were probably the overpowering hatred of suffering of which Gorky so emphatically speaks, combined with a passion for combat that took a curiously impersonal form and made him regard himself as a naked historical force pitted against other such forces. He had disciplined himself in such a way that the emotion always fed the conviction, and the conviction always led to action. This process was brought to a climax when the Tsarist regime involved Russia in the long devastation and slaughter of what Lenin insisted on characterizing as the Imperialist War.

The fact that the Provisional Government of Kerensky desired to continue the war and that it did not seem at all disposed to distribute land or food to the starving Russian masses would thus in itself have been almost enough to make Lenin resolve to overthrow it, even without the mesmeric driving force provided by the Marxist conception of history. People like the Menshevik Martov quite correctly pointed out that Lenin was throwing overboard the procedure expressly prescribed by Marx and formerly accepted by Lenin himself, in not waiting till a bourgeois "democratic" state had made the transition from the Tsarist autocracy to the socialist state of the workers. When Marx had been questioned by young Russians as to whether it would be possible for Russia, with its ancient peasant communes, to pass straight to a socialist economy without traversing all the stages of large-scale capitalist exploitation, he had, despite his earlier approval of the Commune, expressed himself as very doubtful.

But Lenin, for all his endless polemics, was little worried by Marxist theory: he was preoccupied not with ideas, but with actual current events, watching intently for the break, any break, that might make possible the destruction of the Tsardom. When the moment did come during the war, he saw the flimsiness and the impracticability of the bourgeois Provisional Government, and he supplanted it with a new kind of government based on the councils (*soviets*) of workers, peasants and soldiers which, as soon as the grip of the Tsar was relaxed, had been gravitating in 1917, as they had done in 1905, to unofficial positions of authority. But though Lenin disregarded the letter of Marx, he was true to the Armageddon spirit; and it had always been his habit to act first and look up later, when he had the leisure—what, as I have said, is not usually difficult—supporting texts in Marx and Engels.

Lenin's ultimate aims were of course humanitarian, democratic and anti-bureaucratic; but the logic of the whole situation was too strong for Lenin's aims. His trained band of revolutionists, the Party, turned into a tyrannical machine which perpetuated, as heads of a government, the intolerance, the deviousness, the secrecy, the ruthlessness with political dissidents, which they had had to learn as hunted outlaws. Instead of getting a classless society out of the old illiterate feudal Russia, they encouraged the rise and the domination of a new controlling and privileged class, who were soon exploiting the workers almost as callously as the Tsarist industrialists had done, and subjecting them to an espionage that was probably worse than anything under the Tsar. What Lenin had actually effected was a kind of bourgeois revolution; the situation had, in a sense, worked out according to Marx; but it was not at all what Lenin had intended. Lenin himself died, after only six years of power, in great perplexity and anguish of mind, out-maneuvered by one of his lieutenants who knew how to distribute patronage and had no scruples about deceiving the public.

At first, under the dictatorship of Stalin, a serious attempt was made to bring the economy of Soviet Russia up to the level of the capitalist nations, so that socialism might become a reality; but when, due to the mechanical ineptitude and the administrative inefficiency of the Russians, this seemed to be definitely failing, Stalin quickly buried the Leninist ideals, executed or otherwise suppressed all the people who were still disposed to defend them, and consolidated the position of those groups of officials who were doing their best to give Russia the strong bourgeoisie she had lacked and who have ended, it may be, by dominating the dictator Stalin himself.

In the meantime, the short circuit in the capitalist system which Karl Marx had so confidently predicted had actually taken place in Germany, but with results very different from those he had expected. Instead of the processes of capitalism giving rise automatically to a crisis in which a dispossessed proletariat was left facing a small group of capitalists, with nothing to do but to expropriate the expropriators, a new kind of middle class, as in Russia, came out of the petty bourgeoisie and did not find the slightest difficulty in enlisting ambitious members of the working class. This group succeeded in setting up a new kind of state socialism, in which the government planned and directed in the interests of the new governing class, without actually taking over the industrial plant, but eliminating the big capitalists, if necessary, and seeing to it that the working class were well enough off so that they did not become seriously recalcitrant.

III

Karl Marx had arrived at his vision of the working class expelling the capitalists by way of two false analogies. One of these was a probably unconscious tendency to argue from the position of the Jew to the position of the proletarian. The German Jews in Karl Marx's time were just escaping from the restrictions of the ghetto, which meant also the system of the Judaic world; and in this case the former victims of a social and economic discrimination, with their ancient religious discipline and their intellectual training, were quite easily able to take over the techniques and the responsibilities of the outside modern world. The proletariat, however, unlike the Jews, had no tradition of authority; they were, by their very position, kept ignorant and physically bred down. The country—industrial England—in which Marx prophesied that the widening gulf between the owning and the working classes would first bring about a communist revolution, had turned out to be the country where the progressive degradation of the underprivileged classes had simply had the effect of stunting them and slowly extinguishing their spirit. The other false analogy of Marx was his argument from the behavior of the bourgeoisie in the seventeenth and eighteenth centuries to the behavior to be expected of the working class, in their turn, in relation to the bourgeoisie. The European middle classes who finally dispossessed the feudal landlords were, after all, educated people, accustomed to administering property and experienced in public affairs. The proletariat, the true ground-down industrial workers on whom Marx was basing his hopes, were almost entirely devoid of any such experience or education; and what we now know invariably happens when the poor and illiterate people of a modern industrial society first master advanced techniques and improve their standard of living, is that they tend to exhibit ambitions and tastes which Karl Marx would have regarded as bourgeois. We have seen it in the United States, where we have produced what is really the earliest example of that new kind of bourgeoisie that they have been getting in Germany and Russia. But ours is a more highly developed, that is, a more democratic, version; and when I say that it is more democratic, I am using the words not in any loose sense, but in the definite sense that, with us, individual responsibility, the ability to make decisions, is a good deal more evenly distributed than it is in these other countries.

Is there nothing left of Marxism, then? Are there no basic Marxist ideas that may still be accepted as true? I have above, at the risk of banality, discussed it in terms of its historical origins, because it seems to me that the shifting generalities to which the liberal mind is addicted still need to be constantly corrected by the facts of socialist history. But there is, of course, common to the Marxism of Marx and of Engels, of Lenin and of Trotsky, a technique which we can still use with profit; the technique of analyzing political phenomena in social-economic terms. There was this much in the claims of Marx and Engels that they had been able to make socialism "scientific": they were the first to attempt in an intensive way to study economic motives objectively. This does not, of course, mean, however, that we should try to find the key to the events of our time in the conclusions which these men of another time drew from the events of theirs. The Marxist method can get valid results only if applied afresh by men realistic enough to see, and bold enough to think, for themselves.

As for the aims and ideals of Marxism, there is one feature of them that is now rightly suspect. The taking-over by the state of the means of production and the dictatorship in the interests of the proletariat can by themselves never guarantee the happiness of anybody but the dictators themselves. Marx and Engels, coming out of authoritarian Germany, tended to imagine socialism in authoritarian terms; and Lenin and Trotsky after them, forced as they were to make a beginning among a people who had known nothing but autocracy, also emphasized this side of socialism and founded a dictatorship which perpetuated itself as an autocracy.

When all this is said, however, something more important remains that is common to all the great Marxists: the desire to get rid of class privilege based on birth and on difference of income; the will to establish a society in which the superior development of some is not paid for by the exploitation, that is, by the deliberate degradation of others—a society which will be homogeneous and coöperative as our commercial society is not, and directed, to the best of their ability, by the conscious creative minds of its members. But this again is a goal to be worked for in the light of one's own imagination and with the help of one's own common sense. The formulas of the various Marxist creeds, including the one that is common to them all, the dogma of the Dialectic, no more deserve the status of holy writ than the formulas of other creeds. To accomplish such a task will require of us an unsleeping adaptive exercise of reason and instinct combined.

February 22—March 1—March 8, 1941

EPILOGUE, 1952

Edna St. Vincent Millay

ONE IS GRATEFUL to Mr. Vincent Sheean for having written the memoir of Edna Millay that he calls *The Indigo Bunting*, because, since this extraordinary woman's death, no adequate tribute has been paid to either her work or her personality, and Mr. Sheean, though he saw her only a few times in the later years of her life, has been able to bring to the subject his almost novelistic gift for dramatizing contemporary personalities. What sets Mr. Sheean off from the ordinary writer of memoirs, who depends on mere big names or on gossip, is his ardent sense of human greatness. Nothing, for example, could be more different from the way in which celebrities are usually described than the way of Mr. Sheean in such a book as *Between the Thunder and the Sun*. In his account of a house-party on the Riviera, he can give you the colors and contours of Maxine Elliott and Winston Churchill—like a portrait painter in the best old tradition—in such a way as to make them impressive without relinquishing a strong sense of character and personal idiosyncrasy. It is the special Irish faculty, no doubt—which one finds in Yeats's autobiography—for seeing people in their most human, and sometimes in their comic aspects, and yet making them walk the earth like the creatures of heroic legend. In Edna Millay, who had herself so much Irish, Mr. Sheean has an ideal subject, since one needed no romantic temperament, no predisposition to hero-worship, to recognize in her an exceptional being. It is one of the themes of his portrait that

744

she exercised over wild birds what seemed to him a special attraction. This, he says, she pooh-poohed herself—she was not a sentimental or mystical person—explaining that they came to her window or circled about her head simply because she fed them; but what he tells us does show unmistakably that she exercised an enchantment for Vincent Sheean and induced him, for the first time in his life, to become acutely aware of birds, of which he seems hitherto to have been subnormally ignorant. One never forgot the things *she* noticed, for she charged them with her own intense feeling. This power of enhancing and ennobling life was felt by all who knew her.

It was probably a mistake, however, for Mr. Sheean to try to make a small book out of his necessarily slender memoirs. There is a whole chapter on birds in general, which seems little to the purpose and reads like padding —though I believe it is true, as he says and as the following pages will confirm, that Edna Millay had some special affinity with birds; and he runs later to speculations along the lines of his recent interest in Hindu religion, in which she does not seem to have been eager to follow him—not surprising, in view of her exclusive preoccupation with the actual human world. (God never, I think, appears in her works, after such early poems as *God's World* and *Renascence*, except as a mythological property, and her vision of man and the universe is expressed in her *Epitaph for the Race of Man.*) But *The Indigo Bunting* has a certain importance, for Mr. Sheean has recognized and been able to convey something of Edna Millay's qualities, and he has given the lead for others who knew her better and longer and to whom her work has meant more (Mr. Sheean says he read her poetry only after he met her in the forties) to supplement what he has written of his visits to the Boissevains at Austerlitz, New York, and on the island in Maine where they spent their summers. I propose to take advantage of this cue, with apologies to Mr. Sheean for using *The Indigo Bunting* as a pretext for a kind of counter-memoir. I hope that others who knew Edna Millay will also write about her. There ought to be a memorial volume. The wonder is, one realizes with shame, that none of those who were especially indebted to her—with the exception of Mr. Rolfe Humphries, who registered a brief protest in the *Nation* against the stupidity or indifference with which the news of her death was received—has done anything to commemorate this great writer. It is the proof of Mr. Sheean's instinct for spotting and his talent for celebrating what is really important in his own time that he first should have broken the silence.

I

I first met Edna Millay sometime early in 1920, but I had already known about her a long time. A cousin of mine, also a poet, Carolyn Crosby Wilson (now Carolyn Wilson Link), had been in Edna's class at Vassar, 1917, and when I had visited her at college in the spring of 1916, she had given me the April number of the *Vassar Miscellany Monthly*, of which she was one of the editors. I had read it coming back on the train and had been rather impressed by the leading feature, a dramatic dialogue in blank verse called *The Suicide*, by Edna St. Vincent Millay. Sometime later in 1916, my cousin sent me a copy of *A Book of Vassar Verse*, an anthology of poems from the *Miscellany*, in which I found *The Suicide* and another similar poem by Miss Millay called *Interim*. I was then a fifteen-dollar reporter on the New York *Evening Sun* and was sometimes allowed to do book reviews. I tried to give the Vassar girls a little publicity— it must have been sometime in December—by the following two-paragraph notice, which, in view of later developments, has a certain ironic interest:

"The imaginative development exhibited in *A Book of Vassar Verse*, published by the *Vassar Miscellany Monthly*, bears out the editors' prefatory boast that the book has 'a certain significance of symbolism,' which makes apparent 'the widening range of the college girl's emotional and intellectual interest and the quickening of her contact with reality.' The poems which represent the last six years of the last century and the first six of this one seem a little pale and diffident, even when they are ecstatic, but the contemporary verse sounds a new note of frankness, intensity and dramatic feeling. Such things as *The Suicide, The Dragon Lamp* and Miss Ruth Pickering's fresh songs are original poems not unworthy of the American generation which has produced Miss Reese and Miss Teasdale.

"But it is, perhaps, still on the side of paleness and shyness that these lyrics err. It is of moonlight and the sound of the wind that they are fondest of singing, and of the wistful moods of sadness or joy which evaporate before we can examine them. That the Vassar poets have succeeded in giving some of these beautiful expression is not the least merit of a fine collection."

In 1917, when Miss Millay's book *Renascence* came out, I was in France with the A.E.F., and my cousin sent me a copy of the book, which impressed me much more than the Vassar poems. In 1920, when I was back in America again, I read in the March issue of the new literary magazine, the *Dial*, a sonnet called *To Love Impuissant*, which I immediately got by heart and found myself declaiming in the shower:

> Love, though for this you riddle me with darts,
> And drag me at your chariot till I die,—
> Oh, heavy prince! Oh, panderer of hearts!—
> Yet hear me tell how in their throats they lie
> Who shout you mighty: thick about my hair,

Day in, day out, your ominous arrows purr,
Who still am free, unto no querulous care
A fool, and in no temple worshiper!
I, that have bared me to your quiver's fire,
Lifted my face into its puny rain,
Do wreathe you Impotent to Evoke Desire
As you are Powerless to Elicit Pain!
(Now will the god, for blasphemy so brave,
Punish me, surely, with the shaft I crave!)

The fascination that this poem had for me was due partly to its ringing defiance—at that time we were all defiant—but partly also to my liking to think that one who appreciated the poet as splendidly as I felt I did might be worthy to deal her the longed-for dart. This was a different, a bolder voice than the brooding girl of *Renascence*. How I hoped I might someday meet her!

This was finally brought about—sometime in the spring of that year—by Hardwicke Nevin (the nephew of Ethelbert Nevin, the composer), whom my friend John Peale Bishop had known at Princeton. He had further excited my interest by his description of Edna's enchanting personality, and he had invited John and me to an evening party at his apartment in Greenwich Village, to which Edna came, late, from the theater, where she was acting with the Provincetown Players. I think it was just before this that I had seen the double bill there: a play of Floyd Dell's, in which she had acted, and her own *Aria de Capo*, in which her sister Norma played Columbine. I was thrilled and troubled by this little play: it was the first time I had felt Edna's peculiar power. There was a bitter treatment of war, and we were all ironic about war; but there was also a less common sense of the incongruity and the cruelty of life, of the precariousness of love perched on a table above the corpses that had been hastily shoved out of sight, and renewing its eternal twitter in the silence that succeeded the battle. In any case, it was after the theater that Edna came to Hardwicke Nevin's. She complained of being exhuasted, but was persuaded to recite some of her poems. She was dressed in some bright batik, and her face lit up with a flush that seemed to burn also in the bronze reflections of her not yet bobbed reddish hair. She was one of those women whose features are not perfect and who in their moments of dimness may not seem even pretty, but who, excited by the blood or the spirit, become almost supernaturally beautiful. She was small, but her figure was full, though she did not appear plump. She had a lovely and very long throat that gave her the look of a muse, and her reading of her poetry was thrilling. She pronounced every syllable distinctly; she gave every sound its value. She seemed sometimes rather British than American—in her quick way of talking to people as well as in her reading of her poems, and I have never understood how her accent was formed. I suppose it was partly the product of the English tradition in New England, and no doubt—since she had acted from childhood—of her having been taught to read Shakespeare by a college or school elocutionist. She had probably also been influenced by the English Mitchell Kennerleys—Kennerley had been her first publisher—who had taken her up when she was still a girl, and, in a more important way, by the English dramatist Charles Rann Kennedy, who, with his wife Edith Wynn Matthison, the actress, had also been interested in her and had tried to persuade her to go on the stage. In any case, the trueness of her ear made it possible for her to write verse which was really in the English tradition. I believe that our failure in the United States to produce much first-rate lyric poetry is partly due to our flattening and drawling of the vowels and our slovenly slurring of the consonants; and Edna spoke with perfect purity. It may have been partly her

musical training, which came out also in her handling of
her voice. Among poets whose phonograph recordings I
have heard, it seems to me that Edna Millay and E. E.
Cummings and James Joyce give conspicuously the best
performances. Joyce, like Edna Millay, is a musician with
a well-trained voice; Cummings has, like Edna, the New
England precision in enunciating every syllable. All three
are masters of tempo and tone. If you play the recording
of *Renascence*, you will hear how the *r* in the first line
gets just the right little twist—so different from the harsh
or the slighted *r*'s of the American regional accents; and
how the vowels in *long* and *wood* are correctly made,
respectively, short and long. If you play *Elegy*, you will
hear in the closing lines her characteristic cadences that
are almost like song. I do not remember whether she
recited this poem the night that I met her first. If she did
not, I heard it soon after. It was one of a series she had
written for a girl-friend at Vassar who had died, which I
thought among the finest of the things that she showed
me then. What was impressive and rather unsettling
when she read such poems aloud was her power of imposing herself on others through a medium that unbur-
dened the emotions of solitude. The company hushed
and listened as people do to music—her authority was
always complete; but her voice, though dramatic, was
lonely.

My next move was to cultivate her acquaintance by
way of *Vanity Fair*, in the editorial department of which
magazine John Bishop and I were both working then.
She had at that time no real market for her poems; she
sold a lyric only now and then to the highbrow *Dial*, on
the one hand, or to the trashy *Ainslie's*, on the other.
She was hard-up and lived with her mother and sisters
at the very end of West Nineteenth Street. When I would
go to get her there or take her home in a cab, the children
that were playing in the street would run up and crowd

around her. It was partly that she gave them pennies and sometimes taxi-rides, just as she later put out food for the birds, but it was also, I think, the magnetism that Vincent Sheean felt. We published in *Vanity Fair* a good deal of Edna's poetry and thus brought her to the attention of a larger public. This was the beginning of her immense popularity. Frank Crowninshield, the editor of *Vanity Fair*—a clever and extremely entertaining man— was in some ways rather shallow as well as unreliable, but he did have—as it were, as a heritage from his distinguished Boston family—a true instinct about painting and writing and a confidence in his own taste. He deserves a good deal of credit for featuring Edna Millay's poetry and for enabling her later to go abroad. There was nobody else in the publishing world who was both qualified to appreciate her work and in a position to do something to help her in a financial and practical way. As for John Bishop and me, the more we saw of her poetry, the more our admiration grew, and we both, before very long, had fallen irretrievably in love with her. This latter was so common an experience, so almost inevitable a consequence of knowing her in those days, that it is possible, without being guilty of personal irrelevancies, to introduce it into a memoir of this kind. One cannot really write about Edna Millay without bringing into the foreground of the picture her intoxicating effect on people, because this so much created the atmosphere in which she lived and composed. The spell that she exercised on many, of the most various professions and temperaments, of all ages and both sexes, was at that time exactly that which Vincent Sheean imagines she cast on the birds. I should say here that I do not believe that my estimate of Edna Millay's work has ever been much affected by my personal emotions about her. I admired her poetry before I knew her, and my most exalted feeling for her did not, I think, ever prevent me from recognizing or criticizing what was weak or second-rate in her work. Today, thirty years later, though I see her in a different "context," my opinion has hardly changed. Let me register this unfashionable opinion here, and explain that Edna Millay seems to me one of the only poets writing in English in our time who have attained to anything like the stature of great literary figures in an age in which prose has predominated. It is hard to know how to compare her to Eliot or Auden or Yeats—it would be even harder to compare her to Pound. There is always a certain incommensurability between men and women writers. But she does have it in common with the first three of these that, in giving supreme expression to profoundly felt personal experience, she was able to identify herself with more general human experience and stand forth as a spokesman for the human spirit, announcing its predicaments, its vicissitudes, but, as a master of human expression, by the splendor of expression itself, putting herself beyond common embarrassments, common oppressions and panics. This is man who surveys himself and the world in which he moves, not the beast that scurries and suffers; and the name of the poet comes no longer to indicate a mere individual with a birthplace and a legal residence, but to figure as one of the pseudonyms assumed by that spirit itself.

This spirit so made itself felt, in all one's relations with Edna, that it towered above the clever college girl, the Greenwich Village gamine and, later, the neurotic invalid. There was something of awful drama about everything one did with Edna, and yet something that steadied one, too. Those who fell in love with the woman did not, I think, seriously quarrel with her or find themselves at one another's throats and they were not, except in very small ways, demoralized or led to commit excesses, because the other thing was always there, and her genius, for those who could value it, was not something that one could be jealous of. Her poetry, you soon found out, was her real overmastering passion. She gave it to all the world, but she also gave it to you. As in *The Poet and His Book*—at that time, one of my favorites of her poems—with its homely but magical images, its urgent and hurried movement—she addressed herself, not to her lover, by whom, except momentarily, she had never had the illusion that she lived or died, but to everyone whose pulse could throb quicker at catching the beat of her poetry. This made it possible during the first days we knew her for John and me to see a good deal of her together on the basis of our common love of poetry. Our parties were in the nature of a sojourn in Pieria—to which, in one of her sonnets, she complains that an unworthy lover is trying to keep her from returning—where it was most delightful to feel at home. I remember particularly an April night in 1920, when we called on Richard Bennett, the actor, who had been brought by Hardwicke Nevin to the Provincetown Players, in the cheerful little house halfway downtown where he lived with his attractive wife and his so soon to be attractive daughters. I sat on the floor with Edna, which seemed to me very Bohemian. On some other occasion, we all undertook to write portraits in verse of ourselves. John's, under the title *Self-Portrait*, appeared in *Vanity Fair*, and we wanted to publish Edna's, but one of her sisters intervened and persuaded her that it wouldn't do. There was also a trip on a Fifth Avenue bus—we were going to the Claremont for dinner, I think—in the course of which Edna recited to us a sonnet she had just written: *"Here is a wound that never will heal, I know."* For me, even rolling up Fifth Avenue, this poem plucked the strings of chagrin, for not only did it refer to some other man, someone I did not know, but it suggested that Edna could not be consoled, that such grief was in the nature of things.

I used to take her to plays, concerts and operas. We saw Bernard Shaw's *Heartbreak House* together, when it was first done in New York, in the November of 1920. I had not liked it much when I read it and had told her that it was a dreary piece on the model of *Misalliance*. But the play absorbed and excited her, as it gradually did me, and I saw that I had been quite wrong: *Heartbreak House* was, on the contrary, the first piece of Shaw's in which he had fully realized the possibilities of the country-house conversation with which he had been experimenting in *Getting Married* and *Misalliance*. At the end of the second act, Edna became very tense and was rather upset by the scene in which Ariadne—who had just said, "I get my whole life messed up with people falling in love with me"—plays cat-and-mouse with the jealous Randell; and when the curtain went down on it, she said: "I hate women who do that, you know." She must have had, in the course of those crowded years, a good many Randells on her hands, but her method of dealing with them was different from that of Bernard Shaw's aggressive Ariadne. She was capable of being mockingly or sternly sharp with an admirer who proved a nuisance, but she did not like to torture people or to play them off against one another. With the dignity of her genius went, not, as is sometimes the case, a coldness or a hatefulness or a touchiness in intimate human relations, but an invincible magnanimity, and the effects of her transitory feminine malice would be cancelled by an impartiality which was amiably humorous or sympathetic. It is characteristic of her that, in her sonnet *On Hearing a Symphony of Beethoven*, she should write of the effect of the music,

> The spiteful and the stingy and the rude
> Sleep like the scullions in the fairy-tale.

Spitefulness and stinginess and rudeness were among the qualities she most disliked and of which she was least willing to be guilty.

Between John Bishop and me relations were, nevertheless, by this time, becoming a little strained. Frank Crowninshield was complaining that it was difficult to have both his assistants in love with one of his most brilliant contributors. There was a time when, from the point of view of taking her out, I was more or less monopolizing Edna, and John, who, between the office and his perfectionist concentration on his poetry—which he recited in the bathroom in the morning and to which he returned at night—had collapsed and come down with the flu. I went to see him, and afterwards told Edna— no doubt with a touch of smugness—that I thought he was suffering, also, from his frustrated passion for her. The result of this—which I saw with mixed feelings— was that she paid him a visit at once and did her best to redress the balance. I knew that he had some pretty good poetry to read her, and this did not improve the situation.

But her relations with us and with her other admirers had, as I say, a disarming impartiality. Though she reacted to the traits of the men she knew—a face or a voice or a manner—or to their special qualifications—what they sang or had read or collected—with the same intensely perceptive interest that she brought to anything else—a bird or a shell or a weed—that had attracted her burning attention; though she was quick to feel weakness or strength—she did not, however, give the impression that personality much mattered for her or that, aside from her mother and sisters, her personal relations were important except as subjects for poems; and when she came to write about her lovers, she gave them so little individuality that it was usually, in any given case, impossible to tell which man she was writing about. What interests her is seldom the people themselves, but her

own emotions about them; and the sonnets that she pub
lished in sequences differed basically from Mrs. Brown·
ing's in that they dealt with a miscellany of men without.
—since they are all about *her*—the reader's feeling the
slightest discontinuity. In all this, she was not egotistic
in any boring or ridiculous or oppressive way, because it
was not the personal, but the impersonal Edna Millay—
that is, the poet—that preoccupied her so incessantly. But
she was sometimes rather a strain, because nothing could
be casual for her; I do not think I ever saw her relaxed,
even when she was tired or ill. I used to suppose that this
strain of being with her must be due to my own anxieties,
but I later discovered that others who had never been
emotionally involved with her were affected in the same
way. She could be very amusing in company, but the wit
of her conversation was as sharp as the pathos of her
poetry. She was not at all a social person. She did not
gossip; did not like to talk current events; did not like to
talk personalities. It was partly that she was really noble,
partly that she was rather neurotic, and the two things
(bound up together) made it difficult for her to meet the
world easily. When Mr. Sheean met her, late in her life,
she at first, he tells us, seemed tongue-tied; then puzzled
him extremely by thanking him, as if it had happened
yesterday, for his having, in some official connection
about which he had completely forgotten, sent her some
flowers five years before; then analyzed, with a closeness
he could hardly follow, a poem by Gerard Manley Hopkins, the sense of which she insisted, with bitterness and
an "animation" that brought out "her very extraordinary
beauty—not the beauty of every day but apart," had been
spoiled by Hopkins' editor Robert Bridges' having put in
a comma in the wrong place. But although Edna sometimes fatigued one, she was never, as even the most gifted
sometimes are, tyrannical, fatuous or vain. She was either
like the most condensed literature or music, the demands

of which one cannot meet protractedly, or like a serious nervous case—though this side of her was more in evidence later—whom one finds that one cannot soothe.

What was the cause of this strain? From what was the pressure derived that Edna Millay seemed always to be under? At that time I was too young and too much in love to be able to understand her well, and I afterwards saw her only at intervals and in a much less intimate way. But I had found, when I had come into contact with the formidable strength of character that lay behind her attractiveness and brilliance, something as different as possible from the legend of her Greenwich Village reputation, something austere and even grim. She had been born in Rockland, Maine, and had grown up in small Maine towns. I heard her speak of her father only once. He and her mother had not lived together since the children were quite small, and her mother, who had studied to be a singer, supported them by district nursing without ceasing—as I learn from Mr. Sheean—to train the local orchestra and write out their scores. They were poor; the mother was away all day, and the three girls were thrown much on themselves. To Edna, her sisters and her poetry and music must have been almost the whole of life. Such suitors as she had had in Maine she did not seem to have taken seriously. By her precocious and remarkable poem, *Renascence*, written when she was hardly nineteen, she had attracted, at a summer entertainment, the attention of a visitor, Miss Caroline B. Dow, the New York head of the National Training School of the Y. W. C. A., who raised the money to send her to college. She did not graduate, therefore, till she was twenty-five, when she at last emerged into the freedom of a world where her genius and beauty were soon to make her famous, to bring all sorts of people about her, with an intellect and a character that had been developed in solitude and under the discipline of hard conditions. Her human emotional life had, it seemed to me, in her girlhood been rather cramped, but she had herself given her emotions their satisfaction through the objects—the poems—she was able to create, and this life of the mind, this life of art, by which she had triumphed in a little Maine town that offered few other triumphs, was to remain for her the great reality that made everything else unimportant. It is all in the astonishing *Renascence*, which is a study of claustrophobia (as well as, of course, a great affirmation of the stature of the human spirit). Hemmed in between the mountains and the sea of Camden on Penobscot Bay, the girl is beginning to suffocate; she looks up, and the sky seems to offer escape, but when she puts up her hand, she screams, for she finds it is so low that she can touch it, and Infinity settles down on her—she can hear the ticking of Eternity; she is beset by a new ordeal, for she begins to feel all human guilt, experience all human suffering, and this, too, becomes an oppression which is killing her; she now sinks six feet into the ground, and she feels the weight roll from her breast; her tortured soul breaks away, and the comforting rain begins to fall; but she is dead now and she wants to escape from the grave, which itself has become a prison, for she imagines how beautiful the world will be as soon as the rain is over; she prays to God for the rain to wash away the grave, and a storm comes and sets her free to those beauties of the world she has longed for; she springs up, embraces the trees, hugs the ground, feels that nothing can ever hide her from God again; the world, she now knows, is as wide as the heart, the heavens as high as the soul, but East and West will close in and crush you if you do not keep them apart, and the sky will cave in on you if your soul is flat. This poem gives the central theme of Edna Millay's whole work: she is alone; she is afraid that the world will crush her; she must summon the strength to assert herself, to draw herself up to her full stature, to embrace the world with love; and the storm—which stands evidently for sexual love—comes to effect a liberation. Her real sexual experience, which came rather late, was to play in her poetry the role of this storm, for it gives her the world to embrace, yet it always leaves her alone again, alone and afraid of death. Withdrawal is her natural condition: she was always, as Mr. Sheean indicates—and this made itself felt as a part of the strain—extremely shy of meeting people; and she was terrified by New York, of which I do not think she saw much, for she would not cross a street alone. She feels that she is "caught beneath great buildings," and she longs to be back in Maine—though the Maine she is homesick for is never in the least idealized, but, on the contrary, a meager country with threadbare interiors, wizened apples and weedy mussels on rotting hulls. One of her poems of this time that impressed me most was the long *Ode to Silence*, in which she celebrates an inner sanctuary that is like the grave of *Renascence*—a garden which lies "in a lull," like it, "between the mountains and the mountainous sea."

Of the household in which Edna grew up I had a glimpse, in the summer of 1920, when I went at her invitation—she had John Bishop and me on different weekends—to visit her at Truro, near the tip of Cape Cod. It was already dark when I got there—there was in those days a train that went all the way to Provincetown, shuffling along so slowly that it might have been plodding through the sand—and though I was met by a man with a cart, he did not, for some curmudgeonly Cape Cod reason, drive me all the way to the house, but dropped me some distance away from it, so that I somehow got lost in a field and dragged my suitcase through scrub-oak and sweetfern in the breathless hot August night. At last I saw a gleam—a small house—which I approached from the fields behind it, and there I found the Millays: Edna, with her mother and her two sisters, none of whom I had met. The little house had been lent them for the summer by George Cram Cook (always known as "Jig"), the organizer of the Provincetown Players, who with Susan Glaspell lived across the road. It was bare, with no decoration and only a few pieces of furniture; a wind-mill that pumped water and no plumbing. Norma has told me since that, when it rained the first night they got there, before they knew they had neighbors who could see them, they had all taken a shower under the spout from the roof. They gave me a dinner on a plain board table by the light of an oil-lamp. I had never seen any-thing like this household, nor have I ever seen anything like it since. Edna tried to reassure me by telling me that I mustn't be overpowered by all those girls, and one of the others added, "And *what* girls!" Norma, the second sister, was a blonde, who looked a little like Edna; Kath-leen, the youngest, was different, a dark Irish type. Edna was now very freckled. All were extremely pretty. But it was the mother who was most extraordinary. She was a little old woman with spectacles, who, although she had evidently been through a good deal, had managed to re-main very brisk and bright. She sat up straight and smoked cigarettes and quizzically followed the conversa-tion. She looked not unlike a New England schoolteacher, yet there was something almost raffish about her. She had anticipated the Bohemianism of her daughters; and she sometimes made remarks that were startling from the lips of a little old lady. But there was nothing sordid about her: you felt even more than with Edna that she had passed beyond good and evil, beyond the power of hardship to worry her, and that she had attained there a certain gaiety. The daughters entertained me with humorous songs—they sang parts very well together—which they had concocted in their girlhood in Maine. Here are the words of one that I remember, of which Norma has supplied me with an accurate version:

Song to Men

Kathleen, soprano; Vincent, baritone; Norma, tenor

<table>
<tr><td></td><td>Let us sing a little song
To the men we've loved so long—
And to those we've only loved
A little while</td></tr>
<tr><td>Tenor solo:</td><td>A lit-tle while.</td></tr>
<tr><td></td><td>Ti de dee and ta dee da,
We must take them as they are—
Let them spoof us
For they love so
To beguile.</td></tr>
<tr><td>Baritone solo:</td><td>Let them beguile.</td></tr>
</table>

Chorus

<table>
<tr><td></td><td>Oh, darling men!</td></tr>
<tr><td>Baritone:</td><td>Oh, men, men, men.
Oh, men alluring,
Waste not the hours—</td></tr>
<tr><td>Tenor:</td><td>Sweet idle hours—
In vain assuring,
For love, though sweet,</td></tr>
<tr><td>Tenor:</td><td>Love though tho thweet—
Is not enduring.
Ti de da! Ti da dee da!</td></tr>
</table>

Shall we have a smoke? We can—
Oh, a man is just a man
But a little old Fatima
Burns so snug.

Baritone: She burns so snug.
              Should we have another drink,
              Do you think? (*Spoken*) Oh, let's
                      not think!
                  Pour another
                  From the little
                  Earthen jug—(*Sound of cork*)
                      gug-gug-gug
                  gug-gug-gug-gug-gug.

                  Chorus

              Oh, darling men!
              Oh, men, men, men, etc.
          (*Ending*)
                  Ti de da! Ti da dee da!
                  So there you are.

   Edna had been turning into verse, for a collection
called *Folk Songs of Many Peoples,* prose translations of
some European peasant songs, and she sang me her
versions, which enchanted me—especially one from
Esthonia, with a merry and poignant tune:

Piper, pipe a tune, call the dancers out!
Oh, the happy bag-pipes, the laughing shout!
Now the merry step we are treading!
Health to all, and joy bless this wedding!
Tra la la! Tra la la! Youth is all pleasure!
Let the beating foot strike the time of the measure!

Now the master's son, riches spurning,
Weds the farmer maid of his yearning;
Now the girl the rose garland covers,
Leaves her father's house for her lover's.
Tra la la! Lonely my heart, dream laden.
Would that I the bridegroom were, of so sweet a maiden.

The word *lonely* in the second stanza was given a
dramatic emphasis by being put in the place of the second
tra la la, in such a way that the first syllable was prolonged in the two drooping notes.

Since there were only two rooms on the first floor, with
no partition between them, the only way for Edna and
me to get away by ourselves was to sit in a swing on the
porch; but the mosquitoes were so tormenting—there
being then no mosquito control—that we soon had to go
in again. I did, however, ask her formally to marry me,
and she did not reject my proposal but said that she
would think about it. I am not sure that she actually said,
"That might be the solution," but it haunts me that she
conveyed that idea. In any case, it was plain to me that
proposals of marriage were not a source of great excitement.

The next morning she sat on the floor and recited a lot

of new poems—she rarely read her poetry, she knew it by heart. The Millays were rather vague about meals and only really concentrated on dinner, but they never apologized for anything. We played the Fifth Symphony on a primitive old phonograph that had been left with them by Allan Ross Macdougall. She was committing the whole thing to memory, as she liked to do with music and poems; and, raspy and blurred though it sounded, the power of its bold or mysterious motifs came through to me—surcharged with her power—as it never had done before. Jig Cook and Hutchins Hapgood dropped by and sat on the edge of the porch. The conversation was light but learned, and I was rather astonished when Jig quoted a poem in Sanskrit: I did not know at that time that he was a liberated Greek professor. But the things that remain with me most vividly—because she called my attention to them—are the vision of Jig Cook's daughter, Nilla, a handsome and sturdy little girl in a bright red bathing-suit walking along the beach, as we looked down from the cliff above; and a gull's egg we found on the sand—gulls do not build nests—which made Edna stop and stare. It came back to me seven years later when, going up to Cape Cod in the early summer, I found myself alone in Provincetown:

Provincetown

We never from the barren down,
    Beneath the silver-lucid breast
Of drifting plume, gazed out to drown
    Where daylight whitens to the west.

Here never in this place I knew
    Such beauty by your side, such peace—
These skies that, brightening, imbue
    With dawn's delight the day's release.

Only, upon the barren beach,
    Beside the gray egg of a gull,
With that fixed look and fervent speech,
    You stopped and called it beautiful.

Lone as the voice that sped the word!—
    Gray-green as eyes that ate its round!—
The desert dropping of a bird,
    Bare-bedded in the sandy ground.

Tonight, where clouds like foam are blown,
    I ride alone the surf of light,
As—even by my side—alone
    That stony beauty burned your sight.

For I was not "the solution," nor was anyone else she knew; and she had come to a crisis in her life. "I'll be thirty in a minute!" she said to me one day. She moved from the apartment she had shared with her family and where, she complained, the sewing-machine had interfered with her writing, and took two rooms and a bath on West Twelfth Street, where Kathleen eventually joined her. But this made her more accessible and exposed her to the importunities of her suitors, who really besieged her door. She did not want to marry any of them, and, having tried two Greenwich Village ménages, she no longer had any illusions about extra-marital arrangements that were supposed to leave the parties free but, since somebody was always jealous, actually made their relations intolerable. And even with her literary career, she had lately been running into difficulties of a most discouraging kind. Her new book, *Second April*, had been set up a long time before—she showed me the proofs when I first knew her—but Mitchell Kennerley, who was having financial troubles, did not bring the book out and would not even communicate with her. Besides this, her benefactress, Miss Dow, to whom she had dedicated *Second April*, did not approve of her recent work—just as James Joyce's patron, Miss Harriet Weaver, was scandalized by *Ulysses* *—and this worried her very much, for she could not write differently to please Miss Dow, and did not know how to answer her letters. She had one or two depressing illnesses. Her apartment was poorly heated, and I brought her an electric heater. I remember how miserable she seemed— though she never lost a certain liveliness—wrapped up in an old flannel bathrobe and bundled in shabby covers. Above the bed was a modern painting, all fractured geometrical planes that vaguely delineated a female figure, which the Millay girls called *Directions for Using the Empress.*†

It was decided she should go abroad. She had never been in Europe, and she wanted to get away from the Village. She had begun to do for *Vanity Fair* the satirical dialogues and sketches which were published under the pseudonym "Nancy Boyd," and this made it possible for Crowninshield to pay her a regular allowance. He did his best to induce Edna to sign these pieces with her own name—he offered her, in fact, more money; but she never would compromise about her work. No matter how confused her life became, she was always clear about this. If one compares the contents of *Figs from Thistles*, writ-

* See page 794.
† This, I learn from Norma Millay (Mrs. Charles Ellis), was the painter's own name for the picture, which was painted by Charles Ellis. "It was shown," she writes me, "at the Independent Artists' Show and was reviewed under this startling title." The picture, she says, was "an abstract portrait of Vincent's mechanical dressform, the Empress, which gained and lost weight by an intricate system of adjusting nuts and screws. When we later learned that the inventor of the Empress had killed himself, we understood it perfectly."

ten in the same year as the poems in *Second April*, with the contents of the other book, one can see that she imposed on herself a pretty rigorous critical standard. She would not mix with her serious work any of the merely cute feminine pieces that had something in common with the songs that the sisters made up for their own amusement, nor any of the easier lyrics that reflected the tone of the women's magazines. This serious work, never loosely written, was tragic, almost pessimistic (though the best of her lighter verse had the same sort of implications). It was natural that Hardy and Housman should have been among her admirers. From Housman she partly derived (Mr. Sheean, in asserting that Edna Millay owed nothing to any other poet since Shakespeare, has neglected this important exception), and she was closer to this masculine stoicism than to the heartbreak of Sara Teasdale. It was this tough intellectual side combined with her feminine attraction that made her such a satisfactory companion, and that persuaded so many men that they had found their ideal mate. She was quite free from the blue-stocking's showing-off, but she did have a rather schoolmarmish side—which rapped Mr. Sheean's knuckles when he put out a cigarette in his coffee-cup. In just this way I have heard her complain of the vandalisms of Greenwich Villagers who made a point of scorning bourgeois sanctions. And so she reprimanded me once when I tried to fulfil my editorial function by urging her to sign her name to her Nancy Boyd articles. Her attitude was: "Don't you know it's impolite to the teacher and reflects on the home you come from to throw chalk around in class?"

I tried to help her get on with these sketches, at the time when she was not yet well, by typing to her dictation, but she was anything but a facile writer and she insisted on putting in as comic lines remarks I had just made in earnest. We had at this time some wonderful conversations, at which quite a lot of bootleg gin was drunk, and, even in that dreadful form, this exhilarating bitter liquor has always kept for me a certain glamor that others have not acquired. On one of these occasions, she recited to me the fragments of a long poem she had started, called *Epitaph for the Race of Man*. This was something quite different from the sonnet sequence that she published in 1934. It was written, like *Renascence*, in iambic tetrameter; but it was equally evolutionary: there were monkeys, though not yet, I think, dinosaurs. It surprised me, for it was purely philosophical, and it gave me a new idea of her range. One evening we set out to talk French in preparation for her coming trip. I remarked that her ex-admirers ought to organize an alumni association—to which she answered with promptness and point: *"On en parle toujours, mais on ne le fait jamais."* John Bishop and I, who had realized that we were both quite out of the running without, however, we thought, having yet been superseded by a serious rival, had renewed our good relations and spent an evening with her together, just before she left, on our old high and festive basis. But neither of us saw her off. I think that we were both afraid of the possible unknown others we might have to confront on the pier.

That I missed her may be seen from the following poem. I had read the *Georgics* of Virgil in the summer of 1922, and the phrase *in luminis oras*—which he uses in connection with the sprouting plants that reach upwards to "the shores of light"—though a conventional Latin formula that had appeared in the older poets, had echoed in my head with the accent of pathos that haunts even fertility in Virgil, and eventually gave me a motif.

Shut out the Square!
Though not for grayness and the rainy path—
For that intolerable aching air
Of meetings long resolved to silences
And absences like death—
For the throat a moment lifted, the wide brow
    shaken free,
Where there was neither leaf nor wind
A dryad by her tree—
Against the narrow door that closed the narrow hall,
Blank then but for a night that now for all
With blankness wounds the mind.

Gaze out with steady glare!
Present the tough unbroken glove!
For suddenly you heard to-night
Your voice that speaks and saw your hands that write,
Yet never speak nor write the name they love—
And knew the hours were waves that wash away
Farther each day to sea the summer sound
Of children shrill and late, of summer hours that run
Late, late, yet never sleep and never tire
Before they meet the sun.

We spoke the sudden words, the words already
    known—
We spoke, and spoke no more, for tongues were fire.
Now, watching from this shore at last, alone
I seem to wait the turning of that tide
That ebbs for ever.
               Children, waking to the day,
Cry out for joy.
               My stubborn heart to-night
Divines the fate of souls who have not died,
Buried in sullen shadows underground—
That reach for ever toward the shores of light.

II

I saw her in Paris in the summer of 1921. She had made new friends and, both there and in England, was having, I think, a very good time. I had the impression that Europe frightened her less than New York, but she must have continued to live with considerable recklessness, for, at the end of two years abroad, she was in very bad shape again. Returned home at the beginning of 1923, she married, in July, Eugen Boissevain, just before she went to the hospital for a serious operation. She had met him at Croton since she had come back from Europe, and had first got to know him in a round of charades. He was a Dutchman with an Irish mother, the son of the editor of the largest Dutch newspaper and himself a coffee importer, with offices in New York. He had been married to Inez Milholland, a Vassar girl who had practised law and become a famous public champion of labor causes and women's rights, who had died in 1916. He was a gentleman and had once been quite well-to-do. Max Eastman, in his autobiographical *Enjoyment of Living*, describes him at the time of his first marriage as "handsome and muscular and bold, boisterous in conversation, noisy in laughter, yet redeemed by a strain of something feminine that most men except the creative geniuses lack." With no particular talent or bent of his own, it was possible for him only vicariously to express this imaginative and sensitive side, and he was led, as it were, to the special vocation of assisting the careers of gifted women. He was twelve years older than Edna, and, although, as Max Eastman says, he had "the genius, the audacity and the uncompromising determination to enjoy the adventure of life," he made one feel that he had always behind him a stout background of Dutch burgher stability. She had made a very sound choice. He took her on a trip to the Orient and then bought a large farm at Austerlitz, New

York, where they settled in 1925 and lived for the rest of their lives.

I used to see and correspond with her occasionally. I have a memory of calling on her once in January, 1924, in the tiny little house in Bedford Street, 75½, where they lived before they went to the country. I found her absorbed in a paint catalogue, of which she made the special shades of color and their often delightful names start into a relief that seemed almost as vivid as the voices of the Fifth Symphony when she had played it on the phonograph in Truro. From a note-book of 1928—it must have been early in the year, since *The Buck in the Snow* had not yet come out—I learn that she "summoned me to the Vanderbilt to talk about her bobolink poem," about which I seem to have been only moderately enthusiastic. "You mean you think it sounds like Mary Carolyn Davies!" I find she replied to my criticisms. "I said," my record continues, "that, when she had written *Second April*, she had been under so many kinds of pressure that the people who read her poems hardly thought about them as literature at all: there had been an element of panic about them. She said, 'Yes, and I still want to knock 'em cold!' For two cents she would tear up the bobolink proof and not let the *Delineator* have it. . . . She looked quite beautiful, very high pink flush, and brown dress that brought out her color." I noted, also, Boissevain's "protective attitude" and his saying that her recent work was "more objective." He was right, and the volume of lyrics called *The Buck in the Snow*—the first she had published since *The Harp-Weaver* of 1923— which came out later that year, contained work of a much less desperate, a more contemplative kind, which included, along with the bobolink, several of her finest poems: *Dawn, The Cameo, Sonnet to Gath, On Hearing a Symphony of Beethoven.*

This book contained also a piece that I read with both pleasure and embarrassment, for I recognized it—she afterwards confirmed this—as an account of an evening we had spent together (it must have been sometime that same winter), when I had been living in a little room on West Thirteenth Street opposite a taxi-garage and just around the corner from Greenwich Avenue. I had read her the Latin elegiacs that A. E. Housman had prefixed to his Manilius and a translation of them I had made; some of Yeats's latest poems, which she had not seen; James Joyce's *Pomes Penyeach,* as to which I thought her rather old-fashioned for objecting that the title cheapened them, as if he had let them go as the work of some "Nancy Boyd." I do not remember behaving as she describes (as people seem so often to say). I think she must have combined this occasion with some memory from our earlier phase, but it is painful to me to reread this poem today and to feel again, in retrospect, how much I must have hated to part from her.

Portrait

Over and over I have heard,

As now I hear it,

Your voice harsh and light as the scratching of dry leaves
over the hard ground,

Your voice forever assailed and shaken by the wind from
the island

Of illustrious living and dead, that never dies down,

And bending at moments under the terrible weight of the
perfect word,

Here in this room without fire, without comfort of any
kind,

Reading aloud to me immortal page after page conceived
in a mortal mind.

Beauty at such moments before me like a wild bright
    bird
Has been in the room, and eyed me, and let me come
    near it.

I could not ever nor can I to this day
Acquaint you with the triumph and the sweet rest
These hours have brought to me and always bring,—
Rapture, coloured like the wild bird's neck and wing,
Comfort, softer than the feathers of its breast.
Always, and even now, when I rise to go,
Your eyes blaze out from a face gone wickedly pale;
I try to tell you what I would have you know,—
What peace it was; you cry me down; you scourge me
    with a salty flail;
You will not have it so.

She had said to me in the course of this evening that
the only bad feature of Austerlitz was its not being near
the sea, of which she had a permanent need, that the
hills and the woods walled her in and sometimes made
her feel imprisoned (this was, as I now can see, one of
the phases of her recurrent claustrophobia). I suppose
it was to remedy this that they later bought their island
in Maine. In the May of 1928, I had a wire from her
inviting me to Austerlitz for a week-end. I went, and it
was pleasant, as I learn from my notes—the prospect
of seeing her again must, as usual, have stimulated my
perceptions—to find myself on the train, in the widening
landscape of upstate New York, with its dark and thick-
bristling hills, today blurred with mist at the tops and
misted at the bases with fruit-blossoms; and, in intervals
of reading Proust's letters to Mme. Sheikévitch, I looked
out on the long roads leading over these hills, the white
houses and little red cabins and large-looming tarnished

barns, the stone fences that lay in loose meshes, the small faded rural hotels that so often stood opposite the stations—with the soddenly wet gray day superimposed rather queerly on the freshest greenness of spring. There were desolate yellow freightcars trailing along the route, and the timbery marshes were studded with the rank green of skunk-cabbage leaves. The ponds and the streams had a dark smooth luster even under the rain, but the foam of the apple-blossoms, like some dirty sheep in a pasture, seemed yellowed by the turbid weather. A growth of squarish whitish houses in the bowl of one of the valleys seemed almost a product of the damp like the skunk-cabbage in the swamp. At Austerlitz—hirsute hills—the overcast sultry weather seemed brooding like a mother-bird over the not yet quite opening beauties of spring, the little pink fruit-tree buds that were just on the point of bursting. The birds themselves seemed subdued, and Edna, when I reached the Boissevains' place, said that she imagined the farmhands—"ominously silent," also—perched somewhere with their heads under their wings. I had, on my side, been saving for her a simile and remarked that on one of the lawns I had passed the dandelions had looked like grated egg on spinach. We were neither of us, perhaps, at our best, but we always made a certain effort. Above the Boissevains' house—called Steepletop—a big densely green tree-grown hill, with the flat effect of a tapestry, was stitched with distinct white birch.

Gene Boissevain, when I arrived, was planting a border of pansies with a gardener's intent application; but his attention seemed soon to flag, for he began singing cockney songs at the top of his voice. Then he addressed himself to oiling the lawn-mower; then suddenly dropped it and proposed a drink. There was a comfortable living room, in which, as one first came into it, one was startled at being confronted by a dark human head staring fixedly and almost fiercely from eyes that had black irises and glowing whites: a bronze bust of Sappho, painted black, on an immense marble pedestal, which an admirer had sent Edna from Italy. There were also hangings from India, golden birds on a background of green, that she had brought back from her first trip to London. We did a good deal of leisurely drinking, all in the gamut of apple products, on which people who lived in the country much depended under Prohibition: apple brandies and apple wines that ranged in color from citron to amber. Edna was interesting herself in the local animals and birds and trees, which were beginning to turn up in *The Buck in the Snow;* but we decided not to go for a walk, as it had been earlier proposed to do. They had a sensitive German police-dog, who, when Boissevain had given her a scolding, would drag herself into the room, bumping against the chairs, as if her hind legs were paralyzed. They thought she was a case for Freud.

There was a piano in the living room, and the next morning I asked her to play. I had not heard her since years before, when she had taken off her rings and left them on the piano in my apartment in Sixteenth Street, and I had found in my mailbox the next morning a note dated "Three p.m. (out to get food)"—since she lived only a few blocks away—asking me to bring them back. She had now, she told me, taken up music again and was trying to work regularly at it. She was studying a sonata of Beethoven and played parts of it with her bright alive touch, dropping them, however, with impatience at the raggedness of her own performance. Then she got out a lot of new poems, over which we had a long session. It brought her back to her old intensity. She was desperately, feverishly anxious not to let her standard down. She sometimes kept a poem for decades before she got it into satisfactory form. I remember one ambitious piece called *Pittsburgh Rose,* on which she had been working that summer, that impressed me very much at the time but that she never got to the point of publishing—also *Menses,* which was not printed till *Huntsman, What Quarry?* in 1937. I would try to relieve the strain that was inevitably set up between us by talking about current ideas and books—to which at that time she paid little attention—and by telling her a gag of Joe Cook's, which I had also been saving for her, because it was a little in her own vein. Cook, in his latest show, had exhibited to the audience two shower-baths and explained they were his own invention: the remarkable thing about them was that you could have a complete shower without taking off your clothes and without getting them wet. He introduced to the audience two men in full evening-dress, wearing silk hats. They stepped into the showers and pulled the curtains—the sound of water was heard. Joe Cook then jerked open the curtains, and the gentlemen emerged drenched. Cook turned to the audience and said, "I have never been more embarrassed in my life!" But even as I was telling this and Edna was laughing at it, I was chilled by the awful seriousness of the implications it was taking on.

The next summer I was visiting near Austerlitz and called on the Boissevains one afternoon. While we were talking, it began to grow dark, and the living room was half in shadow. There were a number of people there, and the conversation was general. I had a curious and touching impression, as Edna sat quiet in a big chair, that—torn and distracted by winds that had swept her through many seas—she had been towed into harbor and moored, that she was floating at anchor there.

It was difficult for the romantics of the twenties to slow down and slough off their youth, when everything had seemed to be possible and they had been able to treat their genius as an unlimited checking account. One could always still resort to liquor to keep up the old excitement, it was a kind of way of getting back there; the old habit of recklessness was hard to drop, the scorn for safe living and expediency, the need to heighten the sensations of life. Edna had now been led back to something like the rural isolation of her girlhood, and in her retreat she had no children to occupy her, to compel her to outgrow her girlhood. Though I did not see much of her through all these years, I got the impression that she was alternating between vigorously creative periods when she produced the firm-based strong-molded work that represented her full artistic maturity—*Fatal Interview* and *Epitaph for the Race of Man*—and dreadful lapses into depression and helplessness that sometimes lasted for months. I did not encourage her to talk about these; but I remember her telling me on one occasion, not very long after her marriage, when she had apparently spent weeks in bed, that she had done nothing but weep all the time; and on another, she startled me by saying, in the midst of showing me her poetry: "I'm *not* a pathetic character!" This must have been in 1928, at the time when she was still a romantic figure and a fabulously popular poet, imitated, adored and envied all over the United States, who was able to make large fees by reading her poems in public. Through all this, Eugen Boissevain must have been inexhaustibly patient, considerate and comprehending. He had given his whole life to Edna. He dropped his business and seriously worked the farm. He accompanied her on the triumphs of her reading tours and saw her through the ordeals of her hospitals. He arranged for her a social life—it is reflected, I suppose, to some extent, in *Conversation at Midnight*—of a kind that she could never have made for herself, which afforded her more "human" contacts than were

possible in the exhausting relationships that were natural
to her passionate spirit. Yet she continued, from time
to time, to follow her old pattern of escape by breaking
away from her domestic arrangements. The sequence of
sonnets called *Fatal Interview*—certainly one of her most
successful works and one of the great poems of our day—
was evidently the product of such an episode. It is, I
think, unique among her poems in representing the lover
as wanting to end the affair before the poet is willing to
let him go.

I did not see her for nineteen years after my call of
1929. It was not till 1944 that I seem even to have written
her again. I had been astonished and worried by the
poetry she had been publishing during the war, on a
level of wartime journalism of which I had not imagined
her capable. I tried to explain it as partly due to the
natural anxieties of Eugen when Holland was seized by
Hitler, and I remembered Henry James's description, in
his life of William Wetmore Story, of Mrs. Browning's
"feverish obsession" with the Italian Risorgimento. "It is
impossible," says James, "not to feel, as we read, that to
'care,' in the common phrase, as she is caring is to entertain one's convictions as a malady and a doom. . . . We
wonder why so much disinterested passion . . . should
not leave us in a less disturbed degree the benefit of the
moral beauty. We . . . end by asking ourselves if it be
not because her admirable mind, otherwise splendidly
exhibited, has inclined us to look in her for that saving
and sacred sense of proportion, of the free and blessed
general, that great poets, that genius and the high range
of genius, give us the impression of even in emotion
and passion, even in pleading a cause and calling on the
gods." I concluded that when women of genius got carried away by a cause, this was the kind of thing that

deplorably sometimes happened. But I thought that, since she had come to that pass, she probably needed artistic encouragement; the reviewers were giving her plenty of scolding. So I wrote her a letter in which I refrained from mentioning her war-verse at all but congratulated her on the album of her recordings, which, although it had been made some time before, in 1941, I had only recently bought. One of the poems she had recorded was *The Harp-Weaver*, for which I had not much cared when it first appeared. I had told her that it was one of her poems that belonged in a woman's magazine, and was surprised when she defended it strongly, as she did not always do with her work when it verged on the sentimental. I had known that it was about her own mother, and the volume was dedicated to Cora Millay. During the years when Edna had been living in Europe, she had arranged to bring her mother over—which, with her own meager resources at that time, could not have been easy to manage; and I knew how devoted she was to the debonair hard-bitten old lady who had worked for her and educated her. But I did not know with how much effectiveness she had put it into the Harp-Weaver poem—or, at least, into her reading of it, for it is better to hear than to read: the loneliness, the poverty, the unvalued Irish heritage, the Spartan New England self-discipline, the gift of artistic creation and intellectual distinction—she had taught her to write verse at four and to play the piano at seven—that the mother had been able to transmit. She had made of it something dramatic and almost unbearably moving, a record of the closest relationship that Edna, up to then, I suppose—that is, up to her marriage—had ever known. I wrote her something of this, and I told her that John Bishop had died that spring. I heard nothing from her for two years; then, in the summer of 1946, I received from her this strange letter:

Steepletop,

August, 1946.

... It is two years now since I received your letter. You had bad news to tell me: the death of John Bishop. Even now, that seems unlikely. How you must have missed him that summer, and how you still must miss him, is something that I would rather not go into in my mind. For it would make me ache, only to think of it, and I don't like aching, any more than anybody else.

You told me also, in that letter, that you liked my recorded readings from my poems. That pleased me enormously. I had felt pretty sure, myself, that they were good, but your verdict was like an Imprimatur to me.

Your letter reached me at a time when I was very ill indeed, in the Doctors Hospital in New York. I was enjoying there a very handsome—and, as I afterwards was told, an all but life-size—nervous breakdown. For five years I had been writing almost nothing but propaganda. And I can tell you from my own experience, that there is nothing on this earth which can so much get on the nerves of a good poet, as the writing of bad poetry. Anyway, finally I cracked up under it. I was in the hospital a long time.

This does not explain, of course, why, when I got out and came home, after I got well and strong again, still I did not write you. But here, happily for me, and for you, I can save ourselves the cumbersome explaining, by reminding you of a letter of Gerard Hopkins. In this letter he makes apology—I forget to whom; possibly to Robert Bridges, although, somehow, I think not—for having been so slow in answering. And he states—not in these words at all, but this is the meaning of it—: that the driving of himself by himself to make the beginning of a letter, is almost more than his strength can support. When once he has forced himself to begin the letter, he says, the going is not so bad. Well, I, too, suffer from that disease. For it is a disease. It is as real, and its outlines are quite as clear, as in a case of claustrophobia, or agoraphobia. I have named it, just in order to comfort myself, and to dignify this pitiful horror with a name, epistolaphobia. I say, "I, too, suffer from that disease." But I think I have it very much worse than he had. For after all, he did write many letters. And I don't. It is sheer desperation and pure panic—lest, through my continued silence, I lose your friendship, which I prize—that whips me to the typewriter now. I don't know where you are. But I think, and I think it often, "Wherever he is, there he still is, and perhaps some day I shall see him again, and we shall talk about poetry, as we used to do."

I have just finished learning by heart Matthew Arnold's *Scholar Gypsy,*—such a lovely poem. I had wanted for years to know it by heart, but it had always looked a bit long to me. It is not at all difficult, however, to learn by heart, stanza by stanza; it is so reasonable. I have also learned by heart *The Eve of St. Agnes* and *Lamia. Lamia,* let me tell you, is a very long poem. And Keats, in both these poems, makes it as tricky as possible for you, by shifting all the time from "thou" to "you," and by whisking you suddenly from the past tense into the present tense. To get these passages into your memory, and exact, is really quite a chore. I have learned by heart, of Shelley, not only *To the West Wind*—and surely the second stanza of that poem is as fine a thing as ever was written in English—but also the *Hymn to Intellectual Beauty*—a devil to learn by heart. Anyway, I have them all now. And what evil thing can ever again even brush me with its wings?

With love, as ever,
Edna

. . . I am sending you, here—enclosed, three new poems of my own.* I hope, of course I hope very much, that you will like them. But don't—oh, for God's sake, don't for one moment—feel that you must write me something about them, or, indeed, in any way acknowledge this letter at all. I would not put so great a burden upon the shoulders and upon the brain of the person that in all the world I hated the most. I do not need your answer. I am happy enough as it is. For I have at last, after two years of recurring spiritual torment, been able to flog myself into writing a very simple letter to a dear and trusted friend.

E.

I forgot to tell you, even though I was speaking of Father Hopkins, that I have also learned by heart at least one third of his published poetry. Have you ever tried to learn him by heart?—It is great fun, very exciting, difficult.

In the August of 1948, I was attending the Berkshire Music Festival and, discovering that Austerlitz was not far away, I called up the Boissevains and went over with my wife to see them. I had not seen them for nineteen years, and when I had inquired about them of such friends of theirs as I happened to meet, they had not seemed to know much about them either. As we drove through the long tunnel of greenery that led to the Steepletop house, I felt, as I had not done before, that Edna had been buried out there. Gene Boissevain came out in his working-clothes. He shuffled in his leather

* These were *Ragged Island, To a Snake* and a sonnet beginning *Tranquillity at length, when Autumn comes . . .* , which have since appeared in periodicals, but have not yet been collected in a book.

moccasins, he had aged: he was graying and stooped. It seemed to me that he was low in morale. "I'll go and get my child," he said. I did not realize at first that this meant Edna. I found in the living room most of the things that had been there in 1929: the scaring Ethiopian Sappho, the golden birds on the "Tree of Life." But the birds were paler, their background was gray; the couches looked badly worn; the whole place seemed shabby and dim. I had the feeling that it was so long ago that they had set up keeping house together that they had ceased to notice the room, that they never did anything to freshen it up. One saw, standing outside the window, three rusty old tin oil-barrels, on which Edna could put food for birds without having it stolen by the squirrels. In one corner, a litter of copy-books covered table, couch, chair and floor.

In a few minutes, Edna came in, wearing slacks and a white working shirt, open at the neck. It was a moment before I recognized her. She had so changed in the nineteen years that, if I had met her unexpectedly somewhere, I am sure I should not have known her. She had become somewhat heavy and dumpy, and her cheeks were a little florid. Her eyes had a bird-lidded look that I recognized as typically Irish, and I noticed for the first time a certain resemblance to her mother. She was terribly nervous; her hands shook; there was a look of fright in her bright green eyes. Eugen brought us martinis. Very quietly he watched her and managed her. At moments he would baby her in a way that I had not seen him use before but that had evidently become habitual, when she showed signs of bursting into tears over not being able to find a poem or something of the kind. My wife said afterwards that Gene gave the impression of shaking me at her as if I had been a new toy with which he hoped to divert her. She said that she had been writing in the last two months and was very much excited about it, because, for two years before that, she had not been able to work. She talked about her wartime poetry as an error that she frankly confessed to. She knew that she had deserved the reviews she got, but had been hurt by them, nevertheless. She said that she had been dismayed when this handful of political verses—under the title *Make Bright the Arrows*—had been issued in the same format as her other books, as if she meant it to stand beside them, for she had intended a paperbound pamphlet that could circulate quickly and be thrown away. I was confirmed in my supposition that these poems had been inspired by loyalty to Eugen, when he talked about his family in Holland. One of his cousins had been tortured and killed; others had had hairbreadth escapes. Edna now constantly sent them packages. She always spoke of "our relatives," and one could see that she was very much attached to them. She had visited them in Holland and had even learned the language. My wife knows Holland and understands Dutch, and Edna, for her benefit, produced and read a poem she had written in Dutch. She showed us a good deal of her poetry, much of it in an unfinished state. It was of an almost unrelieved blackness. I could see that she was just emerging from some terrible eclipse of the spirit. I had difficulty in adjusting myself to Edna in her present phase. There was something more distressing than the old anxiety that she had shown before in discussing her verse: a pressure that she now put upon you for assurance, approval, praise, and, even in those moments when she sounded like a good-natured healthily laughing elderly woman, this, too, was a person I did not know, and these moments, as it were interpolated, seemed to leave her more nervous still. But the nervousness wore off with the drinks, as did my feeling of strangeness about her. This was, after all, the girl, the great poet, I knew, groping back *in luminis oras* from the night of the underworld. She had tackled Catullus's bitter poem, *Si qua recordanti benefacta priora voluptas . . .* ; and I could see that the last lines,

Ipse valere, opto et taetrum hunc deponere morbum.
O di, reddite mi hoc pro pietate mea!

had for her a special and desperate meaning. She was afraid that the translation she had sketched would not do the poem justice; and she told us that, when she had sat on the judges' committee for the Guggenheim fellowships, she had not been able to bring herself to vote for Horace Gregory, in spite of his list of distinguished supporters, on account of the badness of his translations of Catullus. But she had had some misgivings since—wasn't it better, perhaps, that the Latinless public should be able to get Catullus, even in an imperfect version? Eugen pulled her up: "Remember," he said, "that was the kind of thing you thought about your war poetry—that it was important to rouse the country." I thought this was very shrewd of him. We talked about John Bishop's poetry, of which I had sent her the collected volume, brought out after his death. She said that his poems had "more overtones" than those of any other contemporary poet: "It's like a row of poplars on a river, with another row reflected in the river." I told her how impossible it had been for me, though John had talked about his illness, to realize that the gloom of his poetry had a real and serious cause or to guess that it announced the approach of death. "Yes: he was despairing," she said.

I was reminded of the little Esthonian folk-song that I had loved so when she sang it in Truro, and I asked her about the anthology in which it had appeared. She didn't know where to find it, but, after reflecting a moment, she was able to recover the song, with its sweet little plaintive tune and her own bitter-sweet words. I inquired about the original version of the *Epitaph for the Race of Man*—I had been surprised by its coming out in such a different form from that of the version I had heard in 1920; and she told me that she had lost her first draft, of which she could now recall only scraps. Wanting Elena to hear her read, I asked her to recite *The Poet and His Book*. As she did so, the room became so charged with emotion that I began to find it difficult to bear. I could not weep, I did not want her to weep, and, though Elena thought we ought to have stayed, I soon insisted on leaving.

I told myself that Edna was even more fatiguing than she had been in her younger days, and I reasserted my middle-aged indifference. It was too much for me, at fifty-three, to go back to that old state of mind, so demandingly, imprisoningly personal. The whole thing was like one of those dreams that I had never quite ceased to have, in which I found myself with Edna again—though in these dreams she had sometimes seemed faded and shrunken, never ruddy and overblown as I saw her now. The gap of the almost two decades was something that, encountering the real woman, I could not accept or take in. I had found them there, Edna and Eugen, just as I had left them in 1929, and this latest visit connected itself with my glimpses of that summer long past, not with anything that had happened between. It became like the fears and desires, the revived emotions, of sleep; and the changes in her were like the old images of dreams that come to us exaggerated, distorted, swollen with longing or horror. So she was still, although now in a different way, almost as disturbing to me as she had ever been in the twenties, to which she had so completely belonged—for she could not be a part of my present, and to see her exerted on me a painful pull, as if to drag me up by the roots, to gouge me out of my present personality and to annihilate all that had made it. My own life was now organized and grounded, I had children to worry and divert me; and from my present point of view, besides, it disturbed me to find Edna and Eugen haunting like deteriorated ghosts their own comfortable old house in the country. I tried to imagine their lives. They were evidently very hard-up—a certain income that Gene had from Java had ceased at the time of the war, and Edna could no longer give readings; they never seemed to see anyone or go anywhere. When we asked them to come to Tanglewood—an hour's drive away—and go with us to one of the concerts, I was astonished to find that Edna, who loved music so, had no idea at all of what the festival had become and assumed that the concerts were still held under canvas as they had not been since the very first years. We could not persuade her to go. Gene had said that he would ask us to dinner, but "I'm the only thing in the house—I'm the cook and bottlewasher and maid,"—so I assumed that he attended to the house as well as--with little help nowadays—the farm, and cooked all the meals for Edna. But I could not conceive what their daily existence, month after month, had been like or what it would be like in the future. It did not occur to me, as it had not done in connection with John Bishop, that they were both very soon to die. What had desolated and frightened me there was death, to which Eugen was wearily resigned but against which Edna, when I saw her, with the draughts of her unfinished Erebean poems, was making her last fierce struggle.

Eugen Boissevain died in the autumn of 1949. I had wondered already, at the time of our visit, what would happen to Edna if he should die first. All I was able to learn about her was that she was still living out at Steepletop. The night of October 20, 1950, I had a long dream about Edna. It began with a kind of revival of the longing I had had for her in the twenties, and she came to me in her old dream-shape, which was so much more familiar to me than that in which I had seen her last; but then it turned into a conversation that was taking place in the present. I was telling her about John Bishop's relations with another contemporary poet, who had sat at his feet and learned from him, then later had become better known than John and treated him, I had thought, rather shabbily. The next evening I heard of her death, which had taken place the day before, apparently very early on the morning of the nineteenth (Mr. Sheean gives the erroneous impression that she died the morning of the twenty-first). She had been living alone in the house and had evidently sat up all night reading the proofs of Rolfe Humphries' translation of the *Aeneid,* which were found in the living room on the floor around the chair in which she worked, with her notes on the table beside it. She must have been going upstairs at dawn and have felt faint and sat down on a step. She had set down on the step just above her a glass of wine she was carrying. A man who came in to do the chores found her there the next afternoon.* My dream was probably prompted by Sartre's book on Baudelaire, which I had been reading that night in bed and which must have

* She had at first, I learn, collapsed, after Eugen's death; then had sent away the friends who had come to be with her and insisted on living at Steepletop alone. Her letters show that, as autumn arrived, she had dreaded the winter there. Her sister writes me that when she came there after Edna's death, she found the house "in perfect and beautiful order: the floors were waxed; furniture polished; couches and chairs newly and brightly recovered."

led me to Edna by way of the translation of the *Fleurs du Mal* that she and George Dillon had made, which I had recently reread and thought better of than at the time of my review of *Conversation at Midnight*. My dream was partly motivated, no doubt, by my wanting, in my sleep, to have somebody to listen to my literary gossip and somebody from old times to talk to, but partly, I believe, also, by the impulse to console her in this vicarious way for the neglect that she, too, had been suffering. And I may have had some sort of intuition about what had happened the morning before. I do not mean anything supernatural, but the kind of sympathetic sense of the rhythms of another's life that may sometimes persist in absence, as I had had, in 1944, the feeling that she needed support, at the time of her nervous breakdown.

And she was to speak to me after her death, for the writing of this memoir had a curious sequel. Edna's sister has sent me two letters which Edna had written to me but which I had never seen. The first was dated March 5, 1929, and discussed a novel of mine that I had given her in manuscript. She had not said much about the book the last time I had seen her before she had written, but had promised to send me some notes on it. The letter with these notes had been addressed to a place I had already left and was forwarded to a wrong address, so that it came back to Steepletop when Edna and Gene were abroad and was never sent again. If I had had it, I should have answered it as she asked me to do and might not so completely have lost touch with her for almost twenty years. I thought that she had been offended by a character that was partly derived from her or had so much disliked the book that she had not wanted to write me about it. I now find that she had made careful and copious notes and had good-naturedly undertaken to rewrite in what she thought a more appropriate vein the speeches assigned to the character partly based on herself.

The second letter was an earlier unfinished draught of the one I have given above, which she had written, apparently, the year before and which was in some ways quite different from the one she eventually sent:

. . . I miss you very much. I wish I could see you and talk with you. Not see you just once, and pour out my heart to you, nothing like that. I wish I could see you every once in a while and talk with you, not about war and peace and depressing things like that, but about poetry, which is never depressing, because no matter how many people have done it badly, a few have done it well, and you can't get around that.

Your letter reached me a year ago last summer in Doctors Hospital in New York, where, after years of Painstaking and Pious Prostitution of Poetry to Propaganda, I was relaxing in a complete and handsome nervous breakdown.

("O di, reddite mi hoc pro pietate mea!")

You said in your letter that you liked the recordings of my poems which I had made for Victor. That came at just the right time . . . ; it helped me get well.

I wish I could see you. But if I can't see you, I wish I could write letters. It's too bad you haven't known all this time how much your letter meant to me. That is, if you would have cared, and I think you would have. But I can't write letters. Only when the moon is in perigee and the sun is in at least partial eclipse, can I seem to write a letter. But perhaps you're like that, too. After all, I haven't been hearing from *you* so very often, either, now that I come to think of it.—It's a real sickness, though, and no joking, this dread of writing letters, "Hard for the non-elect to understand," and the fact that one has, infrequently, a lucid interval, makes it no less a mania. Or rather, a phobia: *Epistolaphobia*—quite as real as *agora,* and much more of a nuisance—much more of a public nuisance, anyway.

Did you know that the line I just quoted ("Hard for the non-elect to understand") is from *Lamia?*—I would never have known it, except that I have just finished learning *Lamia* by heart. I am letter-perfect in it now; you can't fault me. It is something of a job, learning *Lamia* by heart; not because it is a long poem, although it is really a rather long poem, nor because Keats is diffi-cult to memorize, for he isn't, except in the few places— and it is astonishing how few those places are, in a poem like *Lamia*—where obviously he could not make up his mind just how to say it, and so you can't make up your mind just how to remember it—but because Keats, like all the other boys then, had such an off-hand inconsequential, irritating way of changing from *thee* to *you* in the flicker of a lid-lash, and of swapping tenses mid-phrase.

> And I neglect the holy rite for thee.
> Even as you list, invite your many guests.
>
> *Lamia*

> . . . Meantime, across the moors,
> Had come young Porphyro, with heart on fire
> For Madeline; beside the portal doors,
> Buttressed from moonlight stands he, and implores—
> *The Eve of St. Agnes*

. . . The stately music no more breathes,
The myrtle sickened in a thousand wreaths.
Lamia

Nor suffer thy pale forehead to be kissed
By nightshade, ruby grape of Proserpine,
Weave not your rosary of yewberries
Ode to Melancholy

Go, for they call you, shepherd, from the hill,
Go, shepherd, and untie the wattled cotes;
No longer leave thy wistful flock unfed
The Scholar Gypsy

The quotation from Catullus shows that the poem I found her translating in 1948 was already much in her mind. The quotations from Keats at the end illustrate the "swapping" of tenses and the inconsistent use of *thou* and *you*, but they seem, also, to echo her own mood. She has written them all down from memory, with variations on the original punctuation, and in the fourth has unconsciously changed *make* to *weave*.

At the time I was writing this memoir, I happened one day, in the country, at Wellfleet on Cape Cod, where I live, to meet my neighbor from Truro, Phyllis Duganne. We talked about Edna Millay, and she told me of a memory she had of seeing her years ago in Greenwich Village running around the corner of Macdougal Street, flushed and laughing "like a nymph," with her hair swinging. Floyd Dell, also laughing, pursued her. Phyllis said she had always remembered it; and I leave this image here at the end to supplement my firsthand impressions—a glimpse of Edna as the fleeing and challenging Daphne of her *Figs from Thistles* poem—from the time when I did not yet know her, when she had first come from Vassar to the Village.

1961. James Joyce's correspondence with Harriet Weaver, which has been published since this book first appeared, shows that my reference to her on page 767 gives rather an unfair impression. She loyally saw Joyce through not only *Ulysses* but also *Finnegans Wake.*

INDEX

An asterisk indicates a reference to an author whose work is mentioned without his being named.